Essentials of
public administration

Essentials of public administration

A text with readings

Larry B. Hill

F. Ted Hebert

University of Oklahoma

Duxbury Press, North Scituate, Massachusetts

Essentials of Public Administration: A Text with Readings
was edited and prepared for composition by Bowden Anderson. Interior design
was provided by Joanna Prudden Snyder. The cover was designed by Oliver
Kline.

Duxbury Press
A Division of Wadsworth, Inc.

Library of Congress Cataloging in Publication Data

Hill, Larry B.   1942-
Essentials of public administration.

Includes bibliographical references and index.
1. Public administration.   I. Hebert, F.   Ted, joint author.   II. Title.
JF1351.H52   350   78-11184
ISBN 0-87872-194-0

Printed in the United States of America
1 2 3 4 5 6 7 8 9 — 83 82 81 80 79

For

Brian and Eric

and

Elizabeth and Becky

Contents

Preface

Introduction:

An orientation to public administration   1

Defining public administration 1 • Why does public administration interest you? 2 • Introducing bureaucrats and bureaucracies 4 • This book's plan 5

PART 1

Perspectives on public administration

Chapter one

The expanding scope of American public administration   11

Classifying public programs 12 • American public programs in historical perspective 16 • Public attitudes toward the public sector 30 • Conclusion 38 • Suggested readings for chapter one 38

Chapter two

Public administration as a field of study   40

Premodern administration 41 • Modern bureaucracy 42 • The environment of administration in early America 43 • The first century of the American public service 44 • The era of reform 46 • Public administration as an academic discipline 48 • Public and private administration 54 • Suggested readings for chapter two 55

PART 2

The environment of public administration

Chapter three
Executive and interbureaucratic involvement

65

Formal executive powers 66 • Tools of executive control 67 • Executive oversight 72 • Interbureaucratic relationships 74 • Selection one *More swelling of the presidency* Thomas E. Cronin 81 • Study questions for selection one 90 • Selection two *The ten commandments of the foreign affairs bureaucracy* Leslie H. Gelb and Morton H. Halperin 91 • Study questions for selection two 100 • Suggested readings for chapter three 100

Chapter four
Legislative and judicial involvement

102

A. Legislators and administrators   102

Administrators as policy makers 103 • Legislators as policy implementors 106 • Sharing policy making and implementation 108 • Selection three *Legislative oversight of bureaucracy* Morris S. Ogul 109 • Study questions for selection three 119

B. Courts and administrators   119

Courts and the substance of administrative decisions 120 • Courts, procedural matters, and administrative law 123 • Rule making and informal adjudication 124 • Selection four *Judicial lawmaking and administration* Roger C. Cramton 126 • Study questions for selection four 134 • Suggested readings for chapter four 134

Chapter five
Group, clientele, and public involvement

136

Clientele groups 139 • Clients and regulation 142 • Professional associations 144 • Sup-

pliers and contractors 144 • Promotional
groups 145 • Selection five *Public interest advocacy
and the regulatory process* Richard C.
Leone 146 • Study questions for selection
five 159 • Suggested readings for chapter five 160

PART 3

The internal dynamics of public administrative agencies

Chapter six

Organization theory and administrative agencies   166

Defining organizations 167 • The scope of organization theory 168 • "Old" and "new" organization
theory 170 • System theories of organization 176 • Selection six *Bureaucracy* Max
Weber 181 • Study questions for selection
six 189 • Selection seven *Changing Organizations* Warren Bennis 190 • Study questions for
selection seven 200 • Suggested readings for
chapter six 200

Chapter seven

Staffing the agency: personnel administration   202

The ubiquity of the personnel function 202 • Merit
systems 203 • The personnel process 204 •
Reforming the federal civil service system 212 •
Continuing education in the public service 213 •
Morale and motivation 214 • The issues today:
unionization and equity 215 • Selection eight
*The implications of collective bargaining for public
administration* Felix A. Nigro 216 • Study questions
for selection eight 226 • Selection nine *Are
merit and equity compatible?* Harry Kranz 227 •
Study questions for selection nine 236 •
Suggested readings for chapter seven 237

Chapter eight

Making the agency's decisions   239

An outline of two decision theories 240 • The ratio-

nal-comprehensive critique of incrementalism 241 • The incremental critique of rationalism 243 • Interfacing rationalism with
incrementalism 246 • Decision models and the context of American politics 247 • The value implications of decision models 249 • Selection ten *The
systems analysis approach* Alain C. Enthoven 251 • Selection eleven *The science of "muddling
through"* Charles E. Lindblom 264 • Study questions for selections ten and eleven 278 • Suggested
readings for chapter eight 279

Chapter nine
Managing the agency: problems of leadership   280

A. Identifying leadership   281

Leadership traits 281 • Styles of leadership 282 • Contingency theories 287

B. Strategies of leadership   290

Reward and punishment 291 • Organizational
humanism 292 • Organization development 294 • Management by objec-
tives 295 • Current tendencies 298 • Selection
twelve *How to choose a leadership pattern* Robert
Tannenbaum and Warren H. Schmidt 300 • Study
questions for selection twelve 314 • Selection thirteen *MBO in state government* George S.
Odiorne 315 • Study questions for selection thirteen 324 • Suggested readings for chapter nine 324

Chapter ten
Securing resources: the politics of the
budgetary process   326

The budget cycle 328 • Budget decision making 335 • Reforming the system 337 • Selection
fourteen *The zero-base approach to government budgeting* Peter A. Pyhrr 342 • Study questions for
selection fourteen 354 • Selection fifteen *Zero-base
budgeting in historical and political context* F. Ted
Hebert 355 • Study questions for selection fifteen 372 • Suggested readings for chapter ten 372

PART 4

Evaluating public bureaucracy

Chapter eleven
Public administration and program evaluation   379

The development of evaluation research 380 • The nature of program evaluation 381 • Research design 383 • The politics of program evaluation 388 • A future for program evaluation 391 • Selection sixteen *Output measurement in urban government* Donald M. Fisk and Richard E. Winnie 392 • Study questions for selection sixteen 407 • Selection seventeen *What can we actually get from program evaluation?* Joseph S. Wholey 408 • Study questions for selection seventeen 417 • Suggested readings for chapter eleven 417

Chapter twelve
The responsibility and the future of American public administration   418

A. Holding government agencies responsible   419

The accountable administrator 420 • Administrative values: the "inner check" 422 • The role of bureaucratic monitoring mechanisms 425 • Unofficial bureaucratic monitoring mechanisms 431 • Internal official bureaucratic monitoring mechanisms 435 • External official bureaucratic monitoring mechanisms 438

B. Public administration's future   451

The slowing of bureaucratic growth 451 • Bureaucracy under attack 453 • A closer interface of the private and the public sectors 454 • International administration 455 • The continuing professionalization of public administration 456 • The future and administrators' democratic values 458 • Suggested readings for chapter twelve 460

xi

Appendix:
How to get a government job 462

Glossary 471

Index 479

Preface

In comparison with other public administration texts, this book is rather slender. The size has deliberately been kept down by including only the essentials of the field. The word *essential* is used in Webster's sense of the "minimal indispensable body, character, or structure of a thing." Public administration is—to say the least—an inexact science, and there is less than complete agreement on what the essentials of the field are. Thus, our approach to the subject is our personal interpretation, and it requires a brief explanation.

Students are likely to approach the subject of public administration from one or more of three motives:

1. Many students see the course as preliminary job training. If they are taking a first, perhaps tentative step in learning how to be a public administrator, their interests are likely to be pragmatic. They want to know what working for government will be like.

2. Many students have an academic curiosity about various aspects of public administration. If they are majoring in political

science, they may be interested in the involvement of public agencies with other actors in the political process. Economics or business majors may be concerned about the comparative efficiency of public and private sector organizations. To students of sociology, the relationship between the bureaucracy's goals and its performance may be of interest. Those majoring in other fields—from agronomy to zoology—are likely to be concerned about the impact of government agencies on their future careers.

3. Many students are concerned about ethical and other philosophical matters. As citizens, they ask questions such as: "Are we actually governed by a new bureaucratic-technical elite?" "How can we make sure that another Watergate does not occur?" "What methods can be used to hold large, bureaucratic agencies politically accountable?" "How has the recent growth of public bureaucracy affected the classical conception of democracy?"

In providing a brief overview of the entire administrative process, we have responded to all three motivations: (1) future civil servants can identify forces that impinge on administrators' jobs and can begin to understand how the managerial problems that arise within public agencies are commonly resolved; (2) as social scientists, we scrutinize administrative behavior, searching for patterns as well as interesting deviations; and (3) from beginning to end, our approach is normative and evaluative—that is, we examine the moral implications of the clash between merit and equity in the personnel process. These three perspectives are interwoven throughout the book.

In the past, there has been considerable competition—even acrimony—between the political science and the business, or management, approaches to public administration, but a rapprochement is occurring as members of both schools realize that each has something to contribute to the study of the administrative process. Recognizing the value of disciplinary cross-fertilization, this text attempts to present a balanced view. For the management specialist, we place the activities of public agencies within a general political context and note some political implications of various management techniques. For the political scientist, we provide an introduction to such currently popular management tools as ZBB, OD, and MBO. If our approach does not satisfy the zealots of either persuasion, we hope it will appeal to a broad range of those who believe, with us, that an introduction to public administration that fails to sensitize students to the value of *both* positions simply is inadequate.

We have not written an encyclopedic text—but we offer a comprehensive introduction to public administration. We have not compiled a collection of readings, but most of our chapters are supplemented with selected readings. We have thus created a combination text-and-reader—apparently the field's first such book.

The selected readings have been chosen not only for appropriateness and quality, but also for student appeal and clarity of expression. A few of the pieces reprinted are considered classics in the field, but the accent is on recent works. Counting even the "classics," three-fourths of the readings have been published within the past six years. Our original materials have been intertwined with the reprinted selections to create a basic text for a beginning course. In addition, because this book's organization and coverage parallel the most popular textbooks, because our brevity and distinctive approach mean that redundancies will be few, and because the reprinted selections provide interesting illustrative materials, this book also can be used to supplement other texts.

Our purpose throughout has been to communicate with students about contemporary public administration, and we applaud the ability of Duxbury Press to support our objectives by producing a book whose design is open and inviting. If our tone is less self-consciously formal than that of other books, this does not imply that we are frivolous. We are highly serious about raising students' levels of understanding of the essentials of American public administration.

Authors tend to incur heavy debts in writing books. In our case, we thank our families for their encouragement and forbearance. Also, we thank our colleagues in political science and public administration at the University of Oklahoma, who have provided a supportive intellectual atmosphere and more direct assistance. Our public administration students have been resonant sounding boards. We are grateful to Donna Lorenson and Gary Parent for research assistance. Stanley Anderson, Dwight Davis, Hugh MacNiven, Kenneth Meier, David Morgan, and Walter Scheffer made useful comments on portions of the manuscript. And Hugh MacNiven generously agreed to write chapter 2 for us. Thanks are also due to the authors who graciously gave us permission to reprint articles, and to their publishers. Once again, we thank our friend Geri Rowden for typing the many drafts, with her customary accuracy and panache. In addition, we have profited from the comments of two people who read the entire manuscript: Jeremy Plant, of the State University of New York at Albany, and David Williams, of West Virginia University. Unfortunately, for reasons of space and time it was not always possible to follow the useful advice we were given, and everyone named above is hereby absolved of any responsibility for the final product.

LARRY B. HILL
F. TED HEBERT

Introduction

An orientation to public administration

Defining public administration

Defining public administration is not easy. For the moment let us simply say that public administration is the authoritative implementation of those policy choices that have been legitimated through political processes. To get a more specific idea of what we mean by "authoritative implementation," consider the following newspaper headlines:

"Energy Policy To Feature Incentives for Conservation and Production"

"Block Grant Assistance Program Expanded"

"Farmers To Get Disaster Relief for Flooded Wheat Crops"

"Students Eligible for Low-Interest Government Loans"

"Oil Companies Must Reveal Assets To Qualify for New Tax Concessions"

"Social Security Payments To Rise 10 Percent"

We are confronted daily with such headlines announcing "solutions" to public problems through the commitment to particular policy alternatives. Because a great deal of publicity often precedes a controversial decision, its announcement captures our attention. But in almost all cases, after a few days the publicity dies down and the issue fades from the public consciousness. This does not mean, however, that the issue is dead. Instead, a new phase of the policy process has begun: implementation. Policies are never self-executing. Complex machinery is required even to handle routine adjustments in the levels of tax or welfare payments, and further political choices always must be made.

To illustrate, let us return to our headlines. Additional questions immediately arise: What will the content be of the energy conservation and production incentives, and will conservation discourage increased production? How have eligibility requirements for block grants been changed? Precisely how are "flooded" farmers to be distinguished from "nonflooded" ones, and what are the boundaries of the disaster area? Can students get out from under their loan obligations by declaring personal bankruptcy? Are the foreign holdings of multinational oil companies to be taken into account in computing assets or only those of the American branch? Is the increase in the Social Security benefit to be treated as income for the purpose of computing other benefits based on income level?

These are only samples of the sorts of important questions that arise. Sometimes the legal provisions of the formal policy proclamation partially answer many such questions. But often the formally ratified policy pronouncements consist of little more than skeletal statements of political goals. It is the process of public administration that translates these vague declarations into actual programs that deeply affect people's lives.

Why does public administration interest you?

To the uninitiated observer, the administrative process may seem less interesting than such dramatic events as the clash among pressure groups over policy issues, a congressional speech advocating a course of action, or a presidential policy statement from the Oval Office. Public administration is not as showy as other kinds of politics, but because the administrative process is less publicized—indeed, parts of it are kept secret—it has added attractions for sophisticated students of politics. The issues that public administrators face are far from prosaic. Public administration involves competitions for power, money, and programs. The resolution of these conflicts, which often involve intense and Byzantine machinations among powerful personalities and social forces, determines a policy decision's real outcome for society.[1] Through administration, policy objectives may be brought to full flower and growth, or they may wither and die.

Not only are the politics of public administration intrinsically interesting, but the actions of administrators have an increasingly important impact on our lives. We are in contact with public administration almost from the moment of birth, when registration requirements are met, and our earthly remains cannot be disposed of without final administrative certification. Our *intermediate* experiences with public administrators have become so extensive that some people believe our society should be labeled the "administered society." An important reason for the renaissance of interest in public administration is that citizens, students, and scholars have come to understand the enormous impact of public administrators on all of us.

There are even stronger motivations to understand this area of public affairs. Many of today's students seek public administration jobs at the local, state, and federal levels. During the decade of the 1960s many activist students looked with disdain on public employees. By this time, however, most college students have rejected revolutionary rhetoric, and increasing numbers believe that they can make personally meaningful contributions to needed social change by working within the administrative process. Moreover, as private-sector jobs become scarce, jobs in government remain relatively plentiful and inevitably draw applicants to new areas.

Whether you read this book from a desire to learn about a possible work setting or for other reasons, we hope it will enhance your understanding of the processes involved and communicate some of the excitement that is so much a part of modern public administration.

---

[1]See Jeffrey L. Pressman and Aaron B. Wildavsky, *Implementation: How Great Expectations in Washington Are Dashed in Oakland; or, Why It's Amazing that Federal Programs Work at All, This Being a Saga of the Economic Development Administration as Told by Two Sympathetic Observers Who Seek to Build Morals on a Foundation of Ruined Hopes* (Berkeley: University of California Press, 1973).

An orientation to public administration/

/**3**

Introducing bureaucrats and bureaucracies

Public administration without living, breathing administrators is, of course, an absurdity. And administrators do not act as individuals; they are agents of organizations. Our next step is to ask: "Through what instrumentalities is public policy implemented?" While a host of institutions are partially involved—including legislatures and courts—most administrative actions are undertaken by *specialized* organizations. It is a fact of American political life that numerous large and complicated public agencies exist. They range from the United States Postal Service to the Department of Defense, from local police departments to state universities. Many of these agencies employ thousands of workers, operate over a wide geographical field, and have missions whose fulfillment affects the lives of hundreds of millions of citizens. These public organizations, commonly labeled bureaucracies, are the principal focus of this book.

Public agencies are complex, professional, highly organized clusters of offices, and our analysis will consider their performance as management-administrative institutions. But their importance to the political system goes far beyond this limited role. They perform multiple functions: agencies not only administer dicta laid down by elected policy makers; they are also active participants in the *making* of public decisions. Many legislative proposals are drafted by administrators long before being seen by most legislators. After legislation is passed, administrators issue rules and regulations to determine application in particular situations. When disputes over meaning arise, administrators interpret the legislation. Rather than being neutral appliers of public policy, these organizations *help determine* the government policies under which we live.

As you read this book, try to draw on your own life experiences with public administration—especially your encounters with administrators—in attempting to analyze the processes. If one is alert to the possibilities, the college or university itself makes an excellent laboratory for observing public administration in action. Whether the institution is public or private, administrators interpret degree requirements; parking violations are handled through a courtlike administrative process; waivers of regulations requiring dormitory residence are granted; grade appeals are processed; and the demands of student and faculty pressure groups are granted or ignored.

In addition to watching your immediate surroundings, be alert to references in the news media to administrative matters or to events that will have an impact on public administrators. For instance, as a part of one safety promotional campaign, the U.S. Consumer Product

Safety Commission ordered from a novelty company 80,000 buttons that showed a toy bear and proclaimed "Think Toy Safety." Unfortunately, the Associated Press reported, "because the buttons have sharp edges, paint with too much lead, and clips that could break off and be swallowed by children," the buttons had to be recalled.[2] The agency had failed to specify in its contract with the novelty company that the buttons themselves should be safe. Of course, you may see this story as merely an amusing and not too costly case of bureaucratic bungling. But we hope that as you proceed with this book you will begin to read a great deal more into what stories like this may reveal about the nature of the administrative process.

Be alert to the goal the agency was *attempting* to accomplish; notice the problems of coordination that can occur (in this case between the administrators responsible for the publicity campaign and those handling the purchasing of the buttons); finally, don't write off administrators as utterly incompetent without first trying to comprehend how it is that complex administrative machinery (even though it may be staffed by well-intentioned and generally competent people) can produce such incongruous results.

This book's plan

In writing a textbook, authors search for ways of conveying to students what is known about a field of study. The common practice is to draw substantially on what others have written, summarizing and often simplifying their materials. The result is a series of chapters that are digests of earlier works, so the reader sees the subject through filters provided by the textbook's author.

Except for our introductory chapters 1 and 2 and our concluding chapter 12, we have taken a different approach. Chapters 3 through 11 open with a summary of much of the prominent literature in the field that provides an integrated conceptual approach to the topic. But this is not simply a "minitext," for, following each chapter's introductory section, selections from important works in the field are reprinted. The selections were chosen to amplify or exemplify points made in the chapter's introductory section. Each selection is preceded by an introduction, which highlights its main points, and followed by questions, which are intended to focus discussion or further study.

In part I the scope of public administration is sketched, and academic and practitioner perspectives on the study of the subject are

---

²Associated Press, 18 November 1974.

An orientation to public administration / **5**

presented. Part II investigates some of the most interesting features of the public administrative process: the involvement of government agencies with environmental actors (the executive and other bureaucratic agencies, legislators and judges, groups, clients, and the public) in the formulation and implementation of policy. In part III treatments of some of the most substantial traditional topics of public administration are presented—including organization theory, personnel administration, decision making, management and leadership, and budgeting. The materials in part IV provide the basis for evaluating the impact of American public administration, for assessing its degree of political accountability, and for looking to the future.

Of course, neither reading this book nor completing an introductory course in public administration will make you fully qualified to practice public administration. Nonetheless, we do hope to provide a foundation, which can be built upon over a long period of time, that will help you to develop an increasingly sophisticated understanding of the essentials of the public administrative process.

Part

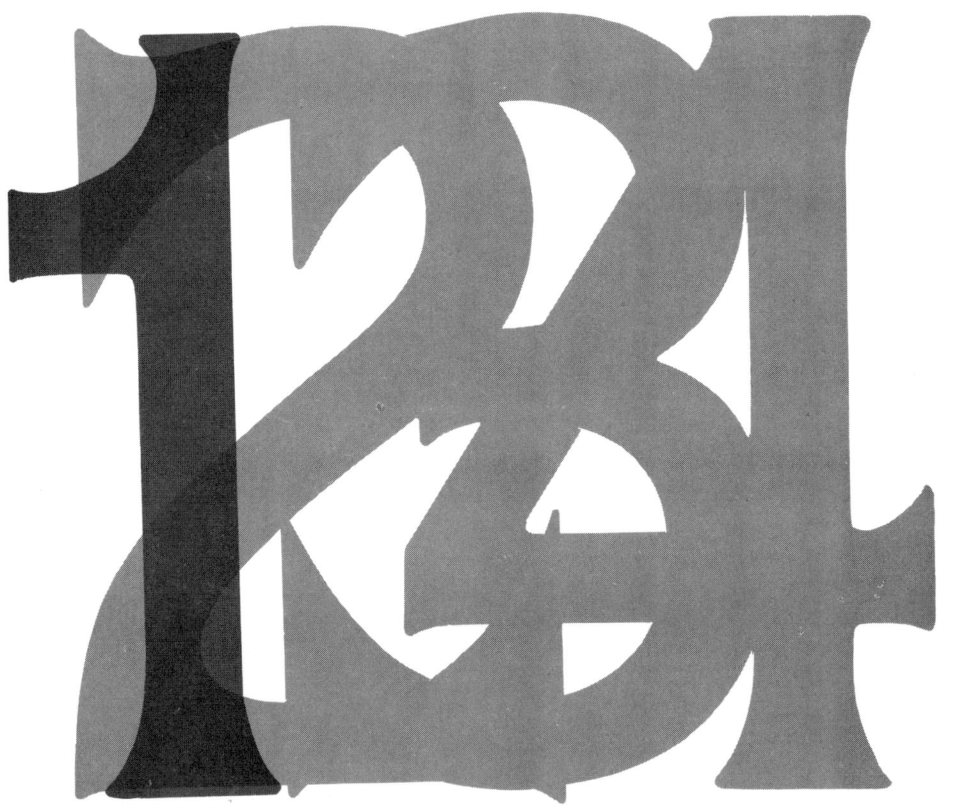

Perspectives on public administration

Each reader of this book brings to it some background information about government and the administering of public programs, information gained through high-school or college courses in political science, through general reading, through conversations with others, and through personal encounters with public administrators. Some of you may even have job experience with a public administration agency. As a starting point for our examination of public administration, it is helpful to see how various observers view the field. The chapters in this part describe the field from several vantage points.

As with any subject of political importance, it is necessary to know something about the views held by the general public. As a result of our experiences, we continually form impressions of public administration and its administrators. These impressions are reinforced or contradicted by our discussions with others about their experiences and by reports from the communications media. From these various sources you approach this book with some more or less fully formulated and more or less deeply imbedded views about public administration. At the extremes, you may perceive government's employees to be loyal, industrious, and efficient servants of the public; or they may appear to be untrustworthy, lazy, incompetent, empire-building bureaucrats. Chapter 1 examines the views Americans hold of their public servants. It also studies the development of government services in the United States and analyzes the changes in American society that helped produce the public administrative apparatus we know today.

Although it is possible to trace the history of American public administration to our earliest days, not until the end of the last century did it emerge as an identifiable field of study. Chapter 2 makes clear that the roots of this emergence are embedded deeply in history. The chapter's focus, however, is upon administration as a process; and most of the significant developments in the administrative process occurred, in the present century, as administrators and students of the process launched many reform efforts. Finally, chapter 2 examines public administration as an academic discipline. Originally joined closely to political science, it enjoys today a semi-independence, with ties not just to political science but also to the disciplines of business administration and management as well.

The expanding scope of American public administration

We can all agree that the activities of public administrators pervade the lives of most Americans. A visitor from a past century, accustomed to a social system in which each individual or family unit was largely self-sufficient, would immediately detect the tightly woven net of public services that undergirds the present version of the "American way." Such a guest from the past would probably be more acute than we at spotting the individual government programs and the specific services performed by public administrators, for we have grown so accustomed to them that they seem a natural part of our lives. Only when controversy develops around one of these programs are Americans sensitized to the role of government and to the performance of public administrators.

As students seeking to understand public administration, however, we need the sensitization without the controversy. We need to examine dispassionately the importance of public administration to

American life. This chapter attempts to accomplish this in three ways. First, governmental activities are grouped, or classified, in such a way that attention is called to the nature of the programs. Second, to show how public agencies reached their present states, the development of the public sector in the United States is traced. Finally, a study of public opinion surveys shows what Americans think about the public sector.

Classifying public programs

Any inventory and analysis of the myriad public programs in existence confronts an apparently chaotic scene. To impose some order on this situation, let us consider some classification schemes that can be applied to the programs.

Level of government classification

Perhaps the first such scheme to come to mind involves classifying programs according to the level of government—federal, state, or local—that supplies them. Unfortunately, the usefulness of this analytical scheme is limited, because many activities of government are now supported by all three levels. Prime examples are education and law enforcement; although these two functions were once almost purely local, today there is extensive state and federal involvement in both. The same can be said about many other programs. Yet because there are still some important distinctions, because public administrators frequently take pride in working for a particular governmental level, and because the public views the three levels differently, it is worthwhile to examine the scope of services that each provides.

Government costs money, and one way of developing an understanding of the roles of federal, state, and local governments is to examine the expenditures of each level. Table 1-1 provides comparative data for 1976. It should come as no surprise that the federal government, which accounts for more than three-fifths of the total, is the biggest spender. The remainder is shared by the state and local levels of government.

One aspect of the table's figures requires explanation: grants from one level to another are treated as expenditures of the granting, *not* the receiving (and ultimately the spending), government. Thus, federal grants to states and localities for highways, hospitals, welfare

Table 1-1. Government expenditures and employment in the United States, 1976

Government levels	Dollars (millions)	Percent	Employees (thousands)	Percent
Federal	389,905	62	4,929	29
State	128,718	21	3,343	20
Local	107,492	17	8,826	52
Total	626,115	100	17,098	101[a]

Source: U.S. Bureau of the Census, *Governmental Finances in 1975–76* (Washington, D.C.: U.S. Government Printing Office, 1977), p. 4; U.S. Bureau of the Census, *Statistical Abstract of the United States: 1977,* p. 306; and unpublished information provided by U.S. Department of Defense.

[a]Percent is greater than 100 because of rounding.

programs, etc., are counted solely as federal expenditures. This helps account for the table's revelation that *local* government employees outnumber those of the other two levels. Furthermore, it should be noted that local employment includes most elementary and secondary teachers. In fact, 55 percent of the local employees work in the field of education. The remainder provide the wide variety of city services (street maintenance, police protection, sanitation services, recreation programs, etc.), county services (rural law enforcement, public welfare, public health services, etc.), and services of special districts (street lighting, garbage collection, flood protection, etc.).

The historical section that follows explores the development of the programs that these figures represent, but it is worth noting here that during the first half of the present century the dominant trend was toward expansion of the *federal* portion of total government expenditures. In 1902, the proportions of total spending accounted for by each level were: federal, 35 percent; state, 11 percent; and local, 55 percent. By 1950, however, the pattern had changed significantly. The federal share had nearly doubled, to 64 percent, as had the state share, to 18 percent; and the local share was 18 percent, only one-third of its former level. As table 1-1 indicates, the federal government's share of total government expenditures has actually shrunk slightly over the last quarter-century. It was state government that took up the slack, and the local government share declined slightly.

Functional classification

A second useful scheme of classifying government programs groups programs into broad functional categories. The Bureau of the Census uses such a method for presenting expenditures of governments. The bureau's categories are displayed in table 1-2, together with the proportion of government funds devoted to each in 1976.

Scanning the list, one can imagine the plethora of specific programs that underlies each functional category. Included under "National defense and international relations," for example, are most of the myriad activities of our armed forces and the many services provided for American citizens and corporations beyond our borders, aid given to other nations, and the conduct of traditional diplomacy by the Department of State. "Education," of course, ranges from earliest childhood to extension programs of continuing education for the elderly, and from traditional classroom instruction to innovative, multimedia efforts. "Old age, survivors, disability, and health insurance" is the Social Security program, which also includes Medicare. Readers in some states might be puzzled by the table's reference to "Liquor stores" as a government program, but the governments of seventeen states operate these institutions as a means of regulating the industry and generating state revenue.

Control or service classification

A third possible classification, which proves useful in conjunction with the functional categories in table 1-2, is to group programs as being either control oriented or service oriented.[1] Notice, however, that some of the functional categories contain both control and service elements. The health and hospitals category, for example, includes both regulatory controls—ranging from local inspection of food-service facilities to federal regulation of foods and drugs—and the provision of service—through clinics, immunization programs, and medical research. Some categories, such as police protection and corrections, are more clearly control oriented, while others, such as education, are primarily service oriented. Similar comments could be made about other functional categories. It is useful to remember that American governments today are deeply involved in both control and service activities.

---

[1]Daniel Katz et al., *Bureaucratic Encounters: A Pilot Study in the Evaluation of Government Services* (Ann Arbor: Institute for Social Research, University of Michigan, 1975).

Table 1-2. Functional distribution of total government expenditures, 1976

Function	Dollars (millions)	Percent
Education	106,255	17
National defense and international relations	100,414	16
Old age, survivors, disability, and health insurance	88,300	14
Public welfare	45,129	7
Interest on general debt	39,575	6
Health and hospitals	27,570	4
Highways	24,201	4
Utilities and liquor stores	19,542	3
Unemployment compensation	19,160	3
Natural resources	16,958	3
Employee retirement	16,774	3
Police protection and corrections	14,739	2
Postal service	13,748	2
General control and financial administration	13,351	2
Housing and urban renewal	5,435	1
Space research and technology	3,691	1
Air transportation	3,359	1
Other	67,914	11
Total	626,115	100

Source: Bureau of the Census, *Governmental Finances in 1975–76* (Washington, D.C.: U.S. Government Printing Office, 1977), p. 13.

Many more classification schemes might help in categorizing government programs. For instance, they could be classified according to whether spending was by general governments, responsible for many services (cities, counties, states), or by special districts, responsible for a single service (lighting districts, water districts, fire protection districts). Another possibility would be a classification according to the population of the governmental jurisdiction providing the programs. While each of these could be useful, the three presented here are sufficient to focus attention on the wide scope of government programs and to point out some of the important services that greatly depend upon public administrators.

American public programs in historical perspective

The two-hundred-year history of the United States reveals a pattern of almost continuous expansion of government programs. Such a historical examination can place current changes in government programs in proper perspective; suggest explanations for the growth of government; and help in evaluating the long-term effects of contemporary efforts to decrease the scope of government programs. Since past events constrain future decisions, a study of history also can provide important insights into the context in which today's public administrator functions.

Because of a lack of solid data, any effort to look back two hundred years is fraught with difficulty. While we know with considerable precision what government programs are like today (their expenditures, their employees, their clients), we lack much basic information about earlier programs. Ironically, the availability of such information today results from the activities of one of the very agencies in which we are interested—the Bureau of the Census. In 1902 this agency became a permanent institution; thereafter it undertook to assemble data on government itself, much as it does on population. For the twentieth century we can rely on census data, but for earlier years we must draw on a variety of sources and attempt to fill gaps through informed speculation.

The beginnings: 1776–1800

During the colonial period, governmental responsibility rested with the individual colonies. The Revolutionary War and the establishment of union under the Articles of Confederation did little to alter that pattern—except that thereafter the responsibility fell to independent states rather than to colonies.

One of the major needs at the time of independence was for a satisfactory communication system—a network of roads and a postal system. Roads had been almost entirely a local or county responsibility, and there was little coordination or consistency as one tried to travel from place to place. Principal roads failed to meet at county boundaries; some were in good repair, others were barely passable. In the previous century some progress had been made in mail service. In 1673, when mail service from Boston to New York began, the trip took three weeks. By 1790, the time had been reduced to five days. Longer distances, however, continued to present great problems: the Philadelphia-to-Georgia trip required a minimum of thirteen days and sometimes took several months.[2] Under the Articles of Confederation little was changed, since the weak central institution—the Congress—had almost no impact on solving such basic domestic problems. The government maintained a Department of Foreign Affairs, and there was a secretary of war assisted by three clerks and a messenger and supported by an army of seven hundred.[3] Although there was a Treasury Board, the central government's income depended on requisitions from the states, which had allowed their contributions to fall almost to zero by 1789, when our present constitution was implemented.

It had become obvious that a system of *national* political and administrative structures was needed to address adequately the many pressing problems. Unfortunately, most colonial regimes afforded few opportunities for the development of administrative expertise among the colony's people. This was just as true of the thirteen American colonies, as it is in the newly independent nations of today. There were few governmental positions in which individuals could gain the experience necessary to take full responsibility for large and elaborate public agencies. In business too there were few places where administrators could have been trained. Most business concerns were tiny; for example, a Connecticut button factory was considered large because it employed twelve people; major shipyards employed no more than fifty workers; the Massachusetts Bank had three employees.[4] The Revolutionary Army was about the only large organization, and not surprisingly, many of the leaders of the new government bureaucracies were former army leaders.

After 1789, then, President Washington and the Federalists had to establish a working central government on this foundation. One of the

---

[2]Leonard D. White, *The Federalists: A Study in Administrative History* (New York: The Macmillan Company, 1948), pp. 480–81.

[3]Jennings B. Sanders, *Evolution of the Executive Departments of the Continental Congress, 1774–1789* (Chapel Hill: University of North Carolina Press, 1935), p. 107.

[4]White, *The Federalists,* p. 470.

first questions to be answered was whether the new central government should administer its own laws or depend on the states to do so. It would have been possible to create a central government that had the power to enact national laws but relied on the state administrative establishments for their enforcement. (Contemporary West Germany is a federal nation that has—in large measure—followed this course.) Although something of a mixed pattern developed at first in the newly united states, the general trend was toward direct federal administration.

Perhaps the most important step for the new federal government was to begin collecting revenue; customs duties were the major source. Individual states had been taxing imports; this possibility was now available to the federal government. In July of 1789, just three months after President Washington assumed office, a Customs Service was established to employ a field staff placed up and down the coast to collect revenues at each port. By 1792, the Treasury Department, of which the Customs Service was a part, had 660 employees.[5] In comparison with the minute size of the business firms mentioned above, this was a gigantic administrative establishment—and it was not alone. In 1790, there were seventy-five post offices, each requiring a postmaster. Total federal government employment in the early 1790s was probably only about 900, but by the year 1800 the total had grown to around 3,000. A principal cause of this expansion was the creation of new post offices, whose numbers jumped from 75 to 903 in just ten years.[6]

In addition to the 3,000 federal employees, state and local employees continued to staff many of the offices created under the Articles of Confederation or under the colonial regime. Precise data are not available, but one estimate made at the time was that there were approximately 12,000 of these subnational employees, mostly elected officials.[7] Despite this seemingly large body of employees and officials, only minimal public services were provided—even in the larger cities, where such services were severely needed. New York City, for example, had a population of approximately 33,000, but it had no municipal water system and no city sewage system. Only the main streets of the principal cities were well maintained, even by the somewhat primitive standards of the day. By 1800, a few cities were making an effort to provide street lighting and a night watch, but none had regular day police or full-time fire departments. Few efforts were made to establish public schools.

To explore more fully the extent of public activity during this early period we can trace the spending of government money. The decision of the federal government to pay off the war debts of the states was per-

---

[5]Ibid., p. 255.

[6]Ibid., pp. 178 and 256.

[7]Ibid., p. 255.

haps one of the most crucial events after the acceptance of the new constitution. During the Revolutionary War most of the states had borrowed heavily to support the army, and they had struggled under this burden during the Confederation period. In 1792, the federal government had expenditures of just over $5 million, and fully 60 percent of this was required to pay interest on the debt. At the turn of the century $3 million was still being spent for debt interest. But total federal spending had more than doubled in eight years: $7 million was being devoted to federal programs.[8]

This money, a huge amount for that time, allowed for some new initiatives and the expansion of some existing programs. Of course, the defense, foreign affairs, and postal establishments continued to be supported; the collection of taxes and management of money consumed some of the resources; a federal court system had been established and needed support; money was spent in governing the western territories and in negotiating with the Indians; public lands had to be managed; and efforts were begun to regulate commerce through the registration of ships and the building of lighthouses. From meager beginnings just eleven years before, the administrative establishment of the federal government had become rather extensive, as had the range of programs it carried out.

Although we are not aware of any study that satisfactorily documents this matter, governmental growth probably occurred at the state and local levels as well. Based on information available for a few states and cities, it seems that all the states together were probably spending about $2 million per year in the 1790s. The larger cities, such as Philadelphia and New York, were spending about two dollars per capita. Most of the population lived a considerable distance from towns and cities and, consequently, benefited little from these meager local expenditures. These expenditure figures for state and local governments probably climbed during our first decade under the present constitution, but it is impossible to say by how much.

A century of growth: 1800–1900

Many of the major developments in nineteenth-century governmental activity necessitated sizable expenditures and the creation of substantial administrative establishments.

— Early in the nineteenth century, states and cities began ambi-

---

[8]Paul Studenski and Herman E. Kroos, *Financial History of the United States,* 2d ed. (New York: McGraw Hill, 1963), p. 54.

Expanding scope of American public administration／

／19

tious efforts to finance the construction of canals; among the first was the highly successful Erie Canal, a model that was rapidly copied in several jurisdictions. Turnpikes also became popular government projects. Later, attention turned to railroads; several states undertook the funding, and the federal government lent its support through land grants and loans to railroad companies. In addition, the federal government spent large sums on other public works projects: roads, lighthouses, and military installations.

— Public education, at the elementary, secondary, and collegiate levels, developed during the century. In some cases, governments gave grants to private institutions, but in other instances, public ones were established.

— Public institutions for the care of the physically and mentally ill and for the incarceration of criminals were established.

— The Civil War was a major expenditure of the last century, and its financial impact upon government lasted for decades through charges for interest and principal on borrowed money and through the payments of veterans' pensions.

— Government regulation of various industries began. For instance, farmers in areas where a particular railroad had a monopoly complained bitterly about the seemingly exorbitant rates charged to ship their goods. States and then the federal government began to regulate the railroads.

— Cities poured considerable money into the paving of streets, the building of water and sewer systems, and the improving of police and fire protection. Public parks were established, as were public museums. The expansion of the cities in both population and geographical area necessitated considerably expanded services.

— Rural areas received such benefits as homestead land grants, grants for agricultural colleges and experiment stations, and rural free delivery by the Post Office Department. The Department of Agriculture was established as a cabinet department.

Most of these programs, begun during the last century, have lived on, with some modifications, into the present. As the twentieth century opened, the growth of government's functions and superstructure had become a pronounced feature of American life.

The twentieth century

Fortunately, better data sources are available for this portion of our history than for the earlier eras. Table 1-3 provides a broad picture of the growth of government as measured by spending and employment levels. Total government spending has grown from considerably less

Table 1-3. Total government spending and employment, 1902–1976

Year	Expenditures[a] unadjusted dollars (millions)	Year	Government employment (thousands)
1902	1,660	1900	1,401
1913	3,215	1910	1,964
1919	22,882[b]	1920	2,920
1922	9,297		
1927	11,220		
1932	12,437	1930	3,667
1938	17,675		
1940	20,417	1940	4,902

Source: Expenditure figures are from the Bureau of the Census as reported in Tax Foundation Inc., *Facts and Figures on Government Finance,* 19th ed. (N.Y.: Tax Foundation, Inc., 1977), p. 17; and from Bureau of the Census, *Government Finances, 1975–76,* p. 4.

Employment figures prior to 1950 are as estimated by Soloman Fabricant, *The Trend of Government Activity in the United States Since 1900* (New York: National Bureau of Economic Research, 1952), p. 198. Those since 1950 are from U.S. Bureau of the Census, *Census of Governments, 1972,* vol. 6, no. 4, p. 59; U.S. Bureau of the Census, *Statistical Abstract of the United States: 1977,* p. 306; and unpublished information provided by U.S. Department of Defense.

[a]Intergovernmental expenditures, such as grants-in-aid, shared taxes, and other payments are counted only once.

[b]Estimated. The expenditure figure for 1919 is taken from James M. Buchanan and Marilyn R. Flowers, *The Public Finance,* 4th ed. (Homewood, Ill.: Richard D. Irwin, Inc., 1975), p. 45.

Expanding scope of American public administration/

Table 1-3.   **Total government spending and employment, 1902-1976** (Continued)

Year	Expenditures[a] unadjusted dollars (millions)	Year	Government employment (thousands)
1942	45,576		
1944	109,947		
1946	79,707		
1948	55,081		
1950	70,334	1950	8,519
1952	99,847	1952	10,664
1954	111,332	1954	10,489
1956	115,796	1956	10,486
1958	134,931	1958	10,894
1960	151,288	1960	11,309
1962	176,240	1962	12,090
1964	196,431	1964	12,746
1966	224,813	1966	14,675
1968	282,645	1968	15,796
1970	332,985	1970	15,974
1972	400,395	1972	16,131
1974	478,325	1974	16,784
1975	556,339	1975	17,083
1976	626,115	1976	17,098

than $2 billion dollars per year at the beginning of the century to over $0.5 trillion dollars at the century's three-quarter mark. The present level of spending, a number almost too large to comprehend, represents an increase of more than 37,600 percent since the beginning of the century.[9]

Although the rate and extent of growth are not nearly as great as the increase in expenditures, the table's employment column presents a similar picture. During three-quarters of a century, government employment has moved from almost 1.5 million persons to over 17 million, a growth of more than 1,100 percent.

In examining this broad sweep of recent history there are several things to note. Most important, the rate of growth of spending and employment over the entire period has fluctuated, especially during wartime, but the trend in both indicators is clearly upward. Table 1-4 presents percentage changes over three consecutive twenty-year periods, beginning with 1902. Expenditures grew fastest in the period from 1902 to 1922 and slowest from 1942 to 1962. The employment data include both civilian and military personnel, so it is not surprising that the interwar period saw the least percentage increase in government employment of the three periods. As we will not complete another twenty-year period until 1982, the table also shows the twenty-year period from 1956 to 1976. During this time, the growth of expenditures was greater than from 1942 to 1962 and from 1922 to 1942, but less than that from 1902 to 1922. Much recent political rhetoric about the multiplication of bureaucrats to the contrary, the percentage increase in the number of employees over the most recent twenty years is the lowest of any of the twenty-year periods studied.

Figure 1-1 presents graphically the rate of growth. Expenditures are plotted on a ratio graph, which is so constructed that attention is focused on growth rates. Notice that on the vertical scale the distance from 2 billion to 4 billion is the same as from 10 billion to 20 billion or from 200 billion to 400 billion. That is, whenever expenditures increase by a certain percentage (100 percent in these examples) the line will rise by the same amount, regardless of the base from which it starts. Consequently, the more nearly vertical the line representing expenditure, the greater the *growth rate*. To provide a base against which to compare the actual growth rate, it is helpful to note that a *constant* annual growth rate of 8.35 percent would have been required for the expenditures to grow from $1.7 billion to $626 billion. Obviously, the

------

[9]Dealing with billions can make comprehension difficult. The following may prove helpful: If one starts counting seconds, it will take approximately twelve days to count one *million* seconds. It will require thirty-two years, however, to count one *billion*, a fact pointed out to the authors by Congressman Tom Steed of Oklahoma, a member of the U.S. House Appropriations Committee.

Table 1-4. Changes in government spending and employment

| Spending | | Employment | |
Period	Percent increase	Period	Percent increase
1902–1922	460	1900–1920	108
1922–1942	390	1920–1940	68
1942–1962	287	1940–1960	131
1956–1976	441	1956–1976	63

Source: Calculated from data in table 1–3.

growth has not been constant. In figure 1-1 both the actual growth rate and this hypothetical constant 8.35 percent growth rate are plotted. Wherever the lines are parallel, the rate of actual growth is 8.35 percent, even if one line is above or below the other. It is the *slope* of the line that reveals the rate of growth. Clearly, it was during World War I and World War II that expenditures grew far more rapidly than the norm; then they actually shrank at the conclusion of the wars. During the 1920s and early 1930s growth was considerably slower than the norm, but otherwise actual growth has been very close to 8.35 percent per year, especially since the mid-1950s. To summarize: although the rates vary somewhat, the level of government expenditure has expanded almost continually.

As we did in the previous section, let us identify certain programs that became responsibilities of public administrators during the first half of the twentieth century. Of course, during this period the United States became a world leader and assumed a growing role in international affairs. This led to increased expenditures both for peaceful and for military purposes. The assumption of this role has been costly and has required the hiring of large numbers of military and civilian employees.

Additionally, there was a considerable expansion of government to regulate various aspects of business and industry. The regulation of railroads, which began in the nineteenth century, continued (although rails have become a less important part of the transportation network), and regulation was extended to other means of transportation, especially shipping, trucks, and aircraft. In the pursuance of these activities, such agencies were created as the Interstate Commerce Commission (1887), the Federal Maritime Commission (1936), and the Civil Aeronautics Board (1938). The advent of radio and television called for some control over use of the limited broadcast spectrum, and the Federal

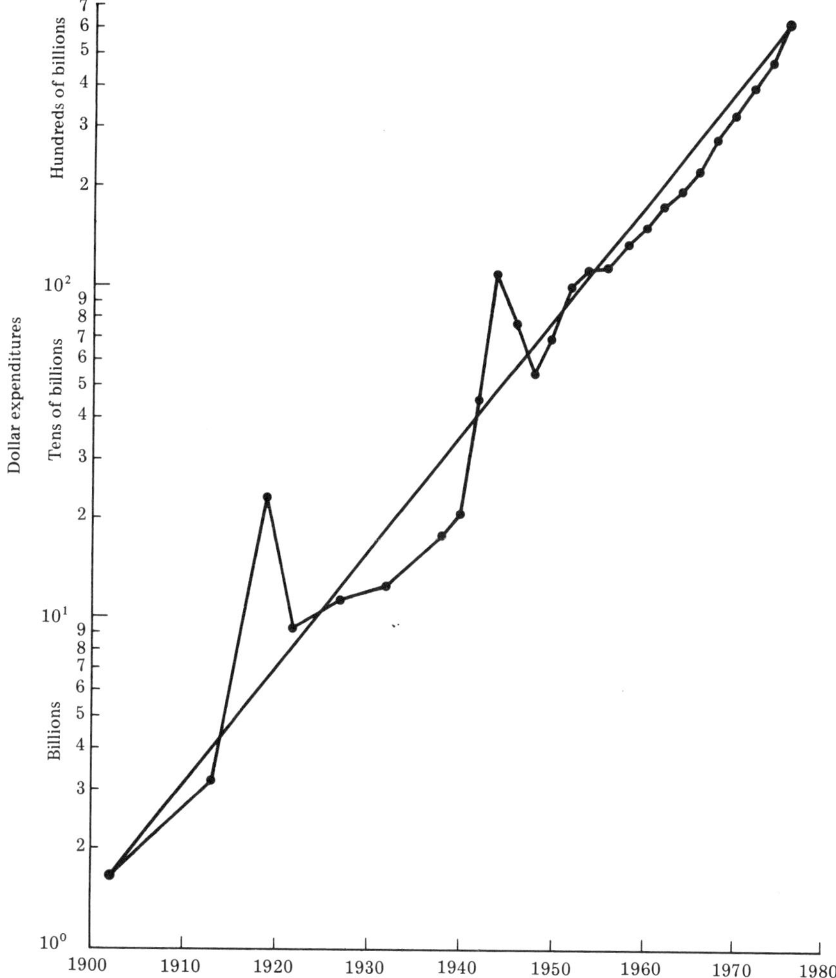

Figure 1-1.   Total government spending and constant annual increase, 1902-1976 (ratio graph)

Communications Commission assumed this responsibility in 1934. The breaking up of industrial monopolies was another important activity of the federal government in the early part of the twentieth century; the Federal Trade Commission, which commenced in 1914, was given jurisdiction over certain antitrust statutes, and the commission—along with the Antitrust Division of the Justice Department—continues to act in this area. All of these efforts to regulate required, and still require, money and personnel.

The single industrial product that probably has done more than any other to shape the lives of Americans and the contemporary face of

Expanding scope of American public administration

the nation is the automobile. Its impact on government programs has been tremendous. Suddenly roads that had seemed satisfactory, if not superb, were obsolete. A huge investment in highways and bridges has been made (the cost of the interstate highway program alone, begun under the Eisenhower administration, has been estimated to exceed $50 billion), and to this must be added government expenditures for law enforcement to control their use. Air transportation also has required a considerable investment, both for airports and for the coordination of air traffic.

Health policy is another area in which government has become increasingly active. An early impetus for government's entry into the field was the potential danger in the mass distribution of tainted food or drugs. Government began by attempting to guard the quality of imported food and gradually expanded the testing and inspection system to cover—at least minimally—most foods and drugs sold in the United States. This would have been an unnecessary activity in earlier times, when many individuals produced much of what they consumed and acquired other foodstuffs locally, usually from people they saw personally. A family—or at most a few dozen people—might die of food poisoning, but with mass distribution, disaster could strike, and many thousands might be killed. The Food and Drug Administration was created in 1931. In another health area, the provision of hospitals continued to be a mixed enterprise, with both government and private involvement, but enlarging upon a trend begun in the nineteenth century, many states moved to establish some health care facilities for those not able to pay.

Education at various levels has been generally identified as a proper enterprise for the public sector, and it has been made available to more and more people. Federal, state, and local governments annually spend enormous sums for the building of classrooms, the paying of teachers, and the support of students (National Defense Educational Loans, Veterans' Assistance).

Programs for the aged and those physically unable to work have grown, especially since the Great Depression of the 1930s. Easy transportation and the development of large cities made it commonplace for younger members of the family to move away from the family home; thus, they were less able to care for parents and grandparents than if they had remained at home. Government stepped into the void and began to provide minimal assistance through the Social Security system and related programs. At the same time, the federal government began to assume a larger role in attempting to manage the economy in order to prevent a recurrence of the serious and lengthy depressions experienced in the past.

While not nearly all of the expanded and new activities of government in the first half of the twentieth century have been mentioned, enough have been cited to provide a general feeling for what has been purchased with expanded governmental spending. We now zero in even closer—to the last quarter-century. Table 1-5, which focuses on this period, indicates that government expenditures have grown from $70 billion dollars to $626 billion, an increase of 790 percent. The table provides three adjustments to these government expenditure figures.

Table 1-5. Government expenditures, 1950–1976

Year	Unadjusted dollars (millions)	Dollars per capita	Adjusted per capita (1976 dollars)	Percent of annual GNP
1950	70,334	468	1,047	25
1952	99,847	646	1,335	29
1954	111,332	696	1,453	30
1956	115,796	697	1,405	28
1958	134,931	784	1,516	30
1960	151,288	846	1,630	30
1962	176,240	955	1,844	31
1964	196,431	1,034	2,000	30
1966	224,813	1,155	2,119	30
1968	282,645	1,423	2,541	33
1970	332,985	1,643	2,725	34
1972	400,395	1,931	2,966	34
1974	478,325	2,270	2,594	34
1975	556,339	2,621	2,742	36
1976	626,115	2,926	2,926	36
Percent increase 1950–1976	790	525	179	

Source: Unadjusted figures are from table 1–3; per capita figures are from Tax Foundation, Inc., *Facts and Figures on Government Finance,* 19th ed. (New York: Tax Foundation, Inc., 1977), p. 18, and were calculated using the population estimate for January of each year, excluding armed forces overseas; figures for per capita 1976 dollars are calculated from first two columns, using the Wholesale Price Index for All Commodities, reported in U.S. Department of Commerce, *Business Conditions Digest* (May 1978), p. 98. Gross National Product figures used in calculation are from U.S. Department of Commerce, *Business Conditions Digest* (November 1977), p. 96.

Expanding scope of American public administration/

First, recognizing that a part of the increased spending has resulted from the need to provide services (health care, police protection, education, etc.) to a larger number of people, a per capita adjustment is made. In isolating growth that occurred *even after* allowing for population expansion, we find that government spending climbed from less than $500 in 1950 to more than $2,900 in 1976. Thus, barring deficit spending, governments must receive in annual revenue more than $2,900 for every individual in the United States; for a family of four, the total is over $11,000. Some of the goods and services provided, such as national defense or regulation of radio and television stations, are not readily measurable by individuals. Others can be more easily evaluated by the individual: streets and highways, sidewalks, buildings and staff of educational institutions, libraries, museums, water supply, sewage and refuse handling, police protection, air traffic safety. Do you get your $2,900 worth? Each person must make an individual judgment.

The second adjustment in table 1-5 converts spending figures to *per capita constant (1976) dollars* and removes the effects of both inflation and population growth. Since recent decades have suffered from considerable inflation, more of today's (less valuable) dollars would be required to provide the same services that fewer 1950 dollars bought then; in fact, over *twice* as many now would be needed. The major conclusion to be drawn from this finding is that once the effects of population change and inflation are removed, the growth of spending has not been as great as the growth in unadjusted dollars would suggest. Instead of a change of 790 percent, there is a change of only 179 percent.

A third way of analyzing the increase in government spending is to relate it to the gross national product.[10] Measured thusly, public spending has increased much less during the period, from one-quarter of the GNP to slightly over one-third of it. Viewed in these terms, the expansion is not as great as the unadjusted figures suggest. To a large extent, the growth of government spending has been simply keeping pace with economic growth. Since 1970, however, a period of recession has slowed economic growth, and the relative size of government has expanded rather sharply.

Government employment figures are presented in table 1-6. The raw employment figures, which reveal much less growth than is often

---

[10]The gross national product is the total market value of the final output of goods and services produced in the economy in a year. It can be argued that comparing total government spending to GNP overstates the size of the public sector. Despite this, total expenditures have been used here because they provide comprehensive coverage of government activities. For further discussion, see Richard A. Musgrave and Peggy B. Musgrave, *Public Finance in Theory and Practice* (New York: McGraw-Hill, 1973), pp. 109–20.

Table 1-6. Government employment, 1950–1976

Year	Employment (thousands)	Percent of labor force
1950	8,519	13
1952	10,664	16
1954	10,489	16
1956	10,486	15
1958	10,894	15
1960	11,309	16
1962	12,090	16
1964	12,746	17
1966	14,675	19
1968	15,796	19
1970	15,974	19
1972	16,131	18
1974	16,784	18
1975	17,083	18
1976	17,098	18
Percent increase	101	

Source: U.S. Bureau of the Census, *Census of Governments, 1972,* vol. 6, no. 4, p. 59; U.S. Bureau of the Census, *Statistical Abstract of the United States, 1977,* p. 306; unpublished data provided by U.S. Department of Defense; unpublished data provided by U.S. Department of Labor.

popularly supposed, are instructive. When government employment is analyzed as a percentage of the labor force, it is apparent that expansion of public employment has been quite small. Although political candidates commonly decry the fact that "almost 20 percent" of the labor force works for government, this is not dramatically different from the middle 1950s. In fact, the level is now below the peak during the Vietnam conflict.

Many aspects of government expansion during the past quarter-century are so familiar—and their consequences so obvious—that a detailed treatment is not necessary for our present purposes. Perhaps it would be useful, however, to list some developments that profoundly affected public programs: the role of the United States in international affairs continued to grow, especially in connection with wars in Korea and Vietnam; educational systems expanded to serve larger numbers of students (although numbers later declined somewhat); the Social Security program, begun during the 1930s, expended large sums as participants reached retirement age; the first humans reached the moon; governments developed programs to cope with the social and fiscal problems of large cities; an interstate highway system was constructed at an enormous cost; the Medicare program was initiated, and governments played an important role in hospital construction. Even more developments could be listed, of course.

Public attitudes toward the public sector

The views that Americans have of their governments, of the public programs provided, and of the administrators who direct them, have been the subject of relatively little research. The few existing surveys of these facets of public opinion have been one-shot efforts, and we have no basis for tracing the development of attitudes. Thus, we know little about how these attitudes are affected by particular political events or encounters. Furthermore, reliable surveys of *any* type are relatively recent; consequently, the few conclusions that can be drawn concerning public attitudes toward government are limited, for the most part, to one fairly recent period.

Attitudes toward levels of government

As the previous section indicates, prior to independence the individual colonies and their local governments had responsibility for the provision of government services. But what did Americans think of such services? Unfortunately, no Gallup, Harris, Roper, or Sindlinger was present to find out. Because the federal experiment endured and federal government programs were established at an increasing rate, we can infer that a substantial number of Americans accepted the central government as a provider of services that formerly had been administered by colonial (then by state) governments, by local governments, or had not been provided at all. Although an important strand of the political culture surely identified with Thomas Jefferson's often quoted dictum, "that government is best which governs least," the almost constant

**Table 1-7. Citizens' perceptions of impact of government, by level
(percents)**

	Local	State	Federal
Great deal	38	39	63
Only somewhat	33	38	21
Hardly at all	26	19	13
Not sure	3	4	3
Total	100	100	100

Source: U.S. Senate Committee on Government Operations, Subcommittee on Intergovernmental Relations, *Confidence and Concern: Citizens View American Government, Part 1* (Washington: U.S. Government Printing Office, 1973), p. 272. *Question:* "In general, how much do you feel local government [state government, federal government] affects your life personally?"

expansion of public programs at the federal level suggests continued public acceptance of those programs.

Since we are trying to understand public administration *today,* it is fortunate that some studies of recent public attitudes toward government programs are available. In a survey of adult Americans conducted in 1973, researchers sought to measure a number of attitudes and perceptions held about government.[11] One of the key questions tried to determine the extent to which Americans felt that government activity had an *impact* on them; table 1-7 reveals the results. While about two-fifths of the respondents felt state and local governments had a "great deal" of impact on their lives, almost two-thirds of the national sample believed the federal government had such an impact. This response says nothing about approval or disapproval of such impact, but it does indicate the important role that people think the federal government has in their lives.

When respondents were asked to indicate the ways each level of government has its impact, their references to the federal government tended to be rather general: "laws," "legislation," "administration not trustworthy." Considering the Internal Revenue Service's apparent insatiability, it is not surprising that by far the most common percep-

[11]U.S. Senate Committee on Government Operations, Subcommittee on Intergovernmental Relations, *Confidence and Concern: Citizens View American Government, A Survey of Public Attitudes, Part I* (Washington: U.S. Government Printing Office, 1973).

tions of the federal government's impact were references—usually negative—to *taxes*. The foundations of the taxpayer's revolt of the late 1970s were already laid.

Taxes also received the greatest attention when the impacts of state and local governments were mentioned, but respondents cited specific programs, too. For states, these included highways, education, driver licensing, and the welfare system. For local governments, the most often cited were police protection, education, streets, zoning, sanitation, and water.[12]

Not only is the federal government's impact seen to be greater than that of states and localities, it also is perceived primarily as a *negative* impact. Although an element of this negative perception is apparent in reported feelings about the other two levels as well, there is also far greater recognition of the *positive* impact of these lower levels. From the public administrator's perspective, the tendency of many Americans to see government as a negative influence can be quite frustrating. It is also striking that even massive programs are given scant mention as having any impact whatsoever, negative or positive.

Contact with government

If Americans are so unlikely to volunteer the feeling that specific programs have a large impact upon their lives, does this mean that citizens actually have little contact with government? The Survey Research Center at the University of Michigan conducted a study that sought to answer this obviously important, but heretofore almost totally neglected, question.[13] Like the study cited above, this one polled adult Americans in 1973. This time, however, the investigators asked respondents if they had sought any help from government agencies in

1. finding a job,

2. training for a better job,

3. getting compensation for accidents or injuries,

4. obtaining unemployment compensation,

---

[12]Ibid., pp. 104–109.

[13]Katz et al., *Bureaucratic Encounters*. But see Herbert Jacob's pioneering article "Contact with Government Agencies: A Preliminary Analysis of the Distribution of Government Services" *Midwest Journal of Political Science* 16 (February 1972): 123–47.

5. receiving help for dependent children or qualifying for other forms of relief or public assistance,

6. getting medical and hospital care, or

7. receiving retirement benefits.

The Michigan researchers found that 58 percent reported utilizing one or more of these specific government services.[14] Since the list presented to the respondents was a greatly abbreviated sample of the total number of problems with which government agencies deal, the amount of reported contact seems impressive. Whether or not they readily list the particular programs affecting their lives, many Americans *do* experience contacts with government agencies and, hence, with public administrators.

Attitudes toward scope of government

Since the scope of government programs has been expanding throughout our national history, it is interesting to ask whether the dominant mood of the country now calls for a halt to such expansion. Several states have considered limitations on state spending. Tennessee passed a constitutional amendment in March of 1978 that ties permissible growth in state spending to growth in personal income. In June of 1978, California passed its *Proposition 13,* which has these main provisions:

1. local governments cannot collect taxes higher than 1 percent of "full cash value," based on 1975–76 assessments;

2. increases in assessments are limited to 2 percent per year;

3. reassessments are allowed only when property is sold;

4. a two-thirds majority vote of both houses of the legislature is required to enact any new revenue-raising taxes;

5. local governments are prohibited from imposing any new property taxes;

6. a two-thirds majority vote of citizens is required to enact other new local taxes.[15]

---

[14]Katz et al., *Bureaucratic Encounters,* p. 20.

[15]See Brigett Rouson, " 'Taxpayers' Revolt': States Vie to Curb Taxes, Spending," *Congressional Quarterly Weekly Report* 36 (8 July 1978): 1729.

In the wake of Proposition 13's passage, several other states and Congress began to pay increased attention to the alleged "taxpayers' revolt."

But are Americans ready to accept the curtailment of services implied by the lowering of taxes? The available data are inconclusive. Data collected in 1973 indicated fairly wide satisfaction with the level of services. Sixty-five percent of the Survey Research Center's respondents replied negatively when asked whether government should do less if such action would result in lower taxes. Eighty-nine percent of the national sample thought that government should do *more,* as long as taxes would not be increased. When the question included the likelihood of increased taxes, however, 57 percent opposed extending services.[16]

More recently, about a month after the passage of Proposition 13, the Associated Press and NBC News conducted a national poll that showed increased concern about the levels of taxation. According to the Associated Press, "about half of those questioned said they supported a one-third reduction in federal and state taxes, even if it means a major cut in government programs." Behind this sentiment was the belief that there is too much waste in government. Again quoting the AP, "This is further reflected by the suggestion, voiced by about half of those interviewed, that taxes at all levels could be cut by one-third without reducing services."[17]

At about the same time, an ABC News-Louis Harris poll asked a national sample of respondents whether they favored a California-scale tax cut if it meant reducing spending on particular policy sectors by 35 percent. When presented with the possibility of such a cut in "aid to the elderly, disabled, and poor," only 24 percent favored such a tax reduction. Given the opportunity to consider similar cuts in "fire protection," "educating children in public schools," "police protection," "service in public hospitals and health care," "the number of teachers in public schools," and "maintaining and repairing roads," those favoring the reductions increased only to 26, 27, 30, 31, 35, and 38 percent, respectively. The highest number, 42 percent, favored such a reduction in spending for "collecting trash and garbage."[18] At least, these surveys indicate that results are highly dependent on the wording of the questions. Furthermore, it is probably also reasonable to conclude that while Americans want taxes to be reduced, most are not willing to support reductions that would require significant cutbacks in basic government services.

---

[16]Katz et al., *Bureaucratic Encounters,* p. 138.

[17]Associated Press, 18 June 1978.

[18]Reported in "People Say: 'Cut Taxes, but . . . ,' " *U.S. News and World Report,* 3 July 1978; p. 17.

Chapter one

Table 1-8. Citizens' evaluations of government offices on various dimensions (percents)

Evaluation	Giving prompt service	Really taking care of problem	Considerate treatment	Fair treatment	Avoiding mistakes	Correcting mistakes
	n=1,422	n=1,419	n=1,419	n=1,418	n=1,420	n=1,414
Bad	18	16	13	12	16	17
Moderate	69	69	69	67	64	59
Good	10	11	15	17	17	19
Don't know	3	4	4	4	4	5
Total	100	100	101[a]	100	101[a]	100

Source: Computed from Daniel Katz et al., *Bureaucratic Encounters: A Pilot Study in the Evaluation of Government Services* (Ann Arbor: University of Michigan Survey Research Center, Institute for Social Research, 1975), p. 119. Katz et al. presented responses along a seven-point scale, ranging from "very bad" to "excellent." Here they are grouped so that responses 1 and 2 are defined as "Bad"; 3, 4, and 5 are "Moderate"; and 6 and 7 are "Good."

[a]Percent is greater than 100 because of rounding.

Satisfaction with government service

Since reductions in programs are not being emphatically demanded, one wonders whether the recipients of government service are generally satisfied, or whether they go along just because they see no alternative. The Survey Research Center study confronted this question in two ways—and got somewhat varied answers.

First, respondents were asked general questions about their views of government services. In response to a question that asked whether "most government offices do a good job," 61 percent gave a positive reply (that means, of course, that—including those who did not have an opinion—nearly two-fifths had something other than a clearly positive opinion).[19] Interviewees also were asked to respond to six statements about the usual performance of the general run of government agencies by rating them on a scale from 1 to 7. Table 1–8 displays their responses,

---

[19]Katz et al., *Bureaucratic Encounters*, p. 118.

Expanding scope of American public administration

which rate agencies according to promptness, "really taking care of the problem," consideration, fairness, and avoiding and correcting mistakes. Most individuals awarded moderate performance ratings, and fewer than one-fifth of the respondents evaluated government performance on any of the dimensions listed as either "good" or "bad." We see Americans, then, as something less than enthusiastic about the job performance of public administrators, and a small proportion are downright negative.

A second way of confronting this matter produced somewhat different results, however. Respondents were asked to evaluate *their own experiences* with specific agencies with which they mentioned having had contacts. Recall that only 61 percent reported feeling that most government offices do a good job; substantially more, 72 percent, reported being either "very satisfied" or "fairly well satisfied" with their own agency contacts. While only 11 percent said government officers are good at taking care of problems, 71 percent reported their own problems were solved. Only 17 percent ranked government "good" in terms of fairness, but 80 percent reported that they, *personally,* were treated fairly. Whereas only 10 percent rated government "good" on promptness of service, 45 percent said their own problems were handled "very efficiently."[20]

This pattern holds for other similar questions. When confronted with *generalized statements* about government services, Americans rate such services much lower than when asked about their *own experiences* with government agencies. It is plain that Americans are ambivalent in their views of government services.

The image of public service

A further complication for public administrators is that the opinions most Americans have of career government employees in general are not highly complimentary. Two questions were asked interviewees, one seeking to identify qualities that Americans feel such career administrators *should* have and the other seeking expressions of opinion regarding qualities that they *do* have. Honesty was seen as the most desirable quality (66 percent), but only 16 percent saw this as an accurate description of career administrators. Fifty-six percent of the respondents said administrators should be dedicated to hard work, but only 25 percent depicted administrators in this fashion. Only 1 percent thought that "just serving time" was a desirable quality, but 21 percent saw this as descriptive of career administrators' actions. Similarly, only 4 per-

---

[20]Ibid., pp. 119–22.

cent thought it was desirable for administrators to "do things by the book," but 23 percent attributed such behavior to public administrators.[21] Public administrators, as a class then, are seen as failing to exhibit the qualities that Americans view as desirable in career government employees. Thus, there exists a substantial expectations-perceptions gap.

Both the generally unfavorable image of public administrators and the ambivalent public attitudes toward government services present problems for public administrators. Seldom does an election occur in which at least one candidate does not attack "the bureaucracy." Yet when pressed for concrete reforms that would control the problems of bureaucracy, few candidates give specific replies; they simply say that "bureaucrats" should be more efficient and more dedicated to their jobs.

In large measure, the ambivalence about government activities rests upon Americans' imprecise and sometimes conflicting expectations of the public sector. Two dearly held American values are "equality of treatment" and "recognition of individualism." On the one hand, Americans insist that any two clients whose *situations* are alike be afforded an *equal level of service,* whether the two clients are patent applicants, welfare recipients, postal patrons, or university students. To assure that service levels are uniform for similar clients, administrators must devise standards, rules, qualifications, etc., that govern the behavior of those providing the service. This process is frequently characterized as "red tape."

To compound the problem, however, Americans also value uniqueness and individuality. Each person is seen as being in some way different from every other, and it is thought that such differences should be recognized and individual attention provided. Of course, to do so impinges on the ability to provide *equality* of service. Consequently, more red tape develops in order to specify particular circumstances that justify special treatment, but if the client's situation is truly unique, provision for the circumstances will not be found in the regulations. Should the service deliverer attempt to provide for them? The value demanding recognition of individualism says, "Yes," but the value demanding equality cries, "That's favoritism!" Since most of us prize both values, it is not surprising that we are often ambivalent in our attitudes about public administrators.

Further contributing to the ambivalence of Americans' evaluations of public sector personnel is the lack of an objective measure of performance. There is not, for example, a quantifiable goal such as "profit" with which to judge performance of the Department of Defense or the Department of Commerce. A political candidate can decry the "gross ineffi-

---

[21]Ibid., p. 306.

ciency" of an agency without the risk of challenge, for few types of data can be used to contest the candidate's claim. Fortunately, progress is being made in requiring agencies to be more precise in specifying their objectives. When this has been done for more programs, it will at least be possible to measure performance against those stated objectives. Nonetheless, we will still lack an objective as broadly applicable as "profit" is in the private sector, and we will not have taken away the candidate's favorite whipping boy (or girl)—the "bureaucrat." Americans will probably remain ambivalent.

Conclusion

Our goal in this chapter was to examine dispassionately the importance of public administration in American life. The impact that public administrators have on us today is unquestionable. Whether the expansion of such impact is "good" or "bad" has not been directly addressed, although it has been shown that American history presents an almost continuous expansion of government's role. Each individual, whether public administrator, elected official, or ordinary citizen, can give consideration to this role, utilizing information presented in all three sections of this chapter: the classification of programs into broad categories, the expansion over time (and forces that may have produced such expansion), and the nature of public attitudes. Through such considerations administrators can better understand their place in society, elected officials can consider possible expansion or contraction of public activities, and ordinary citizens can better cope with relations with administrators and exert pressure for change if desired.

Suggested readings for chapter one

Crozier, Michel. *The Bureaucratic Phenomenon.* Chicago: University of Chicago Press, 1964.

Fabricant, Solomon. *The Trend of Government Activity in the United States Since 1900.* New York: National Bureau of Economic Research, 1952.

Katz, Daniel et al. *Bureaucratic Encounters.* Ann Arbor: Institute for Social Research, University of Michigan, 1975.

Kilpatrick, Franklin P.; Cummings, Milton C., Jr.; and Jennings, M. Kent. *The Image of the Federal Service.* Washington, D.C.: Brookings Institution, 1964.

Medeiros, James A., and Schmitt, David E. *Public Bureaucracy: Values and Perspectives*. North Scituate, Mass.: Duxbury Press, 1977.

Mosher, Frederick C., and Poland, Orville F. *The Costs of American Government*. New York: Dodd, Mead and Co., 1966.

Nathan, Richard P.; Manvel, Allen D.; and Calkins, Susannah E. *Monitoring Revenue Sharing*. Washington, D.C.: Brookings Institution, 1975.

Studenski, Paul, and Krooss, Herman E. *Financial History of the United States*. 2d ed. New York: McGraw-Hill, 1963.

White, Leonard D. *The Federalists: A Study in Administrative History*. New York: Macmillan Co., 1961.

———. *The Jacksonians: A Study in Administrative History—1829–1861*. New York: Macmillan Co., 1963.

———. *The Jeffersonians: A Study in Administrative History—1801–1829*. New York: Macmillan Co., 1961.

———. *The Republican Era 1869–1901*. New York: Macmillan Co., 1963.

Chapter two

Public administration as a field of study

Large-scale administrative organization has existed from early times. The ancient empires of Egypt, Persia, Greece, Rome, China, and Ancient America organized and maintained political rule over wide areas and large populations by the use of more or less skilled administrative functionaries. In later times there was the peculiar entity of the Holy Roman Empire and, more recently, the colonial empires of Spain, Portugal, France, and Britain. All of these relied on sophisticated administrative apparatus and staffs; yet until about the nineteenth century we can hardly speak of the apparatus as bureaucratic or the administrators as bureaucrats. Bureaucracy describes a special type of modern administrative management, but we can learn something about it through comparison with earlier forms and by tracing its development.

---

*This chapter was written by Hugh G. MacNiven, Professor and Chairperson, Department of Political Science, University of Oklahoma.

Premodern administration

In the early years of this century, the great sociologist Max Weber gave us an account of how premodern administration differed from modern bureaucracy; others, too, have given us glimpses of early administration.[1] The Roman Empire illustrates the characteristics of these premodern systems. Over five centuries, under nearly fifty emperors, ruling from 60 to 80 million subjects, the central government of Rome maintained its hold over the Western world. Reading about it today, we are impressed with the personal nature of that rule. Everything depended on the emperor, who in turn had to rely on the personal loyalty of his subordinates, who maintained themselves by the personal support they could muster from their underlings, down to rank-and-file personnel on the fringes of the empire. This was true in the army and in the civil government. Everyone had a claim on the emperor, who spent his time reading or listening to petitions, policy arguments, congratulatory statements, judicial claims, appeals for favors, and the like. Contrary to the picture many of us hold, the emperor carried an enormous work load and dispensed funds almost by whim, in an attempt to keep the vast imperial machine functioning. It was a system of favoritism and patronage.[2]

In such a system, with all major decisions taken by the ruler, there was an inevitable pileup of business at the top and, consequently, a lack of control and supervision at lower levels and at a distance from the center. Power, authority, and accountability thinned out rapidly as one moved farther from the capital, so that there was frequently near anarchy on the borders. Despite a developed legal system, sheer military force supplied what semblance of administrative uniformity prevailed throughout the realm.

In a system based on personal preferment, a change of emperor disrupted the entire arrangements of government. Those who had been in favor might now be out of favor. Presumably a wise ruler chose able subordinates, but he could not ensure that his successor would continue their tenure, nor could he even guarantee that his most basic policy directives would be pursued. The premodern state could not manage succession effectively in either the political or the administrative realms. Weak rulers followed strong rulers, foolish monarchs succeeded wise monarchs—all dependent on the army, which supplied the continuity that enabled the empire to endure so

---

[1]Max Weber, *The Theory of Social and Economic Organization*, trans. A. M. Henderson and Talcott Parsons (New York: Oxford University Press, 1947); and S. N. Eisenstadt, *The Political Systems of Empires* (New York: Free Press, 1963).

[2]Fergus Millar, *The Emperor in the Roman World* (London: Duckworth, 1976).

long. In the absence of institutional, bureaucratic procedures, government moved from stability to near anarchy and back again.

Modern bureaucracy

Contrast the state of affairs sketched above with the description of modern *bureaucracy* given us by Max Weber. Bureaucracy is an administrative system based on objective norms (such as laws, rules, and regulations) rather than on favoritism. It is a system of *offices* rather than officers. Loyalty is owed to the state and the administrative organization, not to those who happen to be the current incumbents of the offices.

Members of the bureaucracy are chosen for their qualification rather than their personal connections with powerful persons. When vacancies occur by death, resignation, or for other reasons, new qualified persons are selected according to clearly defined rules to fill the office. One of the great achievements of the American Republic was the institution of a process of orderly transition from one president to the successor. Bureaucracy, in the administrative realm, has achieved the same thing. Bureaucracy has ensured the continuance without violent fluctuations of the business of government, despite the constant turnover of the membership. In a sense, the modern administrative bureaucracy, whether public or private, has achieved "immortality." It does not die when its members die.

By adherence to laws, rules, and regulations, bureaucracies provide uniformity that earlier administrative structures could not provide. Because personnel are chosen for their competence and are trained to similar standards, because rules and procedures are standardized, and because loyalty is owed the political-administrative system and not powerful persons, administrative functions and services are carried out uniformly throughout the jurisdiction. The taxpayer in Seattle cannot hope that because he is far away from the seat of governmental power in Washington, the Internal Revenue Service will be unable to collect his taxes. Functions and services are managed impartially everywhere in the bureaucratic state.

Bureaucracy, or large, formal, complex organization, is, as Weber thought, one of the great social inventions of the modern world, made possible and necessary by the concomitant development of the nation-state, the moneyed economy, and the industrial system.[3]

---

[3]Reinhard Bendix, *Max Weber: An Intellectual Portrait* (Garden City, New York: Doubleday, 1962).

The environment of administration in early America

A number of themes evident in the early Republic have had important implications for administration in later America. When we consider that at the Revolution the thirteen colonies had a population of about 3.5 million persons sprinkled along the eastern coast for nearly 1,500 miles, it is easy to understand their predilection for decentralization. Every settlement had to be self-reliant, for neighboring communities were distant and communications difficult. The federal system that the Republic's founders established was made necessary by geographical dispersion, but it also reflected the common view that power, and certainly functions, ought to reside with the government nearest the people. So the colonists had a strong sense of home rule based on an experience that had taught them not to expect a distant government to be much concerned with their self-interests.

Along with the commitment to decentralization went a general mistrust of government. Jefferson's idea that the least government was the best was widely held. And it was the executive branch that was to be most feared, for in colonial times the royal governors had resisted local initiatives expressed through the popularly elected legislatures and frequently had attempted to extend their power at the expense of the representatives of the colonists.[4]

These themes, decentralization to the smaller units of government and general mistrust of government, are still in evidence after two hundred years. There is little empirical evidence that local governments are more just, equitable, and efficient than state or national governments. Indeed, the disadvantaged have often turned to the higher levels of government for an impartiality and equity they could not find at home. Yet we still hear comments about funneling a dollar to Washington and getting eighty cents back, and local home rule is an evergreen value in America.

The American colonist had a vigorous regard for justice and freedom inherited from his European forebears but considerably heightened by his emigration to the new world. Governments "ought" to promote justice, liberty, equality, and tolerance, even though often they did not. There was (and still is) a certain contradiction in citizens' attitudes toward their governments. Government had a positive obligation to advance freedom and justice; yet freedom was conceived of as being left alone. Freedom for Americans has always included

---

[4]Leonard D. White, *The Federalists: A Study in Administrative History* (New York: Macmillan, 1961).

freedom from one's own government, both elected and appointed, but in a mobilized and demanding society, it is increasingly hard to leave the citizen alone even in the smallest details of daily routine.

As might be expected in a self-reliant, frontier situation, the early Republic was characterized by a pragmatic approach to public affairs, one that liked to see things work whether the mechanism was traditional or not. A variety of political and administrative forms developed around the country, and the lack of uniformity from jurisdiction to jurisdiction is still a notable feature of our country. For better or worse, structural neatness is conspicuously lacking in the American polity.

In the early days, though, all governments were characterized by the dominance of the legislative branch and the consequent weakness of the executive. In large towns the mayor was likely to be elected only as a member of council and to have no veto and few appointive powers. Functions that we think of as executive today, such as budgeting or personnel appointment and management, were carried out by the council as a collegial body. At the state level, too, the governor's office was weak both in function and prestige. The legislature was the paramount branch, and the governor had few powers of appointment, removal, or veto. What today we would consider as proper gubernatorial appointments at cabinet level were then popularly elected offices, and so attorneys general, secretaries of state, state treasurers, and the like had as much a mandate from the people as the governor himself. The states then, for the most part, had a multiple executive of popularly elected officials, a feature still found in some states.

The legislative branch did not content itself with policy matters. In all of the states the legislature held the power of the purse, and each item of expenditure was carefully detailed by the legislature. Representatives also had important appointment powers either in the form of direct appointment of political favorites to administrative jobs or in the approval of appointments by the governor. At both state and local levels, elected boards and commissions were prominent, again undercutting the powers of chief executives.

The first century of the American public service

His wartime leadership gave President Washington enormous prestige, which helped him establish what was, for those times, a relatively strong and professional public service. He inaugurated a federal public service that can be described as elitist and competent. He thought that federal government posts should go to people with education, with integrity, and with established reputation in their local communities.

With his insistence on community standing and good education, he built a public service made up of gentlemen, a public service both respected at home and admired abroad as one of the most effective and honest of its time. It had a strong class bias, however, and represented the thinking of the landed gentry. Washington also inaugurated the geographical distribution of public offices, which has remained a prominent feature of the American system.[5]

These early bureaucratic arrangements were continued by the Jeffersonian Republicans despite their misgivings about class bias and preference for decentralization. Not until the election of Andrew Jackson in 1828 did a major change take place. President Jackson, representing the new power of the democratic frontier voter, attacked the elitist nature of the old service and called for widespread popular participation in government.

Already the egalitarianism of the frontier had brought about the Tenure of Office Act in 1820, which called for rotating many public offices on a four-year basis. Jackson totally subscribed to the ideas of rotation in office and brief appointment periods. He argued that an honest, intelligent citizen who had given good political service to the party should have access to most government jobs, which he thought required little more than patriotism and common sense. He may have been correct, for the tasks of government were simpler and less complex than they are in our own time.

These two changes—the four-year limitation on the period that offices could be held, and open recruitment from all citizens—had profound effects on the public service. On the positive side can be cited the democratization that took place in the federal bureaucracy and the astounding participation in elected and appointed government by hundreds of thousands of ordinary citizens.

As the years went on, however, the obvious problems with such a system were made manifest. Appointments were made on a partisan basis, and the least qualified could expect public office if they could demonstrate sufficient partisanship. Along with decline in the competence of officeholders came decline in their integrity, and by the middle years of the nineteenth century the United States national government, and certainly the state and municipal governments, could be characterized as politically dominated, inefficient, and in many instances downright corrupt.

---

[5]Paul Van Riper, *History of the United States Civil Service* (Evanston, Ill.: Row, Peterson, 1958).

Shortly after the Civil War, the president was empowered to establish guidelines for the proper operation of the public service. President Grant inaugurated the first Civil Service Commission to oversee the functions of the public service, including the establishment of examinations for determining qualification of applicants. This reform was short-lived, for Congress abolished the commission. It was, however, the forerunner of the structure that pertained in the federal civil service until replaced in 1978.

Demand for reform became overwhelming when President Garfield was assassinated in 1881 by a disappointed office seeker. Following a study of the then recently reformed British Civil Service, the Civil Service Act of 1883 was passed by Congress and signed by the president. This legislation (called the *Pendleton Act* after its sponsor, Senator Pendleton of Ohio) established a three-member *Civil Service Commission* to be appointed by the president, with no more than two members being from the same political party. The commission had responsibility for the promulgation of rules and regulations governing entrance, placement, promotion, discipline, and so forth. Among the reforms instituted was the appointment of persons to jobs according to their qualifications as determined by examinations.

By the second half of the nineteenth century, it had become evident that the United States could no longer be governed by partisan amateurs. The Industrial Revolution had begun, and the complexity of modern society was starting to place a strain on the old Jacksonian spoils system, both in politics and in administration.

The era of reform

Following passage of the Civil Service Act of 1883, a series of waves of reform ebbed and flowed over the United States, bringing fundamental changes in political and administrative life. Demands for change have blended idealism and the crassest kind of efficiency, but the impulses have usually been pragmatic rather than ideological. The movements ran strongly through the last two decades of the nineteenth century and the first two decades of the twentieth century, but in fact pressure for reform never ceased, and the "era" is only a convenient label covering about forty years from passage of the Pendleton Act.

It was during this period that public administration became a recognized field of concern. In 1887, Woodrow Wilson, then professor at Princeton, wrote a now famous essay, "The Study of Administration," which for the first time systematically advocated the operations of government as a proper area for academic study.[6] Whether this article had as much impact at the time as it has had on later readers is doubtful; nevertheless, it can be cited as the beginning of academic interest in what we would today call professional public administration.

Another early contributor to the field was Frank J. Goodnow of Columbia University, the first president of the American Political Science Association. In his book *Politics and Administration,* published at the turn of the century, Goodnow made a clear distinction between politics and administration, which has become known as the *politics–administration dichotomy.* Politics was concerned with policy making, and the task of administrators was to carry out the political mandate efficiently.[7]

The Constitution had made a clear separation between legislative and executive powers. Perhaps it is natural that early writers tended to put a wedge between *executive* and *administrative* functions and to place administration on a routine level of carrying out the day-to-day tasks of government. While this allowed specification of a subject of study, it gave an artificial flavor to early public administration by failing to recognize the constant interaction of politics, policy making, and administration, an interaction in which administrative managers play a significant part.

While the national and state governments were caught up in the movement, the major activities that led to the establishment of a professional public administration field in the United States took place in the large cities. They were the scenes of the most severe problems and also of the most dramatic attempts at remedy. Journalists of the "muckraking" sort, such as Lincoln Steffens in his *The Shame of the Cities,* focused on the inefficiency, corruption, and waste that permeated local government. The most thoroughgoing attempt to do something about these deficiencies was the creation of the New York Bureau of Municipal Research in 1906. This zealous research organization, established by private funding, brought together a staff of competent professionals who analyzed and worked out solutions to policy and administrative questions, and who then were able to mobilize public support for the implementation of suggested changes. Their success in dealing with critical problems in New York City brought them national attention—and brought attention to public administration as a field. Requests poured in for assistance from other city and

---

[6]Woodrow Wilson, "The Study of Administration," *Political Science Quarterly* 2 (June 1887): 197–222.

[7]Frank Goodnow, *Politics and Administration* (New York: Macmillan, 1900).

Public administration as a field of study

47

state governments, and very soon similar organizations were established in other jurisdictions.[8]

Another notable feature of this period of governmental reform was the development of professional associations in various functional fields of public service. To keep in touch with colleagues around the country on matters of common interest, professionals formed associations, and before the turn of the century a number of these were already flourishing. Their purposes were communication, the establishment of professional standards, the advancement of the profession, and support for one another in the struggle for political and administrative reform. Organizations in the fields of public health, municipal engineering, personnel, city management, police, finance, and many others were established. In the 1920s a plan was developed to bring these groups together and funding was found to establish "1313," a central clearinghouse for professional associations located at 1313 East 60th Street in Chicago. These organizations, which included the International City Managers Association, the Civil Service Assembly (later the Public Personnel Administration), the American Municipal Association, the American Public Works Association, and a number of others, created Public Administration Service (PAS). This nonprofit consulting service to governments is still the largest service of its kind.

The "1313" group helped establish new professional associations, such as the Council of State Governments and the Governors Conference, as well as the *American Society for Public Administration,* which was founded in 1939. Today many of the associations that were linked to "1313" have moved their head offices to Washington, where they can be closer to the political power center. It would be hard to overestimate the contribution of professional organizations to public administration over the past century, but any one entering public service today finds an active group by which to keep in touch with developments in the field.

Public administration as an academic discipline

The reform movements had another important meaning for public administration, for they provided the earliest professional training

---

[8]Alice B. Stone and Donald C. Stone, "Early Development of Education in Public Administration," in *American Public Administration: Past, Present and Future,* ed. Frederick C. Mosher (University: University of Alabama Press, 1974), pp. 19–22.

in the field. Shortly after the New York Bureau of Municipal Research was established, it recognized the need to train people for its own use and for other such bureaus that were springing up, and in 1911 the Training School for Public Service was founded as a function of the bureau. The Training School, which maintained quite high standards, undertook the first graduate-level, professional training of public administrators in the United States. The school flourished under the direction of Charles A. Beard, and when the Maxwell School of Citizenship and Public Affairs was founded at Syracuse University in 1924, much of the academic work of the training school was transferred to Syracuse.[9]

Following the model of the Training School, universities quickly developed public administration curricula, for the most part in the municipal area. A full-fledged master's program in municipal administration was inaugurated at the University of Michigan in 1914, and this evolved later into the Institute of Public Administration and then into the present Institute of Public Policy Analysis. Other leading schools established coursework, and some of the largest developed full programs in public administration, most of which were within departments of political science.

The whole period of reform, from the Civil Service Act of 1883 until World War II, is underlaid by the powerful assumption of rationality. Rationality, simply stated, is the belief that by the application of analytical thought and planning we can do things better. Two great streams of rational thought which permeated administration, both professional and academic, were the work of Max Weber and Frederick W. Taylor.

Although Weber's work in the early years of this century was not widely known in America outside a small academic circle, it was compatible with the general tenor of thinking on administrative questions. His legal-rational model of bureaucracy stressed strong, centralized executive power, a clear-cut division of labor, and rational personnel practices based on adequate training and careful selection processes. He stressed professionalism, specialization, and striving for efficiency and economy.[10]

While Weber was a societal theorist who used the national state as his unit of bureaucratic study, Frederick Taylor, as an engineer, came at rationality from the point of view of the factory supervisor. He was interested in how individuals interacted with the work organization, and in his studies from the late 1880s until the publication in 1911 of

---

[9]Ibid., pp. 28–9.

[10]Max Weber, *From Max Weber: Essays in Sociology,* trans. and ed. H. H. Gerth and C. Wright Mills (New York: Oxford University Press, 1946), pp. 196–98.

his great work, *Principles of Scientific Management,* he collected an impressive body of evidence to indicate that by careful observation and analysis of the way in which people work, human beings could identify "the one best way" of doing work. Public administration, like business administration, was influenced powerfully by Taylor and his disciples, and early public administration was marked by a concern for applying their conclusions to practical questions of how best to carry out routine operations. This pragmatic approach, demanding that administrators get things done in an efficient, economical way, gave little attention to questions of value. Management was viewed as an ongoing process, built up on the organization's past experience. It was assumed that administrators should continue to do what they had been doing, only do it better. Early training in the field, then, gave a good deal of attention to techniques and procedures that were thought applicable to almost any administrative situation.[11]

In time, public administrators came to speak of "the principles" of public administration. These were an outgrowth of Taylor's *scientific management* approach. He had stressed observation of what administrators do, analysis of why they do it the way they do, and a restructuring of the task—breaking it into its simplest components. Applied mainly to physical tasks—assembling a product, operating a lathe—scientific management had brought extraordinary productivity gains to industry. The natural question was: If we can apply scientific management to routine labor situations, why cannot we apply it to higher levels of administrative management? "Principles," therefore, were the application of scientific management to a higher level of business and public administration.[12] They were thought to be generalizations that could be made from analyzing many, many cases of real-life experience in administration. The case study was the time-honored approach of legal scholarship, where doctrines and principles had emerged from the analysis of countless cases. This approach was borrowed by the Harvard Business School when it established its case study program in the 1920s and was copied by public administration with the Inter-University Case Program, begun in 1948. It was hoped that by studying scenarios of interesting administrative situations, the student could analyze both the special and the unique elements and see plainly the more widely applicable generalizations that could be drawn from them—the principles.

---

[11]Frederick Taylor, *Principles of Scientific Management* (New York: Harper and Brothers, 1911).

[12]Important contributions and extensions of the principles were made by Henri Fayol, *General and Industrial Management* (London: Pitman, 1930); and James D. Mooney and Alan C. Reiley, *The Principles of Organization* (New York: Harper and Row, 1939).

Chapter two

50

The principles approach at its worst was prescriptive and at times even hortatory. It told the student what he "ought to do" and what he "should not do" in specific situations, as if the practice of administration could be reduced to a series of maxims. At its best, however, it was an attempt to apply rational and scientific approaches to the tasks of management, and an enormous amount was learned during the principles era about the organizing and managing of public agencies. The principles have been severely criticized since, but no satisfactory substitute focus has emerged around which the field of public administration could be organized. In 1946, Herbert Simon wrote an article, which has become famous, on the principles of administration in which he showed that they were little more than proverbs or rules of thumb that sometimes applied and sometimes did not and that the various "principles" even contradicted each other.[13] What was considered good practice by the principles people had not been subjected to careful research and empirical testing, so it was not surprising that rising social scientists attempting to be truly scientific should react strongly to the principles approach. In the 1950s social scientists—especially political scientists—raised an important question: If we do not understand the nature of human organizations, how can we prescribe how they should be run?

Faced with this perplexing issue, public administration in the 1950s began to borrow heavily from sociology, psychology, and social psychology. It was hoped that findings of researchers in the rapidly developing behavioral sciences could help provide the needed understanding. The main stage for bringing psychology and sociology into public adminstration was in the subfield of *organization theory*. Especially important was a merging of concern for the formal, legal side of the organization and the informal, or social side of the organization. Scientific management had emphasized the formal; political science, the legal. It became apparent that dealing with the formal-structural and the informal-behavioral patterns of organizations at all levels, from individuals and small groups to institutions and bureaucracies, would require the insights and methodologies of all the social sciences, sociology and psychology in particular, as well as the experience of management in the private sector. The past decade or more has seen public administration still closely tied to political science, but relying more and more on the findings of many other disciplines.

The 1950s and 1960s witnessed a dramatic upsurge of professional and academic participation in international and comparative administration. This activity was prompted by the growth of new nation-

---

[13]Herbert Simon, "The Proverbs of Administration," *Public Administration Review* 6 (Winter 1946): 53–67.

states—from fewer than 50 to about 150 from World War II to the present—and a growing confidence in cross-cultural analysis, which had been an outgrowth of the behavioral movement.

Much of the work of comparative administration was focused on the developing nations, and development administration became almost synonymous with the term *comparative* public administration. The new international scholars, given a focus by the organization of the *Comparative Administration Group (CAG)* in the early 1960s, were very vigorous and applied methodological and theoretical rigor to their task. Unlike the parent discipline of public administration, which was not strong on theory, comparative administration followed a number of theoretical approaches. It developed elaborate and highly generalized models of development administration, and Fred W. Riggs, one of the founders of CAG, made a major contribution with his analysis of "prismatic" or "transitional" societies.[14] In addition to developing general models that attempted to explain many development situations, there was also considerable activity in studies of particular areas of the world—Latin American administration, for example. Further, there were detailed case-by-case examinations of administrative situations in both the developing countries and the older, established bureaucracies of the industrialized world. In the 1970s, though, there has been some decline in the field, owing partly to reduction in governmental and foundation support for international and cross-cultural activities and partly to a growing resistance on the part of host nations to cooperate in field research. What has been learned from comparative administration, however, has been useful in analyzing developmental problems in different regions of the United States. Another benefit of the comparative administration approach has been to move traditional public administration away from its parochial, American, culture-bound setting. It has also greatly strengthened international interchange in both professional and scholarly public administration and provided a new link with reality for university-based programs by supplying faculty with overseas field experience.

An interesting development in the late 1960s is known as the New Public Administration. In 1968, under the sponsorship of Dwight Waldo, a conference of young public administrators was held at the Minnowbrook Conference Center of Syracuse University, and the publication of that conference report had important effects on administrative thinking.[15] The Vietnam War seemed to reemphasize that the bureaucracy, despite all its stated concern for human betterment, was still a neutral

---

[14]Fred W. Riggs, *Administration in Developing Countries: The Theory of Prismatic Society* (Boston: Houghton Mifflin, 1964).

[15]Frank Marini, ed., *Toward a New Public Administration: The Minnowbrook Perspective* (Scranton, Pa.: Chandler Publishing Co., 1971).

institution, carrying out the mandate of political leaders whether those mandates were sound or unsound, just or unjust. The IRS commitment was still to efficiency and economy.

The new public administration was a reaction against the value-free positivism that had characterized much of public administration thought since World War II. It reasserted the importance of normative values, particularly social justice. It affirmed that public administrators have an obligation to enunciate forcefully and impress upon policy makers the basic values of a free democratic society and actively to advance the causes of equity and justice. The disclosures of the Watergate scandals have reinforced these positions and stressed anew the importance of integrity, openness, and accountability in the conduct of public affairs. This concern for the needs of human beings in the modern world can also be seen in the growth of consumer and environmental protection functions domestically, and its international dimension is manifested in pressure for human rights around the world, a cause being advanced by the Carter administration.

Another innovation that has drawn from both the behavioral and the management science traditions is the emergence of *public policy analysis* as a major branch of public administration studies. Pioneering writings on decision making by Herbert Simon and others raised the possibility of taking a *rational-comprehensive* approach to decision making and policy making. These authors urged that public administrators, faced with a decision, should carefully identify objectives, compare alternative means of reaching those objectives, and then select the best alternative. They criticized decision styles too prone to rely on the argument "That's how we've always done it." During the 1970s, the focus of these efforts to instill rationality has been raised from the organizational decision level, where it resided during the 1960s, to the societal level, where major issues of concern to many organizations and to large sectors of society are examined. What are the various courses of action open to us as a nation? What are the likely consequences of following each of these courses? What will be the impact on various segments of the community? Policy analysis attempts to deal with not only the rational and analytical sides of policy issues, but also with important value considerations. There is an attempt to take into account economic, political, psychological, historical, and even nonrational or irrational processes. It is more than a decade now since the need for a comprehensive policy science was first postulated. In the intervening period, full-fledged policy analysis programs have developed at a number of universities, and coursework is found in almost all modern public administration offerings. The *National Association of Schools of Public Affairs and Administration (NASPAA)* advocates policy analysis as one of the five subject areas that should be included in any comprehensive program in administration.

Public administration as a field of study/

/53

Public and private administration

In conclusion, it is appropriate to look briefly at the question "Just what is the significance of *public* in public administration?" In operational areas of government and business, the blending of functions makes it difficult to tell where the public leaves off and where the private takes up. The widespread use of contracting with private organizations for public services and the blending on a temporary, ad hoc basis of public and private technical staffs for the accomplishment of specific program goals have been significant trends of the past two decades. We see large private enterprises whose output is bought almost entirely by government, and we also see public corporate units managing operations that were formerly run by business. (The federal government recently acquired in a tax settlement—and operated temporarily—a go-go bar in Washington.) Government subsidies, tax incentives, and the like play a major part in the profit picture of many businesses, and government regulations add to the costs of business. Indeed, the very word *profit* almost loses its meaning, a reasonable return being built into an artificial price the consumer must pay.

Another feature of modern organizational life that makes it more difficult to clearly separate what is public from what is private is the development of the voluntary, not-for-profit sector of the economy, organizations that provide services, frequently of a public kind and in accordance with some concept of the public interest, but which are funded from the donations of private individuals and organizations.

The tendency of the past few years, especially in such fields as organization theory, has been to make little distinction between public and private organizations and to focus on the behaviors found in organizations of all kinds or on the common management techniques that can be applied across a broad range of organizations. This has led many to assume that the field of public administration is gradually being absorbed into a larger field of management, and this is evidenced by the growth of public management programs under the umbrella of schools and colleges of business administration.

Yet it is still misleading to suggest that there is little difference between the public and private sectors, even though the old and most obvious distinction—that government does not work for a profit and private business does—does not differentiate as clearly as it once did. The concept of the public interest is a difficult one to define, but it is still powerful. It does mean that a public official may be held publicly accountable for his actions. More and more, public agencies are facing close scrutiny by press, legislatures, and taxpayers, in addition to the traditional surveillance of the courts. In general, the internal activities of private business corporations are not subject to such great public scrutiny, although even here the demands of consumer groups are turning the light of publicity on the corporations more than they would wish sometimes.

It has been said by some that higher moral and ethical standards are expected of public employees than of private employees. Whether or not this is true, the public service ethic is still strong, and the writings of the new public administration, as well as the fallout from Watergate, have reinforced the demand for integrity and high standards in government employment.

Public managers work within very strict limits of legislation, executive orders, and regulations surrounding purchasing, auditing, personnel, budgeting, and other tasks of government. Freedom of information laws and open-meeting legislation subject governmental decision making to public scrutiny. Despite some change, business operations remain somewhat more secret and freer of restrictions.

Clearly, public and private employment will be more intricately intertwined in the future, as business becomes increasingly integrated into the sphere of the public interest and is held accountable in a way that government now is. Yet the word *public* in public administration is still meaningful, and the study of public affairs will have to take into account not only management subjects common to both public and private sectors, but also the special environment in which the public servant has to live, an environment constituted of the volatile mix of administration, policy making, and politics.

It must be apparent by now that public administration is an untidy field of study. Indeed, readers may question whether there is any such discipline at all. It grew up in the household of political science, lives in the management tradition, draws from all the social sciences, and has developed recently along the lines of the policy sciences. As Professor Frederick C. Mosher said of public administration: "It is more an area of interest than a discipline, more a focus than a separate science." Whether there ever was an orthodox approach to the field, even in the days of scientific management and principles of administration, it is certain that there is no single prevailing approach today, nor are discernible patterns of uniformity likely to emerge in the near future.

Suggested readings for chapter two

Appleby, Paul H. *Big Democracy.* New York: Knopf, 1945.

Caldwell, Lynton K. *The Administrative Theories of Hamilton and Jefferson.* Chicago: University of Chicago Press, 1944.

Dahlberg, Jane S. *The New York Bureau of Municipal Research: Pioneer in Government Administration.* New York: New York University Press, 1966.

Dalby, Michael T., and Werthman, Michael S. *Bureaucracy in Historical Perspective*. Glenview, Ill.: Scott, Foresman Co., 1971.

Eisenstadt, S. N. *The Political Systems of Empires*. New York: The Free Press, 1963.

Gladden, E. N. *A History of Public Administration*. London: Frank Cass, 1972.

Goodnow, Frank. *Politics and Administration*. New York: Macmillan, 1900.

Marini, Frank, ed. *Toward a New Public Administration: The Minnowbrook Perspective*. Scranton, Pa.: Chandler Publishing Co., 1971.

Medeiros, James A., and Schmitt, David E. *Public Bureaucracy: Values and Perspectives*. North Scituate, Mass.: Duxbury Press, 1977.

Mosher, Frederick C., ed. *American Public Administration*. University: University of Alabama Press, 1975.

————. *Democracy and the Public Service*. New York: Oxford University Press, 1968.

Ostrum, Vincent. *The Intellectual Crisis in American Public Administration*. University: University of Alabama Press, 1973.

Redford, Emmette S. *Democracy in the Administrative State*. New York: Oxford University Press, 1969.

Riggs, Fred W. *The Theory of Prismatic Society*. Boston: Houghton Mifflin, 1964.

Taylor, Frederick. *Principles of Scientific Management*. New York: Harper and Brothers, 1911.

Waldo, Dwight, ed. *Public Administration in a Time of Turbulence*. Scranton, Pa.: Chandler Publishing Co., 1971.

Weber, Max. *The Theory of Social and Economic Organization*. Trans. A. M. Henderson and Talcott Parsons. New York: Oxford University Press, 1947.

White, Leonard D. *The Federalists: A Study in Administrative History*. New York: Macmillan Co., 1961.

————. *The Jacksonians: A Study in Administrative History—1829–1861*. New York: Macmillan Co., 1963.

————. *The Jeffersonians; A Study in Administrative History—1801–1829*. New York: Macmillan Co., 1961.

————. *The Republican Era 1869–1901*. New York: Macmillan Co., 1963.

Chapter two

Part

The environment of public
administration

When many people—including many otherwise sophisticated people—think of public administration as an activity, they visualize large offices crammed with rows of faceless bureaucrats sitting at desks and churning out an endless stream of paperwork to be filed by yet other functionaries. As we shall see, especially in part III, this view captures few of the important things that professional civil servants actually do. Public administration also has many more participants than this view suggests. Public agencies exist in an environment that contains other actors, such as the executive, the legislature, the courts, and organized groups. Part II examines the involvement of agencies with these environmental actors in the formulation and implementation of public policy.

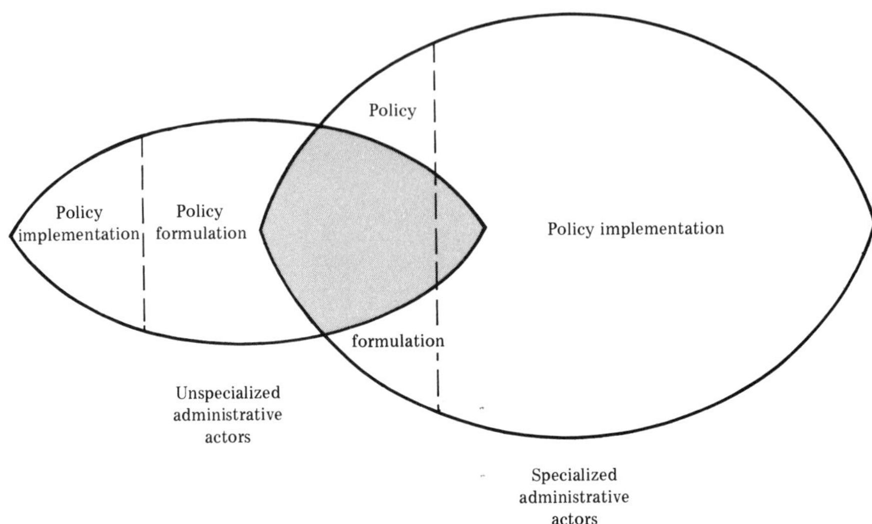

Figure 2–1.   Policy and the administrative process

Our model of policy and the administrative process

We have noted that public administration is a political process involving the authoritative implementation of legitimated policy choices. Furthermore, we recognized that various institutions may become involved in administration, but that in this country, the large, specialized governmental agencies are given responsibility for most public administration. Finally, we observed that these highly differentiated organizations are more than passive "administrators" of decisions made by others; they have become powerful actors in the entire policy process and play important roles in the determination of the *content* of the policies they are assigned to implement.

Figure II-1, a highly simplified model of the administrative process, illustrates the preceding description. Two sets of actors are involved: the unspecialized administrative actors (such as legislatures and courts); and the specialized administrative actors (such as the Department of Agriculture and a state's department of corrections). The specialized actors are depicted as being larger in the figure because their absolute size is usually greater, because they are responsible for making far more administrative decisions, and because they usually are more important to the administrative process than the unspecialized administrative actors.

We assume that two activities, policy *formulation* and policy *implementation,* are sufficiently distinct that one can be differentiated from the other for illustrative purposes.[1] Furthermore, both sets of actors are depicted as engaging in each activity. (The positions of the dotted lines that divide each set of actors into policy formulation and implementation sectors are, of course, arbitrary.) But administrative actors tend to be *mainly* involved with one activity or the other. For example, the Department of Defense (a specialized administrative actor) is more involved with implementing existing policies concerning such matters as the deployment and maintenance of U.S. forces around the world than with recommending what defense policies should be formulated. On the other hand, the Congress (an unspecialized administrative actor) is more involved with formulating new policies concerning such issues as taxation than with direct implementation of the Tax Code.[2]

The figure's large shaded area indicates overlap between the two sets of actors. Such a crude diagram cannot, of course, do justice to the complexity of the interrelationships; there is, for example, no indication in the figure of the directions of influence flow. Nevertheless, the shaded area does call attention to important aspects of the administrative process. The specialized actors participate with enthusiasm in the formulation of public policy; many programs originate from the bureaucracy, and Congress may refuse seriously to consider certain proposed legislation until the attitudes of the responsible administrative agencies are known. Also, the unspecialized actors often penetrate, but usually less deeply, into agencies' implementations of policies; the coming of large-scale bureaucracy has, as we shall see below, greatly complicated the task (traditionally performed by the legislature) of attempting to hold administrative agencies accountable for their actions, but politicians have not abandoned the effort. Scholars long have recognized the importance of the shaded

---

[1]We recognize that when one deals with empirical cases it may be difficult to separate the formulation from the implementation of policy, but the distinction can be made analytically. For a discussion of this point, see Martin Landau, *Political Theory and Political Science: Studies in the Methodology of Political Inquiry* (New York: Macmillan, 1972), pp. 194-202.

[2]Subagencies of "unspecialized administrative actors" may, however, become rather specialized. Recall, for example, that the power base of former Congressman Wayne Hays (of Elizabeth Ray fame) was the House Administration Committee. As committee chairman, Hays directed a large staff and allocated such important perquisites as offices and parking spaces. In addition, the Administrative Office of the United States Courts, a creature of the Supreme Court, has a Bankruptcy Division that regularly makes administrative decisions as it supervises the implementation of the Bankruptcy Act by officers of the bankruptcy courts, including the referees in bankruptcy.

relationships, and they are the principal explanation for the circumstance that public administration often is considered a specialized subfield of the discipline of political science.

Public administration as a political game

The foregoing brief outline of the national administrative process is sketched broadly from what may be called the whole system perspective. Now we shall narrow our perspective and look at the process from the viewpoint of the leaders of large administrative agencies. Their jobs can be compared with those of quarterbacks on professional football teams. Like all analogies, this one has limitations; the major shortcoming, as we shall see, is that football is insufficiently complicated to illustrate fully the complexities administrators face. Nonetheless, the analogy may prove useful in our quest for administrative understanding.

The owners and the fans of professional teams want the players to score points and win games. This is almost certainly also the quarterbacks' chief objective, but other objectives (such as achieving personal glory and avoiding injury) may intrude and even take precedence over winning. If this is true of the quarterbacks, who are designated as the teams' field generals, it is even more true of the remainder of the players. Our quarterbacks' jobs are difficult. In addition to their responsibilities for strategic planning (although they are not always allowed to call plays) and for motivating teammates (who may have quite different ideas about what should be done), the quarterbacks must contend with external variables. Coaches send in both suggestions and binding directives, the opposing teams may unveil devastating offenses and impenetrable defenses, the wind's velocity or direction may shift, crucial injuries may occur, the officials may penalize the teams unfairly, or the crowds' cheers may turn into deafening boos. For all of these reasons, the quarterbacks' leadership responsibilities are extremely challenging.

But the tasks of public administrators are in several respects even more complex than those of our hypothetical quarterbacks. To begin with, the quarterbacks know in advance which teams they will face and when, but our administrators do not even have a fixed schedule. They will become intimately involved with, but will probably not control the process of agenda building or the assigning of priorities to the various public policy issues over which their agencies may have general jurisdiction.

Defining an agency's objectives also may be a difficult problem. Once it is agreed that an issue, such as poverty, should be put on the schedule, it remains to decide exactly what the agency should try to do about it. Is the objective simply to make life more tolerable for those who live in poverty? Is it to assure that we have no marked expansion of the proportion of our citizens living in poverty? Is it to reduce the numbers of the poverty stricken? Or is it to eliminate poverty next year or in a decade? Unlike our football teams' goal of winning the game, the objectives of most public programs are not precisely specified.

Once some working objectives are arrived at (sometimes objectives are never made explicit and can be inferred only from actions), our administrators must develop a game plan or set of tactics for attaining the objectives. Here the quarterbacks' option of referring to the playbook, which contains predetermined solutions for each contingency, would be most welcome. In the course of time, administrative routines do develop, but it is never clear in advance just what actions will produce what results.

Turning to internal team management problems, a given administrative "quarterback" may be responsible for only one small portion of the team. How would our football game look if the quarterback could give instructions only to the backfield, and if the linemen and ends operated independently? Administrators frequently find themselves in this situation, since the agencies involved often are highly decentralized. Sometimes a part of the agency may so disagree with either the proposed objectives or strategies that it may become involved in attempts at sabotage. These intraorganizational problems are the subject of part III.

In the present part, we shall focus on *environmental* relationships. Several actors—especially the executive and other administrative agencies, the legislature and the courts, and organized groups—figure prominently in the administrator's environment, and we are interested in the *linkages* that develop between the agency and these various actors.

To return to the football analogy, the chief executive can be loosely identified as the coach. But if we are to carry out this aspect of the analogy to its conclusion, our coach would be likely to have several teams playing different sports on different fields at the same time. He might constantly give directions to the secretary of state but treat the secretary of housing and urban development with benign neglect. Like the National Football League's governing authority, the Congress is the administrator's rule-making authority; unlike the quarterback, though, the administrator must worry about the rules being changed, perhaps several times, during the game. The lengths of administrative games vary, too, and it is not possible to predict

The environment of public administration

63

with accuracy how long one will last; furthermore, rule makers or officials sometimes accede to demands from opponents and agree to reopen games that administrators thought they had finally won years before. Although officials in a football game may assess damaging penalties, courts sometimes hand down judgments that, in effect, cause the administrator to forfeit the game or otherwise make it impossible to attain objectives. Another difficulty is that the administrator's opponents are not all easily identified in uniforms of contrasting colors. Their identities constantly shift, some are never even known, and several enemies—such as other agencies competing for scarce resources or groups jealously protecting their interests—may have to be confronted all at one time. Finally, just as the stadium crowd's affection may be fickle, so may the agency's clientele groups not be placated easily.

If we have conveyed the impression that the administrative process is extremely complex, then we have already accomplished one of this part's objectives. In the chapters that follow, however, we shall try to sort things out and provide a sampling of the relationships that develop between administrators and other actors during all phases of the policy process.

The need for synthesis

In examining complex processes, scholars tend to proceed in an analytical manner; that is, they try to divide up those processes into their constituent parts in the hope that they can understand the whole by learning more about the parts. The analytical method has much to offer; indeed, academic life as we know it could not be managed without analysis. But there is the danger of forgetting synthesis, of failing to see how the various parts interact and how they relate to the whole—which is greater than the sum of its parts.

The chapters of part II focus on each of several sets of actors in the administrator's environment. As you read these, remember that an administrator usually cannot deal with any one of the environmental actors in isolation. Focusing on relations with one actor may mean that another is neglected, to the possible jeopardy of the entire program. This is, of course, another indication of the complexity and challenge of the administrative game.

Chapter three

Executive and interbureaucratic involvement

This chapter begins our exploration of the links that have been forged between administrative agencies and other actors in the political system. Since any citizen can become involved with an agency, the potential range of actors is enormously wide. But for the administrator, there are major distinctions among the actors in his or her environment. This chapter focuses on two that can be of critical importance: the chief executive and other public agencies. We treat these two together because the executive sponsors policy initiatives that frequently have the effect of encouraging interagency conflict. Also, as the formal superior to most agencies, the executive is responsible for the often arduous job of resolving such conflicts.

Formal executive powers

Article II of the Constitution simply states: "The executive Power shall be vested in a President of the United States of America." Further provisions clearly pertaining to public administration require that the president "faithfully execute" the office; "preserve, protect and defend" the Constitution; command the military forces; require, if he wishes, "the Opinion, in writing, of the principal Officer in each of the executive Departments, upon any Subject relating to the Duties of their respective Offices"; grant reprieves and pardons ("except in Cases of Impeachment"); and—"with the Advice and Consent of the Senate"—make treaties, appoint diplomatic representatives, and "all other Officers of the United States, whose Appointments are not herein otherwise provided for." All of this does not, however, add up to a definite constitutional mandate for a particular pattern of executive-bureaucratic relations. Although later legislation has specified some relationships, an incoming president is left pretty much to his own devices in defining just how he shall deal with the multimillion-member, multibillion-dollar establishment of federal agencies over which he wields "the executive Power."

Executive responsibilities in state constitutions and local charters are also usually defined quite loosely. When bureaucracy was small scale this created few problems, for chief executives could (and often did) take direct charge of administrative matters. This is still sometimes possible in small local governmental units. For example, attempting to interview a small town's city manager, the town's chief executive, one of our students finally found the manager performing the duties of police dispatcher. The town's single police car was normally dispatched by a secretary at city hall, who was ill that day. As the interview progressed—interrupted by occasional radio conversations with the patrolman—the town dogcatcher came in. He told the manager that his truck would not start and absolutely had to be repaired. The manager replied that there was no money for repairs, so the dogcatcher should seek other work. When asked what would be done about stray dogs, he said he was authorized to pay three dollars to anyone who brought in a stray.

This extreme example indicates how directly involved a chief executive could become in administrative affairs. But as government programs have burgeoned, presidents, governors, and local executives have effectively lost most such opportunities. Nonetheless, they remain important features in the environment of administrators. Numerous devices have been created to assure continued executive impact upon administration. An understanding of these devices and an ability to judge how well and under what circumstances they work is important to the administrator. As we shall see in succeeding chapters, it is quite likely that the administrator is being pushed and pulled in different directions by other environmental actors; these inputs demand responses just as do those from the executive.

Tools of executive control

Control is the word often applied to the relationship between executives, who normally are elected,[1] and administrative agencies. In organizational terms, the chief executive is at the top of a hierarchy, and administrators are, to varying degrees, responsible to the executive. As we shall see, much of the executive's "power" is symbolic rather than real, but some tools at the executive's command are useful in attempting to enforce his will.

Appointment of personnel

"If you want it done right, do it yourself." How nice that dictum sounds, but how impractical it is in performing all but the smallest tasks! Next best, perhaps, is to hold absolute powers of appointment and removal of those assigned to the task.

Appointment powers, which lay at the heart of executive control in early American history, have not yet lost their importance. Some of the first debates in the initial Congress concerned appointments and removals. Views expressed ranged from the extreme notion that department heads once appointed by a president should hold their positions for life (unless removed by impeachment) to Madison's belief that if a department head "does not conform to the judgment of the President in doing the executive duties of his office, he can be displaced. This makes him responsible to the great Executive power, and makes the President responsible to the public for the conduct of the person he has nominated and appointed."[2] Although dispute over the removal power has been reopened several times, the power of executives to remove—and also to appoint—was established early and

---

[1] An exception to the practice of electing chief executives is the case of city or county managers, who are chosen by the legislative body—the city council—and can be removed by it.

[2] Cited in Leonard D. White, *The Federalists: A Study in Administrative History* (New York: Macmillan Co., 1948), p. 23.

Executive and interbureaucratic involvement

67

remained for the first one hundred years the major presidential control device. Chapter 7 traces the development of the Civil Service System, which replaced executive appointment for many positions.

The power to appoint and remove—whether held by a president, some lesser federal official, or a state or local official—is such an important tool of executive control that where merit systems have been enacted to restrict these powers, care has been taken to assure that the office of chief executive does not become a hollow shell. The risk of this happening has been especially great in those states that provide for popular election of department heads (secretary of state, secretary of agriculture, etc.) and further restrict governors by placing most remaining positions under the merit system. In one such state, the director of the Budget Office was a merit-system employee. Budgeting is an important means of executive control, but in this case it was almost impossible for the governor to control through budgeting, since his ability to influence the budget director was restricted. Finally, after deciding that he and the director could not work together, a governor convinced the director to accept a transfer to the highway department (with a raise in pay) to a job that required little work and provided a state car for personal use. Should this exercise of executive creativity be viewed as an appalling abuse of the merit system? Perhaps. But another view is that the executive's appointment and removal power had been too far restricted.

Upon taking office in January 1977, President Carter had the opportunity to fill more than two-thousand policy-making positions at the top of the federal bureaucracy.[3] Through his initial appointees, the new president began an attempt to affect the actions of—even to control—a bureaucracy of about five-million persons.

Whether this is an effective device for executive control depends upon answers to two questions: Will the individuals selected respond to the president's wishes and energetically attempt to carry them out? And will this small number of high-level appointees be able to influence enough civil servants so that agency behavior is actually affected?

To assure that their appointees will be responsive, recent presidents have established elaborate selection systems. President Carter's was referred to as TIP (Talent Inventory Process). TIP had a staff of one hundred during the transition between election and inauguration. The staff compiled files on more than 30,000 job prospects; more than 10,000 were possible candidates for positions at the assistant secretary level (assistant secretary of defense, assistant secretary of trans-

---

[3]Including the cabinet, there are about seventy-five major appointments to make; many of the lesser appointments obviously would not be considered by the president personally. See *Congressional Quarterly* 34 (November 20, 1976): 3,196.

Chapter three

68

Drawing by W. Miller; © 197 The New Yorker Magazine, Inc.

portation, etc.) and higher. Obviously, the president could not know all of the job candidates, not even by reputation. He depended on others whom he had already appointed (on the TIP staff as well as in the departments) to screen them before he acted. Final presidential action did not take place until after an FBI investigation, a search of Internal Revenue Service files, clearance with political leaders (including Democratic members of Congress, governors, and party chairpersons of the nominee's home state), and agreement had been reached with the nominee to disclose financial and personal data. Of course, the president had to depend on others to assure him that all these actions had been taken and that the results were satisfactory.[4]

All things considered, then, does the president appoint people who will support and promote the presidential program? Usually, but not always. In addition to problems produced by the process just described, the president is further restrained by the need to reward groups that supported him in the campaign. The principal qualification for some appointments was being a leader of a particular interest group, even if the nominee was known to be lukewarm to some of the president's policy positions; for others, living in certain states was the key qualification, although other nominees whose state voted "wrong" might have promoted the presidential program more vigorously; for yet others, belonging to certain divisions or "wings" of the Democratic

---

[4]Joel Havemann, "The TIP Talent Hunt: Carter's Original Amateur Hour?" *National Journal* 9 (February 19, 1977): 268.

Executive and interbureaucratic involvement

party that supported Carter's election, but that could well fight his policies, insured their appointment.

Thus, the process of appointing even a relatively small number of officials is highly complex, and the president can have only partial confidence that the top-level policy makers he has appointed will devote themselves to carrying out his policies within their agencies. The second question, though, is (assuming that they want to), can the political appointees manage to implement the president's policies?

Any attempt to answer this question must begin with an awareness of the tiny proportion of federal employees appointed through this process—only .04 percent of the bureaucracy. To believe that they can successfully translate the president's hopes into actual programs requires a high trust in the formal aspects of organization. Such trust would seem reasonable if one could assume that the mere issuance of a direct instruction to a subordinate would automatically cause the person to react precisely as the superior wished. Of course, the appointees (and their subordinates down the line) do have sanctions that can be applied to employees who do not perform as instructed. But these sanctions are severely limited, both by the merit system under which most employees are appointed and by the fact that all of the appointees must look in two directions—to their superiors (higher political appointees and the president) and to their own subordinates. Total commitment to presidential desires—if these should conflict with widely held views of subordinates—could result in policy impotency: information and support from merit system employees may vanish. On the other hand, total commitment to departmental views that run counter to those of the president's could result in conflict and even dismissal. Successful political appointees are able to exist between these extremes: they have a talent for seeking out and drawing on those elements in the agency that support presidential actions, while encouraging changes in the positions of others; simultaneously, they also present the agency's case, attempting to get the presidential position modified.

This discussion has focused on the federal level, because it is there that extreme conditions are found. Although the absolute number of political appointees in the federal government is quite large, the executive actually is severely restrained because the number of political appointments relative to the total number of administrators is very small. But state governors, mayors, and city managers face similar problems, if on a different scale. None of these has unrestrained authority to influence administrators. Most administrators were already in their positions when the chief executive assumed office, and most will hold them after he or she leaves. Yet, for the administrators, executives are still important environmental components; their powers over administrators rest on several pillars in addition to those of appointment and removal.

Budgetary control

The budgetary process is considered in chapter 10, but one aspect of it must be mentioned here. Until the twentieth century, government budgeting in the United States was not a tool of executive control. Efforts to estimate systematically the needs of administrative agencies and to secure funding from legislatures were initiated by individual agencies. Chief executives normally did not comment on agencies' budgeting requests or attempt to alter them; also, once money was appropriated by the legislature, agencies were free to spend as they chose.

In most governmental units this has changed. Executives now review agency requests and, in many units, alter them before submission to the legislature. While many state and local governments routinely make available to legislators a tabulation of the agencies' original requests for funds, the federal budgetary process attempts to prevent this. Agency personnel are instructed to defend the executive budget, rather than argue for their own views of agency needs; nonetheless, their personal preferences may emerge—perhaps by prearrangement—when direct questions are asked in congressional hearings.

Although the chief executive may be unable to devote substantial personal attention to the review of agency requests, it is possible to have a relatively small group of appointees look at them in detail. The budget office is an important link between the executive and the agencies. Hence, the programmatic loyalty of budget office personnel is important to the executive, and these officials are crucial to an agency's relations with the executive. Agencies typically learn about new executive programs from budget staffers, and the budget office is also a channel for agencies to communicate their positions to the executive. A good working relationship with the budget office is unlikely to allow the agency to disregard executive wishes, but it can help to avoid unwelcome surprises at budget time.

Once money is appropriated, executives may exercise further control through the spending process. Depending upon statutes governing that process, executives may have the power to approve transfers of funds either among agencies or among programs (or subprograms) within agencies under certain circumstances. This procedure obviously could be used to help or hurt a particular administrative unit, as could the deferring of expenditures—even if

Executive and interbureaucratic involvement

71

only for a few weeks or months. Until 1974, the president was able to impound funds, to simply disallow their expenditure. Even though an agency wanted a program, and Congress had created it and appropriated the money, and the president had signed the bill, the president could later instruct the budget office to forbid spending money for it. Because President Nixon used this power extensively, in 1974 Congress passed the Congressional Budgeting and Impoundment Control Act, which very nearly prohibits such action.

One final comment about executive control through budgeting: *the potential threat of executive action may be more important in affecting the agency's behavior than actual attempts at control.* Administrators know they must return year after year to the chief executive and the budget office for their budgetary infusion. The risk that failure to comply with executive wishes may reduce next year's budget usually is sufficient to secure at least grudging compliance with executive desires.

Public visibility

"Governor Announces Sweeping Investigation of Prison System." Such a headline may merely confirm the undertaking of a study that state prison administrators have long known about, that they have participated in for months, and perhaps that they initiated themselves. What difference does the governor's dramatic announcement make?

The position of chief executive commands public attention. Individuals and groups normally unconcerned about prisons will be mobilized by that headline. Had the warden or prison system director released a similar statement, the headline probably would have been smaller, and public reaction probably would have differed. From their visible positions, executives can issue statements (unfortunately, even half-truths) that sharply affect administrators. The implication of the headline is that the governor thinks something is wrong with the system. Does he? He may have left his actual position ambiguous, but the threat of such headlines acts as an instrument of executive control of public agencies. This is especially so if the executive's prestige is high among those (clientele, interest groups, the public) who matter to the agency.

Executive oversight

Oversight is an important concept in public administration. The following chapter discusses *legislative oversight*—the legislature's pursuit of matters beyond the mere passage of legislation to see that laws are properly enforced. Here we shall briefly explore *executive oversight*.

Although chief executives have formal control over much of public administration and are provided the tools described above, various difficulties are encountered in attempting to exercise that control. Sometimes the tools themselves are nearly unmanageable; for instance, in the case of the president, so many appointees must be selected that he could have little personal confidence that most appointees are loyal to, or even familiar with, his policies. What, then, does a chief executive do? What they seem to do rather uniformly is to assemble a cadre of trusted individuals, chosen on the basis of personal confidence, who serve as extensions of the chief executive. Some members of this cadre are given positions of high personal responsibility (perhaps budget director or press officer); others hold relatively lower-level positions in administrative agencies, but are "detailed" to work directly for the chief executive; yet others may hold no government position, but as long-time advisors and friends of the chief executive, their counsel continues to be sought.

Upon such a cadre, then, many modern chief executives depend for executive oversight, a process that is both less formal and more confidential than the tools of control described above. These individuals keep the executive informed by developing contacts throughout the administrative establishment (even in agencies over which the executive has no formal control) and by observing closely the working of the formal control structures—the budget office, for example.

The use of this cadre for executive oversight is not without its potential hazards. The Watergate affair of the early 1970s argues, of course, for high visibility of the innermost reaches of the executive establishment. In fact, the trend has been to increase gradually such visibility. The creation of a cabinet early in this country's history can be seen as an effort to assemble a cadre of advisors, but this arrangement did not succeed for long. Cabinet members had responsibilities to their departments and often to their own political supporters; thus, frequently they were not very useful as confidential advisors to the president. Later, presidents made use of "kitchen cabinet" advisors, but gradually this arrangement became institutionalized as the White House Office. Over time, the personnel of that office have gradually lost their anonymity and have become almost as visible as the cabinet itself.

Because chief executives are in constant need of information that may not be available through official channels, efforts to provide complete openness are most likely to fail. Carrying such an effort to an extreme, one state legislature recently considered a bill that would have required all conversations between the governor and his or her staff to be open to the press. Even if this extreme step were taken, the governor would find means to secure off-the-record advice; a new cadre for executive oversight would be created.

The agents of executive oversight—operating with varying degrees of visibility—are extensions of the executive; they are eyes and ears and, less frequently, voices. Those involved in executive oversight are also important individuals from the agency perspective, since much of what the chief executive knows of the agency will come from them.

There are numerous strands, then, in the rope that links any agency to the chief executive: those established by constitution or statute, those that devolve from executive status and prestige, and those that are part of the executive oversight system. Frequently this rope is quite long, allowing the agency extensive latitude. Through contacts with other environmental actors (especially the legislature), some agencies are able to stretch the rope ever farther, so that little remains of executive control. For a few agencies, the controls are broken entirely; the agency operates independently of the executive and is responsible only to the legislature. More usually, though, the breaking of formal ties (appointment, budgetary control, etc.) does not eliminate informal ones; the executive remains highly salient in the administrators' environment.

Interbureaucratic relationships

Hierarchy

A fundamental principle underlying the primacy of the chief executive in administrative matters is that of *hierarchy*. According to this principle, each administrative organization is subordinate to the chief executive; and most are subordinate to other organizations between them and the chief executive, while being themselves superior to other organizations. The fundamental structure of the federal government is displayed in figure 3–1. Each of the organizations noted there is itself a complex organization, as indicated in figure 3–2, which is an organization chart for the mammoth Department of Health, Education, and Welfare.

The principle of hierarchy is intended to establish clearly the organizational responsibility of each unit and to make possible the delegation of executive authority. Such delegation is necessary, of course, for it is obviously not feasible for every administrator to report directly

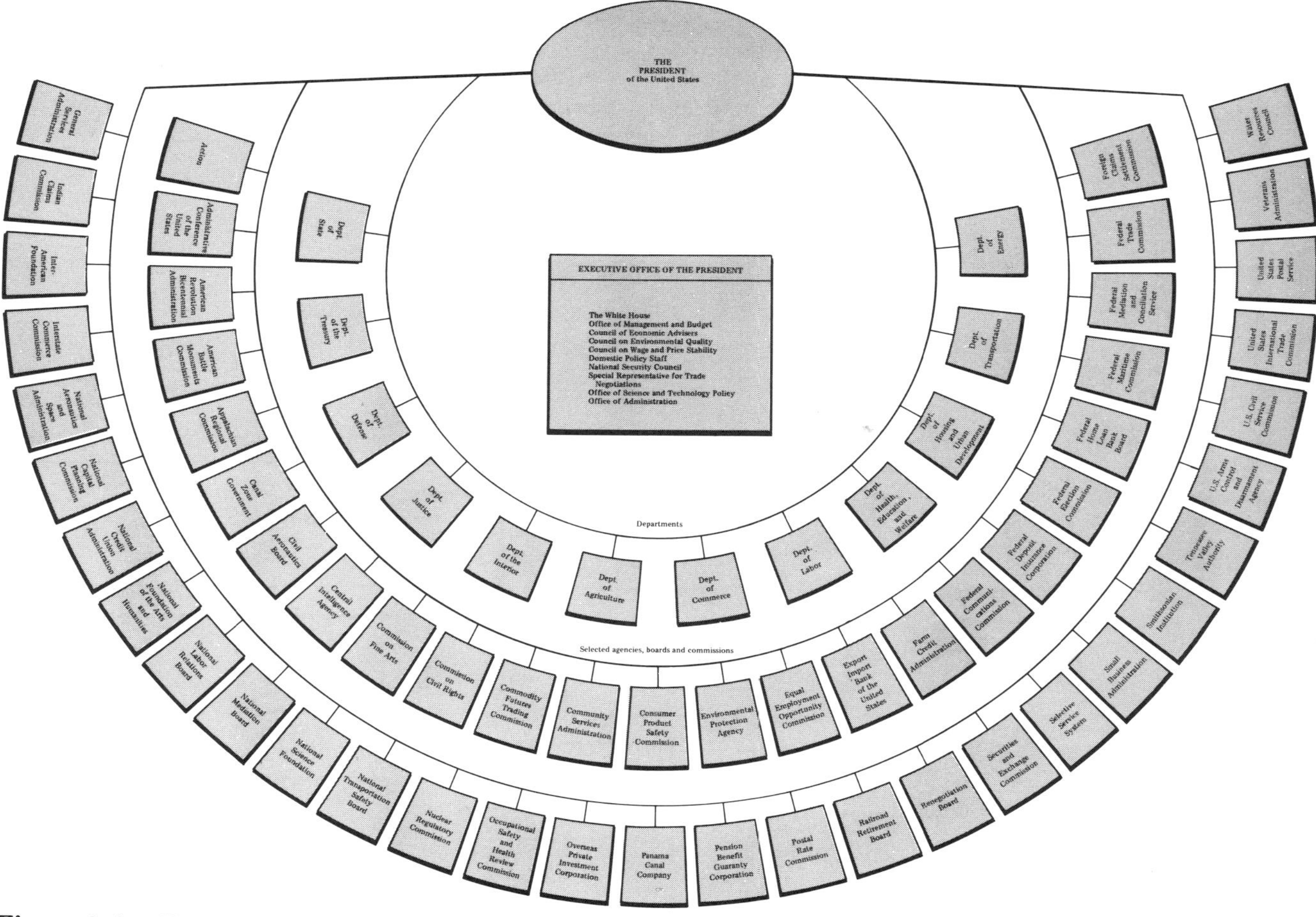

Figure 3–1.   Executive branch of the government

Source: Executive Office of the President, *The United States Budget in Brief, 1979* (Washington: U.S. Government Printing Office, 1978)

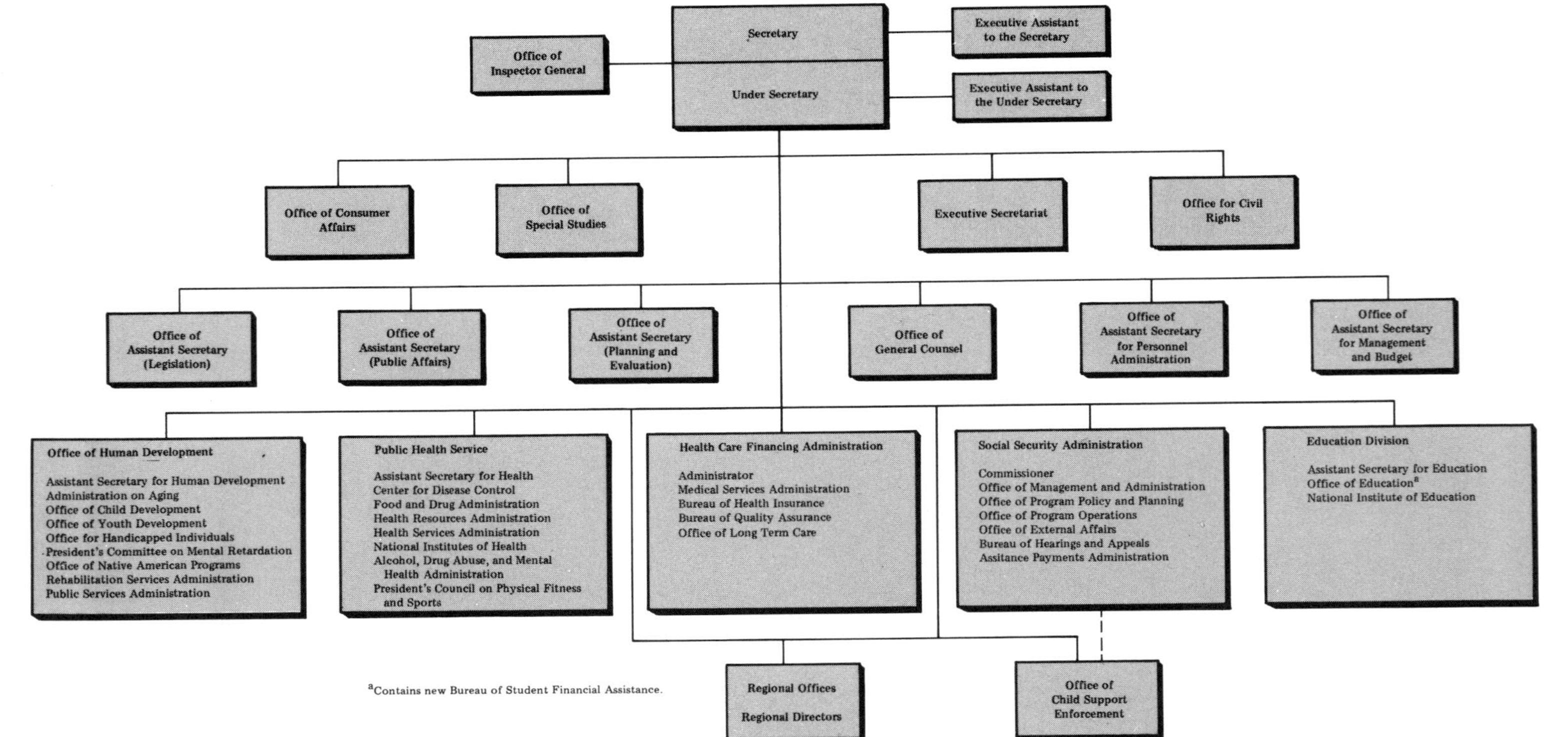

Figure 3–2.   Department of Health, Education and Welfare

aContains new Bureau of Student Financial Assistance

Source: 1977–78 United States Government Manual (Office of the Federal Registrar, 1977), p. 250.

to the chief executive. A first concern of interbureaucratic relationships, then, centers on the administrator's contacts *within* the hierarchy, upward and downward. While the organization chart, which often hangs on the wall, lets each administrator know the unit to which he or she owes formal, hierarchical responsibility, it turns out that the chart is not always right in practice. Often there is an *informal* hierarchical structure that is only partially in accord with the formal one. Examining the formal hierarchy can reveal something about interbureaucratic relationships, but it may not reveal the full picture.

Vertical and horizontal administrative conflict

Throughout part II of this book you will encounter actors who make possible and encourage violations of the formal structure; interest groups, legislators, other administrative employees, and even the chief executive often take actions that allow administrative units to ignore, at least partially, their formal superiors. It is thus that the informal hierarchy is established and that it may also in time be changed. A major feature of interbureaucratic relationships is that they may not be what they at first seem; long-term, intensive observation is often necessary to discover the actual interagency patterns of hierarchical relationships.

For example, after a year of conflict, the director of the General Services Administration, Jay Solomon, reportedly received permission from President Carter to fire the deputy director, Robert Griffin, who had worked for the GSA for thirty-five years. Quoting unnamed administration sources, the *Washington Post* said "Solomon was convinced that he cannot control the agency as long as GSA employees are unsure which of the two men—he or Griffin—is in charge." House Speaker Thomas, "Tip," O'Neill, a personal friend of Griffin's who had tried unsuccessfully to convince Carter to name Griffin as GSA director, intervened with the president—again unsuccessfully—to try to save Griffin's job. The following repercussions are illustrative of the influence of this particular "subordinate" through his patron: Speaker O'Neill cut off relations with the White House congressional liaison man; President Carter met with Griffin, praised him for his work, and said that Vice President Mondale would be detailed to find him another suitable post; a new $50,000-a-year White House staff job was created for Griffin.[5]

The sort of interbureaucratic conflict we have just discussed can be called *vertical conflict* between nominal superiors and nominal subordi-

---

[5]Cited in Associated Press, 26 July 1978, 3 August 1978, and 4 August 1978.

nates. Administrators function in an organizational world of uncertainty, despite its apparent formal precision. Such uncertainty is, of course, not limited to public-sector administrators. Business firms have interbureaucratic struggles that rival any in government—but they usually are less open to public scrutiny. These struggles, in both business and government, often are not irrelevant quarrels among status-seeking, power-mad bureaucrats. Frequently, they concern differences over important policy matters. For example, the controversy about requiring the installation of airbags in automobiles has pitted subunits within the Department of Transportation against each other. Although a considerable body of data is available regarding the utility of airbags, various organizational units interpret these data differently and place differing weights on such values as safety, economics, and freedom of choice for the consumer. While personal pride can be an important motive in attempting to get one's views accepted, quite rational policy considerations can justify a unit trying to circumvent the wishes of its immediate superior.

A second type of interbureaucratic conflict—illustrated by the above example—can be called *horizontal conflict*. Organizational units at various levels, but especially those at similar hierarchical levels, compete against each other for limited resources. The budgetary process described in chapter 10 normally provides for the distribution of funds through formal hierarchical channels. Thus, the unit immediately superior to a given administrator's unit will have a great deal to say about how much that administrator's unit will be allowed to request and then will actually receive. For example, consider the situation of three general hospitals, all operated by a state health department, that prepare preliminary budget requests which finally form part of the department's request to the chief executive and to the legislature. Eventually, a sum of money will be budgeted for the department, which will then have some discretion over how much each hospital receives. Competition arises among the three hospitals; each probably will get less than it requested, but each probably will use whatever political resources it can muster to try to secure special departmental favor. For instance, a hint about a need for a new coronary care unit may be dropped to a friendly local legislator in the hope that he or she will pass it on to the agency head or the chief executive.

Sometimes vertical and horizontal conflicts combine. The Army Corps of Engineers provides much of the funding and supervision for such water resource projects as dams, locks, and harbor facilities. Also involved in some such projects are units of the Department of Interior and Department of Agriculture. Although located in different departments, these units engage in *horizontal competition* for the limited resources available for water resource work. It is not unusual for the Corps of Engineers to be deeply embroiled in *vertical competition* as well. Strong interest groups support its projects, despite the occasional desire of some of its superiors—even of presidents—to reduce the scale of some and to eliminate others. In fighting these vertical battles, the hole card of the Corps is the Congress, whose pork-barrel minded members generally have been quite willing to support the Engineers' projects.

Bureaucratic imperialism

Of course, agencies engage in horizontal or vertical conflict with other members of the executive branch for reasons other than the programmatic ones already discussed. There also is a strong desire to *protect* the agency against aggression from others and to *promote* its interests. Strictly speaking, by using language of this sort we are making the error of anthropomorphizing the agencies, of treating them as if they were persons. We do so because it has become customary to talk of agencies in this way (as scholars of international politics discuss the "national interest" of the United States) and because *many bureaucrats act as if their agencies were persons having interests, goals, etc.*

As the researches of Herbert Kaufman have indicated, agencies die very infrequently.[6] When its life is threatened, an agency may display enormous powers of self-preservation. For example, when President Nixon decided to dispose of the Office of Economic Opportunity (OEO) in early 1973, despite severe budgetary cuts and sophisticated undermining of the agency's programs from on high, many of OEO's staff remained dedicated and the office managed to linger on until early 1975.

OEO's principal allies were nonexecutive actors in its environment, or members of its constituency: friendly congressmen (who continued to appropriate funds, which were promptly impounded by the president) and leaders of interest groups. More will be said of these relationships in chapter 5, but the strength of most agencies' constituency ties (to legislative committees, to producer and consumer groups, to the media) makes us skeptical about the likelihood of very many agencies falling victim to the highly touted "sunset" laws recently adopted in many jurisdictions.

For most agencies most of the time, however, survival is not an important actual concern. Instead, leaders of the organization are deeply involved in maintaining and increasing their power in comparison with that of other organizations. In making just this point, Matthew

---

[6]Herbert Kaufman, *Are Government Organizations Immortal?* (Washington, D.C.: Brookings Institution, 1976).

Executive and interbureaucratic involvement

79

Holden, Jr., elaborates: "This by no means implies that administrative politicians are pirates out for plunder. But it does imply that the most saintly idealist (if a saintly idealist ever could rise to such a high post) could not function if he abandoned the maxim of 'my agency, right or wrong!'"[7] Holden has demonstrated that agencies often act "imperialistically" toward other agencies and try to take over jurisdictions of other agencies or even the agencies themselves. More generally, public agencies have philosophies and orientations that they tend to promote tirelessly. Clearly, they are important forces to be reckoned with in the entire political-administrative system.

Nonconflictive interaction

Thus far, conflict has been featured in our discussion of interbureaucratic relationships. Not all such relationships are conflictive, of course; interaction with staff agencies and cooperative projects undertaken with other agencies often do not involve conflict, although it can and does occur in these cases too.

Superior administrators, all the way to the chief executive, have agencies that assist them; in addition to budget offices (which we have already discussed and whose contacts with agencies often *are* conflictive), legal counsels, personnel offices, purchasing offices, etc., usually exist. Many agencies have more contacts with these staff units than with agencies parallel to themselves. The chore of recruiting and processing new fire fighters, for example, probably will not be handled by the fire department but rather by the city personnel department; the hiring function requires close ties between the two agencies, of course, and such ties are common.

Another type of interbureaucratic link that usually is nonconflictive arises between agencies sharing missions. Putting a man on the moon, for example, required that an enormously large number of agencies cooperate; many of the relations had to be harmonious to achieve the objective. Also, many welfare programs are cooperatively administered. It is not unusual for one agency to determine client eligibility, for another to disburse the funds, and for yet another—often at a lower governmental level—to provide a caseworker for follow-up. Conflict sometimes arises during these interactions, of course; the fact that citizens are often given "the runaround" is a principal impetus for administrative reform proposals. Nonetheless, most such relationships are cooperative; otherwise, much of the administrative process would be bogged down.

---

[7]Matthew Holden, Jr., " 'Imperialism' in Bureaucracy," *American Political Science Review* 60 (December 1966): 944.

More swelling of the presidency*

Thomas E. Cronin

In the past two decades the office of president of the United States has undeniably assumed an ever-growing importance in the nation's political life. In the early 1970s so many powers were being assumed by the president that it became common to talk of the "imperial presidency." Only a part of the disaffection with the office stemmed from the moral lapses of the Nixon administration uncovered during the Watergate investigations; many observers also have been concerned that recent presidents have usurped, or assumed through default, many powers traditionally exercised by Congress.

The expansion of the president's governmental role has required, or has been made possible by, an expansion of the presidential organization. In this section, political scientist Thomas Cronin, who has been a White House Fellow, details the reasons for and the extent of the growth of the presidential role, the office's organizational response to the growth, and the relationship between the president's immediate subordinates and the other executive agencies.

When Jimmy Carter became president, the size and functions of the White House staff and the Executive Office of the President were highly controversial subjects. Carter, campaigning in 1976, pledged to reduce the size of the presidential establishment by 30 percent. Further, he claimed he would reverse the flow of power away from White House staffers back to his cabinet secretaries.

President Carter did succeed in his first year and a half to pare the size of the White House staff. He also tried valiantly to beef up the role of cabinet members. But by 1979 the White House staff had grown again and White House centralization was again a fact of Washington life. In addition to the White House staff there were about 17 support agencies in the Executive Office, such as the National Security Council and Office of Management and Budget.

---

*Prepared for this volume. Copyright, Thomas. E. Cronin, 1979. Parts of this selection are based on "The Swelling of the Presidency," *Saturday Review of the Society* 1 (January 20, 1973): 30–36 and on "The Swelling of the Presidency and Its Impact on Congress," U.S. Congress, House, Select Committee on Committees, *Committee Organization in the House*, vol. 2, part 3, 93d Cong., 1st sess. (1973), pp. 836–44. See also his *The State of the Presidency* (Boston: Little, Brown, 1975).

Executive and interbureaucratic involvement

Table 1. Expanding the White House Staff

Year	President	Full time employees	Employees temporarily detailed to the White House from outside agencies	Total
1937	Franklin D. Roosevelt	45	112 (June 30)	157
1947	Harry S. Truman	190	27 (June 30)	217
1957	Dwight D. Eisenhower	364	59 (June 30)	423
1967	Lyndon B. Johnson	251	246 (June 30)	497
1972	Richard M. Nixon	550	34 (June 30)	584
1975	Gerald R. Ford	533	27 (June 30)	560
1977	Jimmy Carter	480	175 (April 30)	655

Plainly, the experience has been that many in the cabinet have lost power and the Executive Office has grown in status, in size, and in powers. In light of experience, can the performance of the Executive Office be made to conform to Carter's campaign pledges? Can the presidential establishment really be cut back?

The Office of the President increased 13 percent during the Eisenhower and Kennedy years, another 13 percent under LBJ. But it rose approximately another 25 percent under Nixon and the unchecked growth of the White House establishment and its battalion of "faceless ministers" continued to grow even under Gerald Ford, who had always promised to curb bureaucratic growth. His favorite motto was "A government big enough to give you everything you want is a government big enough to take from you everything you have." Ford was unsuccessful in reversing the trend. Midway through his brief presidential term one account indicated there were about seventy-five more White House aides on his staff than when Richard Nixon departed.

The expansion of the presidency, it should be emphasized, is by no means only a recent phenomenon. As table 1 indicates, the number of employees directly under the President has been growing steadily since the New Deal days when only a few dozen people served in the White House entourage, at a cost of less than a few hundred thousand dollars annually.

In the late-1970s the Presidential Establishment embraced nearly a score of support staffs (White House Office, National Security Council, Office of Management and Budget, etc.) and advisory offices (Council of Economic Advisors, Office of Science and Technology Policy, Office of Telecommunications Policy, etc.). It spawned a vast proliferation of ranks and titles to go with its proliferation of functions (Counsel to the President, Assistant to the President, Special Consultant, Director, Staff Director, etc.).

Official figures on the size of the Presidential Establishment, and standard body counts vary widely depending on exactly who is included, but by one frequently used reckoning, between two to three thousand people work directly for the President of the United States. Payroll and maintenance costs for this staff run to several hundred million dollars annually.

Pressures promoting White House concentration

Why has the presidency grown bigger and bigger? There is no single villain or systematically organized conspiracy promoting this expansion. A variety of factors are at work. The most significant is the expansion of the role of the presidency itself—an expansion that for the most part has taken place during national emergencies. The reason for this is that the public and Congress in recent decades have both tended to look to the president for the decisive responses that were needed in those emergencies. The Great Depression and World War II in particular brought sizable increases in presidential staffs. And once in place, many stayed on, even after the emergencies that brought them had faded. Smaller national crises have occasioned expansion in the White House entourage, too. After the Russians successfully orbited Sputnik in 1957, President Eisenhower added several science advisors. After the Bay of Pigs, President Kennedy enlarged his national security staff.

Considerable growth in the presidential establishment, especially in the post World War II years, stems also directly from the belief that critical societal problems require that wise men be assigned to the White House to alert the president to appropriate solutions and to serve as the agents for implementing these solutions. Congress has frequently acted on the basis of this belief, legislating the creation of the National Security Council, the Council of Economic Advisers, and the Council on Environmental Quality, among others. Congress has also increased the chores of the presidency by making it a statutory responsibility for the president to prepare more and more reports associated with what are regarded as critical social areas—annual economic and manpower reports, a biennial report on national growth, etc.

For example, President Nixon responded to a number of troublesome problems that defy easy relegation to any one department—problems like international trade, drug abuse, and the energy crisis—by setting up special offices in the Executive Office with sweeping authority and sizable staffs. Once established, these units rarely get dislodged. And an era of permanent crisis ensures a continuing accumulation of such bodies.

Another reason for the growth of this presidential establishment is that occupants of the White House frequently distrust members of the permanent government. Nixon aides, for example, usually saw most civil servants not only as Democratic but as wholly unsympathetic to such objectives of the Nixon administration as decentralization, revenue sharing, and the curtailment of several Great Society programs. Departmental bureaucracies are viewed from the White House as independent, unresponsive, unfamiliar, and inaccessible. They are suspected again and again of placing their own, congressional, or special-interest priorities ahead of those communicated to them from the White House. Even the president's own cabinet members soon become viewed in the same light.

Not only have recent presidents been suspicious about the depth of the loyalty of those in their cabinets, but they also invariably become concerned about the possibility that sensitive administration secrets may leak out through the departmental bureaucracies. This is another reason why presidents have come to rely more on their own personal groups, such as task forces and advisory commissions.

Still another reason that more and more portfolios have been given to the presidency is that new federal programs frequently concern more than one federal agency, and it seems reasonable that someone at a higher level is required to fashion a consistent policy and to reconcile conflicts. White House aides again and again claim that the presidency is the only place in government where there is a possibility to set and coordinate national priorities. They say it is not done in Congress and should not be left to the departments. Attempts by cabinet members themselves to solve sensitive jurisdictional questions frequently result in bitter squabbling. At times, too, cabinet members themselves have recommended that these multidepartmental issues be settled at the White House. Sometimes new presidential appointees insist that new offices for program coordination be established and located directly under the president.

The presidential establishment has also been enlarged by the representation of interest groups within its fold. Even a partial listing of staff specializations that have been grafted onto the White House in recent years reveals how interest-group brokerage has become added to the more traditional staff activities of counseling and administration. These specializations form a veritable index of American society: budget and management, national security, economics, congressional matters, science and technology, drug abuse prevention, telecommunications, consumers, national goals, intergovernmental relations, environment, domestic policy, international economics, military affairs, civil rights, disarmament, labor relations, District of Columbia, cultural affairs, education, foreign trade and tariffs, the aged, health and nutrition, physical fitness, volunteerism, intellectuals, blacks, youth, women, Wall Street, governors, mayors, "ethnics," regulatory agencies and related industry, state party chairmen, Mexican-Americans.

Both Presidents Ford and Carter, in their efforts to "keep the doors of the White House open" maintained a fairly large staff called the Public Liaison Office. Critics contend that this kind of White House activity is unnecessary, too much of an on-going campaign unit or merely a staff that engages in "stroking" people or groups who want to say they have taken their cause to the White House. White House aides, of course, claim that these staffs that ensure access to the White House for nearly every interest are a requirement of an open presidency.

One of the more fascinating elements in the growth of the Presidential Establishment is the development, particularly under the current administration, of a huge public-relations apparatus. More than 100 presidential aides are now engaged in various forms of press-agentry or public relations, busily selling and reselling the President. This activity — sometimes cynically called the politics of symbolism — is devoted to the particular occupant of the White House, but inevitably it affects the presidency itself, expanding public expectations about the presidency.

Last, but by no means least, Congress, which has grown increasingly critical of the burgeoning power of the presidency, must take some blame itself for the expansion of the White House. Divided within itself and often ill-equipped, or simply disinclined to make some of the nation's toughest political decisions in recent decades, Congress has abdicated significant authority to the presidency. In late 1972 Congress almost passed a grant of authority to the President that would have given him the right to determine which programs are to be cut whenever the budget went beyond the $250 billion ceiling limit — a bill which, in effect, would have handed over to the President some of Congress's long-cherished "power of the purse." Fortunately, Congress could not agree on how to yield this precious power to the executive. In April 1977, Congress restored to President Carter wide powers to propose abolishing or consolidating or modifying organizational bodies within and outside of the departments.

While the number of functionaries is the most tangible and dramatic measure of the White House's expansion, its increasing absorption of governmental functions is more important. President Carter may consider cutting his staff or consolidating a number of agencies, but it is yet another thing to reduce the accumulated prerogatives and responsibilities of the presidency. By 1979 Carter was doing everything he could to strengthen the presidency.

The differentiated White House staff

A proper understanding of the swelling of the presidential office nevertheless requires at least an introductory examination of the central staffs and staff activities that seem now permanently fixed there. Three of these are substantive: (1) *domestic policy,* (2) *economic policy,* and (3) *national security staffs;* three are administrative or procedural: (4) *administrative staffs,* (5) *congressional relations,* and (6) *public relations.* The swelling of the presidency has occurred on all fronts, almost as if designed to offset those institutions that consciously or unwittingly impose limits and constraints on presidential initiatives. In any event, these staffs grow; they are here to stay, and taken collectively, they constitute the very fabric of the modern presidency as an institution (figure A).

Detailed attention should also, indeed must be, devoted to the vast growth in the public relations component of these staffs because much of what passes for public relations work there actually promotes through greater public expectations and demands on the office at least a proportional concentration of powers there. As such it is very central to the swelling. Hence, any discussion of the swelling of the presidency must necessarily also give special attention to the selling and constant reselling of the presidency.

In search of a realistic job description
for the presidency (A GS—118?)

Many, if not all, discussions about the presidency and whether it is too strong or too weak, healthy or pathological, accountable or irresponsible and so forth, suffer from an almost constant shifting from one policy area to another, and from disjointed leaps from one type of decisional activity to a

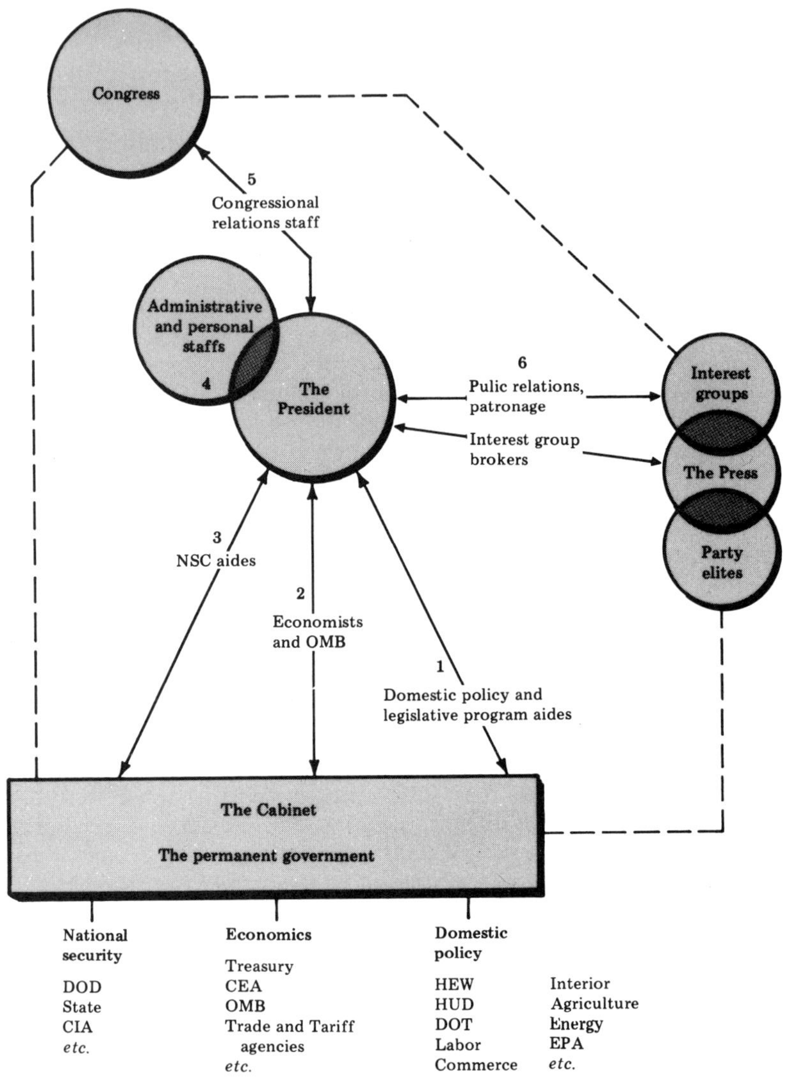

Figure A.   The differentiated White House staff and their constituencies

substantially different type. In fact, of course, a president can be very powerful and near dictatorial in some aspects of his job, whereas in others his condition is more akin to that of a prisoner, hedged in on all sides. Often, too,
the very same act by two different people in the presidency can evoke markedly different acceptance because the nature of the times or political climate
has changed. One is reminded, for example, that when President Hoover suggested that what the nation really needed was a restoration of confidence, he
was greeted by bitter laughter. When Franklin Roosevelt only a little while

later addressed the same nation and declared that "the only thing we have to fear is fear itself," virtually the same message in cliche form, the nation was thrilled and its spirit rallied.

Until recently it has been fashionable to speak of a president as wearing many hats—a commander-in-chief hat, another as chief legislator, one for chief of state, and so on. This simplified metaphor of presidential hats belongs to the days of a simpler past. The swelling of the presidency, in real terms as well as in expectations, has recast that office in numerous ways. First of all, it is now organized around three major but obviously interrelated substantive subpresidencies. These have been outlined: foreign affairs and national security, aggregate economics, and domestic and urban policy. The president's time is constantly absorbed in one or more of these separate but related policy spheres. In addition, a president can be viewed as participating in each of these subpresidencies in one of six functional or task-oriented ways. These are depicted in table 2. This table should be viewed not in one-dimensional, static terms but as a dynamic, weblike assortment of jobs, tasks, and responsibilities.

A president's staff and cabinet are organized around these three substantive subpresidencies. In practice, however, a president must see to it that each is related to the other, and that questions cutting across boundary lines are not ignored just because they fall between jurisdictional cracks. An exclusively domestic or national security problem rarely exists. Inevitably, substantive problems and their corresponding solutions affect each other—often in decidedly counterproductive ways.

It is clear that a president needs to forge majoritarian coalitions, at least temporarily, if he is to move his priorities forward. Presidents Kennedy and Nixon time and again proposed new directions in various policy areas but were unable to secure congressional approval. Nixon, for example, sent Congress a splendid and very idealistic reform message on Indian affairs in 1970 but it occasioned no significant changes. A message was not enough; action and change required partisan and educational leadership, which Mr. Nixon apparently chose not to give or for which he did not have the time or political capital.

Here it must be underscored that many presidents become timid about using the resources of the presidency for partisan leadership. The reason for this, of course, is rather simple. A president wants above all to be "president of all the people" and yet even an outstanding performance as symbolic chief of state cannot relieve a president from the responsibility of initiative and partisan education. A president is obliged to respond to the interests and expectations of the party that nominated and elected him. Having made pledges for which both he and his party will be held to account in future elections, a president must try to win support for his definition of what must be done. As political scientist James M. Burns writes, "The crowning paradox is an old one for the American President. ... He has had to be both a unifier and a divider of the people."

President Nixon's ill-fated Family Assistance Program also died as a result of inadequate political leadership. The president was unable even to win majority support in his own cabinet and among his own White House staff. Failure in his own household made his campaign vulnerable as he tried

Table 2.   Job description for the modern presidency (with examples)

Functional subpresidencies	Symbolic leadership	Priority setting	Crisis management	Chief executive follow-through		
				Legislative and political support and partisan educator	Program implementation and evaluation	Oversight of government routine
Foreign policy/ National security	Hosting visiting dignitaries Chief-of-State rituals	"To preserve a free South Vietnam"	Cuban missile crisis Tet offensive 1968	Winning public support for U.S. fighting in South Vietnam	Affecting the goals of the Alliance for Progress	Overseas base operations Military assistance
Aggregate economics	Being "bullish on Wall Street and the American dollar"	"To reduce unemployment to 4 percent"	Depressions/Dollar devaluations	Passing a tax reform package	Reducing unemployment	IRS-tax collection and enforcement
Domestic policy	Hosting police chiefs at White House to discuss killing of policemen	"To reduce crime"	Detroit riots of 1967 Watergate election conspiracy	Achieving agreement among competing cabinet departments on manpower programs	Regulating polluters	Federal Bureau of Prisons operations

to persuade Congress and the country that this was his number-one domestic initiative. Eventually the measure was removed from his agenda.

Then there is the paramount problem of implementation—the carrying out and realization of presidentially endorsed goals. The vast instruments of the Executive Office which have been created to give presidential control over implementation do not ensure that this happens. Everybody has known that the presidency is limited in its capacity to effect implementation. Strengthening the presidency has been tried. But the presidency is still not as much in charge as most people assume. For the very instruments of presidential control engender in and of themselves new problems. The swelling of the presidency has brought about staff differentiation, overspecialization, compartmentalization, internal conflicts, and considerable conflict with the cabinet and other executive department establishments.

The vast growth in federal grant-in-aid programs and intricate involvement with all levels of government exacerbates problems of implementation. Confusion over goals, inadequate planning, and frequently inept program evaluation all add to the problem.

Implementing policy intentions, then, involves sustained political and chief executive leadership. If any lesson of presidential power has been learned in recent years, it should be that the presidency must stay involved well after the bill-signing celebration is over if White House initiatives are not to be derailed or sabotaged in the labyrinthine modern federalism. Priority setting and budgetary planning are fundamental antecedents to implementation; instrumental leadership involves winning sustained support for new programs and checking to make sure that these programs work as intended. Presidents appear, however, to have been conditioned by a political and journalistic temperament in Washington that prizes the excitement of setting new directions often, though not exclusively, manifest by getting a bill to the Hill. White House staff are usually more interested in generating new policy ideas than in putting a law into operation. Beyond the well-known legislative box score of presidential success in dealing with Congress, there exist neither quick ratings nor glamorous incentives for the tedious job of implementing domestic programs.

Finally, little presidential attention is paid to the routine activities that make up the large bulk of federal government work. Indeed, the latter is almost a contradiction in terms: if a president is involved, the matter must not be routine. But routine activities which are neglected or improperly monitored and evaluated can on occasion be elevated to crisis proportion. For the most part a president must delegate large amounts of discretion to political subordinates and career government professionals; his influence over routine activities is indirect—through appointees, budgetary examinations, legislative clearance. A president may view these activities as self-executing, or he may even attempt to disassociate himself from them. But much of the administrative and chief executive burdens of the presidency consist of far more than merely oversight of routine implementation. In many respects the management of routines is, as V. O. Key pointed out, "between-election politics." That is:

Great administrative decisions, like legislative acts, may involve a reconciliation of conflicting interests and must be made with an

Executive and interbureaucratic involvement

alertness to their general public acceptability. Nor is the task of the President in the leadership of federal administration simply one of the issuance of directions to subordinates: the arts of compromise, of negotiations, of persuasion have as great a relevance in the White House as in Congress.

Moreover, the quality of these "bread and butter" service and assistance programs is important to the average American, and presidents are, like it or not, held responsible for the general quality of government performance.

Only through shrewd monitoring of these routines can a president know whether citizens are getting a fair return on their taxes. Only by more imaginative use of presidential resources in overseeing these routines can we avert these same activities from becoming sources of crises themselves. To be sure, oversight and reform in this area must come not only from presidents but from other quarters as well. But the key is the degree to which a president can fashion an executive management system in which he on the one hand can delegate vast responsibilities to talented managers, and on the other hand benefit from an early-warning system that can alert him through his managers as well as through other monitoring devices about inadequate government performance, about experimentation that yields negative results, and about research and development progress that could serve as feedback correctives to ineffective or counterproductive policies.

Study questions for selection one

1. Could the size of the White House staff be reduced significantly without reducing the scope of the presidential function? Should presidential powers be slashed?

2. Should the individual and collective powers of cabinet members be increased at the expense of the powers of White House officials?

3. Considering the president's multiple responsibilities (as symbolic leader of the nation, as crisis manager, as chief policy maker, etc.), would it be wise or unwise for a president to devote a much larger proportion of his time to policy implementation than recent presidents have?

The ten commandments of the foreign affairs bureaucracy*

Leslie H. Gelb and Morton H. Halperin

As Thomas Cronin mentioned in the previous selection, "departmental bureaucracies are viewed from the White House as independent, unresponsive, unfamiliar, and inaccessible. They are suspected again and again of placing their own, congressional or special-interest priorities ahead of those communicated to them from the White House." Although the chief executive's formal powers make him officially pre-eminent, administrative agencies pursue their own interests—however they may define them—and compete (often successfully) with the "political" actors in formulating public policy.

Among the most independent of America's bureaucrats are those having responsibility for foreign relations. At times, the Central Intelligence Agency, to cite a notorious example, has seemed almost entirely autonomous; in his interview with David Frost broadcast on May 4, 1977, Richard Nixon even mentioned (and did not reject) the possibility of CIA complicity in his downfall. One can, of course, note the influence on policy of administrative agencies without seeing conspiracies everywhere. The following selection, written by a reporter for the *New York Times* (Leslie Gelb) and a former official of the National Security Council (Morton Halperin, who successfully sued Richard Nixon, H. R. Haldeman, and John Mitchell for tapping his telephone), adopts the thesis used in this book—that agencies are powerful actors in the policy system. Such historical events as the formation of the state of Israel, the Bay of Pigs invasion, the Cuban missile crisis, and the bombing of North Vietnam are examined in order to demonstrate *how* the foreign affairs bureaucracies are so frequently able to achieve their objectives, whether or not the president agrees with them.

---

*Reprinted with permission from Leslie H. Gelb and Morton H. Halperin, "The Ten Commandments of the Foreign Affairs Bureaucracy," *Harper's Magazine* 244 (June 1972), pp. 28, 30, 31, 32, 36, 37. Copyright 1972 by Harper's Magazine.

The average reader of the *New York Times* in the 1950s must have asked: Why don't we take some of our troops out of Europe? Ike himself said we didn't need them all there. Later, in 1961, after the tragicomic Bay of Pigs invasion, the reader asked: How did President Kennedy ever decide to do such a damn fool thing? Or later about Vietnam: Why does President Johnson keep on bombing North Vietnam when the bombing prevents negotiations and doesn't get Hanoi to stop the fighting?

Sometimes the answer to these questions is simple. It can be attributed squarely to the president. He thinks it's right. Or he believes he has no choice. As often as not, though, the answer lies elsewhere—in the special interests and procedures of the bureaucracy and the convictions of the bureaucrats.

If you look at foreign policy as a largely rational process of gathering information, setting the alternatives, defining the national interest, and making decisions, then much of what the president does will not make sense. But if you look at foreign policy as bureaucrats pursuing organizational, personal, and domestic political interests, as well as their own beliefs about what is right, you can explain much of the inexplicable.

In pursuing these interests and beliefs, bureaucrats (and that means everyone from cabinet officials to political appointees to career civil servants) usually follow their own version of the Ten Commandments:

1. *Don't discuss domestic politics on issues involving war and peace.*

On May 11, 1948, President Harry Truman held a meeting in the White House to discuss recognition of the new state of Israel. Secretary of State George Marshall and State Undersecretary Robert Lovett spoke first. They were against it. It would unnecessarily alienate forty million Arabs. Truman next asked Clark Clifford, then special counsel to the president, to speak. Arguing for the moral element of U.S. policy and the need to contain Communism in the Middle East, Clifford favored recognition. As related by Dan Kurzman in *Genesis 1948,* Marshall exploded: "Mr. President, this is not a matter to be determined on the basis of politics. Unless politics were involved, Mr. Clifford would not even be at this conference. This is a serious matter of foreign policy determination. . . ." Clifford remained at the meeting, and after some hesitation, the U.S. recognized Israel.

The moral merits of U.S. support of Israel notwithstanding, no one doubts Jewish influence on Washington's policy toward the Middle East. And yet, years later, in their memoirs, both Truman and Dean Acheson denied at great length that the decision to recognize the state of Israel was in any way affected by U.S. domestic politics.

A powerful myth is at work here. It holds that national security is too important, too sacred, to be tainted by crass domestic political considerations. It is a matter of lives and the safety of the nation. Votes and influence at home should count for nothing. Right? Wrong. National security and domestic reactions are inseparable. What could be clearer than the fact that President Nixon's Vietnam troop reductions are geared more to American public opinion than to the readiness of the Saigon forces to defend themselves? Yet the myth makes it bad form for government officials to talk about domestic politics (except to friends and to reporters off the record) or even to write about politics later in their memoirs.

And what is bad form on the inside would be politically disastrous if it were leaked to the outside. Imagine the press getting hold of a secret government document that said: "President Nixon has decided to visit China to capture the peace issue for the '72 elections. He does not intend or expect anything of substance to be achieved by his trip—except to scare the Russians a little." Few things are more serious than the charge of playing politics with security.

Nevertheless, the president pays a price for the silence imposed by the myth. One cost is that the president's assumptions about what public opinion will and will not support are never questioned. No official, for example, ever dared to write a scenario for President Johnson showing him how to forestall the right-wing McCarthyite reaction he feared if the U.S. pulled out of Vietnam. Another cost is that bureaucrats, in their ignorance of presidential views, will use their own notions of domestic politics to screen information from the president or to eliminate options from his consideration.

2. *Say what will convince, not what you believe.*

In the early months of the Kennedy administration, CIA officials responsible for covert operations faced a difficult challenge. President Eisenhower had permitted them to begin training a group of Cuban refugees for an American-supported invasion of Castro's Cuba. In order to carry out the plan, they then had to win approval from a skeptical new president whose entourage included some "liberals" likely to oppose it. The CIA director, Allen Dulles, and his assistant, Richard Bissell, both veteran bureaucrats, moved effectively to isolate the opposition. By highlighting the extreme sensitivity of the operation, they persuaded Kennedy to exclude from deliberations most of the experts in State and the CIA itself, and many of the Kennedy men in the White House. They reduced the effectiveness of others by refusing to leave any papers behind to be analyzed; they swept in, presented their case, and swept out, taking everything with them. But there remained the problem of the skeptical president. Kennedy feared that if the operation was a complete failure he would look very bad. Dulles and Bissell assured him that complete failure was impossible. If the invasion force could not establish a beachhead, the refugees, well-trained in guerrilla warfare, would head for the nearby mountains. The assurances were persuasive, the only difficulty being that they were false. Less than a third of the force had had any guerrilla training; the nearby mountains were separated from the landing beach by an almost impenetrable swamp; and none of the invasion leaders was instructed to head for the hills if the invasion failed (the CIA had promised them American intervention).

Kennedy was told what would persuade him, not the truth or even what the CIA believed to be true. Bureaucrats like Dulles and Bissell are confident that they know what the national security requires. The problem is to convince an uninformed and busy president. To do that you do not carefully explain the reasoning that leads to your position, nor do you reveal any doubts you may have. Rather, you seek to figure out what the president's problem is as he sees it and to convince him that what you want to do will solve it.

3. *Support the consensus—Option B.*

Vietnam policy under President Johnson exemplified the concept of

Option B. The papers to the president went something like this: Option A—Use maximum force (bomb Hanoi and Haiphong and invade North Vietnam, Laos, and Cambodia). Recommend rejection on the ground that the Soviets and the Chinese might respond. Option C—Immediate unilateral American withdrawal. Recommend rejection because it will lead to a Communist victory in Vietnam. Option B—Bomb a little more each time and seek negotiations (even though the bombing was preventing negotiations). Turn more of the fighting over to the Saigon forces and send more U.S. troops (even though the American buildup obviated the need for the South Vietnamese to shoulder more of the burden). Press Saigon for reforms and give them all they want for the war effort (even though aid without conditions gave Saigon no incentive to reform). Option B triumphed.

Option B solves a lot of problems for the bureaucrat. Bureaucrats do not like to fight with each other. Option B makes everybody a winner (by letting everyone do the essence of what he wants), preserves the policy consensus, and provides ultimate comfort to the bureaucrat—deference to his expertise and direct responsibility. Very few will be so dissatisfied as to take their case to the public.

Unfortunately, while this process allows the president to keep his house happy, it also robs him of choice. The alternatives he is given are often phony, two ridiculous extremes and a jumbled, inconsistent "middle course." Unless a president knows enough and has the time to peel off the real alternatives from within Option B, he ends up being trapped by the unanimity of advice.

4. Veto other options.

Former Secretary of State Dean Acheson, summoned by President Kennedy to join the Executive Committee of the National Security Council debate on Soviet missiles in Cuba, favored a "surgical strike," a limited air attack designed simply to destroy the missiles before they could become operational. Each time the military was asked to come in with a plan for a surgical strike, they asserted that a limited air strike could not destroy all the missiles—despite their having the capability to do so. Instead, they produced a plan for their favored option—an all-out air assault on Cuba climaxed by a ground invasion. Their plan had something in it for each service—the Air Force and Navy would pound the island by sea and air, the Marines would storm ashore as the Army paratroopers descended—and the military would be left free to act as they chose. The military insisted that a surgical strike was "infeasible" in part because they assumed that Soviet missiles were "mobile" (i.e., capable of being moved in a few hours) rather than "movable" (i.e., their actual capability of being moved in a few days). Kennedy was intrigued by the surgical-strike option and met with the commander of the Tactical Air Command. When the commander solemnly assured the president face-to-face that the option was "infeasible," Kennedy with great reluctance abandoned it.

"Infeasibility" is one technique to disqualify an option; demanding full authority is another. Early in his administration, Kennedy confronted a deteriorating situation in Laos. He was reluctant to commit any American forces, but neither was he prepared to have Laos overrun. At a critical White House meeting he asked the military what could be done with various levels of force. The Joint Chiefs' answer was clear. They would not recommend any landing of American forces and could guarantee nothing unless the president was prepared to authorize the use of nuclear weapons whenever, in their judgment, that use was required. Kennedy reluctantly decided not to send any forces to Laos.

5. *Predict dire consequences.*

With the Chinese Communist guns firing at the tiny island of Quemoy three miles from the mainland and an invasion expected momentarily, President Eisenhower's principal advisers met to frame a recommendation. The problem, as they saw it, was to formulate an argument that would persuade the president that the U.S. must defend Quemoy. The advisers resorted to the prediction of dire consequences, recognizing that only if the alternative could be shown to be very adverse to American interests would Eisenhower agree to the use of force. They warned the president that in their unanimous judgment, if he permitted Quemoy to be captured, "the consequences in the Far East would be more far-reaching and catastrophic than those which followed when the United States allowed the Chinese mainland to be taken over by the Chinese Communists."

Did Eisenhower reject this prediction as absurd? On the contrary, he accepted it and defended Quemoy.

The uncertainties of international politics are so great that it is difficult to disprove any prediction. This puts the president in a bind. If he fails to act and things go badly, the overruled advisers are likely to leak their warnings. In fact, much of the dialogue within the government is in terms of worst cases. An advocate who does not warn of extreme consequences is often viewed as not seriously supporting his prediction.

6. *Argue timing, not substance.*

Although the advocates of the Bay of Pigs landing had convinced President Kennedy that the invasion of Cuba was worth a try, they recognized that they were not yet in the clear: they still had to persuade the president to act immediately. Presidents are, in the eyes of bureaucrats, notorious for putting off decisions or changing their minds. They have enough decisions to make without looking for additional ones. In many cases, all the options look bad and they prefer to wait. The Bay of Pigs plan called for an effective "now or never" argument, and the CIA rose to the occasion. The agency told Kennedy that the invasion force was at the peak of its effectiveness; any delay, and it would decline in morale and capability. More important, it warned the president that a vast shipment of Soviet arms was on the way to Cuba; the Castro forces would soon have such superior weapons that substantial American combat involvement would be necessary to bail out the anti-Castro Cuban invaders. Faced with these arguments, Kennedy gave the order to proceed.

Conversely, when a president wants to act, bureaucrats can stymie him by arguing that "now is not the time." President Eisenhower reported in his memoirs that he came into office believing, after having served as commander of the allied forces in Europe, that the United States should withdraw most of its forces there; he left office eight years later still believing that the U.S. had far too many troops assigned to NATO. Secretary of State John Foster Dulles knew better than to argue with the military substance of

General Eisenhower's position. Instead he argued timing. Each time Eisenhower raised the issue, Dulles pointed to some current NATO difficulty. This was, he would argue, a critical moment in the life of the alliance in which one or another NATO country was experiencing a domestic crisis. For the U.S. to withdraw troops would be to risk political disintegration. The moment for troop withdrawals never arrived. To this day, pressures for some American withdrawals from Europe have been headed off by the same ploy.

7. *Leak what you don't like.*

We had a glimpse of this phenomenon last January with the publication of the Anderson Papers, in which we read about Henry Kissinger warning his State, Defense, and CIA colleagues: "The President does not believe we are carrying out his wishes. He wants to tilt in favor of Pakistan. He feels everything we do comes out otherwise." And, "The President is under the 'illusion' that he is giving instructions; not that he is merely being kept apprised of affairs as they progress." The president's subordinates disagreed with the president's policy toward the India-Pakistan crisis. They were undermining him by resisting his orders and then by leaking his policy. He knew it and did not like it; but apparently could not do much about it.

Although leaking the texts of many documents, à la Pentagon and Anderson papers, is relatively rare, much classified information regularly makes its way into the press. Presidents are surprised not when something leaks but rather when any hot item remains out of the press for even a few days. Providing information to the press—whether in press conferences, backgrounders, or leaks—is the main route by which officials within the executive branch bring their supporters in the Congress and the interested public into action. Only bureaucrats with potential outside support are tempted to leak. In some cases, it is sufficient to leak the fact that an issue is up for decision: in others, what is leaked is information on the positions of key participants. In many instances sufficient factual material must be leaked to convince Congressmen and others to join the fray.

Presidents don't like leaks by others and complain about them whenever they occur, often asking the FBI to run down the culprit. Such efforts almost always fail.

8. *Ignore orders you don't like.*

On March 20, 1948, President Harry Truman rose from bed early, as was his custom, and began scanning the morning newspapers. He was astonished to read that his ambassador to the United Nations, Warren Austin, had told the Security Council the previous day that "there seems to be general agreement that the plan [for the partition of Palestine] cannot now be implemented by peaceful means." Truman had agreed to no such thing. He was firmly committed to partition and on the previous day had reiterated his support in a private meeting with Chaim Weizmann, the leader of worldwide Zionism. Austin and the Arabists in the State Department did not know about the meeting with Weizmann, but they knew that the president wanted partition and believed that it could be carried out peacefully. Austin and his associates had no doubts about what the president wanted; they simply felt no obligation to do what he wanted them to do.

At the end of his term in office, Truman was acutely conscious of the limited ability of presidents to have their orders obeyed, and he worried about his successor. "Poor Ike," he was heard to muse, "he'll sit here and say do this and do that and nothing will happen." And so it continues.

During the first week of the Cuban missile crisis, in October 1962, an advisor warned Kennedy that the Russians were likly to demand that the United States withdraw its missiles from Turkey in return for the Soviet withdrawal of its missiles from Cuba. Kennedy was astonished. Months before, he had ordered the missiles removed from Turkey and could not believe they were still there.

Most students of the Cuban missile crisis have emphasized the degree to which Kennedy controlled every detail of what the American government did. However, a closer look by Graham Allison, in his book on the crisis, *Essence of Decision,* has shown that the bureaucracy was behaving otherwise, choosing to obey the orders it liked and ignore or stretch others. Thus, after a tense argument with the Navy, Kennedy ordered the blockade line moved closer to Cuba so that the Russians might have more time to draw back. Having lost the argument with the president, the Navy simply ignored his order. Unbeknownst to Kennedy, the Navy was also at work forcing Soviet submarines to surface long before Kennedy authorized any contact with Soviet ships. And despite the president's order to halt all provocative intelligence, an American U-2 plane entered Soviet airspace at the height of the crisis. When Kennedy began to realize that he was not in full control, he asked his Secretary of Defense to see if he could find out just what the Navy was doing. McNamara then made his first visit to the Navy command post in the Pentagon. In a heated exchange, the Chief of Naval Operations suggested that McNamara return to his office and let the Navy run the blockade.

Bureaucrats know that the president and his principal associates do not have the time or the information to monitor compliance with all presidential orders. Often, the bureaucrats can simply delay or do nothing, and no one will notice. If the president is actively involved, they may find it necessary to obey the letter, but not the spirit, of his orders. As Henry Kissinger observed to a journalist recently, the problem is not to know what to do, but rather to figure out how to get the bureaucracy to do it.

9. *Don't tell likely opponents about a good thing.*

The commandments discussed thus far have all dealt with relations between the departments and the White House. When issues get that far, one of the fundamental rules has already been violated: keep issues away from the president. Bureaucrats prefer to be left alone to do their own thing. They will not voluntarily bring issues to the attention of the president (or senior officials) unless they conclude that he is likely to rule in their favor in a conflict with another agency. Consider the case of surplus and long supply arms transfers to other countries.

One of Secretary McNamara's goals in the Pentagon was to reduce the level of military assistance, particularly to countries that did not need the weapons and could afford to pay for what they needed. A prime objective was Taiwan. McNamara and his Office of International Security Affairs engaged in a yearly battle with the State Department and the military over the level of aid to Taiwan. The White House was drawn in because a number of influential congressmen were strong supporters of aid to Taiwan. One year in the late 1960s a battle raged over whether Taiwan would get $30 million or $40 million in military assistance. During the same year, the military quietly shipped to Taiwan more than $40 million worth of military equipment, which the Pentagon had labeled "excess or long supply." No senior civilian official was aware of the fact that these transfers were taking place, and no junior official aware of what was going on felt obliged to report up. Thus, while senior officials argued over irrelevant ceilings on expenditures, Taiwan got more aid than anyone realized.

Observers sometimes assume that the bureaucracy bucks the hard choices to the president. Nothing could be further from the truth. Left alone, the bureaucracy will settle as many issues as it can by leaving each organization free to act as it chooses. When and if the president learns of an issue, bureaucrats will try to incorporate current behavior into "Option B."

10. *Don't fight the consensus and don't resign over policy.*

If an official strongly disagrees with a consensus or dislikes a key man behind the consensus, he might chance a leak to the press. But frontal assaults on a consensus happen only rarely. In the summer of 1965, Undersecretary of State George Ball was among the first to confirm this fact with respect to the policy of bombing North Vietnam. Ball thought U.S. bombing of the North was folly—and worse than that, would only stiffen Hanoi's will. But he did not propose a unilateral cessation. In a TV interview last year, Ball explained himself as follows:

> *What I was proposing was something which I thought had a fair chance of being persuasive . . . if I had said let's pull out overnight or do something of this kind, I obviously wouldn't have been persuasive at all. They'd have said, "The man's mad."*

Ball's remarks express at once the futility of resisting agreed policy and the bureaucrat's concern for his personal effectiveness. Ball knew he could not convince anyone if he revealed his true beliefs. He knew he would have been dismissed as "mad" and would not have been in a position to argue another day. So, he tempered his arguments and went along. Like all other bureaucrats, he hoped to preserve his effectiveness.

As it turned out, Ball's more moderate arguments were not persuasive either, but he did not resign over Vietnam and did not take his case to the public. No one resigned over Vietnam policy. Indeed, there seems to be no evidence that any civilian official has resigned over any foreign-policy matter since World War II.

The only officials with a record for resigning are the professional military. Generals Ridgeway, Taylor, and Powers are notable examples. What is more, they tour the hustings, write books, and complain out loud. Military officers feel strongly about the interests of their military organization and often believe that if the people of the country only knew "the truth," they would support the military's position. With this record on resigning and going to the public, it is no wonder the military has been so influential in presidential decisions.

But again, it is the president and the nation who ultimately suffer. If the president remains confident that none of his civilian advisors will resign and take their case to the public, he has little incentive ever to question his own assumptions.

The Ten Commandments pose a serious problem for a president, who is after all the one who got elected and has the responsibility. Truman understood the problem but feared that Eisenhower would not. But evidence abounds that President Eisenhower, precisely because of his background in Army politics and international military negotiations, was far from a novice. President Kennedy was quite expert and attuned to the ways of the bureaucracy—especially after the Bay of Pigs fiasco. His famous calls to State Department desk officials made the point well. President Johnson was a master of such maneuvering. Even as he stepped up the bombing of North Vietnam he would say, "I won't let those Air Force generals bomb the smallest outhouse north of the 17th parallel without checking with me. The generals know only two words—spend and bomb."

The Nixon-Kissinger team is second to none in its sensitivity to bureaucratic behavior. The elaborate National Security Council decision-making apparatus they established is predicated on tight White House control of the bureaucracy. Their system is designed to neutralize narrow organizational interests (meaning the viewpoints of State and Defense), force the bureaucracy to suggest real alternatives and provide more accurate information (meaning, as has been done, to centralize the intelligence functions around Kissinger).

While this new system has been an improvement in some respects over the past, it has decisive costs and limitations. It has totally demoralized the State Department. The department's expertise has been for naught, and its exclusion has lead to a rash of pointless leaks from disgruntled Foreign Service officers. With all its reins on the bureaucrat, the new system did not prevent part of the bureaucracy from tilting the "wrong way" (meaning against the president, as revealed in the Anderson papers) in the recent India-Pakistan crisis.

The problem, then, boils down to this: given the fact that the president cannot either chain the system or entirely work around it without serious costs, and given the judgment that a president strong enough to collar the bureaucracy would be too strong for the good of the nation, is there a better way to make foreign policy?

The answer is yes—probably. The president, we think, should make a determined effort to use the system. The personal and organizational interests of the bureaucrat are a reality. So are the different viewpoints on what is good policy. The president's main theme of operation should be to force bureaucratic differences out into the open. Pick strong and able men to lead State and Defense. Let them use their judgment and be advocates for their organizations. Encourage debate and contention rather than asking for agreed-upon recommendations. Such tactics may be the only way for the president to ferret out hidden or conflicting information and to leave himself with real choices.

Perhaps, in the end, neither this suggested system nor any system will produce better decisions. Perhaps better decisions really depend on beliefs and events and guesses. But a fuller, more honest and open treatment of the bureaucracy might make for more honest and open treatment of the American people. Presidents might be less inclined to spend a good deal of their time denying differences and hiding policy. This would mean less deception and less manipulation. What better reason for trying it?

Executive and interbureaucratic involvement

Study questions for selection two

1. Pretend that you are a high-ranking bureaucrat. Rank the "commandments" according to how useful you feel they would be: if you were promoting a new policy direction; and if you were defending your agency against threatening proposals.

2. As stated by Gelb and Halperin, the commandments refer to what we have called *vertical* administrative conflicts. How many of the commandments could be slightly reformulated and applied with equal force to *horizontal* conflicts?

3. To what extent do the patterns of administrative behavior described in the article seem to be susceptible to being altered? How likely is it that any change (including a new president, a new secretary of state, a new head of the National Security Council, or an organizational plan that would redefine the relationships among these entities) will significantly reduce the bureaucracy's policy influence?

Suggested readings for chapter three

Cronin, Thomas E., and Greenberg, Sanford D., eds. *The Presidential Advisory System.* New York: Harper and Row, 1969.

Fenno, Richard F., Jr. *The President's Cabinet.* Cambridge, Mass.: Harvard University Press, 1959.

Fisher, Louis. *Presidential Spending Power.* Princeton, N.J.: Princeton University Press, 1975.

Hess, Stephen. *Organizing the Presidency.* Washington, D.C.: Brookings Institution, 1976.

Johnson, Richard Tanner. *Managing the White House: An Intimate Study of the Presidency.* New York: Harper and Row, 1974.

Kaufman, Herbert. *Are Government Organizations Immortal?* Washington, D.C.: Brookings Institution, 1976.

Neustadt, Richard. *Presidential Power.* New York: John Wiley and Sons, 1960.

Powell, Norman John. *Responsible Public Bureaucracy in the United States.* Boston: Allyn and Bacon, Inc., 1967.

Schlesinger, Arthur M., Jr. *Imperial Presidency.* New York: Houghton Mifflin Co., 1973.

Seidman, Harold. *Politics, Position, and Power: The Dynamics of Federal Organization.* 2d ed. New York: Oxford University Press, 1975.

Selznick, Philip. *TVA and the Grassroots: A Study in the Sociology of Formal Organization.* Berkeley: University of California Press, 1949.

Talbot, Allan R. *The Mayor's Game: Richard Lee of New Haven and the Politics of Change.* New York: Praeger, 1970.

Legislative and judicial involvement

In the previous chapter we demonstrated how public administrators become involved with other executive branch actors—especially the chief executive and his or her minions. But the other two branches of government also become implicated in the administrative process. This chapter traces the administrative participation of legislators and judges.

A. Legislators and administrators

Members of legislatures make policy, and administrators carry it out. Right? Well, there is quite a lot of truth in the statement, but the simplistic "politics–administration" dichotomy was rejected by most students of public administration about three decades ago; we now understand that both actors perform multiple tasks. Legislators make policy *and* see to its execution; administrators carry out policy *and* participate in making it. While the dichotomy was once generally accepted by academics, it is safe to say that few legislators ever agreed that administration was beyond their purview, and few administrators ever made a major decision regarding implementation without recognizing that their actions had some effect upon policy outcomes.

The politics-administration dichotomy was enshrined in the United States Constitution, which treated policy making and implementation as distinctive processes separated under different branches of government. The intent was, of course, that the more representative branch, the legislature, should have sole responsibility for establishing law. The administration, while headed by an elected president, would be largely neutral in performing its tasks. Woodrow Wilson's famous essay on public administration, published in 1887, gave considerable support to this view.[1]

Administrators as policy makers

Several aspects of modern legislative-administrative relations challenge the separation of policy making and implementation.

First, administrators are the principal source of *expertise* in policy making. Consider a hypothetical city council member (a local appliance dealer), who must decide whether to vote for a mosquito-control ordinance. The proposed law, written by the city staff would allow city personnel to spray insecticide, permit court orders to force cutting and clearing of vacant lots, and authorize city crews to remove from private property old tires, cans, and other containers where mosquitoes might hatch. A first technical question is simply, "How much of a problem do mosquitoes present?" The council member is likely to find that the answer is rather more complex than expected, especially as he starts considering the costs of eradication. If economic and social costs were zero, the city might as well eliminate mosquitoes simply because they bite people at baseball games. But the costs certainly are not zero and may be quite high, so more knowledge is needed about the *real* danger the mosquitoes present in terms of disease transmission. Consider some pieces of technical information necessary to determine costs: the effects (short and long term) of various insecticides that might be used; the constitutionality of the

---

[1] Woodrow Wilson, "The Study of Administration," *Political Science Quarterly* 2 (June 1887): 197–222.

contemplated actions against private property; the impact that the various cleanup measures would have (including the financial burden on landowners and the costs of expanded city refuse collection).

Our hypothetical council member is unlikely to have the depth of knowledge necessary to resolve satisfactorily issues of this sort, nor does his appliance-selling job leave much time for research. Consequently, the city council, like the state legislature and the U.S. Congress, is heavily dependent upon administrators' written reports and oral briefings. Legislators may even have little basis for evaluating the information provided by administrators.

Second, policy is made through the exercise of *administrative discretion*. As mentioned in chapter 1, Americans seem to demand that government provide equality of treatment, but at the same time recognize individual differences. While some of these differences can be allowed for in statutes, full recognition of others requires choice, or discretion, on the part of administrators. For example, a law concerning public assistance may stipulate that people whose income exceeds a ceiling amount are ineligible for certain benefits. How shall *income* be defined? Normally such matters, sometimes referred to as secondary-policy or implementing-policy matters, are acknowledged to be the primary responsibility of an administrative agency. Perhaps the agency would decide that money received as gifts from relatives and welfare benefits administered by other agencies constituted income; perhaps it would decide otherwise on one or both counts. Some decisions of this sort are codified as regulations, which may be presented to the legislature for ratification and could be (but almost never are) vetoed. Others become formal agency policies, and yet others become informal (but sometimes rigidly followed) practices. Sometimes the codification of an agency's actual policies might prove embarrassing; this is illustrated by Kenneth Culp Davis's attempt to write up as formal rules the narcotics-arrest practices followed—without statutory authority—by many police departments:

> 1. *The arresting officer may release a violator of a narcotics statute, no matter how clear the evidence against him, upon making a finding that he may become an informer.*
>
> 2. *Upon releasing such a violator, no officer shall interfere with his further purchase or sale of narcotics, so long as a finding is made that he is supplying information to the police or may be about to do so.*
>
> 3. *All transactions by which an officer trades nonenforcement for information shall be kept secret, so that the absolute discretion of the officer will be immune to check or review by other governmental authority and immune to criticism by the public.*

4. When two violators of the narcotics laws have committed the same offense in the same circumstances, no principle concerning equal justice under law or equal protection of the laws shall control when an officer chooses to trade nonenforcement for information, all provisions of constitutions, statutes, and ordinances to the contrary are hereby suspended.

5. Whenever an informer becomes recognized as such by the underworld, the officer who has made promises of immunity from arrest shall request another officer to arrest and prosecute the informer, and the second officer shall falsely pretend to have no knowledge of such promises of immunity; as soon as an informer's effectiveness has been spent, considerations of decency and fairness about keeping promises shall be given no weight.[2]

As Davis indicates, many subpolicies, or sub-subpolicies, are left to the discretion of the individual administrator who actually works with citizens. Over time, policemen, caseworkers, etc., develop their own bodies of "case law." Only quite recently have many citizens begun to realize how dependent Americans have become upon the proper exercise of discretion and the good judgment of administrators.

Third, the nature of the administrative process often requires that policy making and implementation be inextricably intertwined. Although it is possible to formulate definitions that distinguish the two, actual practice belies such definitions; often one cannot even identify the content of the policies except by examining how the program is carried out. For example, what is U.S. policy toward the Soviet Union? There are treaties and statutes that can partially answer the question; yet, with little congressional action, the Nixon administration instigated détente, and the Ford and Carter administrations have continued to mold and reshape the policy. The need for flexibility is especially apparent in international politics, but administrative flexibility also is necessary in other policy spheres. Modern administration also requires rapid response; although administrators are often chastised for delay, the volume of work is so great that these delays would only be extended by requiring legislative action at each decision point.

One interesting feature of legislative actions is that they are often intentionally vague. It is frequently politically convenient that much of the actual content of programs be left unclear; sometimes such vagueness is absolutely required as a price for passage of the

---

[2]Kenneth Culp Davis, *Discretionary Justice: A Preliminary Inquiry* (Baton Rouge: Louisiana State University Press, 1969), p. 96.

*"The staff found a few loopholes in your bill, Senator, but nothing that can't
be patched up with a little red tape."*
Copyright © 1978. Reprinted by permission of *Case & Comment* and Brenda
Burbank.

law. Thus, administrators, either with or without the connivance of
legislators, must put flesh on the bill's bare bones. Finally, the vagueness of statutes is, of course, increased by the ambiguities inherent in
any language.

For all of these reasons, then, the rigid distinction between policy making and implementation must be rejected. In numerous ways,
administrators influence the content of policy.

Legislators as policy implementors

Legislators do, however, influence the behavior of public administrators. Especially when matters of implementation have been
points of controversy, many laws specify the procedures to be used in
implementation. During and after the Vietnam conflict, for example,
many complaints were heard about the performance of the Veterans
Administration in making available the benefits due veterans. For
this as well as other reasons, Congress has since altered the statutes
that detail the benefits available and the specific conditions that must
be met to receive them. The agency has been required to undertake
an alteration of its policies.

Changing a statute is not the only way a legislature can influence implementation. In chapter 3 we mentioned the term *legislative oversight*. Various opportunities are presented a legislator to look at the working of an agency. Perhaps the most frequent arises from a constituent complaint. Mr. Rogers calls Senator Thompson and reports that his mother, a patient in a state mental hospital, has told him that conditions are getting worse and worse. Patients, including his mother, who have never needed restraint before, he says, are now being restrained and kept highly sedated; the staff seems to care less and is seen less frequently. Senator Thompson now has an opportunity—she may see it as a responsibility—to check into matters. Since she is a state official, she is likely to conduct an investigation herself. Her investigation may consist of no more than a telephone call to the hospital director reporting the complaint and seeking an explanation. Perhaps the explanation will be satisfactory, and no more will be done. Even this brief contact, however, may influence administrative judgments (even medical judgments) then and in the future.

A related type of involvement, which may differ in intent, is the legislative provision of constituent service. Many of us, when we do not know how to get what we want from an agency or when dissatisfied with the agency's response, contact our legislator for assistance. This is so common at the federal level that the larger agencies have legislative liaison offices to deal with members of Congress and their staffs. Frequently, the citizen's request can be filled without violation of the agency's normal rules. Occasionally, though, legislators seek special treatment for constituents—they seek to specify the implementation process in this particular case. If there is legal flexibility (even if the request may violate agency policy and give the legislator's constituent preferential treatment), the administrator may respond favorably to the request—especially if the legislator's committee assignments give him some authority over the agency's budget.

A more thorough involvement in administrative matters occurs when legislators hold hearings at which administrators are required to testify. These may be routinely scheduled ones—as the appropriations hearings held each year—or they may be investigatory hearings growing out of complaints by individuals or interest groups. In either case, the legislator has a chance to seek information from administrators, but the hearings are also a chance to give administrators the legislator's views; most administrators have learned to take seriously the expression of such views.

One intriguing aspect of legislative oversight at the state and federal levels is that (excepting Nebraska's unicameral legislature) administrators are faced with members of two chambers. Differences in constituency size, term, and time of election can result in marked differences in the demands that members of the two chambers place on the administrator. Some agencies find that one chamber (and its relevant committees) is highly supportive, while the other chamber is antagonistic and would even eliminate the agency if it could. Administrators sometimes find it possible to appeal one chamber's distasteful decisions to the other chamber, in hopes of a reversal.

Elimination of agencies or transfer of functions to other agencies is an extreme result of oversight. Since most agencies have been created under statutory authority (exceptions are states' constitutional agencies and charter-established city agencies), legislatures have considerable formal power to undertake such reorganizations. This may be done for a variety of reasons, but one common reason is to alter the implementation process. So-called *sunset laws* have been passed in several states, and the concept is gaining ground at the federal level. Whether legislatures will actually abolish many agencies that are determined to have outlived their usefulness remains to be seen.

Finally, legislative staff personnel become deeply involved in the implementation process. By providing information, making contacts, and doing research, committee staffs and those of individual legislators play crucial supporting roles in exercising the oversight functions mentioned above. But there are also specialized legislative staff units. At the federal level, the most important is the General Accounting Office, or GAO. Headed by the comptroller general, the GAO is responsible for auditing the performance of administrative agencies. For many years (the agency was created in 1921), the focus was upon the legality of expenditures. More recently attention has shifted from such mundane activities as rechecking travel claims to assessing the performance of agency programs in terms of effectiveness and efficiency. Members of Congress seek reports that evaluate judgments made by administrative personnel. Further developments in this direction (the newly created Congressional Budget Office is likely to be one) could greatly increase the involvement of Congress in the implementation process. State legislatures and city councils lag far behind the federal government in their oversight staff.

Sharing policy making and implementation

In the wide variety of ways described above, administrators find themselves in contact with legislators. The impression may have been left that administrators have little time for anything other than relating to legislators, and for a few, especially when the legislature is considering appropriations, this is sometimes true. For most administrators, however, the legislature is usually simply one more element in the environment. Quite often, it also is rather disinterested.[3] The complexity of the matters with which administrators deal, the passage of money from one level of government to another (especially from federal to state), and sometimes constitutional or charter restrictions—all reduce legislative involvement. Certainly, many lower-level administrators rarely, if ever, have direct legislative contact. Nevertheless, the fact that both policy making and policy implementation are shared processes (if, indeed, they can be sharply distinguished) affects all administrators.

Selection three

Legislative oversight of bureaucracy*

Morris S. Ogul

The 1970s have been a period of legislative resurgence. Spurred by the executive excesses uncovered by the Watergate investigations, legislatures at all levels have been inspired to reassert their powers. Many of the actions taken relate to the policy-making sphere; some relate to the role of administrative watchdog. This selection was written as a background paper for congressional consideration of the state of executive-legislative relations by a long-time student of Congress. A more complete treatment is Morris S. Ogul, *Congress Oversees the Bureaucracy* (Pittsburgh: University of Pittsburgh Press, 1976).

Ogul argues that there are significant barriers to Congress acting as a truly effective monitor of administrative behavior and that the

---

*Reprinted from Morris S. Ogul, "Legislative Oversight of the Bureaucracy," U.S. Congress, House. Select Committee on Committees. *Committee Organization in the House,* Vol. 2, Part 3, 93d Cong., 1st sess. (1973), pp. 701–9.

[3]Noting that congressional interest in monitoring administration is highly intermittent, Allen Schick concludes a citation of several evidences of a resurgence of congressional activity in this area by commenting: "Its 200-year history demonstrates that Congress perfers making laws to overseeing their execution. If oversight is to flourish on Capitol Hill, it will not be at the expense of more traditional legislative activities." Allen Schick, "Congress and the 'Details' of Administration," *Public Administration Review* 36 (September/October 1976): 521.

oversight function is greatly misunderstood. The way to increase congressional effectiveness in this role—if this is desired—lies not in adopting some organizational panacea, he says, but in the members themselves: if members of Congress really want to oversee administrators, they must reallocate their priorities and direct their staff (perhaps they will need to recruit some *better* staff) to concentrate on such matters.

Legislative oversight of bureaucracy involves some of the most complex forms of behavior that the Congress undertakes. Not surprisingly then, legislative oversight is less understood than almost any other aspect of congressional behavior. Both congressmen in interviews and scholars in their writings concede this lack of sustained insight. In this vortex of incomplete knowledge (recognizing that the best experts on congressional behavior are often congressmen), an outsider may make a contribution by looking at familiar questions from a more detached viewpoint than that of the immersed participant.

What follows is based on perspectives derived from a variety of sources, from general reading and observation of the Congress, and especially from intensive research in 1965 and in 1966 into the behavior of several committees and subcommittees. Then, and since, the writer has interviewed in depth some forty House members, an equal number of staff persons, and more than a score of lobbyists and officials in the executive branch concerned with oversight.

Statements embodying general laws about oversight are scarce. It is possible, however, to provide some useful insights into the conduct of oversight. The materials that follow may qualify under this latter heading. Oversight is defined as the behavior of legislators, individually or collectively, formally or informally, which results in an impact on bureaucratic behavior in relation to the structure and process of policy implementation.

Legal expectations and actual behavior

There is a large gap between the oversight the law calls for and the oversight actually performed. The clearest single statement about the oversight that the law requires the Congress to perform comes from that often quoted and seldom heeded statement in the Legislative Reorganization Act of 1946 assigning each standing committee the responsibility to "exercise continuous watchfulness of the execution by the administrative agencies concerned of any laws, the subject matter of which is within the jurisdiction of such committee."

Members of the Congress agree that this provision provides a full and direct legal obligation to act. In addition, all those interviewed saw that obligation as an appropriate one for the Congress. In brief, there is consensus in the Congress that extensive and systematic oversight *ought* to be conducted.

One reason for the gap between expectations and behavior lies in the nature of the expectation. The plain but seldom acknowledged fact is that this task, at least as defined above, is simply impossible to perform. No amount of congressional dedication and energy, no conceivable increase in the size of committee staffs, and even no extraordinary boost in committee budgets will enable the Congress to carry out its oversight obligations in a comprehensive and systematic manner. The job is too large for any combination of members and staff to completely master. Congressmen who feel obligated to obey the letter of the law are doomed to feelings of inadequacy and frustration and are laid open to charges of neglect. Fortunately, at least for their own morale, the members of the Congress tend to focus on the immediate more than on the impossible.

The statements above are not intended to suggest that the Congress ignores the oversight function but rather that it performs it selectively. In fact, the Congress oversees formally and informally in many ways on a daily basis. The most visible and perhaps the most effective way is through the appropriations process; the most unnoticed is latently as it considers authorizations, performs casework, and goes about business not directly labeled as oversight.

The remaining part of the gap between expectations and behavior narrows as one considers why congressmen act as they do. Two topics will be given central attention: the multiple priorities of the members of the Congress, and the impact of their policy preferences on their behavior. A discussion of these topics will reveal that there are sound reasons for this gap to exist and that most members do not really mind too much that the gap is as large as it is. Hence, their lack of willingness to do much about it.

Multiple priorities

Although they seldom seem to articulate it, most members do seem to realize that the performance of oversight is best discussed not in the vacuum of legal expectations but in the more proximate context of multiple priorities and policy preferences. Each member is faced with a variety of obligations that are generally agreed to be legitimate, important, and demanding in time and energy. In principle, he should be working hard at all of them. In fact, since he does not weigh them equally, he is unlikely to give them equal attention.

When any action is perceived to contribute directly and substantially to political survival as well as to other legitimate functions, it is likely to move toward the top of any member's priority list. Extra incentives to oversee come from problems of direct concern to one's constituents or from issues that promise political visibility or organizational support. Conversely, problems not seen as closely related to political survival are more difficult to crowd onto the member's schedule. In the choice phrase of one member: "Our schedules are full, but flexible."

Not all congressional activity is linked directly to political survival. A congressman seems to gain interest in pushing oversight efforts onto his active calendar under the following conditions: new executive requests are forthcoming calling for massive new expenditures or substantial new authorizations in controversial policy areas; a crisis has occurred that has not been met effectively by executive departments; the opposition political party is in control of the executive branch; he has not been treated well either in the realm of personal attention or in the servicing of his requests; he has modest confidence in the administrative capacity of departmental or agency leaders. If key members have confidence in the way that executive department leaders are running their programs, pressure for oversight eases. Comparing the experience of two former heads of the now defunct Post Office Department is instructive. Because most members of the House Post Office and Civil Service Committee had great respect for Postmaster General Lawrence O'Brien, their willingness to give him wide latitude to run his department was immense. Because these same members lacked such confidence in John Gronouski, they probed somewhat more carefully into the affairs of the Post Office Department when he ran it. At issue was not comparative executive competence, but congressional perceptions about that competence.

In making his choices about what to do, each congressman applies his own standards of relevance; all will be doing those things that they consider most important to them at that time. Problems seen as less pressing may be recognized but may remain untouched. In these calculations, oversight frequently falls into the semineglected category. Choice, not accident, governs this decision.

If one judges from the behavior of congressmen rather than from their words alone, the conclusion seems clear that in oversight as in other congressional activities, selection and choice among worthy tasks is always necessary. Absolute mandates, even if accepted as desirable, will be obeyed only in relative terms. The price of effective action in one area may be the neglect of another.

Members of the Congress, like most other people, manage to compartmentalize their various beliefs and behaviors. Even in the face of continuing imperfect performance, congressmen retain their belief in the desirability of doing a good job at oversight. Yet, concurrently, many members seem comfortable while not doing much to narrow the gap between expectations about oversight and the actual performance of it. One might reasonably conclude then that the main spurs to the conduct of oversight do not come from any abstract belief about its necessity or desirability, but from other sources.

Congressmen through their actions implicitly rank their priorities. A glance at the rules that many seem to use provides some help in trying to understand oversight.

All members have many tasks that they feel should be pursued. The finite limits set by time and energy require that some of these expectations will be met more fully than others. If there is widespread agreement about the contents of a list of high-priority tasks, there is less consensus on the relative ranking of them. Only a few things are known about why members choose to give primary attention to some activities and less to others. Even if we can presume that the omnipresent desire to survive politically serves as a major inspiration, still, member selection of other priorities remains a murky area of political analysis.

Chapter four

Because these factors change, the interests of each congressman in oversight will wax and wane despite his continuing adherence to the notion that oversight is an important function for the Congress to be performing.

Policy preferences

Examining the policy preferences of members of the Congress moves us toward a more adequate explanation of the gap between expectations and behavior. From interviews and observation, I conclude that congressmen are seldom anxious to monitor those executive activities of which they approve. Oversight efforts to support administrative programs are the exception. A member essentially indifferent to a program is not likely to press for oversight efforts. One of the most important pressures to oversee flows from disagreements on policies, especially those that are of intense concern to the member. The words of members express the abstract desire to oversee; it is when that desire combines with policy disagreement that oversight is more likely to ensue.

A classic example is the experience of the House Judiciary Committee in 1965 and 1966 with civil rights issues relating to race relations. This committee was an able group vitally interested in civil rights policy making and administration. Emanuel Celler ran the committee as a strong chairman. Superficially, the committee was conducting almost no oversight activity on questions of civil rights. What was strange was that the civil rights concerns of the committee were known to be strong and deep. Several not so obvious factors helped to explain the situation. First, the committee chairman felt that he was having an impact on the activities of the Justice Department through informal consultation. Second, the chairman agreed in essence with what the Justice Department was doing and thus had no desire to interfere. Third, in the judgment of Chairman Celler, the net effect of any formal investigations would be harmful to the cause of civil rights, since antirights forces might find the forum useful to articulate and publicize their views. In this case, the absence of formal oversight could be explained by a simple formula: when policy interests and the obligation to oversee clash, policy preferences will normally prevail as a guide to conduct.

The discussion thus far of member priorities, choices, and policy preferences concerns each member. The fact is that in oversight efforts, as in other activities, all congressmen are not equal. So even an intense desire to oversee, clearly a rarity in the Congress, depends for its fruition on factors other than the individual member's wants. The ability to oversee depends on where one is situated in the legislative process. Individual members, on their own, conduct very little oversight. For reasons of authority, money, and staff, oversight efforts are centered in the standing committees and subcommittees. Where one is placed in the committee system becomes a vital element in translating desires into effective action. A brief look at committees and their oversight activity is thus warranted.

Committees and oversight

One key to understanding oversight can be discovered by examining those places in the Congress where the division of labor and specialization can most easily be found, the committees and subcommittees. Members individually rarely can expect to conduct much legislative oversight. A comment later in the paper will indicate how even individual members can partially overcome this limitation. The heart of legislative oversight lies in the committees and subcommittees. How and why these units function as they do will tell us a great deal about how legislative oversight is performed. How the committees function is related to their structures for decision making.

Perhaps the most effective means to enhance a committee's oversight performance is through the presence of an alert, shrewd, active chairman who wants to conduct oversight broad in scope and profound in depth. Most reforms pale in significance before this seemingly simple solution. No one, of course, really knows how to pretest prospective chairmen for these talents and interests. Nor is it clear that the members would want to pick their chairman on the basis of these criteria even if they could. The best practical bet seems to be to assume that a list of committee chairmen and subcommittee chairmen will include a few who are intensely interested in oversight and highly talented in pursuing it and a larger number who are less keen and less talented.

Assuming some such mix of committee chairmen, is there any way to enhance the oversight efforts of those committees headed by chairmen whose appetites and talents for oversight are unimpressive? At least one suggestion merits discussion. The odds for active oversight are better, in the absence of an eager chairman, if there are some semiautonomous subcommittees with established jurisdictions, budgets, and staffs. The objective is to create additional fields in which ambition may flower. Visibility and ambition are as effective stimulants for subcommittee chairmen as for any other members. An active subcommittee within a quiescent full committee is not an unknown phenomenon in the Congress.

Innovation always has its price. The flexibility of the full committee chairman, his personal power, and perhaps even committee efficiency could possibly suffer. Whether enhancing the prospects for oversight may be worth these costs has to be decided by the congressmen themselves.

What promotes the personal power of the chairman is not necessarily good for committee oversight efforts. Fixed subcommittee jurisdictions may indeed remove some flexibility from the full committee chairman, but the price may be right: promoting the competence prerequisite to oversight activity. Numbered subcommittees without fixed jurisdictions may impede the development of expertise. Besides, from an odds maker's perspective, the presence of several subcommittee chairmen with defined jurisdictions, separate staffs, and separate budgets increases the field from which an interest in oversight may emerge. This analysis does not ignore the problems that may arise in some decentralized communities, but merely adds another weight to the scales.

Committee leaders may not dominate all committee behavior, but they do control much of it. What they are willing to do is central. Of course, committee members may press committee leaders to act. One type of situation minimizes the likelihood of member pressure for leadership action: where the members of a committee are there involuntarily. Members view some committee assignments as highly desirable; other assignments are viewed as burdens to be endured. Members appointed to unsought committees frequently transfer to more satisfactory assignments as soon as they can muster sufficient seniority. Given the normal problems in allotting their time and energy, we can expect that few members who see their assignments as undesirable are likely to exert maximum effort on such committees. Some oversight behavior, or the lack of it, is explainable in part by the priority that members assign to their work on a particular committee. In low-status committees, those few members who choose to remain probably do so for reasons unrelated to any desire to actively pursue oversight.

Some grist for contemplation and discussion

Four myths about oversight

Perhaps the first necessity in thinking more generally about oversight is to suggest that some widely held and deeply cherished ideas are myths. The first of these is that the Congress lacks sufficient authority to oversee properly. In fact, one can argue that the Congress has all of the authority that it needs to oversee much more extensively and effectively.

A second myth holds that the Congress lacks the budget to oversee effectively. With few exceptions, committees have the money that they need even if they wish to sharply augment their oversight efforts. One can uncover, of course, some relatively deprived committees or subcommittees, but these are the exceptions.

A third cherished belief states that the answer to how to improve oversight efforts is more staff. This answer might hold in a few cases, but not generally. Committee staff persons are hired to satisfy a variety of needs. If committee chairmen choose to take on staff exclusively for subject-matter competence, research skills, and investigative talents, they can quickly improve the prospects for oversight. But even then, staff behavior is largely a function of member preferences. A chairman passive about oversight is unlikely to have staff persons, however talented, who view oversight as a high priority. With a few conspicuous exceptions, staff behavior is more a function of member preferences than a determinant of them.

The Legislative Reorganization Act of 1970 spelled out some relationships between the Congress, its committees, and the GAO. The actual impact of the GAO on legislative oversight would be an intriguing study in itself. Such an analysis might well suggest useful paths in a rethinking of how the oversight function is performed.

Legal authority, staff, and money are all important prerequisites to congressional action, but none of these are grossly lacking now. Genuflections before the trilogy of authority, money, and staff do not reach the basic problems.

In my judgment, a fourth myth about oversight is that members of the Congress and their staffs lack the experience, training, intelligence, or creativity to conduct more and better oversight. To put it more bluntly, some critics charge that the members and their staff simply lack the competence, defined broadly in the terms just mentioned, to do the necessary work. One can unearth situations where members lack the competence needed for specific tasks, but one finds little evidence to support the proposition that these deficiencies are universal or, when found, that normally they are beyond remedy. As has been demonstrated in actual performance, useful oversight is practicable in the Congress. Deficiencies in competence in specific circumstances can frequently be remedied if the committees or subcommittees desire to do so.

It is true that even talented generalists (viz., the members of the Congress) can be intimidated by mountains of data, by exotic or technical vocabularies, or by arcane analyses. It is also true that some technical experts at times seem to relish prolix analyses presented in nearly incomprehensive language. The expert may indeed understand that obfuscation is his first line of defense. But legislators and their staffs are predestined neither to succumb nor to be deceived. Effective legislative oversight does not require that all members and all staff persons be competent in all aspects of public policy. If that were necessary the task indeed would be hopeless. The dual practices of division of labor and specialization provide the classical solution to this problem.

Some summary propositions

1. Oversight is neither comprehensive nor systematic because that goal is beyond achievement.

2. Oversight is performed intermittently because the factors most relevant to stimulating it are not constantly present. Thus the quality and quantity of oversight varies between the two branches of the Congress, among the committees and subcommittees within each house, and in the same committees and subcommittees from session to session and from issue to issue.

3. It is not too difficult to produce a syndrome of factors which tend to maximize the possibilities for effective oversight. The elements might be: there is a legal basis for committee activity and there is an adequate budget for it; adequate staff resources, defined in terms of numbers, skills, and attitudes are present; the subject matter is not unusually complex or technical; the issue involved has high political visibility; the committee with relevant jurisdiction is decentralized in structure unless the chairman is a strong advocate of oversight in the given area; key committee members are unhappy with their treatment by executive personnel; key committee members lack confidence in top executive personnel; committee senior members harbor per-

sonal antipathy toward executive officials; the executive proposes vast changes in existing programs; committee control rests in the political party opposite to that of the president.

The ease of creating such a list obscures the more difficult problem of assigning weights to each element and to predicting the possible consequences of its presence or absence. Perhaps that is because the primary elements of explanation may well vary from case to case. There seems to be no single pattern which explains legislative oversight in all circumstances. There are only common factors which combine in different ways under specified sets of circumstances. Moreover, even casual inspection of congressional behavior suggests that all the conditions which are part of this syndrome are rarely present simultaneously.

4. Oversight is not a high priority much of the time for most members.

5. Congressional staff behavior is primarily determined by member priorities and policy preferences. The best way to alter staff behavior is to focus on its major determinant.

6. A sense of realism demands recognition of the fact that most members are relatively satisfied with the conduct of legislative oversight of the bureaucracy. They feel little stimulus to alter existing patterns.

Some proposals perhaps worthy of discussion

1. Casework and oversight.

For very fundamental reasons, most oversight activity will come from congressmen acting not as individuals, but as members of committees and subcommittees. But congressmen acting as individuals in their own offices can do something that most do not do now. Priorities are basic. Most members now view the mountains of casework processed in their offices simply as service for constituents. Members could instruct their caseworkers to be more alert to the patterns of problems revealed in cases so that this information could be passed on to the appropriate committees and subcommittees. Congressmen collect routinely a mother lode of information potentially useful for oversight. Members either have not understood the value of what they have or have not cared enough to order the modest effort that would make this information more useful.

2. Committee structure and oversight.

Committees that are serious about improving their potential for oversight should carefully examine their subcommittee structure to see if more autonomy might be provided.

3. Recognition of the full dimensions of oversight.

Much oversight that now occurs in the Congress is not recognized. Because a session is called a legislative hearing or because processing of constituent complaints is called casework does not mean that these activities are unrelated to oversight. Oversight should be viewed from a broader perspective than that of formal investigations.

4. Are oversight subcommittees worthwhile?

Perhaps the most obvious step taken by a few standing committees to enhance their oversight efforts has been to create specific oversight subcommittees. To my knowledge, no one has systematically or intensively looked at whether having such subcommittees makes any appreciable difference in the conduct of oversight. Here is a structural solution which one could suspect has not had any great impact. But nobody knows for sure. The topic does deserve attention.

A final note

The standard answer to improving the conduct of the congressional oversight function usually seems to be: elect smarter people to the Congress, make them work harder, and give them bigger staffs. After extensive observation of the Congress at work, it seems to me that most members have the talent necessary to perform their jobs well; many congressmen probably cannot work much harder than they do now, although they can change what they do if they want to; few congressmen argue that increasing staff size would have any significant impact on the conduct of oversight. Apparently, those members who publicly proclaim the general virtue of having more staff seemingly do not have the improvement of oversight specifically in mind.

Surely a more accurate answer than the standard one (although still not a fully satisfactory one) might be: if more and better oversight is to be achieved, members need to alter their priorities for allocation of their time and they need to insist on *better* staffs. In practice, how to achieve either of these objectives is far from obvious.

The idea that no problem, given human effort and enough money, is beyond solution stands at the center of the American ethos. As a goad to improve things, this view may have great utility; as an observation about reality, it may be sadly defective. If the goal is to increase the quantity of oversight and to improve its quality, one needs to look at underlying causes. From this perspective, structural changes in the Congress, by themselves, are unlikely to do the job. The basic limits to more adequate oversight seem to me to lie not in defective structures but peripherally in excessive expectations and centrally in an imperfect will to act. The latter comment necessarily implies neither a general criticism nor a weakness. Congressmen do what they do and slight what they slight for reasons that seem persuasive to them.

In the words of an astute Senate staff member discussing staff behavior on oversight matters:

> *Specialists in departmental interference must judge both the merits of the case and the costs in time, effort, and their own or the congressman's "credit" with the agency, of attempting to achieve a given solution.*

In other words, reality is complex. The bases for choice are many. Balancing reasonable requests for time and action is central. Most congressmen feel that they can justify much of what they do in terms that their constituents would find quite acceptable. Most staff members feel that what they are doing is what their employers, the members of Congress, want them to do. Merely telling members or staff persons to do something else is just not much help. The incentives for conducting more intensive and extensive oversight are great in the abstract and yet are modest in most concrete situations. Any analysis of legislative oversight has to be grounded in these stern facts.

Study questions for selection three

1. How convinced are you of the truth of the following statement, in which Ogul argues that Congress is incapable of really effective oversight of the bureaucracy? "No amount of congressional dedication and energy, no conceivable increase in the size of committee staffs, and even no extraordinary boost in committee budgets will enable the Congress to carry out its oversight obligations in a comprehensive and systematic manner."

2. Are oversight and legislation necessarily mutually exclusive functions, so that if Congress were to devote an increasing proportion of its energy to oversight, less would be available to spend on legislation?

3. Regardless of your answer to the previous question, *should* Congress—and other legislative bodies as well—devote more attention than at present to administrative oversight?

B. Courts and administrators

While many people think that the courts operate merely to see that laws are properly applied and to act as neutral arbiters, the administrator had best take a different view. Judges have the power to make judgments that seriously affect the substance of the agencies' programs and the general operation of the administrative process.

During the 1960s, civil rights groups successfully used the court system to overturn policies they opposed; the school-bussing decisions probably were the most dramatic assertions of judicial power over the political-administrative process. The 1970s have seen other groups (including those concerned about environmental protection, product safety, the treatment of prisoners, and the punishment of school children) turn to the courts for relief. Both substantive and procedural questions are posed to the courts. The substantive issues concern the interpretations that agencies place on particular statutes; the central question is: "Does the agency's program conform to the legislature's intent?" The procedural issues concern how the agencies behave in the course of implementing a statute; the court is asked: "Are citizens being afforded due process of law?"

Courts and the substance of administrative decisions

For many purposes it makes sense to think of the courts as a partner in the administrative process, rather than an entirely separate authority that occasionally reviews isolated administrative actions. In many areas of administration, the judge's determination can be thought of as simply another phase of the administrative process, one that is expected to recur with considerable regularity.

Consider, for example, the role of state courts in the local planning and zoning process. Since local government units can take actions that vastly alter the value of private property, courts often are called upon to decide just how far state statutes and state and federal constitutions allow local authorities to go in drafting laws. What options are available to a city that wants to adopt a "no-growth" or "controlled-growth" policy? Can it impose a population ceiling and simply refuse to issue building permits? Can it cite limitations on the capacity of the water treatment plant (and refuse to improve it) as an excuse for denying building permits? Can it allow expansion on a phased basis, when the development is congruent with the city's planned improvements (parks, schools, streets, sewers)? Can it declare a piece of property part of a "green belt" and allow it to be used only for purposes that will produce little revenue for the landowner?

Of course, the developers' reactions to these questions are that the courses of action mentioned are illegal or unconstitutional for various reasons. It is often alleged especially that the actual effect of any of the policies would be to take property without due process of law. Having laboriously put together several parcels of land at great expense and risk over the years and having waited until the time was propitious for a development project that should be worth millions of dollars, it is understandable that the developers would be incensed at the actions of the "liberal-elitist" city planners in forming an alliance with environmental groups to block their project, which would, they feel, also provide jobs and benefit the community in other ways. The result of the conflict is that a judge is asked to participate in the administrative process, and the names of Ramapo, New York, and Petaluma, California, for example, are now famous among local planning officials, because these are towns in which judges have made landmark decisions affecting growth policy. As they make decisions that are likely to be controversial, administrators know that expensive and lengthy court action may follow and that the final decision may not be made until a judge somewhere provides his input. This knowledge is likely to color administrators' decisions.

Judges also affect substantive policy at the federal level, of course. For example, the authority of the so-called *independent regulatory commissions* (the FCC, the ICC, the FTC, and CAB, etc.) frequently has been challenged in the courts. Throughout the histories of several of these agencies there have been recurrent struggles over the validity of Congress's attempt to delegate to them broad rule-making power. This struggle was intensified by the grant to the agencies of *quasi-judicial authority* as well—the power to perform a courtlike function in determining if the agency's own rules have been violated. In the early decades of this century, federal courts hesitated to accept fully the notion that Congress could delegate its authority, but gradually—especially during and after the depression years—court opposition declined. Not only the independent agencies, but many ordinary executive agencies also have wide rule-making power today. Nevertheless, the power of courts to influence the specifics of agency policies remains considerable.

In his studies of the relationship between administrators and courts, Martin Shapiro has concentrated especially on executive agencies' top administrators, who are likely to be high-ranking civil servants—just below those appointed by the president. Shapiro refers to these administrators, together with federal appellate court judges, as *supplementary lawmakers,* who "accept general statutes and fill them in with sufficient supplementary and explanatory rules to make them adequate guides to the myriad specific decisions in the individual cases which the 'administration' of law requires."[4] In several ways, courts and

---

[4]Martin Shapiro, *The Supreme Court and Administrative Agencies* (New York: The Free Press, 1968), p. 45.

agencies are similar: both have hierarchical structures, both operate under rather elaborate regulations and rules, both have developed their own conventional languages, and both are inclined to place considerable weight on past practices and make decisions incrementally.[5]

Courts and agencies are, in fact, parallel structures performing similar functions. Yet it is obvious that conflicts between them do occur. The Cramton article reprinted below, as well as your daily newspaper, presents evidence that the conflicts can be quite severe. Shapiro suggests that the conflicts are a product of three factors. First, the judges are likely to be generalists, whereas agency personnel are specialists; the judges are, in a sense, more political and bring to supplementary lawmaking a broader perspective—that of the layman. Second, imprecision of statutes may lead to judicial involvement; in such situations, judges find it possible to influence greatly the substance of policy, and they take the opportunity to do so. (There is, of course, no objective reason to expect judges' decisions to be better than those of administrators.) Third, statute makers may allow administrators considerable discretion within broad guidelines and depend upon the courts to see that reasonable boundaries are not violated; this is, of course, an invitation to conflict.[6]

In point of fact, the policy roles of courts and agencies are inextricably intertwined. Shapiro has commented about the sharing of responsibility between the two institutions:

> *In effect, then, what* [Congress] *has often done is to commission the agency to use its discretion in policy exploration and commission the courts to use their discretion in determining when the problem should be returned to Congress for another look by a court decision saying that the agency has gone further than it legally could under the old statute.*[7]

Although the involvement of courts in matters of administration is important to civil servants, it is not necessarily to be feared greatly. On occasion administrators may feel fortunate to be able to rely on the court to provide an interpretation of otherwise vague statutory language and even to take the blame for doing so. Of course, there are also those frustrating times when the judicial decision runs counter to what the administrator wants and what, to him or her, seems perfectly obvious statutory language. While the courts and the administrators are, indeed, both trying to flesh out the statute, the differences in their perspectives can lead to considerable conflict.

---

[5]Ibid., pp. 44–45.

[6]Ibid., pp. 97–101.

[7]Ibid., p. 102.

Courts, procedural matters, and administrative law

It is not unusual for the courts to become involved in reviewing the procedures agencies have used in rule making or in adjudication. In fact, this is the most frequent basis for judicial involvement, even when the final result is a change in substantive policy. Although the courts now accept that administrative agencies have a legitimate role to play in establishing and enforcing regulations, the courts have continued to monitor the process and to impose procedural requirements upon the agencies. Of central importance to federal courts have been the due process clauses of the Fifth and Fourteenth amendments to the Constitution:

> *No person shall . . . be deprived of life, liberty, or property, without due process of law. . . .*
> *No state shall . . . deprive any person of life, liberty, or property, without due process of law. . . .*

In attempting to define what "due process of law" is, courts usually require agencies to: give formal notice and hold a hearing before taking action that adversely affects an individual, if that person contests the decision; maintain a record of events, evidence, statements, etc., concerning a particular matter; and allow the individual or organization concerned to be represented by counsel.[8]

The federal government and many states have gone beyond the rules established by courts and have adopted statutes that specify what proper administrative procedures are. One of the most important features of such federal requirements, first passed as the *Administrative Procedure Act* in 1946, is the provision of *administrative law judges.* (They were originally called *hearing examiners;* the name was changed in 1972.) Although these personnel are assigned to particular agencies, they have considerable independence from agency supervisors.[9] Their task is to conduct such hearings as are necessary and to recommend a decision on the basis of briefs presented by agency personnel and by the

---

[8]See Robert S. Lorch, *Democratic Process and Administrative Law* (Detroit: Wayne State University Press, 1969), pp. 128–44.

[9]In describing the administrative law judge's degree of independence, a distinguished judge (now retired) has said, "His appointment is absolute, he is not subject to agency efficiency ratings, promotions, or demotions, and his compensation is established by the Civil Service Commission independent of agency recommendations." See Merritt Ruhlen, *Manual for Administrative Law Judges* (Washington, D.C.: Administrative Conference of the United States, 1974), pp. 1–2.

individuals or organizations contesting the agency position. Although this is not a purely judicial procedure totally independent from the agency, it does afford a degree of impartiality. Use of these judges is widespread, but not universal; in effect, at some agencies it is still possible for a client to be prosecuted and judged by the same individual. For these reasons, a considerable movement—especially favored by administrative lawyers—is campaigning for separate administrative courts on the European model.

Under some circumstances, although not all, agency decisions can be appealed to the ordinary courts. Since such cases frequently go directly to appeals courts, the judges have the power to refuse to review them, in which event the original agency decision stands. Only a very small percentage of agency adjudicatory decisions actually reach the ordinary courts, however. The ones that do tend to concern alleged procedural or *substantial* factual error, or cases in which agencies may have exceeded their statutory or constitutional authority. Furthermore, judges usually require that all appeals within the agency be exhausted before access to the courts is granted.[10]

Rule making and informal adjudication

As noted above, agencies not only *enforce* laws and regulations, they also *make* many of the rules themselves. As with the processes of formal adjudication just considered, in making formally published regulations or rules, agencies are required to take certain actions. But the rule-making process is much less structured than is true of law making by legislators. For example, the Administrative Procedure Act requires agencies to file notice of their intent in the Federal Register and lists a number of encouragements to broad public participation in the rule-making process, but it also contains an escape clause that eliminates the notice requirement under certain circumstances: "When the agency for good cause finds (and incorporates the finding and a brief statement of reasons therefor in the rule issued) that notice and public procedure thereon are inpracticable, unnecessary, or contrary to the public interest."[11]

Commenting upon the greater informality of the administrative

---

[10]Lorch's book (note 8) is an excellent synopsis of the extremely complex processes of administrative law, written from a political viewpoint. His treatment of such topics as the prerogative writs (including mandamus, certiorari, prohibition, injunction, and habeas corpus), standing, ripeness, and exhaustion of remedies is very helpful for the uninitiated; see especially chapter 7.

[11]Section 553 (b) (3) (B).

Chapter four

rule-making process as compared with that of adjudication, Robert Lorch has said that administrators have

> *far fewer constitutional and statutory "t's" to cross and "i's" to dot. The law is more zealous about protecting people as individuals than people as part of the public. Courts seldom question the* procedure *of a legislature (partly for political reasons) and they seldom try to impose any particular procedure on the rule-making function of agencies except those few procedures required by statutes. This contrasts with the great concern of courts over* adjudicatory procedures.[12]

Most agencies usually do not hold formal hearings or undertake broad consultations before setting the rules that statutes allow them to make. Instead, they are likely to rely on the expertise of their own personnel and contacts with interest groups that they consider to have a legitimate interest in the subject under consideration and a friendly orientation toward the agency. In some cases there are statutes that require formal consultation, but these are exceptions; ordinarily, it is through these informal methods that the merits and political acceptability of proposed rules are judged.

Administrators might shudder at the possibility of wider consultation in rule making, for the claim is that such a change would slow the rule-making process to the crawl of legislative statute making. College campuses provide many examples of rule making with no consultation and some with a bit of consultation. Admissions requirements may have been set by the governing board after consultation with administrators and with some faculty—but probably not with students, prospective students, parents, or high-school teachers. Deviations from the stated requirements probably occur daily, as individual departmental chairpersons, deans, and admissions officers apply their own special rules. Requirements that students live in college dormitories may be set after consultation with banks that hold bonds to be paid off with rent, but not with private apartment owners in the community who may go bankrupt from loss of student residents. Rules governing the use of library materials may be set with a view to preserving the materials and are not likely to involve broad consultations that might result in wider availability and use. In defense of the status quo, it does appear that the following of elaborate and formal consultative procedures before making all administrative rules could result in deadlock and stagnation. Although the present practice falls far short of any democratic ideal, there may be little choice but to continue to allow the administrators themselves to consider (through whatever procedures they may choose)

---

[12]Lorch, *Democratic Process*, p. 95.

the possible ramification of their rules; those who challenge the results can go to court when they feel it is worth the trouble.

The adjudication process described above is the formal one; it often involves hearings, evidence, and representation by counsel. Not all adjudication is so complex and time consuming. Far more takes place as an informal process. Returning to the rules of the campus, consider the applicant for admission who is denied, but who then visits the admissions office and the academic department, claiming that the poor grades received during his or her senior year in high school could be explained by the difficulties associated with the death of a brother and working thirty hours per week to help support the family. Chances are, no formal hearing will be held and no written evidence taken, although there may be a phone call to confirm the facts. At the end of the interview, the applicant may well be admitted on probation—especially if he or she has made a good impression and the administrator is in a good mood. The lack of formal procedures probably results in unfair treatment of some individuals, but hundreds of adjudicatory decisions of this type must be made on every large campus each week.

Thus, what must be balanced against the obvious shortcomings of the informal adjudication process is that adoption of more rigid procedures increases the possibility of slowing down and eventually strangling the administrative process so that many decisions cannot be made at all.

Selection four

Judicial law making and administration*

Roger C. Cramton

Some years ago the John Birch Society decorated the highways of the South and the West with "Impeach Earl Warren" billboards. It is not necessary to approve of their politics to give the group high marks for understanding before many others did that the effect of the

*Reprinted from *Public Adminstration Review* 36 (September/October 1976): 551–555. © 1976 by The American Society for Public Administration, 1225 Connecticut Avenue, N.W., Washington, D.C. All rights reserved.

Supreme Court's activism during the 1950s and 1960s—particularly on racial issues—was to realign the functions of the branches of government so as to give the courts a prominent law-making role. This new judicial function now has been elaborated so that administrative duties are added on to those of law making; federal judges decide how much paper and supplies a school system will order for the following year and how many square feet of living space convicts will be given. However one may feel about the increasing power of judges (Harvard sociologist Nathan Glazer refers to "the imperial judiciary"), it is apparent that the involvement of the courts in determining and administering social policy is one of the most important constitutional developments of recent decades.

Roger Cramton, the author of this selection, is dean of the law school at Cornell University; previously he occupied that position at the University of Michigan, was chairman of the Administrative Conference of the United States, and was assistant attorney general in charge of the Office of Legal Counsel at the Department of Justice. Thus, Cramton has been favorably situated to observe the development of this new phase of judicial activism, which he analyzes below. It is Cramton's thesis that the courts became deeply involved in the law making and administrative roles reluctantly, because elected officials were immobilized by political fear. He warns that an excess of judicial activism could cause a backlash of popular opinion against the courts and that such a development could be so dangerous as to threaten even the general acceptance of the authority of law in society.

Seventy years ago in St. Paul, Roscoe Pound gave a famous speech on "The Causes of Popular Dissatisfaction with the Administration of Justice." Recently, a prestigious group of lawyers and judges, assembled by Chief Justice Burger, reconvened in St. Paul to reconsider Pound's theme. A surprising conclusion was that, although the professionals—the lawyers and judges themselves—have many problems with the administration of justice, the tide of popular dissatisfaction is at a relatively low ebb.

In contrast to other agencies of the government, the people have confidence in the fairness and integrity of the courts. True, there is continuing complaint over the law's cost and delay. But, apart from this perennial complaint, popular dissatisfaction appears to stem from two perceptions: first, that decisions in criminal cases turn too often upon procedural technicalities rather than upon the guilt or innocence of the offender; and second, that some judges, and especially the federal judiciary, have been too actively engaged in law making on social and economic issues that are better handled by other institutions of government. The layman, on scanning his newspaper or viewing the television screen, discovers to his surprise that judges are running schools and prison systems, prescribing curricula, formulating budgets, and regulating the environment.

Causation is a tricky matter. A student theme has reported that, since Smokey the Bear posters were displayed in the New York subways, forest fires have disappeared in Manhattan. Despite the risks, I hazard the generalization that several fundamental changes in the nature of our society may have altered the role of the judiciary.

Foremost among those changes is that suggested by the title of this article. The Leviathan is upon us, and it has implications for all branches of government, including the judiciary. Government now attempts so much! Every technical, economic, and social issue seems to end up in the hands of government; and the demand for further government action is combined with charges that existing government is inefficient, heavy-handed, and ineffective. This is one field in which the appetite for nostrums does not fade with the demonstrated failure of prior cures. Each reformer, after criticizing the failure and inefficiency of government, then concludes that the remedy is—more of the same!

But our attitudes about ourselves and about conflict have also changed. The confrontational style of contemporary America assures that social conflict will increase. "Doing your own thing" is the central value of a hedonistic, self-regarding society; and patience is a nearly extinct virtue. Nowadays no one takes "no" for an answer, whether it is a job aspirant or a welfare claimant or a teacher who has been denied tenure. We perceive our society as having grown old; the enthusiastic and venturesome spirit that prompted the unchartered growth of the American past is now suffering from hardening of the arteries. As we experience slower economic development and approach zero population growth, organized groups contend with each other with increasing ferocity for larger shares of a more static pie. There is a declining sense of a common purpose; the prevailing attitude is "What's in it for me?"

These trends give lawyers and judges an even more central role in our society than they have had in the past. The decline of moral consensus and of institutions of less formal control, such as the family and the church, places much more strain on the law as an instrument of conflict resolution and social control. And the increasing contentiousness of groups organized for their own advantage has made conflict resolution a growth industry. If you could buy stock in law firms, I would advise you to do so. Lawyers have a legal monopoly on the conflict resolution industry, and it is the boom industry of today.

To these developments—the increasing reliance on law as an instrument of social control and the rapid growth of group conflict—must be added another factor: the failure of the executive and the legislature to meet the challenge of today's inflated expectations. The public perception that these branches of government have failed—a perception greatly abetted by the debacles of Vietnam and Watergate—has led the people to turn increasingly to the courts for solutions to their problems.

Models of judicial review

Consider in the context of the Leviathan State two models of judicial review of administrative action. The traditional model is one of a restrained and sober second look at what government has done that adversely affects a citizen. The controversy is bipolar in character, with two parties opposing each other; the issues are narrow and well defined; and the relief is limited and obvious. Has a welfare recipient been denied a benefit to which he is entitled by statute? Was fair procedure employed by the agency? Were constitutional rights violated?

Judicial review in this model serves as a window on the outside world, a societal escape valve which tests the self-interest and narrow vision of the specialist and the bureaucrat against the broader premises of the total society. Every bureaucracy develops its own way of looking at things and these belief patterns are enormously resistant to change. In time an agency acquires a tunnel vision in which particular values are advanced and others are ignored. An independent judiciary tests agency outcomes against the statutory framework and the broader legal context.

Judicial review in this form is an absolute essential, especially in a society in which the points of contact between officials and private individuals multiply at every point. The impartial and objective second look adds to the integrity and acceptance of the administrative process rather than undermining it. If the administrator is upheld, as usually is the case, citizen confidence in the fairness and rationality of administration is enhanced. In the relatively small number of cases in which the administrator is reversed, the administrator is forced to readjust his narrower view to the larger perspective of the total society.

During the last twenty years the pace of constitutional change, especially in judicial review of government action, has been astounding. The values implicit in general constitutional provisions such as due process, equal protection, and free speech have been given expanded content and new life. Even more important, constitutional rights have been extended to persons who were formerly neglected by the legal system—blacks, aliens, prisoners, and others. One can disagree with the merits of particular decisions. But the general trends—implementation of fundamental values by the courts and the inclusion of previously excluded groups in the application of these values— constitute a great hour in the long struggle for human freedom.

There is, however, a second model of judicial review that is growing in acceptance and authority. This model of the judicial role has characteristics more of general problem solving than of dispute resolution. Simon Rifkind speaks of a modern tendency to view courts as modern handymen—as jacks of all trades available to furnish the answer to whatever may trouble us. "What is life? When does death begin? How should we operate prisons and hospitals? Shall we build nuclear power plants, and if so, where? Shall the Concorde fly to our shores?"[1]

Thoughtful observers believe that controversies of this character strain the capacities of our courts and may have debilitating effects on the self-reliance of administrators and legislators. At the risk of appearing more reactionary than I am, let me focus not on the achievements of the past but on the possible dangers that arise when the judiciary succumbs to pressures to attempt too much.

---

[1]Simon H. Rifkind, "Are We Asking Too Much of Our Courts?" paper prepared for the National Conference on the Causes of Popular Dissatisfaction with the Administration of Justice, St. Paul, Minn., April 8, 1976, p. 5.

The court as administrator

The traditional judicial role, earlier described, envisions a lawsuit which is bipolar in character, seeks traditional relief (usually damages), and applies established law to a relatively narrow factual situation. The relief given is backward-looking and does not order government officials to take positive steps in the future.

The traditional model still persists in much private litigation and in many routine cases challenging official action, but in many other constitutional and statutory controversies radical changes have occurred. The changes have led Abram Chayes to argue that the basic character of public litigation has changed.[2] In today's public litigation, a federal judge often is dealing with issues involving numerous parties; indeed, everyone in the community may be affected. Moreover, the issues are complex, interrelated, and multifaceted; and they turn less on proof concerning past misconduct than on complex predictions as to how various social interests should be protected in the future. Since the remedy is not limited to compensating named plaintiffs for a past harm, the judge gets drawn, for example, into coercing school officials to close schools, bus pupils, change curricula, and build new facilities. The federal judge becomes one of the most powerful persons in the community; on the particular issue, he is the one who decides.

Consider the role of one man, Frank Johnson, in the governance of the once sovereign state of Alabama. Johnson, a distinguished United States district judge in Alabama, is supervising the operation of the prisons, mental hospitals, highway patrol, and other institutions of the state. His decrees have directed the state to hire more wardens with better training, rebuild the prisons, and even extend to such details as the length of exercise periods and the installation of partitions in the men's rooms.

What is the authority of a federal judge to take such far-reaching actions? Why isn't the Alabama legislature the proper body to determine what prison or hospital care should be provided, and at what cost, through agencies administered by the state's executive branch? The answer is that all of these actions are designed to remedy violations of the constitutional rights of prisoners, mental patients, and others. And the Alabama legislature and executive have defaulted on their obligation to remedy these violations.

We are caught on the horns of a terrible dilemma. It is unconscionable that a federal court should refuse to entertain claims that state officials have systematically violated the constitutional rights of prisoners, mental patients, or school children. On the other hand, the design of effective relief may draw the court into a continuing role as an administrator of complex bureaucratic institutions. The dangers of the latter choice are worth brief exploration.

First, the judge who assumes an administrative role may gradually lose his neutrality, becoming a partisan who is pursuing his own cause. In one

---

[2]Abram Chayes, "The Role of the Judiciary in a Public Law System," *Harvard Law Review* 89 (May 1976): 1281–1316.

recent class action, a federal judge not only appointed expert witnesses, suggested areas of inquiry, and took over from the parties a substantial degree of the management of the case, but also went so far as to order that $250,000 from an award required of the defendants be paid for social science research on the effectiveness of the decree. That may be good government, but is it judicial justice?

A further problem arises from the tentativeness of our knowledge about such matters as minimum standards in operating a prison or mental hospital. We fervently hope that civilized and humane treatment will be provided to all of those who are confined to public institutions. But is it desirable to take the view of the current generation of experts, especially those self-selected by the plaintiffs or the judge, and to give their views of acceptable standards the status of constitutional requirements, with all that implies concerning their fixed meaning and difficulty of change?

Here as elsewhere, our capacity to anticipate the future or to discern all relevant facets of polycentric problems is limited. Thus, for example, when a federal judge ordered New York City to close the Tombs as a city jail or to rebuild it, the city, faced with an extraordinary financial crisis, opted to close it, and prisoners confined to the Tombs were transferred to Riker's Island. The crowded conditions of the Tombs were immediately duplicated on Riker's Island. But a further result was not anticipated: Riker's Island is much less accessible to the families and attorneys of prisoners; and there is reason to believe that the vast majority of prisoners prefer the convenience of the Tombs, despite its problems, to the inaccessibility of Riker's Island.

The underlying truth is that court orders cannot by judicial decree achieve social change in the face of the concerted opposition of elected officials and public opinion. In a representative democracy, the consent of the people is required for lasting change.

The impulse to reform, moreover, is not limited to courts nor to constitutional law. A vigilant press, an informed populace, and the leadership of a committed minority have mobilized forces of change and reform throughout our history. A representative democracy may move slowly, but if we lack patience we may undermine the self-reliance and responsibility of the people and their elected officials.

The danger of confrontation between branches of government is yet another concern. What happens, for example, if Alabama refuses to fund its mental hospitals or prisons at the level required to achieve the standards specified in Judge Johnson's decrees? The next step, Judge Johnson has said, is the sale of Alabama's public lands in order to finance, through court-appointed officers, the necessary changes.

A degree of tension is a necessary concomitant of the checks and balances of a federal system. But in our urge to check we should not forget that balance is involved as well. One of the lessons of the Watergate era is that cooperation, restraint, and patience among the various branches and levels of government is necessary if our system is to survive in the long run. As Ben Franklin said many years ago, we must hang together or we will hang separately.

Pressures for judicial action

Why have the courts undertaken these more expansive functions? They have not done so as volunteers desirous of expanding their own powers, but reluctantly and hesitantly in response to public demands for effective implementation of generally held values.

The American people today have little patience or restraint in dealing with social issues. An instant problem requires an instant solution that provides instant gratification. Playing this game under those rules, the executive and legislature have done their best—grinding out thousands of laws and regulations, many of them ineffective and some of them intrusive and harmful. The public, while demanding even more action from legislators and administrators, perceives these bodies as inept, ineffective, and even corrupt. Moreover, issues on which there is a deep social division, such as school busing or abortion, are avoided by elected officials, who view them as involving unacceptable political risks.

Nature abhors a vacuum, and the inaction of the executive and law-making branches creates pressures for judicial action. A prominent federal judge put it succinctly at the recent St. Paul conference: "If there is a serious problem, and the legislature and executive don't respond, the courts have to act."

And they have done so on one after another burning issue. The mystery is that they have been so successful and that there has been so little popular outcry. The desegregation of southern schools, of course, is a success story of heroic proportions. Legislative reapportionment is also generally viewed as a success despite the mathematical extreme to which it was carried in its later years. Organs of opinion, especially the TV networks and major newspapers, support the Court's actions in general and especially in such areas as civil rights and criminal procedure. There is no institution in our society that has as good a press as the Supreme Court. Judicial activism, it appears, has the approval of the intellectual elite who have become disillusioned with the effectiveness of social change by other means. It is more doubtful, however, whether the common man concurs either in the elite's support of judicial law making or of its substantive results.

Long-term effects

Neither popular acclaim nor criticism, of course, can answer the long-term question of the appropriate law-making role of the judiciary and the desirable limits on the scope of judicial decrees. More fundamental considerations must be decisive.

First, the practical question of comparative qualifications. Do judges, by training, selection, or experience, have an aptitude for social problem solving that other officials of government lack? And are the techniques of adjudication well designed to perform these broader policy-making functions? Professor Abram Chayes of the Harvard Law School has answered these questions with a confident affirmative.[3] I am inclined to disagree.

Second, what will be the long-term effects of this trend on the credibility of the courts and on the sense of responsibility of administrators and legislators?

After completion of this article, my fears on this score received support from an unlikely source—Anthony Lewis in the *New York Times*. After acknowledging, as I do, that the Boston School Case "presented exceptional difficulties," that "a judge could [not] in conscience remit the complaining black families to their political remedy," and that District Judge Garrity's lonely efforts should be viewed with sympathy, Lewis nevertheless concludes that Garrity's involvement in the day-by-day administration of school affairs "has not worked well" and " is a serious philosophical error:"

> *American judges have to handle many controversial problems with political implications – redistricting, prisons and the like. Their object should always be to nudge elected officials into performing their responsibility. [Excessive intervention by the judge] tends to take responsibility away from those who ought to be seen to bear it.*[4]

And finally, as Simon Rifkind has put it, there is "the ancient question, *quo warranto?* By what authority do judges turn courts into mini-legislatures?"[5]

The critical question in a republic is how government by nonelected, lifetime officials can be squared with representative democracy. The magic of the robe, the remnants of the myth that law on these matters is discovered by an elaboration of existing rules (rather than by personal preference), and the prudence of the judiciary in picking issues on which it could command a great deal of popular support—perhaps these factors explain why the judges have been as successful as they have.

I fear, however, that the judiciary has exhausted the areas where broad majoritarian support will sustain new initiatives and that the tolerance of local communities for "government by decree" is fast dissipating. If so, caution is in order lest a depreciation of the esteem in which we hold the courts undermines their performance of the essential tasks that are indisputably theirs and that other institutions cannot perform.

The authority of the courts depends in large part on the public perception that judges are different from other policy makers. Judges (but not elected officials) are impartial rather than willful or partisan; judges utilize special decisional procedures; and they draw on established general principles in deciding individual cases. In short, traditional ideas concerning the nature, form, and

---

[3]Ibid.

[4]*New York Times*, 24 May 1976, p. 29. © 1975 by the New York Times Company. Reprinted by permission.

[5]Rifkind, p. 20.

functions of adjudication as a decisional technique underlie popular acceptance of judicial outcomes.

While the precise boundaries of the adjudicative technique are flexible rather than fixed, if they are abandoned entirely the judge loses credibility as a judge. He becomes merely another policy maker who, in managing prisons or schools or whatnot, is expressing his personal views and throwing his weight around. When that point is reached, the judge's credibility and authority is no greater than that of Mayor White in Boston or Mayor Rizzo in Philadelphia.

With the credibility of the legislature and executive branches of government in such disrepair, we cannot afford any further depreciation in the judicial currency. General acceptance of the authority of law is a necessary bulwark of our otherwise fragile social order. If it disappears, the resulting collapse of order may put the American people in the mood for that "more effective management" which is likely to characterize any distinctly American brand of authoritarianism.

Opportunities for charismatic and authoritarian leadership, it has been said, derive in considerable measure from the ability to "accentuate [a society's] sense of being in a desperate predicament." If the courts, by overextension and consequent failure, contribute to our growing sense of desperation, our liberties may not long survive. When a people despair of their institutions, force arrives under the masquerade of ideology.

Study questions for selection four

1. What are some advantages judges bring to their new role of political administrator? What are some liabilities of judges in this role?

2. If judges were less willing to intervene, do you think elected officials and administrators would be more likely to assume their proper responsibilities in disputes about such matters as prison conditions?

3. Do you think that judicial law making and administration as it now exists is a passing phase or a permanent part of a new constitutional arrangement?

Suggested readings for chapter four

Berger, Raoul. *Impeachment: The Constitutional Problems.* Cambridge, Mass.: Harvard University Press, 1973.

Bowhay, James H., and Thrall, Virginia D. *State Legislative Appropriations Process.* Lexington, Ky.: Council of State Governments, 1975.

Brown, Richard E. *The GAO: Untapped Source of Congressional Power.* Knoxville: University of Tennessee Press, 1970.

Davis, Kenneth Culp. *Administrative Law and Government.* St. Paul, Minn.: West Publishing Company, 1960.

———. *Discretionary Justice: A Preliminary Inquiry.* Baton Rouge: Louisiana State University Press, 1969.

Fenno, Richard F., Jr. *The Power of the Purse. Appropriations Politics in Congress.* Boston: Little, Brown, 1966.

Freeman, J. Leiper. *The Political Process: Executive Bureau-Legislative Committee Relations.* New York: Random House, 1965.

Harris, Joseph P. *Congressional Control of Administration.* Garden City, N.Y.: Doubleday, 1964.

Holtzman, Abraham. *Legislative Liaison: Executive Leadership in Congress.* Chicago: Rand McNally and Co., 1970.

Horn, Stephen. *Unused Power: The Work of the Senate Committee on Appropriations.* Washington, D.C.: Brookings Institution, 1970.

Lorch, Robert S. *Democratic Process and Administrative Law.* Detroit: Wayne State University Press, 1969.

Loveridge, Ronald O. *City Managers in Legislative Politics.* Indianapolis: Bobbs-Merrill, 1972.

Ogul, Morris S. *Congress Oversees Bureaucracy.* Pittsburgh: University of Pittsburgh Press, 1976.

Ripley, Randall B., and Franklin, Grace A. *Congress, the Bureaucracy and Public Policy.* Homewood, Ill.: The Dorsey Press, 1976.

Schwartz, Bernard, and Wade, H. W. R. *Legal Control of Government: Administrative Law in Britain and the United States.* New York: Oxford University Press, 1972.

Shapiro, Marshall. *The Supreme Court and Administrative Agencies.* New York: Free Press, 1968.

Group, clientele, and public involvement

The title of this chapter points to three categories of people who are *outside* of the formal government structure but who are, nonetheless, highly important to administrators. First let us treat *pressure groups,* or *interest groups,* which we consider to be "collection[s] of individuals who seek, through coordinated activity, to influence the political system without attempting to place group members in formal government offices."[1] Almost 150 years ago the perceptive French social theorist Alexis de Tocqueville commented upon the importance of groups in America:

Americans of all ages, all stations in life, and all types of disposition are forever forming associations. There are not

---

[1]L. Harmon Zeigler and G. Wayne Peak, *Interest Groups in American Society,* 2d ed. (Englewood Cliffs, N.J.: Prentice-Hall, 1972), p. 3.

*only commercial and industrial associations in which all
take part, but others of a thousand different types—religious,
moral, serious, futile, very general and very limited, im-
mensely large and very minute. Americans combine to give
fetes, found seminaries, build churches, distribute books, and
send missionaries to the antipodes. Hospitals, prisons, and
schools take shape in that way. Finally, if they want to proclaim a truth or propagate some feeling by the encouragement of a great example, they form an association. In every
case, at the head of any new undertaking, where in France
you would find the government or in England some territorial magnate, in the United States you are sure to find an
association.*[2]

Little has changed since Tocqueville's day; Americans are still
internationally famous for belonging to a multitude of groups. Political scientists routinely examine the clearly political activities of these
organizations that openly lobby to affect legislation and try to deliver
the votes of their members to friendly candidates at election time.
This chapter traces some group activities directed toward administrators and indicates the importance of groups to the administrative
process.

Second, our chapter title refers also to *clientele* involvement. The
clients of an agency are those who are under its protection or control,
or those who receive services from it. From the viewpoint of clients,
their relationship with the agency is a *dependency* relationship. In
many cases, the dependency is extreme: often recipients of assistance
from the Veterans Administration and the Social Security Administration, for example, could not obtain food, clothing, and shelter if
their payments were cut off. Thus, clientele-agency linkages are
usually much more important for the clients than for the agency.

The relationship between clients and agencies obviously varies
enormously. Several ways of classifying the relationships have been
suggested. Let us briefly discuss one based on the nature of agency
contacts with ordinary citizens.[3] Three types of organizations—"client-
serving," "client-processing," and "non-client-oriented"—can be identified. *Client-serving agencies* such as a neighborhood service center or
a county health clinic, exist to help citizens as individuals, who are
perceived as objects of concern in themselves. *Client-processing agen-*

---

[2]Alexis de Tocqueville, *Democracy in America,* eds. J. P. Meyer and Max Lerner,
trans. George Lawrence (New York: Harper and Row, 1966), p. 485.

[3]See Larry B. Hill, *The Model Ombudsman, Institutionalizing New Zealand's Democratic Experiment* (Princeton, N.J.: Princeton University Press, 1976), pp. 87–93.

cies such as the police and the tax department, also come into contact with large numbers of individual citizens, but they are not valued personally; instead, they are attended to (often involuntarily) as a by-product of pursuing a broader public purpose. *Non-client-oriented agencies*, such as the Department of State or the Atomic Energy Commission,[4] seldom come into contact with individual citizens. The goods or services they produce affect society as a whole, or some segment of it, but are not ordinarily divisible so that they can be consumed by individuals.

The character of an agency's relationship with citizens is very important in determining its structural development and its orientation. But, perhaps ironically, regardless of the type of organization involved, citizens, as individual clients, are often not very important actors in the administrative environment. As we shall see, individual clients may be most important to an agency as potential recruits for an organized group. The clients of an agency can become a vocal interest group that may demand radical changes (even the abolition) of an agency or lend important support for the development of stronger programs.

Finally, the *public* to which our title refers is at once the most obvious and most elusive feature in the administrative environment. Politicians and administrators talk glibly of "public opinion" or "what the public wants," but usually they realize that they are certain of neither public opinion nor the public's desires. Experts agree that elections are poor reflections of the public's opinions on specific political-administrative issues. Although some change may be underway, studies show that party loyalty has an important influence on citizens' votes, and most voters have simply assumed the party identification of their parents. A few issues become critical campaign themes that influence the outcomes of elections and thus give an administrator a little guidance, but only rarely does this occur. Even in the cities, a fire chief or director of a sanitation department can seldom obtain much guidance from an electoral outcome—unless fire station location or frequency of garbage removal was a dominant campaign issue and candidates took clearly opposing positions.

More commonly, the administrator depends upon his or her own perceptions of public views, gets information (not unbiased) from elected officials and interest groups, and receives some input from the agency's unorganized clientele. This book's final chapter will return to the linkages between administrators and the public when the concept of administrative accountability is examined.

---

[4]Note that the terminology "non-client-oriented" refers to relations with individual citizens. Of course, a clientele group, such as organized electricity producers, may be very important actors in the administrative environment of the Atomic Energy Commission.

Clientele groups

While the above discussion distinguished between interest groups and clientele, the interest groups confronting an agency are often composed of its clientele, of those organizations or individuals who receive the agency's services. Whether wheat farmers or manufacturers of computers, they may well form an interest group to deal collectively with the Department of Agriculture or the Department of Commerce.

In some cases, organized *clientele groups* are older than the agency, and some have even been instrumental in the agency's creation. For example, as an outgrowth of World War I, the American Legion was formed in 1919. The Legion rapidly became an effective advocate of government action to aid veterans and succeeded in 1921 in getting Congress to create the Veterans Bureau, which was given specific responsibility for veterans' affairs.[5] This agency became the Veterans Administration (VA) in 1930. In addition to having been the prime mover in the agency's creation, the American Legion has vigorously represented veterans' causes before the VA and other government agencies. On occasion, the Legion has sought congressional and presidential action to override the VA and other agencies' decisions. Thus, from its inception, administrators of the VA have been under the vigilant eye of this highly organized and active clientele group. Furthermore, other powerful groups (such as the Veterans of Foreign Wars and various Vietnam veterans groups) lobby the VA to insure that their voices are heard too.

In contrast to the VA's situation (and that of other agencies, such as the Department of Agriculture), some agencies are able virtually to ignore their large clientele groups. Many agencies that provide services to the disadvantaged in society have been of this type. The ability of a clientele to form an effective interest group depends, in considerable measure, upon its financial resources, general respectability or status, and its members' knowledge of governmental processes. Recipients of public assistance (welfare), for example, usually lack one or all of these qualities; consequently, they have had little to say about the programs of which they are clients. Instead, for the social service agencies serving them, an important interest group has been the agencies' own employees and their national organizations. For example, the National Association of Social Workers sets a code of ethics for members of the social work profession and provides guidance for administrators. The association is not only a voice for the employees; it also addresses the interests of clients as it sees them.

---

[5]William Pyrle Dillingham, *Federal Aid to Veterans: 1917–1941* (Gainesville: University of Florida Press, 1952), pp. 38–57.

The positions it takes on such matters as competing modalities of client treatment can be important influences upon administrators of programs.[6] For example, the association's endorsement of a Children's Advocate (an official within a social agency whose job it is to review cases, watching out for the welfare of children) will cause administrators to override their caseworkers' possible opposition to the creation of such a position.

Important changes in the social welfare field, however, have modified, to some extent, the importance of employees and their associations. The springboard for these changes was the phrase in the Equal Opportunity Act of 1964 (the Poverty Program) which demanded that programs be "developed, conducted, and administered with the *maximum feasible participation of residents* of the area and members of the groups served."[7] The clientele was to be heard and even encouraged to speak. This provision was a stimulus to the formation in 1966 of the National Welfare Rights Organization (NWRO), whose charter indicates its purpose: "To seek adequate income, dignity, justice and democracy for persons on public assistance and other low-income people."

During the late 1960s and early 1970s, similar groups were created, stimulated by the doctrine of "maximum feasible participation" of the poor, which was especially relevant to the Office of Economic Opportunity's Community Action Programs (CAP), and by the "widespread citizen participation" doctrine of the Model Cities Program. In its various forms, the theme of citizen participation also excited academicians; for example, during 1972, the *Public Administration Review* published "Symposium on Neighborhoods and Citizen Involvement" (May/June 1972); "Citizens Action in Model Cities and CAP Programs: Case Studies and Evaluation" (September 1972); and "Curriculum Essays on Citizens, Politics, and Administration in Urban Neighborhoods" (October 1972). Despite the political and academic interest in the subject (or perhaps *because* of the interest), the two programs that were the backbone of the citizen participation movement, Model Cities and CAP, were casualties of the political process during the Nixon administration. Even at the height of the movement, however, the citizen participation concept did not pervade all agencies or programs, and citizen action groups often felt they were only marginally a part of the decision-making process. For example, when revisions to the Food Stamp program are under consideration, the NWRO is unlikely to be consulted by the Department

---

[6] Harleigh B. Trecker, *Social Work Administration: Principles and Practices* (New York: Association Press, 1971), pp. 97–99.

[7] Ibid., p. 124, emphasis added.

Chapter five

140

of Agriculture as fully as such traditionally powerful producer groups as the National Farm Bureau Federation.

If citizen participation is less visible than it was a few years ago, this does not mean it is dead. An intensive effort to obtain citizen input is a requirement of most recently initiated federal programs. For example, the Department of Health, Education, and Welfare's 1975 regulations, made under Title XX of the Social Security Act, require that states shall publish a service plan for the following year. According to the regulations:

> *The primary purpose of this plan is to provide the citizenry of each State comprehensive and meaningful insight into each State's services plan so that they, as an informed citizenry, can interact with the State decision-making process. In order to achieve this purpose, the State shall meet the following requirements.*
>
> *A news release shall be issued by the approving official on the proposed services plan prior to its publication . . .*
>
> *A description of the proposed services plan shall be published as a display advertisement in the newspaper of widest circulation (and in foreign language newspapers, as appropriate) in each geographic area described in the proposed services plan for three consecutive days in daily newspapers; in three consecutive editions if published other than daily. Publication of the proposed services plan shall begin at least 90 days prior to the beginning of the program year.*

Under the program, states have the option of holding formal hearings, which are important forums of citizen access; hearings are routinely held in connection with many programs, such as appeals to the Environmental Protection Agency concerning environmental impact statements. If citizen groups have to rely on written statements and testimony at formal hearings or organizing welfare recipients to hold protest demonstrations, however, these are likely to be signs of weakness. Many of the most important decisions may have been made through prior consultation with groups the agency considers "legitimate."[8]

---

[8]This is not to disparage the importance of clientele participation in formal hearings. Believing that agencies are too responsive to well-financed producer groups and insufficiently aware of the interests of community groups, consumers, the poor, etc., Senators Kennedy and Mathias have introduced "The Public Participation in Federal Agency Proceedings Act." The bill would allocate $10 million annually in federal funds to pay the expenses of citizens and their lawyers and expert witnesses who wish to testify before agencies about rule making, rate making, and licensing issues.

Clients and regulation

Beyond the close tie of the VA to the American Legion and the developing power of welfare recipients and students, there are other types of relationships between agencies and clients. One is the special relationship of regulatory agencies to those being regulated (or perhaps we should say those *allegedly* being regulated). Beginning with the Interstate Commerce Commission, which was created in 1886 to monitor railroads, Congress has established a number of independent regulatory commissions with broad powers to establish regulations and see to their enforcement. Most of these deal with a single industry—or closely allied industries—and must often confront such highly technical questions as: Is it feasible to require that CB radio transmitters include features that decrease the production of interference for television receivers? What fare would an airline need to charge on certain routes in order to make a reasonable profit, recognizing that some flights will have few passengers? What is the actual cancer risk of cyclamates, saccharin, and newer artificial sweeteners? Could they be approved as prescription drugs if they are found too dangerous as food additives? Congress has determined that there is a public interest in seeing that such matters are regulated and has charged these commissions to regulate in the public interest.

In the course of establishing regulations, administering their application, and performing courtlike functions in hearing appeals concerning the regulations, these agencies are perpetually in contact

Drawing by Oliphant; © 1978 Washington Star. Dist. Los Angeles Times Synd.

with those being regulated. Can we say, then, that the regulated corporations are their clients? The answer appears to be affirmative, and the clientele relationship is a continuous one, beginning long before and continuing long after any particular attempt at regulation might occur.

Legal requirements (imposed by Congress and the courts) demand that the agencies hold formal hearings in many circumstances, that proper prior notice be given of pending actions, and that independent hearing examiners conduct many of the courtlike agency functions. But despite the existence of elaborate administrative machinery designed to discourage favoritism, charges are frequently made that the regulators respond to *industrial* interests rather than to the *public* interest. It is often said that regulatory agencies have been "captured" by their clients.

Those being regulated are undoubtedly quite influential in the regulatory process, but this does not in itself suggest that corruption—including bribery or other illegal activity—has occurred. Far more important, in this situation in which the regulated industry and the staff of the regulatory agency may be the sole sources of information about many technical matters, are the backgrounds of the agency's staff and the intimate nature of agency-industry interaction. Many regulatory officials gained their expertise from their former industrial employers; and if they learned about the industry from American Airlines, the National Broadcasting Corporation, or Upjohn, it would be surprising if their work for the CAB, the FCC, or the FDA were not colored by that experience.

Possible proindustry orientations are reinforced by the nature of the regulatory process, which requires that agency personnel interact closely and frequently with those of businesses. This relationship includes social interaction, of course. At industry association meetings, for example, regulators are included in discussions of industry problems at cocktail parties and dinners. Louis Kohlmeir, Jr., quotes an airline lobbyist describing his strategy at a meeting when his airline was awaiting a route decision from the CAB:

> *Of course, we never bring up a pending case. Let's say we have pending a case concerning a route application. Of course I wouldn't mention the route matter. I talk about equipment, about new airplanes, new hangars. I know and the board member knows that the only reason we're talking about equipment is the use we hope to make of it on the new route.*[9]

---

[9]Louis M. Kohlmeier, Jr., *The Regulators: Watchdog Agencies and the Public Interest* (New York: Harper and Row, 1969), p. 71.

Group, clientele, and public involvement /

143

Many employees of regulatory agencies hope to move back into an industry job (with a promotion) after serving a stint with the agency; we are not so uncharitable, however, as to suggest that those who have this ambition necessarily let it affect their regulatory decisions.

There is another type of regulation in which those regulated are even more salient to the administrator: the regulation by state governments of professions and occupations. States license (and minimally regulate) such diverse professions as beauticians, accountants, plumbers, detectives, physicians, nurses, embalmers, lawyers, and real estate salesmen. In many cases the regulation is supervised by a board *composed of members of the profession regulated.* Operating under broad guidelines set by the legislature, this board establishes procedures and requirements for obtaining a license to practice the profession. In fact, limiting entrance to the profession is often the board's principal reason for existence; does anyone believe that the citizens of those states that require barbers to take a course in anatomy receive better haircuts as a result? It is obvious that organized clientele groups (such as bar and medical associations) play very important roles in the regulatory process, and it would not be a gross exaggeration to assert that with the sanction of the state, professions are for the most part self-regulating.

Professional associations

Not all interest groups important to administrators are clientele groups. Another type has already been mentioned in connection with clientele: the professional associations of the agencies' employees. Examples would be the National Education Association, the American Library Association, and the Fraternal Order of Police. Often these groups bring to the agency demands that national standards be met, standards set by the employee groups themselves. With the recent increase in unionization of public employees, several of these groups have taken the additional responsibility of serving as bargaining agents for employees. College and university administrators find, for example, that the American Association of University Professors, a long-established interest group watching over the affairs of higher education, now is becoming a faculty union as well. (Chapter 7 has more to say about public-sector unions.)

Suppliers and contractors

In addition to employees and office space, agencies also need supplies and equipment—sometimes quite expensive equipment. Suppliers of such commodities find it helpful to maintain good relationships with administrators, in hope of securing contracts. These suppliers, then, become a type of interest group that is quite important for some agencies. While these contractors may supply school textbooks, laboratory rats, or gravel for county roads, the most dramatic examples come from the national defense field, where some large contractors are nearly 100 percent dependent upon continued weapons business. The "military-industrial complex" that President Eisenhower warned against in his farewell address in 1960 is a reality. Many contracts are awarded on a negotiated rather than a bid basis, making previously established agency-supplier links extremely important. One feature of this interest-group-administrator relationship is the movement of people from industrial positions to agency positions and back to industrial positions. At the height of the Vietnam War, Senator Proxmire found 2,124 retired high-ranking military officers (colonel and above) working for major defense contractors.[10] Civilian personnel, too, flow between defense agencies and their suppliers. In this manner, then, the suppliers become important interest groups in the environment of defense administrators.

Promotional groups

Some interest groups champion causes that cut across the activities of many agencies. The National Organization for Women defends its view of women's rights, and this brings it into contact with administrators in almost every field. The National Association for the Advancement of Colored People and other organizations supporting causes of minority groups are similar in this respect, as are such relatively specialized groups as Citizens for Clean Air and the Sierra Club. Additionally, groups that champion "better government," such as the League of Women Voters and the Pennsylvania Economy League, interact with a variety of administrators on many topics. So do groups that promote a political ideology, such as the Americans for Democratic Action. Finally, a recent innovation (one treated in the selection to follow) is the creation of self-styled *"public interest"* groups or advocates, such as Common Cause and Ralph Nader's Center for the Study of Responsive Law.

These promotional groups are so varied that few generalizations about them are possible. Certainly their levels of success vary. Probably the highest ambition of many of these groups would be to become accepted by administrators as a given part of the agency's environment; to be consulted in advance of decisions and treated as many clientele

---

[10]William Proxmire, *Report from Wasteland: America's Military Industrial Complex* (New York: Praeger, 1970), p. 153.

groups are treated would be perceived as heaven by most promotional groups.

Additional typologies for groups can always be constructed, but those that are most often suggested have been mentioned. We can summarize our brief discussion of agency-interest group relations as follows: Administrators are confronted by a wide variety of groups. Moving from those that are closest to agencies to those that are more distant, these include employee and professional organizations, clientele groups, suppliers, and cause-oriented or promotional groups. Not every administrator is confronted by all of these, certainly not on most issues, but upon reflection, nearly all administrators would confirm that one or more groups are important environmental features and exercise a degree of influence and constraint over their actions.

Selection five

Public interest advocacy and the regulatory process*

Richard C. Leone

At the beginning of the chapter we mentioned the difficulty of defining the opinions and interests of the "public." One of the interesting features of the politics of the late 1960s was the development of groups that professed to know what the public interest was and, indeed, to embody it. During the 1970s these "public interest" groups have flowered and become a force with which administrators, as well as other political actors, must come to terms.

The regulatory agencies have become a special target of these public interest advocates, who are led by Ralph Nader. Perhaps because the regulatory agencies were themselves created as official watchdogs of society's interests, their shortcomings are especially galling to the new public interest advocates. Not only, the critics charge,

---

are the agencies lethargic, ensnarled in red tape, and so attuned to their own bureaucratic imperatives that individual citizens cannot get fair hearings, but also the agencies subvert the public interest by responding to the selfish—usually economic—interests of those allegedly being regulated. What is new about the public interest advocates is that they take this rather standard critique of the regulatory process (detailed earlier in the chapter) as their starting point: after monitoring the activities of the agencies, the advocates file legal actions and publicize those activities with which they disagree.

This selection's analysis of the relationships among the new public interest advocates—especially the Nader forces—and the agencies and their "natural" constituency groups—the regulated industries—is written by Richard Leone, who has had a varied career as lecturer at Princeton University, executive director of a Presidential Task Force on the Cities, administrative assistant to the governor of New Jersey, consultant to the Ford and Carnegie Foundations, candidate for U.S. Senator from New Jersey, and director of the Center for Analysis of Public Issues, a public interest research organization.

Modern America is characterized by the expansion of government and corporate power. To monitor and condition these concentrations of power, particuularly in the private sector, we have created a complex of public regulatory mechanisms. These organizations for administrative regulation are, one would hope, the foremost institutionalized advocates of the public interest. They are the watchdogs we have set on an economic system we have difficulty controlling and sometimes even understanding.

Many regulatory agencies are expected to ensure that in vital areas of private activity, the interest of the public is not overridden by private considerations of economic gain. Other agencies monitor the use of scarce resources, some of which are, by their nature, public. And still other aspects of administrative regulation affect the workings of governments themselves at all levels. Most of the areas in which regulatory agencies are involved—pure foods, safe water, transportation, product safety, protection against deceptive advertising, safe working conditions, and the like—are of great potential significance for most people most of the time. In this sense, regulatory agencies fill one of the most immediately vital and sympathetic roles of government. The policy decisions they make and the way in which they are implemented can have a direct impact on the quality and safety of people's lives. Delay or failure to act can have an equally important consequence.

Yet, no one could claim that the regulatory agencies are among the cherished institutions in our society. They have been subjected to sharp criticism throughout their history. The agencies involved, in theory, should have responded to these criticisms as translated by various checks on the regulatory process, including the Congress, the courts, the press, and the political parties. Each of these groups, in theory, provides a mechanism for bringing individual grievances, public opinion, and widely shared community values to bear on the regulatory process. Perhaps out of disenchantment with these mechanisms, as much as with the regulatory agencies themselves, a new group of activists have established themselves in recent years as persistent and unyielding critics of administrative regulation.

The public interest advocates, as they frequently are called, have set out to watch the watchdogs. In conception and approach, their leader is Ralph Nader. He has given the movement inspiration, even a name, "Naderism." The term *public interest advocate* lumps together a variety of groups and individuals who have emerged in recent years as critics of government and corporate activity. Some are directly imitative of Nader's across-the-board gadfly approach; others confine their activities to discrete areas, such as civil liberties and environmental protection.

More specialized in their approach but basically of the same genre are the public interest law firms, such as the Center for Law and Social Policy in Washington, D.C. These groups hope to redress some of the imbalance between the legal resources available to the government and private corporations and those available to private citizens attempting to promote the public interest. They probably are a direct outgrowth of poverty law programs and the general movement within the legal profession toward greater relevancy to pressing social problems. They also are a response to the conclusion—not unreasonable, given the history of the last twenty years—that one major way to bring about social change is through the courts.[1]

With regard to administrative regulation generally, public interest advocates, lawyers or not, have one thing in common: they all seek the reform and reorientation of regulatory agencies. Although their methods differ, all of them tend to bring more scrutiny and publicity to bear on these agencies. Since most people agree that powerful government agencies should be subjected to a maximum amount of scrutiny, these efforts have been widely applauded—a reaction made all the more likely by the varying degrees of disrepute into which regulatory agencies have fallen. A look at almost any agency's history, for example, reveals a series of studies or commission reports indicting the agency for numerous failures and calling, typically, for sweeping reorganization. These indictments, in a sense, provide an ideal context for public interest advocates. In fact, few specific problems of administrative regulation were discovered by public interest advocates. They simply have given focus and substance to difficulties which long have been recognized by scholars as characteristic of the American regulatory experience.

The public interest advocacy movement is, in a sense, a second round of

---

[1] More specifically, the public interest lawyers are emerging in response to a perceived need for "public" legal counsel in the regulatory process. In the challenge filed by the *United Church of Christ* v. *FCC,* for example, 359 F2D. 944 (DC ct. app. 1966 at 1003–4), Warren E. Burger, then of the U.S. Court of Appeals for the District of Columbia, concluded: "The theory that the Commission can always effectively represent the lesser interest . . . without the aid and participation of legitimate listener representatives fulfilling the role of private attorneys general, is one of those assumptions we collectively try to work with so long as they are reasonably adequate. When it becomes clear, as it does now, that it is no longer a valid assumption which stands up under the realities of actual reference, neither we nor the Commission can continue to rely on it. The gradual expansion and evolution of concepts of standing of administrative law attest that experience rather than logic or fixed rules have been accepted as the guide."

regulatory reform, following the New Deal era criticism which concentrated on achieving procedural safeguards and minimizing arbitrary actions. Its most important and obvious result was the Administrative Procedure Act. Before this act was passed in 1946, it was sometimes impossible to ascertain the basic procedural and substantive actions involved in a regulatory decision.

Current criticism, though it includes complaints about access to information, focuses on administrative apathy, abuse of discretionary authority, disregard for citizen's rights, bureaucratic stultification, and cozy relationships with special interests. These criticisms of the agencies, familiar to those who have thought about regulation, have shaped the development of public interest advocacy in this field. Perhaps more important, they may be crucial to the prospects for the long-term effectiveness of the movement.

Isolation of the regulatory process

One of the most common observations about the regulatory bodies is that they are somewhat isolated from the general political process or, perhaps more precisely, that their relative independence means that only selective "political pressures" affect them. This is so partly by design; architects of the regulatory process intended to fashion a quasi-judicial system functioning above the rough-and-tumble of partisan conflict. But that inherent immunity has been reinforced by factors perhaps not foreseen by early regulatory proponents. Disincentives have emerged which discourage other public institutions from acting as monitors, critics, and reformers of the regulatory structure.

Legislators, chief executives, and press alike have been frustrated by the sheer size of the regulating bureaucracy. Once considered a daring and legally questionable application of the delegation of power, the regulatory apparatus has flourished and expanded until now the establishment of new agencies, endowed with sweeping discretionary powers, is a predictable response to any new technologies or professional services. No one can stay abreast of all the regulatory activity at any given level of government—federal, state, or large urban.

At the legislative level, only the members of the appropriate substantive committees have a chance to become genuinely familiar with the work of a major agency. As a result, other members of Congress or state legislatures rely heavily on these members to oversee and finance regulatory operations. And, knowing this, the affected economic interests attach highest priority to seeing that sympathetic officials are named to these key committees. Their efforts in this regard have been generally successful at the federal level, particularly in the House of Representatives, and spectacularly successful at the state level.

Chief executives are discouraged from attempts to reorient public agencies, in part because of the potentially high political costs of such efforts and the lack of offsetting public demands for change.

The printed press, which we expect to resist outside political influences, often has yielded to internal copy-room pressures. The vicious circle which overtakes many state newspapers finds news editors unable to free reporters for

long-term investigative projects, while these same reporters, under relentless
pressure to produce usable copy, become dependent on the daily press releases of
regulatory agencies and increasingly reluctant to bite the hand that feeds
them.

The courts have been so reluctant to second-guess agency decisions that an
entire, course-length body of law has sprung up to describe the "standing" and
"ripeness" required to sustain a complainant's petition for review. When regulatory decisions are overruled at the judicial level, it is almost always at the
behest of an aggrieved company or trade group. They alone have the legal
resources, the detailed knowledge of agency decisions, and the common interest
necessary to launch a costly and extended litigation.

Industry influence

The one group which does oversee agency activities with a keen, critical
eye is the regulated industry. It expends considerable effort in lobbying agencies
and Congress to make its position known and to see that it is accepted. Industries have the resources to assign someone to cover agency rule making on a
full-time basis. Over time, they develop channels for obtaining preferential
access to the early stages of decision making, when it is usually easier to affect
outcomes. Their pressure tactics are refined, focused, and effective. The long-
term personal relationships they nurture with key regulatory personnel are
likewise aids to successful lobbying.

Given the context in which most regulatory agencies operate, industry has
other built-in advantages. On questions of rate regulation, for example, regulatory decisions frequently are made on the basis of industry figures and forecasts.
Indeed, most state departments of insurance, to pick an obvious case, have far
too few staff members even to review adequately the figures provided by the
large and expert staffs of the underwriters' associations. In the area of product-
testing, regulators must depend heavily on the results of industry tests. In fact,
given the magnitude of the tasks assigned to them, many agencies must depend
on the good will and good intentions of industry—which presumably are
expressed through voluntary compliance—in order to accomplish the missions
assigned to them by legislative bodies.

Many legislators, in turn, apply pressure to regulatory agencies on behalf
of the special interests of powerful constituents. Until an alternative method for
campaign financing is discovered and implemented, most officeholders will have
important relationships with industrialists and others with a direct interest in
administrative regulation. In many cases, legislators themselves have business
interests which impact directly on the actions of administrators. Since they are
the source not only of agency authority but also of financing, legislators are
highly effective in getting their points across.

By contrast, the group which is least represented in this system is the
private citizenry. Because of the nature of many of the industries regulated—
food, consumer products of all kinds, health services, and the like—policy decisions and the efficiency and fairness with which they are implemented are of
tremendous concern to the private citizen. Yet, for most citizens most of the

time, no individual regulatory action seems important enough to cause reorganization of their lives and reordering of personal priorities in order to monitor and pressure the agency involved. Recent attempts, such as Common Cause, have tried to pool citizen concern and thus create the possibility of a citizens' lobby. Mass membership environmental groups are similar attempts to represent the affected citizen in the process. To be effective, such groups must educate the public about the extent to which their interests are involved in administrative decisions.

Among the obstacles to organizing citizens is lack of knowledge. Agencies are reluctant to disseminate information, and comprehensive press coverage of regulatory affairs does not exist. The day-to-day operations of most regulatory agencies are not very newsworthy; or, rather, they are newsworthy only to the specialized industry press. People, not surprisingly, fail to perceive the broader implications of specific grievances or how they relate to regulatory inaction or action. The regulatory process remains invisible for most citizens. Altered train schedules seldom are related to the Interstate Commerce Commission or a bad chicken to the Food and Drug Administration. And even if they are so inclined, most private citizens lack the training and time to monitor agency decisions of relevance to them. When a citizen does act, he soon discovers the procedural delays and complexity of rule making and hearings. Due process requires the intervention of a lawyer and that, in turn, requires expense.[2] And, the question of court standing has seriously hampered individual attempts to force agencies to be responsive to particular needs.

In the absence of coherent public pressure, administrative agencies are free to respond to their own internal pressures. Government bureaucracies, like any other large institutions, develop a life of their own with certain internal pressures and goals—pressures which often have little to do with protecting the interests of any other group. Large bureaucracies, after all, are designed to carry out—to prolong and extend—existing policies. They are meant to keep operating in the absence of outside interference. They build up their own internal systems of rewards and punishments and seek to reduce internal conflict. One of the ways such values are maximized is also to avoid unfavorable attention from outside. This means, in part, minimizing conflicts with special interests and powerful legislators.

Regarding publicity, industry enjoys another advantage over public interest advocates. The regulated industry seldom desires to damage the public image of the agency. It poses no threat to the bureaucracy—indeed, it shares an interest in low visibility and even secrecy. This common interest fits in well with the agency's bureaucratic imperative to minimize external pressures. True, the advocate may be pressing the same public interest which is the agency's presumed mission but, imprudently, advocates want "to make it all public."

Created and designed to preserve existing policies, agencies often are one of the last groups to respond to altered circumstances. Because of their internalized perspective, they frequently fail to see their role in terms of broader social goals, society at large, or even the government in general.

---

[2]Yet due process safeguards are essential in the context of necessary agency discretion. Protection of this sort has other costs. Due process can be the enemy of public necessity, and it certainly is the father of large regulatory bureaucracies—bureaucracies which swallow individual complaints rather than respond to them.

A role for public interest advocacy

In a system of balancing interests and pressures, a group incapable of articulating its needs and without significant organized power is seen as less important to satisfy than those like the industries, which effectively make their influence felt. One objective of public interest advocacy is to mitigate this imbalance by providing private citizens with the information and analysis needed to perceive common interests and, potentially, to organize common pressures. Public interest advocacy operates from the premise that the only way regulation will be more responsive is for more people to become aware of the extent to which their interests are bound up in regulatory decisions.

In this sense, the first task of public interest advocates is to educate. They must develop materials which break complex issues down into a form which is comprehensible to the public. They must discover, for example, what the operating policies of regulatory agencies are, what impact they have on the parties involved, who benefits, who gets hurt, which groups or individuals are most affected by these policies, how they are affected, who pays for them, who stands to lose or gain by proposed changes, how the decision-making process works, and how pressure is applied.

In this effort to make such complex questions understandable to the layman, there is clearly a danger of oversimplification; thus not infrequently, public interest advocates have been, in an absolute sense, unfair in an attempt to arouse public ire. They are likely to dramatize; there is a bit of "theatre" involved in arousing public indignation and even outrage.[3] On occasion, they hold up a mantle of righteous indignation which can be a mask for malice and carelessness. Advocates, on the other hand, should be blunt, even harsh, in their criticism, particularly when compared with political leaders. And in so doing, they can "run interference" for officeholders or even a timid press.

Working properly, public interest advocacy goes beyond straight reporting to analysis of existing policies. It examines alternative approaches and assesses the likely public impact of variations in agency operation. Ideally, publication of studies will force legislative bodies and the press—"official" guardians of the public interest in the area—to take a more aggressive role.

In this context, an important role of a public interest advocate is to make the patterns of agency action clear. He can, in this way, provide something of a check on its arbitrary use or misuse of discretionary power. In attempting to fulfill this mission, he runs into the problem that much discretionary action is not rule-governed and, therefore, is not covered by the disclosure provisions of the Administrative Procedure Act and the Freedom of Information Act. Much of the difficulty encountered in any attempt at finding information involves learning the facts about decisions made in discretionary areas. In response, public interest advocates seek to have patterns of action, tacit principles, and policies made explicit. Thus, private citizens—indeed, the advocates themselves—have a

---

[3]One of Nader's investigators once complained about the caution of middle-level staff personnel in a regulatory agency. He emphasized their fear of reprisal from above. But what about their fear of Nader's approach—the need for a headline, the impetus to find the "dirt" which will expose the agency's failure or venality?

chance to understand what is at stake and make choices about where to press for change. Publicity is the best available check on the misuse of discretionary powers.

The Administrative Procedure Act did not make agencies completely open in their operations, but it did make it possible for determined investigators and researchers to learn about major policy changes and procedures. Under section 3 of the act, "public information" agencies are required to make available statements on organization, procedure, and substantive rules. All matters of official record now should be available to concerned persons. Today, regulatory agencies spew forth an almost overwhelming amount of information and paper. One of the paradoxical consequences of the Freedom of Information Act is that the volume of information has in itself become an obstacle to citizen knowledge.[4] Most states have passed acts similar to the Administrative Procedure Act, although at the state level the information available is on a much smaller scale.

Public interest advocates today have contradictory feelings about the Administrative Procedure Act. On the one hand, it has failed to provide information in usable form to the public; but, on the other hand, without it and its state counterparts there might have been no Ralph Nader and no public interest advocacy.

Nader's role

Talking about advocacy as we know it today is tantamount to talking about Nader; he is universally regarded as the prototype of the public interest advocate. He provides, if not always the model, at least the inspiration for most other advocacy operations. Public interest groups frequently identify themselves as "Nader-type" organizations.

In addition to being the best known, Nader is of course the most respected and the most powerful. It may be overstating the case to say, as a *New York Times Magazine* reporter did, "He has become an institution, at least as formidable as General Motors."[5] But there is no denying that his access to media, his credibility, and his influence are enormous. Credited to his legislative account is the chief responsibility for passage of six major laws for protecting the public interest: the Natural Gas Pipeline Safety Act of 1968, the Radiation Control for Health and Safety Act of 1968, the Coal Mine Health and Safety Act of 1969, the 1970 Comprehensive Occupational Health Safety Act, the Motor Vehicle Safety Act of 1966, and the 1967 Wholesome Meat Act (portions of which were applied to poultry products in 1968).

On the administrative ledger, Nader's 1968 FTC study resulted in President Nixon commissioning an American Bar Association investigation, the find-

---

[4]A sampling of materials made available before a recent FCC rule making revealed that several individuals could be kept busy for several weeks simply organizing it into usable form and discovering the points of particular interest to the public interest advocacy group involved.
[5]*New York Times Magazine,* 21 March 1971. © 1971 by the New York Times Company. Reprinted by permission.

ings of which produced top-level staff changes in the commission. His critique of FDA operations led to the ban of cyclamates from soft drinks and the discharge of three top agency officials. Nader regards such responses as mere "cosmetics." "We always fail," he says. "The whole thing is limiting the degree of failure."[6]

His own misgivings aside, Nader has had an undeniable impact on the regulatory process. He has created a presence, a feeling of scrutiny, under which all regulators now operate; and he has launched a movement which draws on his prestige for its form and respectability. Still, Nader is a unique phenomenon, and an extensive concentration on him as a model for other groups is misleading. He can do things that a less well known and credible group could not, and perhaps should not, attempt. His enormous public support—a recent Harris poll reported that 69 percent of the American public think "it's good to have critics like Nader to keep industry on its toes"—allows him to speak from a base of limited information and be sure that his utterances will be taken seriously. His enormous skills at making and shaping news enable him to command media coverage of his comments on virtually any issue. He can step in and have an impact on an already well-developed controversy where an unsupported statement from another group would be lost in the dispute.

Without his special relationship with the press or his wide public credibility—or the good fortune to be tailed by a General Motors private investigator— other advocate groups are confronted with serious legal and practical limitations which Nader can and does ignore.

The aspect of Nader's day-to-day operation which is perhaps most envied by others involved in public interest advocacy is his apparent freedom from restraints, imposed either by collegiate decision making or, more important, by nonprofit tax status. Most public interest advocacy groups are nonprofit organizations, tax-exempt under section 501(c)(3) of the Internal Revenue Code. Maintenance of this status is imperative for foundation funding. The code specifically excludes from exemption as a nonprofit group any organization that, as a substantial part of its activities, attempts to influence legislation. According to the Internal Revenue Service, any organization is attempting to influence legislation when it contacts or urges the public to contact members of a legislative body to support or oppose legislation or when it otherwise advocates the adoption or rejection of legislation. In effect, this means that such groups are prohibited from lobbying, endorsing, or recommending a particular piece of legislation or bill. A group can urge general reforms and regulations and it can appear as an advocate at a hearing as long as the appearance is in response to a specific written invitation to testify as an expert.

Several of Nader's operations are tax-exempt. The Center for the Study of Responsive Law, his "parent group," receives support from several foundations. On the other hand, his Public Interest Research Groups are not tax-exempt and are free to lobby. Recently, Nader has launched Ralph Nader, Public Citizen, Inc., a Common Cause-like mass membership organization to support his proj-

---

[6]Ibid.

Chapter five

154

ects.[7] Nader himself makes no attempt to limit his personal lobbying, even calling senators and threatening to denounce them to the press if they fail to go his way.

The Nader experience notwithstanding, there is no question that the limitations imposed by the IRS regulations place public interest advocates so affected at a distinct disadvantage in affecting public decisions. Nonetheless, some groups are credited with having an impact and, even with the limitations of the IRS, they have played a major role in the shaping of certain policies and decisions.

Lawyers predominate

One of the conspicuous aspects of Nader's methodology is his reliance on attorneys. It is only a slight exaggeration to say that he believes that if three or four lawyers are brought together, they can solve almost any problem. He sees many of the basic questions confronting society as essentially legal in nature.

Nader's approach is, of course, responsive to the social and political history of the last twenty years, when the courts, the litigation process, and lawyers were the cutting edge of social change. Nader's statements imply that since other parts of the political process have been generally unresponsive to those causes we hold dear, he will continue to depend heavily on the courts. Yet, Nader's own work is much more that of publicist, popularizer, and spokesman for causes than it is that of practicing lawyer, reflecting his own impatience with the limits of the law firm approach.

In many cases, particularly those involving regulatory agencies, it is difficult to find a client with standing to bring a suit to court, or with a grievance which involves the precise substantive issue the advocate wants to raise. It is difficult, for example, to make a court case on the basis of someone habitually not showing up for work—the kind of "no show" political jobs which are common in some state and local governments. But the advantage, and it is a big one, to the litigation approach, is that when a public interest lawyer can find a client and take on an issue, there will be a definite determination. If victorious, the advocates have a hard victory with a court action behind them. The great appeal of his approach is that there is no way for an agency to "slide off." The problem is getting jugular cases in the right form, in spite of the difficult problems of timing, standing, and jurisdiction which may block access to the courts.[8]

---

[7]Nader also is the founder of The Center for Auto Safety and The Professionals for Auto Safety. In addition, he is starter of the Project for Corporate Responsibility, which included "The Campaign to Make General Motors Responsible." While not directly related to Nader, the Center for Law and Social Policy handles much of the litigation which emerges from his work.

[8]One of the best examples of the potential of class actions in the consumer area was the 1970 settlement of the *Virginia* v. *Charles R. Pfizer and Co.* suit. Under the agreement, Pfizer agreed to pay $100 million for price fixing on the drug tetracycline, dating back to 1954. But state courts generally have been unsympathetic, and a specific violation of a federal standard is usually a prerequisite for bringing such a suit.

Group, clientele, and public involvement/

155

The muckraking method

The nonlitigating advocate groups face a different set of problems. They need not hunt for a client or worry about timing. They can make a "case" on the basis of anything that will appeal to the public's sense of outrage. They, however, are almost totally dependent on the press to get their story across and to develop sufficient public awareness about problems. They rely on others for direct pressure group tactics on legislators. The importance of sympathetic press coverage to some extent determines both the issues dealt with and the research methods employed. Public interest research groups are dependent on shock techniques. For, if the newspapers run their story once and then drop it, they have lost most chances to be effective. Extra headlines are brought about only by controversy and response. The "muckraking" release, which is applauded by a patronizing local press but successfully ignored by the agencies or interests attacked, is considered an unqualified failure.

In New Jersey, a study of auto negligence cases which recommended no-fault insurance might have been brushed aside by a calmer legal community. Instead, it resulted in the trial lawyers' association hiring a public relations firm to present the lawyers' point of view. The consequence of this act was a protracted public controversy about no-fault insurance which otherwise might have been carried out on a much lower key with much less publicity.

Unlike Nader, second-generation advocate groups are not in a position simply to give journalists a report and rely on them to wade through and interpret it. Groups like these in New Jersey, Ohio, and Connecticut must educate the press about their story in order to obtain acceptance and demonstrate a point. They frequently confront the problem of making their message digestible without having it become meaningless.

No advocate group boasts a 100 percent record in seeing its recommendations adopted. When their impact seems insubstantial, most of these groups find comfort in the tentative but widely held proposition that publicity and continual scrutiny of public agencies is a desirable end in itself. Nader puts it well.

In our polity, where the ultimate power is said to rest with the people, a free and prompt flow of information from government to people is essential to achieve the reality of citizen access to a more just governmental process. It is especially essential to provide this informational flow in the Washington regulatory agencies, which are essentially unaccountable to any electorate or constituency.[9]

The exposure of overall agency operations becomes a necessity when, as in the present circumstances, public confidence in regulatory agencies is low and studies of their performance are highly critical. Ralph Nader, perhaps more than any other individual, has helped to suggest the gap between the agencies' perceptions of themselves and their actual operations. His studies show ineffi-

---

[9]Ralph Nader, "Freedom from Information: The Act and the Agency," article adapted from a statement released publicly on August 26, 1969.

ciency, ineptness, and willful failure to act on the part of the federal agencies. The Center for Analysis of Public Issues discovered similar problems with such minor agencies as the New Jersey Office of Consumer Protection and Department of Agriculture. Indeed, when an agency is failing to do a good job in terms of its own goals, the possibility for reform is obvious, for reform in this sense is little more than holding an agency or group to account against its own standards. When these standards or values are shared widely in the society, public support for reform is possible and even easy to obtain.

This attempt to enforce accountability, a key notion for public interest advocacy, is much easier in an area in which public expectations and regulatory standards are set. While policies are still in formation—a good current example is cable television—it is much more difficult to identify deficiencies and place blame. The FCC has failed for more than a decade to develop a coherent policy on CATV, but only recently has the commission been subjected to criticism from public-interest-oriented groups.

Funding and the future

Despite public acceptance of the "product" of public interest advocacy, few are willing to pay the costs of "production." The resource constraint ultimately will end the current round of public interest advocacy. Many groups, as indicated, are heavily dependent on foundation support—a short-term solution at best. Indeed, for each group which succeeds in obtaining the minimal support necessary to commence operations, many others are stillborn because of failure in the competition for scarce foundation resources—a competition made keener by the reluctance of the vast majority of foundations to support such potentially controversial activities as public interest advocacy.

Some groups, particularly in the environmental field, are finding an alternative—and sometimes one that, because of non-tax-exempt status, permits overt lobbying—in mass membership support. Clearly, this route offers the most promising hope for long-term assistance. A special case of this approach is the student-funded Public Interest Research Groups springing up from Nader-planted seeds in several states.

The contingent fee may answer some of the financial questions with regard to public interest law firms. The possibility of sharing, say, 25 percent of the settlement may induce attorneys to risk their own time and money on the suit in question. A cynic, however, would see most of this activity as a mere transient response to a trend. It's "in" to be for advocacy, as it was "in" a few years ago to work for civil rights or, later, the poverty program, the Peace Corps, or the antiwar movement. It is no accident, in this sense, that the movement is dominated by well-educated white middle-class advocates, or even that most of its concerns are white middle-class. The movement also is elitist, made up principally of top law school graduates, Ph.D.'s, and the like. The foundations, after all, have some of the most sensitive antennae to current trends in "do-goodism" in America.

One way to perceive the whole public interest advocacy movement, then, is simply as another manifestation of the cyclical surges of reform in America. At times, the activities of institutions and individuals, both public and private, become so much at variance with widely held community values that criticism receives ready acceptance and encouragement. When such a period includes a feeling of powerlessness and frustration, individual reformers come to symbolize the needs and anger of millions of unhappy citizens. Almost every American agrees that the trouble with our society is that "nothing works anymore." Products appear shoddy, institutions unresponsive. We are bombarded by media reports of our failures and our problems. We perceive government agencies as not living up to standards they themselves have set. We fear that our national goals and values are unrealistic or, perhaps worse yet, unfashionable.

It is little wonder that the personification of the current reform movement, Ralph Nader, has some of the aspects of an Old Testament prophet calling the people back from their idolatry. It is little wonder that when he is pushed to define how to bring about the changes he desires on the massive scale required, he incants an almost romantic vision of the future, complete with a new professionalism and a renewed code of self-enforced personal behavior.

> *We're interested in the development of initiatory democracy and this is more fundamental than participatory or representative democracy. We need a fundamental change in our structure so that people can initiate actions to make sure public officials are acting responsibly. I'm talking about the rights and remedies, plus legal responsibilities, so it can be a citizen versus the ICC or the FDA. A civil servant should be forced to make the law work and, if he won't do it, he should be censured or expelled from the government.*[10]

When, in 1902, *McClure's* magazine blossomed briefly as the consumer's advocate, it began a period of muckraking that set standards of investigative journalism in the public interest seldom equalled in the history of the American press. It also signaled a turning in the political reform movement of the times— Populism, the Progressive movement, trust-busting, the labor movement, and so on.

It is barely possible that "Naderism" will affect the present rapid evolution of the political process. We may be struggling toward a new alignment of parties and a new partisan agendum. Some candidates are groping for new "populist" themes. Perhaps this is saying no more than that they seek to share some of Nader's public magic. The pressures to take a strong line on administrative regulation and consumer protection are real. One suspects that, though the emphasis may fade, its effects will be real—in terms of both statutory results and political behavior.

At this stage it is impossible to fix with any certainty the place and significance of the current surge of public interest advocacy. Much of what it has accomplished is episodic, journalistic. Even in the area of litigation, the cases have more often been demonstrative of what can be done on a specific issue than

---

[10]*New York Times Magazine,* 21 March 1971. © 1971 by the New York Times Company. Reprinted by permission.

Chapter five

precedent-setting in their consequences for administrative regulation.

In terms of the overall political movement in this society, it is hard to identify the present period as a reform era. Rather, the country is lurching toward some new accommodation with a set of forces which have reacted to and rejected much of American life. These attitudes, and this movement, do not seem likely to blow over. There will probably be important changes in the way corporations and administrative agencies operate, but whether public interest advocacy groups become institutionalized and play a continuing role in this process or not is an unanswerable question.

Some radicals argue that instead of changing the system, public interest advocacy is tinkering. Indeed, they go further and claim that its marginal adjustments in the system tend to make the system more tolerable and tend to reduce the chances for real change. Even rejecting that argument—which logically requires that we let things get as bad as possible, or even help them along—one cannot say that much of what is being done by the advocates will bring about permanent change. Perhaps in another sense they are only responding to more limited goals, to the more limited world of the possible. Their fights, even when they are small ones, frequently are tangible. And perhaps this approach—more generally familiar as *incrementalism*—in time will bring about changes in the regulatory process. Although it is much too early to assess the impact of public interest advocacy, it is quite possible that, in a decade or two, the current period will be seen as a time of dramatic change in the regulatory process. We may then identify this era as marking a turning away from sole reliance on due process and similar safeguards toward more forceful, independent policy development in the public interest. If such changes occur, public interest advocates will have a strong claim to any credit or blame.

Study questions for selection five

1. If you were betting whether industry groups or public interest groups were likely to win the most battles over a period of, say, ten years, which would you put your money on? Why?

2. What appear to be the relative advantages and disadvantages of the two principal weapons of the public interest advocates: publicity and legal remedies?

3. Regardless of your own feelings about the matter, construct an argument that defends the present roles of industry groups in the regulatory process and that criticizes the interference of public interest advocates.

Suggested readings for chapter five

Alford, Robert R. *Bureaucracy and Participation: Political Cultures in Four Wisconsin Cities*. Chicago: Rand McNally, 1969.

Altshuler, Alan. *Community Control: The Black Demand for Participation in Large American Cities*. New York: Pegasus, 1970.

Berry, Jeffrey M. *Lobbying for the People: The Political Behavior of Public Interest Groups*. Princeton, N.J.: Princeton University Press, 1977.

Cole, Richard L. *Citizen Participation and the Urban Policy Process*. Lexington, Mass.: Heath, 1973.

Cox, Edward F., et al. *Nader's Raiders*. New York: Grove Press, 1969.

Frederickson, H. George, ed. *Neighborhood Control in the 1970s*. New York: Chandler, 1973.

Herring, E. Pendleton. *Public Administration and the Public Interest*. New York: McGraw-Hill Book Co., 1936.

Kohlmeier, Louis M., Jr. *The Regulators: Watchdog Agencies and the Public Interest*. New York: Harper and Row, 1969.

Krislov, Samuel. *Representative Bureaucracy*. Englewood Cliffs, N.J.: Prentice-Hall, 1974.

Lipsky, Michael. *Protest in City Politics: Rent Strikes, Housing, and the Power of the Poor*. Chicago: Rand McNally, 1970.

Marini, Frank, ed. *Toward a New Public Administration*. Scranton, Pa.: Chandler Publishing Co., 1971.

McConnell, Grant. *Private Power and American Democracy*. New York: Vintage Books, 1966.

Moynihan, Daniel P. *Maximum Feasible Misunderstanding*. New York: Free Press, 1969.

Proxmire, William. *Report from Wasteland: America's Military Industrial Complex*. New York: Praeger Publishers, 1970.

Selznick, Philip. *TVA and the Grass Roots*. New York: Harper and Row, 1949.

Zeigler, Harmon. *The Political Life of American Teachers*. Englewood Cliffs, N.J.: Prentice-Hall, 1967.

Part

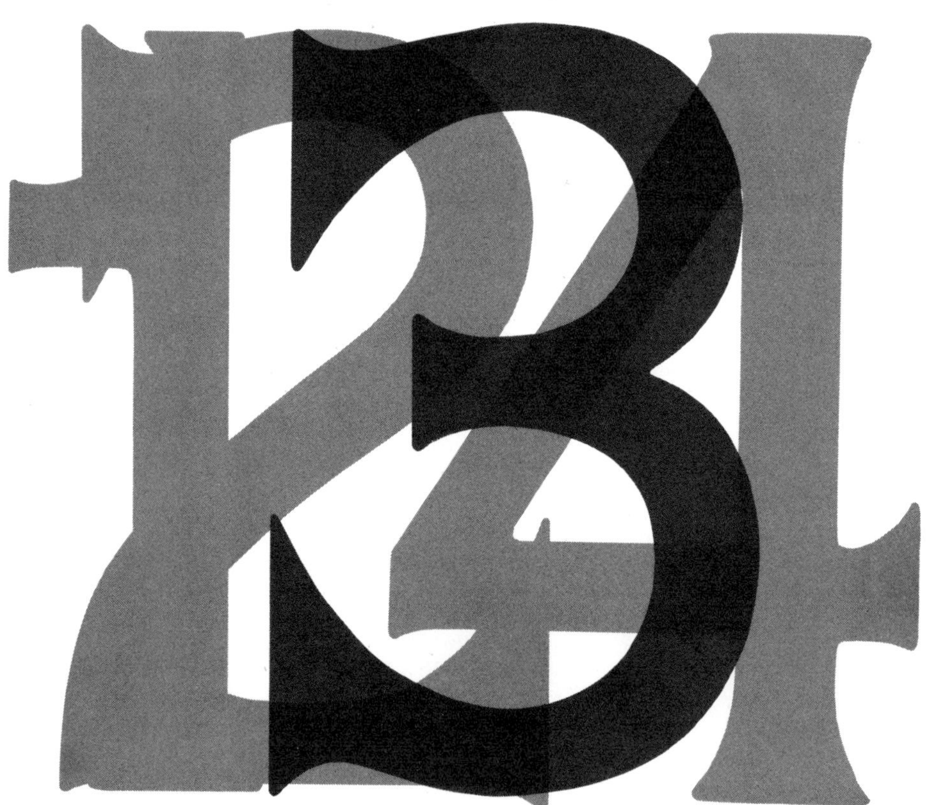

The internal dynamics of public administrative agencies

I don't think I can work in this place another day! Every time I turn around somebody tells me something different. First they tell me that private secretaries are good for executive morale; then they say the old typing pool was more efficient. Do this! Do that! How am I supposed to keep the office staff working smoothly when everything else in the agency is falling apart?—John Doe, office manager

Why won't anyone do what I say? I sent Jones and Smith a memo telling them exactly the kind of reorganization plan I wanted them to come up with, but instead of complying, they went over my head and got an authorization for exactly the plan I was fighting. Aren't workers supposed to obey orders from the boss?—Daniel Poe, regional director

It's that time again, when every program director is pleading his case for more money. I do my damnedest to help the boss judge which requests are really important, and then in the end, the secretary tells

us to change everything we've done and put in the very programs we think are least needed.—Richard Roe, agency budget officer

Let's get this place organized! A union, that's what I mean. First place I ever worked with no union. I ain't a plumber and I ain't paid a plumber's wages. Next time that john overflows, I'm gonna blow it up. If we had a union we'd get paid for what we do or we'd do nothing!— Robert Coe, custodian.

These brief, somewhat strident monologues illustrate some aspects of administrative life that this book has hardly touched thus far. We have viewed the public's administrative agencies as one set of participants in the policy process. Although some glimpses have been offered of the complex inner workings of the agencies, our general approach has been to see them as *entities* that conflict and cooperate during the development and administration of policy with other *entities* (executive, legislative, judicial, or interest group).

This approach provides insight, but it is a limited view. So long as we look principally at what may be called the *foreign relations* of administrative agencies, some oversimplifications are likely to distort our analysis. What is missing, of course, is an analysis of the *domestic politics* of the agencies. In terms of the issues raised in part V, an examination of the internal dynamics of these usually complicated and always fascinating organizations will help to explain *why* agencies behave as they do in the larger political arena.

The above complaints by imaginary public administrators show particular problems that arose out of their work experience and that affected them personally. The discussions in part III will help prospective recruits to the ranks of public administrators understand in advance some of the issues in which they are likely to become intimately involved. A careful reading of the complaints reveals that they do raise general administrative issues which go beyond the particular individual's problem. Not coincidentally, our hypothetical workers' complaints mention public administration's most traditional topics, which are the subjects of the chapters to follow.

This part's chapters utilize the concepts of *organization theory* as a perspective for analyzing public agencies (chapter 6); focus on the agencies' staffing procedures and other aspects of *personnel administration* (chapter 7); explore the patterns of agency *decision making* (chapter 8); indicate some of the techniques employed and point to some of the leadership problems that arise in the *management* of public agencies (chapter 9); and emphasize the importance for the agency of the *budgeting process,* the securing of resources to pursue its ends, however well defined they may be (chapter 10).

The word *dynamics* in this part's title emphasizes that we are studying nonstatic patterns of interaction. Students of administration have not discovered any absolute laws governing the working of bureaucracy, although some interesting generalizations (really tendency statements) have been made. Our understanding of the administrative process will continue to grow, but any generalizations developed must allow for the dynamism of our subject matter.

Chapter six

Organization theory and administrative agencies

That ours is an organizational society has become a commonplace observation. Citizens can hardly avoid contacts with organizations, if only as consumers of the services of such organizations as fast-food franchises, communications agencies, and hospitals. Most of us have worked—at least on a part-time basis—for a large or small, public or private, profit or nonprofit organization. Thus, most everyone has some perceptions of what organizations are like and how they work, based on actual experience. If many readers already know quite a lot about the subject, why should organization theory be given featured treatment?

The inclusion of a chapter on organization theory reflects the extent to which the subject has become a part of the discipline of public administration. Furthermore, we endorse the view of an increasingly large group of social scientists, called organization theorists, who believe that citizens' general impressions about organizations, based on occasional encounters with them, are inadequate as a basis for understanding the important role these structures play in modern society.

For some years now, scholars—most of them sociologists—have been hard at work attempting to fathom organizational behavior. Their objective has been to move toward formalized theories and empirically based studies of the organizational phenomenon. In the first sentence of his prominent text, *Principles of Organization,* Theodore Caplow clearly states his thesis: "Human organizations are a class of natural phenomena the attributes of which are not time bound or culture bound and the workings of which are orderly, so that the sociology of organization is more susceptible to development as a science than other branches of sociology."[1] Developing a science of organization is highly important to most theorists, although some might be less optimistic about the prospects for success than Caplow.

Defining organizations

Just what is an organization? Unfortunately, no consensus exists about a precise definition of *organization.* Definitions from five influential books about organizations are presented below.[2] In reading these, think about groups with which you have some experience, perhaps the "junior class" of your college or university. Does the class qualify as an organization under any or all of these definitions?

The definition of a formal organization . . . is: A system of consciously coordinated activities or forces of two or more persons (Chester I. Barnard).

Organization is the form of every human association for the attainment of a common purpose (James D. Mooney and Alan C. Reiley).

An organization is a social system that has an unequivocal collective identity, an exact roster of members, a program of

---

[1]Theodore Caplow, *Principles of Organization* (New York: Harcourt, Brace and World, 1964), p. v.

[2]Chester I. Barnard, *The Functions of the Executive* (Cambridge, Mass.: Harvard University Press, 1938), p. 81; James D. Mooney and Alan C. Reiley, *The Principles of Organization* (New York: Harper and Brothers, 1939), p. 1; Caplow, *Principles of Organization,* p. 1; Amitai Etzioni, *Modern Organizations* (Englewood Cliffs, N.J.: Prentice-Hall, 1964), p. 3; Anthony Downs, *Inside Bureaucracy* (Boston: Little, Brown, 1966), p. 24.

activity, and procedures for replacing members (Theodore Caplow).

Organizations are social units (or human groupings) deliberately constructed and reconstructed to seek specific goals (Amitai Etzioni).

An organization is a system of consciously coordinated activities or forces of two or more persons explicitly created to achieve specific ends (Anthony Downs).

Attempting to strictly apply such definitions to collectivities when one is not sure whether they are organizations is a use of the definitional approach; thus, applying Barnard's definition, it is possible to evaluate the extent to which activities are "consciously coordinated," for example, and decide whether an organization exists or merely a conglomeration of people. Another use of the definitional approach is in *building* an organization; if one is given a small budget and some people, precisely what must be done to create an organization? In such circumstances, the value of definitions as blueprints can be tested.

This list of definitions may not be entirely representative, but we believe it to be reasonably so. Few authors in this field are willing to rely on the assumptions of others, and a much longer and more diverse list of definitions could have been provided. Of course, the large public administrative agencies that are our objects of study would definitely qualify as organizations by every definition with which we are familiar. It is necessary to move beyond definitions to understand how organization theory has enriched public administration.

The scope of organization theory

The contribution of organization theory to public administration lies not in the discovery that public agencies are organizations, but in the opportunity to apply the insights that investigators of various types of organizations provide. Much of the material in previous sections of this book has been influenced by research on formal organizations—whether public or private. Chapter 2 indicated that public administration became a self-conscious discipline just as various writers (to be discussed in a bit more detail below) were devoting their efforts to the discovery of ways of getting the most from human interaction. Furthermore, our view that public agencies participate in multiple relationships with other participants in the political process reflects the influence of theorists who have contended that organizations are dependent on exchanges with their environments. But many more insights have emerged from study of formal organizations; some of these will become evident in succeeding chapters on decision making, leadership, and staffing.

An important feature of what we have called organization "theory" is that it is not a single theory, but rather a large grab bag of theories and perspectives used to study organizations. Ralph Stogdill surveyed much of the literature and selected nine basic premises, or orientations. His list provides some indication of the field's diversity:

1. organization as a cultural product;

2. organization as an exchange agent with its environment;

3. organization as an independent agency;

4. organization as a system of structures and functions;

5. organization as a structure in action over time;

6. organization as a system of dynamic function;

7. organization as a processing system;

8. organization as an input-output system;

9. organization as a structure of subgroups.[3]

Even this list is not exhaustive; one could easily unearth from the mountain of recent writing on the subject several additional orientations that have come into widespread use. As a further means of emphasizing the scope of the field, we note that Henry Triandis has inventoried as many as two hundred variables (which he groups under input, structural, functional, and output headings) that are used by organizational theorists and that would have to be taken into account by a truly comprehensive theory of organizations.[4] This catalogue of the diversity in current organization theory is not to indicate that such theorizing is futile. Rather, it is to show that the field is alive with possibility and likely to continue to have an important impact on what we know about why humans behave as they do when they interact with each other.

---

[3]Ralph M. Stogdill, "Dimensions of Organization Theory," reprinted from *Approaches To Organizational Design* edited by James D. Thompson by permission of the University of Pittsburgh Press. © 1966 by the University of Pittsburgh Press, p. 4.

[4]Henry C. Triandis, "Notes on the Design of Organizations," ibid., p. 97.

"Old" and "new" organization theory

Chapter two sketched the early origins of public administration. No doubt, even in ancient times some thought was given to organizational arrangements. It is impossible to know just how far back into history *formal* theories of organization might be traced. Certainly, the Egyptian and Mayan pyramid builders had developed highly workable theories of organization. Illustrative of the venerable status of organization theorizing is the Old Testament quotation (Exodus 18:25–26) that Mooney and Reiley chose as the epigraph for their successful textbook:

> *And Moses chose able men out of all Israel, and made them heads over the people, rulers of thousands, rulers of hundreds, rulers of fifties, and rulers of tens. And they judged the people at all seasons:* the hard causes they brought unto Moses, but every small matter they judged themselves [*Mooney and Reiley's emphasis*].

The quotation was a fitting introduction to the *Principles of Organization,* for it is an apt illustration of some of the authors' main concerns. According to Mooney and Reiley, there are three main principles of organization. The first is the *coordinative principle,* which is the "orderly arrangement of group effort, to provide unity of action in the pursuit of a common purpose."[5] Authority, mutuality of interest, doctrinal objective, and discipline are key elements in the understanding of coordination. The second principle is the *scalar, or hierarchical, principle* of organization, which involves leadership, delegation of authority, and functional definition of tasks. Third is the *principle of functional differentiation.* This principle refers to the division of labor rather than hierarchy: "To employ a military illustration, the difference between generals and colonels is one of gradations in authority and is, therefore, *scalar.* The difference between an officer of infantry and an officer of artillery, however is *functional,* because here we have a distinct difference in the nature of these duties."[6] Finally, Mooney and Reiley emphasize the importance of distinguishing between the functions of organization members who have *staff* responsibilities (that is, they offer advice, information, ideas to top management) and those who have *line* responsibilities (that is, they have authority over a particular segment of the organization's operations). The staff/line distinction apparently is

---

[5]Mooney and Reiley, *Principles of Organization,* p. 5 (their italics deleted).
[6]Ibid., p. 25.

intended to be a special feature of the functional principle rather than a separate principle.

The Mooney and Reiley book epitomizes what we shall call the "old" organization theory. It would be convenient if we could provide a simple test for sharply differentiating between the "old" and the "new" theories; unfortunately we cannot, for there is considerable blending of the two. Nonetheless, some distinctions between them often can be drawn. On the one hand, the thrust of old organization theory is primarily structural and descriptive; it has high hopes—mentioned in chapter 2—for finding universal principles that can be learned and used to promote efficiency, centralize control of the organization, etc. On the other hand, new organization theory tends to be less structural and more dynamic, less descriptive and more analytical. Perhaps these distinctions will be made clear as the following brief discussion unfolds.

Bureaucracy

Several sources for the views on organizations expressed by Mooney and Reiley might be identified. One would be the brilliant German social theorist Max Weber's analysis of the modern bureaucratic form of organization. Weber offered a sophisticated interpretation of the complex dynamics of bureaucracy. (This is why his analysis remains valuable today, and it explains our inclusion of an excerpt from his work later in this chapter.) He also felt that bureaucracies could be distinguished from other sorts of organizations by testing for the presence of a combination of such structural characteristics as hierarchy and professionalism. In this sense, Weber had an important influence on "old" organization theorists, but we stress that most of these authors were far more mechanistic than he.

Scientific management

The "scientific management" school of administration, which originated in the industrial setting, was a very important source for the "old" organization theory. The most influential member of the school was Frederick Taylor, whose book *The Principles of Scientific Management* gave the field both its character and its name. Taylor laid out what he regarded as the basic elements of the mechanism for implementing his science:

> *time study, with the implements and methods for properly making it;*

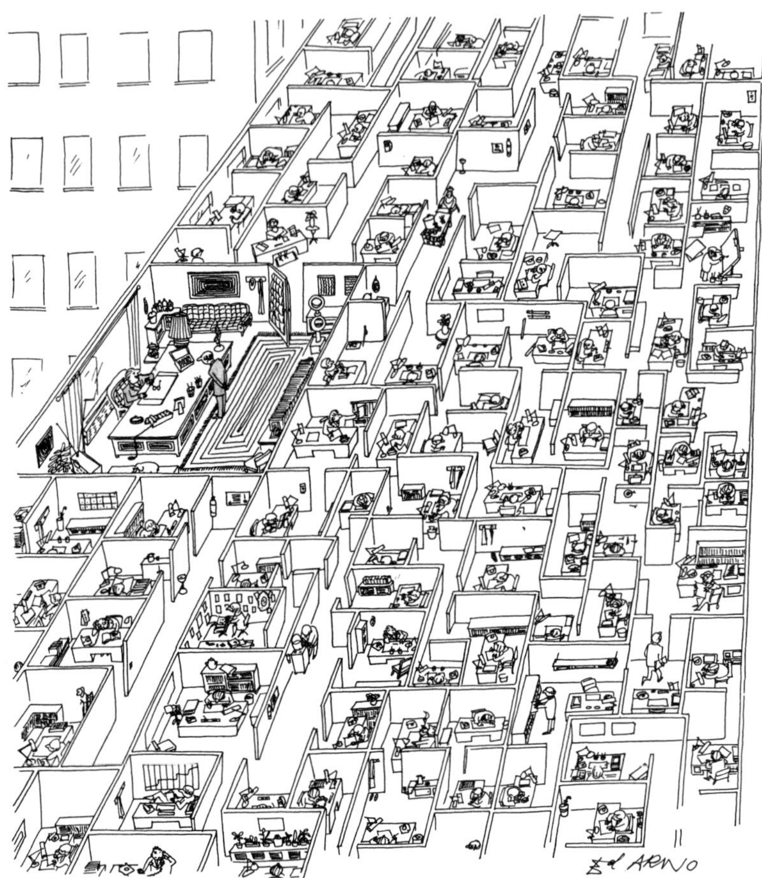

"I'm afraid a raise is out of the question, Benton, but in view of your sixteen years of service we are advancing you two spaces."
Drawing by Ed Arno; © 1977 The New Yorker Magazine, Inc.

functional or divided foremanship and its superiority to the old-fashioned single foreman;
the standardization of all tools and implements used in the trades, and also of the acts or movements of workmen for each class of work;
the desirability of a planning room or department;
the "exception principle" in management;
the use of slide-rules and similar time-saving implements;
instruction cards for the workman;
the task idea in management, accompanied by a large bonus for the successful performance of the task;
the "differential rate";

*mnemonic systems for classifying manufactured products as
well as implements used in manufacturing;
a routine system;
modern cost system, etc., etc.*[7]

Taylor hastened to add, however, that one could not turn around a slipshod workplace simply by hiring someone with a stopwatch to do time-and-motion studies. It was also necessary, he said, to have a commitment to the four principles on which his theory was based: *"First. The development of a true science. Second. The scientific selection of the workman. Third. His scientific education and development. Fourth.* Intimate friendly cooperation between the management and the men."[8] Although organization theorists who followed Taylor hoped to create a "true science," many neglected his *theoretical principles* and concentrated instead on the *elements of his mechanism,* which gave managers some apparently clear-cut rules.

Administrative management

The Mooney and Reiley book discussed above is a prominent representative of what we might call the "administrative management" approach.[9] One point on which exponents of administrative management were in general agreement was their insistence that administration was a generic process. They believed that there were overarching principles equally applicable to factories, schools, hospitals, prisons, insurance companies, or welfare agencies—*whether these organizations were public or private.* This belief was shared by Gulick and Urwick, who were students of public administration and advisors to Franklin D. Roosevelt but who, nonetheless, deliberately left the word *public* out of the title of their landmark book, *Papers on the Science of Administration.* This insistence that private and public administration really are at most slightly different aspects of the same process explains the current location of some "public administration" programs within schools of management or business administration.

---

[7]Frederick Winslow Taylor, *The Principles of Scientific Management* (New York: Harper and Brothers, 1911), pp. 129–30.

[8]Ibid., p. 130.

[9]For other authors sharing the approach, see: Mary Parker Follett, *Creative Experience* (Gloucester, Mass.: Peter Smith, 1951), original edition, 1924; W. F. Willoughby, *Principles of Public Administration* (Washington, D.C.: Brookings Institution, 1927); Henri Fayol, *General and Industrial Management* (London: Pitman, 1930); Luther Gulick and Lyndall Urwick, eds., *Papers on the Science of Administration* (New York: Institute of Public Administration, 1937).

No discussion of the administrative management movement would be complete without mentioning Gulick and Urwick's seven administrative principles, which have become famous—or infamous, depending upon one's point of view. Whole generations of students of public administration were forced to memorize the anagram, *POSDCORB*. *P*lanning, *O*rganizing, *S*taffing, *D*irecting, *CO*ordinating, *R*eporting, and *B*udgeting were the principles represented by this most infelicitous memory device. For many later students, however, POSDCORB became an epithet that conveniently summarized what they saw as the intellectual sterility of the entire "principles" approach to public administration.

Administrative behavior

Disillusionment with administrative management began to peak during the late 1940s. Perhaps the best-known critique of the school was Herbert Simon's book *Administrative Behavior*. Simon sifted through a number of the so-called principles of administration and selected for special attention four that commonly appeared in the literature: task specialization; hierarchy of authority; limited span of control; and the grouping of workers according to purpose, process, clientele, or place. Simon's close examination showed these alleged principles to be vague, ambiguous, and often contradictory. For example, hierarchy (sometimes called "unity of command") is frequently in conflict with another principle, specialization: "If an accountant in a school department is subordinate to an educator, and if unity of command is observed, then the finance department cannot issue direct orders to him regarding the technical, accounting aspects of his work."[10] Such conflicts occur frequently, and as Simon observes, "What evidence there is of actual administrative practice would seem to indicate that the need for specialization is to a very large degree given priority over the need for unity of command."[11] Having reviewed all of the principles and having found all of them inadequate, Simon summarized his dissatisfactions:

Administrative description suffers currently from superficiality, oversimplification, lack of realism. It has confined itself too closely to the mechanism of authority, and has failed to bring within its orbit the other, equally important, modes of influence on organizational behavior. It has refused to undertake

---

[10]Herbert A. Simon, *Administrative Behavior: A Study of Decision-Making Processes in Administrative Organization* (New York: Macmillan, 1947), pp. 23–24.

[11]Ibid., p. 25.

the tiresome task of studying the actual allocations of decision-making functions. It has been satisfied to speak of "authority," "centralization," "span of control," "function," without seeking operational definitions of these terms.[12]

Simon's prescription for these maladies was given in the title of his book: the object of study should be *administrative behavior.* From about the beginning of the 1950s onward, Simon's admonition has been followed.[13] Scholars have branched out in an enormous number of directions, but in the course of formulating their theories they have become far more interested in what actually happens in organizations than in abstract theorizing. Even contemporary theoretical models of organizations tend to be based on studies of the decision-making processes, etc., of real organizations.

Human relations

The roots of the new organization theory actually reach somewhat beyond Simon's critique of administrative management to efforts during the 1930s to test the effectiveness of several of scientific management's prescriptions. Those working in this tradition developed the *human relations* approach to organization. Despite the label "scientific," apart from some physiological studies, Taylor and other advocates actually undertook few efforts to experiment with and test their postulates prior to urging them upon administrators. The most famous attempt at testing was a set of studies conducted at the Hawthorne plant of Western Electric, near Chicago. According to the scientific management approach, certain working conditions (light, heat, etc.) and pay procedures should induce maximum productivity; many examples could be cited of plants where the prescribed changes were made and productivity increases followed. At Hawthorne, however, Elton Mayo and the team of researchers went further: they tried making changes *opposite* to those prescribed by the theory. For example, the light level was lowered in steps; each time illumination was lowered, production increased—just as it had when the lights had been raised. Even when the experimenters returned to the original lighting level, productivity again increased.

It did not seem reasonable to Mayo and his colleagues that *any*

---

[12]Ibid., p. 38.

[13]There were in addition to Simon several other critics of the "principles" approach. See as prominent examples Robert A. Dahl, "The Science of Public Administration: Three Problems," *Public Administration Review* 7 (Winter 1947): 1–11; and Dwight Waldo, *The Administrative State* (New York: Ronald Press, 1948).

change should increase productivity, until they realized that the workers were putting out more effort not because of a new management technique, but because a great deal of *attention* was being paid to them. This sort of result is now well known as the *Hawthorne effect*. The lesson students of administration have learned from the experiments, a lesson that has greatly influenced modern organization theory, is that people's attitudes can have a major impact on the way they behave. Without knowing the subtleties of the experiment, the workers knew they were being given special attention; their positive reaction to this knowledge was of far greater importance than the mechanistic changes scientific management prescribed.[14]

The findings of Mayo and others were slow to be incorporated into our understanding of organizations. Gradually, though, we have learned that, in addition to the structure prescribed by the formal organization chart, there is an informal one, based on the way people relate to people—perhaps in direct violation of the formal chain of command. Furthermore, we now know that people work not only for money: workers are motivated also by such intangible factors as pride, status, and even curiosity. Also, apart from the main goal of the organization (e.g., profit making), other goals grow up (e.g., security for workers) that may even detract from the ability to accomplish the main goal. Simon's critique of administrative management and the efforts of others to focus more sharply on the actual behavior of individuals in organizations have broadened the study of organizations by requiring consideration of the complex, human creatures of which they are composed.

System theories of organization

In briefly indicating the scope of current thinking about organizations earlier in this chapter, we noted that the range of available theories is a very wide one. For that reason, we shall not attempt a comprehensive survey of recent developments. Instead, we shall introduce the approach that has become most influential—the system approach to organizations.

In our daily lives we are likely to encounter a transportation *system*, the college or university's course registration *system*, and various *systems* of communication. And, if we listen, we can hear radicals fulminating against the machinations of "the System." This word, so com-

---

[14]Fritz J. Roethlisberger and W. J. Dickson, *Management and the Worker* (Cambridge, Mass.: Harvard University Press, 1939).

monplace in modern life, also has its scientific uses, and various schools of system theory have grown up. The one we shall discuss is called *general system theory (GST)*. The originator of GST, Ludwig von Bertalanffy, has remarked upon the ubiquity of systems:

> *Conceptions appear in contemporary science that are concerned with what is somewhat vaguely termed "wholeness," i.e., problems of organization, phenomena not resolvable into local events, dynamic interactions manifest in the difference of behavior of parts when isolated or in a higher configuration, etc.; in short, "systems" of various orders not understandable by investigation of their respective parts in isolation. Conceptions and problems of this nature have appeared in all branches of science, irrespective of whether inanimate things, living organisms, or social phenomena are the object of study.*[15]

According to GST, similar principles apply to the operations of all systems, including the single cell studied under the biologist's microscope, the individual organism, and human society.

Social psychologists Daniel Katz and Robert Kahn have described, in rather esoteric language, their system conception: "Our theoretical model for the understanding of organizations is that of an energic input-output system in which the energic return from the output reactivates the system."[16] Thus, their system is an "open" system in the sense that the "input of energies and the conversion of output into further energic input consist of transactions between the organization and its environment."[17] Restating these views in somewhat more conventional terms, we can say that a system consists of elements, or parts, that are interrelated and dependent on each other, so that any change in one has an impact on other parts; furthermore, it is possible to distinguish the system from the nonsystem. A boundary separates the system under analysis from any other elements that may be parts of another system, and those elements that impact on the system under analysis belong to its environment. Such a system imports energy of various types (inputs) from the environment, and the system's structural elements (the processor) convert the energy into products (outputs) that have further consequences (feedback) for the system and the environment.

---

[15]Ludwig von Bertalanffy, *General System Theory: Foundations, Development, Applications* (New York: George Braziller, 1968), p. 37.

[16]Daniel Katz and Robert L. Kahn, *The Social Psychology of Organizations* (New York: John Wiley, 1966), p. 16.

[17]Ibid., pp. 16–17.

Just what are the properties of systems? How can systems be distinguished from nonsystems? Can system theorizing improve our understanding of organizational life? As we list and briefly discuss the properties of systems, using some organizational examples, at least partial answers to these questions will be provided. Katz and Kahn say that all open systems are defined by the following nine characteristics:[18]

1. *Importation of energy.* No organization is completely self-sufficient or self-contained. Members, whether employees or volunteers, have to be recruited from the outside and motivated to work. Also, material resources must be acquired to support the organization's operations. The Central Intelligence Agency needs reports from its spies, and the National Science Foundation needs grant applications from scientists. Of course, every agency requires a budget.

2. *The through-put.* The system does something that alters the energy and materials fed into it. This is usually called the processing or conversion function. Universities try to transform their raw—professors sometimes think *very* raw—materials into educated men and women, and welfare agencies devise ways of combining their workers' skills and the legislature's appropriations to deliver services to clients.

3. *The output.* As a result of the processing or conversion or through-put function, something is produced and exported to the environment. The Army Corps of Engineers builds dams, Customs officials conduct drug raids, and Health, Education, and Welfare makes student loans—all three are outputs.

4. *Systems as cycles of events.* The output typically stimulates the production of sources of energy for a repetition of the cycle of activities. This is easy to see in the case of manufacturers when proceeds from the sale of the product pay for the raw materials and production costs of additional outputs. But the phenomenon also can be traced for other types of organizations. To return to the instance of the Corps of Engineers, certain consequences will flow from the completion of a dam: on the one hand, perhaps neighboring landowners who are impressed with the new structure's usefulness for flood control will demand that their own marauding river be similarly tamed; on the other hand, ecology-minded agitators (who sometimes call the Engineers the Damnable Corps and who may be concerned with how few free-flowing rivers remain and with the alleged environmental damages of dams) may campaign vigorously against further dams.

5. *Negative entropy.* It seems to be a law of nature that closed systems move toward entropy; that is, they become disorganized—through death, the organism's molecules eventually become randomly

---

[18]The source of most of the following treatment is ibid., pp. 19–26.

distributed in the environment. But *open* systems have the capacity to import more energy from the environment than is expended. Although organizations constantly go out of existence, many are successful in combating entropy; this latter circumstance explains the recent appeal of "sunset" laws, which are designed to insure reviews of the continuing usefulness of public agencies.

6. *Information input, negative feedback, and the coding process.* Energy is not the only type of input to a system; information inputs that enable the system to judge how it is doing in relation to the environment also are necessary. The most important such informational inputs are negative ones that help to correct the organization's course. Furthermore, every organization has a coding process that enables it to select those informational inputs that are appropriate. Thus, an agency's legislative liaison office is likely to strongly advise against persisting in courses of action that legislators have criticized, especially if budget time is near.

7. *The steady state and dynamic homeostasis.* Those systems that are successful in importing energy and combating entropy so that they survive are characterized by a steady state. It would be a mistake to believe that the term *steady state* is synonymous with a static or motionless condition. Organizations exist in a dynamic situation in which transactions with the environment occur constantly, but there is a strong tendency to maintain the basic character of the system or to maximize its character and mission through organizational growth. Herbert Kaufman did not frivolously choose the title of his recent book—*Are Government Organizations Immortal?*[19]

8. *Differentiation.* Systems tend to become more elaborate over time; ours is the age of professionalization, and specialization of function and structural differentiation—along with at least some absolute growth—are commonplace organizational phenomena. For confirmation, compare the organization charts of any large federal agency that has been in existence for at least two decades, let us say, during five-year intervals in the *Government Organization Manual.*

9. *Equifinality.* The principle, stated by von Bertalanffy in 1940, suggests that an open system's fate is not necessarily determined by conditions applying at a given time. Whereas knowledge of the initial situation enables one to predict outcomes in a closed system, if we compare two particular open systems, different outcomes may result from identical initial situations; or the same outcomes might be reached even though the systems began from different initial situations. The principle of *equifinality* as applied to organizations is another way of saying that

---

[19]Herbert Kaufman, *Are Government Organizations Immortal?* (Washington, D.C.: Brookings Institution, 1976).

these open systems are able to create regulatory mechanisms for adapting their behavior to fit the circumstances.

System theorizing is a complex subject, and this brief explanation has mentioned only some of its most basic concepts. Among the other subjects most often discussed by theorists, the notion of subsystems is a prominent one. Much system analysis occurs at the subsystem level, and theorists debate about the analytical relationships between subsystems (which often are factored out on the basis of their alleged performance of systemic functions) and the environment.[20] Another controversial topic in the field is the matter of whether individuals or organizational roles should be the objects of analysis.

Although systems concepts are helpful in structuring our thinking about organizations (indeed, we have drawn from the concepts in developing the framework for this book), we cannot leave the topic without emphasizing again that it is only one of numerous perspectives on organizations. We are sensitive to the criticism of some scholars and practitioners who claim that much system theorizing—especially elementary discussions, such as the one presented above—really accomplishes little more than recasting in a new language concepts that long have been studied. Students of public administration, however, have frequently *failed* to be sufficiently aware of agencies' environments, of agencies' efforts to survive, and of agencies' needs for resources obtained from outside their boundaries. Systems theory calls attention to these phenomena. Whether systems theory is merely a faddish analogy or whether it genuinely advances the scientific understanding of organizations, there can be no denial that it has had an enormous impact on the discipline of public administration. Such currently popular and diverse topics as organization development, zero-base budgeting, and program evaluation—all discussed below—are all based on system theory.

---

[20]For example, Katz and Kahn (p. 39) suggest that five basic organizational subsystems can be identified: "(1) production subsystems concerned with the work that gets done; (2) supportive subsystems of procurement, disposal, and institutional relations; (3) maintenance subsystems for tying people to their functional roles; (4) adaptive subsystems, concerned with organizational change; (5) managerial subsystems for the direction, adjudication, and control of the many subsystems and activities of the structure."

Bureaucracy*

Max Weber

In its various manifestations, bureaucracy is the distinctively modern form of organization. Although it seems omnipresent and is so pervasive that it is often taken for granted as the apparently "natural" form of organization, bureaucracy as we have come to know it developed only in the last century. In this selection, the distinguished social theorist Max Weber sets out the essential aspects of the bureaucratic form of organization.

Weber's analysis probably will seem very familiar. One reason is that bureaucracy impinges upon many aspects of life, and it is evident that Weber's analysis of the beast is essentially correct: hierarchical subordination, professionalization, expertise, impersonalism, etc., all are part of the ethos of large organizations as we know them. The second reason Weber seems familiar is the impact of his analysis; his work was truly seminal. Our teachers and the authors we read have been so influenced (either at first or second hand) by Weber's analysis that all of us can hardly think about the bureaucratic phenomenon except by using his categories.

Weber is sometimes criticized as being overly static and descriptive and for using ideal-type analysis (that is, he sought to capture the conceptual essence of *all* bureaucracies without seeking to explain the workings of any *particular* organization). Also, he is chided for not dwelling on the deficiencies of bureaucracy and for failing to foresee the *changes* that time would bring. Furthermore, some writers dislike Weber because they hate bureaucracy! Parenthetically, we observe that Weber is more dynamic than is sometimes appreciated; note, for example, his insights into the technical advantages of bureaucracy at the end of the selection. But Weber does not need to be defended: the value of his analysis is apparent.

Organization theory and administrative agencies/

Characteristics of bureaucracy

Modern officialdom functions in the following specific manner:

I. There is the principle of fixed and official jurisdictional areas, which are generally ordered by rules, that is, by laws or administrative regulations.

1. The regular activities required for the purposes of the bureaucractically governed structure are distributed in a fixed way as official duties.

2. The authority to give the commands required for the discharge of these duties is distributed in a stable way and is strictly delimited by rules concerning the coercive means, physical, sacerdotal, or otherwise, which may be placed at the disposal of officials.

3. Methodical provision is made for the regular and continuous fulfillment of these duties and for the execution of the corresponding rights; only persons who have the generally regulated qualifications to serve are employed.

In public and lawful government these three elements constitute "bureaucratic authority." In private economic domination, they constitute bureaucratic "management." Bureaucracy, thus understood, is fully developed in political and ecclesiastical communities only in the modern state, and, in the private economy, only in the most advanced institutions of capitalism. Permanent and public office authority, with fixed jurisdiction, is not the historical rule but rather the exception. This is so even in large political structures such as those of the ancient Orient, the Germanic and Mongolian empires of conquest, or of many feudal structures of state. In all these cases, the ruler executes the most important measures through personal trustees, table companions, or court servants. Their commissions and authority are not precisely delimited and are temporarily called into being for each case.

II. The principles of office hierarchy and of levels of graded authority mean a firmly ordered system of super- and subordination in which there is a supervision of the lower offices by the higher ones. Such a system offers the governed the possibility of appealing the decision of a lower office to its higher authority, in a definitely regulated manner. With the full development of the bureaucratic type, the office hierarchy is monocratically organized. The principle of hierarchical office authority is found in all bureaucratic structures: in state and ecclesiastical structures as well as in large party organizations and private enterprises. It does not matter for the character of bureaucracy whether its authority is called "private" or "public."

When the principle of jurisdictional "competency" is fully carried through, hierarchical subordination—at least in public office—does not mean that the "higher" authority is simply authorized to take over the business of the "lower." Indeed, the opposite is the rule. Once established and having fulfilled its task, an office tends to continue in existence and be held by another incumbent.

III. The management of the modern office is based upon written documents ("the files"), which are preserved in their original or draft form. There is, therefore, a staff of subaltern officials and scribes of all sorts. The body of officials actively engaged in a "public" office, along with the respective apparatus of material implements and the files, make up a "bureau." In private enterprise, "the bureau" is often called "the office."

In principle, the modern organization of the civil service separates the bureau from the private domicile of the official, and, in general, bureaucracy segregates official activity as something distinct from the sphere of private life. Public monies and equipment are divorced from the private property of the official. This condition is everywhere the product of a long development. Nowadays, it is found in public as well as in private enterprises; in the latter, the principle extends even to the leading entrepreneur. In principle, the executive office is separated from the household, business from private correspondence, and business assets from private fortunes. The more consistently the modern type of business management has been carried through, the more are these separations the case. The beginnings of this process are to be found as early as the Middle Ages.

It is the peculiarity of the modern entrepreneur that he conducts himself as the "first official" of his enterprise, in the very same way in which the ruler of a specifically modern bureaucratic state spoke of himself as "the first servant" of the state. The idea that the bureau activities of the state are intrinsically different in character from the management of private economic offices is a continental European notion and, by way of contrast, is totally foreign to the American way.

IV. Office management, at least all specialized office management—and such management is distinctly modern—usually presupposes thorough and expert training. This increasingly holds for the modern executive and employee of private enterprises, in the same manner as it holds for the state official.

V. When the office is fully developed, official activity demands the full working capacity of the official, irrespective of the fact that his obligatory time in the bureau may be firmly delimited. In the normal case, this is only the product of a long development, in the public as well as in the private office. Formerly, in all cases, the normal state of affairs was reversed: official business was discharged as a secondary activity.

VI. The management of the office follows general rules, which are more or less stable, more or less exhaustive, and which can be learned. Knowledge of these rules represents a special technical learning which the officials possess. It involves jurisprudence, or administrative or business management.

The reduction of modern office management to rules is deeply embedded in its very nature. The theory of modern public administration, for instance, assumes that the authority to order certain matters by decree—which has been legally granted to public authorities—does not entitle the bureau to regulate the matter by commands given for each case, but only to regulate the matter abstractly. This stands in extreme contrast to the regulation of all relationships through individual privileges and bestowals of favor, which is absolutely dominant in patrimonialism, at least in so far as such relationships are not fixed by sacred tradition.

The position of the official

All this results in the following for the internal and external position of the official:

I. Office holding is a "vocation." This is shown, first, in the requirement of a firmly prescribed course of training, which demands the entire capacity for work for a long period of time, and in the generally prescribed and special examinations which are prerequisites of employment. Furthermore, the position of the official is in the nature of a duty. This determines the internal structure of his relations, in the following manner: Legally and actually, officeholding is not considered a source to be exploited for rents or emoluments, as was normally the case during the Middle Ages and frequently up to the threshold of recent times. Nor is officeholding considered a usual exchange of services for equivalents, as is the case with free labor contracts. Entrance into an office, including one in the private economy, is considered an acceptance of a specific obligation of faithful management in return for a secure existence. It is decisive for the specific nature of modern loyalty to an office that, in the pure type, it does not establish a relationship to a *person*, like the vassal's or disciple's faith in feudal or in patrimonial relations of authority. Modern loyalty is devoted to impersonal and functional purposes. Behind the functional purposes, of course, "ideas of culture values" usually stand. These are *ersatz* for the earthly or supramundane personal master: ideas such as "state," "church," "community," "party," or "enterprise" are thought of as being realized in a community; they provide an ideological halo for the master.

The political official—at least in the fully developed modern state—is not considered the personal servant of a ruler. Today, the bishop, the priest, and the preacher are in fact no longer, as in early Christian times, holders of purely personal charisma. The supramundane and sacred values which they offer are given to everybody who seems to be worthy of them and who asks for them. In former times, such leaders acted upon the personal command of their master; in principle, they were responsible only to him. Nowadays, in spite of the partial survival of the old theory, such religious leaders are officials in the service of a functional purpose, which in the present-day "church" has become routinized and, in turn, ideologically hallowed.

II. The personal position of the official is patterned in the following way:

1. Whether he is in a private office or a public bureau, the modern official always strives and usually enjoys a distinct *social esteem* as compared with the governed. His social position is guaranteed by the prescriptive rules of rank order and, for the political official, by special definitions of the criminal code against "insults of officials" and "contempt" of state and church authorities.

The actual social position of the official is normally highest where, as in old civilized countries, the following conditions prevail: a strong demand for administration by trained experts; a strong and stable social differentiation, where the official predominantly derives from socially and economically privileged strata because of the social distribution of power; or where the costliness of the required training and status conventions are binding upon him. The possession of educational certificates . . . are usually linked with qualification for office. Naturally, such certificates or patents enhance the "status element" in the social position of the official. For the rest this status factor in individual cases is explicitly and impassively acknowledged; for example, in the prescription that the acceptance or rejection of an aspirant to an official career depends upon the consent ("election") of the members of the official body. This is the case in the German army with the officer corps. Similar phenomena, which promote this guild-like closure of officialdom, are typically found in patrimonial and, particularly, in prebendal officialdoms of the past. The desire to resurrect such phenomena in changed forms is by no means infrequent among modern bureaucrats. For instance, they have played a role among the demands of the quite proletarian and expert officials (the *tretyj* element) during the Russian Revolution.

Usually the social esteem of the officials as such is especially low where the demand for expert administration and the dominance of status conventions are weak. This is especially the case in the United States; it is often the case in new settlements by virtue of their wide fields for profit making and the great instability of their social stratification.

2. The pure type of bureaucratic official is *appointed* by a superior authority. An official elected by the governed is not a purely bureaucratic figure. Of course, the formal existence of an election does not by itself mean that no appointment hides behind the election—in the state, especially, appointment by party chiefs. Whether or not this is the case does not depend upon legal statutes but upon the way in which the party mechanism functions. Once firmly organized, the parties can turn a formally free election into the mere acclamation of a candidate designated by the party chief. As a rule, however, a formally free election is turned into a fight, conducted according to definite rules, for votes in favor of one of two designated candidates.

In all circumstances, the designation of officials by means of an election among the governed modifies the strictness of hierarchical subordination. In principle, an official who is so elected has an autonomous position opposite the superordinate official. The elected official does not derive his position "from above" but "from below," or at least not from a superior authority of the official hierarchy but from powerful party men ("bosses"), who also determine his further career. The career of the elected official is not, or at least not primarily, dependent upon his chief in the administration. The official who is not elected but appointed by a chief normally functions more exactly, from a technical point of view, because, all other circumstances being equal, it is more likely that purely functional points of consideration and qualities will determine his selection and career. As laymen, the governed can become acquainted with the extent to which a candidate is expertly qualified for office only in terms of experience, and hence only after his service. Moreover, in every sort of selection of officials by election, parties quite naturally give decisive weight not to expert considerations but to the services a follower renders to the party boss. This holds for all kinds of procurement of officials by elections, for the designation of formally free, elected officials by party bosses when they determine the slate of candidates, or the free appointment by a chief who has himself been elected. The contrast, however, is relative: substantially similar conditions hold where legitimate monarchs and their subordinates appoint officials, except that the influence of the followings are then less controllable.

Where the demand for administration by trained experts is considerable, and the party followings have to recognize an intellectually developed, educated, and freely moving "public opinion," the use of unqualified officials falls back upon the party in power at the next election. Naturally, this is more likely to happen when the officials are appointed by the chief. The demand for a trained administration now exists in the United States, but in the large cities, where immigrant votes are "corraled," there is, of course, no educated public opinion.

Organization theory and administrative agencies/

Therefore, popular elections of the administrative chief and also of his subordinate officials usually endanger the expert qualification of the official as well as the precise functioning of the bureaucratic mechanism. It also weakens the dependence of the officials upon the hierarchy. This holds at least for the large administrative bodies that are difficult to supervise. The superior qualification and integrity of federal judges, appointed by the president, as over against elected judges in the United States is well known, although both types of officials have been selected primarily in terms of party considerations. The great changes in American metropolitan administrations demanded by reformers have proceeded essentially from elected mayors working with an apparatus of officials who were appointed by them. These reforms have thus come about in a "Caesarist" fashion. Viewed technically, as an organized form of authority, the efficiency of "Caesarism," which often grows out of democracy, rests in general upon the position of the "Caesar" as a free trustee of the masses (of the army or of the citizenry), who is unfettered by tradition. The "Caesar" is thus the unrestrained master of a body of highly qualified military officers and officials whom he selects freely and personally without regard to tradition or to any other considerations. This "rule of the personal genius," however, stands in contradiction to the formally "democratic" principle of a universally elected officialdom.

3. Normally, the position of the official is held for life, at least in public bureaucracies; and this is increasingly the case for all similar structures. As a factual rule, *tenure for life* is presupposed, even where the giving of notice or periodic reappointment occurs. In contrast to the worker in a private enterprise, the official normally holds tenure. Legal or actual life-tenure, however, is not recognized as the official's right to the possession of office, as was the case with many structures of authority in the past. Where legal guarantees against arbitrary dismissal or transfer are developed, they merely serve to guarantee a strictly objective discharge of specific office duties free from all personal considerations. In Germany, this is the case for all juridical and, increasingly, for all administrative officials.

Within the bureaucracy, therefore, the measure of "independence," legally guaranteed by tenure, is not always a source of increased status for the official whose position is thus secured. Indeed, often the reverse holds, especially in old cultures and communities that are highly differentiated. In such communities, the stricter the subordination under the arbitrary rule of the master, the more it guarantees the maintenance of the conventional seigneurial style of living for the official. Because of the very absence of these legal guarantees of tenure, the conventional esteem for the official may rise in the same way as, during the Middle Ages, the esteem of the nobility of office rose at the expense of esteem for the freemen, and as the king's judge surpassed that of the people's judge. In Germany, the military officer or the administrative official can be removed from office at any time, or at least far more readily than the "independent judge," who never pays with loss of his office for even the grossest offense against the "code of honor" or against social conventions of the salon. For this very reason, if other things are equal, in the eyes of the master stratum the judge is considered less qualified for social intercourse than are officers and administrative officials, whose greater dependence on the master is a greater guarantee of their conformity with status conventions. Of course, the average official strives for a civil-service law, which would materially secure his old age and provide increased guarantees against his arbitrary removal from office. This striving, however, has its limits. A very strong development of the "right to the office" naturally makes it more difficult to staff them with regard to technical efficiency, for such a development decreases the career opportunities of ambitious candidates for office. This makes for the fact that officials, on the whole, do not feel their dependency upon those at the top. This lack of a feeling of dependency, however, rests primarily upon the inclination to depend upon one's equals rather than upon the socially inferior and governed strata. The present conservative movement among the Badenia clergy, occasioned by the anxiety of a presumably threatening separation of church and state, has been expressly determined by the desire not to be turned "from a master into a servant of the parish."

4. The official receives the regular *pecuniary* compensation of a normally fixed *salary* and the old age security provided by a pension. The salary is not measured like a wage in terms of work done, but according to "status," that is, according to the kind of function (the "rank") and, in addition, possibly, according to the length of service. The relatively great security of the official's income, as well as the rewards of social esteem, make the office a sought-after position, especially in countries which no longer provide opportunities for colonial profits. In such countries, this situation permits relatively low salaries for officials.

5. The official is set for a *career* within the hierarchical order of the public service. He moves from the lower, less important, and lower-paid to the higher positions. The average official naturally desires a mechanical fixing of the conditions of promotion: if not of the offices, at least of the salary levels. He wants these conditions fixed in terms of "seniority," or possibly according to grades achieved in a developed system of expert examinations. Here and there, such examinations actually form a character *indelebilis* of the official and have life-long effects on his career. To this is joined the desire to qualify the right to office and the increasing tendency toward status group closure and economic security. All of this makes for a tendency to consider the offices as "prebends" of those who are qualified by educational certificates. The necessity of taking general personal and intellectual qualifications into consideration, irrespective of the often subaltern character of the educational certificate, has led to a condition in which the highest political offices, especially the positions of "ministers," are principally filled without reference to such certificates. . . .

Technical advantages of bureaucratic organization

The decisive reason for the advance of bureaucratic organization has always been its purely technical superiority over any other form of organization. The fully developed bureaucratic mechanism compares with other organizations exactly as does the machine with the nonmechanical modes of production.

Precision, speed, unambiguity, knowledge of the files, continuity, discretion, unity, strict subordination, reduction of friction and of material and personal costs—these are raised to the optimum point in the strictly bureaucratic administration, and especially in its monocratic form. As compared with all collegiate, honorific, and avocational forms of administration, trained bureaucracy is superior on all these points. And as far as complicated tasks are concerned, paid bureaucratic work is not only more precise but, in the last analysis, it is often cheaper than even formally unremunerated honorific service.

Honorific arrangements make administrative work an avocation and, for this reason alone, honorific service normally functions more slowly; being less bound to schemata and being more formless. Hence it is less precise and less unified than bureaucratic work because it is less dependent upon superiors and because the establishment and exploitation of the apparatus of subordinate officials and filing services are almost unavoidably less economical. Honorific service is less continuous than bureaucratic and frequently quite expensive. This is especially the case if one thinks not only of the money costs to the public treasury—costs which bureaucratic administration, in comparison with administration by notables, usually substantially increases—but also of the frequent economic losses of the governed caused by delays and lack of precision. The possibility of administration by notables normally and permanently exists only where official management can be satisfactorily discharged as an avocation. With the qualitative increase of tasks the administration has to face, administration by notables reaches its limits—today, even in England. Work organized by collegiate bodies causes friction and delay and requires compromises between colliding interests and views. The administration, therefore, runs less precisely and is more independent of superiors; hence, it is less unified and slower. All advances of the Prussian administrative organization have been and will in the future be advances of the bureaucratic, and especially of the monocratic, principle.

Today, it is primarily the capitalist market economy which demands that the official business of the administration be discharged precisely, unambiguously, continuously, and with as much speed as possible. Normally, the very large, modern capitalist enterprises are themselves unequalled models of strict bureaucratic organization. Business management throughout rests on increasing precision, steadiness, and, above all, the speed of operations. This, in turn, is determined by the peculiar nature of the modern means of communication, including, among other things, the news service of the press. The extraordinary increase in the speed by which public announcements, as well as economic and political facts, are transmitted exerts a steady and sharp pressure in the direction of speeding up the tempo of administrative reaction towards various situations. The optimum of such reaction time is normally attained only by a strictly bureaucratic organization.[1]

Bureaucratization offers above all the optimum possibility for carrying through the principle of specializing administrative functions according to purely objective considerations. Individual performances are allocated to functionaries who have specialized training and who by constant practice learn more and more. The "objective" discharge of business primarily means a discharge of

---

[1]Here we cannot discuss in detail how the bureaucratic apparatus may, and actually does, produce definite obstacles to the discharge of business in a manner suitable for the single case.

business according to *calculable rules* and "without regard for persons."

"Without regard for persons" is also the watchword of the "market" and, in general, of all pursuits of naked economic interests. A consistent execution of bureaucratic domination means the leveling of status "honor." Hence, if the principle of the free market is not at the same time restricted, it means the universal domination of the "class situation." That this consequence of bureaucratic domination has not set in everywhere, parallel to the extent of bureaucratization, is due to the differences among possible principles by which polities may meet their demands.

The second element mentioned, "calculable rules," also is of paramount importance for modern bureaucracy. The peculiarity of modern culture, and specifically of its technical and economic basis, demands this very "calculability" of results. When fully developed, bureaucracy also stands, in a specific sense, under the principle of *sine ira ac studio.* Its specific nature, which is welcomed by capitalism, develops the more perfectly the more the bureaucracy is "dehumanized," the more completely it succeeds in eliminating from official business love, hatred, and all purely personal, irrational, and emotional elements which escape calculation. This is the specific nature of bureaucracy and it is appraised as its special virtue.

The more complicated and specialized modern culture becomes, the more its external supporting apparatus demands the personally detached and strictly "objective" *expert,* in lieu of the master of older social structures, who was moved by personal sympathy and favor, by grace and gratitude. Bureaucracy offers the attitudes demanded by the external apparatus of modern culture in the most favorable combination. . . .

Study questions for selection six

1. Do you see much evidence that Weber's analysis of bureaucracy is limited by most of his illustrations being of Prussian government agencies?

2. Are you convinced that hierarchical control, a principle much extolled by Weber, really is necessary to the existence of bureaucracy?

3. If an agency actually possessed the characteristics of Weber's ideal bureaucracy, would the organization be efficient, just, and adaptive?

Changing organizations*

Warren Bennis

According to Bob Dylan, "The times, they are a changin'." Many of the changes that are such a noticeable feature of modern society are likely to be reflected in our organizations. Furthermore, since organizations are social artifacts, they can be deliberately restructured to conform to whatever values society wishes to promote. As we look around us, we still see a great many offices that look very much like those Weber dubbed "bureaucracies," and it seems rather premature to talk of a "postbureaucratic" age, as some do. But many current theorists of organizations contend that organizations are changing in significant respects, that they should be changed to correct certain shortcomings, and that organizations of the future will look very different from those we have come to know.

The ideas of Warren Bennis (immediate past president of the University of Cincinnati), who has written extensively on the subject of organizational change, have had an important impact upon other theorists; we will refer to his human-relations-based concepts of organization development in chapter 9. In this selection, Bennis sketches Weber's "bureaucratic machine" model and declares that it needs replacing—indeed, that it is being replaced—with new organizational forms now in the process of development. Many contemporary organizations are becoming "revitalized," Bennis says, and organizations of the future will be increasingly concerned with what Douglas McGregor (the theorist in whose honor this selection was written) has called the "human side of enterprise."

Some aspects of Bennis's evolving "organic adaptive structures" (which were popularized by Alvin Toffler in *Future Shock* as "ad-hocracies"), especially their temporary and rapidly changing character, are likely to place strains on workers' psychological coping mechanisms, but he believes that compensations can be found in the increased scope the new structures allow for creativity and freedom.

---

*Abridged from Warren G. Bennis, "Changing Organizations," speech delivered at the First Annual Douglas McGregor Memorial Lecture, Massachusetts Institute of Technology, 1965. Reprinted by permission of the author.

The idea of change

Not far from where the new Government Center is going up, in down-town Boston, a foreign visitor once walked up to an American sailor and asked why the ships of his country were built to last for only a short time. According to the foreign tourist

> *the sailor answered without hesitation that the art of navigation is making such rapid progress that the finest ship would become obsolete if it lasted beyond a few years. In these words, which fell accidentally from an uneducated man, I began to recognize the general and systematic idea upon which your great people direct all their concerns.*

The foreign visitor was that shrewd observer of American morals and manners, Alexis de Tocqueville, and the year was 1835. He would not recognize Scollay Square today. But he caught the central theme of our country—its preoccupation, its *obsession* with change. One thing, however, is new since Tocqueville's time: the prevalence of newness, the changing scale and scope of change itself, so that, as Oppenheimer said, "The world alters as we walk in it, so that the years of man's life measure not some small growth or rearrangement or moderation of what was learned in childhood, but a great upheaval."

Numbers have a magic all their own, and it is instructive to review some of the most relevant ones. In 1789, when George Washington was inaugurated, American society comprised fewer than 4 million persons, of whom 750,000 were Negroes. Few persons lived in cities; New York, then the capital, had a population of 33,000. In all, 200,000 individuals lived in what were then defined as "urban areas"—places with more than 2,500 inhabitants. In the past ten years, Los Angeles has grown by 2,375,000, almost enough to people present-day Boston. In July 1964, the population of the U.S. was about 192 million. The U.S. Census Bureau estimates that the population in 1975 will be between 226 and 235 million and that in 1980 it will be between 246 and 260 million. World population was over 3 billion in 1964. If fertility remains at present levels until 1975 and then begins to decline, the population of the world will reach 4 billion in 1977, 5 billion by about 1990.

Observe the changes taking place in education. Thirty years ago only one out of every eight Americans at work had been to high school. Today four out of five attend high school. Thirty years ago 4 percent or less of the population attended college. Now the figure is around 35 percent, in cities about 50 percent.

"Everything nailed down is coming loose," a historian said recently, and it does seem that no exaggeration, no hyperbole, no outrage can realistically appraise the extent and pace of modernization. Exaggerations come true in only a year or two. Nothing will remain in the next ten years—or there will be twice as much of it.

And it is to our credit that the pseudo-horror stories and futuristic fantasies about *accelerations* of the rate of change (the rate of obsolescence, scientific and technological unemployment) and the number of "vanishing" stories (the vanishing salesman, the vanishing host, the vanishing adolescent, the vanishing village)—it is to our credit that these phenomenal changes have failed to deter our compulsive desire to invent, to overthrow, to upset inherited patterns and comfort in the security of the future.

No more facts and numbers are needed to make the point. We can *feel* it on the job, in the school, in the neighborhood, in our professions, in our everyday lives.

Changing organizations

How will these accelerating changes in our society influence human organizations?

Let me begin by describing the dominant form of human organization employed throughout the industrial world. It is a unique and extremely durable social arrangement called "bureaucracy," a social invention, perfected during the industrial revolution to organize and direct the activities of the business firm. It is today the prevailing and supreme type of organization wherever people direct concerted effort toward the achievement of some goal. This holds for university systems, for hospitals, for large voluntary organizations, for governmental organizations.

Corsica, according to Gibbon, is much easier to deplore than to describe. The same holds true for bureaucracy. Basically, bureaucracy is a social invention which relies exclusively on the power to influence through rules, reason, and the law. Max Weber, the German sociologist who developed the theory of bureaucracy around the turn of the century, once described bureaucracy as a social machine: "Bureaucracy," he wrote, "is like a modern judge who is a vending machine into which the pleadings are inserted together with the fee and which then disgorges the judgment together with its reasons mechanically derived from the code."

The bureaucratic "machine model" Weber outlined was developed as a reaction against the personal subjugation, nepotism, cruelty, and capricious and subjective judgments which passed for managerial practices in the early days of the industrial revolution. The true hope for man, it was thought, lay in his ability to rationalize, to calculate, to use his head as well as his hands and heart. Bureaucracy emerged out of the need for more predictability, order, and precision. It was an organization ideally suited to the values of Victorian Empire.

Most students of organizations would say that the anatomy of bureaucracy consists of the following "organs": a division of labor based on functional specialization, a well-defined hierarchy of authority, a system of procedures and rules for dealing with all contingencies relating to work activities, impersonality of interpersonal relations, and promotion and selection based on technical competence. It is the pyramidal arrangement we see on most organizational charts.

Allow me to leap-frog to the conclusion of my paper now. It is my premise that the bureaucratic form of organization is out of joint with contemporary realities; that new shapes, patterns, and models are emerging which promise drastic changes in the conduct of the corporation and of managerial practices in general. In the next twenty-five to fifty years we should witness, and participate in, the end of bureaucracy as we know it and the rise of new social systems better suited to twentieth-century demands of industrialization.

Reasons for organizational change

I see two main reasons for these changes in organizational life. One has been implied earlier in terms of changes taking place in society, most commonly referred to as the population and knowledge explosions. The other is more subtle and muted—perhaps less significant, but for me profoundly exciting. I have no easy name for it, nor is it easy to define. It has to do with man's historical quest for self-awareness, for using reason to achieve and stretch his potentialities and possibilities. I think that this deliberate self-analysis has spread to large and more complex social systems, to organizations. I think there has been a dramatic upsurge of this spirit of inquiry over the past two decades. At new depths and over a wider range of affairs, organizations are opening their operations up to self-inquiry and analysis. This really involves two parallel shifts in values and outlooks, between the men who make history and the men who make knowledge. One change is the scientist's realization of his affinity with men of affairs, and the other is the latter's receptivity and newfound respect for men of knowledge. I am calling this new development *organizational revitalization*. It is a complex social process which involves a deliberate and self-conscious examination of organizational behavior and a collaborative relationship between managers and scientists to improve performance.

I can assure you that this development is unprecedented, that never before in history, in any society, has man, in his organizational context, so willingly searched, scrutinized, examined, inspected, or contemplated—for meaning, for purpose, for improvement.

I think this shift in outlook has taken a good deal of courage from both partners in this encounter. The manager has had to shake off old prejudices about "eggheads" and long-hair intellectuals. More important, he has had to make himself and his organization vulnerable and receptive to external sources and to new, unexpected, even unwanted information—which all of you know is not such an easy thing to do. The academician has had to shed some of his natural hesitancies. Scholarly conservatism is admirable, I think, except to hide behind, and for a long time caution has been a defense against reality.

It might be useful to dwell on the role of academic man and his growing involvement with social action, using the field of management education as a case in point. Until recently, the field of business was disregarded by large portions of the American public, and it was unknown to or snubbed by the academic establishment. Management education and research were at best regarded there with dark suspicion, as if contact with the world of reality—particularly monetary reality—was equivalent to a dreadful form of pollution. In fact, academic man has historically taken one of two stances toward The Establishment, *any* Establishment—that of rebellious critic or of withdrawn snob.

It is probably true that we in the United States have had a more pragmatic attitude toward knowledge than anyone else. Many observers have been impressed with the disdain European intellectuals seem to show for practical matters. Even in Russia, where one would least expect it, there is little interest in the "merely useful." Harrison Salisbury, the *New York Times*' Soviet expert, was struck during his recent travels by the almost total absence of liaison between research and practical application. He saw only one great agricultural experimental station on the American model. In that case, professors were working in the fields. They told Salisbury, "people call us Americans."

There may not be many American professors working in the fields, but they can be found, when not waiting in airports, almost everywhere else: in factories, in government, in less advanced countries, more recently in backward areas of our own country, in mental hospitals, in the State Department, in educational systems, and in practically all the institutional crevices Ph.D. recipients can worm their way into. They are advising, counseling, researching, recruiting, interpreting, developing, consulting, training, and working for the widest variety of client imaginable. This is not to say that the deep ambivalence which some Americans hold toward the intellectual has disappeared, but it does indicate that academic man has became more committed to action, in greater numbers, with more diligence, and with higher aspirations than at any other time in history.

Indeed, Fritz Machlup, the economist, has coined a new economic category called the "knowledge industry," which, he claims, accounts for 29 percent of the gross national product. And Clark Kerr, the president of the University of California, said not too long ago.

What the railroads did for the second half of the last century and the automobile did for the first half of this century may be done for the second half of this century by the knowledge industry: that is, to serve as the focal point of national growth. And the university is at the center of the knowledge process.

Changes in managerial philosophy

Now let us turn to the main theme and put the foregoing remarks about the reciprocity between action and knowledge into the perspective of changing organizations. Consider some of the relatively recent research and theory concerning the human side of enterprise which have made such a solid impact on management thinking and particularly upon the moral imperatives which guide managerial action. I shall be deliberately sweeping in summarizing these changes as much to hide my surprise as to cover a lot of ground quickly.

Chapter six

1. A new concept of *man,* based on increased knowledge of his complex and shifting needs, which replaces the oversimplified, innocent push-button idea of man.

2. A new concept of *power,* based on collaboration and reason, which replaces a model of power based on coercion and fear.

3. A new concept of *organizational values,* based on humanistic-democratic ideals, which replaces the depersonalized mechanistic value system of bureaucracy.

Please do not misunderstand. The last thing I want to do is overstate the case. I do not mean that these transformations of man, power, and organizational values are fully accepted or even understood, to say nothing of implemented, in day-to-day affairs. These changes may be light-years away from actual adoption. I do mean that they have gained wide intellectual acceptance in enlightened management quarters, that they have caused a tremendous amount of rethinking and search behavior on the part of many organizations, and that they have been used as a basis for policy formulation by many large-scale organizations.

I have tried to summarize all the changes affecting organizations, resulting both from the behavioral sciences and from trends in our society, in table 1 of human problems confronting contemporary organizations. These problems (or predicaments) emerge basically from twentieth-century changes, primarily the growth of science and education, the separation of power from property and the correlated emergence of the professional manager, and other kinds of changes which I will get to in a minute. The bureaucratic mechanism, so capable of coordinating men and power in a stable society of routine tasks, cannot cope with contemporary realities. The chart shows five major categories, which I visualize as the core tasks confronting the manager in coordinating the human side of enterprise:

1. The problem of integration grows out of our "consensual society," where personal attachments play a great part, where the individual is appreciated, in which there is concern for his well-being—not just in a veterinary-hygiene sense but as a moral, integrated personality.

2. The problem of social influence is essentially the problem of power, and leadership studies and practices reveal not only an ethical component but an *effectiveness* component: people tend to work more efficiently and with more commitment when they have a part in determining their own fates and have a stake in problem solving.

3. The problem of collaboration grows out of the same social processes of conflict, stereotyping, and centrifugal forces which inhere in and divide nations and communities. They also employ the same furtive, often fruitless, always crippling mechanisms of conflict resolution: avoidance or suppression, annihilation of the weaker party by the stronger, sterile compromises, and unstable collusions and coalitions. Particularly as organizations become more complex they fragment and divide, building tribal patterns and symbolic codes which often work to exclude others (secrets and noxious jargon, for example) and on occasion to exploit differences for inward (and always, fragile) harmony. Some large organizations, in fact, can be understood only through an analysis of their cabals,

Table 1.

	Problem	Bureaucratic solutions	New twentieth-century conditions
Integration	The problem of how to integrate individual needs and management goals.	No solution because of no problem. Individual vastly oversimplified, regarded as passive instrument or disregarded.	Emergence of human sciences and understanding of man's complexity. Rising aspirations. Humanistic-democratic ethos.
Social influence	The problem of the distribution of power and sources of power and authority.	An explicit reliance on legal-rational power but an implicit usage of coercive power. In any case, a confused, ambiguous, shifting complex of competence, coercion, and legal code.	Separation of management from ownership. Rise of trade unions and general education. Negative and unintended effects of authoritarian rule.
Collaboration	The problem of managing and resolving conflicts.	The "rule of hierarchy" to resolve conflicts between ranks and the "rule of coordination" to resolve conflict between horizontal groups. "Loyalty."	Specialization and professionalization and increased need for interdependence. Leadership too complex for one-man rule or omniscience.
Adaption	The problem of responding appropriately to changes induced by the environment of the firm.	Environment stable, simple, and predictable; tasks routine. Adapting to change occurs in haphazard and adventitious ways. Unanticipated consequences abound.	External environment of firm more "turbulent," less predictable. Unprecedented rate of technological change.
"Revitalization"	The problem of growth and decay.	?	Rapid changes in technologies, task, manpower, raw materials, norms and values of society, and goals of enterprise and society all make constant attention to the processes of the firm and revision imperative.

cliques, and satellites, their tactics resembling a sophisticated form of guerrilla warfare, and a venture into adjacent spheres of interest is taken under cover of darkness and fear of ambush.

4. The real *coup de grace* to bureaucracy has come as much from our turbulent environment as from its incorrect assumptions about human behavior. The pyramidal structure of bureaucracy, where power was concentrated at the top—perhaps by one person or group who had the knowledge and resources to control the entire enterprise—seemed perfect to "run a railroad." And undoubtedly, for tasks like building railroads, for the routinized tasks of the nineteenth and early twentieth centuries, bureaucracy was and is an eminently suitable social arrangement.

Nowadays, due primarily to the growth of science, technology, and research and development activities, the organizational environment of the firm is rapidly changing. Today it is a turbulent environment, not a placid and predictable one, and there is a deepening interdependence among the economic and other facets of society. This means that economic organizations are increasingly enmeshed in legislation and public policy. Put more simply, it means that the government will be in about everything, more of the time. It may also mean, and this is radical, that maximizing cooperation, rather than competition between firms—particularly if their fates are correlated—may become a strong possibility.

5. Finally, there is the problem of revitalization. Alfred North Whitehead sets it neatly before us: "The art of free society consists first in the maintenance of the symbolic code, and secondly, in the fearlessness of revision. . . . Those societies which cannot combine reverence to their symbols with freedom of revision must ultimately decay." Organizations, as well as societies, must be concerned with those social conditions that engender buoyance, resilience, and fearlessness of revision. Growth and decay emerge as the penultimate problem where the environment of contemporary society is turbulent and uncertain.

Forecast of organizations of the future

A forecast falls somewhere between a prediction and a prophecy. It lacks the divine guidance of the latter and the empirical foundation of the former. On thin empirical ice, I want to set forth some of the conditions that will dictate organization life in the next twenty-five to fifty years.

1. *The Environment.* Those factors already mentioned will continue in force and increase. Rapid technological change and diversification will lead to interpenetration of the government—its legal and economic policies—with business. Partnerships between business and government will be typical. And because of the immensity and expense of the projects, there will be fewer identical units competing for the same buyers and sellers. The three main features of the environment will be interdependence rather than competition, turbulence rather than steadiness, and large-scale rather than small-scale enterprises.

2. *Population Characteristics.* The most distinctive characteristic of our society is, and will become even more so, its education. Peter Drucker calls us

the "educated society," and for good reason: within fifteen years, two-thirds of our population living in metropolitan areas will have attended college. Adult education is growing even faster. It is now almost routine for the experienced physician, engineer, and executive to go back to school for advanced training every two or three years. Some fifty universities, in addition to a dozen large corporations, offer advanced management courses to successful men in the middle and upper ranks of business. Before World War II, only two such programs existed, both new and struggling to get students.

All of this education is not just "nice" but necessary. For as W. Willard Wirtz, the secretary of labor, recently pointed out, computers can do the work of most high-school graduates—and they can do it cheaper and more effectively. Fifty years ago education used to be regarded as "nonwork," and intellectuals on the payroll (and many staff workers) were considered "overhead." Today, the survival of the firm depends, more than ever before, on the proper exploitation of brain power.

3. *Work Values.* The increased level of education and mobility will change the values we hold about work. People will be more intellectually committed to their jobs and will probably require more involvement, participation, and autonomy in their work.

Also, people will tend to be more "other-directed," taking cues for their norms and values more from their immediate environment than from tradition. We will tend to rely more heavily on temporary social arrangements, on our immediate and constantly changing colleagues. We will tend to be more concerned and involved with relationships rather than with relatives.

4. *Tasks and Goals.* The tasks of the firm will be more technical, complicated, and unprogrammed. They will rely more on intellect than muscle. And they will be too complicated for one person to comprehend, to say nothing of control. Essentially, they will call for the collaboration of specialists in a project or team form of organization.

There will be a complication of goals. Business will increasingly concern itself with its adaptive or innovative-creative capacity. In addition, metagoals—that is, supragoals which shape and provide the foundation for the goal structure—will have to be articulated and developed. For example, one metagoal might be a system for detecting new and changing goals; another could be a system for deciding priorities among goals.

Finally, there will be more conflict and contradiction among diverse standards of organizational effectiveness, just as in hospitals and universities today there is conflict between teaching and research. The reason for this is the increased number of professionals involved, who tend to identify more with the goals of their profession than with those of their immediate employer. University professors can be used as a case in point. More and more of their income comes from outside sources, such as foundations which grant them money and industries for whom they consult. They tend not to be good "company men" because they divide their loyalty between their professional values and organizational goals.

5. *Organization.* The social structure of organizations of the future will have some unique characteristics. The key word will be "temporary"; there will be adaptive, rapidly changing *temporary* systems. These will be problem-oriented "task forces" composed of groups of relative strangers who represent a

diverse set of professional skills. The groups will be arranged on an organic rather than a mechanical model; they will evolve in response to a problem rather than to programmed role expectations. The "executive" thus will become a coordinator or "linking pin" between various task forces. He must be a man who can speak the diverse languages of research, with skills to relay information and to mediate between groups. People will be differentiated not vertically according to rank and status but flexibly and functionally according to skill and professional training.

Adaptive, problem-solving, temporary systems of diverse specialists, linked together by coordinating and task-evaluating specialists in an organic flux—this is the organizational form that will gradually replace bureaucracy as we know it. As no catchy phrase comes to mind, I call this an organic-adaptive structure.

6. *Motivation.* The organic-adaptive structure should increase motivation, and thereby effectiveness, since it will enhance satisfactions intrinsic to the task. There is a harmony between the educated individual's need for meaningful, satisfactory, and creative tasks and a flexible organizational structure.

There will, however, also be reduced commitment to work groups, for these groups, as I have already mentioned, will be transient and changing. While skills in human interaction will become more important, due to the growing needs for collaboration in complex tasks, there will be a concomitant reduction in group cohesiveness. My prediction is that in the organic-adaptive system people will have to learn to develop quick and intense relationships on the job and learn to bear the loss of more enduring work relationships. Because of the added ambiguity of roles, more time will have to be spent on the continual search for the appropriate organizational mix.

In general, I do not agree with those who emphasize a new utopianism in which leisure, not work, will become the emotional-creative sphere of life. Jobs should become more rather than less involving; man is a problem-solving animal, and the tasks of the future guarantee a full agenda of problems. In addition, the adaptive process itself may become captivating to many.

At the same time, I think the future I describe is not necessarily a "happy" one. Coping with rapid change, living in temporary work systems, developing meaningful relations and then breaking them—all augur social strains, and psychological tensions. Teaching how to live with ambiguity, to identify with the adaptive process, to make a virtue out of contingency, and to be self-directing will be the task of education, the goal of maturity, and the achievement of the successful manager. To be a wife in this era will be to undertake the profession of providing stability and continuity.

In these new organizations, participants will be called on to use their minds more than at any other time in history. Fantasy, imagination, and creativity will be legitimate in ways that today seem strange. Social structures will no longer be instruments of psychic repression but will increasingly promote play and freedom on behalf of curiosity and thought.

Bureaucracy was a monumental discovery for harnessing the muscle power of the industrial revolution. In today's world, it is a lifeless crutch that is no longer useful. For we now require structures of freedom to permit the expression of play and imagination and to exploit the new pleasure of work.

One final word: While I forecast the structure and value coordinates for organizations of the future and contend that they are inevitable, this should not bar any of us from giving the inevitable a little push here and there. And while the French moralist may be right that there are no delightful marriages, just good ones, it is possible that if managers and scientists continue to get their heads together in organizational revitalization, they *might* develop delightful organizations—just possibly.

I started with a quote from Tocqueville and I think it would be fitting to end with one:

> *I am tempted to believe that what we call necessary institutions are often no more than institutions to which we have grown accustomed. In matters of social constitution, the field of possibilities is much more extensive than men living in their various societies are ready to imagine.*

Study questions for selection seven

1. Having read Bennis, do you think any "bureaucracies" will be left by the year 2000? If so, which ones?

2. Have you seen many examples of what Bennis calls "revitalization" within organizations that you know something about?

3. To what extent does Bennis's view of the future depend on economic growth and technological development?

Suggested readings for chapter six

Barnard, Chester I. *The Functions of the Executive.* Cambridge, Mass.: Harvard University Press, 1938.

Bennis, Warren. *Beyond Bureaucracy: Essays on the Development and Evolution of Human Organization.* New York: McGraw-Hill, 1973.

Downs, Anthony. *Inside Bureaucracy.* Boston: Little, Brown, 1967.

Golembiewski, Robert T. *Organizing Men and Power: Patterns of Behavior and Line-Staff Models.* Skokie, Ill.: Rand McNally, 1967.

Gulick, Luther, and Urwick, L., eds. *Papers on the Science of Administration.* New York: Augustus M. Kelley Publishers, 1937.

Katz, Daniel, and Kahn, Robert L. *The Social Psychology of Organizations,* 2d ed. New York: John Wiley and Sons, 1966.

Likert, Rensis. *The Human Organization: Its Management and Value.* New York: McGraw-Hill, 1967.

March, James G., and Simon, Herbert. *Organizations.* New York: John Wiley and Sons, 1958.

Mayo, Elton. *The Human Problems of an Industrial Civilization.* New York: The Viking Press, 1933.

Presthus, Robert. *The Organizational Society,* 2d ed. New York: St. Martin's Press, 1962.

Scott, William G., and Mitchell, Terence R. *Organization Theory: A Structural and Behavioral Analysis.* Homewood, Ill.: Irwin, 1972.

Simon, Herbert. *Administrative Behavior,* 3d ed. New York: Free Press, 1976.

Taylor, Frederick. *Principles of Scientific Management.* New York: W.W. Norton, 1911.

Waldo, Dwight. *The Administrative State.* New York: Ronald Press, 1948.

Staffing the agency: personnel administration

An important task in the management of any enterprise, private or public, is the recruiting, selecting, promoting, and terminating of personnel. Personnel management stretches far beyond these four actions, however, to include such matters as employee training, the development of morale, and the handling of union-management relations.

The ubiquity of the personnel function

The extent to which administrators become involved in personnel matters depends, of course, on their organizational specializations and positions. The scientist who directs a government research laboratory might wish to devote full attention to the organization's research projects and avoid becoming bogged down with staff problems; but personnel problems are likely to intrude, as when a research chemist is attracted by the offer of a faculty position at a university, when technicians quarrel over the assignment of cleanup chores, or when everyone is dissatisfied with the annual salary increase. Similarly, from the worker's perspective, a government employee in a heavy-equipment maintenance shop may have fairly precise duties assigned, work on a fixed schedule, and have satisfactory pay and working conditions; yet, at the same time he may deal on a daily basis with shop rules that conflict with union rules and with a supervisor who acts as though he has the power to fire any employee for the smallest infraction. No administrator can afford the luxury of total ignorance of public employment administration, and all personnel are involved in it, at least minimally, through their own relationships to the agency as employees.

For those in supervisory positions, the knowledge of personnel administration must be especially great. Understanding the employer-employee relationship requires a grasp of what Herbert Simon has called the inducements-contributions balance that exists between the agency and each employee.[1] What is it that attracts the individual to a given position? And what is the worker willing and able to contribute to the enterprise in return? Although the widespread use of merit systems has constrained the administrator in selecting subordinates, discretion is not eliminated completely; nor are other opportunities to influence personnel administration destroyed. We can briefly examine in this chapter only a few of the currently important issues in public employment administration, but the centrality of the personnel task to the total administrative process should be kept in mind.

M erit systems

Of the 2.8 million civilian employees of the federal government, about 90 percent are now employed under some form of *merit system*.[2] By merit system we mean a set of procedures that limits the impact of partisan politics on public employment, that provides competitive examinations for job seekers, and that prohibits firing of employees on political grounds. Former president Nixon took the most recent important step to assure that federal personnel are employed on the

---

[1] Herbert A. Simon, *Administrative Behavior,* 3d ed. (New York: Macmillan, 1976), pp. 110–22.

[2] O. Glenn Stahl, *Public Personnel Administration,* 7th ed. (New York: Harper and Row, 1976), p. 48.

basis of such a system when he extended merit system coverage to more than 60,000 postmasters and rural letter carriers. Previously, getting one of these federal jobs depended principally upon the applicant's political affiliation and connections with particular candidates. Before making an appointment, the president or postmaster general would seek specific recommendations from members of the president's party in Congress. When filling vacancies in areas where the president's party held no congressional seats, the president would usually accept recommendations of key party officials, such as state or county party chairmen. During the 1950s, when Republicans controlled the White House for eight years, lifelong Democrats in some areas of the Deep South went so far as to reregister as Republicans in order to increase their chances of appointment. Doing so might have helped them considerably, since some counties had only ten to twenty Republicans—most of whom were not applying for the same job.

The extension of coverage to postmasters is only the most recent of many steps. Well into the present century, the prime means of securing most governmental positions was to support the winning political candidate; the degree of support was a main determinant of the level of position that one could reasonably expect.

State and local governments have been slower than the federal government in expanding the coverage of their merit systems. Since 1940 there has been federal pressure on the states to do so. Requirements, instituted in that year, stipulated that personnel of many state agencies receiving federal grants-in-aid must be employed on the basis of merit. Failure of a state to provide a merit system, covering at least these employees, meant risking withdrawal of federal funds. Consequently, all states have at least partial merit system coverage. By 1975, thirty-four states had gone even further than required and implemented relatively thorough statewide merit systems. Among local governments the variation is wider. Some large cities have highly developed systems and many have at least partial ones. Most county employees, however, are still politically appointed.[3]

The personnel process

As merit systems at all levels expanded, their operating procedures became increasingly complex and detailed. Although they accomplished many of the same basic tasks performed under the system of political appointment, their operations were now formalized and subject to public

---

[3]Ibid., pp. 49–50.

scrutiny. Personnel administration has become a profession. Several of its activities can be mentioned briefly.

Position classification

Of central importance to the functioning of a personnel system is the scheme of *position classification*. If individuals are to have their qualifications for government jobs systematically evaluated according to universal criteria, clear and precise descriptions of the jobs in question must be available. Usually it is possible to group similar individual positions into a category, referred to as a *class*. Personnel managers and the staff of central personnel agencies participate in evaluating responsibilities associated with each job in order to assure proper classification. The job characteristics considered might include the level and difficulty of duties, the qualification requirements (skills, education, etc.), and the degree of supervisory responsibility.

Compensation plan

The establishment of a *compensation plan* is a partial responsibility of personnel administrators. Frequently, another agency—especially the budget agency—may participate in compensation decisions, but the need for close correspondence between job classification and pay makes this essentially a personnel function. Recently, the growing role of unions among public sector employees has resulted in compensation plans being set largely through negotiations.

Recruiting

Once jobs have been created and classified and compensation for the positions has been set, what more remains of personnel administration? Obviously, finding people to fill those jobs—the recruitment of personnel. Public administration in the United States has come a long way from the time of Andrew Jackson, when, in the popular view, government jobs could be performed by any individuals (or at least any *men*) with normal intelligence. As indicated in chapter 2, under Jackson and his successors, frequent rotation in office was encouraged; no particular prior training or experience was necessary for most jobs. According to Jackson:

<blockquote>The duties of all public officers are, or at least admit of being made, so plain and simple that men of intelligence may readily qualify themselves for their performance; and I can not but believe that more is lost by the long continuance of men in office than is generally to be gained by their experience.[4]</blockquote>

Jackson thus defended both his appointment of "common" people and his removal of his predecessors' appointees.

These views persisted for many decades, changing only gradually, partly in reaction to the corrupt aspects of "spoils politics." In time, public employers began to be urged to seek well-educated, trained, and experienced personnel. But the egalitarian thrust persisted, too. For a long time, the recruitment efforts of the federal government were mainly limited to the posting of job notices in post offices. State and local governments continued to operate under spoils systems or quite rudimentary merit systems that undertook hardly any recruitment. Where used, merit systems were designed for the most part to *keep out* the grossly incompetent, not to *attract* the highly qualified.

Gradually, the pattern changed. The federal government, followed by the state and local governments, began attempting to attract especially competent applicants. Openings were more highly publicized, recruiting visits were made to college and university campuses, and wages were made more nearly competitive with those in the private sector. Congress established procedures for regular comparisons of public with private pay, and a system of advisory bodies to recommend changes was created. Table 7–1 presents the pay rates in effect in 1978.

Even with efforts to approach pay comparability, however, a problem persisted. The relatively low popular image of public employment discouraged some from applying. Studies indicate that citizens view federal employment less favorably than employment in the private sector, and state and local employment is held in lower esteem than federal.[5] Even though almost one-fifth of the labor force is employed by government, the view that government employment is not quite respectable persists. For instance, faculty members of state universities, who often make derogatory remarks about public employment, seem to ignore

---

[4]James D. Richardson, ed., *A Compilation of the Messages and Papers of the Presidents 1789–1908* (New York: Bureau of National Literature and Art, 1909), vol. 2, p. 449.

[5]George Frederickson, "Understanding Attitudes toward Public Employment," *Public Administration Review* 27 (December 1967): 411–20. An earlier study, based on a broader sample, is Franklin K. Kilpatrick, Milton C. Cummings, Jr., and M. Kent Jennings, *The Image of the Federal Service* (Washington, D.C.: Brookings Institution, 1964).

Table 7–1. **Annual pay rates of general scheduled federal employees by grade, 1977**

Grade	Pay range
GS 1	$ 6,219–8,082
GS 2	7,035–9,150
GS 3	7,930–10,306
GS 4	8,902–11,575
GS 5	9,959–12,947
GS 6	11,101–14,431
GS 7	12,336–16,035
GS 8	13,662–17,757
GS 9	15,090–19,617
GS 10	16,618–21,604
GS 11	18,258–23,739
GS 12	21,883–28,444
GS 13	26,022–33,825
GS 14	30,750–39,975
GS 15	36,171–47,025
GS 16[a]	42,423–53,735
GS 17[a]	49,696–56,324
GS 18[a]	58,245

Source: U.S., Civil Service Commission, *Salary Table No. 63, Executive Branch of the Government* (Washington, D.C.: U.S. Government Printing Office, 1977).

[a]Despite the scheduled amounts, the actual pay of these employees is presently limited by congressional action to a maximum of $47,500.

totally the fact that they and everyone around them are public employees—even "bureaucrats."

Recent events have added a new dimension to the recruitment effort. Legislatures and courts have increasingly required that active efforts be made to attract individuals who, in earlier times, would have been excluded from public employment because of their ethnic or racial backgrounds or because they were women. These *affirmative action* efforts have been the center of considerable controversy.

The famous *Bakke* case *(Regents of the University of California* v. *Allan Bakke)*, though concerning university admission rather than employment, is an important example of such controversies. On July 3, 1978, the U.S. Supreme Court, divided five to four, ruled that affirmative action plans can be lawful, but that the rigidity with which they are applied and the specific circumstances surrounding their application are open to legal challenge. For instance, such plans may include race as one factor in a university's admissions policy (and presumably also in an employer's hiring policy). Furthermore, such plans may be particularly appropriate (even if they require hiring certain percentages of minority race individuals) if the employer had in the past explicitly discriminated against such individuals. Furthermore, they may be legal as efforts to remedy the injustice done by society to all members of minority races and women if they do not require specific numbers or percentages (quotas). In examining the policy of the University of California at Davis, where Bakke had been excluded from medical school because sixteen places were reserved for minorities, the Court found the particular plan too rigid and ruled that Bakke must be admitted. It should be noted, however, that the various aspects of the *Bakke* ruling just discussed were decided upon by a shifting majority on the Court. Thus, more time is necessary to be sure about how to interpret the ruling; and if membership on the Court should change, so might the ruling. Coming months and years will bring more challenges and more court rulings as governments seek equity in hiring practices and protection of merit systems, but simultaneously try to overcome effects of past discrimination.

Examining

Once applications have been received, the next step in the personnel process is examination. The term *examination* does not refer only to a pencil-and-paper test. Some judgments are made on the basis of an *unassembled examination*. That is, the application form itself may require sufficient information to permit the assignment of a score based on reported experience and education and on references. Another possibility, especially important for jobs requiring particular skills, is a *performance examination*. Perhaps the most familiar is a "words per minute" typing test, but performance examinations are used also for a variety of other equipment operator positions. Furthermore, some jobs call for an *oral examination,* particularly those for which communication skills are especially important. One examination of special importance is the *Professional and Administrative Career Examination (PACE)*. Open to college graduates who majored in almost any field, PACE is intended to select candidates for federal government *careers* rather than for particular jobs. Some of these will be careers in general administration, but others will be careers in a specific profession.

A problem in the examination process, as in recruiting, is the need to avoid discrimination against minorities or women. Complicating this issue is that, until recently, very few efforts were made by any governmental units to validate the tests employed. Did they measure what they were supposed to measure? Were the measured characteristics really important for the job to be filled? In most cases, no definite answer could be given. A 1971 study of all large state and local personnel systems revealed that only 54 percent of them systematically validated *any* of their tests. That means, of course, that nearly half validated none at all.[6]

Charges that examinations discriminate illegally have led to a flow of litigation that is likely to continue and result in further modifications of the examination process. Because of their less well-developed personnel systems, the pressure will be particularly great on state and local governments.

Selecting

Following the establishment of examination scores, based on any or all of the examination types referred to above, the selection process begins—if the position is to be filled by a person recruited from outside the agency. An alternative, of course, is to fill a vacancy by promotion or transfer, procedures that lead to their own problems of equity and morale. For present purposes, however, we assume that the position is to be filled from the outside. In this case, the most common practice is for the personnel agency (e.g., Civil Service Commission) to supply a list of those eligible for the job. Most commonly, the list includes the names of the three individuals with the highest examination scores. There can be, however, a complicating factor. A number of governmental jurisdictions, including the federal government, use a device called *veterans' preference* to award bonus points to all veterans and even more to disabled veterans, provided they pass the examination with some minimum score. The federal government awards all veterans five points and disabled veterans ten. Thus, the three names the agency official receives

---

[6]Jean J. Couturier, "Court Attacks on Testing: Death Knell or Salvation for Civil Service Systems?" *Good Government* 87 (Winter 1971): 10–12.

Why does a fireman wear red suspenders?
A. ☐ *The red goes well with the blue uniform.*
B. ☐ *They can be used to repair a leaky hose.*
C. ☐ *To hold up his pants.*
Drawing by D. Fradon; © 1974 The New Yorker Magazine, Inc.

might not be those who performed best on the examination; they may have been overtaken by three veterans. Some states carry veterans' preference even further, moving them all the way to the top of the list if they minimally pass the examination. It is obvious that these practices may result in the employment of less well qualified individuals; they also result in discrimination against women, since women are less likely to be veterans.

With or without veterans' preference, the typical agency official finally has a list of three names from which to choose the new employee. Interviews may then be held, and considerable discretion is allowed in making the final choice—as long as it is from the three-person list. Following selection, the new employee is likely to serve a probationary period, often six months, during which removal is relatively easy. Personnel managers encourage supervisors to see this as an extension of the testing procedure, but few employees are, in fact, dismissed during this period.

Evaluation

The evaluation of employee performance is a further personnel function. Recently, the trend has been to formalize rating schemes and to regularize feedback to employees.[7] Where possible, objective measures of the work completed are employed. In jobs where this is not possible, supervisors are encouraged to judge performance as accurately as possible using impressionistic techniques and to avoid being unduly influenced by such employee characteristics as age, sex, race, religion, physical appearance, or personality type.

The formalization of evaluation can serve both the agency and the employee. Obviously, the provision of helpful (not always negative) feedback to employees can improve morale and otherwise serve management purposes. By supplying a continuing record of performance, such formalization can also protect employees from capricious actions. Previously, if a supervisor suddenly declared that an employee's performance had been below standard for three years, there was nothing the employee could do to challenge the charge of long-standing poor performance. With regular evaluation, the record of earlier judgments can be used as a defense against capricious action.

Discipline

Finally, to cope with problems arising after employment, a personnel system must provide for disciplinary actions.[8] These range from formal or informal reprimands, through suspension, reassignment, and demotion, to dismissal. As with recruitment and selection—and, for that matter, throughout the personnel process—a fine line must be drawn between the rights and needs of the employee and the responsibility of the public agency, and various safeguards and checks—including rights of appeal—have been developed in an attempt to strike the necessary balance.

---

[7]N. Joseph Cayer, *Public Personnel Administration in the United States* (New York: St. Martin's Press, 1975), p. 82.

[8]Additionally, several peripheral activities are associated with personnel administration, such as the management of insurance and retirement programs and the maintenance of personnel records.

Reforming the federal civil service system

In March of 1978, President Carter proposed a series of civil service reforms, which he labeled "the centerpiece of government reorganization" during his term in office.[9] Congress approved these organizational and procedural changes in October of 1978.

This new legislation replaced the Civil Service Commission, which previously directed the main federal merit system, with two entities. A Merit Systems Protection Board will hear appeals from government employees regarding conflicts with the agencies employing them. A second agency, the Office of Personnel Management, would be responsible for developing and implementing policies regarding the recruitment, testing, and hiring of employees. Formerly, the Civil Service Commission was responsible for the tasks of both of these new agencies. A further organizational change has created a Federal Labor Relations Authority to oversee labor-management relations in federal employment, much as the National Labor Relations Board does in the private sector.

The procedural changes congress passed are too numerous to cover in a brief discussion, but some important ones should be mentioned. Two changes were designed to increase the initiative of managerial level employees. A Senior Executive Service, consisting of about 8,000 top-level administrators, was created. These persons, at the level of GS 16 or higher, will be able to be transferred from agency to agency as needed, will have their salaries adjusted on the basis of their performance, and can be demoted to the lower-level positions if their work is not satisfactory; furthermore, bonuses will be available to superior performers. The second change enacted of this type, which also deviates from the present practice of basing pay increases on length of service, would apply to managers at levels GS 13 through GS 15. A portion of their pay increases will now come in the form of incentive pay based on performance evaluations. President Carter's hope appears to be that these changes will encourage managers to use greater initiative in improving their own and their agencies' services.

A second procedural change will make it easier for managers to discipline employees, even to fire them. Furthermore, the new Merit Systems Protection Board will hear appeals of disciplined employees more rapidly than formerly was so and will render speedier judgments.

Finally, the president's proposals included a request to reduce the

---

[9]"Civil Service Reform," *Congressional Quarterly Weekly Report* 36 (11 March 1978): 658–60. This article reproduces the text of President Carter's message to Congress of March 2, 1978.

benefits accorded veterans. As noted above, all veterans applying for civil service jobs have been receiving a five-point bonus, while disabled veterans have received ten points. Under the president's proposals, the treatment of disabled veterans would have been unchanged, but for others the five-point bonus would have been available for only ten years. High-ranking retired officers would have received no bonus points, and other retirees would have had theirs limited to three years. The veterans' interest groups succeeded in defeating most of these proposed reductions in veterans' preference. Instead, Congress eliminated preference points only for retired military officers at or above the rank of major, leaving them available for other veterans.

Overall, Congress gave the president most of what he wanted. Taking all of the provisions into account, these changes mark the most extensive revisions in the federal personnel system since passage of the Pendleton Act in 1883.

Continuing education in the public service

Government is, of course, deeply involved with the further education and training of the employees in whom it has such a large investment. This involvement may range from relatively simple, in-house training sessions—even on-the-job training—to the financing of undergraduate or graduate education. Many universities, in cooperation with government agencies, have developed special programs for public employees. Federal and, to a lesser extent, state agencies have contracted with these universities to provide a variety of short courses for their employees. These courses, which typically last about one week, may be conducted either at a university campus or at an agency site. Topics covered range from managerial subjects, such as human relations or leadership, to highly technical matters, such as innovations in engineering or medicine. In addition, many agencies provide similar short courses taught by their own personnel.

A milestone in continuing education for public administrators was the establishment of the *Federal Executive Institute* in Charlottesville, Virginia, in 1968. Operated by the Civil Service Commission, this institution provides managerial training for high-level federal executives. The commission also has regional training centers located throughout the country. An important step, taken in 1970, was the passage of the Intergovernmental Personnel Act, which authorized federal agencies to include state and local personnel in their training programs and facilitated temporary personnel exchanges among governmental units. Furthermore, the law authorized grants to state and local governments for their own training programs.

Another important contribution has been the willingness of universities to modify their traditional course systems to meet more adequately the needs of public employees. For example, the public administration programs of both the University of Oklahoma and the University of Southern California offer master's degrees at locations where there are high concentrations of federal employees, most notably in Washington, D.C. These programs are based on course work taken as intensive seminars. Rather than leaving their jobs for several semesters, under programs such as these students can take off work for one week at a time to attend individual courses, but they spend thirty or more hours in the classroom during that week and engage in extensive preliminary study. Southern California has recently extended its program to the doctoral level (the Doctor of Public Administration is offered), while Oklahoma offers its master's program at locations both in the Far East and in Europe. Other universities vary their schedules by offering evening courses at military installations and state capitols and by offering courses with weekend classroom work. All of these have been important additions to the many standard-format university programs available for public personnel, who are often given leaves for a semester or a year by their agency to pursue a degree.

Morale and motivation

One important development in the field of personnel administration during the last two decades has been the decentralization of responsibility from the central personnel agency (Civil Service Commission in the federal government) to individual agencies. In classifying, setting compensation, recruiting, examining, selecting, evaluating, and disciplining, the agencies must, of course, operate under regulations provided by the central personnel system. As the personnel function has been strengthened within agencies, the decentralized personnel offices have in many cases assumed responsibility for assisting top-level administrators in attempting to motivate employees and encourage high morale. The offices often undertake studies of employee attitudes about their jobs and develop recommendations for modifying their responsibilities, reassigning their tasks, etc.

Morale and motivation, which are often closely linked to traditional personnel concerns, can be greatly affected by decisions regarding the filling of vacancies—promotion from within or recruitment from without. Compensation plans that assure relatively equal pay for equal work can also be important, as can job security and fringe benefits. Since personnel offices become involved in determining all of these, it is logical that they be advisors regarding morale and motivation.

The issues today: unionization and equity

While all the sections of this chapter touch on important issues that confront personnel administrators, two currently controversial issues cut across all of the topics discussed: unionization and equity.

The face of American private industry began to change during the last century as unions were formed, but not until much later in the present century was the power of unions felt in certain industries and some sections of the country. Today, it is apparent that unions have had and continue to have an enormous impact on working conditions in this country. It is difficult to imagine, for example, an American automobile industry without the United Auto Workers.

Despite such important gains in the private sector, and despite a legal right to organize granted in 1912, unions of federal government employees have grown only slowly. The growth has been even slower in most states and localities. But as the Nigro article below indicates, unions are now a major feature of public employment systems. Matters previously considered "management" prerogatives are now subject to negotiations. Since 1962, federal employees have had a guarantee of the right to bargain collectively. Some states have afforded similar rights to their employees and those of local jurisdictions. Formal negotiations, covering not just salaries but working conditions, fringe benefits, training programs, and vacation schedules are becoming commonplace. While many jurisdictions formally prohibit strikes, unions sometimes openly violate such statutes or engage in *"job actions"*: slowdowns, rigid adherence to rules and regulations (which bog down work in red tape), or "sick-ins." Furthermore, the unions use their political powers and lobby legislative bodies to achieve their demands. There can be no doubt that these developments are changing the merit system.

Equity—or the lack of it—is the second major issue. As with the issue of unionization, the public sector does not stand alone. Private employees, too, are confronted by questions of equity, but public employees bear special responsibilities. A democratic system that seeks to assure equal treatment under law for its citizens would be severely remiss if its own personnel practices discriminated on the basis of sex, race, or religion. Public agencies at all levels have, on occasion, done just that—sometimes intentionally, sometimes not. The challenge today is to eliminate such discrimination while preserving valuable features of the personnel system.

Some theorists promote equity because they see it as a means of attaining a broader goal: a *representative bureaucracy*. This goal is pursued for a variety of reasons. Among the most common is the hope that a public service that was, in effect, a microcosm of the society at large would be more likely to make decisions faithfully reflecting society's views than an unrepresentative, elitist public service. In his investigation of the subject, Kenneth Meier said the test of representative bureaucracy is "whether or not the social characteristics—the education, occupation, social status, and similar measures of the bureaucracy—mirror those exhibited by the American public."[10] After subjecting the federal bureaucracy to this test, Meier concluded: "The evidence clearly contradicts the existence of representative bureaucracy in the United States."[11] The rarity of nonwhites and women among the higher GS ratings is particularly striking. Whether a more socially representative bureaucracy really would be attentive to the views of the populace and whether the decisions made by such bureaucrats really would be better in various senses of the term than those made by the present bureaucrats (whose socioeconomic status is higher than that of most of the population) is questionable. Nonetheless, representative bureaucracy has become an article of faith for many theorists and personnel officials.

The selections that follow elaborate on the impacts of unionization and demands for equity. They provide a background against which the reader can judge particular controversies—teacher strikes, demands that universities hire more minority-group faculty members—and assess the changes occurring in public personnel systems.

Selection eight

The implications of collective bargaining for public administration*

Felix A. Nigro

In recent years, an important new element has been added to the public personnel process. Whereas personnel officials and other admin-

---

[10]Kenneth John Meier, "Representative Bureaucracy: An Empirical Analysis," *American Political Science Review* 69 (June 1975): 528.

[11]Ibid., p. 541.

istrators, the civil service commission (where one existed), and the chief executive once were the principal actors in determining classification and hiring practices, public employee unions have become very important actors in these decision processes. As Felix Nigro (Professor of Political Science at the University of Georgia) points out in this selection, unions also have gained quite substantial influence in determining workers' pay and fringe benefits: three-fifths of the federal work force is represented by unions that are exclusive bargaining agents. On the state and local levels as well, the unions are in many cases supplanting the role of the legislature as the chief influence in determining the pay of public employees. Nigro examines several effects of the rising tide of unionization upon public administration and evaluates the implications of the changes for the relative influence of the actors in the policy-making process and for what Nigro understands the public interest to be.

The four years since publication of the March/April 1968 PAR symposium on "Collective Negotiations in the Public Service" make a big difference. The developments are clearer to identify, although not surprising, and there is more documentation to support predictions about the future. In this article, we will: (1) present in detail *eight* specific ways in which public administration has been affected; (2) consider the resulting changes in the relative influence of different participants in the public policy-making process; (3) discuss the concern about the public interest; and (4) conclude with a final, evaluative balance sheet.

Eight specific effects

First, bilateral determination of the conditions of work is now well-established for very large numbers of public employees. Fifty-eight percent of the federal work force is now represented by unions recognized as exclusive bargaining agents, which is "far greater than the coverage in private employment."[1] Furthermore, contrary to a lingering misconception, 35 percent of all federal white-collar employees are so represented; indeed, there are now more white-collar than blue-collar workers so represented. Of the more than a million state and local government employees in New York, 900,000 are exercising their collective bargaining rights under legislation passed in 1967. In New York City, about 280,000 of the some 370,000 municipal workers are represented by the six major unions. Some education authorities consider that

---

[1] *Labor Management Relations in the Federal Service, Executive Order 11491 As Amended by Executive Order 11616 of August 26, 1971, Reports and Recommendations United States Federal Labor Relations Council* (Washington, D.C.: The Council, 1971), p. 38.

collective bargaining is now the "prevailing decision-making style" in the public school systems.[2]

The rapidly growing membership base justifies employee leaders' optimism about winning representation rights for even higher percentages of the total work force. About one million federal employees are members of employee organizations, while,

> *Membership in unions and employee associations currently totals about two million, or more than one-third of all non-instructional fulltime employees of states, cities, counties, school districts and other local authorities, as compared with less than 30 percent organization of nonagricultural workers in the private sector.[3]*

Second, public officials are increasingly being policed through binding grievance arbitration clauses in collective contracts. Four years ago such clauses were far less common, and management often resisted them tooth and nail. Executive Order 11616 continues the provision in Executive Order 11491 permitting union-negotiated grievance procedures with binding arbitration; and it also requires *all* new agreements to contain negotiated grievance procedures for resolving disputes over interpretation of contract terms.

The significance of binding grievance arbitration was clear in the recent school teacher strike in Newark, New Jersey. The strike became inevitable when the Newark school board announced it would not agree to a new contract containing the provision for binding arbitration. Teachers who grieve transfers can get them canceled if the arbitrator agrees that management's action violates the contract or is otherwise unfair. Many teachers fear transfers to slum neighborhoods, and the whites are apprehensive that black-dominated school boards may transfer them out of their jobs. A compromise on this issue was reached as part of the final strike settlement in Newark.[4] While this was a dramatic confrontation, grievance arbitration is now curbing the discretion of numerous public officials in many routine and nonroutine matters, depending on the coverage of the contracts. The truth is that grievance arbitration, based on the principle of fairness guaranteed by final decision making by a neutral third party, is an important part of the "new public administration."

Third, unions are widening their participation in program policy making, whether or not they have this role in the contract. Many public officials are strongly opposed to contract provisions calling for joint management-union determination of program questions, such as class sizes, caseloads, and number of police in patrol cars. While management should not, and legally cannot, abdicate its role in many program areas, it is obvious from recent

---

[2]See George R. La Noue and Marvin R. Pilo, "Teacher Unions and Educational Accountability," in Robert H. Connery and William V. Farr, eds., *Unionization of Municipal Employees* (New York: The Academy of Political Science, Columbia University, 1971), p. 147.

[3]Jack Stieber, "State, local unions pass industry and still going," *LMRS Newsletter*, 2 (July 1971): 1.

[4]See Fox Butterfield, "At Root of Newark Teacher Strike: Race and Power," *New York Times*, 8, April 1971.

Chapter seven

218

developments, particularly in state and local government, that strong unions can influence and even determine certain program decisions even though denied such a role in the contract.

The instrument, both simple and blunt, is the "job action," threatened or actual. New York City is a good example; on repeated occasions, Mayor Lindsay and some of his department heads have insisted on their "management prerogatives"—but eventually made decisions which represent important concessions to union demands. Although it is thunderously proclaimed that management alone determines the budget, later it is quietly announced that the number of new positions requested for a particular department has been substantially increased. Management both decided—and listened to the unions!

According to one analysis, the

> *controversy over the establishment of an independent New York City Health and Hospitals Corporation to take over the city's decaying municipal hospital system remained insoluble until the union representing hospital workers gave its blessing—at a price in increased power for the union and its members that is not yet fully known.*[5]

Unions have always sought to influence decisions of this kind through lobbying and the political process, but now, despite antistrike laws, they have added the new wallop of the "job action."

Fourth, . . . the unions have intensified their political activities. Success in collective bargaining, far from causing diminished political activity, has been accompanied by stepped-up political action to capitalize on the power of expanded union memberships and a record of success in contract settlements. Political activity coalitions are constantly forming, with doctrinal differences submerged in the interest of greater impact in lobbying and in rewarding or punishing elective officials at the polls. The alliance between the AFL-CIO-affiliated AFSCME and the NEA, with the latter's history of disdain for "labor," is a strange one, dubbed an "odd-couple" arrangement by the AFT (the NEA's big competitor), which claims that, although it also is AFL-CIO, it was not even consulted on the pact by AFSCME.

Fifth, collective bargaining settlements are substantially increasing the personal service budget and contributing to the financial crisis in government, particularly at the state and local level. While comprehensive research findings in this area are still in the preparation stage,[6] the relationship between contract settlements and soaring budgets is obvious in many places.

With large numbers of public employees, even moderate increases can raise the wage bill by hundreds of thousands of dollars. Wages, pensions, and other "fringes" accounted for 56 percent of New York City's $7.8 billion budget in one recent fiscal year, with rising labor costs accounting for half of

---

[5]John M. Leavens et al, "City Personnel: The Civil Service and Municipal Unions," in pamphlet published for Institute of Public Administration in New York by Sage Publications, p. 17.
[6]The Brookings Institution will publish a monograph on this subject.

Staffing the agency

219

the budget increase. This rise in the wage bill, in a period of declining revenues, has naturally led to increased taxpayer interest in worker productivity, with management now in a better position to insist that the workers put out more. A beneficial result is that management is spurred to give greater attention to methods of evaluating program results and measuring worker productivity, whereas previously it tended to neglect these areas. At the same time, the unions, aware of the taxpayer discontent, know that they cannot expect the productivity question to be overlooked in contract negotiations.[7]

Sixth, the political environment of government makes collective bargaining different in important ways from bargaining in the private sector. While the role of "market discipline" in preventing excessive wage settlements has been exaggerated in the present era of giant companies and lessened competition, it is still true that consumers can elect to buy less expensive, nonunion-made products, or substitute products, of which many are available. The consumers of public (government) services have no such choice. Companies can move or go out of business; government agencies cannot.[8]

If this argument seems like theoretical economics not applicable today, evidence from the real world is clear, based upon the performance of principal "actors" in the political process—elective officials. When strikes in essential services are threatened or occur, chief executives and other politicians are very sensitive to the angry protests of the inconvenienced public which often hates the strikers but the inconvenience more. The tendency is to make substantial, relatively quick concessions to the government unions. Walkouts are not very extended, and, as the private sector experience shows, it is the *long* strikes which are the hardest for the unions to win.

Private companies sometimes manage to operate during massive walkouts by using supervisors to provide at least limited service. In some governmental jurisdictions the supervisors have full collective bargaining rights (not permitted supervisors under Taft-Hartley), and they may walk out with the nonsupervisory employees or overlook slowdowns—which means they cannot be counted on to side with the top management during labor disputes.[9]

Public employee leaders like AFSCME president Jerry Wurf insist that many politicians are hostile and that the government unions do not have excessive power. This certainly is true in many parts of the country, particularly in the small towns and the rural areas. It is in the big cities with heavily unionized employees and a record of resort to strikes that the potential for excessive union power appears greatest. Those proposing solutions for public employee disputes sometimes fail to take into account these variations. New

---

[7]On educational productivity, see Myron Lieberman, "Professors Unite!" *Harper's Magazine*, 243, no. 1457 (October 1971): 69.

[8]See Harry H. Wellington and Ralph K. Winter, Jr., "The Limits of Collective Bargaining in Public Employment," *Yale Law Journal*, 78 (June 1969); and John F. Burton, Jr., and Charles Krider, "The Role and Consequences of Strikes by Public Employees," and Wellington and Winter, "More on Strikes by Public Employees," *Yale Law Journal*, 79 (January 1970).

[9]See Anthony C. Russo, "Management's View of the New York City Experience," in Connery and Farr, pp. 87–88.

York City may be ripe for compulsory arbitration, but countless other jurisdictions do not need this last-ditch machinery.

The different environment in government does not justify denial of collective bargaining rights or even of a limited right to strike. To deny, however, the potential for undue union power in government under certain circumstances is simply to disregard the reality. The search for workable solutions in the public interest proceeds best when that reality is clearly understood and accepted.

Seventh, the decline in the power of civil service commissions, which are buffeted by forces besides the unions anyway, is continuing. The role of the commission, based on the civil service law, in recommending pay plans and revisions does not mean much when, as provided by another law, or on a de facto basis, pay and fringes are negotiated by management and union representatives. For various good reasons, the commissions, with rare exceptions, do not represent management at the bargaining table, and they usually are not in a position to influence the management stands greatly. Suffice it to say that a settlement desired by the chief executive and/or legislators will likely be concurred with by the commission, but it may not even be seriously asked for its opinion.

When collective bargaining agreements provide for final-step binding grievance arbitration, the civil service commission also loses its prestigious role as principal court of appeal for the aggrieved employee. Increasingly, important provisions of the civil service rules and regulations are negotiated along with economic benefits, which reduces the commission's policy-making role. It is not surprising that some labor relations experts, anxious to solidify management strength for dealing with the unions around the chief executive, are happy with the recommendation in the National Civil Service League's new Model Public Personnel Administration Law to abolish civil service commissions.

While the commissions decline, the position of many personnel directors is both clarified and strengthened. Frequently, they are either the chief spokesmen, or members, of the management's negotiating team, which makes it clear that they *are* part of management. The critical nature of labor relations, and their prominent role in it, give them an importance many have not had in the past. Their background for labor relations thus becomes a key consideration in their employment and training.

Eighth, the budgetary process is being affected in several ways. Negotiations and budgetary time tables should be synchronized; this is being attempted, but with not too much success since bargaining deadlocks often extend beyond budget submission and adoption dates. Somehow, chief executives and legislatures must make good estimates of the amounts needed in the budget to finance the labor contracts, so as to eliminate or reduce the need for supplementary appropriations, or for reductions-in-force or other cuts in already funded programs. Contrary to the long-expounded postulate of honesty in budgets, ways must be found to "hide" the estimated funds for the settlements in unsuspected parts of the estimates. The expectation is that the unions, if they knew the maximum amounts management would settle for, would ask for more.

Staffing the agency/
/**221**

Public administration and collective bargaining: one impression of changed roles

Policies governing pay and fringes		Other personnel policies[a]	
Before C B	**After C B**	**Before C B**	**After C B**
1. Legislature	1. Unions Chief executive	1. Legislature	1. Legislature
2. Chief executive	2. Legislature	2. Civil service commission	2. Unions Chief executive
3. Pressure groups (excluding unions)	3. Pressure groups (excluding unions)	3. Chief executive	3. Civil service commission
4. Unions	4. Budget director and department heads	4. Department heads	4. Department heads
5. Civil service commission and budget director	5. Civil service commission	5. Pressure groups (excluding unions)	5. Pressure groups (excluding unions)
6. Department heads	6. General public	6. Unions	6. General public
7. General public		7. General public	

[a]Recruitment, promotion, transfer, layoff, reinstatement, service rating, training, disciplinary, and other personnel processes.

[b]Determination of the content of legislation dealing with substantive programs of government.

[c]Policies made in carrying out substantive program authorized by the legislature.

Relative roles in the power game

Collective bargaining in government is visibly altering the relative shares of different individuals and groups in the formulation and implementation of public policy. An agenda for research to identify these changes in selected jurisdictions is presented in the table included in this article. Based on this writer's analysis of kinds of changes which have occurred, a scheme of rankings is proposed for verification by researchers in different communities. The rankings show relative roles for different participants *before* and *after* the introduction of collective bargaining (CB). Since there are different phases of policy making influenced by labor relations, the rankings are separate for these phases, as defined in the footnotes in the table.

Formulation of program policy[b]		Implementation of program policy[c]	
Before C B	**After C B**	**Before C B**	**After C B**
1. Legislature	1. Legislature	1. Chief executive	1. Chief executive
2. Pressure groups (excluding unions)	2. Pressure groups (excluding unions)	2. Department heads (including budget director)	2. Department heads (including budget director)
3. Chief executive	3. Chief executive	3. Pressure groups (excluding unions)	3. Pressure groups (including unions)
4. Department heads	4. Unions	4. Legislature	4. Legislature
5. Unions	5. Department heads	5. Unions	5. General public
6. General public	6. General public	6. General public	

There is no precise agreement by the participants and observers as to these relative shares, even before CB, and, of course, the picture varies by place, depending upon the extent of unionization, strength of the labor movement in the area, and other factors. While civil service commissions have had important influence in recommending pay and fringe benefit plans, their greatest power has been in recommending and implementing the rules and regulations which cover all aspects of the technical personnel program. Although these rules and regulations usually require the approval of the chief executive and sometimes of the legislative body, such approval without major change is generally much easier to obtain than for recommendations in the economic benefit area. (If this assumption is wrong, its inaccuracy would be revealed by the projected research.) If the investigations in a particular community reveal that the unions have jumped in influence, not only in determinations on economic benefits but also in general personnel policy formulation, this would document one of the "impressions" in the table. Another "impression" to be tested is that the unions also have climbed up several notches in program policy implementation, but not quite as many in program policy formulation.

Undoubtedly, some of the rankings in the table of other participants such as department heads and the general public will look "wrong" to many PAR readers; the idea, however, is to provide a usable guide for launching much-needed research in the volatile, emotion-laden area of labor relations. As to research methodology, interviewing and analysis of recorded decisions and of positions taken by the respective participants, and newspaper and other written accounts of the effective factors in the decisions would be used. While the influence process is obscure in some aspects, there is plenty of information in the hearing and other records of civil service commissions, and in the briefs and published statements of unions and taxpayer and other groups. The collective contracts themselves will provide much of the data. Quite a few insightful public officials are available to contribute opinions to the "before" and "after" comparisons; the "before" is not so long ago.

The public interest question

When, in the flush of their successes of the 1960s, some public employee leaders proclaimed the doctrine that collective contracts supersede provisions in existing laws and regulations, the "public interest" question came to the fore in an unprecedented way. If the price of bilateralism in determination of employment conditions was to be the shunting aside of the public and its legislative representatives in such decisions, then the net impact would be less democracy in the total political system.

Worries on this score have since lessened; as the result of court decisions, the resistance of appointed and elected officials, and a modification of the unions' own stand on this matter, the agreements generally are not wiping out laws and regulations.[10] It is now the *process* of collective bargaining in government which causes much of the concern about the public interest.

In an era of great pressures to reform existing institutions and make them "open," to some people the collective negotiations now taking place in government are unduly secretive. Too often the final "package," announced by management and union representatives after a long "blackout" period during which the press and the public are told very little, represents a very important commitment of community resources about which even legislators have had nothing to say.

Abe Raskin, the labor editor of the *New York Times*, knows that an essential element of private sector collective bargaining is closed negotiating sessions, but he and others believe that the public should be told in detail about management and union stands on proposals by mediators. Since the negotiations continue or resume after mediators intervene and make proposals, Raskin's position basically is that collective bargaining in government is different and requires divulgences to the public. "The people of New York are entitled to know what they are being asked to pay and what increased efficiency they can expect to get in return—before the deal is made, not after."[11]

---

[10]See Felix A. Nigro, "Collective Bargaining and the Merit System," ibid., pp. 55–67.
[11]*New York Times,* editorial page, 19, March 1971. © 1971 by The New York Times Company. Reprinted by permission.

Raskin may be wrong about making public mediators' recommendations, but his argument that the full costs, present and future, of settlements should be revealed to the public is unassailable. Management has sometimes been able to reduce the unions' demands for increased wages and other benefits by agreeing to liberal increases in pensions, to be funded, and therefore paid for, by the taxpayers at some future time.

Frank P. Zeidler, former mayor of Milwaukee, has suggested the possibility of public referenda on proposed contracts, just as on bond issues.[12] If the Rhode Island court interpretation, cited by Van Asselt above, is accepted, namely, that private arbitrators become public officials when they issue awards fixing government salaries, then it can be argued that there is clear justification for giving the public the opportunity to vote on arbitral awards and proposed settlements.

While collective bargaining in government has in recent years moved closer to the industrial model, there are many unresolved perplexing questions of how to modify that model to meet the special needs of government. The view is spreading that mediators, fact-finders, arbitrators, and the personnel of supposedly "neutral" labor relations agencies favor the "private" interests of the unions over those of the general public. The challenge is to create, in all necessary detail, a special kind of collective bargaining for government which will give sufficient protection to the public interest and thus allay these fears.

The balance sheet

The tendency is either to be for the unions or against, but the picture is a mixed one, as is so often the case with complicated developments. Our conclusions are:

1. Collective bargaining has proved itself a salutary check on public employer arbitrariness and paternalism. No review group analyzing the experience under existing collective bargaining programs in government has recommended their termination. Whatever the shortcomings found, the desirability of collective bargaining has been upheld by such groups as proved in practice.

2. Collective bargaining is an excellent antidote for the evils of bureaucracy. The employee feels that he counts for something through the strength of his union: now management *must* listen. It is possible that the unions have done more to alleviate the much-discussed conflict between organization and individual needs than any other force or technique.

3. Curbs on excessive union power *are* needed, and, in some places, compulsory arbitration may be the answer.

4. The difficulties in financing contract settlements have made the need for tax reform very clear; indeed, union leaders with vision are pushing efforts for such reform. They have a common interest with local officials in ending the

---

[12]Frank P. Zeidler, *New Roles for Public Officials in Labor Relations,* Public Employee Relations Library, no. 23 (Chicago: Public Personnel Association), p. 20.

heavy reliance on property taxes which has caused the virtual bankruptcy of so many cities.

5. Legislatures must assert their role, else chief executives and the unions may relegate them to an increasingly minor role in labor relations. Since the collective bargaining process does contribute to executive power, this is another point at which the modern legislature should hold firm against encroachment on its powers.

6. Civic groups and individual citizens can get in the act by developing strong positions in advance on contract negotiations. At present, they are usually silent and inactive while public management and the unions busily negotiate in private. Surely there is a way for the public to be heard before it is too late; the trouble is that too few people have as yet figured out when and how to inject themselves effectively into the changed decision-making processes.

There is no inexorable force which will make collective bargaining turn out one way or another, nor are the developments so swift as to make it problematic that humans can shape the future picture. Dramatic as the unionism is, its significance has not yet been appreciated by enough of the public or, for that matter, of public management.

Study questions for selection eight

1. Do you see any differences between the proper role of unions in the private sector and in the public sector?

2. How do you balance the following statements? (a) Unions protect workers from arbitrary behavior by employers and make workers feel their individual needs are being taken into account; (b) Unions have so much political power that they can force fat contract settlements which are unjustified and can bring some jurisdictions to the verge of bankruptcy.

3. Should public employee unions—especially those for police and fire-fighters—be allowed to go out on strike?

4. Is compulsory arbitration the solution to the strike or "job action" problem?

Are merit and equity compatible?*

Harry Kranz

Traditionally, the promoters of merit systems have been opposed to the intrusion of "political" factors into the public personnel process. Displays of favoritism toward political allies, friends, and relatives have drawn the reformers' greatest ire, because such behavior was in obvious conflict with the commonly expressed goal of filling public service positions with the best people available for the job. Recently, however, a new breed of reformers has questioned whether truly neutral, universal criteria have ever been applied systematically to a very large proportion of the American public service and even whether some degree of certain types of discrimination might not be a good thing.

In this selection, political scientist Harry Kranz of the U.S. Department of Labor argues that for a variety of reasons (relating mainly to considerations of social justice) it is desirable for the public service to be a "representative bureaucracy," more or less accurately reflecting the racial, ethnic, and sex composition of the nation. Furthermore, after a review of the operation of "merit" systems, he concludes that a number of factors unrelated to merit as it might be defined in a purely objective sense have, in fact, intruded into such systems. Veterans' preference discriminates against women, for example, and demanding formal educational qualifications for many jobs whose duties do not actually require them discriminates against members of minority groups. Kranz believes these and other discriminatory selection methods should be abolished and the public service should achieve proportional representation for currently underrepresented groups, especially minorities and women. Following his discussion of such controversial topics as "selective certification," "reverse discrimination," "affirmative action goals," and "compensatory preferential treatment," Kranz concludes that various means are available to increase the representation of these groups in the public service, which would increase social equity, without necessarily sacrificing the merit principle, properly understood.

Can we have both a "representative bureaucracy" in which minorities and women are equitably distributed, and a "merit system" of selecting government employees?

The presumed conflict between "merit" and "equity" arises out of two myths which have grown up about the functions of the bureaucracy and the accomplishments of the "merit system" in selecting the "most qualified" bureaucrats. Careful analysis disproves both.

During the past seventy-five years most discussion of bureaucracy has focused on its "service" function—whether the decisions and actions of the bureaucrats were good or bad for the public. This emphasis on bureaucratic "service" has tended to override two other significant functions of bureaucracy—as a source of jobs and economic betterment for citizens, and as a form of group representation in a democracy.

The quantity, quality, and impact of jobs with federal, state, and local governments can no longer be overlooked. More than 16 million Americans—nearly 19 percent of the work force—are now employed by government.[1] Not only is this the largest single "industry" in the United States, but it is also the fastest growing, with at least 4,000,000 more jobs projected for the public sector by 1980. Moreover, comparable jobs in government now pay higher wages than in the private sector, and those very groups, women and black men, heretofore excluded from full participation, benefit most from public employment.[2]

A variety of federally funded manpower programs ranging from the relatively small Public Service Careers to the relatively large Emergency Employment (PEP) Program, and the recently launched Comprehensive Employment and Training Act of 1973, gave priority in employment to the "disadvantaged," and permitted state and local governments to hire the "disadvantaged" outside the merit system, if necessary. By definition, most minority group members were included within the "disadvantaged" because of their high incidence of poverty, unemployment, and underemployment. Thus, a significant number of minorities have entered the public service since 1965 as a result of these federally subsidized programs.

In the past, the representative function of bureaucracy has received relatively little attention, because we tend to think of "representation" as a responsibility of the legislator elected to speak, vote, or act for the constituents of a geographical area. However, a second meaning can apply to both the legislator and the bureaucrat; each may "re-present" (i.e., present again) a social, economic, ethnic, or religious group whose characteristics and views he shares and reflects. Geographic representation is usually direct, overt, and conscious, but group representation may also be indirect, unconscious, and symbolic. It exists whenever the legislator or bureaucrat sees himself or is seen by "his" reference group or by others as mirroring that group in his public role.

The relevant question today is whether all racial ethnic and sex groups are adequately represented. By a "representative" bureaucracy, I refer to one

---

[1]U.S. Department of Labor, *The Employment Situation: February 1974,* Tables A-1 and B-1.

[2]Bennett Harrison, *Public Employment and Urban Poverty* (Washington, D.C.: The Urban Institute, 1971).

in which the ratio of each minority group in a particular government agency equals that group's percentage in the population in the area served by that office. Thus, a Washington office of a federal agency would be rated on the basis of the national population ratios (e.g. percent Spanish-speaking), and a city department on the basis of minority percentages in that city. Moreover, it must include equitable distribution of minorities at all levels of appointive positions, not just at the low entry levels.

In these terms, my own research has shown that women and minorities, including blacks, Chicanos, American Indians, and Orientals, are not equitably represented in most federal, state, and local government departments and agencies, particularly in their higher-paying professional jobs.[3]

[s a "representative bureaucracy" desirable?

My contention is that a "representative bureaucracy" is desirable for political, economic, and social reasons: it would have beneficial effects on minorities, on consumers and clients, on bureaucratic organizations, and on the American governmental system.

For minorities and women, increased public employment would provide greater income, job security, and living standards, as well as increased power, influence, and participation in government decision making. Increased economic and political status would lead to increased social status, both in their own eyes and in the eyes of others, within the organization and outside it.

Second, a more representative bureaucracy would benefit the recipients of public services, particularly members of minority groups, whether those services were directly furnished by minority staff or not. Clearly, no direct cause-and-effect relationship has been shown between increased representation for a social group and the policies advocated, decisions made, or services performed by a particular "representative" of that group in the bureaucracy.

However, we do expect that minority and female "representatives" *as a group* will more closely mirror the needs and wishes of *their* group, whether overtly or subconsciously, than nonminorities do, and that on *most* decisions and services, a bureaucracy with "ideal-type" representation of minorities and women will govern "better" than one which is unrepresentative. The decisions will be "better" because we subjectively believe democracy is "better" than oligarchy.

Third, equitable minority and female representation would be beneficial for the bureaucratic organizations themselves. By increasing the opportunities for decision making by a broader cross-section of the population, it would tend to dilute the discretionary power and influence currently vested in unrepresentative elites. Propinquity reduces ignorance and rejection; increased bureaucratic understanding of minority views and feelings would lead to greater responsiveness to minority problems and needs. Moreover, the

---

[3]Harry Kranz, "How Representative is the Public Service?" *Public Personnel Management 2,* (July-August 1973): 242–55.

infusion of new blood should increase internal democracy by stimulating diversity, egalitarianism, conflict, and change. While the organization might eventually co-opt the new employees to its norms, the increased reliance on equity and individual human factors could also lead to reduced bureaucratic pathology.

Finally, a more representative bureaucracy would increase the legitimacy of the entire American system by making the predominant arm of government—the nonelected bureaucracy—a closer reflection of the diverse population it represents, both actually and symbolically. For some consumers, it will mean improved services, decisions, and policies; for others, there would be increased acceptance of the legitimacy of policies and decisions rendered by a government *believed* to be more representative. Exclusion is morally and ethically wrong; equal opportunity is not only legally required, but socially just. Moreover, a representative bureaucracy would also provide a more efficient, as well as just, use of America's human, manpower resources, and would increase domestic tranquility and stability by reducing minority alienation, anomie, apathy, and antisocial behavior.

The "merit" myth

The second major myth creating an artificial conflict between equity and merit is the belief that virtually all public servants are chosen largely on the basis of "merit," usually evidenced by fair written tests, and that only the "best and the brightest" survive this scientific process to be appointed to federal, state, and local jobs.

Throughout American history, the concept of "merit" in public employment has had a rubbery texture, stretching or contracting to cover the prevailing ethos, but at no time either before[4] or after[5] adoption of the civil service reforms of the 1880s has *actual* merit (defined as the ability to perform a specific job) prevailed as the predominant or exclusive method of selecting the American bureaucracy.

In 1883 the "merit principle" simply meant determining who was minimally competent to perform a job of work, without regard to such irrelevancies as political considerations, but this soon was embroidered by the "scientific management" tools of position classification and psychological testing. As government activity and employment grew under the New Deal, job specialism blossomed and selection methods became less job-oriented.

Contrary to popular belief, most public employees in the United States today are not under a "merit system," and were not selected in accordance with "merit principles." Of the 16.4 million federal, state, and local govern-

---

[4]See, e.g., Sidney H. Aronson, *Status and Kinship in the Higher Civil Service: Standards of Selection in the Administrations of John Adams, Thomas Jefferson, and Andrew Jackson* (Cambridge: Harvard University Press, 1964).

[5]See, e.g., David H. Rosenbloom, *Federal Service and the Constitution: The Development of the Public Employment Relationship* (Ithaca, N.Y.: Cornell University Press, 1971).

ment employees, only 3.5 million, or 21 percent, are covered by authentic merit systems.[6] The rest are in the military services (2.3 million), education (6 million), skilled and unskilled laborers and postal employees governed by collective bargaining agreements, political appointees, and professionals whose selection is determined outside the "system." Moreover, for those included within what we loosely call "merit systems," nonmerit selection factors have persisted and grown.

These nonmerit selection factors have included both negative discrimination requirements and positive, preferential provisions. Among the discriminatory extrinsic considerations have been race, religion, sex, evidence of formal education, family relationship, friendship, and personality attributes. For example, overt, legal discrimination barred blacks from jobs well into the twentieth century, and women could legally be excluded from federal appointments as late as 1962.[7]

Similarly, not merit, but social equity has been the motivating ideology behind the many preferential provisions in civil service law and regulations. Best known is the preference given veterans, particularly disabled veterans and their families, in appointments and promotions, which tends to severely discriminate against women and disadvantaged minorities. In addition, however, age, physical handicaps, economic needs, and representation for regions and states, as well as particular interest groups, have diluted the merit concept.[8]

The new mandates

The key to the compatibility of merit and equity may be found in the historic *Griggs* decision,[9] in which Chief Justice Burger, speaking for a unanimous Supreme Court, struck down non-performance-related tests and educational requirements for appointment and promotion. In effect, *Griggs* held:

1. Where a particular minority (race, religion, nationality, or sex) is underrepresented in a job category in a government agency, it is evidence of de facto discrimination, regardless of whether or not the employer intended to discriminate, and the burden of proof shifts to the employer to prove the validity of his employment practices, including all of his "merit system" selection and promotion methods, requirements, procedures, and devices. These must be proven to be "a reasonable measure of job performance"; they "must measure the person for the job and not the person in the abstract." If they are not performance-related, they are illegal, and must be removed.

---

[6]This includes 2.2 million state and local government noneducation employees and 1.3 million federal general schedule employees.

[7]Don Hellriegel and Larry Short, "Equal Employment Opportunity in the Federal Government: A Comparative Analysis," *Public Administration Review* 32 (January/February 1972): 18–29.

[8]Eugene B. McGregor, Jr., "Social Equity and the Public Service," *Public Administration Review* 34 (January/February 1974): 18–29.

[9]401 U.S. 424 (1971).

Staffing the agency

231

2. Where selection procedures have not been or cannot be validated to measure job performance, the employer must rectify underrepresentation by accelerated hiring and promotion of members of the disadvantaged group.

A year after the *Griggs* decision there was another significant mandate, this time from Congress. The Equal Employment Opportunity Act of 1972 extended coverage of the Civil Rights Act of 1964 to federal, state, and local government employees, barring discrimination and requiring affirmative action to end it.

Changing the "system"

A variety of selection methods, whose feasibility has already been demonstrated, are available to increase minority and female employment.[10] Changes are needed in three major areas: (1) the policies and structure of the civil service and merit system agencies; (2) qualifications, requirements, and recruitment techniques; and (3) the selection methods utilized, particularly written tests.

The first of seven essential policy changes would require establishment and enforcement of specific numerical goals and timetables for the hiring and promotion at each salary/grade level of each minority group currently underrepresented in proportion to its percentage of the population served by the agency.[11] While the Civil Service Commission originally opposed establishing "goals and timetables" as a means of increasing minority and female representation, it now *permits* them, but has surrounded this permission with rhetoric against "quotas," has hedged the definition of "goals" with impossible requirements that minimize their utility, and has taken little action to ensure that agencies are progressing toward their goals on schedule.[12]

Although goals are not quotas,[13] even stringent goals and harsh methods to ensure their achievement, which would be tantamount to "quotas," may be

---

[10]Harry Kranz, "Government By All The People: The Why and How of a More Representative Public Service," *Good Government* 89 (Fall 1972): 1–7.

[11]Initiated by the U.S. Department of Labor's Office of Federal Contracts Compliance as part of the "Philadelphia Plan" to increase minority representation in the building and construction trades, this formula has been upheld as constitutional by the U.S. Supreme Court in *The Contractor's Association of E. Pa.* v. *Shultz et al.*, 404 U.S. 854, *cert. denied*, Oct. 12, 1971, affirming 442 F.2nd 159, 3 FEP Cases 395 (3rd Cir. 1971).

[12]M. Weldon Brewer, Jr., *Behind the Promises: Equal Employment Opportunity in the Federal Government* (Washington, D.C.: Public Interest Research Group, 1972).

[13]"A 'goal' is a realistic objective which an agency endeavors to achieve on a timely basis within the context of the merit system of employment. A 'quota' on the other hand would restrict employment or development opportunities to members of particular groups by establishing a required number or proportionate representation which agency managers are obligated to attain without regard to merit system requirements" (CSC Chairman Hampton, Memo to Federal agency heads, 11, May 1971). But see, e.g., the letter of 27 October 1972, by the EEOC chairman to all EEOC staff: "Such terms as 'quotas' and 'preferential hiring,' 'goals and timetables,' and 'proportional representation' mean different things to different people .... [W] here the facts have established ... that discrimination exists, a remedy must be devised .... Numerical proportions might well be included ...."

necessary where there is gross underrepresentation.[14] Thus, where agencies have not achieved their hiring goals and schedules and have failed to make "good faith" efforts to do so, the enforcement agency should require and institute four additional changes:

1. Establishment of rewards and punishments for individual managers based on their EEO performance;[15]

2. Restriction of hiring and promotion of overrepresented employees until equitable representation is attained for each relevant minority group;[16]

3. Providing automatic promotions for minority employees who complete relevant training programs, regardless of available "slots";[17]

4. In the case of federal grants to state and local governments, requiring that the grants be targeted on recruitment, selection, and training procedures designed to achieve the goals promptly.[18]

Moreover, since few civil service exams, whether written or unassembled, have ever been validated on the basis of the skills and ability required for the particular position,[19] comprehensive and accurate job analyses should be conducted to determine the performance requirements. Once these are known, pre-employment training programs can be established to train candidates for the jobs and at the same time evaluate their performance on a sample of the work to be done.[20]

The second area requiring change is the screening out of minority candidates through restricted recruitment and arbitrary qualifications requirements. Outreach to minority communities and institutions, utilizing empathetic personnel and appropriate media, are essential to effective recruitment. Similarly, all non-performance-related requirements for appointment or promotion should be eliminated, including age, sex, height, weight, residence, voting,

---

[14]Remedies already sanctioned or ordered by the courts include specific hiring "goals" and time-tables; minority preference in hiring and promotion; changes in recruitment, selection, placement, testing, systems of transfer, promotion, seniority, and lines of progression; and provision of back pay and legal costs. See R. Edison Elkins and Marvin Rogoff, "Collective Bargaining and Affirmative Action," *Public Management* 55 (July 1973): 17–19.

[15]Agency heads can be sued, even if the U.S. government can't, to remedy racial discrimination (Penn v. Schlesinger [5th Cir. No. 72–3684] Dec. 18, 1973).

[16]Carter v. Gallagher, 452 F.2nd 9th Cir., 1972; NAACP v. Allen, 4 EPD para, 7669, 1972. "An interim requirement that hiring and promotion be effected on the basis of at least one black for every two whites does not amount to the imposition of a quota system as such, nor does it discriminate against whites. It merely means that, unless and until the defendants can justify excluding a disproportionate number of blacks, they are not permitted to do so" (Penna. v. O'Neill, 473 F.2nd 1029).

[17]As is done in the "corps" career systems, but not for equity reasons.

[18]In 1971 the federal merit standards were amended to require affirmative action by state and local grant recipients to eliminate discrimination in employment and utilization of minorities and women covered by grants (U.S. Civil Service Commission, *Annual Report,* 1971 [Washington, D.C.: U.S. Government Printing Office], pp. 51–53). Instead of withholding federal grants from discriminating jurisdictions, the current unused drastic sanction, CSC should be empowered to direct use of the funds in ways designed to achieve equitable representation.

[19]"Survey of Current Personnel Systems for State and Local Governments," *Good Government* (Spring 1971), pp. 12–19. E. S. Savas and Sigmund G. Ginsburg, "The Civil Service: A Meritless System?" *The Public Interest* (Spring 1973): 74.

[20]Examples of such programs include Peace Corps, VISTA, Project CAUSE, New Careers.

arrest record, nonrelevant convictions, and degrees or years of education.

The third and most effective barrier against equitable minority and female representation has been the inequitable selection methods utilized. Surprisingly, most government employees covered by "merit systems" are no longer appointed or promoted following a written test;[21] however, it is still the largest single method and the principal means of excluding minorities, despite overwhelming evidence that written "merit" tests are useless for many jobs, are poorly constructed and unreliable, and are rarely able to predict successful performance on specific jobs.

While "unassembled" (noncompetitive) ratings of training and experience and work sample or performance tests are now the predominant means of selection, less than half of the federal and only 10 percent of the state and local exams appear to meet the *Griggs* requirement.[22] In rating candidates without written tests, the same mistakes are being repeated—setting arbitrary qualification requirements, basing job requirements on ancient or nonexistent job analyses, and failing to determine that the required education and experience is reasonably related to job performance.

Where the essential tasks to be performed can be recorded through careful job analysis, any one of three equitable selection methods can be utilized to determine relative ability:

1. Competitive performance tests of a sample of the job to be done (e.g. typing or driving), and unassembled evaluations of samples of the applicants' work products (e.g. a writer's articles).

2. "Unassembled" bio-data forms to determine and rate experience and training relevant to the specific job and obtain accurate appraisals of the candidate's qualifications from past employers, trainers, and associates.

3. Structured oral interviews by selection boards containing minority and female representatives, particularly where, as in telephone switchboard and receptionist positions, public speaking is a job requirement.

On the other hand, where it is not feasible to determine relative ability to perform the job, two other methods are available for use where minorities and women are underrepresented. Recognizing that all tests are subject to a statistical margin of error (even if the test is valid), and that there is no sanctity to "passing marks" or relative rankings, these methods are:

---

[21]At the federal level, only 80,000 or 44 percent of the 180,000 persons selected from Civil Service registers for appointment in fiscal year 1973 in the general service and wage board pay systems received a written test as part of the selection process. (Estimate derived from U.S. Civil Service Commission data furnished the author, March 1974). Only 47 percent of the state and local classes of jobs were filled by written tests in fiscal 1972. (U.S. Civil Service Commission, *Statistical Summary of Reviews of Personnel Operations: State and Local Agencies*, 1973, p. 5).

[22]Of the 100,000 federal appointees (56 percent) in the GS and wage board systems selected without written tests in fiscal 1973, about 42,000 skilled and unskilled laborers were admitted as a result of an "unassembled" review matching their experience with relevant "job elements," while the remainder were mainly professionals whose appointments followed an "unassembled" review of their education and experience. Only the performance test for typists and the unassembled job element matching for skilled laborers appear to meet the *Griggs* test. Of the 53 percent of state and local job classes filled without written tests, only 10 percent of the state and 7 percent of the local job categories were filled by performance tests in fiscal 1972 *(ibid)*.

1. Pass-fail tests (written, oral, or unassembled), whereby only the minimum essential requirements for the job are established, and priority in appointment from among all those with "pass" grades goes to those individuals whose group (race, sex, nationality, etc.) is most underrepresented in the particular position.[23] If a representative work force has been attained in that bureau, or if more members of the underrepresented minority are eligible than there are positions open, selection can be based on such neutral criteria as random lottery, order of application, or (in the case of promotions) seniority.

2. Allowing extra "points" toward appointment or promotion to candidates with minority backgrounds or qualifications, or instituting "selective certification" of minorities and women,[24] where warranted.

Some have contended that such preference is "reverse discrimination" against innocent members of the majority group (i.e., white males). Selective perception appears to be at work here, since minorities and women have been discriminated against in public employment as a *group* and *their* individual abilities and skills ignored for nearly two hundred years without audible protest by the favored groups.

Second, the notion of compensating a group for social inequities is not a new one—either in American law or in public employment. Courts have not only ordered rectification for groups in class action suits where individual damages could not be estimated, but the Supreme Court has ruled that race may be considered in formulating a remedy, when racial discrimination has been shown. In public employment, white male veterans, Indians, and the needy have been among the past beneficiaries of compensatory preferential treatment.

Third, even where an innocent majority group member is denied a job or promotion because social justice impels preference to an underrepresented minority group member, such balancing of the equities is warranted. It is still easier for members of majority groups to obtain public employment and other privileges than it is for a minority group member; hence, the individual majority group member will suffer lesser damages than the minority person would if denied appointment or promotion. Of course, no one would be discharged or demoted to give preference to minorities, and once a particular bureau achieves proportional representation, special preferences would not apply.

Finally, it should be remembered that there is no discrimination, reverse or otherwise, if the performance requirements of the job have not or cannot be determined accurately. In that case, it cannot be contended that one candidate is "better qualified" than another, because we do not know what qualifications are needed. Both are in the same eligible pool, equally qualified, and the desirabil-

---

[23]National Civil Service League, *A Model Public Personnel Administration Law* (Washington, D.C.: National Civil Service League, 1970), sec. 3(d)(4). "This means 'pass-fail' certification. Our survey of civil service systems shows that about 1/3 of the nation's civil services now use 'pass-fail' certification" (National Civil Service League, "Policy Statement on Equal Employment Opportunity in the Public Sector," November 1972).

[24]See U.S. Civil Service Commission, Bureau of Intergovernmental Personnel Programs, *Guidelines for Reevaluation of Employment Requirements and Practices Pursuant to Emergency Employment Act* (Washington, D.C.: U.S. Civil Service Commission, 1972), p. 11. Federal civil service rules permit selective certification and have been used to increase Spanish-speaking representation.

ity of a more representative work force sanctions priority to the most underrepresented group.

The last point is the hardest of all for friends of merit to comprehend. I do not want to lower relevant standards or hire the incompetent when we *know* the standard required for performance of the job (e.g., typist, writer) and can adequately measure the skills and aptitudes needed. Unfortunately, for most public-sector jobs today, we do not have or aren't using performance-related criteria. If this means that some specialists and some supervisors will be appointed or promoted who will have to learn to do their jobs better through training and further experience, it is the price we will have to pay for having tolerated so long discriminatory and invalid selection methods which perpetuated social injustice.

Thus, it is clear that merit and equity *are* compatible. By insisting that any selection method measure the ability of a person to perform a specific job, we would be faithful to the original intent of the civil service laws, professional test standards, and the requirements of civil rights law. At the same time, by discarding discriminatory selection devices and criteria and substituting methods designed to achieve social equity for underrepresented minorities and women, we will be achieving a truly meritorious public service—one *by*, as well as for, all the people.

Study questions for selection nine

1. Let us imagine that two candidates apply for a manhole-cover-counting department's typist position, for which the single qualification of being able to type sixty words per minute has been set. The candidates are apparently equal except in the following ways: one applicant is a male member of the green race, has one year of college, and types seventy-five words per minute; the other applicant is a female member of the blue race, is a high-school dropout, and types sixty words per minute. If male greenies are already overrepresented in the department, which applicant would Kranz probably hire? Which one would you hire?

2. How might a more representative bureaucracy increase the legitimacy of the political system?

3. Are there advantages for an agency in hiring people who are "overqualified" for their job?

4. Do you think affirmative action goals represent reverse discrimination or justifiable compensatory treatment?

Suggested readings for chapter seven

Anderson, Arvid, and Jascourt, Hugh D., eds. *Trends in Public Sector Labor Relations.* Chicago: International Personnel Management Association, 1975.

Byers, Kenneth T., ed. *Employee Training and Development in the Public Service.* Chicago: International Personnel Management Association, 1970.

Cayer, N. Joseph. *Public Personnel Administration in the United States.* New York: St. Martin's Press, 1975.

Harvey, Donald R. *The Civil Service Commission.* New York: Praeger Publishers, 1970.

Jascourt, Hugh D. *Public Sector Labor Relations, Recent Trends and Developments.* Lexington, Ky.: Council of State Governments, 1975.

Kilpatrick, Franklin P.; Cummings, Milton C., Jr., and Jennings, M. Kent. *The Image of the Federal Service.* Washington, D.C.: Brookings Institution, 1964.

Kranz, Harry. *The Participatory Bureaucracy: Women and Minorities in a More Representative Public Service.* Lexington, Mass.: Lexington Books, 1976.

Krislov, Samuel. *The Negro in Federal Employment. The Quest for Equal Opportunity.* Minneapolis: University of Minnesota Press, 1967.

————. *Representative Bureaucracy.* Englewood Cliffs, N.J.: Prentice-Hall, 1974.

Macy, John W., Jr. *Public Service: The Human Side of Government.* New York: Harper and Row, 1971.

Meier, Kenneth John, "Representative Bureaucracy: An Empirical Analysis." *American Political Science Review* 69 (June 1975): 526-42.

Mosher, Frederick C. *Democracy and the Public Service.* New York: Oxford University Press, 1968.

Murphy, Thomas P., ed. *Government Management Internships and Executive Development.* Lexington, Mass.: Heath, 1973.

Nigro, Felix A., and Nigro, Lloyd G. *The New Public Personnel Administration.* Itasca, Ill.: F. E. Peacock, 1976.

Sasso, Carmen, and Tanis, Earl. *Disciplinary Policies and Practices.* Chicago: International Personnel Management Association, 1973.

Spero, Sterling, and Capozzola, John M. *The Urban Community and its Unionized Bureaucracies: Pressure Politics in Local Government Labor Relations.* New York: Dunellen, 1973.

Stanley, David T. *The Higher Civil Service: An Evaluation of Federal Personnel Practices.* Washington, D.C.: Brookings Institution, 1964.

Steiber, Jack. *Public Employee Unionism, Structure, Growth, Policy.* Washington, D.C.: Brookings Institution, 1973.

Taylor, Vernon R. *Test Validity in Public Personnel Selection.* Public Employment Practices Bulletin No. 2. Chicago: International Personnel Management Association, 1971.

Van Riper, Paul P. *History of the United States Civil Service.* New York: Harper and Row, 1958.

Warner, E. Lloyd; Van Riper, Paul P.; Martin, Norman H.; and Collins, Orvis F. *The American Federal Executive.* New Haven, Conn.: Yale University Press, 1963.

Zagoria, Sam, ed. *Public Workers and Public Unions.* Englewood Cliffs, N.J.: Prentice-Hall, Inc., 1972.

Chapter seven

Chapter eight

Making the agency's decisions

Somehow, hard decisions must be taken by every organization. The Ford Motor Company must decide whether or not to invest in electric power as an alternative to the internal-combustion engine, and the Department of Defense must come to a decision about the practicality of certain military applications of laser beams. This chapter investigates the decisional processes of public administrative agencies. The literature on this topic is replete both with descriptions of the decision-making process and with prescriptions for what it ought to be. In general, there are two traditions of thought: the *rational-comprehensive* school and the *incremental* school. After describing the main tenets of these two schools, we shall consider briefly some features of the setting of American public administration that strongly influence the ways decisions are made.

An outline of two decision theories

The first school sees administrators as rational—or at least potentially rational—beings, who are capable of setting out clearly defined objectives and then selecting from among many alternatives the one that maximizes the achievement of those objectives. In most conceptualizations, this means selecting the alternative that will achieve the objective *with the least cost*. Many writers of this genre deride administrators for failing to exploit the potential for such rational processes. The rationalists insist that before an existing program is continued or expanded and before any new program is established, those responsible should clearly state the goals the program is expected to reach. In fact, the ideal procedure would be to set the objectives *before* even considering the structure of possible programs. Thus, a hypothetical city police department that decided it wanted to reduce the crime rate in a particular area would establish a definite target (such as a 10 percent reduction), would state precisely how the crime rate was to be measured, and would proceed to search for alternative programs that might accomplish the goal. From among the alternatives discovered, one would be selected for implementation.[1]

The second tradition of decision theorists, the incremental school, perceives administrators as making decisions through a process far less rigorous than that associated with pure rationality. In its place they suggest a process that emphasizes the roles of bargaining and negotiation among officials and interest groups.[2] New programs begin slowly in order to allow experience to accumulate, and modifications are made as needed. Rather than attempting to determine in advance the total impact of a program, the decision maker monitors the impact as the program evolves. Under this scheme, the police department might decide that one method they could try in their attempt to halt crime would be to increase patrol frequency. After a period of negotiation with the police union, with neighborhood protection associations, and with the city council (some of whose members really are more interested in paving streets than fighting crime), the change is made in one precinct. Feedback is then awaited—from officers, from

---

[1]An excellent presentation of the rational decision process, as applied to the public sector, is found in E. S. Quade, *Analysis for Public Decisions* (New York: American Elsevier, 1975).

[2]Prominent statements of the incremental school include Aaron B. Wildavsky, *The Politics of the Budgetary Process*, 2d ed. (Boston: Little, Brown, 1974); and Charles E. Lindblom, *The Policy-Making Process* (Englewood Cliffs, N.J.: Prentice-Hall, 1968).

citizens, and from city council members. Depending on the reaction, the practice might or might not be continued and expanded. If expansion is undertaken, it would be in step-by-step fashion, slowly including additional precincts and monitoring feedback, negotiating at each step.

Authors representing each of these schools have set out numerous reasons for the unacceptability of the alternate approach. We shall summarize the main contentions of each side and make some brief explanations.

The rational-comprehensive critique of incrementalism

Proponents of the rational decision model have declared the incremental process to be unacceptable on several grounds.

1. Since it allows for only small changes, incrementalism is *status quo* oriented; there is a presumption that present programs and procedures are superior to, or at least more practicable than, those that might be established using rational processes.

2. Precise objectives or goals usually are not specified; thus, later program evaluation is difficult or impossible.

3. Important factors that should influence the decision often are not considered by the decision maker; furthermore, personal or professional bias often enters into decisions.

4. Interest group pressures are too influential; this is undesirable because all individuals are not adequately represented by interest groups, and all groups that might have a stake in the decision are not necessarily asked for their advice.

5. Coordination is difficult; one decision may influence many others, but systematic attention usually is not given to the prediction of such impacts.

6. Ordinarily, insufficient attention is given to the need for efficiency; money is spent with no measure of return.

7. It is too easy to ignore the need for planning and to begin new programs on a small-scale or trial basis; later they may develop sufficient political clout that even worthless programs can survive and possibly develop into large agencies.

8. It is often difficult or impossible to convey to others the reason for the decision made.

Devotees of the rational decision model find evidence of the "evils" of incrementalism nearly everywhere. Henry S. Rowen, former president of the RAND Corporation, has actively engaged in trying to move the federal government's decision-making processes toward the rational comprehensive model. He has cited examples of incrementally based government policies that he believes turned out badly because the steps of the rational model were not followed:

We invest quite a lot to move air passengers from airport to airport but have paid little attention to the increasingly significant links in the journey from portal to and from airports. Our maritime policies, which have traditionally been worked out via the bargaining mode, include an operating subsidy which is structured so as to create a positive incentive to overmanning of ships. Our water resources policies favor expensive means of reducing water pollution over less expensive means. These policies have also produced flood control projects which have generated incentives for people to overbuild in still vulnerable flood plains. In Agriculture we pay both to take land out of agricultural production while bringing reclaimed land in. We have a sugar subsidy program which seems to cost three times the net incomes of the sugar producers. We spend ten times on urban roads as on urban mass transit without the balance between these two types of transportation being examined.[3]

Adoption of the rational choice model, its advocates feel, would help to overcome the obvious faults of incrementalism enumerated earlier and detailed in Rowen's statement.

Beyond the basic steps of rational decision making mentioned above (stating the objective, developing a measure of its attainment, finding alternatives, and selecting the best one), proponents of rational-comprehensive decision making place great emphasis on *analysis*. By this they mean an effort to systematically collect and present information for decision makers. Especially heavy weight is likely to be given to information presented in quantitative form. The actual procedures can become highly technical, but the stress is on finding measures of both the costs and the benefits of each alternative course of action.

The costs of a government program are not, of course, all reflected in money. For example, a good analyst, brought in as a consultant to our mythical police department that was considering increasing patrol frequency, would inform them that such a change

---

[3]Henry S. Rowen, "Bargaining and Analysis in Government," in *Planning Programming Budgeting Inquiry*, Subcommittee on National Security and International Operations, Committee on Government Operations, U.S. Senate, 91st Cong., 2d sess., 1970, p. 612.

Chapter eight

242

might cause morale problems in the department. Officers compelled to spend more time in high-crime areas might well resist exposing themselves to greater personal risk. Such analyses attempt to specify the costs—both monetary and nonmonetary—of alternative courses of action. Another crime-reduction alternative might be to infiltrate a neighborhood with undercover agents. If this approach were taken, the loss of privacy suffered by residents would have to be considered a cost—one to which it might be impossible to attach a dollar value.

On the benefit side of the equation, the obvious objective sought is a reduction in the crime rate, but other benefits may flow from adopting certain alternatives. Reinstating foot patrols, for example, might do much to improve the image of the police department and, perhaps, help unify neighborhoods by providing a common focal point. Such a benefit would be included in the computations. Under the rational-comprehensive decision-making system, the analyst, by developing reports on the costs and benefits of each alternative and presenting the findings to the decision maker for determination, plays a crucial role.

The incremental critique of rationalism

All of this sounds most worthy. Are the antirationalists simply perverse in refusing to accept such an exemplary process? The defenders of incrementalism plead innocent to the charge. According to them, flaws in the rational-comprehensive scheme make its adoption not only unwise, but impossible. These critics claim rationalism is unacceptable on, at least, the following grounds.

1. The political process thrives on imprecision, and more than mere intent is necessary to produce clearly defined goals. Requiring agreement on precisely stated objectives could result in deadlock at the very beginning of the decision process.

2. The complexity of the decision process is overwhelming. Considering (all at the same time) multiple goals, multiple alternatives, and multiple impacts of each alternative (all within the context of limited resources) is beyond human capacity—even with computer assistance. One might as well admit in advance that shortcuts, which would undermine the rational character of the decision process, inevitably would be taken.

3. The time required to reach a decision following the rationalist credo is simply too great; the prescribed data collection and analysis procedures are more appropriate for academic ivory towers than for the pressure-cooker environments of public administrators.

4. The financial costs of the purely rational process are too high.

Assembling and analyzing some of the information an analyst might want if all avenues were to be explored is prohibitively expensive, and some information is not available at any cost.

5. Rationalism promotes conflict. The rational choice method encourages each decision maker to be rigid and defensive about his or her version of "scientific truth"; there are likely to be clear winners and losers in each battle, whereas incrementalism facilitates compromise and accommodation.

6. The rational model has a centralizing bias. Upper-level administrators, who often become dependent on computer models and hardware, frequently come to view the line officials, who are close to the problems and who may be capable of solving them, as mere providers of inputs for sophisticated information-processing systems. Thus, rationalism narrows the circle of decision makers—which may or may not be desirable, depending on one's assumptions.

7. Too much attention is given to economic costs, with a consequent overlooking of important political considerations. Interest groups having legitimate concerns about issues often are not given an opportunity to voice them—especially if their concerns do not fit neatly into the rational model employed.

During the last two decades the incrementalists have been kept busy defending themselves against several concerted efforts to install rational-comprehensive decision systems. The most vigorous "reform" effort was in the Department of Defense, where the rational model developed great momentum under Secretary Robert McNamara in the early 1960s. The effort was facilitated by the "hardware" orientation of modern military services; this orientation made the specification of objectives and the conduct of analyses easier than in such "people"-oriented areas as social services, education, or health.

Perhaps the most outspoken opponent of this effort in the Defense Department was Admiral Hyman G. Rickover, the father of the atomic submarine. In testimony before a Senate subcommittee, Rickover made the following comments about the attempts to decide on a propulsion system for the aircraft carrier *John F. Kennedy:*

> *I think that cost-effectiveness studies are occasionally used to kill something—to kill it by studying it to death. The use of studies for this purpose is well known in Washington . . . .*
>
> *Making the* John F. Kennedy *nuclear powered would have added substantially to the capability of the fleet. However, the decision on this one ship was delayed a year while the Navy attempted to respond to a request to "undertake a comprehensive, quantitative study" of whether "the future Navy will, indeed, make full use of nuclear power." It was requested that the study "consider the design of the future*

carrier striking force in the broadest possible context." Questions were asked such as: How many escort vessels of what type should be included? Should ASW escort be provided in the conventional manner, or should it envision added emphasis on nuclear submarines? How is replenishment of aviation fuel and ordnance to be accomplished? Should the underway replenishment ships also be nuclear? How should the Navy be deployed around the world? Would nuclear power speak for a modification of the present concept of the 1st, 2d, 6th, and 7th Fleets? Realizing that we will have a large number of conventionally powered surface vessels in the inventory for some time to come, how should we approach the ultimate design? What are the implications on force size? Would nuclear propulsion allow us to reduce the total number of carriers and/or carrier task forces?

Each time one of these questions was answered, more were asked. The scope of these studies is so vast and vague that all participants could spend their lifetime at it.

As you know, a decision was finally made by the Department of Defense against putting nuclear propulsions in this carrier in order "to avoid further delay" in the construction of the ship. But is it really necessary to engage in cost-effectiveness studies on the whole future of the Navy before we can decide to put nuclear propulsion in a single ship?[4]

Admiral Rickover was voicing the views of many who have worked under an incremental decision system and are generally satisfied with it. Furthermore, they argue that the piecemeal character of the incremental process helps to assure that adjustments can be made when "dysfunctional" impacts are noted. Although the rational-comprehensive scheme would seek to avoid undesirable consequences by anticipating them, as a practical matter this may be impossible. As Rickover indicates, the complexity of the task may be too great; analyses can continue for years beyond the time a decision is needed.

In addition, the defenders of incremental decision making contend that their model *does* provide for coordination. As agencies, legislators, and interest groups interact with each other, exert influence to insure that their interests are taken into consideration, and reach compromises, a degree of coordination is achieved. The coordination imposed in a rational-comprehensive decision system depends on someone at the top exercising a veto over lower levels. Since such a centralized system

---

[4]Excerpt from testimony May 11, 1966, hearings, Department of Defense Appropriations for 1967, Subcommittee on Department of Defense, House Committee on Appropriations, 89th Cong., 2d sess., part 6, p. 99.

Making the agency's decisions/

/245

© 1974 by NEA, Inc.

demands the comprehension of more information about more variables than any individual or staff could really master, the system may actually be a less effective coordinating mechanism than the incremental system.

Interfacing rationalism with incrementalism

Not surprisingly, the rational-comprehensive model and the incremental model have not remained pure types. Those who write about the decision process, and practitioners of public administration as well, long have recognized the high probability that any particular decision process will have elements of both models.

Herbert Simon, a prominent administrative theorist, has used the word "satisfice" to describe what an administrator really attempts to accomplish by his decisions. That is, the administrator "looks for a course of action that is satisfactory or 'good enough.' "[5] The pressure of time often leaves little choice. Even the systems analysts in the Depart-

---

[5]Herbert A. Simon, *Administrative Behavior: A Study of Decision-Making Processes in Administrative Organizations,* 2d ed. (New York: Macmillan, 1957), p. xxv.

ment of Defense, strong supporters of the rational-comprehensive process, once had the motto: "It is better to be roughly right than exactly wrong." They and Simon were both recognizing the limited human capability to secure purely rational decisions.

Another important theorist of administration, Amitai Etzioni, has described a process that he refers to as *mixed scanning*.[6] Etzioni maintains that it both describes decision-making procedures used in some situations and prescribes appropriate procedures for others. Mixed scanning suggests that decision makers should systematically review (perhaps at set intervals) their entire areas of responsibility. Since highly detailed comprehensive coverage may be impossible, however, Etzioni recommends that the scope of the review be intentionally "truncated." That is, agency resources could be invested in detailed analyses of important decisions (those with the broadest impact); the systematic overview would provide a context for application of the incremental model in reaching less important decisions.

Decision models and the context of American politics

The acceptability of these various models, either as descriptions of present decision-making processes or as blueprints for "proper" ones, will depend substantially on one's interpretation of how the political system functions and on one's own political preferences. Since both the incrementalists and the rationalists generally agree that the former model best describes past and present processes, a convenient way to analyze the political implications of choosing decision models is to imagine the impact that the adoption of the rational-comprehensive model would have on the American political system. Let us begin by mentioning three of the system's structural and attitudinal components that might be affected by such an adoption.

Divided authority

The American system divides decision-making authority. The separation of powers is the most obvious manifestation of this tendency. Constitutionally, at state and federal levels and in many cities, the executive, the legislature, and the courts all participate actively in decision making and have more or less clearly defined roles to play in the

---

[6]Amitai Etzioni, "Mixed Scanning: A 'Third' Approach to Decision Making," *Public Administration Review* 27 (December 1967): 385-92.

process. We are well aware that specialized administrators also play important roles. Not only does such separation accurately describe the American system, but the separation is highly valued by Americans, who may be inclined to consider carefully a claim that one branch of government is overstepping its authority and assuming functions that are the prerogative of another branch.

In addition to this division of authority produced by separation of powers, authority is further divided according to levels of government: federal, state, and local. Again, this is a division that Americans value; complaints about encroachments by higher levels of government are prominent political issues.

The primacy of representation

A second feature of the American political system that is relevant to a discussion of decision models is the system's great reliance on elected representatives. Representatives chosen from and residing in single-member districts are the acceptable linkage between the public and public decision making.

According to one prominent theory of representation, these officials (members of Congress, of state legislatures, and of local governing bodies) have a responsibility to speak for the specific needs of their constituents. Legislators from agricultural areas, for example, are expected to take positions favorable to agriculture and to defend them vigorously, while city council members from wards populated by union members are expected to sympathize with efforts to unionize city employees. There is even an expectation that representatives will "deliver the goods" by seeing that government spends money in the district.

According to a rival theory of representation, however, elected officials should consider the interests of the country (or state or city) at large and should vote according to the impact they think a proposed program would have on the total governmental area—even if the impact might run counter to the wishes (and immediate interests) of constituents. Each of these theories of representation is familiar and has a place in American political thinking. Our purpose in discussing them is not to underscore the ambiguity of American values, but to point to the importance of some kind of theory of representation—whatever position the particular theory may take.

Confidence in science and technology

The third aspect of the American political context we shall mention is the appreciation of (often infatuation with) technological innovation. The United States was created while the Industrial Revolution was occurring in Western Europe. As increasingly sophisticated technology developed, it became possible to employ it to help solve many of our day-to-day problems, from medical problems to transportation problems and from communication problems to food problems. Although in the last decade some have questioned the continued ability of science and technology to cope with human difficulties, others remain quite optimistic about the prospects. Many optimists continue to hope that, as in the past, a "technological fix" will be found to deal with such immediate problems as food and energy shortages.[7]

The value implications of decision models

The rational-comprehensive decision model would seem to be congruent with one of the structural and attitudinal components of the American system mentioned above—our predisposition to place a high value on science and technology. Simply engaging in something called "analysis," especially quantitative analysis, seems reasonable and certainly respectable to most Americans. Furthermore, the rational model is at least sympathetic to experimentation. Although it is obvious that important measurement and evaluation difficulties arise, the notion of a more or less formal experiment, perhaps including control groups, is congruent with our appreciation of science.

The other two aspects of the American political context discussed above (divided authority and the importance of representation) are, however, less compatible with rationalism. In fact, sharp clashes may arise.

The rational model suggests that after data collection and analysis, one way of solving a problem will emerge as superior to others and will be adopted. This would require, however, a high degree of cooperation among decision makers in the "branches" of government and among the various "levels." Perhaps unfortunately, institutional jealousy works against such cooperation, and, more important, differences in perspective often prevent agreement on even the system's fundamental objectives. A national effort to combat crime may look quite different to a Justice Department administrator in Washington than it does to a

---

[7]For the pessimistic view, see Donella Meadows et al., *The Limits to Growth: A Report for the Club of Rome's Project on the Predicament of Mankind* (New York: Universe Books, 1972); for the optimistic view, see Herman Kahn, William Brown, and Leon Martel, *The Next 200 Years: A Scenario for America and the World* (New York: William Morrow, 1976).

police chief in Sheboygan, Wisconsin. If a thorough analysis should suggest, for example, that an appropriate action would be to abolish local police departments and to replace them with statewide law enforcement agencies, it is likely that the views taken of this proposal would differ widely. The federal structure and the division of powers—and the values we place on them—also work against the implementation of the rational-comprehensive decision process, in its pure form at least.

Furthermore, the nature of our representative system also impedes the acceptance of rationalism. A city council member is expected to be devoted to his or her ward. Many Americans would find it difficult to understand or accept a council member who supported zoning changes permitting massage parlors and porno-movie houses in the ward's prime residential areas because "careful analysis showed this to be the best place in the city for their location, given the pattern of growth likely to occur over the next decade." Similarly, the political need of a senator to secure a particular facility for the state may outweigh all other considerations—even those resulting from careful analysis of alternatives.

Where, then, does this leave the rational-comprehensive decision-making method? Does it succumb completely to the demands of immediate political concerns? Not necessarily, but it must function within the political context. While the mode's proponents have generally accepted the fact that the analyst will not make final decisions, they believe, nonetheless, that analytic results are sure to carry considerable weight.[8] It seems to us that their hopes probably are too high. Some decision makers will base their own decisions upon the analytic conclusions and use them as tools for influencing others. Sometimes this effort will be successful; sometimes it will fail. There will still be room for political maneuver, room for the representative to "represent," and room for other participants in the decision-making process to support, modify, or oppose particular alternatives. While the results of careful consideration of alternatives and measurement of potential results will carry some influence, analysts should recognize that their results are likely to function as merely one more input to an already highly complex decision process.

---

[8]An excellent study of policy analysts and the ways they see their jobs is Arnold J. Meltsner, *Policy Analysts in the Bureaucracy* (Berkeley: University of California Press, 1976).

The systems analysis approach*

Alain C. Enthoven

This selection describes and promotes systems analysis, the variety of rational-comprehensive decision theory dominant in the Pentagon during the McNamara era. Mr. Enthoven, an economist who was then assistant secretary of defense for systems analysis and a leading theoretician of the concept, presented the following testimony to a subcommittee of the Senate's Labor and Public Welfare Committee. Any puzzlement the reader may feel about why an assistant secretary of defense would be asked to testify before such a committee is likely to be cleared up by noting the full title of the bill under consideration: "A Bill to Mobilize and Utilize the Scientific and Engineering Manpower of the Nation to Employ Systems Analysis and Systems Engineering to Help to Fully Employ the Nation's Manpower Resources to Solve National Problems."

The exchanges between Mr. Enthoven and Senator Gaylord Nelson (chairman of the subcommittee and principal author of the bill) and Senators Jacob Javits and George Murphy (members of the subcommittee) are enlightening because they help to clarify the participants' perceptions of the virtues and the possible nondefense applications of systems analysis. But the exchanges also illustrate one of the senses in which the relationships between legislators and bureaucrats are often symbiotic: some legislators find an administrator who shares their enthusiasm for a proposal; then the administrator is brought in as an expert witness to a hearing; and the legislative sponsors guide the discussion of the proposal so as to produce a favorable impression.

This testimony was given more than ten years ago. Nevertheless, it accurately reflects the views of those today who continue to promote rational-comprehensive systems.

Mr. Chairman, it is a great pleasure for me to appear before you this morning and to have the opportunity to make a contribution to the use of systems analysis on problems of state and local governments. I believe that this is a most worthwhile objective and that there are clear possibilities for

---

*Reprinted from U.S., Congress, Senate, Special Subcommittee on the Utilization of Scientific Manpower of the Labor and Public Welfare Committee, *Scientific Manpower Utilization, 1965–66: Hearings on S2662,* 89th Cong., 2d sess., May 17, 1966, pp. 146–62.

making major contributions to the public welfare through the broader use of systems analysis at all levels of government.

What I have to say will be based on our experience in the Department of Defense. But, I want to emphasize at the outset my conviction that the problems of state and local government and the problems of education, natural resources management, pollution of the environment, and public health and welfare are no more complex and no less amenable to systematic, rational analysis than are the problems of defense. I need only mention our current problems in NATO and in defeating aggression in southeast Asia to illustrate the point that we have our share of complex problems. While I would not want to suggest that systems analysis has solved these problems, I think that it is fair to say that a systematic and integrated approach to the gathering and presentation of information on the alternatives available to our government has made the work of our responsible decision makers easier and more productive than it might otherwise be.

I understand that you are interested in identifying and making available useful literature on the systems analysis approach. I am very happy to be able to call to your attention and to submit for the record a prepublication copy of "A Modern Design for Defense Decision," an anthology on Defense management, programming, and systems analysis, including speeches and articles on these subjects by Secretary McNamara, former Assistant Secretary of Defense (Comptroller) Charles Hitch, and myself. This volume is being published by the Industrial College of the Armed Forces and the hardbound printed version will be available late in June.

Senator Nelson. You are submitting a copy of this for use by the subcommittee?

Mr. Enthoven. Yes.

Senator Nelson. That will be put in the subcommittee files.

Mr. Enthoven. There is a great deal that might be said about the systems analysis approach. In this statement, I would like to pick out a few of the aspects that seem to me to be especially relevant and to make these points largely by the use of excerpts from "A Modern Design for Defense Decision."

In my statement, I would like to expand on the following points:

1. Systems analysis is a reasoned approach to problems of decision, accurately described as "quantitative common sense."

2. Systems analysis is an application of scientific method, using that term in its broadest sense.

3. There are limitations in the application of systems analysis, although these have often been overstated.

4. In 1961, the Defense planning and budgeting system had to be changed to permit the application of systems analysis.

5. Systems analysis is a regular working contributor to the annual Defense decision-making cycle.

6. Two necessary conditions for the successful application of systems analysis as a working part of an operating organization are that it be used by decision makers, and that it be fed with ideas by a broadly based interdisciplinary research program.

7. Systems analysis can be applied to the problems of state and local government, including programs for social welfare.

Senator Nelson. Will you elaborate a little bit on that? In what way do you use the interdisciplinary approach in the development of your systems analysis in the Defense Department? What disciplines are involved in the Defense Department development of a program?

Mr. Enthoven. The main disciplines that we draw on in our weapons systems and strategy studies are the military profession; that is, officers experienced in military operations; physics, engineering, and other physical sciences, economics, political science, and other social sciences. The men from these professions work together in collaboration, oriented toward the solution of the problems at hand. The main focus has to be the problem itself, and not the prerogatives or the use of this or that particular discipline.

It is very important to make sure that the physics used in our weapons systems analysis is good physics. So you want to have good physicists. But once the physicists are working on the problem, they have to be willing to transcend the traditional boundaries of their academic background.

Senator Nelson. In deciding on a particular weapon, for example, where it might be used or where it might be based, does the Defense Department use the counsel of political and foreign relations experts for some advice on what the effect might be? In other words, the development of a weapons system may require the use of a certain weapon, an airplane or something else, based on foreign soil; and as long as it is there, it may be most effective and the best weapon we have. But if something developed politically that required the withdrawal of the weapon and you could not use it at all, what effect would that have on the weapons systems you have developed?

Are political experts used to raise these questions so that the decision maker or makers in the Defense Department can at least evaluate that problem in making a determination as to the weapons system?

Mr. Enthoven. Yes, sir. We do that, both in our research program and in our staffing of specific decisions that have to be made by the Secretary of Defense and with the help of the State Department. We go through a process very much along the lines of what you described. That is, a group working on the choice of weapons systems might well include a political scientist who would observe that the different basing concepts associated with different weapons would have substantial implications for our relations with foreign countries. He would raise and identify the issues and clarify what the implications are for the decision makers.

Senator Nelson. How is the system set up? You do have to have an analysis of the overall weapons system. It has a thousand parts. What are the mechanics for setting up the analysis of the weapons system?

Mr. Enthoven. Let me take an example from the research program, one in which Mr. Rowen was a leading participant back in the early 1950s, when the Rand Corporation embarked on a major study of the basing and operation of the Strategic Air Command.

One of the main problems that study identified was the fact that our basing of strategic bombers on overseas bases close to the U.S.S.R. and outside our warning net left these bombers vulnerable to surprise nuclear attack. The study examined a number of alternatives for the solution of this problem, alternatives for guaranteeing the security of our strategic retaliatory power. The alternatives were described and evaluated primarily from the point of view of our strategic retaliatory capability, but also from the point of view of what implications and requirements they would have for overseas bases and therefore for our dependence on other countries.

Actually, this particular study, which is an example of the best of this kind of research, was done mainly by a group of four men within a larger organization from which they could draw for assistance on particular pieces of the work by aeronautical engineers, physicists, political scientists, and the like.

Senator Nelson. All part of the Rand Corporation?

Mr. Enthoven. All part of the Rand Corporation; yes, sir.

Senator Nelson. Did they also use whatever they needed from the whole military establishment?

Mr. Enthoven. Yes. In fact, we had very good assistance and cooperation from the Air Force; in this case, the Strategic Air Command. Air Force officers were present at the Rand Corporation, participating in and contributing to the studies, and providing very necessary and most valuable advice on the practicability of the operations and the realistic aspects of the operational problems.

Senator Nelson. Senator Murphy, we have testifying presently Mr. Enthoven, of the Defense Department, and Mr. Rowen, of the Budget Bureau, with him.

Senator Murphy. Thank you.

Senator Nelson. You may proceed.

Systems analysis approach

Mr. Enthoven. Systems analysis is nothing more than quantitative or enlightened common sense aided by modern analytical methods. What we seek to do in the systems analysis approach to problems is to examine an objective in its broadest sense, including its reasonableness or appropriateness from a national policy point of view, and then develop for the responsible decision maker information that will best help him to select the preferred way of achieving it. This process of selection requires that we first identify alternative ways of achieving the objective and then estimate, in quantitative terms, the benefits (effectiveness) to be derived from, and the cost of, each alternative. These aspects of the problem that cannot easily be quantified are explicitly stated. Of course, this would include the foreign policy aspects. In principle, we strive to identify the alternative that yields a specified degree of effectiveness for the least cost or, what is the same thing, the greatest effectiveness for a given cost. In essence, it is a way of dealing with the basic economic problem—how best to use our limited national resources. So much for what systems analysis is. A few words on what it is not.

Systems analysis is not synonymous with the application of computers. There is no essential connection between the two. Certainly the development of the former in no way depends on computers. Some researchers, working within the limits of the systems analysis approach, try to do their analyses by means of large-scale computer simulations. Actually, the computer simulation approach so far has not been particularly fruitful as a method of weapon systems analysis. However, the potential advantages offered by high-speed electronic computers are very great. One of the primary advantages of the computer to the systems analysis function is to permit us to examine a much larger number of alternatives in a shorter period of time than would be otherwise possible. This is especially important in the case of very complex and interrelated systems where hand calculations would limit the time available for the more important work of analysis. I intend to try to exploit more fully the potential of high-speed computers. But I would like to make it clear that I view the computer as a mechanical aid in my work and not as the substance of my work.

Moreover, systems analysis is not mysterious or occult. It is not performed with the help of a mysterious black box. A good systems analyst should be able to give a clear nontechnical explanation of his methods and results to the responsible decision makers.

Application of the scientific method

I would like now to turn to what I believe are some of the basic characteristics of the systems analysis method. Systems analysis is at once eclectic and unique. It is not physics, engineering, mathematics, economics, political science or military operations, and yet it involves elements of all of the above disciplines. But regardless of its makeup, the art of systems analysis—and it is an art—like the art of medicine, must be based on the scientific method, useing this term in its broadest sense.

What are the relevant characteristics of scientific method as applied to the problem of choosing strategies and selecting weapon systems, or, for that matter, to the analysis of any problem of public policy involving allocation of the nation's scarce resources? I would like to answer this by quoting a passage from an address I gave before the Naval War College in 1963.

> *First, the method of science is an open, explicit, verifiable, self-correcting process. It combines logic and empirical evidence. The method and tradition of science require that scientific results be openly arrived at in such a way that any other scientist can retrace the same steps and get the same results. Applying this to weapon*

I might add, Mr. Chairman, that it was a possible misconception when
we brought system's analysis into the Pentagon that this somehow was going
to be a substitute for and an end to debate. In fact, it has not turned out that
way at all. Rather, I think it might be better described as a sophisticated,
logical set of ground rules for conducting a debate, ground rules which help
the debate to converge on some useful conclusions and to eliminate the
unsupportable arguments as you go along.

appropriate method for dealing with some aspects of problems of choice of weapon systems and strategies requires numbers. Nonquantitative judgment is simply not enough. What is at issue here really is not numbers or computers versus words or judgment. The real issue is one of clarity of understanding and expression. . . .

Numbers are a part of our language. Where a quantitative matter is being discussed, the greatest clarity of thought is achieved by using numbers instead of by avoiding them, even when uncertainties are present. This is not to rule out judgment and insight. Rather, it is to say, that judgments and insights need, like everything else, to be expressed with clarity if they are to be useful.

Let me emphasize the point about uncertainties. Many people seem to feel that quantitative analysis is not possible if there are any uncertainties. But this view is incorrect. In fact, there is substantial literature on the logic of decision making under uncertainty going back at least as far as Pascal, Bernoulli, and Bayes in the seventeenth and eighteenth centuries. Moreover, there are simple practical techniques for dealing with uncertainty which make it possible to do analyses that point up the certainties for the decision maker and indicate their significance. In fact, rather than conceal uncertainties, a good analysis will bring them out and clarify them. If it is a question of uncertainties about quantitative matters such as operational factors, it is generally useful to examine the available evidence and determine the bounds of the uncertainty. In many of our analyses for the secretary of defense, we carry three estimates through the calculations: an "optimistic", a "pessimistic", and a "best" or single most likely estimate. If there are uncertainties about context, at least one can run the calculations on the basis of several alternative assumptions so that the decision maker can see how the outcome varies with the assumptions.

The limitations of systems analysis

I have frequently been asked about the shortcomings and limitations of the systems analysis approach. Let me refer to an article I wrote for the Naval Review, 1965, reprinted in "A Modern Design for Defense Decision."

What's wrong with systems analysis? What are its particular limitations and biases? One criticism I have heard is that emphasis on quantitative analysis risks ignoring those factors that cannot be reduced to numbers, or at least overemphasizing those that can.

Suppose, for example, that the problem is to choose between two alternative ways of destroying a certain set of targets. The less costly way is to base short-range missiles on the territory of an ally; the more costly way is to cover the targets with long-range missiles based in the United States. But suppose basing the missiles on the ally's territory would lead to political difficulties, to the embarrassment and possible fall of a

Making the agency's decisions/

/257

friendly government. How does one take account of such political aspects in a quantitative analysis? The answer is that one doesn't. There is no way of "grinding in" the potential difficulties of an ally. The most the analysis can do is make clear to the decision maker the differences in cost and effectiveness between the two approaches so that he can make an informed judgment about their weight in relation to the political problems.

I would not want to deny that there is potential danger here, even though there is nothing about the systems analysis approach that prevents an assessment of the political or other nonquantitative factors from being included in the staff work. I am confident that the top-level leaders of the Department of Defense who use systems analyses as one of their sources of information, are careful to give balanced consideration to all factors, whether quantitative or not.

Another criticism sometimes made is that application of the "flat of the curve" argument—that the extra effectiveness is small in relation to the extra cost—to force or performance requirements may lead people to ignore the decisiveness of a narrow edge in superior performance. There is a danger here if an unwary analyst confuses performance and effectiveness. There is no question but that, in some cases, a narrow edge in performance may have a very great impact on effectiveness. The performance advantage of the Japanese Zero fighter over American aircraft at the beginning of World War II is a good case in point. But there are other cases in which even a substantial increase in performance, purchased at a high price, may have a small impact on effectiveness. For example, many Navy aviators believe that under today's conditions, a substantial speed advantage in attack aircraft may mean rather little in terms of increased effectiveness. It is easy to confuse performance and effectiveness. But this mistake is clearly not peculiar to the systems analysis approach. The only way to avoid it, and to relate performance to effectiveness properly, is with the help of good analysis.

Next, it is argued that the systems analysis approach may be biased against the new and in favor of the old. I am sometimes concerned that our analyses may be subject to such bias, but I think that the method of open explicit analysis is much less likely to be so biased than is reliance on judgment or intuition or experience unsupported by analysis. The reason for the bias is that we all tend to compare the old and the new in the current mission that happens to have been optimized for the old. . . .

Finally, sometimes it is said that systems analyses oversimplify complex problems. Of course, we have to simplify the complex problems we face; no one could possibly understand most problems of modern weapon systems and strategy in all their complexity. And it is a natural human failing to oversimplify. But I believe the facts are that the systems analysis approach is much less prone to oversimplification than any alternative approach. For it is part of systems analysis to bring to bear all of the best of modern analytical techniques for organizing data and summarizing clearly its most relevant aspects. Moreover, reliance on the method of open, explicit analysis is our best guarantee against persis-

Some important preconditions for success

Two conditions seem to me to be necessary to the successful development and functioning of a systems analysis group within a policy-making organization. The first is that the responsible decision makers make use of systems analysis and take it seriously. Without this, the professional personnel will recognize in time that their work is not influencing the course of events and their motivation is likely to be destroyed. By using systems analysis and taking it seriously, I do not mean that the decision makers must accept the results of the analyses uncritically or that they must rely exclusively on the systems analysis input. Far from it.

Every analysis must be based on many assumptions, and a responsible decision maker may not choose to accept the assumptions that his analysts have made. What is important is that the analyses be given a fair hearing and be acted upon if they successfully stand up under reasonable debate and criticism; or, if they are not acted upon, that the analysts are told why so that they can correct their work in the future. The analysts must have this "feedback" from the decision makers, if they are to know which issues are considered relevant or significant, which objectives the decision makers wish to pursue, and which assumptions appear to them to be plausible. A systems analysis capability installed as "window dressing" is not likely to develop into a good one.

The second necessary condition is that the systems analysis operation be fed with ideas growing out of a broadly based interdisciplinary research program. A research program is necessary in order to develop analytical tools, to define criteria and objectives for programs, and to invent new alternatives for achieving the objectives. Certainly, in defense, the research program must be interdisciplinary, because the scope and complexity of defense problems is too great to be encompassed within any single discipline. I am sure that this would also be true of systems analysis applied to major social problems outside of defense.

One practical implication of this is that, generally speaking, research funds in these fields are likely to be better spent supporting research institutes containing groups of scholars from a variety of relevant disciplines oriented toward the problems, rather than on individual scholars who are more likely to be oriented toward the exercise of their academic specialties.

Making the agency's decisions/

I might add a third necessary condition for success in this kind of work is that the studies be conducted with continuity and depth. In almost every area that I have seen studies by systems analysts, the studies in the first year or two that the particular group was working tended to be very superficial and weak. It is usually only after a good group has worked continuously for a period of several years that they begin to develop the true continuity and the depth required to understand the problem adequately.

Systems analysis nondefense applications

Finally, let me repeat my conviction that systems analysis can be applied fruitfully to social problems. I feel certain that good analysis can assist in the design, development, and consideration of alternative approaches to education, health, urban transportation, justice and crime prevention, natural resources, environmental pollution, and numerous other problems. In fact, there is already a great deal of useful research going on in these areas, some of which you pointed out, Mr. Chairman.

It is often suggested that these problem areas will be resistant to systematic analysis because they do not lend themselves to quantification. In commenting on that, I would like to point out that we, in the Defense Department, also have our own imponderables to deal with. We try to measure those things that are measurable, and, insofar as possible, to define those things which are not, leaving to the responsible decision makers the job of making the difficult judgments about the imponderables. It has been our experience that in those areas most difficult to quantify, years of research and the application of a good deal of ingenuity will often yield ways of measuring and making comparisons that were not available at the outset.

Ultimately, policy decisions will be based on judgments about relative values, the likelihood of uncertain future events, which risks we should and should not run, et cetera. But, in defense, and in these other areas as well, good analysis can do a good deal to sharpen the issues, clarify the alternatives available to the decision makers, and narrow substantially the range of uncertainty, thus freeing the responsible officials to concentrate their attention on the crucial judgments.

Mr. Chairman, that completes my presentation. I would be happy to attempt to answer any questions you may have.

Senator Nelson. One of the purposes of conducting these hearings on this bill is to explore, as you know, the possibility of using the systems analysis approach in terms of evaluating social problems that confront all levels of government with the ultimate objective of seeking an adequate or best-possible solution to the problem.

You raised the question a moment ago about the difficulty of quantifying the statistics in the social problem field. I am wondering if it is really any more difficult in meeting social problems than it is Defense Department problems.

For example, if you were going to tackle the various problems that confront a state government; welfare problems, transportation problems, education problems, recreation problems—isn't there a substantial amount of this that can be quantified in the same way that you do in your analysis of the defense problem? For example, in any system analysis approach to these problems you would need to start out and locate certain statistics. You would have to start out with a comprehensive state evaluation, comprehensive population plan; because all of the rest of the problems you are concerned with also involve the population.

So you would have to do an analysis of how many people you are going to have in your states in the year 1980, and how many in the year 2000. You can come up with pretty good predictions by starting with the year 1930 and going to 1940, 1950, 1960. Then you see the population shift within your state after making this analysis. You then make a qualitative analysis of the population. That is, what are the age groupings? Where are they going to be located in the state? How many are going to be mentally retarded? How many are you going to have in primary and secondary schools? How many are going to be elderly citizens and need some type of care?

Then when we get all through with this basic study of the population, which again you would, if completed in 1966, you would continue to project in 1967 for another forty years and in 1968 for another forty years. Then you need to tackle the question of what is the long-range problem in terms of building adequate institutions for, say, the mentally retarded. We know now that a certain fraction of 1 percent of all the children born will be mentally retarded. If that factor did not change, you can predict in the year 2000 how much personnel you need, how much institutional space you need.

Of course, the factor you raise about needing interdisciplinary advice here comes into play, because you would need the experts in the field of mental retardation to qualify your statistics by pointing out that maybe we are making some headway in reducing retardation on births, which we are.

Then you project how many are going to be age eighteen and then how many are going to go to college. So you can predict for the year 1980 and the year 2000 how many institutions you have to have, how many students you have, and then where the institutions should be located to best service the state.

You move with your statistics over to the transportation problem, making analysis and projection of what air transportation you need, what bus transportation you need, what railroad transportation you need, what mass transportation you need, based again on the predictions of your location of the population, location of industry, the necessity for moving products and people.

So, it seems to me that you can certainly quantify a tremendous amount of information which then you begin to analyze, and give the decision makers; that is, your city council, county boards, legislatures, and the Congress—good information for making determinations and predictions as to how you meet that problem.

You apply, it, then, not only to your college institutions, your welfare institutions, your transportation, but you move over into the field of recreation. And then you have to get into the land-use field. You make a prediction on how many people are going to be water skiers, fishermen, and so forth. What demands are going to be made for parks.

I just want to emphasize at this point, it does seem to me that a tremendous amount of information can be quantified in the social field which would be creatively useful to the administrators and legislative bodies that have to face up to these problems.

Mr. Enthoven. Mr. Chairman, I am very much in agreement with you on that. It seems to me that a great deal of considerable value can be done. Many people seem to look at this problem of quantification in an all or nothing way. That is, they reason that if you can't completely reduce the problem to numbers and calculations, then it must not be useful at all to develop numbers and do calculations. I think this kind of intellectual extremism, if you like, is a mistake. The fact that you can't quantify everything does not mean that it is not useful to do some. Most of the problems that we analyze involve interpenetration between measurable calculable things and unmeasurable things. A good systems analysis will organize and calculate the calculable, and then leave it to the responsible public officials to judge the other parts.

Senator Nelson. Doesn't exactly the same theory and the same scientific method and the same approach apply in the case of systems analysis with equal force to social problems as they apply to the development of a defense system?

Mr. Enthoven. Yes, sir. I might give a couple of examples. My mentor in this business, former Assistant Secretary of Defense Charles Hitch, from whom I learned a great deal about systems analysis, is now the financial vice-president of the University of California. He is starting to develop similar methods of long-range planning and analysis for application to the problems of the University of California system.

There, it is very necessary, as you pointed out, Senator, to project pretty far into the future. If I recall correctly, Mr. Hitch told me a few weeks ago that the leadtime on a new campus in the University of California system is twelve years.

Senator Murphy. Even then, they are behind schedule. At a new campus down at Irvine, they found that they are 20 percent off now in their prognostications. They have to upgrade it continuously, as you say, from the action which is really taking place.

Senator Nelson. If I could comment on that, I think the fact of the matter is that in all states the failure has been that they really haven't used this type of systems analysis in order to make accurate predictions on how many young folks are going to show up in college. So we have ended up with a shortage of space on the campuses and a shortage of personnel.

It would have been pretty easily predictable. But every prediction they have made has been kind of an ad hoc one which ended up with them underpredicting the number of students that wanted to come in.

Senator Murphy. This is one of the outputs of bigness. Whenever you get into an industry, government, state, or local problem, you have to have an accumulation of all the skill, all the knowledge, all the statistics, and put them together and then evaluate them quantitatively and come out with the right answer, which is exactly what we are talking about.

There is no question in my mind that this is the right approach if properly applied, not only the right approach, but it must be applied in the future.

May I be excused, Mr. Chairman? I have another committee meeting.

Senator Nelson. Certainly.

Senator Javits. I have one question.

Chapter eight

262

Senator Nelson. Yes, Senator Javits.

Senator Javits. Would it be feasible, Mr. Enthoven, for you or your colleague Mr. Rowen, to ask you to submit an outline for how you would go about applying systems analysis to a specific subject?

For example, I would give you a choice of three. One, would be the medical care facilities of the United States which are under very great debate right now, especially in view of the imminence of the impact of the Medicare legislation. Second, concerning this very discussion on education, what are the demands on elementary or secondary education? We have higher education legislation and we have more coming. Third, unemployment. We have a bill going through this very committee which deals with new techniques for the Department of Labor in dealing with unemployment, consolidating the various functions which are intended to serve the unemployed in the state employment offices.

It seems to me it would strengthen enormously the case for Senator Nelson's bill if we could have some outline of the applicability of the systems analysis technique to a specific social subject. Naturally, you would not make a systems analysis of it, but you would tell us how you go about doing it.

I remember reading a book which impressed me enormously, possibly the most important book I ever read, which was called "An Introduction to the History of Civilization in England," written by Thomas Buckle in the middle-nineteenth century. He outlined how you would go about taking a scientific approach to the writing of history. That is what I had in mind with you.

In other words, would it be feasible to apply this technique to a subject by outlining how you would go about making a systems analysis that would be applicable to that subject?

I make that as a suggestion, Mr. Chairman. I think it might strengthen your case enormously.

Senator Nelson. I think it is a good question. I will be happy to have Mr. Rowen or Mr. Enthoven handle that. We have asked the aerospace industry to do exactly that. They will be testifying later on. We have had some preliminary testimony from them in California last fall.

As I mentioned, I think before you came, the state of California made four contracts with the aerospace industry. One of them deals with waste management, for example; one with the field of crime. We have asked them to testify, to explain how to use the systems analysis technique as applied to social problems. So that will be in the testimony.

But I will be very happy, if the gentlemen have the time, to have them add examples of their own, because I think it is a necessary part of the testimony.

Mr. Rowen. We will be very happy to prepare, to take one of these and prepare an outline of how to tackle the problem, how to structure it, recognizing as you have said that we can't do it very quickly, because these are very complex matters.

Senator Nelson. If I may add one that may or may not be similar. I would just add this one. The question of pesticides. This is not the whole question of pollution, but is a very narrow and significant part of pollution.

I think if would be relatively simple to apply the systems analysis approach to the use of pesticides; that is, we could even just take one pesticide, or DDT. We know how much DDT we are putting into the atmosphere each year. We discover it is showing up in the Antarctic, in the fatty tissue of the penguin. We find it is showing up in the egg of the eagle. We find it is showing up in the fatty tissue of the muskie. We find it is having some effects on insects and worms in soil.

Now we are using it in this country in great quantity, but we have no notion of what the social and economic cost of using this particular pesticide is in terms of the damage it is doing to marine life and to birds and animals, and so forth.

I think it would be fairly simple to set up a systems analysis approach to weigh the value of this versus the damage it is doing. If that one turns out to be a simple one to apply—

Mr. Rowen. Let me look into it to see if it is possible.

Senator Javits. Thank you so much.

Selection eleven

The science of "muddling through"*

Charles E. Lindblom

Through means that sometimes seem bizarre and often seem anything but rational, public agencies do make decisions. The burden of this well-known essay by Charles Lindblom, Yale University political economist, is that there is, in fact, an underlying rationality to the traditional way of making public decisions. Operations research, statistical decision theory, systems analysis, and other rational-comprehensive, or "root," decision-making models are of little value in making public choices of any consequence, Lindblom says. Instead, he staunchly defends the pluralistic, incremental, successive limited comparisons, or "branch" decision models. Pay particular attention to Lindblom's argument that the traditional decision method is not as formless as it seems on the surface and that it does indeed constitute a "system"—for making the public's decisions—albeit of a rather different type than the one advocated by Enthoven.

---

*Reprinted from *Public Administration Review* 19 (Spring 1959): 79-88. © 1959 by The American Society for Public Administration, 1225 Connecticut Avenue, N.W., Washington, D.C. All rights reserved.

Chapter eight

264

Suppose an administrator is given responsibility for formulating policy with respect to inflation. He might start by trying to list all related values in order of importance, e.g. full employment, reasonable business profit, protection of small savings, prevention of a stock market crash. Then all possible policy outcomes could be rated as more or less efficient in attaining a maximum of these values. This would of course require a prodigious inquiry into values held by members of society and an equally prodigious set of calculations on how much of each value is equal to how much of each other value. He could then proceed to outline all possible policy alternatives. In a third step, he would undertake systematic comparison of his multitude of alternatives to determine which attains the greatest amount of values.

In comparing policies, he would take advantage of any theory available that generalized about classes of policies. In considering inflation, for example, he would compare all policies in the light of the theory of prices. Since no alternatives are beyond his investigation, he would consider strict central control and the abolition of all prices and markets on the one hand and elimination of all public controls with reliance completely on the free market on the other, both in the light of whatever theoretical generalizations he could find on such hypothetical economies.

Finally, he would try to make the choice that would in fact maximize his values.

An alternative line of attack would be to set as his principal objective, either explicitly or without conscious thought, the relatively simple goal of keeping prices level. This objective might be compromised or complicated by only a few other goals, such as full employment. He would in fact disregard most other social values as beyond his present interest, and he would for the moment not even attempt to rank the few values that he regarded as immediately relevant. Were he pressed, he would quickly admit that he was ignoring many related values and many possible important consequences of his policies.

As a second step, he would outline those relatively few policy alternatives that occurred to him. He would then compare them. In comparing his limited number of alternatives, most of them familiar from past controversies, he would not ordinarily find a body of theory precise enough to carry him through a comparison of their respective consequences. Instead he would rely heavily on the record of past experience with small policy steps to predict the consequences of similar steps extended into the future.

Moreover, he would find that the policy alternatives combined objectives or values in different ways. For example, one policy might offer price-level stability at the cost of some risk of unemployment; another might offer less price stability but also less risk of unemployment. Hence, the next step in his approach—the final selection—would combine into one the choice among values and the choice among instruments for reaching values. It would not, as in the first method of policy making, approximate a more mechanical process of choosing the means that best satisfied goals that were previously clarified and ranked. Because practitioners of the second approach expect to achieve their goals only partially, they would expect to repeat endlessly the sequence just described, as conditions and aspirations changed and as accuracy of prediction improved.

Making the agency's decisions/

/**265**

By root or by branch

For complex problems, the first of these two approaches is of course impossible. Although such an approach can be described, it cannot be practiced except for relatively simple problems and even then only in a somewhat modified form. It assumes intellectual capacities and sources of information that men simply do not possess, and it is even more absurd as an approach to policy when the time and money that can be allocated to a policy problem is limited, as is always the case. Of particular importance to public administrators is the fact that public agencies are in effect usually instructed not to practice the first method. That is to say, their prescribed functions and constraints—the politically or legally possible—restrict their attention to relatively few values and relatively few alternative policies among the countless alternatives that might be imagined. It is the second method that is practiced.

Curiously, however, the literatures of decision making, policy formulation, planning, and public administration formalize the first approach rather than the second, leaving public administrators who handle complex decisions in the position of practicing what few preach. For emphasis I run some risk of overstatement. True enough, the literature is well aware of limits on man's capacities and of the inevitability that policies will be approached in some such style as the second. But attempts to formalize rational policy formulation—to lay out explicitly the necessary steps in the process—usually describe the first approach and not the second.[1]

The common tendency to describe policy formulation even for complex problems as though it followed the first approach has been strengthened by the attention given to, and successes enjoyed by, operations research, statistical decision theory, and systems analysis. The hallmarks of these procedures, typical of the first approach, are clarity of objective, explicitness of evaluation, a high degree of comprehensiveness of overview, and, wherever possible, quantification of values for mathematical analysis. But these advanced procedures remain largely the appropriate techniques of relatively small-scale problem solving where the total number of variables to be considered is small and value problems restricted. Charles Hitch, head of the Economics Division of RAND Corporation, one of the leading centers for application of these techniques, has written:

> *I would make the empirical generalization from my experience at RAND and elsewhere that operations research is the art of suboptimizing, i.e., of solving some lower-level problems, and that difficulties increase and our special competence diminishes by an order of magnitude with every level of decision making we attempt to ascend. The sort of simple explicit model which operations researchers are so proficient in using can certainly reflect most of the significant factors influencing traffic control on the George Washington Bridge, but the proportion of the relevant reality which we can represent by any such*

---

[1] James G. March and Herbert A. Simon similarly characterize the literature. They also take some important steps, as have Simon's recent articles, to describe a less heroic model of policy-making. See *Organizations* (John Wiley and Sons, 1958), p. 137.

Rational-comprehensive (root)	**Successive limited comparisons (branch)**
1a. Clarification of values or objectives distinct from and usually prerequisite to empirical analysis of alternative policies.	1b. Selection of value goals and empirical analysis of the needed action are not distinct from one another but are closely intertwined.
2a. Policy formulation is therefore approached through means-end analysis: first the ends are isolated, then the means to achieve them are sought.	2b. Since means and ends are not distinct, means-end analysis is often inappropriate or limited.
3a. The test of a "good" policy is that it can be shown to be the most appropriate means to desired ends.	3b. The test of a "good" policy is typically that various analysts find themselves directly agreeing on a policy (without their agreeing that it is the most appropriate means to an agreed objective).
4a. Analysis is comprehensive; every important relevant factor is taken into account.	4b. Analysis is drastically limited: 1.) Important possible outcomes are neglected. 2.) Important alternative potential policies are neglected. 3.) Important affected values are neglected.
5a. Theory is often heavily relied upon.	5b. A succession of comparisons greatly reduces or eliminates reliance on theory.

model or models in studying, say, a major foreign-policy decision, appears to be almost trivial.[2]

Accordingly, I propose in this paper to clarify and formalize the second method, much neglected in the literature. This might be described as the method of *successive limited comparisons*. I will contrast it with the first

---

[2]"Operations Research and National Planning—A Dissent," *Operations Research* 5 (October 1957): 718. Hitch's dissent is from particular points made in the article to which his paper is a reply; his claim that operations research is for low-level problems is widely accepted.

For examples of the kind of problems to which operations research is applied, see C. W. Churchman, R. L. Ackoff, and E. L. Arnoff, *Introduction to Operations Research* (John Wiley and Sons, 1957); and J. F. McCloskey and J. M. Coppinger, eds., *Operations Research for Management*, vol. 2, (The Johns Hopkins University Press, 1956).

approach, which might be called the rational-comprehensive method.[3] More impressionistically and briefly—and therefore generally used in this article—they could be characterized as the branch method and root method, the former continually building out from the current situation, step-by-step and by small degrees; the latter starting from fundamentals anew each time, building on the past only as experience is embodied in a theory, and always prepared to start completely from the ground up.

Let us put the characteristics of the two methods side by side in simplest terms. (See table p. 267)

Assuming that the root method is familiar and understandable, we proceed directly to clarification of its alternative by contrast. In explaining the second, we shall be describing how most administrators do in fact approach complex questions, for the root method, the "best" way as a blueprint or model, is in fact not workable for complex policy questions, and administrators are forced to use the method of successive limited comparisons.

Intertwining evaluation and empirical analysis (1b)

The quickest way to understand how values are handled in the method of successive limited comparisons is to see how the root method often breaks down in its handling of values or objectives. The idea that values should be clarified, and in advance of the examination of alternative policies, is appealing. But what happens when we attempt it for complex social problems? The first difficulty is that on many critical values or objectives, citizens disagree, congressmen disagree, and public administrators disagree. Even where a fairly specific objective is prescribed for the administrator, there remains considerable room for disagreement on subobjectives. Consider, for example, the conflict with respect to locating public housing, described in Meyerson and Banfield's study of the Chicago Housing Authority[4]—disagreement which occurred despite the clear objective of providing a certain number of public housing units in the city. Similarly conflicting are objectives in highway location, traffic control, minimum wage administration, development of tourist facilities in national parks, or insect control.

Administrators cannot escape these conflicts by ascertaining the majority's preference, for preferences have not been registered on most issues; indeed, there often *are* no preferences in the absence of public discussion sufficient to bring an issue to the attention of the electorate. Furthermore, there is a question of whether intensity of feeling should be considered as well as the number of persons preferring each alternative. By the impossibility of doing otherwise, administrators often are reduced to deciding policy without clarifying objectives first.

---

[3] I am assuming that administrators often make policy and advise in the making of policy and am treating decision making and policy making as synonymous for purposes of this paper.
[4] Martin Meyerson and Edward C. Banfield, *Politics, Planning and the Public Interest* (The Free Press, 1955).

Even when an administrator resolves to follow his own values as a criterion for decisions, he often will not know how to rank them when they conflict with one another, as they usually do. Suppose, for example, that an administrator must relocate tenants living in tenements scheduled for destruction. One objective is to empty the buildings fairly promptly, another is to find suitable accommodation for persons displaced, another is to avoid friction with residents in other areas in which a large influx would be unwelcome, another is to deal with all concerned through persuasion if possible, and so on.

How does one state even to himself the relative importance of these partially conflicting values? A simple ranking of them is not enough; one needs ideally to know how much of one value is worth sacrificing for some of another value. The answer is that typically the administrator chooses—and must choose—directly among policies in which these values are combined in different ways. He cannot first clarify his values and then choose among policies.

A more subtle third point underlies both the first two. Social objectives do not always have the same relative values. One objective may be highly prized in one circumstance, another in another circumstance. If, for example, an administrator values highly both the dispatch with which his agency can carry through its projects *and* good public relations, it matters little which of the two possibly conflicting values he favors in some abstract or general sense. Policy questions arise in forms which put to administrators such a question as: Given the degree to which we are or are not already achieving the values of dispatch and the values of good public relations, is it worth sacrificing a little speed for a happier clientele, or is it better to risk offending the clientele so that we can get on with our work? The answer to such a question varies with circumstances.

The value problem is, as the example shows, always a problem of adjustments at a margin. But there is no practicable way to state marginal objectives or values except in terms of particular policies. That one value is preferred to another in one decision situation does not mean that it will be preferred in another decision situation in which it can be had only at great sacrifice of another value. Attempts to rank or order values in general and abstract terms so that they do not shift from decision to decision end up by ignoring the relevant marginal preferences. The significance of this third point thus goes very far. Even if all administrators had at hand an agreed set of values, objectives, and constraints, and an agreed ranking of these values, objectives, and constraints, their marginal values in actual choice situations would be impossible to formulate.

Unable consequently to formulate the relevant values first and then choose among policies to achieve them, administrators must choose directly among alternative policies that offer different marginal combinations of values. Somewhat paradoxically, the only practicable way to disclose one's relevant marginal values even to oneself is to describe the policy one chooses to achieve them. Except roughly and vaguely, I know of no way to describe—or even to understand—what my relative evaluations are for, say, freedom and security, speed and accuracy in governmental decisions, or low taxes and better schools than to describe my preferences among specific policy choices that might be made between the alternatives in each of the pairs.

In summary, two aspects of the process by which values are actually handled can be distinguished. The first is clear: evaluation and empirical analysis are intertwined; that is, one chooses among values and among policies at one and the same time. Put a little more elaborately, one simultaneously chooses a policy to attain certain objectives and chooses the objectives themselves. The second aspect is related but distinct: the administrator focuses his attention on marginal or incremental values. Whether he is aware of it or not, he does not find general formulations of objectives very helpful and in fact makes specific marginal or incremental comparisons. Two policies, X and Y, confront him. Both promise the same degree of attainment of objectives *a, b, c, d, and e*. But X promises him somewhat more of *f* than does Y, while Y promises him somewhat more of *g* than does X. In choosing between them, he is in fact offered the alternative of a marginal or incremental amount of *f* at the expense of a marginal or incremental amount of *g*. The only values that are relevant to his choice are these increments by which the two policies differ; and, when he finally chooses between the two marginal values, he does so by making a choice between policies.[5]

As to whether the attempt to clarify objectives in advance of policy selection is more or less rational than the close intertwining of marginal evaluation and empirical analysis, the principal difference established is that for complex problems the first is impossible and irrelevant, and the second is both possible and relevant. The second is possible because the administrator need not try to analyze any values except the values by which alternative policies differ and need not be concerned with them except as they differ marginally. His need for information on values or objectives is drastically reduced as compared with the root method; and his capacity for grasping, comprehending, and relating values to one another is not strained beyond the breaking point.

Relations between means and ends (2b)

Decision making is ordinarily formalized as a means-ends relationship: means are conceived to be evaluated and chosen in the light of ends finally selected independently of and prior to the choice of means. This is the means-ends relationship of the root method. But it follows from all that has just been said that such a means-ends relationship is possible only to the extent that values are agreed upon, are reconcilable, and are stable at the margin. Typically, therefore, such a means-ends relationship is absent from the branch method, where means and ends are simultaneously chosen.

Yet any departure from the means-ends relationship of the root method will strike some readers as inconceivable. For it will appear to them that only in such a relationship is it possible to determine whether one policy choice is better or worse than another. How can an administrator know whether he has made a wise or foolish decision if he is without prior values or objectives by which to

---

[5]The line of argument is, of course, an extension of the theory of market choice, especially the theory of consumer choice, to public policy choices.

judge his decisions? The answer to this question calls up the third distinctive difference between root and branch methods: how to decide the best policy.

The test of "good" policy (3b)

In the root method, a decision is "correct," "good," or "rational" if it can be shown to attain some specified objective, where the objective can be specified without simply describing the decision itself. Where objectives are defined only through the marginal or incremental approach to values described above, it is still sometimes possible to test whether a policy does in fact attain the desired objectives; but a precise statement of the objectives takes the form of a description of the policy chosen or some alternative to it. To show that a policy is mistaken one cannot offer an abstract argument that important objectives are not achieved; one must instead argue that another policy is more to be preferred.

So far, the departure from customary ways of looking at problem solving is not troublesome, for many administrators will be quick to agree that the most effective discussion of the correctness of policy does take the form of comparison with other policies that might have been chosen. But what of the situation in which administrators cannot agree on values or objectives, either abstractly or in marginal terms? What then is the test of "good" policy? For the root method, there is no test. Agreement on objectives failing, there is no standard of "correctness." For the method of successive limited comparisons, the test is agreement on policy itself, which remains possible even when agreement on values is not.

It has been suggested that continuing agreement in Congress on the desirability of extending old age insurance stems from liberal desires to strengthen the welfare programs of the federal government and from conservative desires to reduce union demands for private pension plans. If so, this is an excellent demonstration of the ease with which individuals of different ideologies often can agree on concrete policy. Labor mediators report a similar phenomenon: the contestants cannot agree on criteria for settling their disputes but can agree on specific proposals. Similarly, when one administrator's objective turns out to be another's means, they often can agree on policy.

Agreement on policy thus becomes the only practicable test of the policy's correctness. And for one administrator to seek to win the other over to agreement on ends as well would accomplish nothing and create quite unnecessary controversy.

If agreement directly on policy as a test for "best" policy seems a poor substitute for testing the policy against its objectives, it ought to be remembered that objectives themselves have no ultimate validity other than they are agreed upon. Hence agreement is the test of "best" policy in both methods. But where the root method requires agreement on what elements in the decision constitute objectives and on which of these objectives should be sought, the branch method falls back on agreement wherever it can be found.

In an important sense, therefore, it is not irrational for an administrator to defend a policy as good without being able to specify what it is good for.

Making the agency's decisions/

271

Noncomprehensive analysis (4b)

Ideally, rational-comprehensive analysis leaves out nothing important. But it is impossible to take everything important into consideration unless "important" is so narrowly defined that analysis is in fact quite limited. Limits on human intellectual capacities and on available information set definite limits to man's capacity to be comprehensive. In actual fact, therefore, no one can practice the rational-comprehensive method for really complex problems, and every administrator faced with a sufficiently complex problem must find ways drastically to simplify.

An administrator assisting in the formulation of agricultural economic policy cannot in the first place be competent on all possible policies. He cannot even comprehend one policy entirely. In planning a soil bank program, he cannot successfully anticipate the impact of higher or lower farm income on, say, urbanization—the possible consequent loosening of family ties, possible consequent eventual need for revisions in social security and further implications for tax problems arising out of new federal responsibilities for social security and municipal responsibilities for urban services. Nor, to follow another line of repercussions, can he work through the soil bank program's effects on prices for agricultural products in foreign markets and consequent implications for foreign relations, including those arising out of economic rivalry between the United States and the U.S.S.R.

In the method of successive limited comparisons, simplification is systematically achieved in two principal ways. First, it is achieved through limitation of policy comparisons to those policies that differ in relatively small degree from policies presently in effect. Such a limitation immediately reduces the number of alternatives to be investigated and also drastically simplifies the character of the investigation of each. For it is not necessary to undertake fundamental inquiry into an alternative and its consequences; it is necessary only to study those respects in which the proposed alternative and its consequences differ from the status quo. The empirical comparison of marginal differences among alternative policies that differ only marginally is, of course, a counterpart to the incremental or marginal comparison of values discussed above.[6]

Relevance as well as realism

It is a matter of common observation that in Western democracies public administrators and policy analysts in general do largely limit their analyses to incremental or marginal differences in policies that are chosen to differ only incrementally. They do not do so, however, solely because they desperately need some way to simplify their problems; they also do so in order to be relevant.

---

[6]A more precise definition of incremental policies and a discussion of whether a change that appears "small" to one observer might be seen differently by another is to be found in my "Policy Analysis," *American Economic Review* 48 (June 1958): 298.

Chapter eight

272

Democracies change their policies almost entirely through incremental adjustments. Policy does not move in leaps and bounds.

The incremental character of political change in the United States has often been remarked. The two major political parties agree on fundamentals; they offer alternative policies to the voters only on relatively small points of difference. Both parties favor full employment, but they define it somewhat differently; both favor the development of water power resources, but in slightly different ways; and both favor unemployment compensation, but not the same level of benefits. Similarly, shifts of policy within a party take place largely through a series of relatively small changes, as can be seen in their only gradual acceptance of the idea of governmental responsibility for support of the unemployed, a change in party positions beginning in the early 1930s and culminating in a sense in the Employment Act of 1946.

Party behavior is in turn rooted in public attitudes, and political theorists cannot conceive of democracy's surviving in the United States in the absence of fundamental agreement on potentially disruptive issues, with consequent limitation of policy debates to relatively small differences in policy.

Since the policies ignored by the administrator are politically impossible and so irrelevant, the simplification of analysis achieved by concentrating on policies that differ only incrementally is not a capricious kind of simplification. In addition, it can be argued that, given the limits on knowledge within which policymakers are confined, simplifying by limiting the focus to small variations from present policy makes the most of available knowledge. Because policies being considered are like present and past policies, the administrator can obtain information and claim some insight. Nonincremental policy proposals are therefore typically not only politically irrelevant but also unpredictable in their consequences.

The second method of simplification of analysis is the practice of ignoring important possible consequences of possible policies, as well as the values attached to the neglected consequences. If this appears to disclose a shocking shortcoming of successive limited comparisons, it can be replied that, even if the exclusions are random, policies may nevertheless be more intelligently formulated than through futile attempts to achieve a comprehensiveness beyond human capacity. Actually, however, the exclusions, seeming arbitrary or random from one point of view, need be neither.

Achieving a degree of comprehensiveness

Suppose that each value neglected by one policy-making agency were a major concern of at least one other agency. In that case, a helpful division of labor would be achieved, and no agency need find its task beyond its capacities. The shortcomings of such a system would be that one agency might destroy a value either before another agency could be activated to safeguard it or in spite of another agency's efforts. But the possibility that important values may be lost is present in any form of organization, even where agencies attempt to comprehend in planning more than is humanly possible.

Making the agency's decisions

The virtue of such a hypothetical division of labor is that every important interest or value has its watchdog. And these watchdogs can protect the interests in their jurisdiction in two quite different ways: first, by redressing damages done by other agencies; and, second, by anticipating and heading off injury before it occurs.

In a society like that of the United States in which individuals are free to combine to pursue almost any possible common interest they might have and in which government agencies are sensitive to the pressures of these groups, the system described is approximated. Almost every interest has its watchdog. Without claiming that every interest has a sufficiently powerful watchdog, it can be argued that our system often can assure a more comprehensive regard for the values of the whole society than any attempt at intellectual comprehensiveness.

In the United States, for example, no part of government attempts a comprehensive overview of policy on income distribution. A policy nevertheless evolves, and one responding to a wide variety of interests. A process of mutual adjustment among farm groups, labor unions, municipalities and school boards, tax authorities, and government agencies with responsibilities in the fields of housing, health, highways, national parks, fire, and police accomplishes a distribution of income in which particular income problems neglected at one point in the decision processes become central at another point.

Mutual adjustment is more pervasive than the explicit forms it takes in negotiation between groups; it persists through the mutual impacts of groups upon each other even where they are not in communication. For all the imperfections and latent dangers in this ubiquitous process of mutual adjustment, it will often accomplish an adaptation of policies to a wider range of interests than could be done by one group centrally.

Note, too, how the incremental pattern of policymaking fits with the multiple pressure pattern. For when decisions are only incremental—closely related to known policies, it is easier for one group to anticipate the kind of moves another might make and easier too for it to make correction for injury already accomplished.[7]

Even partisanship and narrowness, to use pejorative terms, will sometimes be assets to rational decision making, for they can doubly insure that what one agency neglects, another will not; they specialize personnel to distinct points of view. The claim is valid that effective rational coordination of the federal administration, if possible to achieve at all, would require an agreed set of values[8]—if "rational" is defined as the practice of the root method of decision making. But a high degree of administrative coordination occurs as each agency adjusts its policies to the concerns of the other agencies in the process of fragmented decision making I have just described.

For all the apparent shortcomings of the incremental approach to policy alternatives with its arbitrary exclusion coupled with fragmentation, when compared to the root method, the branch method often looks far superior. In the root

---

[7]The link between the practice of the method of successive limited comparisons and mutual adjustment of interests in a highly fragmented decision-making process adds a new facet to pluralist theories of government and administration.

[8]Herbert Simon, Donald W. Smithburg, and Victor A. Thompson, *Public Administration* (New York: Alfred A. Knopf, 1950), p. 434.

Chapter eight

274

method, the inevitable exclusion of factors is accidental, unsystematic, and not defensible by any argument so far developed, while in the branch method the exclusions are deliberate, systematic, and defensible. Ideally, of course, the root method does not exclude; in practice it must.

Nor does the branch method necessarily neglect long-run considerations and objectives. It is clear that important values must be omitted in considering policy, and sometimes the only way long-run objectives can be given adequate attention is through the neglect of short-run considerations. But the values omitted can be either long run or short run.

Succession of comparisons (5b)

The final distinctive element in the branch method is that the comparisons, together with the policy choice, proceed in a chronological series. Policy is not made once and for all; it is made and remade endlessly. Policy making is a process of successive approximation to some desired objectives in which what is desired itself continues to change under reconsideration.

Making policy is at best a very rough process. Neither social scientists, nor politicians, nor public administrators yet know enough about the social world to avoid repeated error in predicting the consequences of policy moves. A wise policy maker consequently expects that his policies will achieve only part of what he hopes and at the same time will produce unanticipated consequences he would have preferred to avoid. If he proceeds through a *succession* of incremental changes, he avoids serious lasting mistakes in several ways.

In the first place, past sequences of policy steps have given him knowledge about the probable consequences of further similar steps. Second, he need not attempt big jumps toward his goals that would require predictions beyond his or anyone else's knowledge, because he never expects his policy to be a final resolution of a problem. His decision is only one step, one that if successful can quickly be followed by another. Third, he is in effect able to test his previous predictions as he moves on to each further step. Lastly, he often can remedy a past error fairly quickly—more quickly than if policy proceeded through more distinct steps widely spaced in time.

Compare this comparative analysis of incremental changes with the aspiration to employ theory in the root method. Man cannot think without classifying, without subsuming one experience under a more general category of experiences. The attempt to push categorization as far as possible and to find general propositions which can be applied to specific situations is what I refer to with the word "theory." Where root analysis often leans heavily on theory in this sense, the branch method does not.

The assumption of root analysis is that theory is the most systematic and economical way to bring relevant knowledge to bear on a specific problem. Granting the assumption, an unhappy fact is that we do not have adequate theory to apply to problems in any policy area, although theory is more adequate in some areas—monetary policy, for example—than in others. Comparative analysis, as in the branch method, is sometimes a systematic alternative to theory.

Making the agency's decisions/

/275

Suppose an administrator must choose among a small group of policies that differ only incrementally from each other and from present policy. He might aspire to "understand" each of the alternatives—for example, to know all the consequences of each aspect of each policy. If so, he would indeed require theory. In fact, however, he would usually decide that, *for policy-making purposes,* he need know, as explained above, only the consequences of each of those aspects of the policies in which they differed from one another. For this much more modest aspiration, he requires no theory (although it might be helpful, if available), for he can proceed to isolate probable differences by examining the differences in consequences associated with past differences in policies, a feasible program because he can take his observations from a long sequence of incremental changes.

For example, without a more comprehensive social theory about juvenile delinquency than scholars have yet produced, one cannot possibly understand the ways in which a variety of public policies—say on education, housing, recreation, employment, race relations, and policing—might encourage or discourage delinquency. And one needs such an understanding if he undertakes the comprehensive overview of the problem prescribed in the models of the root method. If, however, one merely wants to mobilize knowledge sufficient to assist in a choice among a small group of similar policies—alternative policies on juvenile court procedures, for example—he can do so by comparative analysis of the results of similar past policy moves.

Theorists and practitioners

This difference explains—in some cases at least—why the administrator often feels that the outside expert or academic problem solver is sometimes not helpful and why they in turn often urge more theory on him. And it explains why an administrator often feels more confident when "flying by the seat of his pants" than when following the advice of theorists. Theorists often ask the administrator to go the long way round to the solution of his problems, in effect ask him to follow the best canons of the scientific method, when the administrator knows that the best available theory will work less well than more modest incremental comparisons. Theorists do not realize that the administrator is often in fact practicing a systematic method. It would be foolish to push this explanation too far, for sometimes practical decision makers are pursuing neither a theoretical approach nor successive comparisons, nor any other systematic method.

It may be worth emphasizing that theory is sometimes of extremely limited helpfulness in policy making for at least two rather different reasons. It is greedy for facts; it can be constructed only through a great collection of observations. And it is typically insufficiently precise for application to a policy process that moves through small changes. In contrast, the comparative method both economizes on the need for facts and directs the analyst's attention to just those facts that are relevant to the fine choices faced by the decision maker.

With respect to precision of theory, economic theory serves as an example. It predicts that an economy without money or prices would in certain specified ways misallocate resources, but this finding pertains to an alternative far removed from the kind of policies on which administrators need help. On the other hand, it is not precise enough to predict the consequences of policies restricting business mergers, and this is the kind of issue on which the administrators need help. Only in relatively restricted areas does economic theory achieve sufficient precision to go far in resolving policy questions; its helpfulness in policy making is always so limited that it requires supplementation through comparative analysis.

Successive comparison as a system

Successive limited comparisons is, then, indeed a method or system; it is not a failure of method for which administrators ought to apologize. None the less, its imperfections, which have not been explored in this paper, are many. For example, the method is without a built-in safeguard for all relevant values, and it also may lead the decision maker to overlook excellent policies for no other reason than that they are not suggested by the chain of successive policy steps leading up to the present. Hence, it ought to be said that under this method, as well as under some of the most sophisticated variants of the root method—operations research, for example—policies will continue to be as foolish as they are wise.

Why then bother to describe the method in all the above detail? Because it is in fact a common method of policy formulation, and is, for complex problems, the principal reliance of administrators as well as of other policy analysts.[9] And because it will be superior to any other decision-making method available for complex problems in many circumstances, certainly superior to a futile attempt at superhuman comprehensiveness. The reaction of the public administrator to the exposition of method doubtless will be less a discovery of a new method than a better acquaintance with an old. But by becoming more conscious of their practice of this method, administrators might practice it with more skill and know when to extend or constrict its use. (That they sometimes practice it effectively and sometimes not may explain the extremes of opinion on "muddling

---

[9]Elsewhere I have explored this same method of policy formulation as practiced by academic analysts of policy ("Policy Analysis," *American Economic Review* 48 [June 1958]: 298). Although it has been here presented as a method for public administrators, it is no less necessary to analysts more removed from immediate policy questions, despite their tendencies to describe their own analytical efforts as though they were the rational-comprehensive method with an especially heavy use of theory. Similarly, this same method is inevitably resorted to in personal problem solving, where means and ends are sometimes impossible to separate, where aspirations or objectives undergo constant development, and where drastic simplification of the complexity of the real world is urgent if problems are to be solved in the time that can be given to them. To an economist accustomed to dealing with the marginal or incremental concept in market processes, the central idea in the method is that both evaluation and empirical analysis are incremental. Accordingly, I have referred to the method elsewhere as "the incremental method."

through," which is both praised as a highly sophisticated form of problem solving and denounced as no method at all. For I suspect that in so far as there is a system in what is known as "muddling through," this method is it.)

One of the noteworthy incidental consequences of clarification of the method is the light it throws on the suspicion an administrator sometimes entertains that a consultant or advisor is not speaking relevantly and responsibly when in fact by all ordinary objective evidence he is. The trouble lies in the fact that most of us approach policy problems within a framework given by our view of a chain of successive policy choices made up to the present. One's thinking about appropriate policies with respect, say, to urban traffic control is greatly influenced by one's knowledge of the incremental steps taken up to the present. An administrator enjoys an intimate knowledge of his past sequences that "outsiders" do not share, and his thinking and that of the "outsider" will consequently be different in ways that may puzzle both. Both may appear to be talking intelligently, yet each may find the other unsatisfactory. The relevance of the policy chain of succession is even more clear when an American tries to discuss say, antitrust policy with a Swiss, for the chains of policy in the two countries are strikingly different and the two individuals consequently have organized their knowledge in quite different ways.

If this phenomenon is a barrier to communication, an understanding of it promises an enrichment of intellectual interaction in policy formulation. Once discuss, say, antitrust policy with a Swiss, for the chains of policy in the two countries are strikingly different and the two individuals consequently have organized their knowledge in quite different ways.

This raises again a question only briefly discussed above on the merits of like-mindedness among government administrators. While much of organization theory argues the virtues of common values and agreed organizational objectives, for complex problems in which the root method is inapplicable, agencies will want among their own personnel two types of diversification: administrators whose thinking is organized by reference to policy chains other than those familiar to most members of the organization and, even more commonly, administrators whose professional or personal values or interests create diversity of view (perhaps coming from different specialities, social classes, geographical areas) so that, even within a single agency, decision making can be fragmented and parts of the agency can serve as watchdogs for other parts.

Study questions for selections ten and eleven

1. Are you convinced by Enthoven's and the senators' argument that systems analysis can be as useful for solving such social problems as crime and unemployment as it has proven to be for developing such defense projects as the C-5A aircraft and major weapons systems?

2. Do you agree with Lindblom that the "branch," or "incremental," or "successive limited comparisons" decision method he advocates actually is a system rather than a "failure of method for which administrators ought to apologize?"

3. Is Enthoven's systems approach precisely the sort of rational-comprehen-

sive theory that Lindblom flatly rejected, saying, "It cannot be practiced except for relatively simple problems and even then only in a somewhat modified form"? What common ground do you find between Enthoven and Lindblom?

4. How much truth is in the claim that the rational decision method supports a politically neutral or even a radical philosophy, while incrementalism supports status quo conservatism?

5. All things considered, are you more sympathetic to the rational-comprehensive or the incremental decision-making model? What are the most important reasons for your conclusion?

Suggested readings for chapter eight

Byrd, Jack, Jr. *Operations Research Models for Public Administration.* Lexington, Mass.: Lexington Books, 1975.

Dror, Yehezkel. *Public Policymaking Reexamined.* San Francisco: Chandler Publishing Co., 1968.

Hatry, Harry P. *Practical Program Evaluation for State and Local Government Officials.* Washington, D.C.: Urban Institute, 1973.

Hitch, Charles. *Decision Making for Defense.* Berkeley: University of California Press, 1965.

Jones, Charles O. *An Introduction to the Study of Public Policy.* Belmont, Calif.: Wadsworth, 1970.

Lindblom, Charles E. *The Intelligence of Democracy: Decision Making through Mutual Adjustment.* New York: Free Press, 1965.

————. *The Policy-Making Process.* Englewood Cliffs, N.J.: Prentice-Hall, 1968.

Lynch, Thomas D. *Policy Analysis in Public Policymaking.* Lexington, Mass.: Lexington Books, 1975.

Quade, E. S. *Analysis for Public Decisions.* New York: American Elsevier Publishing Company, 1975.

Rivlin, Alice M. *Systematic Thinking for Social Action.* Washington, D.C.: Brookings Institution, 1971.

Scioli, Frank P., Jr., and Cook, Thomas J., eds. *Methodologies for Analyzing Public Policies.* Lexington, Mass.: Lexington Books, 1975.

Wade, Larry L., and Curry, R. L., Jr. *A Logic of Public Policy: Aspects of Political Economy.* Belmont, Calif.: Wadsworth, 1970.

Wildavsky, Aaron. *The Politics of the Budgetary Process.* 2d ed. Boston: Little, Brown, 1974.

Managing the agency: problems of leadership

Leadership has to do with the direction and guiding of other participants in the organization. This component of management is so central to the manager's job that the terms *management* and *leadership* sometimes are used interchangeably. We shall not do so, for we conceive of the total management process as consisting of other activities as well, including such matters as staffing and decision making, which are discussed in other chapters in this part. Certainly, these other activities are a means of getting people to do what the manager wants, so they too require leadership. This chapter, however, focuses upon leadership as a generalized phenomenon consisting of a set of psychologically based relationships between managers and subordinates. The chapter is divided into two sections: the first examines various means of identifying leadership, and the second examines strategies for promoting better leadership.

A. Identifying leadership

The *American Heritage Dictionary of the English Language* defines leadership as: "(1) The position, office, or term of a leader. (2) A group of leaders. (3) The capacity to be a leader; ability to lead." It is not very difficult to identify leaders according to definitions one and two, but definition three poses problems. How can we tell who has the capabilities of leadership and what circumstances generate leadership? In this section we investigate the personal traits, the styles, and the situational characteristics of leadership.

Leadership traits

Over many years, investigators who have hoped to identify sets of personality characteristics that produce effective leadership have devoted great effort to the attempt to discover *leadership traits*. Can we determine which job candidates are "natural born" leaders? Or can we train employees so that they develop the required personality characteristics (or at least the appropriate techniques) to become effective leaders?

Although the possibility of discovering generic leadership traits is an alluring prospect, some simple reflection will remind us that it would be difficult to know precisely what traits such diverse political leaders as George Washington, Napoleon Bonaparte, Abraham Lincoln, Theodore Roosevelt, Joseph Stalin, Lyndon Johnson, Martin Luther King, Indira Ghandi, and Jimmy Carter shared in common. Despite these obvious difficulties, many researchers have attempted to identify universal characteristics of leadership. Ralph Stogdill, who assembled the results from more than two hundred of the studies, classified the leadership traits that were suggested:

1. capacity (intelligence, alertness, verbal facility, originality, judgment);

2. achievement (scholarship, knowledge, athletic accomplishments);

3. responsibility (dependability, initiative, persistence, aggressiveness, self-confidence, desire to excel);

4. participation (activity, sociability, cooperation, adaptability, humor);

5. status (socioeconomic position, popularity);

6. situation (mental level; status; skills, needs, and interests of followers; objectives to be achieved, etc.).[1]

Each reader will probably react differently to the list. Some items will seem consistent with his or her understanding of what is necessary for an individual to be a "good leader," while others will seem markedly less important. On the one hand, we may think of people who are not very intelligent and not blessed with verbal facility but who are, nonetheless, obvious leaders. On the other hand, we may know brilliant thinkers and glib talkers who are, in spite of these advantages, quite clearly not leaders. It appears that particular traits are neither necessary or sufficient for producing leaders. Although many leaders do possess several of the traits indicated, the relationships among the traits are unclear, and the list of traits is not very useful as a management tool for predicting the leadership capability of any single individual. (In addition, very serious problems of trait definition and measurement arise.) For these reasons, for some years the search for universal leadership traits has not been a popular area of study, although many managers are convinced they know intuitively how to spot the job candidate who will be a true leader.

Styles of leadership

During the 1950s, many researchers who were frustrated with the difficulties of identifying leadership traits began instead to examine particular styles of leadership in the hope of identifying those styles that were especially effective. This trend was given impetus by the emergence (especially over the previous two decades) of the new approach to organizations discussed in chapter 6: the human relations movement. Under the traditional scientific management approach, leadership was a mechanistic function, provided for by the formal structure. A production worker employed under scientific management might verbalize his experiences with leadership as follows:

There's no doubt who the leader is—it's my boss, the supervisor. He's got all the cards. When he's told: "You get those guys busy," he does just that. If we don't get busy, there are plenty of things he can do about it. He's got the authority to say how much money we make—not just our rate, but overtime and bonuses; he says how fast we have to work; he can

---

[1]Ralph M. Stogdill, *Handbook of Leadership: A Survey of Theory and Research* (New York: Free Press, 1974).

"Faster!"

Drawing by Whitney Darrow, Jr.; © 1977 The New Yorker Magazine, Inc.

cut our break time; and most of all, he can fire all of us. But there's something else: he's just like we are; his supervisor tells him what to do.

The advocates of the human relations approach contended that, despite the leader's formal power, he or she did not always get from subordinates the performance that was desired. It was obvious that some managers were better leaders than others, and if clear differences in managers' social psychological traits did not explain the variations, what was the explanation? Many students of human relations believed that some behavioral variables, particularly alternative leadership styles, provided the explanation.

An early exploration in this field was a series of landmark studies by psychologist Kurt Lewin and his associates at the University of Iowa. Lewin recruited twenty ten-year-old boys and organized them into clubs that engaged in activities of interest to all of the children, including mask making, soap carving, and model airplane construction. The central purpose of the experiments was to see what differences in group performance, interaction patterns, satisfaction, etc. occurred when alternative leadership styles were tried. Each group

Table 9-1. Kurt Lewin's leadership styles

Authoritarian	Democratic	*Laissez-faire*
1. All determination of policy by the leader.	1. All policies a matter of group discussion and decision, encouraged and assisted by the leader.	1. Complete freedom for group or individual decision, without any leader participation.
2. Techniques and activity steps dictated by the authority, one at a time, so that future steps were always uncertain to a large degree.	2. Activity perspective gained during first discussion period. General steps to group goal sketched, and where technical advice was needed the leader suggested two or three alternative procedures from which choice could be made.	2. Various materials supplied by the leader, who made it clear that he would supply information when asked. He took no other part in work discussions.
3. The leader usually dictated the particular work task and work companions of each member.	3. The members were free to work with whomever they chose, and the division of tasks was left up to the group.	3. Complete nonparticipation by leader.
4. The dominator was "personal" in his praise and criticism of the work of each member, but remained aloof from active group participation except when demonstrating. He was friendly or impersonal rather than openly hostile.	4. The leader was "objective" or "fact-minded" in his praise and criticism, and tried to be a regular group member in spirit without doing too much of the work.	4. Very infrequent comments on member activities unless questioned, and no attempt to participate or interfere with the course of events.

Reprinted with permission from Kurt Lewin, Ronald Lippitt, and Ralph K. White, "Patterns of Aggressive Behavior in Experimentally Created 'Social Climates,'" *Journal of Social Psychology* 10 (May 1939): 273.

was given an adult leader, whose job it was to create a particular social atmosphere using one of three leadership styles: authoritarian, democratic, or *laissez-faire*. Table 9-1 elaborates the meaning of the three styles. The group leaders were changed every six weeks, and the new leader used a different leadership technique, so that during the study each group was exposed to each of the styles. Various controls were built in to insure that the results were as reliable as possible (e.g. particular leaders used alternative leadership styles with different groups), so one could know that the children were not merely reacting to the leaders' personalities; and after psychological testing the children were assigned to groups in such a way that balances were created, and insurance was provided that some groups were not composed of dominant personalities while others were composed of submissive ones.

The results indicated that leadership styles *do* make a difference. After brief periods of transition, the groups accepted a move from autocratic to democratic rule, for example, and group interaction tended to take on the tinge of the new style. As one might expect when boys were allowed to "run wild," the number of aggressive actions per meeting was highest in the *laissez-faire* atmospheres. Democracy produced moderate amounts of aggressive behavior, but authoritarianism was paradoxical: sometimes the boys reacted to autocracy with high degrees of hostility and aggression; at other times they were nonaggressive and apathetic. The authors summarized their interpretation of this latter phenomenon:

> *Four types of evidence indicate that this lack of aggression was probably not caused by lack of frustration, but by the repressive influence of the autocrat: (a) outbursts of aggression on the days of transition to a freer atmosphere; (b) a sharp rise of aggression when the autocrat left the room; (c) other indications of generalized apathy, such as an absence of smiling and joking; and (d) the fact that 19 out of 20 boys liked their democratic leader better than their autocratic leader, and 7 out of 10 also liked their "laissez-faire" leader better.*[2]

The results of Lewin's study do not provide a clear mandate for particular theories of management (although they give some support to the human relations approaches discussed below), but they do prove that leadership styles matter. Furthermore, leadership styles can be

---

[2]Kurt Lewin, Ronald Lippitt, and Ralph K. White, "Patterns of Aggressive Behavior in Experimentally Created 'Social Climates,' " *Journal of Social Psychology* 10 (May 1939): 298–99.

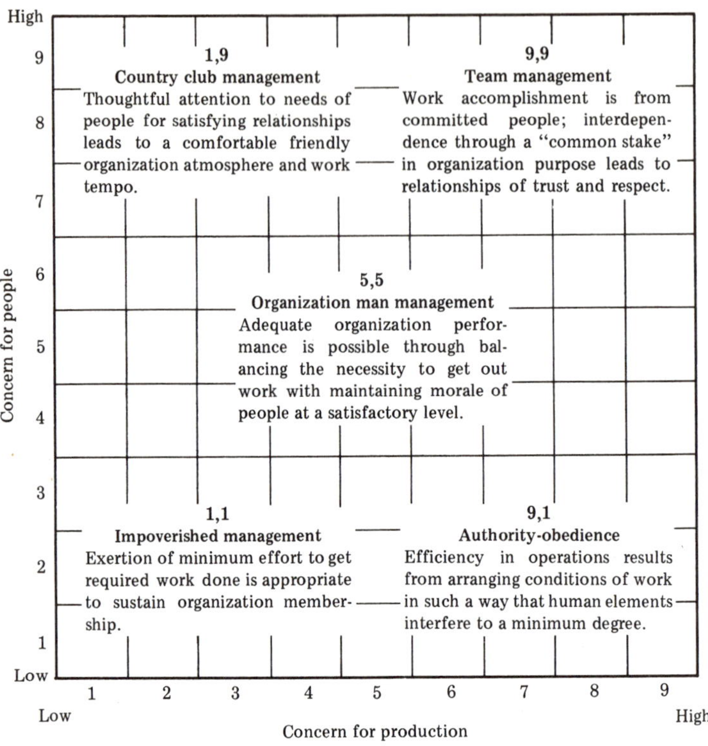

Figure 9-1. The New Managerial Grid®

Source: The Managerial Grid from *The New Managerial Grid,* by Robert R. Blake and Jane Srygley Mouton. Houston: Gulf Publishing Company, Copyright © 1978, page 11. Reproduced by permission.

manipulated; they are not necessarily bound to the personality of a particular manager.

The most widely cited shorthand description of leadership styles is Robert Blake and Jane Mouton's *Managerial Grid*®, shown in figure 9-1. The first edition of their book, published in 1964, sold nearly one million copies. They argue that leadership style rests principally upon the relative emphasis on *concern for production* on the one hand and *concern for people* on the other hand. A leader may be highly interested in increasing production, or this may be of relatively low importance. The same may be true of concern for people. Blake and Mouton's Grid is basically a table in which high, intermediate, and low degrees of each orientation are plotted against each other. Consequently, a large range of positions, which they believe actually exist in functioning organizations, is possible. Some leaders, "authority-obedience" managers, may be production oriented to an extreme degree and have little concern for the impact such goal striving has upon subordinates. Conversely, there are leaders, "country club managers," who have as a principal goal the maintenance of good relations with subordinates and who are very concerned that subordinates relate well to each other.

The combination of the variables that Blake and Mouton call the "best way to manage" is "team management" (the 9,9 management orientation in terms of the grid), which combines high concern for production with high concern for people. According to Blake and Mouton, from the organizational perspective, adopting a 9,9 orientation can increase profitability, improve relations between headquarters and other organization units and reduce interpersonal frictions and misunderstandings, and increase individual effort and creativity as well as commitment. From the individual manager's perspective, they report that a 9,9 orientation is positively associated with mental and physical health (whereas adverse mental and physical health consequences are associated with all other grid styles) and with career success. Blake and Mouton have so much confidence in team management that they conclude the revised edition of their book with the following thought: "Achievement of such a 9,9 orientation may be the key to strengthening the free enterprise system and the political democracy on which it rests."[3]

It may be interesting to think of yourself in an organizational setting. Would you push for goal attainment as the foremost objective? Would you strive for a happy relationship with others above all? Would you try to strike a middle ground? Or would you seek both goal attainment *and* the best in personal relationships? Through asking themselves such questions, leaders can assess their own behavior and perhaps seek to alter it.

Lewin and Blake and Mouton are, of course, not the only authors to have sought an understanding of leadership by looking at styles.[4] In fact, this type of analysis has come to surpass the trait theories as a focus of research.

Contingency theories

A third group of investigators emphasize the *situational* character of leadership. That is, they have concluded that there may not be a single set of traits or a single behavior pattern that can be certified as

---

[3]Robert R. Blake and Jane Srygley Mouton, *The New Managerial Grid* (Houston: Gulf Publishing Co., 1978), pp. 119, 128, and 217.

[4]See, for example, Ralph M. Stogdill and Alvin E. Coons, eds., *Leadership Behavior: Its Description and Measurement*, Research Monograph No. 98 (Columbus: Ohio State University, Bureau of Business Research, 1957); and Rensis Likert, *New Patterns of Management* (New York: McGraw-Hill, 1961).

Table 9-2.   Summary of Fiedler's investigations of leadership

| Condition | Group situation | | | Leadership style correlating with productivity |
	Leader-member relations	Task structure	Position power	
1 . . . . .Good		Structured	Strong	Directive
2 . . . . .Good		Structured	Weak	Directive
3 . . . . .Good		Unstructured	Strong	Directive
4 . . . . .Good		Unstructured	Weak	Permissive
5 . . . . .Moderately poor		Structured	Strong	Permissive
6 . . . . .Moderately poor		Structured	Weak	No data
7 . . . . .Moderately poor		Unstructured	Strong	No relationship found
8 . . . . .Moderately poor		Unstructured	Weak	Directive

Source: Fred E. Fiedler, *A Theory of Effective Leadership* (New York: McGraw-Hill, 1967), as summarized in James H. Donnelly, Jr., James L. Gibson, and John M. Ivancevich, *Fundamentals of Management,* rev. ed. (Dallas, Texas: Business Publications, Inc., 1975, © 1975), p. 226. Reprinted with permission.

resulting in "good" leadership. Rather, the appropriate traits and behaviors depend on the situation. To understand leadership, these theorists contend, one must describe relevant characteristics of the situation, including the nature of the task to be performed (highly structured or relatively unstructured), the amount of formal power or authority assigned to the leader, the value systems of all concerned, the nature of the problems presented, the size of the organization, and many similar features. To take just two examples, the traits and style needed to lead an infantry battalion are probably quite different from those needed to lead a university department. While some individuals might be able to adjust to either role, many would not. Similarly, differences in the total situation may be more important in explaining the rise of Hitler in Germany and Churchill in Britain than differences in traits or style. Both were leaders, but the particular situations in which they lived, including the prevalent values, defined the appropriate leadership traits and style.

Chapter nine

Accepting this understanding of leadership means that we cannot talk about individuals as being simply "good" or "bad" leaders. Such judgments are appropriate only after considering the situations in which the people are functioning at the time. The Tannenbaum and Schmidt article reprinted below is an example of the thinking of those who see leadership as situational.

Fred E. Fiedler, another author working in the situational tradition, argues that three elements define any situation:

1. *position power:* the degree to which the leader's official position enables him to get group members to comply with and accept direction and leadership; the potential power that the organization provides for the leader's use;

2. *task structure:* the degree to which the jobs of the followers are well defined, rather than unstructured or ambiguous; for instance, work on an assembly line is highly structured, whereas participation in a committee meeting is relatively unstructured;

3. *leader-member relations:* acceptance of the leader by members (liking, trusting) and loyalty of members to the leader.[5]

If these elements are, in fact, sufficient for defining the situation, then in a given situation there should be a leadership style that is especially effective. Fiedler contends he has found just that. Group productivity can be increased by particular styles of leadership, he says, but choice of style depends on the situation. Table 9–2 lists eight combinations of Fiedler's three elements of the situation, and the table's right column indicates the leadership style (directive or permissive) that would be most productive. Notice that all three of the items describing the situation must be considered; it would be convenient if we could conclude, for example, that mainly structured situations need directive leaders and mainly unstructured situations need permissive ones, but Fiedler found that matters are more complicated.

Not all researchers agree that Fiedler's method of "measuring the situation" is acceptable, but his findings and similar ones do emphasize the need to consider the situation—even if we have not yet found means for precisely describing it and even if we have not yet definitely learned how to react once it is defined.

Few public administrators, either in their own leadership roles or as participants in the selection of other leaders, would be so foolish as to rely totally on simple trait measures ("she has a master's degree in business administration," or "he is intelligent and a good speaker"). It is generally recognized that these traits, as well as particular leadership

[5]Fred E. Fiedler, *A Theory of Leadership Effectiveness* (New York: McGraw-Hill, 1967), pp. 22–23.

styles, may be quite appropriate in some situations, but inappropriate in others. For example, some cities have experienced difficulty when their city councils have hired managers mainly on the basis of a single trait: the holding of a degree in urban management. Without degrading such degrees (in fact, we heartily encourage prospective managers to take them), the holding of one simply does not say enough about the holder. Furthermore, the degree itself says almost nothing about just how that individual would fit into a particular urban situation. In some cities the manager's superior education may be resented by less well educated council members. It is critical that all involved in the selection process take such possibilities, as well as other features of the situation, into account at the time of selection.

B. Strategies of leadership

The student who decides to study leadership in organizations will learn quickly that scholars of business administration are the authors of most research and writing on the subject. We do not quarrel in essential respects with the thesis of these authors that there are important similarities between the private and public sectors with regard to the leadership component of the management task. At some point in their careers, public administrators, like business administrators, often find themselves functioning within large, complex organizations (which are characterized by a relatively rigid hierarchical structure) and charged with the task of "leading" others toward some objectives.

Consider the example of an acquaintance of ours who had worked for ten years in the personnel office of a federal agency, serving in such varied positions as classification specialist, interviewer, and job counselor. One day her supervisor offered her the opportunity of becoming the director of a twelve-person team responsible for implementing a new personnel management system. Her first reaction was to worry that her technical knowledge was far too limited for such a position. The job called for her to work closely with nationally prominent consultants in designing a program for improving employees' morale and then to educate the agency's managers in implementing it. Despite her worries, she accepted the post, determined to work hard to educate herself and develop a workable program. As the position evolved, though, her concerns for her lack of technical knowledge paled in comparison to a new worry: she doubted her ability to lead twelve people effectively and to get them to lead others. Personality clashes that had developed among workers in the unit during the past decade, which previously had seemed inconsequential, were suddenly of direct concern; thus far, her experience had taught her to do her own job well and not worry about others, but now *her job was to see that others did their jobs well.* She found that technical expertise could be gained rather easily; the consultants played key roles in devising the program. But her principal task was to see that the unit functioned smoothly and worked toward the established goal.

Important questions for our friend and for many public and business administrators are "Just how does one lead?" and "What strategies can be used to *assure* effective leadership?" Investigators of both the private and the public sectors have attempted to meet this demand by prescribing particular modes of leadership. Some of these prescriptions are linked closely to the various theories of organization presented in chapter 6.

Reward and punishment

Closely tied to Frederick Taylor's scientific management, and never completely abandoned, is the attempt to motivate workers by reward and punishment—promises of higher pay and the threat of job loss. Taylor's scheme, applied especially in the private sector, incorporated payment on a piece-rate basis so that the employee knew in advance precisely what financial reward would be given for each increment of production. Higher production levels resulted not only in greater *total pay* but also in a higher *pay rate;* the employee should thus be doubly motivated.[6]

Although justly criticized as failing to recognize other human aspirations and failing to realize that many individuals will stop short of producing up to their capabilities, the use of material rewards certainly has not been abandoned. The pay schedules in the public sector, which are linked to the position classes of the personnel system, normally allow for several steps within each pay grade. Using these, a supervisor has a means of financially rewarding a subordinate without giving a promotion to a higher grade, at least until the employee reaches the top level of the present grade. Whether or not such pay steps are so used depends on the practice of the particular supervisor and governmental unit. From the point of view of those who support material reward as a means of motivation, it is unfortunate that many units have fallen into the practice of basing salary increases on longevity rather than performance. Doing so avoids the difficulty of evaluating employees; only those whose performance is so unsatisfactory as to warrant dismissal are

---

[6]Frederick W. Taylor, "A Piece Rate System: Being a Step Toward a Partial Solution of the Labor Problem," in Clarence Bertrand Thompson, ed., *Scientific Management* (Cambridge: Harvard University Press, 1914), pp. 636–65.

sanctioned. Recent changes in the federal government's civil service system are designed to increase opportunities for leaders to hand out rewards and penalties. Some governments use of special bonuses, prizes for money-saving suggestions, commendations, etc., but these rewards are less predictable (hence, presumably less efficient motivators) than those discussed above.

Organizational humanism

Out of the human relations movement of the 1930s grew a group of leadership strategies, sometimes called *organizational humanism,* that focus upon the interpersonal relationships between managers and workers and among workers themselves and upon the nonmonetary needs of workers. James A. Lee has given the label Modern Human Resources Management (MHRM) to this group of strategies developed by such authors as Lewin and Blake and Mouton, discussed earlier in the chapter, and by others to be discussed such as McGregor and Maslow. Synthesizing these theories, Lee says MHRM has three main parts:

1. managers should trust their subordinates to be more responsible in the performance of their jobs;

2. managers should permit subordinates to participate in the making of their own jobs; and

3. managers should replace much of the mechanistic structure, characteristic of most institutions, with an organic approach to organization.[7]

One leading theorist of organizational humanism was Douglas McGregor, who felt that the repressive structure of bureaucratic organizations often discouraged workers from motivating themselves to do their best work. To illustrate his thinking, he developed two polar conceptions of organization: *Theory X and Theory Y.* McGregor said that Theory X assumes that most people do not like to work, and when they must, they prefer to be led; furthermore, they are autonomous individuals indifferent to the organization, noncreative, opposed to change, easily manipulated, and motivated by threat of punishment. In contrast, Theory Y assumes that in favorable circumstances most people can

---

[7]James A. Lee, "Behavioral Theory vs. Reality," *Harvard Business Review* (March–April 1971): 21.

enjoy work as much as play, that they prefer to assume responsibility for their work, that (especially through group interaction) they can identify with the goals of the organization, that they can be creative and flexible, and that they are intelligent beings motivated by a variety of monetary and particularly nonmonetary factors. Of course, McGregor advised that Theory Y was a superior managerial tool, particularly because of its self-motivating features.[8]

Since any effort by a leader to meet the organization's goals could be thwarted by disagreement and tension among subordinates, a human relations consultant might recommend, for example, that individual and group counseling be adopted to aid employees in coping with such difficulties. Furthermore, in the hope that employees who are involved in the decision-making process will come to feel they are a part of the "team," leaders have been encouraged to employ democratic decision-making techniques. A number of authors—including Rensis Likert, Frederick Herzberg, and Chris Argyris—have stressed the importance of *participatory management*.[9] Because workers can identify with their work and with the goals of the organization and because they feel that their contribution to the organization is recognized and rewarded, they are motivated to do their best; the end result of this strategy (as with material reward or punishment) should be higher productivity.

Abraham Maslow, a prominent humanistic psychologist, suggested that each individual has a *hierarchy of needs*. Thus, any effort to lead that individual must begin with the recognition of just which needs have been previously satisfied and which needs are presently most critical. Maslow's five needs, in ascending order, are:

1. physiological needs—including the need for food, sleep, and other basic requirements for survival;

2. safety needs—consisting of the need for freedom from fear, for structure, for security, and for stability;

3. belongingness and love needs—the necessity for a place in a group or family, for friends, for contact and intimacy;

4. esteem needs—including the need for self-esteem and the respect of others, for mastery and competence, and for reputation and status;

---

[8]Douglas McGregor, *The Human Side of Enterprise* (New York: McGraw-Hill, 1960).

[9]See Rensis Likert, *New Patterns of Management* (New York: McGraw-Hill, 1961); Herbert Herzberg, *Work and the Nature of Man* (Cleveland: World Publishing Co., 1966); Chris Argyris, *Interpersonal Competence and Organizational Effectiveness* (Homewood, Ill.: Dorsey Press, 1962).

5. need for self-actualization—a requirement for achieving one's potential, using his or her talents fully.[10]

According to Maslow, only after lower order needs are satisfied can the individual be motivated by the promise of satisfaction of the higher needs.

While the conception of the importance of workers' needs does not provide the leader a precise strategy, it does give a guide in selecting the means of motivation to be employed. For example, monetary rewards might be quite appropriate for some employees, who could then use that money to satisfy needs 1 and 2. For those employees who already find those needs basically satisfied, however, the promise of somewhat more money may not be sufficiently motivating. Clearly, the "happy worker" theme is aimed principally at satisfying needs 3 and 4.

Organization development

Perhaps the distinctive feature of modern organizations is the establishment of hierarchies of authority. Max Weber saw the existence of such hierarchies as central to the accomplishment of organizational goals. But what happens when important changes occur in the organization's goals or when the basic technologies for accomplishing its work are altered? How do leaders continue to lead when such fundamental changes make old hierarchical arrangements and statements of formal authority anachronistic?

Warren Bennis and others have urged that specific strategies be adopted for *organization development (OD)*.[11] They have urged leaders to recognize the need for change and to undertake it systematically. Many leaders have decided to employ outside OD consultants, who are asked to examine the organization's present functioning and then to work with the leaders to produce changes both in the organization and in its individual members. Sometimes the consultant finds it useful to establish mechanisms for feedback of views from one part of the organization to another; questionnaires may be distributed and the results analyzed; face-to-face meetings may be arranged. Also, training groups (T-groups), in which participants are encouraged to examine both their own attitudes and those of others, are commonly created; as a result, the

---

[10]Abraham H. Maslow, *Motivation and Personality,* 2d ed. (New York: Harper and Row, 1970), pp. 35–46. Maslow mentioned also the "desire to know and understand" and aesthetic needs, but indicated that little is known about these.

[11]Warren G. Bennis, *Organization Development: Its Nature, Origins and Prospects* (Reading, Mass.: Addison-Wesley Publishing Co., 1969).

participants may become more sensitive to the needs of other organizational units and members. "Team-building," bringing together those eight to ten people who work together in order to discuss their needs and problems and their proposed solutions, is also often attempted. Through these processes, it is hoped that organizational members will learn about themselves and each other, and from them changes in individual behavior and in the organization itself are expected to emerge.

There has been no single approach to organization development. Some consultants have brought with them a package of prepared plans, which were simply applied to the organization in question (perhaps after some modification); others have allowed a particular plan to develop through interchanges within the organization, after its needs have been assessed. In both cases, though, a major effort is made to look simultaneously at the individuals and at the organization. The OD specialist sees neither formal structure nor individual needs as dominant.

Management by objectives

Drawing on several of the strategies mentioned above, management consultant Peter Drucker has proposed that leaders should perform their tasks by focusing attention on organizational objectives; the objectives of each lower-level manager should be derived from the grand objectives. This approach to leadership is called *management by objectives (MBO)*. Although much of MBO is compatible with the human relations approach to management, Drucker has criticized one aspect of it: "To 'give [a worker] a *sense* of participation' (to use a pet phrase of human relations jargon) is not enough. It is the wrong thing. Being a manager means *having* responsibility."[12] While the goals of the total organization remain paramount for Drucker, the process of arriving at specific objectives for each lower level is one of communication and exchange of information between leader and subordinate. The result should be an objective upon which both agree and a commitment by the subordinate to pursue that objective. The leader, in turn, agrees to judge performance on the basis of the attainment of the objectives. The expectation of this management philosophy is that the process will result in individual commitment to particular goals and a real feeling of being a part of the organization. The exchange of information necessary for agreement on goals is highly important in this approach. Attaining goal agreement may itself require more communication than leaders would

---

[12]Peter Drucker, *Management: Tasks, Responsibilities, Practices* (New York: Harper and Row, 1973), p. 438.

otherwise have with their subordinates over an entire year, and some critics of MBO see this as an artificial and time-wasting exercise.

It was, of course, the scientific management, rather than the human relations, aspects of MBO that made it attractive to the Nixon administration; the technique was officially mandated for twenty-one federal agencies by presidential memoranda on April 18, 1973. Sherwood and Page have noted that MBO

> was part of an orientation that found societal good in the private sector and evil in the public. Harvard Business School became newly glorious. The attitude of the Nixon top management was one of low trust and contempt toward civil servants. Control and dominance of the system became particularly central concerns in [Nixon's] second term. There was a drive to introduce managerial techniques to assure continued control of policy, money, and manpower according to the classic business model.[13]

Officials of the newly revitalized *Office of Management and Budget (OMB)* were supposed to conduct frequent objectives-setting sessions with heads of agencies, who were instructed to thresh out their own objectives with their subordinates in earlier meetings. Within a few months, however, difficulties became apparent. The installation of MBO in the private sector has been facilitated by wide agreement on such relatively unambiguous goals as *profit making,* but for reasons we have mentioned elsewhere (especially in chapter 2) it is much more difficult for government agencies to develop precise objectives that are nontrivial. Apparently, MBO's sponsors at OMB came to realize that the concept for which they had such great hopes was simply a management tool (and a rather cumbersome one at that) which had no mystical powers to force agencies to implement Nixon policies.

According to Richard Rose, who has conducted a study of the program, as it became apparent that MBO was *apolitical,* directors at OMB gradually lost interest in the technique, as evidenced, for example, by the frequent cancellation of meetings between them and the responsible officials in the government agencies. Rose's analysis of the formal objectives that agencies were required to file with OMB in 1973 and 1974 found that four-fifths of them were apolitical; for instance, they agreed to file a report by a certain date (without saying what the content would be), or they pledged to implement a newly minted law. Although MBO no longer exists as a definite program in the federal government, this

---

[13]Frank P. Sherwood and William J. Page, Jr., "MBO and Public Management," *Public Administration Review* 36 (January/February 1976): 7. Reprinted from *Public Administration Review.* © 1976 by The American Society for Public Administration, 1225 Connecticut Avenue, N.W., Washington, D.C. All rights reserved.

does not mean that it has sunk without a trace. Richard Rose's concluding observations are apt, and the implications extend beyond MBO:

> *To ask today—"What's happened to MBO?"—is to raise fundamental questions about the implementation of management innovation within the federal government. Are we to say that MBO was institutionalized when there was a paper exercise in full swing in 1973–74? Are we to say that it has disappeared in default of political interest, even though there remain staff in many agencies still carrying on MBO-type activities? Perhaps it is better to turn from a legalistic determination of its status to a more atmospheric one, concluding that MBO has evaporated, becoming a part of the climate of management, albeit a part whose specific influence is limited and incapable of precise measurement. For better or worse, it thus stands in the tradition of a long line of management improvement schemes launched under the auspices of the Bureau of the Budget and OMB in the past quarter century or more.*[14]

Devoted advocates of MBO claim that it was not given a fair trial by the federal government and that some state and local governments and private businesses also have adopted the technique in *name but not in spirit*. Total implementation requires that supervisors be willing to give their subordinates wide latitude and to use achievement of objectives as the basis for judging performance. Many supervisors find it difficult if not impossible to overlook personal characteristics and work practices that they find objectionable. Especially hard for many old-line managers is the setting of subordinates' objectives only through consultation, rather than through issuance of instructions. One supervisor of our acquaintance, a high-ranking federal official who handled in-service education programs, addressed a group of subordinates and announced the implementation of management by objectives for the coming year. Then he proclaimed:

> *Here are your objectives: (1) We are going to cooperate with each other this year rather than compete; (2) We are going to follow proper procedures in handling matters that impact upon the contracts we have with universities; (3) The universities that have contracts with us are going to establish an association to make contract negotiation easier . . . .*

Totally missing were any efforts to specify *precisely* the organizational objectives, to set *jointly* the objectives of subordinates, to specify means

---

[14]Richard Rose, "Implementation and Evaporation: The Record of MBO," *Public Administration Review* 37 (January/February 1977): 68–70.

of measuring the *attainment* of objectives, or to provide subordinates broad *discretion* in reaching objectives. While this example is extreme, such corruptions of MBO are not uncommon.

Current tendencies

The sometimes intense disagreements about what produces "good leadership," whether it be traits or styles or both in varying situations, illustrate the complexity facing students of organizational behavior. Despite this complexity (or perhaps because of it), theorists are under strong pressure to provide prescriptions for the obvious maladies of organizations. Most of us who observe government agencies or private firms conclude that all too often these organizations do not perform up to the level we would desire: they are inefficient, ineffective, or unresponsive.

Fortunately for the families of management consultants, hope springs eternal in the reformer's breast. Despite failures in many cases, confidence that performance can be improved through organizational restructuring or through the introduction of some new leadership technique continues. Change efforts are frequent; innovations are often adopted in the desperate *hope* that they will work, but with little real basis for *believing* they will work. Sometimes the desire to demonstrate that an effort at improvement is being made is the actual motivating factor.

The scientific management approach is of more than historical interest; efforts to apply it continue today. A new area in which the techniques are now being applied, for example, is higher education. We are not aware that any of the new breed of business-trained academic administrators have actually conducted time-and-motion studies with stopwatches, but as the number of high-school graduates declines, student count (number of majors, credit hour load, faculty-student ratios, etc.) is increasingly being used as a principal basis for funding academic departments. To the applause of state legislatures, managers are telling departments that rewards will be dispensed to those who attract students; in some cases, the salaries of individual faculty members are even determined in this way. While universities do not generally go so far as to pay on a piece-rate basis, the link of this present trend to the scientific management philosophy is clear. But there was more to scientific management than the piece-rate basis of payment. In general, it encouraged managers to make decisions on the basis of carefully specified organizational objectives. Student count meets that requirement—although we doubt that most academicians would agree that it is the *appropriate* objective. Throughout much of government, scientific management is alive and well, even if it is not always so labeled.

Perhaps more apparent in government agencies today, however, are efforts to incorporate in management practices the teachings of the human relations school. Especially notable are efforts to increase employee satisfaction by opening avenues for them to express their views and by making possible their participation in decision making. Simple *decentralization* is a step toward this, and many government agencies have taken that step. So, too, have they *expanded communication channels* by establishing employee newsletters and holding regular meetings, often conceived of as "rap sessions," between employees and upper-level managers. Few would have dreamed twenty years ago that army generals, commanding large units, would meet regularly with enlisted personnel and hear their comments on the unit's operation. But today they sometimes do, and comparable practices exist in civilian agencies as well.

The introduction of management by objectives (MBO) is especially interesting because it incorporates important elements of both scientific management and human relations. It encourages a clear and fixed focus on organizational objectives (as does scientific management), but it also encourages significant participation by subordinate personnel in setting their own objectives and in selecting the means of achieving them. It seems likely that such techniques as MBO will continue to dominate leadership training and development, at least in the near future. But as public administrators, consultants, and university scholars all seek effective cures for organizational maladies, the variety of prescriptions will continue to expand. Many will be tried; the results of most will be inconclusive, but some probably will prove valuable—even if the cure is not likely to be miraculous.

How to choose a leadership pattern*

Robert Tannenbaum and Warren H. Schmidt

As its title indicates, this selection is highly programmatic. The authors, both professors of management at UCLA, undertake to tell managers how "authoritarian" or how "democratic" they should be in exercising leadership under varying circumstances. Three factors, or "forces," should be considered, they believe: forces in the manager, such as the extent to which he or she is inclined to be directive or can tolerate ambiguity; forces in the subordinates, such as their identification with the organization's goals or their degrees of competence; and forces in the situation, such as the pressure of time or the need to keep plans confidential. Constructing a continuum between what they prefer to label "boss-centered" and "subordinate-centered" leadership, Tannenbaum and Schmidt say that the successful leader is the one who in any given case understands the configuration of the forces and is sufficiently flexible to pick a leadership pattern—any point on their continuum—that is appropriate to the occasion.

The main part of the selection was first published in 1958. Because of its insights, the article is considered a classic statement on the subject. The *Harvard Business Review* republished the piece fifteen years after its original appearance, and the authors contributed a retrospective commentary, which is included here.

"I put most problems into my group's hands and leave it to them to carry the ball from there. I serve merely as a catalyst, mirroring back the people's thoughts and feelings so that they can better understand them."

"It's foolish to make decisions oneself on matters that affect people. I always talk things over with my subordinates, but I make it clear to them that I'm the one who has to have the final say."

"Once I have decided on a course of action, I do my best to sell my ideas to my employees."

"I'm being paid to lead. If I let a lot of other people make the decisions I should be making, then I'm not worth my salt."

---

*Robert Tannenbaum and Warren H. Schmidt, "How to Choose a Leadership Pattern," *Harvard Business Review*, May–June 1973, Copyright © 1973 by the President and Fellows of Harvard College; all rights reserved.

"I believe in getting things done. I can't waste time calling meetings. Someone has to call the shots around here, and I think it should be me."

Each of these statements represents a point of view about "good leadership." Considerable experience, factual data, and theoretical principles could be cited to support each statement; even though they seem to be inconsistent when placed together. Such contradictions point up the dilemma in which the modern manager frequently finds himself.

New problem

The problem of how the modern manager can be "democratic" in his relations with subordinates and at the same time maintain the necessary authority and control in the organization for which he is responsible has come into focus increasingly in recent years.

Earlier in the century this problem was not so acutely felt. The successful executive was generally pictured as possessing intelligence, imagination, initiative, the capacity to make rapid (and generally wise) decisions, and the ability to inspire subordinates. People tended to think of the world as being divided into "leaders" and "followers."

Gradually, however, from the social sciences emerged the concept of "group dynamics" with its focus on *members* of the group rather than solely on the leader. Research efforts of social scientists underscored the importance of employee involvement and participation in decision making. Evidence began to challenge the efficiency of highly directive leadership, and increasing attention was paid to problems of motivation and human relations.

Through training laboratories in group development that sprang up across the country, many of the newer notions of leadership began to exert an impact. These training laboratories were carefully designed to give people a firsthand experience in full participation and decision making. The designated "leaders" deliberately attempted to reduce their own power and to make group members as responsible as possible for setting their own goals and methods within the laboratory experience.

It was perhaps inevitable that some of the people who attended the training laboratories regarded this kind of leadership as being truly "democratic" and went home with the determination to build fully participative decision making into their own organizations. Whenever their bosses made a decision without convening a staff meeting, they tended to perceive this as authoritarian behavior. The true symbol of democratic leadership to some was the meeting—and the less directed from the top, the more democratic it was.

Some of the more enthusiastic alumni of these training laboratories began to get the habit of categorizing leader behavior as "democratic" or "authoritarian." The boss who made too many decisions himself was thought of as an authoritatian, and his directive behavior was often attributed solely to his personality.

The net result of the research findings and of the human relations training based upon them has been to call into question the stereotype of an effective leader. Consequently, the modern manager often finds himself in an uncomfortable state of mind.

Often he is not quite sure how to behave; there are times when he is torn between exerting "strong" leadership and "permissive" leadership. Sometimes new knowledge pushes him in one direction ("I should really get the group to help make this decision"), but at the same time his experience pushes him in another direction ("I really understand the problem better than the group and therefore I should make the decision"). He is not sure when a group decision is really appropriate or when holding a staff meeting serves merely as a device for avoiding his own decision-making responsibility.

The purpose of our article is to suggest a framework which managers may find useful in grappling with this dilemma. First, we shall look at the different patterns of leadership behavior that the manager can choose from in relating himself to his subordinates. Then, we shall turn to some of the questions suggested by this range of patterns. For instance, how important is it for a manager's subordinates to know what type of leadership he is using in a situation? What factors should he consider in deciding on a leadership pattern? What difference do his long-run objectives make as compared to his immediate objectives?

Range of behavior

Exhibit 1 presents the continuum or range of possible leadership behavior available to a manager. Each type of action is related to the degree of authority used by the boss and to the amount of freedom available to his subordinates in reaching decisions. The actions seen on the extreme left characterize the manager who maintains a high degree of control, while those seen on the extreme right characterize the manager who releases a high degree of control. Neither extreme is absolute; authority and freedom are never without their limitations.

Now let us look more closely at each of the behavior points occurring along this continuum.

The manager makes the decision and announces it. In this case the boss identifies a problem, considers alternative solutions, chooses one of them, and then reports this decision to his subordinates for implementation. He may or may not give consideration to what he believes his subordinates will think or feel about his decision; in any case, he provides no opportunity for them to participate directly in the decision-making process. Coercion may or may not be used or implied.

The manager "sells" his decision. Here the manager, as before, takes responsibility for identifying the problem and arriving at a decision. However, rather than simply announcing it, he takes the additional step of persuading his subordinates to accept it. In doing so, he recognizes the possibility of some resistance among those who will be faced with the decision, and seeks to

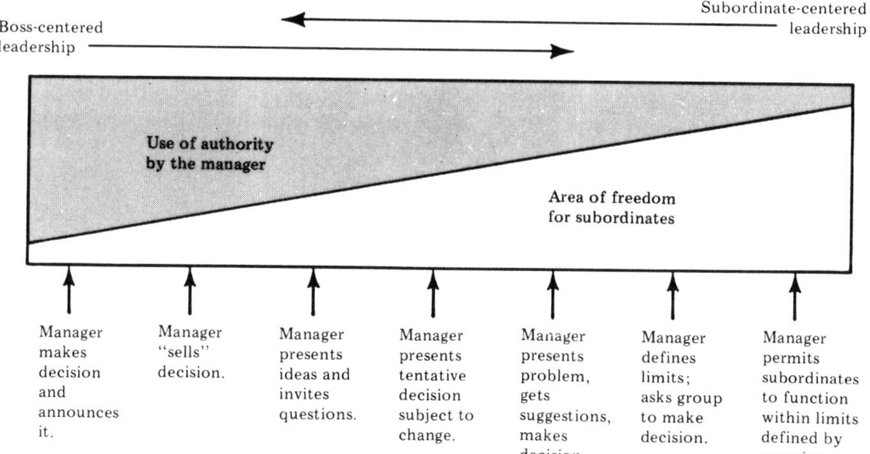

Exhibit 1. Continuum of leadership behavior

reduce this resistance by indicating, for example, what the employees have to gain from his decision.

The manager presents his ideas, invites questions. Here the boss who has arrived at a decision and who seeks acceptance of his ideas provides an opportunity for his subordinates to get a fuller explanation of his thinking and his intentions. After presenting the ideas, he invites questions so that his associates can better understand what he is trying to accomplish. This "give and take" also enables the manager and the subordinates to explore more fully the implications of the decision.

The manager presents a tentative decision subject to change. This kind of behavior permits the subordinates to exert some influence on the decision. The initiative for identifying and diagnosing the problem remains with the boss. Before meeting with his staff, he has thought the problem through and arrived at a decision—but only a tentative one. Before finalizing it, he presents his proposed solution for the reaction of those who will be affected by it. He says in effect, "I'd like to hear what you have to say about this plan that I have developed. I'll appreciate your frank reactions, but will reserve for myself the final decision."

The manager presents the problem, gets suggestions, and then makes his decision. Up to this point the boss has come before the group with a solution of his own. Not so in this case. The subordinates now get the first chance to suggest solutions. The manager's initial role involves identifying the problem. He might, for example, say something of this sort: "We are faced with a number of complaints from newspapers and the general public on our service policy. What is wrong here? What ideas do you have for coming to grips with this problem?"

The function of the group becomes one of increasing the manager's repertory of possible solutions to the problem. The purpose is to capitalize on the knowledge and experience of those who are on the "firing line." From the

Managing the agency/

expanded list of alternatives developed by the manager and his subordinates, the manager then selects the solution that he regards as most promising.[1]

The manager defines the limits and requests the group to make a decision. At this point the manager passes to the group (possibly including himself as a member) the right to make decisions. Before doing so, however, he defines the problem to be solved and the boundaries within which the decision must be made.

An example might be the handling of a parking problem at a plant. The boss decides that this is something that should be worked on by the people involved, so he calls them together and points up the existence of the problem. Then he tells them:

"There is the open field just north of the main plant which has been designated for additional employee parking. We can build underground or surface multilevel facilities as long as the cost does not exceed $100,000. Within these limits we are free to work out whatever solution makes sense to us. After we decide on a specific plan, the company will spend the available money in whatever way we indicate."

The manager permits the group to make decisions within prescribed limits. This represents an extreme degree of group freedom only occasionally encountered in formal organizations as, for instance, in many research groups. Here the team of managers or engineers undertakes the identification and diagnosis of the problem, develops alternative procedures for solving it, and decides on one or more of these alternative solutions. The only limits directly imposed on the group by the organization are those specified by the superior of the team's boss. If the boss participates in the decision-making process, he attempts to do so with no more authority than any other member of the group. He commits himself in advance to assist in implementing whatever decision the group makes.

Key questions

As the continuum in Exhibit 1 demonstrates, there are a number of alternative ways in which a manager can relate himself to the group or individuals he is supervising. At the extreme left of the range, the emphasis is on the manager—on what *he* is interested in, how *he* sees things, how *he* feels about them. As we move toward the subordinate-centered end of the continuum, however, the focus is increasingly on the subordinates—on what *they* are interested in, how *they* look at things, how *they* feel about them.

When business leadership is regarded in this way, a number of questions arise. Let us take four of especial importance:

1. *Can a boss ever relinquish his responsibility by delegating it to someone else?* Our view is that the manager must expect to be held responsible by his superior for the quality of the decisions made, even though operationally these decisions may have been made on a group basis. He should, therefore,

---

[1]For a fuller explanation of this approach, see Leo Moore, "Too Much Management, Too Little Change," *Harvard Business Review*, January–February 1956, p. 41.

be ready to accept whatever risk is involved whenever he delegates decision-making power to his subordinates. Delegation is not a way of "passing the buck." Also, it should be emphasized that the amount of freedom the boss gives to his subordinates cannot be greater than the freedom which he himself has been given by his own superior.

2. *Should the manager participate with his subordinates once he has delegated responsibility to them?* The manager should carefully think over this question and decide on his role prior to involving the subordinate group. He should ask if his presence will inhibit or facilitate the problem-solving process. There may be some instances when he should leave the group to let it solve the problem for itself. Typically, however, the boss has useful ideas to contribute, and should function as an additional member of the group. In the latter instance, it is important that he indicate clearly to the group that he sees himself in a *member* role rather than in an authority role.

3. *How important is it for the group to recognize what kind of leadership behavior the boss is using?* It makes a great deal of difference. Many relationship problems between boss and subordinate occur because the boss fails to make clear how he plans to use his authority. If, for example, he actually intends to make a certain decision himself, but the subordinate group gets the impression that he has delegated this authority, considerable confusion and resentment are likely to follow. Problems may also occur when the boss uses a "democratic" façade to conceal the fact that he has already made a decision which he hopes the group will accept as its own. The attempt to "make them think it was their idea in the first place" is a risky one. We believe that it is highly important for the manager to be honest and clear in describing what authority he is keeping and what role he is asking his subordinates to assume in solving a particular problem.

4. *Can you tell how "democratic" a manager is by the number of decisions his subordinates make?* The sheer *number* of decisions is not an accurate index of the amount of freedom that a subordinate group enjoys. More important is the *significance* of the decisions which the boss entrusts to his subordinates. Obviously a decision on how to arrange desks is of an entirely different order from a decision involving the introduction of new electronic data-processing equipment. Even though the widest possible limits are given in dealing with the first issue, the group will sense no particular degree of responsibility. For a boss to permit the group to decide equipment policy, even within rather narrow limits, would reflect a greater degree of confidence in them on his part.

Deciding how to lead

Now let us turn from the types of leadership which are possible in a company situation to the question of what types are *practical* and *desirable*. What factors or forces should a manager consider in deciding how to manage? Three are of particular importance: forces in the manager, forces in the subordinates, forces in the situation.

We should like briefly to describe these elements and indicate how they might influence a manager's action in a decision-making situation.[2] The strength of each of them will, of course, vary from instance to instance, but the manager who is sensitive to them can better assess the problems which face him and determine which mode of leadership behavior is most appropriate for him.

Forces in the manager.   The manager's behavior in any given instance will be influenced greatly by the many forces operating within his own personality. He will, of course, perceive his leadership problems in a unique way on the basis of his background, knowledge, and experience. Among the important internal forces affecting him will be the following:

1. *His value system.* How strongly does he feel that individuals should have a share in making the decisions which affect them? Or, how convinced is he that the official who is paid to assume responsibility should personally carry the burden of decision making? The strength of his convictions on questions like these will tend to move the manager to one end or the other of the continuum shown in Exhibit 1. His behavior will also be influenced by the relative importance that he attaches to organizational efficiency, personal growth of subordinates, and company profits.[3]

2. *His confidence in his subordinates.* Managers differ greatly in the amount of trust they have in other people generally, and this carries over to the particular employees they supervise at a given time. In viewing his particular group of subordinates, the manager is likely to consider their knowledge and competence with respect to the problem. A central question he might ask himself is: "Who is best qualified to deal with this problem?" Often he may, justifiably or not, have more confidence in his own capabilities than in those of his subordinates.

3. *His own leadership inclinations.* There are some managers who seem to function more comfortably and naturally as highly directive leaders. Resolving problems and issuing orders come easily to them. Other managers seem to operate more comfortably in a team role, where they are continually sharing many of their functions with their subordinates.

4. *His feelings of security in an uncertain situation.* The manager who releases control over the decision-making process thereby reduces the predictability of the outcome. Some managers have a greater need than others for predictability and stability in their environment. This "tolerance for ambiguity" is being viewed increasingly by psychologists as a key variable in a person's manner of dealing with problems.

The manager brings these and other highly personal variables to each situation he faces. If he can see them as forces which, consciously or unconsciously, influence his behavior, he can better understand what makes him prefer to act in a given way. And understanding this, he can often make himself more effective.

---

[2]See also Robert Tannenbaum and Fred Massarik, "Participation by Subordinates in the Managerial Decision-Making Process," *Canadian Journal of Economics and Political Science,* August 1950, p. 413.

[3]See Chris Argyris, "Top Management Dilemma: Company Needs vs. Individual Development," *Personnel,* September 1955, pp. 123–34.

Forces in the subordinate.   Before deciding how to lead a certain group, the manager will also want to consider a number of forces affecting his subordinates' behavior. He will want to remember that each employee, like himself, is influenced by many personality variables. In addition, each subordinate has a set of expectations about how the boss should act in relation to him. (The phrase "expected behavior" is one we hear more and more often these days at discussions of leadership and teaching.) The better the manager understands these factors, the more accurately he can determine what kind of behavior on his part will enable his subordinates to act most effectively.

Generally speaking, the manager can permit his subordinates greater freedom if the following essential conditions exist:

1. If the subordinates have relatively high needs for independence. (As we all know, people differ greatly in the amount of direction that they desire.)

2. If the subordinates have a readiness to assume responsibility for decision making. (Some see additional responsibility as a tribute to their ability; others see it as "passing the buck.")

3. If they have a relatively high tolerance for ambiguity. (Some employees prefer to have clear-cut directives given to them; others prefer a wider area of freedom.)

4. If they are interested in the problem and feel that it is important.

5. If they understand and identify with the goals of the organization.

6. If they have the necessary knowledge and experience to deal with the problem.

7. If they have learned to expect to share in decision making. (Persons who have come to expect strong leadership and are then suddenly confronted with the request to share more fully in decision making are often upset by this new experience. On the other hand, persons who have enjoyed a considerable amount of freedom resent the boss who begins to make all the decisions himself.)

The manager will probably tend to make fuller use of his own authority if the above conditions do *not* exist; at times there may be no realistic alternative to running a "one-man show."

The restrictive effect of many of the forces will, of course, be greatly modified by the general feeling of confidence which subordinates have in the boss. Where they have learned to respect and trust him, he is free to vary his behavior. He will feel certain that he will not be perceived as an authoritarian boss on those occasions when he makes decisions by himself. Similarly, he will not be seen as using staff meetings to avoid his decision-making responsibility. In a climate of mutual confidence and respect, people tend to feel less threatened by deviations from normal practice, which in turn makes possible a higher degree of flexibility in the whole relationship.

Forces in the situation.   In addition to the forces which exist in the manager himself and in his subordinates, certain characteristics of the general situation will also affect the manager's behavior. Among the more critical environmental pressures that surround him are those which stem from the organization, the work group, the nature of the problem, and the pressures of time. Let us look briefly at each of these:

Type of organization. Like individuals, organizations have values and traditions which inevitably influence the behavior of the people who work in them. The manager who is a newcomer to a company quickly discovers that certain kinds of behavior are approved, while others are not. He also discovers that to deviate radically from what is generally accepted is likely to create problems for him.

These values and traditions are communicated in numerous ways—through job descriptions, policy pronouncements, and public statements by top executives. Some organizations, for example, hold to the notion that the desirable executive is one who is dynamic, imaginative, decisive, and persuasive. Other organizations put more emphasis upon the importance of the executive's ability to work effectively with people—his human relations skills. The fact that his superiors have a defined concept of what the good executive should be will very likely push the manager toward one end or the other of the behavioral range.

In addition to the above, the amount of employee participation is influenced by such variables as the size of the working units, their geographical distribution, and the degree of inter- and intra-organizational security required to attain company goals. For example, the wide geographical dispersion of an organization may preclude a practical system of participative decision making, even though this would otherwise be desirable. Similarly, the size of the working units or the need for keeping plans confidential may make it necessary for the boss to exercise more control than would otherwise be the case. Factors like these may limit considerably the manager's ability to function flexibly on the continuum.

Group effectiveness. Before turning decision-making responsibility over to a subordinate group, the boss should consider how effectively its members work together as a unit.

One of the relevant factors here is the experience the group has had in working together. It can generally be expected that a group which has functioned for some time will have developed habits of cooperation and thus be able to tackle a problem more effectively than a new group. It can also be expected that a group of people with similar backgrounds and interests will work more quickly and easily than people with dissimilar backgrounds, because the communication problems are likely to be less complex.

The degree of confidence that the members have in their ability to solve problems as a group is also a key consideration. Finally, such group variables as cohesiveness, permissiveness, mutual acceptance, and commonality of purpose will exert subtle but powerful influence on the group's functioning.

The problem itself. The nature of the problem may determine what degree of authority should be delegated by the manager to his subordinates. Obviously he will ask himself whether they have the kind of knowledge which is needed. It is possible to do them a real disservice by assigning a problem that their experience does not equip them to handle.

Since the problems faced in large or growing industries increasingly require knowledge of specialists from many different fields, it might be inferred that the more complex a problem, the more anxious a manager will be to get some assistance in solving it. However, this is not always the case. There will be times when the very complexity of the problem calls for one person to work it out. For example, if the manager has most of the background and factual data relevant to a given issue, it may be easier for him to think it through himself than to take the time to fill in his staff on all the pertinent background information.

The key question to ask, of course, is: "Have I heard the ideas of everyone who has the necessary knowledge to make a significant contribution to the solution of this problem?"

The pressure of time. This is perhaps the most clearly felt pressure on the manager (in spite of the fact that it may sometimes be imagined). The more that he feels the need for an immediate decision, the more difficult it is to involve other people. In organizations which are in a constant state of "crisis" and "crash programming," one is likely to find managers personally using a high degree of authority with relatively little delegation to subordinates. When the time pressure is less intense, however, it becomes much more possible to bring subordinates in on the decision-making process.

These, then, are the principal forces that impinge on the manager in any given instance and that tend to determine his tactical behavior in relation to his subordinates. In each case his behavior ideally will be that which makes possible the most effective attainment of his immediate goal within the limits facing him.

Long-run strategy

As the manager works with his organization on the problems that come up day by day, his choice of a leadership pattern is usually limited. He must take account of the forces just described and, within the restrictions they impose on him, do the best that he can. But as he looks ahead months or even years, he can shift his thinking from tactics to large-scale strategy. No longer need he be fettered by all of the forces mentioned, for he can view many of them as variables over which he has some control. He can, for example, gain new insights or skills for himself, supply training for individual subordinates, and provide participative experiences for his employee group.

In trying to bring about a change in these variables, however, he is faced with a challenging question: At which point along the continuum *should* he act?

Attaining objectives. The answer depends largely on what he wants to accomplish. Let us suppose that he is interested in the same objectives that most modern managers seek to attain when they can shift their attention from the pressure of immediate assignments:

1. To raise the level of employee motivation.

2. To increase the readiness of subordinates to accept change.

3. To improve the quality of all managerial decisions.

4. To develop teamwork and morale.

5. To further the individual development of employees.

In recent years the manager has been deluged with a flow of advice on how best to achieve these longer-run objectives. It is little wonder that he is often both bewildered and annoyed. However, there are some guidelines which he can usefully follow in making a decision.

Most research and much of the experience of recent years give a strong factual basis to the theory that a fairly high degree of subordinate-centered behavior is associated with the accomplishment of the five purposes mentioned.[4] This does not mean that a manager should always leave all decisions to his assistants. To provide the individual or the group with greater freedom than they are ready for at any given time may very well tend to generate anxieties and therefore inhibit rather than facilitate the attainment of desired objectives. But this should not keep the manager from making a continuing effort to confront his subordinates with the challenge of freedom.

Conclusion

In summary, there are two implications in the basic thesis that we have been developing. The first is that the successful leader is one who is keenly aware of those forces which are most relevant to his behavior at any given time. He accurately understands himself, the individuals and group he is dealing with, and the company and broader social environment in which he operates. And certainly he is able to assess the present readiness for growth of his subordinates.

But this sensitivity or understanding is not enough, which brings us to the second implication. The successful leader is one who is able to behave appropriately in the light of these perceptions. If direction is in order, he is able to direct; if considerable participative freedom is called for, he is able to provide such freedom.

Thus, the successful manager of men can be primarily characterized neither as a strong leader nor as a permissive one. Rather, he is one who maintains a high batting average in accurately assessing the forces that determine what his most appropriate behavior at any given time should be and in actually being able to behave accordingly. Being both insightful and flexible, he is less likely to see the problems of leadership as a dilemma.

Retrospective commentary

Since this [article] was first published in 1958, there have been many changes in organizations and in the world that have affected leadership patterns. While the article's continued popularity attests to its essential validity,

---

[4]For example, see Warren H. Schmidt and Paul C. Buchanan, *Techniques that Produce Teamwork* (New London: Arthur C. Croft Publications, 1954); and Morris S. Viteles, *Motivation and Morale in Industry* (New York: W. W. Norton and Company, Inc., 1953).

we believe it can be reconsidered and updated to reflect subsequent societal changes and new management concepts.

The reasons for the article's continued relevance can be summarized briefly:

1. The article contains insights and perspectives which mesh well with, and help clarify, the experiences of managers, other leaders, and students of leadership. Thus it is useful to individuals in a wide variety of organizations—industrial, governmental, educational, religious, and community.

2. The concept of leadership the article defines is reflected in a continuum of leadership behavior (Exhibit 1 in original article). Rather than offering a choice between two styles of leadership, democratic or authoritarian, it sanctions a range of behavior.

3. The concept does not dictate to managers but helps them to analyze their own behavior. The continuum permits them to review their behavior within a context of other alternatives, without any style being labeled right or wrong.

(We have sometimes wondered if we have, perhaps, made it too easy for anyone to justify his or her style of leadership. It may be a small step between being nonjudgmental and giving the impression that all behavior is equally valid and useful. The latter was not our intention. Indeed, the thrust of our endorsement was for the manager who is insightful in assessing relevant forces within himself, others, and the situation, and who can be flexible in responding to these forces.)

In recognizing that our article can be updated, we are acknowledging that organizations do not exist in a vacuum but are affected by changes that occur in society. Consider, for example, the implications for organizations of these recent social developments:

> the youth revolution that expresses distrust and even contempt for organizations identified with the establishment;
>
> the civil rights movement that demands all minority groups be given a greater opportunity for participation and influence in the organizational processes;
>
> the ecology and consumer movements that challenge the right of managers to make decisions without considering the interest of people outside the organization; and
>
> the increasing national concern with the quality of working life and its relationship to worker productivity, participation, and satisfaction.

These and other societal changes make effective leadership in this decade a more challenging task, requiring even greater sensitivity and flexibility than was needed in the 1950s. Today's manager is more likely to deal with employees who resent being treated as subordinates, who may be highly critical of any organizational system, who expect to be consulted and to exert influence, and who often stand on the edge of alienation from the institution that needs their loyalty and commitment. In addition, he is frequently confronted by a highly turbulent, unpredictable environment.

In response to these social pressures, new concepts of management have emerged in organizations. Open-system theory, with its emphasis on subsystems' interdependency *and* on the interaction of an organization with its environment, has made a powerful impact on managers' approach to problems. Organization development has emerged as a new behavioral science approach to the improvement of individual, group, organizational, and interorganizational performance. New research has added to our understanding of motivation in the work situation. More and more executives have become concerned with social responsibility and have explored the feasibility of social audits. And a growing number of organizations, in Europe and in the United States, have conducted experiments in industrial democracy.

In light of these developments, we submit the following thoughts on how we would rewrite certain points in our original article.

The article described forces in the manager, subordinates, and the situation as givens, with the leadership pattern a resultant of these forces. We would now give more attention to the *interdependency* of these forces. For example, such interdependency occurs in: (a) the interplay between the manager's confidence in his subordinates, their readiness to assume responsibility, and the level of group effectiveness; and (b) the impact of the behavior of the manager on that of his subordinates, and vice versa.

In discussing the forces in the situation, we primarily identified organizational phenomena. We would now include forces lying outside the organization, and would explore the relevant interdependencies between the organization and its environment.

In the original article, we presented the size of the rectangle in Exhibit 1 as a given, with its boundaries already determined by external forces—in effect, a closed system. We would now recognize the possibility of the manager and/or his subordinates taking the initiative to change those boundaries through interaction with relevant external forces—both within their own organization and in the larger society.

The article portrayed the manager as the principal and almost unilateral actor. He initiated and determined group functions, assumed responsibility, and exercised control. Subordinates made inputs and assumed power only at the will of the manager. Although the manager might have taken into account forces outside himself, it was *he* who decided where to operate on the continuum—that is, whether to announce a decision instead of trying to sell his idea to his subordinates, whether to invite questions, to let subordinates decide an issue, and so on. While the manager has retained this clear prerogative in many organizations, it has been challenged in others. Even in situations where he has retained it, however, the balance in the relationship between manager and subordinates at any given time is arrived at by interaction—direct or indirect—between the two parties.

Although power and its use by the manager played a role in our article, we now realize that our concern with cooperation and collaboration, common goals, commitment, trust, and mutual caring limited our vision with respect to the realities of power. We did not attempt to deal with unions, other forms of joint worker action, or with individual workers' expressions of resistance. Today, we would recognize much more clearly the power available to *all* parties, and the factors that underlie the interrelated decisions on whether to use it.

In the original article, we used the terms *manager* and *subordinate*. We are now uncomfortable with *subordinate* because of its demeaning, dependency-laden connotations and prefer *nonmanager*. The titles *manager* and *nonmanager* make the terminological difference functional rather than hierarchical.

We assumed fairly traditional organizational structures in our original article. Now we would alter our formulation to reflect newer organizational modes which are slowly emerging, such as industrial democracy, intentional communities, and "phenomenarchy."[5] These new modes are based on observations such as the following:

Both manager and nonmanagers may be governing forces in their group's environment, contributing to the definition of the total area of freedom.

A group can function without a manager, with managerial functions being shared by group members.

A group, as a unit, can be delegated authority and can assume responsibility within a larger organizational context.

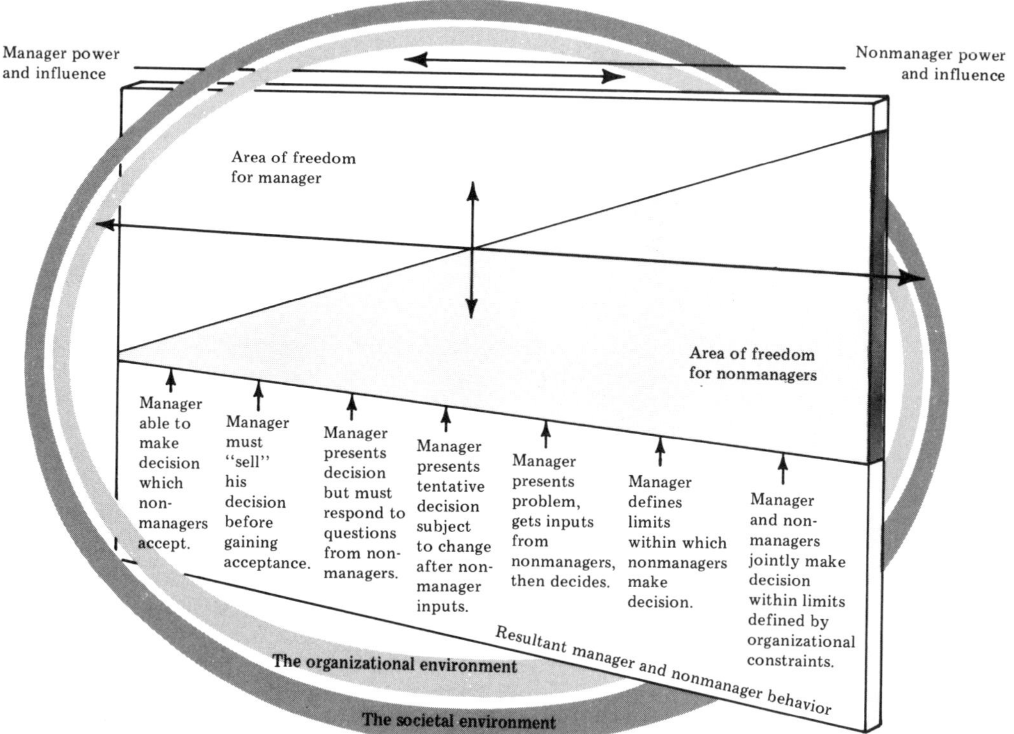

Exhibit 2.   Continuum of manager-nonmanager behavior

---

[5]For a description of phenomenarchy, see Will McWhinney, "Phenomenarchy: A Suggestion for Social Redesign," *Journal of Applied Behavioral Science,* May 1973.

Our thoughts on the question of leadership have prompted us to design a new behavior continuum (see Exhibit 2) in which the total area of freedom shared by manager and nonmanagers is constantly redefined by interactions between them and the forces in the environment.

The arrows in the exhibit indicate the continual flow of interdependent influence among systems and people. The points on the continuum designate the types of manager and nonmanager behavior that become possible with any given amount of freedom available to each. The new continuum is both more complex and more dynamic than the 1958 version, reflecting the organizational and societal realities of 1973.

Study questions for selection twelve

1. Tannenbaum and Schmidt teach us that factors relating to the manager personally, to the subordinates, and to the situation are important and that a successful manager will perceive them accurately and "behave appropriately in the light of these perceptions." But do they tell us anything about how to know what appropriate behavior is, about how to weight the various factors, about how to choose a *particular* leadership pattern?

2. In the "Retrospective Commentary" the authors mention some changes they would make if they were writing on the same subject for the 1970s. How many of the points they list occurred to you as criticisms or things that needed updating as you read the selection?

3. Apart from updating, is it correct that the "Retrospective Commentary" reflects the authors' increased understanding of the importance of including *political* factors in analyses of managerial leadership?

4. Please comment on the following assertions: "Tannenbaum and Schmidt are entirely Machiavellian. Their interest in how much authority the manager should use in leading does not go beyond a desire to manipulate; they don't care about either managers or nonmanagers as people."

M^{BO} in state government*

George S. Odiorne

Although the federal government's experiment with MBO has been for the most part discontinued, at least as a formal program, the concept's popularity for state and local governments continues. This selection was written by George Odiorne, dean of the School of Business at the University of Massachusetts, Amherst, who has been called "management's modern healer" and whose book *Management by Objectives: A System of Managerial Leadership* has been an important document in promoting MBO.

In this "constructed case study," Odiorne draws on his experiences in advising governments and businesses and discusses the successes and problems of an imaginary state, Old West, in implementing MBO.

A constructed case study probably provides the best object lessons on managing public affairs by objectives. This is a composite of experience with MBO in three different states compiled into a single illustrative case example.

Recently the state of Old West opted in the direction of MBO and decentralized management of the state tied to MBO. It broke itself into a half dozen or more "ministates." Each area was headed by a professional public administrator, quite similar in education and experience. Most had MPA degrees; most were old enough to have had some solid experience, but young enough to be energetic and ambitious. All were males. All were informed that they would be in charge of their own area of the state in all respects except higher education and one or two other areas. All were solemnly informed that they would be managed "by objectives" and that they were admonished to do likewise with their own responsibilities. Extensive training in MBO accompanied the program. The basic pattern of MBO as it was defined consisted of a five-part program:

1. *Goal Setting:* Each administrator would strike agreements with his or her superior about what was expected in terms of results, and such statements would be made in advance of the period.

2. *Budgeting:* The objectives would be related to resources which would be released to achieve the job. That is, the budgets would be forthcoming for the

---

Managing the agency/

tasks to be achieved, or the results would be amended if resources were for some reason not forthcoming.

3. *Autonomy:* Each person would be left alone to make decisions affecting his or her territory or responsibility, except that reporting periods and forms were agreed upon in advance. It was also agreed that each would obey the law and the policies affecting the various responsibility areas.

4. *Feedback:* Since the managers would know how well they were doing in their work while it was going on, they were expected to know when their results were faulty, to initiate corrective action upon learning of such shortcomings, and to *notify or ask for help* if things went clearly beyond permitted exceptions in a serious fashion.

5. *Payoffs:* There would be rewards in proportion to achievement. For one thing, the merit system would reflect achievements rather than personality or political affiliation. Furthermore, performance reviews would be related to achievements against goals. A proposed incentive plan for managers was not strong enough to survive the political buffeting encountered, and was abandoned before birth.

As a theoretical example, Old West's MBO had much to commend it. Yet it was not without its troubles, most of which comprise a cautionary tale to those in public administration wishing to use this most useful and stimulating method of management. In each of the five basic precepts which comprised the system, problems and lessons emerged.

"Tell me what's expected in advance"

From the beginning when the area managers sat down with their boss to discuss objectives, it was apparent that the superiors and cabinet ranks didn't really have a clear fix on what they expected from such line managers. "When I find out what we are here for, I'll try to let you know" was one kind of response. This of course was not a defect in MBO, but in the existing state of management, for it described what had been going on for some time. In areas like conservation the results sought were clearer than in the prison system, where nobody could agree on what prisons were supposed to produce. In environment the law was reasonably clear, but the development of strategies for getting to compliance wasn't all that lucidly defined. A major corporation and large employer in one region stated baldly that to live within the state air quality laws would put the organization out of business. It was agreed that more thought would have to be given to this case, since unemployment in that sector was already over the national average. The state unemployment service, the welfare chief, and the director of economic development of the state broke into a rather noisy argument over what the environmental objectives should be.

This led to the conclusion that each ministate must have a person responsible for shaping and recommending objectives in each functional area for its own geographical area. The bureaucracy in the state office building resisted this flowing away of their power and personnel out to the field. This battle came to a head when the state chief of mental health services went to the press over an unfortunate death of a mentally retarded child in a program initiated at the ministate level. MBO had killed this child, he charged. The governor backed the decentralization system in this case, and the MBO program survived.

Object lesson: Decentralization, or the moving of important decisions to lower levels in the organization is not a natural phenomenon in political organizations, and when it occurs will meet resistance from those in the bureaucracy whose power flows away from them.

There are other important lessons which were learned about goal setting in this case. First, while operational objectives must be measurable, many of the best strategic goals were not reduced to measurement, but to verbal statements of conditions which would exist if the goal were attained. Strategic objectives require criteria, but not all criteria will be measurable. . . . This distinction between strategic and operational goals is an important one in government.

The patent and staple argument against MBO in public administration that "my most important responsibilities can't be measured" is of course true, not only in government but in business. The similarities between strategic staff work in corporations and government are startling. Neither relates to the production of things. Neither in fact directly and immediately relates to profits. Neither is free of unexpected changes in the world. Both work in multiyear time frames. Both produce software rather than hardware. Both entail judgments of small groups of experts and professionals rather than short-term leadership of large corps of workers.

Yet all of these conditions have not prevented the best-run organizations from using staff MBO superbly well. Service organizations, it was discovered in the ministate's case at hand, can state their goals if they abide with some guidelines which have evolved in practice.

1. Anticipate strategic missions as much as is possible, in defining objectives, but adjust as often as necessary.

2. Developing indicators to be watched is a means to improving output and should not become an end in itself. The indicators themselves should be changed if needed, and no manager should have more than a dozen key indicators to be watching, and probably less than that. If there are more, there should be somebody helping watch and respond to them.

3. It is important to answer the question "are we doing the right things" prior to answering the more explicit questions of measurement, and "doing things right."

4. Timing is of the essence in goal setting. Those objectives which are multiyear in character (to clean up the pollution in the Cupcake River to federal standards by June 1978) need to be stated before the budget allocations are decided, not after. Those of an operational character can be stated at the beginning of an operating period after the budget allocation and not before (to buy a new patrol boat for the Cupcake River by June 1, 1976).

The best MBO programs in government will probably have two sets of objectives, one long-range set stated prior to budgeting or resource movement, and the second or short-range set after the budget is decided.

5. Any operational indicators should be related to some kind of important output and should contain some element of time (such as park visitors per month).

6. It is a mistake to expect too much precision in operating objectives. The

Managing the agency/

317

most exact science consists of approximations, and goal setting is far from an exact science. This need for reasonableness in goals can be achieved by stating them in *ranges* ("between 22,000 and 23,000 violations processed during the coming six months"). If some precision-obsessed soul insists upon a single number, pick the middle of the range and state it as the target.

7. Despite the special character of government objectives which often makes them difficult to measure, a *rule of rigor* can be applied: "measure that which is measurable, describe that which is describable, and eliminate that which is neither."

8. There is a division of labor in goal setting and management. A final lesson is that higher-level people who constantly are interfering in operational management will cause the MBO program to abort. The proper function of cabinet or policy-level positions is to define strategic goals. The function of operating heads is to be responsible for operations and commit to short-term (one-year) goals. The case of the cabinet person who insists upon knowing every operational detail is commonplace in government. In addition to being a serious handicap to management by objectives, it is also easily recognized as bad management in general.

Give me the resources to do the job

Precept two of the case study at hand was the provision of resources to do the job. This meant that the manager at the lower level was given budgetary resources. But it meant more than simply getting *more* resources, it also meant some latitude in moving resources. Many state and local governmental accounting systems are labyrinths of regulations which prevent such movement ("01 funds can be spent for 01 purposes only, but 03 funds may be spent for personnel or for any other purpose exclusive of travel and entertainment").

A strategic planning system within the MBO system provided much flexibility in moving resources, for it required that for each program four questions be answered:

1. Where is this program now? Statistically, factually, and in judgments about strengths and weaknesses?

2. What trends are apparent? If we didn't do anything differently where would we be in five years?

3. What mission statements could be shaped for this program?

4. What would be the financial consequences of each mission?

These budgetary-mission statements were prepared about January of each year and forwarded upward to the state level, where they comprised working papers for the compilation of the immediate budget requests and for multiyear budget planning.

The most successful application of this plan was executed by one ministate area manager who moved personally and individually with each of the key subordinates through an interview using these four questions as an agenda. Each manager prepared some notes, but the process was operated basically on a face-to-face basis. The superior then dictated the results of the interview with the subordinate and the resulting memorandum became the strategic goals position paper for the two to make their budgetary-allocation decisions upon. The questions are not simple. For example, in one discussion these kinds of questions came about:

Superior: "Let's look at the first topic: Where is your program now? What statistics are generated for your program? Who creates them? Are we well enough informed about the present situation? Do you have enough information to know what your strengths, weaknesses, and problems are? Do there seem to be any impending threats? What risks are we exposed to in your area? What are some opportunities which you see that might be pursued in the coming year or five years?"

Note that these are probing questions which force the subordinate to dig deeply into his or her own business before sitting down with the superior. It requires judgments about threats, risks, and opportunities. It also requires that people begin to think about new and original things as well as thinking about unthinkable possibilities.

Among the more interesting questions overheard in one such discussion were the following:

"Imagine that your budget were suddenly cut 20 percent. What would you be forced to stop doing? Then imagine after that move were completed that budget was restored again. What would you then add? Is it the same as the thing you dropped? If not, why not? Why can't you just do the new things within the existing resources?"

"Are there skills in your organization, or even that you yourself possess, that aren't being fully used? Is there any way you could use them more fully, given the existing resources?"

"What resources could be used well in your job that you don't now have? For example, what could I do, do differently, or stop doing to help you succeed?"

The most important single reason for failure of MBO in government is the tendency to treat it as a paperwork system, rather than a face-to-face management system.

Memoranda are essential to verify and follow up on agreement made face to face. When used in the absence of such face-to-face dialogue, they can be poisonous. The MBO system becomes bogged down in a morass of forms, memoranda, and unintelligible evasions. The logic of MBO alone won't carry it off if the system is depersonalized and mechanistic. This is especially true in the movement of resources, for such shifts often require human ingenuity, managerial support, and some confidence which comes with personal assurances that risks are worth taking.

This is even more valid when the manager in state government must interface with local and county officials. For them, there is no compulsion which requires that they cooperate, and only personalized and face-to-face discussions have any hope for getting mutual information, cooperation, and commitment. A random sample of the relationships which system people call "interfaces" shows that in most government agencies they are not interfaces at all, but a crossing of memorandum.

Object lesson: The allocation of resources and their movement should always be done on a face-to-face basis.

Managing the agency/

/**319**

Leave me alone as much as possible to do my job

Because steps I and II are necessary, step III is not possible until I and II have been completed. If subordinate managers know what is expected, and what resources and help are available, they can then be relied upon to show self-control, and govern their actions to achieve the commitments they have made. People who make commitments to somebody else whose opinion is important to them are practically obliged to do something about those commitments. This is especially true if those commitments have been made in face-to-face discussion, and have been confirmed in writing.

The power of commitment is what makes MBO work, and the absence of such commitment can cause it to fail.

The objectives and constraints are known in advance. Thus, the subordinate knows that he is to "achieve my commitments, and stay within my constraints," and thus can operate freely within these boundaries. This is significantly different from "doing what you are told to do." Under such a constraining rule, innovation and variations in methods require lengthy requests for permission, funneled through the hierarchy, and producing three effects:

1. Decision making is slowed down.

2. Innovation is dampened and ultimately dies.

3. There can be no excellence at lower levels.

The problem of managerial control remains, however. The higher-level official is always responsible for the actions of subordinates, and it would be unrealistic not to expect that higher-level persons will be concerned about lower-level performance. Yet, through the completion of explicit goals, stated in far more detail than ever was thought necessary or possible, managerial control through subordinate self-control is possible. The tightest form of control is self-control.

The exception principle requires four major rules for subordinates if it is to function as a tool of managerial control in an MBO system:

1. The subordinate must be clear on the goals and know when they are not being met, and know earlier than anybody else.

2. The subordinate should know the reasons those goals are not being achieved.

3. The subordinate should be able to initiate corrective action as soon as a deviation appears and he or she knows its reason, even before the boss learns of the problem.

4. The subordinate should be able to call for help, and thereby notify the superior early enough. Most bosses do not favor unpleasant surprises, and should be protected against them.

In the case study at Old West State, one manager described his rules for deciding whether to call the boss for help for notification purposes: "If the boss

could hear about it from some third party, I make sure I get there first. That
third party could be a peer, a higher up, or simply an indignant client."

In one instance a highway patrol team ran into a dispute with the Air
Police from an Air Force base in the area. On the supposition that the commanding colonel might call the state capital, the regional manager called his boss and
explained the situation. When the complaint arrived in due course, no adrenalin
flowed at the higher levels.

The boss, on the other hand, must show some restraint when receiving a
single isolated report from a citizen. Such letters to the governor or a legislator
should be bucked down through the channels for more grass-roots information,
and not become a basis for tearing down the management system and recen-
tralizing all decision making.

In one highly publicized incident the entire decentralization MBO process
was nearly scuttled because a state truck ran over a cow. The owner wrote an
indignant letter to the legislature, and the state office bureaucracy attempted to
use the incident as proof that MBO produced reckless and irresponsible behavior
at lower levels, implying that every cow in the state was endangered by MBO.
Fortunately the director of administration for the state was able to resolve the
question quickly. One of the major influences was the fact that a speedy
response was forthcoming. Within an hour of the report's reaching the state
capital, a responsible official from the region was on the scene, viewing the
bovine's remains, and making specific arrangements with the farmer for fair
reimbursement from local funds. Under a more centralized system the payment
would have been years in coming, for the state capital was more than a hundred
miles from the cow.

*MBO should produce a more personalized responsive system of government
for citizens, by placing decision making over small matters affecting citizens in
the hands of lower level organizations.*

Delegation, and leaving lower-level subordinates alone once their objectives are established clearly and resources defined accordingly, produces a more
localized decision system to allow for local variances.

Let me know how well I am doing in my work

Objectives, properly defined, should comprise an instrument panel of vital
signs of the organization. These vital signs are analogous to the pulse, body
temperature, blood pressure, and other vital signs of the human organism. Such
a vital sign as body temperature could be "normal" within a range as follows:

normal at rest	98.6
after exercise	99.9
in cool climate	98.0

The physician doesn't demand that every temperature be identical with
the at-rest norm. Nor should managers expect precision in measuring their own

performance, nor should their superiors demand such uniformity. Take the case of the park system in Old West. Records of parks use by summer months for the past four years showed the following:

1968–7,601

1969–7,950

1970–8,310

1971–8,734

For planning purposes it was noted that a secular trend upward in excess of 300 to 400 a year was observed. Thus, it could be anticipated, "other things being equal," that a rise of another 400 to 500 could be expected in 1972. This became the *normal* objective. This meant that the preparation of staff assignments, preparation of park sites, tons of refuse disposal planned, and similar demands upon the park management and staff could be anticipated.

Yet, the purpose is *not to forecast nor to predict.* The prediction is that park use in 1972 will be at a rate of about 9,200 persons per month, and the *prediction itself is a means to better management.* It affords the management a vital sign. If it goes above 9,500, then some kind of response is indicated. If it goes below 8,700, then some kind of investigation and possible response should be made by management.

The idea of measurement is not to punish the people for being poor forecasters. The forecast is created to provide vital signs for management to make managerial responses.

Thus, when the energy crisis came along and cut sharply into the park use, for motorists could not obtain gasoline, the use of the park went down to 3,165 per month. The park manager used this opportunity to move personnel from planned services to other approved projects within the park, and to other projects which had not been thought feasible outside the park.

Reward my accomplishments

Perhaps the major distinction between government and business applications of MBO is not in the profit motive for the firm, but in the willingness of industry to relate achievement to pay. This is achieved in several ways, and the experience of those municipalities who have developed and installed performance payment systems has been sufficiently good that it proves such incentive compensation is viable for government.

Clearly, managerial or professional compensation in government cannot be related to *profit.* But it can be related to *performance* if these performance objectives exist.

1. There must be a norm or standard of performance which is related to the public purposes of the organization and the specific performance objectives of the job.

2. Such standards must be related to *output* for a period of time, usually a year.

3. The standard should be written as a form of performance contract for that year, which require objectives to be carefully negotiated.

4. There should be statements of special conditions under which the incentive pay will not apply. If the job holder is penalized for hard luck, or rewarded for windfalls not of his own doing, the system can fail.

5. Provision for review at the highest levels must be made, both of the goals used as standards, and of the results actually achieved. This assures uniformity of treatment among equals, and prudent use of public funds.

6. Selective application of incentive payments is possible without destroying the system. For example, in one city the incentive pay principle was applied to revenue-producing positions. Where the revenues went beyond historic normal standards, an ascending scale of compensation was awarded, provided certain other kinds of objectives were also met.

7. Incentives for innovative objectives can be managed through suggestion award plans. Under current systems, it would seem to be more prudent to relate the award to the achievement by rewarding only proved savings or demonstrated innovations which increase yield from resources.

8. Relating rewards to achievement requires a change in many performance reviews or appraisal forms and procedures. The old form of adjective rating of performance against a list of personality traits, if related to pay increases or merit ratings, will compete and perhaps extinguish achievement-centered behavior.

In an MBO management system, performance review and merit rating must be directly related to goals and results statements, and adjective rating systems abandoned.

Summary

MBO in government is confronted with the same kinds of bureaucratic and political traps which every new program runs into. Strong administrative overtures are met with equal and opposite countermoves. When power flows from one place to another, people from whom it is flowing will resist that flow away from themselves. The political leader tends to seek ever-increasing amounts of power, in contrast with the economic sector where leaders operate on a principle of acquisition. It is difficult to say which is loftier. Procedures which were once important, perhaps even noble, persist long after their useful life has ended. Activity for its own sake becomes a false goal, becomes firmly embedded, and ultimately becomes a religion. Changing behavior of bureaucrats is not done easily, for their security lies in doing what has worked in the past. There is a general reluctance to invest heavily in training which is innovative in character, for it promises to produce an unwanted change, and perhaps new centers of power. Finally, the culture of government, especially state government, is more *affiliation centered* than achievement centered. Ideology seldom dominates state government, nor is there a strong culture of performance on behalf of the constituency, with some notable exceptions.

These are the lessons of MBO in Old West state's program of applying MBO. It does not prove that MBO has procedural nor logical flaws, nor that government is evil. It does demonstrate, however, that some special efforts are required to make it work. Turning a government into an achieving organization is never easy.

Study questions for selection thirteen

1. In order for MBO to be applied in Old West, was it necessary for the state to be divided into several geographically based "ministates"? Might analytical divisions, based on welfare policy, agricultural policy, etc., have been as useful?

2. To what extent is MBO a technique for reaching and carrying out decisions? To what extent does it tell the manager what decisions to make?

3. Do you think that MBO will be more useful in dealing with short-term, small, and noncontroversial problems or with perennial, large, and politically hot problems? Why?

Suggested readings for chapter nine

Argyris, Chris. *Personality and Organization.* New York: Harper and Row, 1957.

Bennis, Warren G. *Organization Development: Its Nature, Origins and Prospects.* Reading, Mass.: Addison-Wesley Publishing Co., 1969.

Blake, Robert R., and Mouton, Jane S. *Corporate Excellence Through Grid Organization Development.* Houston: Gulf Publishing Co., 1968.

Carlisle, Howard M. *Situation Management: A Contingency Approach to Leadership.* New York: AMACOM, 1973.

Drucker, Peter F. *Management: Tasks, Responsibilities, Practices.* New York: Harper and Row, 1974.

Fiedler, F. E. *A Theory of Leadership Effectiveness.* New York: McGraw-Hill, 1967.

French, Wendell L., and Bell, Cecil H. *Organization Development.* Englewood Cliffs, N.J.: Prentice-Hall, 1973.

Herzberg, Frederick. *Work and the Nature of Man.* Cleveland: World Publishing, 1966.

McGregor, Douglas. *The Human Side of Enterprise.* New York: McGraw-Hill, 1960.

Maslow, Abraham H. *Motivation and Personality*. 2d ed. New York: Harper and
Row, 1970.

Odiorne, George S. *Management by Objectives: A System of Managerial Leadership*. New York: Pitman, 1965.

Selznick, Phillip. *Leadership in Administration: A Sociological Interpretation*.
New York: Row, Peterson, 1957.

Stogdill, Ralph M. *Handbook of Leadership: A Survey of Theory and Research*.
New York: Free Press, 1974.

Securing resources: the politics of the budgetary process

By now it should be clear that the management of a public organization cannot be accomplished by attending to internal considerations alone. In at least one essential respect, the management task of the public administrator stretches far outside the confines of a particular administrative unit. Resources—especially monetary resources—must be secured in quantity sufficient to enable the organization to conduct its business. Many public administrators find significant portions of their working hours devoted to various phases of the effort to obtain from other administrators, from the chief executive, and from the legislature the financial support crucial for the expansion or continued existence of particular programs, or even of the agency itself.

In this budgetary process, perhaps more than in any other administrative activity, the actions of environmental actors and of the public managers who command the organization's internal administrative processes converge in a way that is conducive to ready observation. Because resources are scarce and there is competition—usually cutthroat rather than genteel—for those resources, difficult decisions about funding must be made. The environmental actors recognize that money, the most negotiable form of resources, translates eventually into programs; therefore, they seek a role in the budgetary process. Furthermore, the centrality of budgetary decision making for the agency causes its leaders to undertake major initiatives at "budget time" and focuses attention on the questions of appropriate decision-making style discussed in the previous chapter. Of course, the expertise of administrators who are close to budgetary requests gives them an important competitive advantage over their inter- and intra-agency colleagues who know less about financial matters.

Operating under a constitutional provision that specified that "no money shall be drawn from the Treasury, but in consequence of appropriations made by law," the Congress managed for much of the nineteenth century to dominate financial decision making at the federal level. During most of this period, however, resources often were relatively plentiful, thanks especially to the tax surpluses generated by restrictive tariffs. Ordinarily, agencies had but to ask in order to receive appropriations. Many could safely spend even more than was appropriated without bothering to ask, confident that Congress would take care of the bills when next it met. Around the turn of this century several events converged (not the least of which was a series of federal deficits), and they led to an important expansion of the chief executive's participation in matters concerning financial resources. Not until 1921, however, did Congress finally provide for the preparation of an *executive budget* for the entire federal government. States and cities were taking similar steps at about the same time, assigning budgetary responsibilities to their chief executives. At the federal level, the task of actual budget preparation was given to the Bureau of the Budget (which was responsible to the president), and the president was instructed to present to Congress each year his budget request and budget message. The public administrative agencies thus found themselves required to serve two masters in matters financial: the chief executive and the legislature.

Agencies begin preparing their budgets as much as two years before the beginning of a new fiscal year, which runs from October 1 to September 30. (Until 1976, the fiscal year ran from July 1 to June 30.) A crucial deadline for the executive branch is the necessity for the president to submit to Congress in mid-January of each year his executive budget, which presents detailed proposals for spending and revenue raising during the ensuing fiscal year. Although the Office of Management and Budget (OMB), the successor to the Bureau of the Budget and a division of the Executive Office of the President, has primary responsibility for preparing the executive budget, it does not act alone. In fact, administrators at all levels are deeply involved in the budgetary process and provide the basic financial data upon which decisions are based. More important, most of the decisions actually are *made* at various levels within the administrative agencies; many highly important issues never come to the attention of OMB or the president.

The budget cycle

Preparation

The basic outline of the federal government's budgetary process has changed but little since 1921. The processes of most state and local governments are essentially similar to the federal process, although budget preparation time is usually somewhat shorter. Figure 10–1 indicates the formal steps in the federal budget preparation process that lead up to submission of the president's budget.

Careful examination of the figure reveals important exchanges that take place between the Office of Management and Budget and any given agency. The OMB maintains a staff responsible for contact with agencies, and there are frequent formal and informal exchanges throughout the process. Events of particular importance are the instructions issued by OMB to all agencies in the spring, the submis-

"Please, Major! Our critics *call it the old flim flam game. We refer to it as the* budget."
© 1978 Mort Gerberg

sion of formal estimates by the agencies in the early fall, the presidential review in November, and the transmission of the Budget to Congress in January.

Appropriation

Figure 10–2 exhibits the process by which Congress considers the budget and enacts *appropriation bills.* The passage of the *Congressional Budget and Impoundment Control Act* in 1974 introduced a new set of procedures, involving newly created Budget Committees in each chamber and a new Congressional Budget Office. Many of the procedures involving these new institutions are designed to provide Congress with a mechanism by which it can better monitor the impact of the budget on the nation's economy. Previously, since only the president (through OMB) had an opportunity to view the total budget, major responsibility for considering its economic impact rested with him. Congressional appropriations committees and those concerned with taxation examined the budget only as it was reflected in numerous separate appropriation and revenue bills. As figure 10–2 indicates, the appropriation bills continue to be considered separately, but first a maximum spending figure is set for the total budget and for each of several broad functional categories; this helps to assure that members of Congress are aware of the potential impact which each appropriation bill has on those spending totals. Although the appropriations committees still consider spending bills for each agency and program, the budget committees, the Congressional Budget Office, and—in a sense—all members of Congress watch over their shoulders.

Since the budget for fiscal year 1977 (October 1, 1976–September 30, 1977) was the first to be considered under the new congressional procedure, scholars are just beginning to determine the impact of the new procedure on the budget process. No doubt, it will be several years before we can know just how seriously Congress will take this opportunity to become more deeply involved in using the total budget as a tool of economic management.

Execution

After preparation and appropriation comes the third phase of the budget process: carrying out the programs for which appropriations have provided the resources. Before discussing execution, however, the *program authorization,* which is not technically a part of the budget process, should be mentioned parenthetically. Throughout the

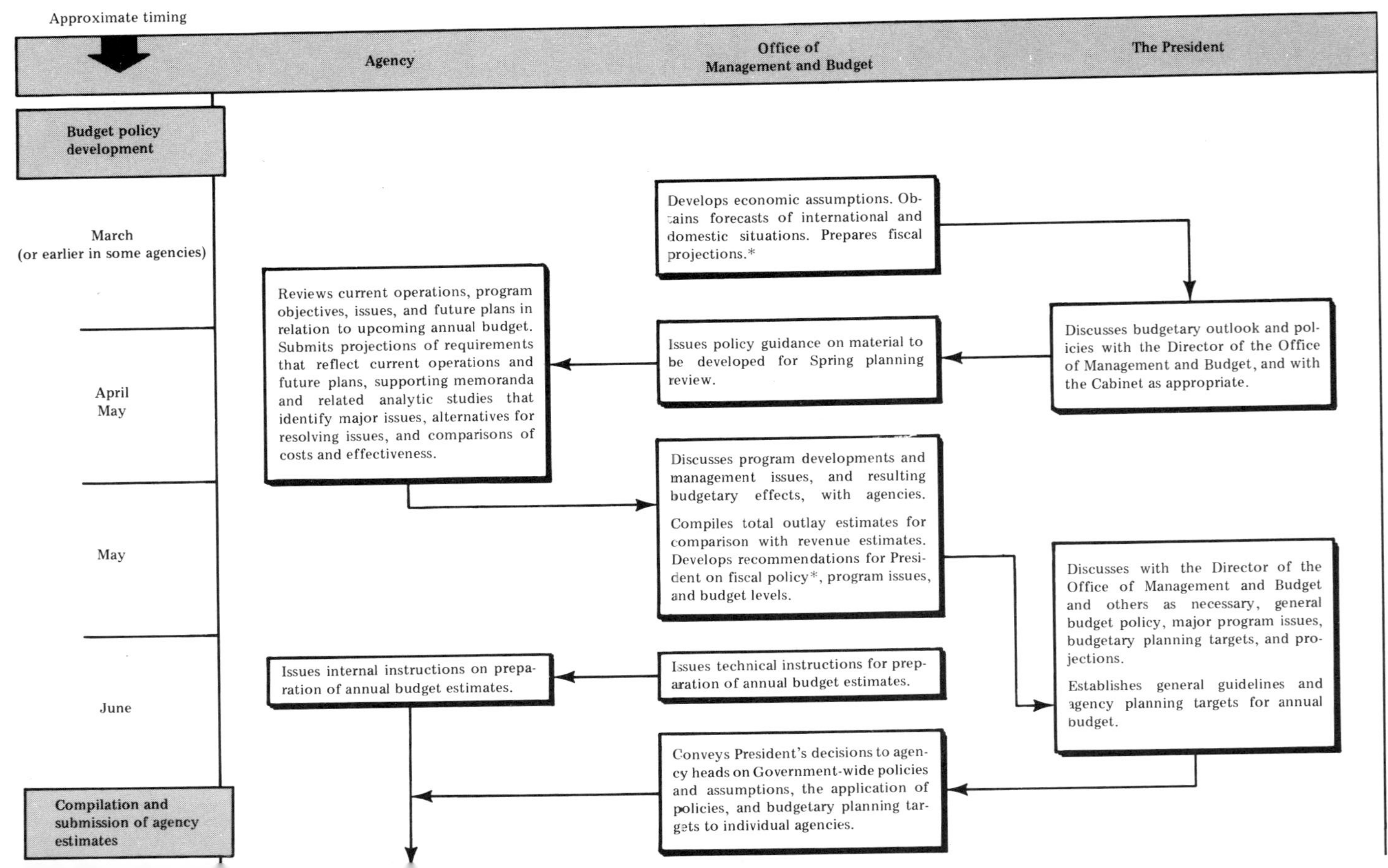

Approximate timing
Agency
Office of Management and Budget
The President
Budget policy development
March (or earlier in some agencies)
April May
May
June
Compilation and submission of agency estimates
Develops economic assumptions. Obtains forecasts of international and domestic situations. Prepares fiscal projections.*
Reviews current operations, program objectives, issues, and future plans in relation to upcoming annual budget. Submits projections of requirements that reflect current operations and future plans, supporting memoranda and related analytic studies that identify major issues, alternatives for resolving issues, and comparisons of costs and effectiveness.
Issues policy guidance on material to be developed for Spring planning review.
Discusses budgetary outlook and policies with the Director of the Office of Management and Budget, and with the Cabinet as appropriate.
Discusses program developments and management issues, and resulting budgetary effects, with agencies.
Compiles total outlay estimates for comparison with revenue estimates. Develops recommendations for President on fiscal policy*, program issues, and budget levels.
Discusses with the Director of the Office of Management and Budget and others as necessary, general budget policy, major program issues, budgetary planning targets, and projections.
Establishes general guidelines and agency planning targets for annual budget.
Issues internal instructions on preparation of annual budget estimates.
Issues technical instructions for preparation of annual budget estimates.
Conveys President's decisions to agency heads on Government-wide policies and assumptions, the application of policies, and budgetary planning targets to individual agencies.

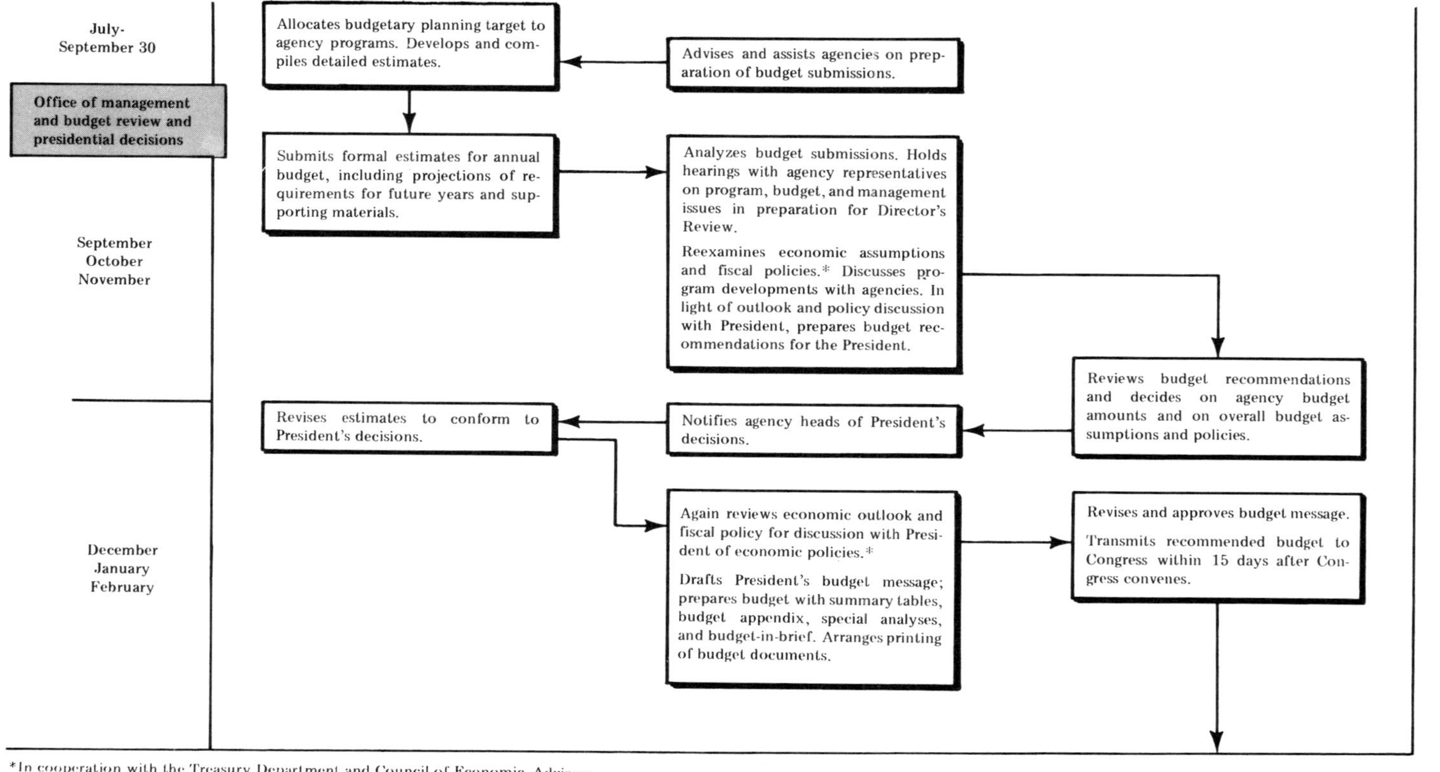

*In cooperation with the Treasury Department and Council of Economic Advisors

Figure 10–1. Formulation of the president's budget

Source: U.S. Executive Office of the President, Office of Management and Budget

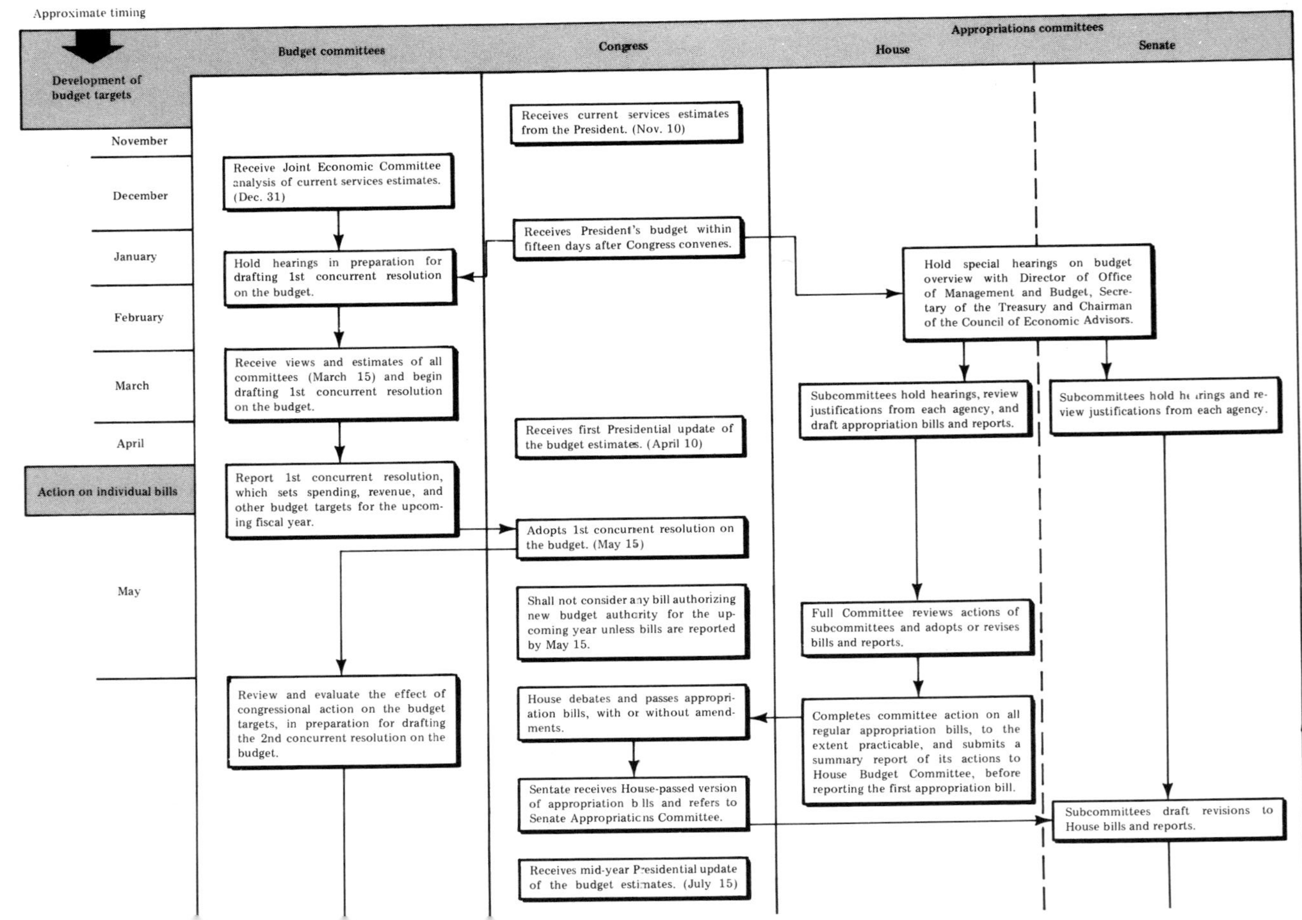

Approximate timing

Budget committees

Congress

Appropriations committees

House

Senate

Development of budget targets

November

December

January

February

March

April

Action on individual bills

May

Receives current services estimates from the President. (Nov. 10)

Receive Joint Economic Committee analysis of current services estimates. (Dec. 31)

Hold hearings in preparation for drafting 1st concurrent resolution on the budget.

Receives President's budget within fifteen days after Congress convenes.

Hold special hearings on budget overview with Director of Office of Management and Budget, Secretary of the Treasury and Chairman of the Council of Economic Advisors.

Receive views and estimates of all committees (March 15) and begin drafting 1st concurrent resolution on the budget.

Subcommittees hold hearings, review justifications from each agency, and draft appropriation bills and reports.

Subcommittees hold hearings and review justifications from each agency.

Receives first Presidential update of the budget estimates. (April 10)

Report 1st concurrent resolution, which sets spending, revenue, and other budget targets for the upcoming fiscal year.

Adopts 1st concurrent resolution on the budget. (May 15)

Shall not consider any bill authorizing new budget authority for the upcoming year unless bills are reported by May 15.

Full Committee reviews actions of subcommittees and adopts or revises bills and reports.

Review and evaluate the effect of congressional action on the budget targets, in preparation for drafting the 2nd concurrent resolution on the budget.

House debates and passes appropriation bills, with or without amendments.

Completes committee action on all regular appropriation bills, to the extent practicable, and submits a summary report of its actions to House Budget Committee, before reporting the first appropriation bill.

Sentate receives House-passed version of appropriation bills and refers to Senate Appropriations Committee.

Subcommittees draft revisions to House bills and reports.

Receives mid-year Presidential update of the budget estimates. (July 15)

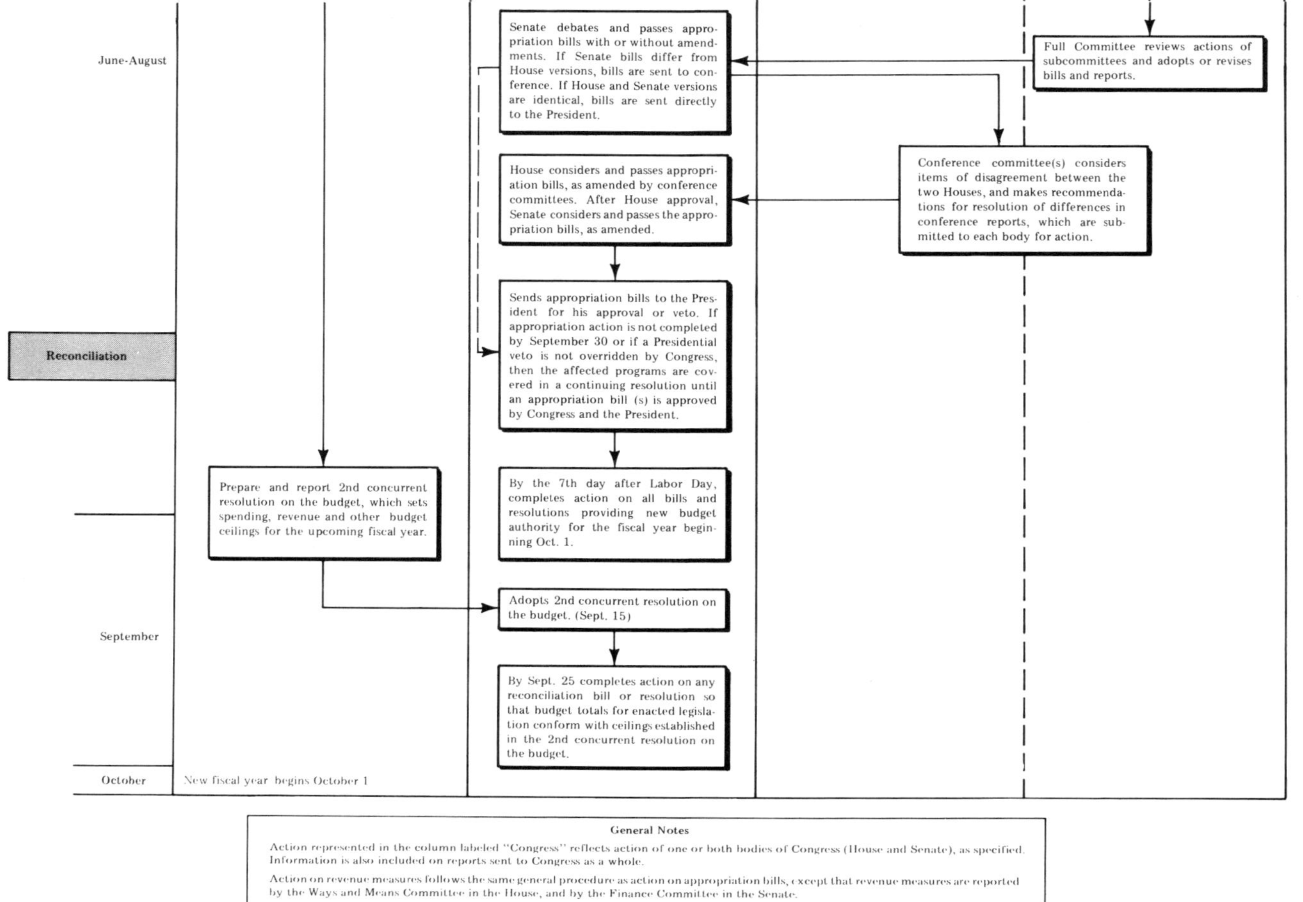

Figure 10–2. Congressional budget process
Source: Executive Office of the President, Office of Management and Budget

year, as it carries on its programs and prepares the budget for a coming year, an agency is likely also to be seeking program authorizations for the future. Before Congress will appropriate money for any program, it first passes a statute granting the agency authority to operate the program. For example, if the Department of Transportation wanted to begin construction of a high-speed mass-transit system linking New York and Chicago, it would first have to find in present statutes a provision that permitted such expenditure or seek new authorization from Congress; without such legislation, no appropriation would be made. In the case of our example, the authorizing legislation probably would be considered by the House and Senate Commerce Committees. Even if the department got the legislation passed and signed by the president, no rails could yet be laid. Now that the project was authorized, however, Transportation could try to get an appropriation bill passed to fund their scheme. This bill would go to the House and Senate Appropriations Committees, which have little membership overlap with the committees that handled the authorizing legislation. As a result, the program could be stopped before it begins if it does not receive an appropriation, and the following phrase is frequently heard in Washington: "The program is authorized but not funded." Some claim (and it probably has occurred) that authorizing committees sometimes approve legislation that they do not really want in the confidence that, when funding is sought, the Appropriations Committees will be the "bad guys" and say, "No!"

Only after an agency is successful in getting *both authorization and appropriation* can its budget process move to the execution phase—though it still is not free of all restraint. As mentioned in chapter 3, the Office of Management and Budget can act for the president and establish a schedule for granting the agency permission to spend. Furthermore, some of the appropriated funds may be *reserved,* not immediately apportioned to the agency. Apportionments by OMB are normally provided on a quarterly basis, with reserved funds being released late in the fiscal year.

As a result of all of the processes described above—budget preparation, passage of authorization and appropriation bills, and OMB apportionment—the successful agency finally has available the authority to obligate the federal government (for that is what an appropriation really is). As it hires people, acquires the supplies and equipment it needs, contracts to build facilities, etc., such obligations are created. By processing vouchers and invoices, the agency requests the Treasury Department to issue checks to whomever the agency owes money. (A few agencies issue their own checks.) The program is now under way.

The complexity of this budget process may seem overwhelming. To some administrators that adjective describes it well. Of course, federal agencies and larger state and local agencies establish separate budget offices to cope with the complexity. Why is it so complex? Two reasons account for much of the complexity. One is our constitutional principle of separation of powers. Administrative agencies, otherwise responsible to the chief executive, find themselves at budget time reporting to the legislature as well; neither the executive nor the legislature will give the other full fiscal responsibility. Both insist on being deeply involved. The second reason for the complexity is that the total process (including authorization) is designed to *control* agencies' programs and expenditures; hence the multiple hurdles that must be jumped before a new program can begin.

Auditing

In chapter 4 reference was made to the General Accounting Office (GAO) as an agency of Congress that audits administrative agencies. From time to time an operating agency will have contact with GAO. Of prime importance to GAO is assurance that obligations created and money paid out have been handled legally. Was the expenditure authorized? Were proper procedures followed, such as competitive bidding, where required? Today the GAO depends heavily on agencies to control themselves. All agencies must have systems for monitoring their expenditures as they occur, and the large agencies have created internal audit divisions for this purpose. But beyond this, the GAO has the authority to probe deeply into the operations of any agency and to review its procedures on a periodic basis. As chapter 4 indicated, auditors today are concerned with matters of managerial efficiency and effectiveness—they go beyond mere legality. The agency must be prepared to respond to queries from GAO as the fiscal year progresses. That is, auditing is not sequential as are the preparation, appropriation, and execution phases; rather, it is an ongoing process that may include examination of present and planned activities as well as those already completed.

Budget decision making

In his book *The Politics of the Budgetary Process,*[1] Aaron Wildavsky describes in considerable detail many of the most important

---

[1] Aaron Wildavsky, *The Politics of the Budgetary Process,* 2d ed. (Boston: Little, Brown, 1974).

considerations that enter into agency budgetary decisions. To be sure, considerations include programming concerns (how can we best carry out the statutory mandate under which we operate?). But perhaps more important they also include: getting a "fair share" of new money available (how can we be sure to get a percentage increase similar to that of other agencies?); satisfying demands (how can we respond to important interest group pressures?); and allowing for later cuts (how much should we "pad" our request so that OMB and the Congress will have something to cut and thus feel confident that they are doing their jobs?). On this final point, one of the authors had the following discussion with a departmental budget officer in one state:

Budget Officer: Well, they did it again!

Interviewer: Oh, who did what?

Budget Officer: That Legislative Budget Committee. They took my microfilm reader out of the budget again this year.

Interviewer: Oh? Does that cause you a big problem?

Budget Officer: Hell, no—we ain't got no damn microfilm. I just put that in every year so they'll have something to cut.

This is not to suggest that "padding" is always that glaring, or that it is necessarily bad. In fact, as Wildavsky suggests, "in many cases 'padding' consists of programs the agency wants badly but can do without, a matter of priorities."[2] A further factor to consider is that, over time, various norms, or expected forms of behavior, have developed. Agencies believe that they are *expected* to pad; if an agency does not do so, OMB and Congress will probably cut its budget anyway—because that is what is expected.

Because the budget cycle is repeated each year, administrators and other participants develop firmly held expectations about each other's behavior. For example, formal rules issued by a state budget office may require the submission of elaborate documentary support for budget requests. But experience may have taught the administrator that such material receives little attention, since the budget office is severely understaffed. The administrator may have learned that mobilizing interest group support is far more important than the documents submitted. Similarly, the rules may require that any appropriated money not spent during a fiscal year should be allowed to revert to the treasury, but the administrator may have learned from experience that failure to spend one year's appropriation is sure to lead to a severe cut the next year. The feeling is, "If you didn't need what we gave you last year, you can probably get by with even less this time."

---

[2]Ibid., p. 23.

Chapter ten

In addition to padding, generating interest group support, and spending all money appropriated, there are other strategies employed by agencies to secure funding of their programs. Most agencies carefully monitor actions and statements of the chief executive and key legislators (especially members of the appropriations committee) in order to design programs that appeal to their biases. Also, agencies usually try to assure that administrators who must defend the agency's budget are well informed and prepared for questions asked by legislators at hearings; they may even go so far as to "plant" questions for friendly legislators to ask.

For their part, the central budget office and legislators also adopt strategic approaches to budget decisions. These decision makers are responsible for looking beyond the single agency, for considering (at least in a limited way) the impact that decisions that concern one agency will have on the funding and programs of others. Most frequently, their task is to *cut* the requests agencies have submitted. Just how do these reviewers decide where to cut? There is no single answer, but one thing is clear. Limitations on time and resources preclude a thorough study of each agency's real needs; reviewers must depend heavily on information the agencies themselves provide. Budget reductions are often based on rather simple decision rules, sometimes as simple as using the "meat axe," such as cutting 15 percent from each request. Alternatively, they might zero in on particular expenditure item requests and reduce them sharply. A favorite for such treatment is "travel." Another, as the microfilm reader example indicates, is equipment. And some reviewers are prejudiced against "consultants." Actions such as these may seem irrational; surely there must be a better way. During the last two decades there have been two major attempts to implement a "better way" in federal, state, and local governments.

Reforming the system

In chapter 8 you encountered the controversy concerning the appropriate decision-making mode for the public sector—the "rational-comprehensive" or the "incremental" mode. Students of budgeting are found in the thick of this battle. Wildavsky argues that incrementalism is not only descriptive of the most widely employed decision mode in the public sector, but furthermore, the incremental process "is in many ways superior to the proposed alternatives."[3]

---

[3]Ibid., p. 146.

Although there is little reason to question the descriptive accuracy of the incrementalist view of total agency budgets and appropriations, several researchers have pointed out that there are frequently some rather large changes *within* agencies, as the priorities given to particular programs are altered.[4] The total agency appropriation may change little, but this apparent stability may conceal large shifts of funds within the agency. Such a possibility accentuates the role that administrators heading particular programs play in the budgetary decision process. One study argues that this makes "the program director, the operating level bureaucrat, . . . a central figure in the determination of public policy."[5] It is this administrator who, by using technical expertise, interest group support, and shrewd political strategies, may be able to secure relatively large funding increases. Of course, failure to maximize such influence may result in sizable funding cuts for the agency.

Planning Programming Budgeting System

While Wildavsky supports incrementalism as an appropriate basis for budgetary decision making, this view has been frequently challenged. The first extensive effort to move public sector decision making *away* from incrementalism and toward the rational-comprehensive mode was that undertaken at the direction of President Lyndon Johnson in 1965, who called for the establishment of the *Planning Programming Budgeting System (PPB)* in the federal government. By 1968, this massive effort, which was modeled on the procedures Robert McNamara had established in the Defense Department, involved 1,594 employees of major agencies working full time on PPB and 2,135 working part time (these figures exclude secretarial and clerical personnel).[6] Numerous state and local governments followed the federal lead and sought to implement their own PPB systems. Among those making the most progress were the states of Pennsylvania and Hawaii.

It is important to understand that PPB is but one manifestation of a theme that runs through several efforts to increase the level of rationality in public-sector decision making. As presented in chapter 8, this

---

[4]See Peter B. Natchez and Irvin C. Bupp, "Policy and Priority in the Budgetary Process," *American Political Science Review* 67 (September 1973): 951–63.

[5]Ibid., p. 963.

[6]Comptroller General of the United States, *Survey of Progress in Implementing the Planning-Programming-Budgeting System in Executive Agencies* (Washington: Comptroller General of the United States, 1969), pp. 46–47.

theme can be described as demanding that public-sector decision makers take the following actions:

1. specify government goals with precision;

2. develop means of measuring the degree of attainment of those goals;

3. consider a wide range of alternative means of achieving (or moving toward) those goals;

4. conduct an economic analysis of each alternative, looking at potential costs and benefits of each;

5. select the alternative to be implemented primarily upon the basis of a comparison of the economic analyses.

One further feature of such efforts, which is implied but not specifically stated in the above list, is that considerations are to reach well beyond a single year—to include long-range planning. In some agencies it is necessary to consider the impacts of programs (e.g., construction and use of a large system of canals) as stretching over many decades. This contrasts sharply with the essentially year-to-year nature of incremental budgeting. A second feature, which may not be so evident, is that there is no guarantee that each goal will fall neatly within the province of a particular agency. If it does not, efforts to highlight the goal may intensify interagency territorial disputes and may centralize decision making at the next higher organizational level. This happened in the Defense Department. When Robert McNamara became secretary, all three services (Army, Navy, and Air Force) were developing long-range missiles and other strategic hardware. Analyses revealed a number of these programs to be competitive or duplicatory. Whereas in an earlier day disputes about the ownership of programs might have been resolved through compromises among officers of the uniformed services, in this case *departmental level* personnel stepped in and made the decisions.[7]

Zero-base budgeting

Recent efforts to improve the budgetary process have focused on *zero-base budgeting (ZBB)*. Advocates of this system express their alarm

---

[7]Allen Schick suggests the following reasons for the demise of PPB: Processes of planning and analysis were not incorporated into the budget process—even in the Bureau of the Budget; there was insufficient financial and personnel support; Congress was given little consideration; rigid organizational boundaries made program coordination difficult; once they discovered PPB had little budgetary impact, agencies gave little support; and information systems were insufficient. See Allen Schick, "A Death in the Bureaucracy: The Demise of Federal PPB," *Public Administration Review* 33 (March/April 1973): 146–56.

at the tendency of some government programs to continue—and even expand—for many years after their apparent usefulness has ended. It appears that even major programs—the construction of dams, the acquisition of new weapons systems, or the distribution of aid to dependent children—may continue to be funded although superior alternatives are available. Like PPB and other efforts to install rational-comprehensive decision systems, ZBB encourages decision makers to specify objectives and consider alternatives for reaching them. ZBB advocates especially emphasize, though, the need to examine *presently functioning* programs.

In many elections during the mid-1970s, ZBB became an important item of campaign rhetoric. Several gubernatorial candidates throughout the country promised to install such a system, and a successful candidate in Georgia, Jimmy Carter, did so. His system required agency directors to specify objectives and present to their superiors alternative ways of moving toward those objectives. Once a particular alternative was selected, the agency would construct *decision packages,* each representing a different level of funding, for instance, 10 percent less than the previous year, the same level as the previous year, and 10 percent more than the previous year. Packages from various programs and agencies were merged into a ranked list by upper-level budget decision makers. When the amount of money available was determined, a line simply was drawn through the rankings at the appropriate point.[8] Thus, the central budget office might draw a line that would fund three packages of one agency, five of another agency, but only one of a third agency.

Ironically, the Georgia system has been criticized for failing to require a full *examination from zero.* It remained probable that major portions of agencies' programs would be funded without a thorough examination. Furthermore, ZBB in Georgia—and in local governments where it has been tried—does not demand precise statements of objectives and thorough consideration of alternatives. In this sense, it fails to approach the rational-comprehensive model as closely as did PPB. Of course, if the incrementalists are correct, this would make it easier to implement than was PPB.

Shortly after assuming office, President Carter fulfilled a campaign promise and took an initial step to introduce ZBB in federal agencies. Figure 10-3 is a reproduction of his memorandum ordering agencies to develop a zero-base system. Since then the Office of Management and Budget and other federal agencies have developed procedures for implementing the system, which closely follows the Georgia model.

---

[8]See Peter A. Pyhrr, *Zero-base Budgeting: A Practical Management Tool for Evaluating Expenses* (New York: John Wiley and Sons, 1973). Pyhrr played a major role in design and implementation of the Georgia system.

February 14, 1977

MEMORANDUM FOR THE HEADS OF

EXECUTIVE DEPARTMENTS AND AGENCIES

During the campaign, I pledged that immediately after the inauguration I would issue an order establishing zero-base budgeting throughout the Federal Government. This pledge was made because of the success of the zero-base budget system adopted by the state of Georgia under my direction as Governor.

A zero-base budgeting system permits a detailed analysis and justification of budget requests by an evaluation of the importance of each operation performed.

An effective zero-base budgeting system will benefit the Federal Government in several ways. It will

- Focus the budget process on a comprehensive analysis of objectives and needs.

- Combine planning and budgeting into a single process.

- Cause managers to evaluate in detail the cost-effectiveness of their operations.

- Expand management participation in planning and budgeting at all levels of the Federal Government.

The Director of the Office of Management and Budget will review the Federal budget process for the preparation, analysis, and justification of budget estimates and will revise those procedures to incorporate the appropriate techniques of the zero-base budgeting system. He will develop a plan for applying the zero-base budgeting concept to preparation, analysis, and justifications of the budget estimates of each department and agency of the Executive Branch.

I ask each of you to develop a zero-base system within your agency in accordance with instructions to be issued by the Office of Management and Budget. The Fiscal Year 1979 budget will be prepared using this system.

By working together under a zero-base budgeting system, we can reduce costs and make the Federal Government more efficient and effective.

Jimmy Carter

The zero-base approach to government budgeting*

Peter A. Pyhrr

The important role of Peter Pyhrr in designing and promoting the present-day version of ZBB makes his description of it required reading for administrators who are interested in understanding the approach or, more important, who face a mandate to begin using it. This selection is an excellent summary of Pyhrr's views.

Pyhrr's ZBB system is highly structured. It requires the central budget office (OMB at the federal level) to issue precise instructions to agencies regarding their budget submissions. Central to the system are agency-prepared decision packages that can be ranked in such fashion that when the total amount of money to be appropriated is determined, it is clear just which programs will be funded and which will not.

Some governmental units have approached ZBB in ways different from Pyhrr's. One city simply instructed each agency to select 25 percent of its programs and consider their elimination and, if they were to be retained, consider alternative means of conducting them. The results, as might be expected, were mixed. Some agencies took the task more seriously than others, and some had superior capability for conducting the necessary analyses.

Closely related to ZBB, and perhaps a third version of it, is the "sunset" law approach. Under these laws, passed by a number of states, each program or agency is scheduled to cease operation on a certain date unless the legislature takes specific action to continue it. Under most such laws, the "sunsets" for agencies are scheduled on a periodic (e.g. five years) rotating basis. Like Pyhrr's ZBB, these laws are efforts to cope with what is seen as an inordinate tendency of agencies and programs to be perpetuated and expanded without sufficient study of their activities and results.

Zero-base budgeting is an emerging process, which has been adopted by a variety of industrial organizations in many sectors of the economy, as well as state and local governments.

---

*Reprinted from *Public Administration Review* 37 (January/February 1977): 1–8. © 1977 by The American Society for Public Administration, 1225 Connecticut Avenue, N.W., Washington, D.C. All rights reserved.

As it is generally practiced today, zero-base budgeting was developed at Texas Instruments, Inc. during 1969. The process was first adopted in government by Governor Jimmy Carter of Georgia for the preparation of the fiscal 1973 budget, and the process is still being used today in Georgia. It would appear at this point that zero-base budgeting will be adopted in the federal government, sponsored by both the president and Congress. The Government Economy and Spending Reform Act of 1976 (S. 2925) was introduced by Senator Muskie, and co-sponsored by more than 50 percent of the Senate when it was reported out of the Government Operations Committee. The bill required a congressional zero-base review and evaluation of every government authorization for programs and activities every five years, and requires the director of OMB to develop a program for the zero-base budgeting for all departments and agencies of the executive branch.

There are three key users of the zero-base analysis in government:

1. Legislative (Congress, state legislature, city council)

2. Executive (president/OMB, governors, mayor/city manager)

3. Agency (agency director, program and department managers).

The focus of each user is obviously different with the legislature requiring more summarization and focusing on public priorities and objectives, the agencies requiring more detailed information and focusing on program implementation and efficiency, and the executive straddling the needs of legislature and agency. However, regardless of specific information needs and focus, the legislature, executive, and agencies must all address themselves to two basic questions:

1. Are the current activities efficient and effective?

2. Should current activities be eliminated or reduced to fund higher-priority new programs or to reduce the current budget?

These two questions are the focus of the zero-base budgeting process.

The zero-base approach

On December 2, 1969, at the Plaza Hotel in New York City, Arthur F. Burns, then counselor to the president of the United States, addressed the annual dinner meeting of the Tax Foundation on the "Control of Government Expenditures." In this speech, Dr. Burns identified the basic need for zero-base budgeting; but he also expressed his concern that such a process would be difficult if not impossible to implement:

> *Customarily, the officials in charge of an established program have to justify only the increase which they seek above last year's appropriation. In other words, what they are already spending is usually accepted as necessary without examination. Substantial savings could*

Dr. Burns was advocating that government agencies reevaluate all programs
and present their requests for appropriation in such a fashion that all funds can
be allocated on the basis of cost/benefit or some similar kind of evaluative
analysis.

The fears of Dr. Burns that a zero-base approach "will add heavily to the
burdens of budget-making" are unwarranted, as I view the matter. None of the
organizations that I am familiar with that have implemented the approach have
added additional time onto their calendar for the preparation of a zero-base budget (other than design and training prior to the budget preparation process,
which is a normal start-up requirement of any new process). To be sure, zero-
base budgeting usually involves more managers and takes more management
time than the traditional budget procedures. However, it must be taken into
account that the zero-base approach includes objective setting, program evaluation, and operational decision making, as well as budget making, whereas traditional budgeting procedures often separate these management aspects. In the
worst case, the traditional budget process is merely a way to obtain an appropriation with the operational decision making and operating budgets determined
after the total appropriation has been obtained. If we added the total time of
these additional management elements to the time used by the traditional budgeting process, then the time requirements of zero-base budgeting do not add to
management's burdens. In fact, after the initial year's implementation, the zero-
base approach can actually reduce management's burden as the zero-base
thought process and methodology become ingrained into management's normal
way of problem solving and decision making.

Zero-base budgeting procedures

The zero-base approach requires each organization to evaluate and review
all programs and activities (current as well as new) systematically; to review
activities on a basis of output or performance as well as cost; to emphasize managerial decision making first, number-oriented budgets second; and to increase
analysis. However, I should stress that zero-base is an approach, not a fixed
procedure or set of forms to be applied uniformly from one organization to the
next. The mechanics and management approach has differed significantly
among the organizations that have adopted zero-base, and the process must be
adapted to fit the specific needs of each user. In governmental jurisdictions, for
example, certain expenditures may be fixed by law.

Although the specifics differ among organizations, there are four basic steps to the zero-base approach that must be addressed by each organization:

1. Identify "decision units."

2. Analyze each decision unit in a "decision package."

3. Evaluate and rank all decision packages to develop the appropriations request.

4. Prepare the detailed operating budgets reflecting those decision packages approved in the budget appropriation.

Defining decision units

Zero-base budgeting attempts to focus management's attention on evaluating activities and making decisions. Therefore, the "meaningful elements" of each organization must be defined so that they can be isolated for analysis and decision making. For the sake of terminology, we have termed these meaningful elements "decision units." The definition of decision units in most organizations is straightforward, and the decision units may correspond to those budget units defined by traditional budget procedures.

For those organizations with a detailed budget unit or cost center structure the decision unit may correspond to that budget unit. In some cases, the budget unit manager may wish to identify separately different functions or operations within his budget unit if they are significant in size and require separate analysis. He may therefore identify several "decision units" for a budget unit. If an organization has a well-developed program structure, the decision unit may correspond to that lowest level of the program structure (program element, activity, function). Decision units may be defined at the subprogram level if there are separate organizational units within that program element. The resulting decision packages at the subprogram element level can then be grouped to evaluate the program element. In the same manner, decision packages for each program element (or subprogram element) can be grouped to evaluate each program.

The decision packages built around each decision unit are the building blocks of the budget and program analysis. These building blocks can be readily sorted either organizationally or programmatically. For those organizations without a detailed program structure, the information and analysis developed by zero-base provides a readily usable data base from which a program structure can be developed.

Decision units can also be defined as major capital projects, special work assignments, or major projects. Each organization must determine for itself "what is meaningful." In practice, top management usually defines the organization or program level at which decision units must be defined, leaving it to the discretion of each manager to identify additional decision units if appropriate.

The decision package concept

The "decision package" is the building block of the zero-base concept. It is a document that identifies and describes each decision unit in such a manner that management can (a) evaluate it and rank it against other decision units competing for funding; and (b) decide whether to approve it or disapprove it.

The content and format of the decision package must provide management with the information it needs to evaluate each decision unit. This information might include:

1. Purpose/objective

2. Description of actions (What are we going to do, and how are we going to do it?)

3. Costs and benefits

4. Workload and performance measures

5. Alternative means of accomplishing objectives

6. Various levels of effort (What benefits do we get for various levels of funding?)

The key to developing decision packages is the formulation of meaningful alternatives. The steps that should be used in developing decision packages include:

1. Alternative methods of accomplishing the objective or performing the operation: Managers should identify and evaluate all meaningful alternatives and choose the alternative they consider best. If an alternative to the current method of doing business is chosen, the recommended way should be shown in the decision package with the current way shown as the alternative not recommended.

2. Different levels of effort of performing the operation: Once the best method of accomplishing the operation has been chosen from among the various alternative methods evaluated, a manager must identify alternative levels of effort and funding to perform that operation. Managers must establish a minimum level of effort, which must be below the current level of operation, and then identify additional levels or increments as separate decision packages. These incremental levels above the minimum might bring the operation up to its current level and to several multiples of the current level of effort.

The identification and evaluation of different levels of effort is probably the most difficult aspect of the zero-base analysis, yet it is one of the key elements of the process. If only one level of effort were analyzed (probably reflecting the funding level desired by each manager), top management would be forced to make a yes or no decision on the funding request, thus funding at the requested level, eliminating the program, making arbitrary reductions, or recycling the budget process if requests exceeded funding availability.

A decision package is defined as one incremental level in a decision unit. There may be several decision packages for each decision unit. It is these incremental levels that get ranked. By identifying a minimum level of effort, plus additional increments as separate decision packages, each manager thus presents several alternatives for top-management decision making:

Elimination. Eliminate the operation if no decision packages are approved.

Reduced Level. Reduce the level of funding if only the minimum level decision package is approved.

Current Level. Maintain the same level of effort if the minimum level, plus the one or two incremental levels (bringing the operation from the minimum level to the current level of effort) are approved. (*Note:* The current level of effort refers only to the level of output or performance sometimes referred to as a "maintenance level." However, even at the current level of effort, managers may have changed their method of operation and made operating improvements, so that the current level of effort may be accomplished at a reduced cost.)

Increased Levels. Increased levels of funding and performance if one or more increments above the current level is approved.

The minimum level of effort is the most difficult level to identify, since there is no magic number (i.e., 75 percent of the current level) that would be meaningful to all operations. The minimum level must be identified by each manager for his/her operations. The minimum level must be below the current level of effort. The minimum level should attempt to identify "that critical level of effort, below which the operation would be discontinued because it loses its viability of effectiveness." There are several considerations which can aid managers in defining the minimum level of effort:

1. The minimum level may not completely achieve the total objective of the operation (even the additional levels of effort recommended may not completely achieve the objective because of realistic budget and/or achievement levels).

2. The minimum level should address itself to the most critical population being served or attack the most serious problem areas.

3. The minimum level may merely reduce the amount of service (or number of services) provided.

4. The minimum level may reflect operating improvements, organizational changes, or improvements in efficiency that result in cost reductions.

5. Combinations of 1 through 4.

By identifying the minimum level, each manager is not necessarily recommending his operation be funded at the minimum level, but is merely identifying that alternative to top management. If a manager identifies several levels of effort, he is recommending that all levels be funded.

Air quality laboratory. The following example of the Georgia Air Quality Laboratory (Air Quality Control) illustrates the type of analysis that each manager needs to make in order to prepare decision packages. The Air Quality Laboratory tests air samples collected by field engineers throughout Georgia. It identifies and evaluates pollutants by type and volume, then provides reports and analyses to the field engineers. The manager involved made the typical two-part analysis; first, identifying different ways of performing the function; and second, identifying the different levels of effort.
I. Different ways of performing the same function:
    A.) Recommended decision package: Use a centralized laboratory in Atlanta to conduct all tests. Cost—$246,000. This expenditure would

allow 75,000 tests and would determine the air quality for 90 percent of the population (leaving unsampled only rural areas with little or no population problem).

    B.) Alternatives not recommended:

       1. Contract testing to Georgia Tech. Cost—$450,000. The $6 per test charged by the University exceeds the $246,000 cost for doing the same work in the Air Quality Laboratory, and the quality of the testing is equal.

       2. Conduct all testing at regional locations. Cost—$590,000 the first year due to set-up cost and purchase of duplicate equipment, with a $425,000 running rate in subsequent years. Many labs would be staffed at a minimum level, with less than full utilization of people and equipment.

       3. Conduct tests in Central Laboratory for special pollutants only, which require special qualifications for people and equipment, and conduct routine tests in regional centers. Cost—$400,000. This higher cost is created because regional centers have less than full workloads for people and equipment.

The recommended way of performing this laboratory function was chosen because the alternatives did not offer any additional advantages and were more expensive. The manager therefore recommended the level of 75,000 tests, at $246,000. Each manager has complete freedom to recommend either *new ways* or the current way of doing business.

Once the manager had defined the basic alternatives and selected the one he considered best, he completed his analysis by describing different levels of effort for his chosen alternative. For the recommended Central Laboratory in Atlanta, the Air Quality Laboratory manager described and evaluated decision packages that called for different levels of effort for air quality tests. In this case, the manager believed that he could reduce the level of testing to 37,300 samples and still satisfy the minimum requirements of the field engineers who used his services. Therefore, he completed his analysis by identifying the minimum level and additional levels of effort for his recommended way of performing the testing as follows:

II. Different levels of effort of performing the function:

    A.) Air Quality Laboratory (1 of 3), cost—$140,000. Minimum package: Test 37,300 samples, determining air quality for only five urban areas with the worse pollution (covering 70 percent of the population).

    B.) Air Quality Laboratory (2 of 3), cost—$61,000 (Levels 1 + 2 = $201,000). Test 17,700 additional samples (totaling 55,000, which is the current level), determining air quality for five additional problem urban areas plus eight counties chosen on the basis of worst pollution (covering 80 percent of the population).

    C.) Air Quality Laboratory (3 of 3), cost—$45,000 (Levels 1 + 2 + 3 = $246,000). Test 20,000 additional samples (totaling 75,000), determining air quality for 90 percent of the population, and leaving only rural areas with little or no pollution problems unsampled.

The Air Quality Laboratory manager thus prepared three decision packages (levels 1 of 3, 2 of 3, and 3 of 3).

Development of different levels as separate decision packages indicates that the functional manager thinks all levels deserve serious consideration within realistic funding expectations. He identifies three possible levels and leaves it to higher management to make tradeoffs among functions and level of effort within each function.

An example from city operations.   The decision package analysis can be applied to any federal, state, or local operation or program. The questions raised by the decision package, and the analysis required, are similar even for extremely diverse programs and operations.

To demonstrate this point, I have taken an example of residential refuse collection from the city of Garland, Texas. Garland was the first city to my knowledge to have successfully implemented zero-base budgeting throughout all city departments. The residential refuse example clearly illustrates the zero-base analysis and identifies the alternatives and funding decisions faced by city managers.

"Residential Refuse Collection" is the city operation responsible for collecting and transporting all residential solid waste for disposal. The manager of this function made the typical two-part analysis: first, identifying alternative means for accomplishing this activity; and second, identifying different levels of effort.

I. Different ways of performing the same function:
    A.) Recommended means: City provides the collection service, requiring the use of plastic sacks for all refuse. Plastic sacks are purchased by each resident. Refuse trains are used for heavily populated areas. Front-loading refuse trucks are used to empty the refuse trains on the route to transport the refuse to the landfill. Other types of trucks are used for the less-populated areas and country runs. Cost — $790,300.
    B.) Alternatives not recommended:
    1. Collection without the use of plastic sacks: Additional man required on each crew if garbage cans are used in place of plastic sacks. Added cost of $96,000.
    2. Collection of all refuse by the trains. Use of other types of equipment (shu-packs and barrel trucks) are more efficient in less densely populated areas. Purchase of three additional refuse trains and two front-loaders would be required, plus eight additional personnel, for an additional cost of $150,000.
    3. Contract city refuse collection to a private contractor: Cost $1,108,800 for twice-a-week collection; $900,000 for once-a-week collection.

The recommended means was chosen because the alternatives did not offer any additional advantages and were more expensive.

The residential refuse collection manager completed his zero-base analysis by identifying different levels of effort for performing the function. In this case, the manager believed he could reduce the level of refuse collection from twice a week to once a week and still satisfy the minimum sanitary requirements. Therefore, he completed his analysis by identifying the minimum level and additional levels of effort for his recommended means of refuse collection as follows:

II. Different levels of effort for performing the function:

    A.) Residential Refuse Collection (1 of 3): cost—$607,000 minimum level: Collect residential refuse once per week; brush pickup on Thursday and Friday.

    B.) Residential Refuse Collection (2 of 3): cost—$142,800 (Levels 1 + 2 = $750,300). Add one additional collection per week, so that refuse is collected twice per week.

    C.) Residential Refuse Collection (3 of 3): cost—$40,500 (Levels 1 + 2 + 3 = $790,300). Collection of brush and white goods an additional two days per week, so that brush is collected every collection day (Mon., Tues., Thurs., and Fri.).

The manager thus prepared three decision packages.

It should be pointed out that there is no magic number of funding levels, but two to five levels are most common. It is also common in many cases to have a great deal of back-up information and analysis, which the decision package itself displays in summary form. In the residential refuse case, there was extensive information and analysis regarding different types of equipment, detailed city maps with an analysis of different route alternatives, and an evaluation of different types of equipment for different routes. The city manager in this case reviewed the detailed analysis, and there were several revisions before the recommendations were put into final form.

The ranking process

The ranking process provides management with a technique to allocate its limited resources by making management concentrate on these questions: "How much should we spend?" and "Where should we spend it?" Management constructs its answer to these questions by listing all the decision packages identified in order of decreasing benefit to the organization. It then identifies the benefits to be gained at each level of expenditure and studies the consequences of not approving additional decision packages ranked below that expenditure level.

The ranking process establishes priorities among the incremental levels of each decision unit (i.e., decision packages). The rankings therefore display a marginal analysis. If the manager of the Air Quality Program in Georgia developed decision packages for the Air Quality Laboratory, Reviews and Permits, Source Evaluation, Registration, and Research, his ranking might appear as shown in the table on p. 351.

From a practical standpoint, the rankings of the minimum levels for Reviews and Permits, Source Evaluation, Air Quality Laboratory, and Registration may be requirements, so that the absolute ranking of those decision packages (ranked 1–4) are not meaningful. However, the priority of the packages with a lower ranking becomes significant since management will ultimately make a decision on which packages will be funded. If packages one through eight are funded, management would approve a budget for Air Quality Control

Rank	Decision package	Incremental cost	Cumulative program cost
1	Reviews and permits (1 of 2)	$116,000	$116,000
2	Source evaluation (1 of 4)	103,000	219,000
3	Air quality laboratory (1 of 3)	140,000	359,000
4	Registration (1 of 3)	273,000	632,000
5	Source evaluation (2 of 4)	53,000	685,000
6	Air quality laboratory (2 of 3)	61,000	746,000
7	Source evaluation (3 of 4)	45,000	791,000
8	Air quality laboratory (3 of 3)	45,000	836,000
9	Reviews and permits (2 of 2)	50,000	886,000
10	Research (1 of 2)	85,000	971,000

of $246,000. Management would have funded all three levels of the Air Quality Laboratory, thus increasing that budget; funded only the minimum level of Registration, thus decreasing that budget; and not funded any Research, thus eliminating that function. Discretionary programs may have the minimum level ranked at the medium or low priority, while increased levels for other programs may be given a high priority. Therefore, the rankings can produce dramatic shifts in resource allocations.

The key to an effective review and ranking process lies in focusing top management's attention on key policy issues and discretionary expenditures. In a small organization such as the City of Garland, Texas, all decision packages were reviewed by the city manager. The city manager took the lower-priority packages from each organization that he thought were somewhat discretionary and concentrated his ranking efforts on developing a consolidated ranking across all city organizations for those discretionary decision packages.

In large organizations, top management may be forced to rely primarily on management summaries in lieu of concentrating on the decision packages. In the state of Georgia, decision packages are ranked to the program level in each agency. The Budget Office prepares executive summaries based on the decision packages and program rankings submitted by each agency for the governor's review.

It is also possible to prepare "activity decision packages" (an activity being the lowest element in the program structure). Activity decision packages would then be ranked for each program. "Program decision packages" could then be prepared based on the activity decision packages and the ranking at the program level. The program decision packages could have a format and content similar to the activity decision package, but provide a summary and program analysis for use by top agency management and the executive and legislative review process.

Regardless of organizational size and form of top management review, the decision packages and rankings form the backbone of analysis and decision making. The nature of each review process must be specifically designed to fit the size and personality of each organization.

Preparing the detailed operating budget

The budget or appropriation requests prepared by each organization are usually subject to some form of legislative review and modification. If the legislative appropriation differs markedly from the budget request, many organizations that have used traditional budgeting techniques are forced to recycle their entire budgeting effort to determine where the reductions should be made. Under the zero-base budgeting approach, the decision packages and rankings determine specifically the actions required to achieve any budget reductions. If the legislature defines reductions in specific program areas, we can readily identify the corresponding decision packages and reduce the appropriate program and organizational budgets. If the legislature identifies an arbitrary reduction (e.g. reduce budget five percent), each agency can use its rankings and eliminate those decision packages that it considers to be the lowest priority.

In the final analysis, each organization will have a number of approved decision packages which define the budget of each program and organizational unit. The decision packages also define the specific activities and performance anticipated from each program and organizational unit. This information can provide the basis for both budget and operational reviews during the year.

Practices and problems

The term "zero-base" has many different connotations. To those who have merely heard the term, it tends to mean "the process of throwing everything out and starting all over again from scratch," or "reinventing the wheel." These connotations are incorrect and imply an effort of impractical magnitude and chaos.

In a more practical vein, "zero-base" means the evaluation of all programs. The evaluation of alternatives and program performance may occasionally lead us to completely rethink and redirect a program, in which case we do "throw everything out and start all over again." However, in the great majority of cases, programs will continue, incorporating modifications and improvements. For the majority of programs, we will concentrate our analysis on evaluating program efficiency and effectiveness and the evaluation and prioritization of different levels of effort.

This pragmatic approach offers us an extremely flexible tool. Managers can "reinvent the wheel" in those situations where preliminary investigation indicates the need and potential benefits of such an approach, and can concentrate their effort on improving programs that appear to be headed in the right direction.

The zero-base approach has led to major reallocation of resources. For example, the state of Georgia experienced a $57 million (5 percent of general funds) revenue shortfall. Governor Jimmy Carter used the zero-base analysis to reduce budgets across 65 agencies, with reductions ranging from 1 percent to 15 percent. Program reductions within each agency ranged from no change to elimination.

In a political environment, the expectations for major shifts in resource allocations must be qualified. The major reallocations of resources will normally take place within major agencies, such as shifting administrative and maintenance cost savings into direct program delivery. However, it is unrealistic to expect a 20 percent decrease in the Department of Education to fund a 40 percent increase in Mental Health. The political realities do not usually allow such shifts. It is also unrealistic to expect an automatic tax reduction due to zero-base budgeting. When cost reductions are achieved, the overriding political tendency is to plow the money back into increased services in other programs.

If we can't realistically expect major funding reallocations among major agencies, and if we can't expect a tax decrease, then why do zero-base budgeting? I believe that there are four overriding reasons that make the zero-base approach worthwhile:

1. Low-priority programs can be eliminated or reduced. How the savings are used is a completely separate question.

2. Program effectiveness can be dramatically improved. Such improvements may or may not have a budgetary impact.

3. High-impact programs can obtain increased funding by shifting resources within an agency, whereas the increased funding might not have been made available had the agency merely requested an increase in total funding.

4. Tax increases can be retarded. The first three benefits can significantly reduce the necessity for increased taxes by allowing agencies to do a more effective job with existing revenues. For the hard-nosed executive or legislature, budgets can be reduced with a minimum of reduced services.

The zero-base approach is not without its problems. The major problem is the threat that many bureaucrats feel towards a process that evaluates the effectiveness of their programs. The zero-base process also requires a great deal of effective administration, communications, and training of managers who will be involved in the analysis. Managers may also have problems in identifying appropriate decision units, developing adequate data to produce an effective analysis, determining the minimum level of effort, ranking dissimilar programs, and handling large volumes of packages. For many programs, workload and performance measures may be lacking or the cause/effect and program impact may not be well defined so that the analysis will be less than perfect. Therefore, zero-base budgeting should be looked upon as a longer-term management development process rather than a one-year cure-all.

If done properly, the zero-base approach is not subject to the gamesmanship one might anticipate. The traditional budget approach offers maximum opportunity for gamesmanship because current operations are seldom evaluated and many discreet decisions are never explicitly identified and get "buried in the numbers." However, the zero-base approach removes the umbrella covering current operations and requires managers to clearly identify operating deci-

Securing resources/

353

sions. In zero-base, most obvious forms of gamesmanship would be to avoid identifying reasonable alternatives, to include the pet projects within the minimum level package, and to rank high-priority programs low in the ranking in order to obtain additional funding. If the decision packages are "formatted" adequately to display the alternatives considered, workload and performance data, descriptions of actions, and enough cost data so that discretionary items cannot be built into the cost estimate, it becomes very obvious when such gamesmanship is attempted. Also, because the entire ranking of decision packages must be displayed, it is very easy to challenge a high-priority item that received a low ranking or a low-priority item that received a high ranking.

The problems in implementing zero-base budgeting are not to be minimized. The specific needs, problems, and capabilities of each organization must be considered in adapting the zero-base approach. Although most of the basic concepts of the zero-base approach have been maintained, the specifics of administration, formats, and procedures have been different for each organization that has adopted the approach. Zero-base can be applied on an intensive basis throughout all levels of an organization, applied only to selected programs, or applied only at major program levels rather than involving all operating managers. The strategy of implementing the zero-base approach must be developed for each organization, depending on its specific needs and capabilities. It should be considered a management and budgetary improvement effort that may require several years to reach full utilization and effectiveness.

Study questions for selection fourteen

1. Once ZBB decision units have been identified, managers are required to establish a "minimum level of effort" decision package. What is the significance of this first package? What factors should a manager consider in setting it?

2. Under ZBB, as under most budget schemes, the review process is important. Reviews are conducted by agency superiors, by the chief executive, and by the legislature. What is the significance of package rankings for this review process?

3. It is generally understood that agencies "pad" their requests and that budgetary decision makers expect them to pad. How are these expectations likely to be affected by implementation of ZBB?

Chapter ten

354

Zero-base budgeting in historical and political context*

F. Ted Hebert

Executive budgeting was born in an era of reform. Ever since, reformers seeking to improve the procedures and functioning of government agencies have looked at the budgetary process. The ZBB reform should be examined in the context of earlier reform efforts, as well as in the context of present political realities.

Zero-base budgeting, as now being implemented, incorporates features of several earlier proposals. Particularly important is the pursuit of efficiency through attaching costs to work-load information, yielding "costs per order processed," "cost per case handled," etc. This is very similar to requirements of performance budgeting promoted in the 1950s.

In the article reprinted here, Hebert describes this and other links between ZBB and earlier reforms. He then questions whether ZBB will be found politically acceptable, given our failure to fully implement earlier reform proposals.

The much heralded zero-base budgeting system, a matter of interest to public administrators and politicians alike, is certainly not a new idea to students of government budgeting. Its history reaches back almost as far as the history of American executive budgeting itself. Writing in 1924, just three years after passage of the Budget and Accounting Act, E. Hilton Young and N. E. Young describe the start of a British budget cycle as follows:

> *On October 1st [the Treasury] sends a circular letter to the officers responsible for the preparation of the estimates in each civil department, requesting them to prepare estimates of the expenses of the departments in the coming year. There are two stereotyped admonitions in this circular: one is general, that the state of the public revenue demands the utmost economy; the other is a particular warning against assuming last year's estimates as the starting point for those of the next. The latter is a necessary warning. It must always be a temptation to one drawing up an estimate to save himself trouble by taking last year's estimate for granted, adding something to any item for which an increased expenditure is fore-*

---

*Reprinted with permission from F. Ted Hebert, "Zero-Base Budgeting in Historical and Political Context," *Midwest Review of Public Administration* 11 (September 1977): 163-181.

Securing resources/

355

seen. Nothing could be easier, or more wasteful and extravagant. It is in that way that obsolete expenditure is enabled to make its appearance year after year in the estimates, long after all reason for it has ceased to be. By this warning and by the general admonition as to the need for economy the departments are no doubt duly impressed.[1]

In a ten-year-later examination of the budgetary systems of the United States and of other nations, A. E. Buck quotes the Youngs with apparent sympathy[2] and asks:

Do current or past requirements have any value in [expenditure estimations]? Undoubtedly so; they are facts which should be regarded as elements in the calculation, although they should not be accepted as inevitably indicative of future needs and the necessity for a sustained level of expenditure.[3]

Although not using the terms *zero-base budgeting* (ZBB), these early authors were calling attention to the very same concern that has captured the interest of budgetary system reformers today.

Zero-base budgeting today

Before undertaking further efforts to trace historical roots of ZBB it is useful to attempt a description of the recent reforms initiated under that rubric. Doing so requires examination of efforts made in several state and local jurisdictions.

The place with which to begin is the state of Georgia. Here Governor Carter undertook to implement ZBB with the help of Peter A. Pyhrr, whose 1970 article in *Harvard Business Review* is generally credited with sparking the flames of renewed interest in the approach.[4] The objective sought by the ZBB effort is well stated by George Minmier in his evaluation of Georgia's experience: "Zero-base budgeting is a technique whereby the total cost of every item included in the proposed budget must be justified and approved."[5] This means that items carried forward from previous years are subject to review just as are new recommendations. This understanding of ZBB accords well with the desires of the Youngs and of Buck quoted above, and with a 1969 statement of Arthur F. Burns, now chairman of the Federal Reserve Board, when he said: "Substantial savings could undoubtedly be realized if [it

---

[1]E. Hilton Young and N. E. Young, *The System of National Finance*, 2nd ed. (London: John Murray, 1924), pp. 23-24. Emphasis added.

[2]A. E. Buck *The Budget in Governments of Today* (New York: Macmillan, 1934), pp. 171–72.

[3]Ibid., p. 175.

[4]Peter A. Pyhrr, "Zero-Base Budgeting," *Harvard Business Review* 48 (November-December, 1970): 111–21.

[5]George Samuel Minmier, *An Evaluation of the Zero-Base Budgeting System in Governmental Institutions* (Atlanta: Georgia State University School of Business Administration, 1975), p. 10.

were required that] every agency ... make a case for its entire appropriation request each year, just as if its program or programs were entirely new."[6] Pyhrr began his 1970 article with that quotation, clearly indicating that such was the goal of ZBB as he conceived it.

What remains is to see how the Georgia budgetary system was reformed to achieve that goal. Of prime importance was a requirement that all concerned with the budgetary process begin to focus their attention upon the *activities* performed by state agencies, to "identify the current year's activities and operations."[7] The costs of the activities were to be carefully calculated, a procedure which may be new in some governmental units accustomed to focusing upon objects of expenditure only. Frequently, though, the activities corresponded with the lowest organizational level within an agency and cost may thus equal its budget.

The second step which the procedure requires is the formulation of decision packages identified with each activity. These are of four types:

1. A "business as usual" package, supporting both the present means of performing the activity and the present performance level.

2. A "different level" package considering an increase or decrease in the performance and funding level of the activity.

3. An "alternative means" package suggesting a different approach to the task which the present activity is designed to perform.

4. A "new activity" package. This would relate only tangentially, if at all, to present activities.

Each organizational unit is expected to develop one or more such decision packages for each activity under its responsibility. Pyhrr suggests that one package should indicate a "minimum level of effort"—the basic amount of funds and number of employees necessary to keep the activity functioning, even though failing to meet goals or solve problems for which it is intended. Additional packages would suggest alternative means or levels which, added to the minimum level package, would move toward goal attainment. Each organizational unit, after preparing a justification for each package, is required to rank its packages from the one most desired, that which should be funded even in event of the most severe financial constraint, to that least required, which should be eliminated first if funding levels are not sufficient.

Although Pyhrr stresses the importance of cost/benefit analysis as a basis for ranking, he makes few references to any effort to determine the goals of activities or to measure goal accomplishment.[8] This possible shortcoming will be returned to below.

Once an individual unit has ranked its own packages, these are forwarded to the next higher organizational level where rankings from various

---

[6]Quoted in Pyhrr, "Zero Base Budgeting," p. 111, from a speech delivered by Mr. Burns at the Plaza Hotel, New York, 2 December 1969.

[7]Peter A. Pyhrr, *Zero Base Budgeting: A Practical Management Tool for Evaluating Expenses* (New York: John Wiley, 1973), p. 12.

[8]Ibid., pp. 62–70.

Securing resources/

/357

subunits are consolidated into a department-wide ranking. Finally, these departmental rankings are submitted to the executive budget office for consideration. Matters can become highly complex, with thousands of individual decision packages.[9] Various efforts at simplification have been undertaken including the establishment of a cutoff at, for example, 60 percent of the current budget. There is then no need to review those packages that fall below that level, and efforts can concentrate on ranking only those that move to higher funding levels.[10] For the 1978 fiscal year, agencies are instructed to prepare packages at these levels: minimum objective level (something below current funding); current objective level (service the same with costs usually somewhat higher); and improvement objective level (service closer to achieving activity goals). Departments then will rank these packages. Some activities may find their improvement objective level packages ranked above the current objective level packages of other activities. Minmier indicates that in recent years no effort has been made to prepare a ranking at an organizational level higher than the department.[11]

To support the rankings, various forms for data presentation have been developed in Georgia and in other jurisdictions attempting ZBB.[12] Although there are obvious differences among these (even within the Georgia system from year to year), there are significant similarities. One is the inclusion of a statement of purpose of the activity. This allows for a brief narrative description of the goal(s) of the activity. There is a similar space for a narrative description of the activity itself, which is then elaborated upon by a quantitative presentation of work-load data, typically for three fiscal years. Another important feature of the presentation is a statement of the consequences which would result from failure to approve the package—the impact that such failure would have upon goal achievement. This is accompanied by a brief statement of alternatives, which are usually the subjects of other decision packages. Consequently, from the forms supporting any one decision package the reviewer can get a superficial look at the total consideration given to that activity. Finally, the forms include specific financial and personnel requests.[13]

Although this comment is probably more severe than evidence presented so far justifies, the zero-base budgeting efforts being made today probably do not deserve to be labeled "zero-base budgeting." Pyhrr's sympathetic description of the Georgia system, as well as Minmier's more critical examination, leave doubt that any real effort was made to justify and approve in total every item in the budget. This is not to say that the reforms may not be important, a matter to be addressed below, but to argue that all activities or programs are considered from zero, that new proposals have the same chance to be funded (given equal merit) as old programs, is not justified.

---

[9]Ibid., p. 64.

[10]Ibid., pp. 83–86.

[11]Minmier, p. 105.

[12]Among the ZBB forms examined were those of Georgia, included in Pyhrr and in Minmier and those of Wilmington, Delaware and Garland, Texas.

[13]Although this description of ZBB is based heavily upon the Georgia experience, it captures the fundamental features of reforms being promoted generally.

\Chapter ten

358

What, then, is ZBB all about? If it is not simply a "justify from zero" effort, what is it? This can best be answered by seeing how it fits into the development of public budgeting in the United States.

Zero-base budgeting in historical context

ZBB: A secondary goal of earlier reforms

The most complete presentation of earlier reform efforts is found in Allen Schick's excellent article, "The Road to PPB," published in 1966.[14] Schick maintained that we have seen the emphasis of reform placed, successively, upon the control, management, and planning purposes of budgeting.[15] Each of these foci was accompanied by a particular budgetary scheme: object classification budgeting, performance budgeting, and the planning programming budgeting system, respectively. How orderly matters would be if one could identify a fourth purpose which the budgetary process might serve and then proceed to identify ZBB with that purpose. Such is not the case, however. As shown above, the demand that budget makers justify from zero reaches back well into the "control-oriented" period. It was not totally overlooked during either the "management" or the "planning" periods. The thrust of the Hoover Commission recommendation, which was the capstone of performance emphasis, clearly encompassed an effort to justify from zero. The following recommendation from the commission is not very different from a portion of the Georgia budget process.

Supporting [budgetary] detail submitted initially would include a narrative explanation of the significance and scope of each subprogram—by activity or subunit when appropriate—changes in emphasis over previous years, together with a progress report of work accomplished or under way. Additional data would be set forth in tabular form showing comparative work load, unit costs, and such other yardsticks as might be necessary to evaluate any elements of the appropriation request.[16]

Later, as the focus of reform shifted to planning, concern for justification from zero persisted. The most noteworthy effort to implement a zero-base budget process was undertaken by the Department of Agriculture in preparation of the 1964 budget. Wildavsky and Hammann have provided an excellent

---

[14]Allen Schick, "The Road to PPB: The Stages of Budgetary Reform," *Public Administration Review* 26 (December, 1966): 243–58.
[15]Ibid., pp. 244–45.
[16]Commission on Organization of the Executive Branch of Government, "Budgeting and Accounting" (Washington, D.C.: Government Printing Office, 1949), p. 78.

description and evaluation of this exercise.[17] In the USDA budget preparation instructions, subunits were told, "All programs will be reviewed from the ground up and not merely in terms of changes proposed for the budget year."[18] This was followed by an effort (not altogether successful, according to Wildavsky and Hammann) to use these justifications as a basis for allocating resources.

Still later, the planning programming budgeting system which was introduced throughout most of the federal government in 1965 clearly demanded that budget preparation include consideration of the contribution which each program (or program component) made to accomplishment of a specific end or objective.[19] PPB, as implemented by the federal government, required that agencies prepare program memoranda which provided a justification for the program in terms of its contribution to a stated objective. As with ZBB, agencies were told to "compare the effectiveness and the cost . . . of alternative *types* of programs designed to meet the same or comparable objectives, and of different *levels* within a given program category."[20] These alternatives were to be compared with present programs for which, of course, complete cost and benefit data would be needed. Clearly this process required examining *total* costs and benefits of current programs, an examination from a zero base. A later instruction told federal agencies that program memoranda should "be prepared with as much attention paid to reducing and modifying obsolete and low priority programs as expanding others and introducing new ones."[21]

The desire to achieve zero-base budgeting, then, has been a motivating force behind most of the budget reform efforts of the twentieth century. As Schick correctly indicates, budgets are expected to serve multiple purposes.[22] The desire to review ongoing programs from zero, to thereby curtail or eliminate outdated or nonproductive programs, is one of those purposes, and it has persisted as an objective of governmental budgeting throughout all the decades of reform. The present ZBB effort is its latest manifestation and gives it greater emphasis than ever before. Yet, it remains to be seen whether the current effort can succeed where others have failed, whether the ZBB scheme

---

[17]Aaron Wildavsky and Arthur Hammond, "Comprehensive Versus Incremental Budgeting in the Department of Agriculture," *Administrative Science Quarterly 10* (December, 1965): 321–46. (The correct spelling of the second author's name is Hammann, but was spelled incorrectly in the original publication).

[18]Ibid., p. 326.

[19]See Melvin Anshen, "The Federal Budget as an Instrument for Management and Analysis," in David Novick, ed., *Program Budgeting: Program Analysis and the Federal Budget* (Cambridge: Harvard University Press, 1967), pp. 3–23. See also other selections in this excellent volume on PPB.

[20]Executive Office of the President, Bureau of the Budget, "Bulletin No. 66–3" (October 12, 1965), as reprinted in Fremont J. Lyden and Ernest G. Miller, *Planning Programming Budgeting: A Systems Approach to Management* (Chicago: Markham Publishing Company, 1968), p. 413. Emphasis added.

[21]Executive Office of the President, Bureau of the Budget, "Supplement to Bulletin No. 66–3" (February 21, 1966), as reprinted in Lyden and Miller, p. 422.

[22]Allen Schick, *Budget Innovation in the States* (Washington, D.C.: The Brookings Institution, 1971), pp. 1–13.

as introduced in Georgia is sufficiently different from earlier reforms to make such success even likely.

The Georgia system and earlier reforms

To judge the potential for success of the current ZBB effort, one must see just how it relates to previous reforms. The brief presentation of the Georgia scheme given above provides insufficient information for such an examination, but a slightly more detailed look at certain features will facilitate fitting this latest effort into the historical pattern of reform. (While comments here refer specifically to Georgia, they apply equally to other ZBB efforts that follow Pyhrr's design.)

A first question to ask is whether ZBB is an extension of the planning programming budgeting movement. If it were, a significant feature of it should be heavy emphasis upon the stating of a concrete objective, the attainment of which is measurable. It was this specification of objectives, and the formal presentation of the relationships between program activities and attainment of those objectives, which characterized PPB. A look at Pyhrr's description and Minmier's evaluation of the Georgia system, as well as at other ZBB efforts, reveals little emphasis upon the ultimate ends which government programs are designed to serve. Pyhrr devotes one chapter of his book to specifying the inadequacies of PPB and to showing that ZBB is capable of filling certain gaps therein. Fundamental to his criticism is a contention that PPB is designed for long-range planning and provides little help with short-term decisions, that PPB "focuses on the effect that a group of activities has in achieving certain objectives rather than the efficiency in which each activity is carried out," and that PPB focuses primarily upon new programs or program changes rather than on current programs.[23]

Certainly Pyhrr is correct. Zero-base budgeting and planning programming budgeting are quite distinct systems. Although Pyhrr in several places stresses the requirement that a ZBB process focus attention upon the benefits of activities, there is little in the Georgia process which facilitates this. For example, he says that in constructing decision packages, managers should stress those things which the program accomplishes, being interested in the "benefits achieved for a given expenditure."[24] Elsewhere he says that each decision package should, at a minimum, provide a cost/benefit analysis—clearly a focus on program objectives.[25] However, an examination of the Georgia budget forms (and, for that matter, forms used in other ZBB systems) reveals little emphasis on previous statement of objectives or presentation of cost/benefit analyses. Drawing from an example Pyhrr presents, a decision package of the Highway Patrol-Field Operation includes the following Statement of Purpose:

---

[23]Pyhrr, p. 150.
[24]Ibid., p. 51.
[25]Ibid., p. 62.

> *To patrol the rural and public roads and highways throughout the
> State, to prevent, detect and investigate criminal acts, and to arrest
> and apprehend those charged with criminal offenses appertaining
> thereto, and to safeguard the lives and property of the public.*[26]

A package of the Air Quality Laboratory presents the following:

> *Ambient air laboratory analysis must be conducted for identification
> and evaluation of pollutants by type and by volume. Sample analysis
> enables engineers to determine effect of control and permits use of an
> emergency warning system.*[27]

Neither of these statements even approaches the degree of precision necessary for a cost/benefit study nor provides higher-level decision makers with a
clear understanding of the contribution which the activity makes to a higher
purpose. Even granting that other sections of the form, especially one headed
"Consequences of Not Approving Package," supply some supplementary information, there is still a vast gap between what is provided and what would be
necessary for a precise (quantitative or nonquantitative) evaluation of the
package.

Since Pyhrr has made clear his dissatisfaction with the planning programming budgeting reform, it is perhaps unfair to evaluate his ZBB proposal
against the criteria for implementation of PPB—especially since few, if any,
PPB efforts met those criteria. One simply needs to discount Pyhrr's suggestions
that ZBB would permit cost/benefit analysis or really focus attention upon program accomplishments.

If ZBB is not an extension of the PPB reform, what might it be? One possibility is that it is a revival of the earlier marginally successful reform effort
generally known as "performance budgeting." This, of course, is the reform
Schick associated with a management emphasis in budgeting and which was
promoted by the Hoover Commissions. Under these proposals there was an effort
to lessen the rigidity of control by the executive budget office and the legislature. Administrators of programs were to gain latitude to take steps which, it
was hoped, would produce greater efficiency. The desire for *efficiency* was the
driving force behind the performance budgeting movement.[28]

To encourage efficiency, budget makers were required to focus attention
upon the activities of their organizations rather than upon the traditional inputs
represented by line items. In the words of Jesse Burkhead, "Performance classification provides the link between the things bought and the things done or
accomplished."[29] He goes on to give examples of "things done," to include roads
built, tons of food transported, acres of trees planted, tax returns audited or

---

[26]Ibid., p. 42.

[27]Ibid., p. 66.

[28]For a discussion of performance budgeting, see Schick, pp. 44–85.

[29]Jesse Burkhead, *Government Budgeting* (New York: John Wiley and Sons, Inc., 1956), p.
140.

Chapter ten

362

pennies minted.[30] Each of these may be seen as an end product of a government activity.

The next step in performance budgeting was to attach costs to each of these activities, determining appropriate unit costs. It is here that many performance budgeting schemes broke down. To establish the *full* unit cost required a more elaborate accounting system than most agencies or governments had; it required an ability to assign overhead as well as direct costs to performance units.

Despite this difficulty, many governments in the United States implemented a performance budgeting system, at least in name. A look at the Budget of the United States today reveals the inclusion of activity measures. In many cases, though, these innovations were but an overlay upon the older budgetary process. This author's experience in the state of Louisiana may be indicative of widespread practice.

The Louisiana Budget Office in 1965 was employing, in part, a performance budget. Agencies were required to submit, on the first page of their budget requests, a statement of purpose and measures of their activities. Frequently, the statement of purpose provided was merely a quotation from the statutory authority of the agency. Activity measures were of the crudest sort and were supplied only by those agencies which had activities readily quantifiable. Even more significant is the fact that when the budget request forms reached the budget office, this author received the first page (containing the performance information) while the responsible budget examiner received the request presented in an *object* classification. All decision making from that point on was done through examination of the object requests. Not until time to print the budget was the performance information (edited to take up a half-page) turned over to a secretary for typing along with the governor's recommendation—presented in an object classification.

Schick's description of the "hybridization" of performance budgeting in many states accords well with that found in the Louisiana budget system. There are reasons, then, for severe reservations about "classification by activities" having had any large impact on state or federal budgeting.

As was indicated above, the data employed in ZBB seem to provide little information about objectives or ends, or the accomplishment of those objectives. As examples, information required by both the Georgia and the Garland, Texas, forms is work-load information quite similar to that demanded by performance budgeting. Further, the brief narrative "statements of purpose" are quite like the statements that accompanied Louisiana's performance forms. As an example of activity measures, the Garland instruction Manual for 1976-77 provides a completed form for a Fleet Maintenance Center, General Office.[31] Work-load data are provided for the following:

Work Orders Processed

---

[30]Ibid., p. 142.

[31]Budget Office, City of Garland, *Annual Budget Instruction Manual,* 1976–77 (Garland, Texas: City of Garland, n.d.), p. 23.

Mainstem Report Terms

Parts Orders Processed

Parts Issue Transactions

In each case, work-unit data are provided for three years.

The Georgia forms have sought to have agencies go one step further, if possible, and calculate unit-cost data and man-hour data in relation to the work-load statistics. In both cases, the similarity to the requirements of performance budgeting schemes is most marked. Even the weaknesses are similar. Both Pyhrr and Minmier decry the lack of adequate cost information that is applicable at the activity level.[32]

This focus upon work-load data and upon brief descriptions of the purposes of activities is so strikingly similar to the performance budgeting reform that it cannot be overlooked. In both cases there is, it appears, an assumption that the budgetary process has little to do with the selection of the objectives of government programs. For both, budgeting is primarily a process through which an attempt is made to assure that those goals which are sought are pursued in the most efficient manner. It seems that ZBB may be a bit more open to consideration of alternative activities for pursuit of given goals than some formulations of performance budgeting may have been, but a basic similarity remains. It is the *activity* which is important to budget makers and the efficiency with which that activity is carried out.

Despite this obvious similarity, there is a distinction which must be noted. This distinction could be, if ZBB were to be fully implemented (and implemented differently from the way it seems to have been so far), more important than the similarities. It is the feature that proponents of ZBB talk about most: that budget makers must justify their activities from zero. Although other reforms have included this demand, none has given it much emphasis. As best can be told so far, neither does ZBB. The formal requirements, the forms, and the results do not indicate any truly concerted effort to justify activities from zero, let alone *every* activity *every* year.[33]

If ZBB does not really promote justification from zero and seems to have some of the same weaknesses as performance budgeting, is there anything about it which might justify the attention it is receiving? One possibility is the fact that ZBB has revived interest in an approach to budgeting which was suggested in 1952 by Verne B. Lewis and labeled the "alternative budget system."[34] Lewis explicitly declined to suggest the mechanism through which his approach to budgeting might be implemented but did describe the system's major features. Each preparer of a budget would be required to consider the services which could be provided at, perhaps, five different funding levels. These levels might be varied to take account of particular situations, but would adhere to the gen-

---

[32]Pyhrr, p. 132, and Minmier, p. 101.

[33]On the impact of ZBB upon budgets, see Minmier, pp. 118 and 154.

[34]Verne B. Lewis, "Toward a Theory of Budgeting," *Public Administration Review* 12 (Winter 1952): 42–54.

eral pattern. At each level the "nature, quantity, and quality of services" which the agency could provide would be specified.[35] Each higher administrative level would have opportunity to review the alternatives. The highest levels, and even the legislature, would have access to a group of alternatives.[36]

A slight variation of the alternative budget scheme was suggested in 1971 by Merewitz and Sosnick. They proposed that three levels of funding might be sufficient. These levels would provide, in comparison to the present year, "the same-dollar amount," "the same-performance amount," and "the recommended amount."[37] Justifications, including quantitative supporting data if available, would be provided for the recommended amount and to support conclusions regarding the impact which would result from funding at the alternative levels. Higher administrative units would consolidate these reports into alternatives similarly defined, but covering the entire higher-level agency. Additionally, the higher-level request would indicate the distribution of funds which would be made to subordinate agencies. For example, if the department received the same-performance amount, some of the lower agencies might get as much as or more than their recommended amounts, while others could get less than their same-dollar amounts. The process would compel budget reviewers to consider such trade-offs.[38] Merewitz and Sosnick comment:

> *The alternative budget approach ... has important advantages over zero-base budgeting. Both procedures encourage officials to consider curtailing or terminating ineffective or obsolete programs. The alternative budget approach, however, does not throw away information about last year's appropriation and does not demand justifications that cannot be given. It recognizes that what is the best allocation of funds is a matter of judgment, and it seeks to provide decision-makers with the information needed to pass judgment. This information consists of a description of what would be gained in one program and lost in another if funds were reallocated.[39]*

This description of the alternative budget system does not differ markedly in some of its features from the ZBB system as proposed by Pyhrr. In fact, the ZBB procedures implemented in Georgia and elsewhere can be seen as an effort to institutionalize an alternative budget system in combination with important features of performance budgeting. Admittedly, the focusing of attention at the activity level (perhaps lower than Lewis or Merewitz and Sosnick had in mind) is an important variation of alternative budgeting. However, doing so ties this recent reform more closely to the performance budget approach. It is at the

---

[35]Ibid., p. 49.

[36]Ibid., pp. 53–54.

[37]Leonard Merewitz and Stephen H. Sosnick, *The Budget's New Clothes: A Critique of Planning-Programming-Budgeting and Benefit-Cost Analysis* (Chicago: Markham Publishing Company, 1971), p. 66.

[38]Ibid., pp. 68 and 69.

[39]Ibid., p. 70.

activity level that there are likely to be countable work units to which costs can be attached. Decisions under the ZBB system are apparently to be made in terms of the impact which various funding levels, represented by the decision packages, have upon performance of the activities and, especially, upon the accomplishment of units of work.

What is new in ZBB is not the goal or focus of budgeting but rather it is the concerted effort to institutionalize earlier reform proposals. By requiring the presentation of performance information and by requiring the preparation of decision packages which are comparable to alternatives, ZBB establishes procedures which compel decision makers to consider issues and data frequently overlooked. The ranking process, even if not adhered to rigidly, at least focuses attention upon possible effects which funding decisions may have. The effects are not, however, stated precisely in terms of achieving objectives. Compared to an ideal of PPB, the ZBB system stops far short of addressing the attainment of objectives. It does facilitate consideration of the efficient conduct of activities and of a possible trade-off between one activity and another.

As with efforts to implement performance budgeting, the accumulation of cost and activity data is limited. Although Pyhrr gives assurance that, once in place, the ZBB system should not add significantly to time and money costs of budgeting, there can be little doubt that assembling the data required for full implementation would be costly indeed.

In addition to these money costs, there are important political costs of ZBB implementation. These can be suggested by examining the political history of the earlier reforms which ZBB seems to encompass. In addition to fitting into an historical context, the emergence of ZBB at this particular time—after its having been around for at least fifty years—is of political significance.

Zero-base budgeting in political context

No examination of political considerations associated with budgetary reform would be complete without reference to the work of Aaron Wildavsky.[40] His description of the politics of the budgetary process provides the base from which to begin a discussion of reform proposals. That description unabashedly admitted that public budgeting is a political matter and, further, Wildavsky judged that it *ought* to be political. He recognized that the budgetary process itself, as well as the decisional outputs of that process, are influenced by partisan considerations, by interest groups, and by strategies devised by participants and, further, that the process and outputs *should* be so influenced.[41]

Any attempt to reform the process will succeed or fail, in part, on the basis of how well its proponents recognize the political forces at work and design the reform to gain sufficient support. One of the difficulties with which the current

---

[40]Aaron Wildavsky, *The Politics of the Budgetary Process*, 1st ed. (Boston: Little, Brown and Company, 1964).

[41]Mention should be made of one earlier work which did show sensitivity to political considerations, that of Burkhead cited above.

ZBB reforms must contend is the still present negative reaction to the earlier PPB reform effort. As a means of considering the effect of this as well as other political matters, it is helpful to look at the politics of earlier reforms.

According to Schick, the performance budgeting movement which caught on after World War II was really an extension of prewar developments. Attention had been diverted by the war, but at its close energies could be used to implement reforms which had been discussed by students of public administration during the 1930s. Of special importance was the focus upon work units, which grew quite naturally from the scientific management movement.[42] This concern, coupled with the postwar desire to assure efficiency in public spending (a matter of little interest during the war years), combined to produce a receptive political environment for performance budgeting. This environment was at least hospitable for a *discussion* of performance budgeting. It may have been less hospitable for its *actual implementation*.

Schick points out that there was no real urgency to budgeting reform in the early 1950s; neither the general public nor public administrators felt there was a crisis that might be resolved through changes in budgetary procedures. There was a general concern over rising government spending, but that did not necessarily suggest sweeping changes in budgetary practices.[43] Neither executives nor legislatures stood to enhance their political strengths through adoption of performance budgeting. Neither would gain markedly, as the executive may have gained with adoption of the executive budget system thirty years earlier.[44] This time many participants simply did not see the value in institutionalization of the reforms. Obviously, if one set of participants (the legislature, for example) had decided that there was much to gain, there would have been a willingness to commit political capital, to engage in a struggle to insure true implementation and thus reap the benefits. This did not occur. Implementations were partial, at best, and were usually simple overlays upon traditional budgeting. The traditional pattern of bargaining over incremental changes in line-items remained the major pattern.

In describing the political considerations which may have influenced the adoption or rejection of PPB, Schick explains the benefits various participants gain from preservation of the traditional process. With regard to the preparers of budgets, the spending agencies, Schick notes that the proposed reforms would have inhibited the agencies' abilities to "sell" their programs. The agencies generally prefer a subjective evaluation process within which they can make use of interest group and clientele support as defenses of funding. With line-item budgeting, agencies find it easier to manipulate the facts to their advantage.[45] Lest one immediately react negatively to such an explanation for the rejection of budget reform, note that Wildavsky defends such subjective techniques as both simplifying devices and as means of assuring input of various political interests. Frequently, matters to be decided are of such great complexity that a reviewer will not have the technical expertise to make a decision based on a presentation

---

[42]Schick, pp. 30–31.
[43]Ibid., p. 63–64.
[44]Ibid., p. 64.
[45]Ibid., pp. 172–173.

of material which seeks to justify a total program. He or she simply will not be able to comprehend and to consider all implications of major program changes.

In defending incremental decision making as a means of furthering representation, Wildavsky treats favorably a partial-view-of-the-public-interest in which, through the budgetary process, various participants contend heatedly, each defending their own interests, with no one participant trying to take into consideration the interests of all groups in society. No preparer of a program and no reviewer is required to think of himself or herself as speaking for some vague public will. The competition and struggle engendered by each agency and each interest group seeking its own advantages are seen as appropriate.[46]

Earlier reforms did not dramatically alter the general nature of budgetary politics. With regard to central budget offices, Schick notes that their prime responsibility is budget cutting. This persists despite earlier reform efforts. These earlier efforts have attempted to force the budget cutters to consider the impacts their cuts have upon activities or programs. Such a demand has greatly complicated the task of the budget cutters and made them resistant to reforms.[47] Wildavsky notes that precise cutting of specific programs demands far greater knowledge than the budget cutters usually have.[48] Further, it demands that the budget cutters be explicit about the activities or programs which will not be funded. The possibility of simply eliminating a small percentage of total budget from many programs (a meat-axe approach) is precluded. Reformers assume that analyses have a high degree of precision, perhaps higher than can be provided. In short, the tasks of budget cutters are complicated by performance budget or PPB type reforms.

The legislative branch can be considered somewhat similar to other budget cutters. Certainly it plays a cutting role and is benefitted in the same way by traditional techniques. Further, however, the traditional techniques provide the line-items which are important simplifying devices to many legislators. As generalists (with the exception of certain committee members), the legislators would have little basis for detailed consideration of fundamental program changes. Complexities of programs are frequently so great that no legislator can thoroughly understand all aspects of the process by which a particular activity leads to an accepted objective. Simplifying devices are important. Looking at and questioning sharp growth in personnel costs or in travel expenses can afford the legislator an opportunity to elicit responses from agency representatives and to probe more deeply if necessary. It might seem ideal for a legislator to vote directly upon the implementation of a major new treatment modality at a state institution, but his or her understanding of the implications of that change would be sharply limited. Little would be gained over noting the associated increase in personnel expenses and, perhaps, compelling the agency to absorb some of these increases through attrition in other activities.

With all of these factors operating against earlier reforms, performance

---

[46]Wildavsky, pp. 165–67.
[47]Schick, pp. 173–77.
[48]Wildavsky, p. 148.

budgeting and PPB, it is not terribly surprising that neither was widely accepted despite partial implementation by many governmental units.[49] But what of ZBB? Is there reason to expect its acceptance?

Zero-base budgeting in Washington

To this point most references have been to ZBB systems that have been in place for several years. It is appropriate, though, that a few comments be made on the federal government's ZBB system, presently being implemented.

Most important, the federal system varies little from that of Georgia. In a memorandum dated February 14, 1977, President Carter stated, "A zero-base budgeting system permits a detailed analysis and justification of budget requests by an evaluation of the importance of each operation performed." He instructed the director of the Office of Management and Budget (OMB) to issue revised procedures incorporating ZBB techniques.

Under federal ZBB (as under other systems), agencies are required to specify *decision units*—"the program or organizational entity for which a manager makes significant decisions on the amount of spending and the scope or quality of work to be performed."[50] For each of these decision units there is a set of *decision packages,* each of which is a "brief justification document that includes the information necessary for managers to make judgments on program or activity levels and resource requirements."[51]

Application of these features can be shown by a couple of examples. Guidance distributed within the Department of Housing and Urban Development listed sixty-one decision units including "payments for operation of low income housing projects," "urban renewal grants," "community development grants," and "housing counseling assistance." Some of these are consolidations of other, lower-level decision units. Following OMB guidance, it is required that there be for each unit a *minimum level* decision package—a request for the minimum amount of funds, for support at a level below which it would not be feasible or practical to continue the program or activity. Second, there is to be a *current level* package, indicating funds needed to continue the present level of activity through the budget year; it is recognized that such continuance might require more funds than provided at present. Finally there can be an *improved level* package, indicating the manager's recommended level of activity and associated costs.

These packages are supported by brief justification statements—and it is required that they be brief, normally limited to two pages.[52] Statements of goals and objectives (as shown in instructional examples of OMB and several agen-

---

[49]Schick concludes that these political factors seem to have produced less resistance to PPB than to performance budgeting.

[50]Office of Management and Budget, Bulletin No. 77–9, 19 April 1977, p. 1.

[51]Ibid., p. 1.

[52]Joel Havemann, "Zero-Base Budgeting," *National Journal 9* (2 April 1977): 517.

cies) are quite general. In Bulletin 77-9, OMB provided the following example for a community mental health grant program.

> Goal: *To ensure needy citizens access to community based mental health services, regardless of ability to pay. Services should be of high quality, provided in the least restrictive environment, and in a manner assuring patients' rights and dignity.*
> Objective: *To assist in the establishment and operation of a nationwide network of 1,200 qualified community mental health centers (CMHCs) by 1984 to ensure availability and accessibility of services to residents of each mental health catchment area.*

In its instructions, HUD used the following example:

> Goal: *Provide decent housing.*
> Objective: *Over the next five years approve grants for construction of 70,000 units of multi-family housing in 30-unit and 40-unit structures.*

As in Georgia, little emphasis is placed on systematic evaluation of program contributions to any goals or objectives that are more general than those most obviously associated with the program. Also as in Georgia, instructions place little emphasis upon seriously considering program or activity elimination. Such might happen as a result of the ranking process, but the possibility does not receive major attention.[53]

Conclusion

If the description of ZBB presented above is accurate and if what is occurring is an effort to institutionalize a combination of performance budgeting and alternative budgeting, there is ample reason to question whether ZBB will be widely accepted (in more than in name) and will have any truly marked impact upon the budgetary process. There may be, however, some features about public attitudes today which could facilitate implementation. We have witnessed the election of a presidential candidate who campaigned as an outsider to Washington and as a strong supporter of ZBB. While it is doubtful that his specific support for ZBB contributed greatly to his victory, his more general criticism of "Washington bureaucrats" may have helped, especially in the primaries. There may exist a reservoir of public support for a concerted effort to reduce government programs and employment and, hence, to support a budgetary scheme that purports to facilitate that. On the other hand, economic considerations will probably prevent sharp curtailment of either government spending or employment.

---

[53]See this author's letter and Peter Pyhrr's response in *Public Administration Review 37* (July/August 1977): 438–39. See also Donald F. Haider, "Zero Base; Federal Style," *Public Administration Review 37* (July/August 1977): 400–407.

Any results from immediate implementation of a ZBB system would need to be demonstrated through the transferring of resources among activities. Such results would be difficult to communicate to the public, and support for ZBB might be short lived.

If there may be support from the public, it is doubtful that much support will be found among participants in the budgetary process. The memory of PPB is still fresh and many agencies have continued to improve upon their cost/benefit studies and program evaluations. Of course, the federal budget process already includes activity measurements. What can be added would be the formal presentation of alternatives in the form of decision packages. Unlike Georgia, many federal agencies have available fairly adequate data bases for creation of supporting documentation. The particular forms employed would need to be far more elaborate than those used in Georgia to take advantage of such data. The complexity imposed upon reviewers would be many times larger.

On the legislative side, Congress is still implementing its own new budgetary process. One must doubt that there will be much enthusiasm from members or staff for an extensive revision of executive budget procedures.

At the federal level, then, despite some possible support from the public, it seems doubtful that ZBB will make any real headway. The likely gain for various participants does not seem great enough to justify elimination of the traditional process and modification of the remnants of PPB to accord with the demands of ZBB.

In state and local governments a flurry of activity labeled "implementation of ZBB" continues. Although there is a general familiarity with the Georgia system, many of these governmental units may be devising their own procedures and, in fact, may be taking more literally the "justify from zero" prescription. For example, Oklahoma City, after examining the various attempts being made in Georgia and elsewhere, elected to instruct agencies simply to provide justifications from zero for 25 percent of their operations. Few additional instructions were supplied, although Budget Office staff members consulted with the agencies. What will result from such an unstructured process is difficult to determine. No doubt, there will be wide variation in the justification efforts.[54]

One fact is clear. The data problems encountered by Georgia are likely to be fairly common among state and local governments. It is significant that Georgia encountered problems even though the data requirements were quite minimal. Whether budget participants in state and local governments can justify the investment of time and money to meet even the level demanded by the Georgia system remains to be determined.

Zero-base budgeting, then, is something other than what the name implies, and probably less than what the name implies if the Georgia system is taken as the archetype. ZBB is an attempt to institutionalize a combination of older proposals for budget reform. This would be an accurate description, of course, even if actual justification from zero were required. Does this conclusion

---

[54]I am indebted to the staff of the Oklahoma City Budget Office and its director, Joe Clytus, for the use of their library and numerous conversations during the course of preparing this paper.

make the ZBB effort any less significant? Not necessarily, but it does place upon the proponents of ZBB a responsibility to demonstrate that (1) there have been political changes which now make institutionalization possible or (2) that the failure of earlier efforts resulted from improper approaches to institutionalization rather than from weaknesses inherent in the reform proposals themselves.

Study questions for selection fifteen

1. In what ways is ZBB similar to the performance budget and PPB reforms that preceded it? How does it differ from them?

2. In what ways is the American political process likely to be changed by adoption of ZBB? Or is it likely to change at all? One question to consider is whether certain political actors might gain power relative to others.

3. Is it accurate to say that ZBB, like PPB, represents an effort to make government decision making conform to the rational-comprehensive model? Would it be possible to have ZBB, but continue to follow the incremental model?

Suggested readings for chapter ten

Anton, Thomas J. *The Politics of State Expenditures in Illinois.* Urbana: University of Illinois Press, 1966.

Brown, Richard E. *The GAO: Untapped Source of Congressional Power.* Knoxville: University of Tennessee Press, 1970.

Friedman, Lewis B. *Budgeting Municipal Expenditures: A Study in Comparative Policy Making.* New York: Praeger Publishers, 1975.

Howard, S. Kenneth. *Changing State Budgeting.* Lexington, Ky.: Council of State Governments, 1973.

Lee, Robert D., Jr., and Johnson, Ronald W. *Public Budgeting Systems.* 2d ed. Baltimore: University Park Press, 1977.

Merewitz, Leonard, and Sosnick, Stephen H. *The Budget's New Clothes: A Critique of Planning-Programming-Budgeting and Benefit-Cost Analysis.* Chicago: Markham Publishing Company, 1971.

Mowitz, Robert J. *The Design and Implementation of Pennsylvania's Planning, Programming, Budgeting System.* State College: Institute of Public Administration, Pennsylvania State University, 1970.

Pyhrr, Peter A. *Zero-Base Budgeting*. New York: John Wiley and Sons, 1973.

Schick, Allen. *Budget Innovation in the States*. Washington, D.C.: Brookings Institution, 1971.

Sharkansky, Ira. *The Politics of Taxing and Spending*. Indianapolis: Bobbs-Merrill, 1970.

Steiss, Alan Walter. *Public Budgeting and Management*. Lexington, Mass.: Lexington Books, 1972.

Wildavsky, Aaron. *Budgeting, A Comparative Theory of Budgetary Processes*. Boston: Little, Brown, 1975.

————. *The Politics of the Budgetary Process*. 2d ed. Boston: Little, Brown, 1974.

Part

Evaluating public bureaucracy

As public policies are implemented through administrative proce-dures, they have certain consequences, or impacts. Furthermore, these consequences will be observed by clients (who are likely to feel the most immediate impacts), by the general public, and by other official and unofficial policy makers. And there will be *reactions*—in systems language feedback—to the administrators' actions.

The reactions to administrative activity will be evaluations of the worth, fairness, responsiveness, efficiency, etc. of the policy as implemented. Sometimes public reactions are expressed as complaints, either directly or through an intermediary (letters of praise are sel-dom received); sometimes more direct action, such as individual or group lobbying efforts (even sit-ins) with administrators occur; some-times there seems to be little public reaction, in which case the feed-back message received by administrators is that the public is at least acquiescent. Policy makers—including administrative policy makers—

also make their own assessments of programs. Their reaction, especially in the case of elected officials, may be largely based on their perception of the public reaction.

To be sure, the public, policy makers, and academic analysts are involved in judging not only particular programs—what we might call microevaluation—but also they continually engage in macroevaluation; that is, they assess the extent to which the entire administrative apparatus is responsible and responsive.

Further consequences flow from both microevaluations and macroevaluations: a particular program may be killed, or its budget may be greatly expanded; and citizens' alienation may be increased, or the public may be inspired, at least, to pay their taxes more willingly. Conceptually, both levels of evaluation are important elements of the administrative process in a democracy, and as a practical matter, interest in applying both has increased greatly during the 1970s. Chapter 11 treats the evaluation of particular programs, and our final chapter assesses the accountability and responsibility of modern American bureaucracy and tries to look into the future.

Professionalism, evaluation, and accountability

Before examining the topics of evaluation and accountability in some detail, it is useful to explore selected aspects of the relationship between them and the administrator's professional expertise. Our traditional understanding of democratic theory suggests that as administrators implement and then assess their programs, they should be responsive to public desires and expectations. At the same time, modern administrators are likely to have received technical training on the same subject that has aroused the citizen feedback; administrators must be held accountable for their competence and for the extent to which their actions reflect the norms of their profession.

Depending on the situation, these twin aspects of administrative accountability (responsiveness to citizens and responsiveness to professional norms) can either operate in tandem to keep administrative actions moving in a particular direction, or they can compete, making further action difficult, if not impossible. As chapter 11 shows, systematic evaluation of program impact can tell an administrator much about the general direction the program is taking and about managerial matters that might move the agency more quickly toward some goal. If that goal is well articulated and widely agreed upon, the twin forces of political accountability reinforce each other. If powerful actors in the administrator's environment have competitive goals or if they fundamentally challenge the administrator's interpretation of the extent to which current programs contribute to the reaching of shared goals, then the administrator can be torn between professional and political responsibility.

Let us illustrate these comments with the following scenario about the town of Pleasantville's recently appointed superintendent of schools, who was hired by a seven-to-two vote of the local school board. The new superintendent's professional training and stature are of the highest level: she has a doctorate in education from a distinguished university, has a solid administrative record in previous school systems, and has been active in state and national organizations of school administrators.

Although the circumstances under which she was hired were not altogether auspicious, she welcomed the job as a challenge and did not learn the full extent of the controversy that preceded her hiring until she arrived in town to begin work. The previous superintendent had been released, after a two-year battle with the board, by a vote of five-to-four. A vociferous group of parents had sought his removal, saying he was out of touch with the community's educational needs. The group claimed that changes in the high-school curriculum had eliminated traditional requirements and introduced so many electives and "fluff" courses that graduates were prepared for neither college or a trade.

After carefully examining the curriculum through the lenses of her professional training and experience, the new superintendent sees much to commend and little she would change. As nearly as she can tell, the curriculum has been at least reasonably well applied in this community; she suspects that the overall performance of the school system has been about average. Most important, she feels certain that adoption of the "back-to-basics" changes being publicly demanded would result in little, if any, real educational gain. She has learned that five board members now share this view, but they are under great political pressure to support a restructuring of the curriculum. (Of the two others who voted to hire her, one apparently found her shapeliness a decisive consideration; the other was pledged to vote for any female candidate.)

Thus, our superintendent has two conflicting responsibilities: to her profession and to the public. One ameliorating fact, however, is her knowledge that she and even that vocal interest group segment of the public share the same goals. Nonetheless, the dilemma remains: Where does her ultimate responsibility lie, to her professional judgment or to the public?

Unfortunately, no particular course of action can guarantee that our superintendent will escape the dilemma. Perhaps she will con-

Evaluating public bureaucracy/

377

clude that the public would approve of the curriculum if it could be demonstrated that the schools' programs *are* effective in promoting learning. Systematically evaluating the educational program may give her the needed evidence. And it may be necessary to undertake an aggressive campaign to sell parents on the results of the evaluation and the merits of their school system.

But if the results of the evaluation are negative or inconclusive and if a substantial body of citizens remains highly dissatisfied, then our superintendent's predicament remains. In this case the predicament's moral roots lie deeper than the question of whether she will manage to keep her job, for it is an accepted principle of democratic theory that the desires of citizens should be weighted heavily in the making of public decisions. If citizens frequently choose not to participate in policy making—as every student of government knows they do—this does nothing to make their input illegitimate on those occasions when they do choose to participate.

If an administrator concludes, on the basis of professional expertise and personal belief, that a course of action demanded by the public is wrong and possibly harmful, then resignation may be the most honorable and perhaps most convenient course of action. Under most circumstances, however, less drastic measures are more appropriate. Our hypothetical superintendent might create, for example, an alternative curriculum with highly structured classrooms, which emphasize traditional "basic" approaches to education, alongside the more innovative classrooms currently in existence; parents could choose either program for their children, and over time a comparative evaluation of the educational effectiveness of the two programs could be undertaken. Such a solution, actually tried in several school districts around the country, incorporates the twin aspects of administrative accountability (responsiveness to citizens and responsiveness to professional norms). Rather than sacrificing either aspect, the alternative curriculum is itself responsive to citizen desires, but in support of professional norms, the existing programs are retained. And the evaluation that will follow sets up a structure to insure further accountability of both types. Administrators can never escape the dual nature of accountability.

Public administration and program evaluation

From time to time, the director of a state agency with responsibility for a particular program is likely to wonder: "How well is this program working?" This director may not spend much time pondering the question, and perhaps it can be quickly put out of mind with the answer: "It's working more or less as it should; I wouldn't be here if I thought otherwise!" Pressed to defend that answer, the agency head might reply simply: "I know my job; I've been working in this field for twenty-five years, and I can tell when things are right or wrong, what works and what doesn't." To accept such an answer, based on impressionistic assessments and intuitive feelings, requires blind faith in the administrator's judgments. In the present "age of accountability," responses of this kind are seen as unsatisfactory. Citizens want to know what return is received for their tax dollar, and increasing attention is being given to the evaluation of public programs.

Evaluation is no easy task. Consider, for example, some of the practical problems faced by state corrections department administrators. The possible treatment programs applicable to convicts have multiplied dramatically in recent years; individual and group counseling, vocational education, work release, drug and alcoholic treatment, and many more programs are touted as effective strategies for rehabilitation. Faced with this plethora of programs to choose from, the administrator is hard pressed to be certain just what program or combination of programs will most promote rehabilitation. Conversely, when prisoners are successfully returned to society, it may be very difficult to know just which program did work. Evaluation studies are increasingly seen as the solution to such problems.

The development of evaluation research

Program evaluation has both a general and a technical meaning. In general terms, it refers simply to any process of judging the value of a program. Throughout administrative history, the question "How well is the program working?" has been the subject of street-corner debate and newspaper editorials, and it has, of course, been a central point of conflict in election campaigns. Such informal evaluative considerations have been a traditional part of the democratic process, in which citizens have attempted (with varying degrees of success) to hold legislators, executives, and administrators accountable for the programs they install.

It seems frustrating to many citizens that the success or failure of a program is seldom obvious. Two programs whose consequences were clear cut show the infrequency of this happening: following the development of polio vaccines, the nearly universal delivery of immunizations brought about a decline in the disease so dramatic that the success of the program was apparent; and the failure of the "noble experiment"—the Eighteenth Amendment, which prohibited "the manufacture, sale, or the transportation of intoxicating liquors"—was equally obvious. But how can citizens measure the consequences of bussing school children, of revenue sharing, of the negative income tax as a substitute for welfare payments, etc.? Often it may seem to citizens that the programs have ambiguous, contradictory, or marginal impact on the problem they were designed to address. Sometimes the only definite impact may seem to be a contribution to government's budget and to the growing army of its employees. Although the difficulties of arriving at consensus about the merits of competing solutions to problems may be frustrating, resolving such conflicts is, of course, central to the operation of the political process.

Government activity is at a level that was hardly dreamed of just a short while ago; thus, today's public administrators have a special responsibility to demonstrate the effectiveness of their ever more expensive programs. While general evaluations of the sort just described will continue to be significant, for more than a decade now administrators in many fields have been applying the term *program evaluation* in a technical fashion to refer to the application of a particular set of techniques of data collection and analysis to determine how well programs are working.

Spurred by legislation such as the Elementary and Secondary Education Act of 1965, which began the big push to require evaluations of new social programs, evaluation research has become a growth industry: agencies are creating evaluation units; experienced practitioners can have their choice of job offers; and since governments do not have enough trained evaluators, outside consultants are eating well. Also, program evaluation has gained academic respectability: universities are beginning to offer courses on the subject; a spate of literature has appeared; and—a sure sign of the "arrival" of a specialization—an academic journal, called *Evaluation Quarterly,* has been inaugurated by Sage Publications.

The nature of program evaluation

Most of the techniques used by evaluation researchers were developed by political scientists, sociologists, psychologists, economists, and other students of public policies. Usually these earlier studies had only an abstract analytical focus, however; they ordinarily were not meant to have an immediate influence upon policy. The practitioners in the burgeoning field of evaluation research *do* want to contribute to policy making, so they have picked up the analytical techniques, while dropping the detached perspective of the "scientific" observer. A leading exponent of program evaluation asserts that its purpose is "to measure the effects of a program against the goals it set out to accomplish as a means of contributing to subsequent decision making about the program and improving future programming."[1]

Thus, the programmatic nature of program evaluation is quite clear. This discussion of evaluation is in the part of our book that examines bureaucratic accountability, *but program evaluation also is a management tool,* and we might have followed the lead of some other authors

---

[1]Carol H. Weiss, *Evaluation Research: Methods of Assessing Program Effectiveness* (Englewood Cliffs, N.J.: Prentice-Hall, Inc., 1972), p. 4.

who treat the subject as a management problem (like employee motivation and budgeting) and located this chapter in the previous part. We choose the present organization in order to emphasize the normative implications of program evaluation, but we certainly do not mean to neglect the managerial implications.

As a management tool, evaluation research is another effort to instill a greater degree of rationality in the administrative process. In this, it is similar to rational-comprehensive decision making described in chapter 8. The kinds of analyses discussed there (necessary in order to decide upon which of several possible programs to implement) must, however, be *prospective* analyses: they must project program impact to some future date. The task of evaluation research is *retrospective:* its task is to examine the actual accomplishments of completed or ongoing programs. As a consequence, the techniques used by evaluators can be somewhat more precise than those used by the program's designers, who cannot measure changes the program has yet to produce.

Although the approach of program evaluation is retrospective, increasing efforts are being made to build evaluation into the program's design from the beginning. If the program's creators must say just what its objectives and benefits are supposed to be and indicate specifically how it is intended that they be measured, then it is likely that the entire conception of the program will be far better planned than it otherwise would be—so say the rationalist proponents of evaluation research.

In getting any evaluation effort underway, it is first necessary to establish some measurement standards: the program's goals must be specified. As indicated above, this should be done before a program's initiation, but if it is not, the apparent goals of the ongoing program must be discovered and articulated at the beginning of the evaluation exercise. The evaluator probably will be either an outsider whom the agency has hired as a consultant for this purpose or an insider given a degree of autonomy. If the program's director cannot produce a set of unambiguous goals whose degree of accomplishment is sufficiently measurable, the evaluator, after careful study of the program, may ask penetrating questions, collaborate in goal setting, or even specify the goals.[2] From this point onward, the evaluation task rests principally with the evaluator, although continued agency cooperation is absolutely essential.

---

[2]Ibid., p. 28.

Research design

Designing a sound research strategy is critical to the success of any evaluation effort. The nature of the design will depend on many things, not the least of which is the amount of money available for the evaluation. Sometimes scientific considerations might specify, for example, that a large sample of the program's clients be interviewed in order to obtain a certain level of reliability of the results; if the money is simply unavailable, however, science may have to bow to practicality, and a lower level of confidence in the data may have to be accepted.

In some designs, data collection may extend over several years; for example, the Manhattan Bail Bond experiment (an effort to determine if releasing certain carefully selected defendants without bail could be as effective as normal bonding practices in assuring appearance at trial) cost $200,000 during a three-year period.[3] Unfortunately, high costs often discourage the design of adequate evaluation efforts. One text refers to a "bargain basement" evaluation design, which simply calls for measurement before the program is instituted and again after it has been functioning for a reasonable time.[4] But even such seemingly straightforward projects can become expensive as time is devoted to specifying objectives, selecting or designing measurement tools, taking measurements (interviewing, judging street cleanliness, checking on encounters with the law, etc.), analyzing the results, and drawing policy-relevant conclusions.

Too much concern should not be shown for costs, because there are other equally critical design problems. Prominent among these is the demand that the evaluation focus precisely on those changes that result from the operation of the program under study. To illustrate this difficulty, let us assume that Academic University decided to implement a new freshman advisory system whose goal was to increase by 5 percentage points the number who remain at the university until graduation. An evaluator following the "bargain basement" design just mentioned would simply compare the graduation rate of the class entering immediately before the implementation of the new system with the graduation rate of the following class. Unfortunately, if the evaluator were to attribute to the new advisory procedure the 7 percentage points increase in

---

[3]Henry W. Riecken and Robert F. Boruch, eds., *Social Experimentation: A Method for Planning and Evaluating Social Intervention* (New York: Academic Press, 1974), pp. 1 and 10.

[4]Harry P. Hatry, Richard E. Winnie, and Donald M. Fisk, *Practical Program Evaluation for State and Local Government Officials* (Washington, D.C.: The Urban Institute, 1973), p. 41.

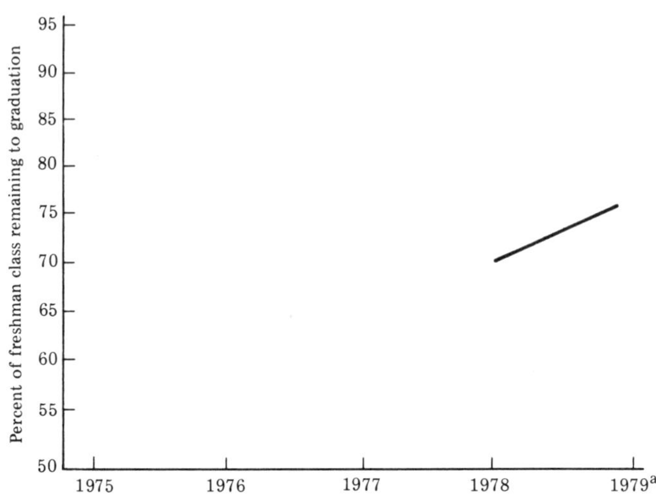

**Figure 11–1. Before and after test of Academic University's freshman gradu-
ation rate**

ᵃFirst class advised under new procedure

those graduating (figure 11-1) without further extensive investigation,
such a conclusion might be invalid. For example, there may have been
simultaneous changes whose precise nature and extent are unknown to
the evaluator. Perhaps the university's fees may have been raised
enough to force some students to drop out; perhaps the new advising
system was even more successful than is indicated, and without the
increase in fees the graduation rate would have gone up by 10 percentage points. Alternatively, the appeal of fraternities and sororities may
have increased and been the real cause of more of the 1979 class stay-
ing. Or perhaps the economy began to boom and encouraged more students to stay in school. It is even possible that one of these classes
happened to behave, for unknown reasons, in an unusual fashion; the
researcher has no way to detect such phenomena.

Thus, bargain basement evaluation has its problems, yet it is better than none at all. The techniques it features are especially useful if
the measurements can be taken over a long period, before and after the
implementation of the program whose impact is the object of study.
Such operations make it possible to search for trends and note any
marked change that coincides with the introduction of the new procedure. This is referred to as *time series analysis*. Again, the evidence of
program effectiveness cannot be conclusive, but if we add a time series
dimension to our analysis of the university's graduation rate (figure
11-2) we have much more information than if only the 1978 and 1979
classes were examined. When we learn that, as the figure indicates, the

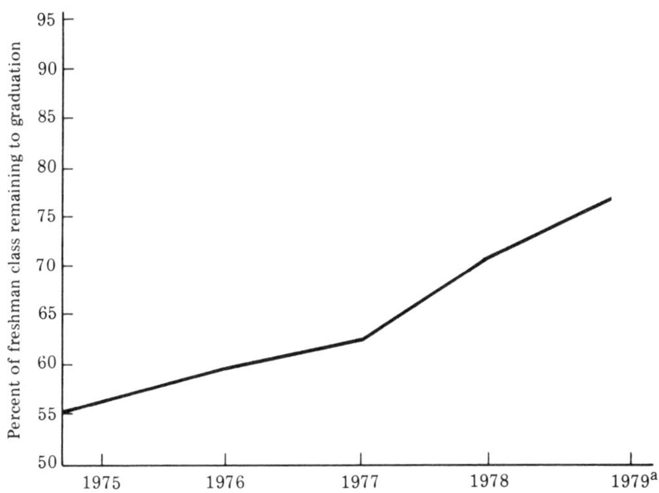

Figure 11–2. Time-series analysis of Academic University's freshman graduation rate

[a]First class advised under new procedure

increase between 1978 and 1979 was part of a long-range increase, there is less reason to give much credit to the new program.

Another possibility, and one that might be used in conjunction with a time series analysis, is a comparison with external norms. Returning to Academic University's freshmen, data are collected on dropout rates for universities of different types in various regions of the country. If the evaluator were to find that AU's classes participating in the new procedures had completion rates significantly higher than the appropriate norms would predict, this would be additional evidence of program effectiveness. Furthermore, these comparisons would help control for any environmental changes, such as reinstitution of the military draft or an economic decline or recovery.

It might be apparent now that what program evaluators really desire is to conduct an *experiment*. This word is frequently used in the natural sciences, where chemists, for example, might subject two samples of the same substance to different treatments (or one to none at all) in order to determine the impact of the treatment. Natural scientists stress the importance of keeping *all other things constant;* only the specific treatment under study is allowed to vary. Life scientists operate on the same model. An effort to determine the nutritional needs of cats, for example, might involve maintaining two groups under identical conditions and feeding them equivalent diets, except that the one nutrient under study at the time is withheld from one group. Over time, the impact of this one omission can be assessed. Life scientists, though, have some problems that physical scientists are able to avoid; most especially, the animals being studied have individual (even if quite similar) hereditary characteristics, so some may need more or less of the nutrient. Consequently, large groups usually are studied, in order to establish an average level of need.

Academic University's program evaluator has these problems, and more, in attempting to construct an experimental evaluation of the advisement program. An experimental design in this case would call for the assignment of freshmen to either an *experimental group* or a *control group*. Such assignments must be made in a way that minimizes the likelihood of there being important differences in the groups. Obviously, given what we know about the usual graduation rates of males and females, the sexual composition of the two groups is likely to matter. Similarly, high-school grade-point averages, scores on nationally standardized tests of ability and achievement, and family income might affect the likelihood of remaining to graduation. In an experimental design, the evaluator solves these problems by *random* assignment; the experimenter's goal is to give every student an absolutely equal opportunity to be assigned to either group—through such procedures as flipping coins and using tables of random numbers. If successfully done, and if the groups are sufficiently large, the chance of group-to-group differences in important characteristics will be minimized.[5] After assignment, one group of freshmen is provided the experimental advising program, while the other receives traditional advising—which sometimes constitutes "benign neglect."

The fate of those students not receiving the new program raises moral problems concerning the design of experimental evaluations. Conducting tests on people rather than chemical components or cats raises ethical questions. Presumably, administrators have a strong hunch that the new advising system will help more students complete a college education. *Is it morally justifiable to provide no additional advising to the control group while giving elaborate attention to the experimental group?* As evaluators have wrestled with such problems, a near consensus has been reached that it is not ethical to reduce levels of service below what clients would have received if the experiment had not been undertaken, but that it is not ethically necessary to deliver the new program to all clients at the same time, which would, of course, contaminate the control group and negate the experiment. In our university examples, as

---

[5]When groups are small, or time or money is at a premium, it might be wise to *structure* the groups by matching the occurrence of salient characteristics, for instance, insure that x percent of both groups are male, y percent from low educational achievement backgrounds, z percent from high socioeconomic backgrounds, etc. Evaluation researchers have relied heavily on the recommendations made by Donald T. Campbell and Julian C. Stanley, *Experimental and Quasi-Experimental Designs for Research* (Chicago: Rand McNally and Co., 1966).

Chapter eleven

386

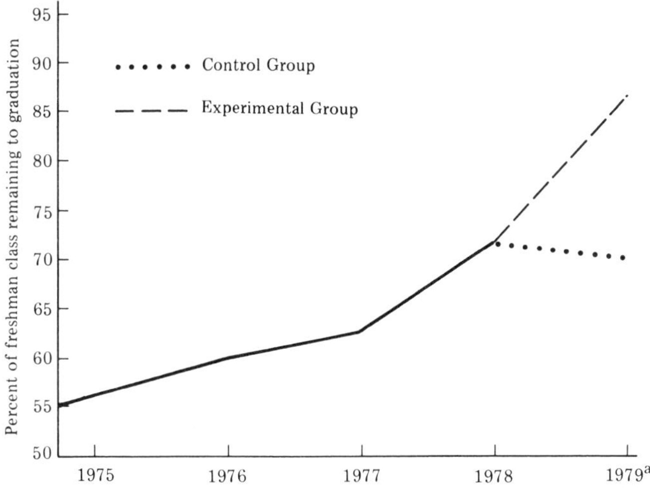

Figure 11–3. Experimental design for Academic University's freshman graduation rate

[a]First class advised under new procedure

the elaborate advisory program being afforded those in the experimental group is not an assured success (it may just waste students' time) and as the control group is no worse off than all freshmen were before the experiment and many freshmen at other campuses remain, our evaluator does not face a moral dilemma.

If an experimental design is feasible for the program in question, many of the evaluator's problems are solved. If the experimental and the control groups were properly selected, any changes in university or national policy or even any changes in student life-styles or attitudes should have an equal impact on the two groups. While the percentage of the students graduating may change from the percentage graduating during the base period in both groups, the *differences between the groups* can reasonably be attributed to the new procedure. If there should be no differences, beyond those that might randomly occur, the new procedure can be declared a failure—at least as far as this goal is concerned.[6] But figure 11-3 indicates that the advisory program was an apparent success: there were dramatic differences in the graduation rates of the experimental and the control groups. Unless other factors intervened during the study, it seems that only the new program saved A.U. from having a decline in its graduation rate. This example illustrates the

---

[6]Evaluators should bear in mind that programs may have unanticipated consequences, possibly of a long-term sort. For example, even if the advisory program had little effect upon retention rate, perhaps its personalizing aspects would convince students that their alma mater cared for them individually and would cause more of them to send unusually large checks to the alumni association in later years.

Public administration and program evaluation/

possible managerial value of sophisticated evaluation efforts. Without the results of figure 11-3, A.U. officials might have concluded from figure 11-2 that the new advisory program did not increase the graduation rate significantly more than it had been increasing in recent years without the program.

There do remain some potential difficulties for the evaluator to consider. One is the Hawthorne effect referred to in chapter 9; those in the experimental group might remain in school in large numbers because of their knowledge that they are being studied, rather than because of the substance of advising; the increased attention they receive might increase their determination and self-confidence. Another difficulty is the possibility that the control group members will talk with those in the experimental group and get some of the possible benefits at second hand. A further difficulty in attempting to analyze the results is that conclusions drawn from one experiment may not be generalizable; they may hold true only in one particular time and place.

A variety of designs have been successfully employed in evaluation research that have not been described in this brief introduction; of course, no single design can eliminate all of the potential problems. As administrators learn more about evaluation, further means of controlling for factors that contaminate experiments are sure to be developed. Various experimental and *quasi-experimental* techniques (the time series design mentioned earlier can be classed as a quasi-experiment) seem to offer the most promise as evaluation tools.

The politics of program evaluation

If you reflect on the nature of public administration's political environment, discussed in part I, you will recognize that program evaluation might have a potent impact upon an administrator and his or her organization. It provides a formalized opportunity for other participants in policy making to demand that administrators present evidence of program accomplishment, evidence far more substantial than the administrators' simple assertion, "We know it works." In the future, as agencies compete for funds and other support, those able to produce the most convincing evaluations may have an advantage—even if their programs really accomplish less than others.

A crucial decision the administrator must make (in reality, the decision may be shared with other policy makers) is a determination of the amount of resources to be devoted to evaluation. The harried, underpaid, understaffed director of the Johnson County Health Department, for example, when she is told that henceforth she is responsible for seeing that all programs are formally evaluated according to a complex, time-consuming, and costly set of guidelines (some of which are irrelevant to her programs) is likely to retort: "This agency was not established to evaluate programs, but rather to provide health care!" The question of how much health care or social welfare or police money should be used for evaluation is just as political a matter as the establishment of the programs themselves. It can be answered only in the context of particular programs. As citizens, we might demand that the worth of every program be proved by a thorough evaluation. Unfortunately, doing so would be so costly as to destroy many of the ongoing programs. As the so-called "sunset" laws (which require that every agency justify its existence periodically) are implemented around the country, it will be very interesting to examine the evaluation documents from the point of view of thoroughness.

Another crucial element of the politics of evaluation is the matter of goal setting. To return to our freshmen, while Academic University certainly has as a paramount interest in the retention of entering students for their entire college programs, it is also hoped that the advisory system will serve other goals as well: giving appropriate career counseling, assisting in choices of course sequence, and so on. Sometimes these goals conflict. Career counseling, for example, may cause a student to decide on a major that the university does not offer, with the result that the student may go elsewhere. Does the evaluator conclude that the system has succeeded or failed in this case? From the point of view of maximizing the student's self-realization, the program was a success, but the student is more likely to be counted as a failure by the university. Success and failure are labels awarded on the basis of how the goals have been set and defined. Determining the goals and specifying them for evaluation purposes are political processes; considerable leeway often exists so that administrators who want the evaluation to have a certain outcome can manipulate the results by helping to define the goals.

Conducting successful evaluations depends on having the cooperation of the agency, but this can be a political problem, because sometimes its personnel may be unwilling to cooperate: perhaps they resent the intrusion; perhaps they object to a particular experiment on ethical grounds; perhaps they are fearful of an evaluation's possible results; or perhaps they consider the exercise a waste of everyone's time and money. Even if the evaluation project has been formally blessed by top-level administrators, this is no guarantee of actual cooperation. Evaluators must recognize the necessity of establishing rapport with agency personnel; they also must even accept that some evaluative projects just cannot be accomplished.

It is acutely frustrating for evaluators that their efforts frequently fail to have any apparent impact on policy. The report they issue may

demonstrate conclusively that Program X is accomplishing nothing, yet it continues to be funded year after year. This sometimes can be attributed to the fact that evaluations may require years to complete and often provide little feedback in the interim. During this time, the program establishes a clientele, a budgetary base, and probably some political allies. Thus, when a program's elimination or curtailment is attempted, those who benefit from it (perhaps not in the way that was intended) may be able to marshall superior political forces. Perhaps the program has a congressional protector; perhaps it is a large employer in an economically depressed area; or perhaps the program is a hobbyhorse of one of the agency's top administrators, who argues the program was not given a fair trial.

Acceptance of the evaluator's results also may be discouraged if the evaluation was imposed from above, perhaps by another level of government. For instance, the federal government requires that certain federally funded state and local programs be evaluated. Related to this problem is the question of to whom the evaluation is directed. Evaluations done under federal requirements and addressed to federal agencies may be of little help to state program administrators.[7] Obviously, a well-done evaluation may not come to a simple positive or negative conclusion about a program's value; it is more likely to contain comments

---

[7]Carol H. Weiss, "Evaluating Educational and Social Action Programs: A 'Treeful of Owls,'" in Carol H. Weiss, ed., *Evaluating Action Programs: Readings in Social Action and Education* (Boston: Allyn and Bacon, Inc., 1972), p. 13.

on particular aspects of the program and their contributions to goal achievement. At various levels of the administrative hierarchy there are individuals who have the power to adjust these program components, and they may welcome the opportunity to do so if the proposed changes are congruent with their own interpretations and their goals.

A future for program evaluation

In this "age of accountability," the public sector is not likely to back away from the current determination to improve on evaluative techniques. Goal specification, research design, data collection, and analysis will all improve during the 1980s. The critical question concerns the impact that evaluations will have on policy. As Joseph Wholey's article reprinted below indicates, evaluations can be done for different purposes. To have an impact on policy, they must provide the right kind of evaluation to the right person. Because of their prejudices, job assignments, or organizational positions, some administrators could hardly care less about dry, highly quantitative, multivolume evaluation reports. Others do care and will use them. This does not mean, though, that the evaluator's recommendation will be followed. Other information, including information on political considerations, will continue to be influential; political considerations may, however, be somewhat less dominant in the future. Persons holding a wide range of views about the program will have the evaluation to use as a tool for strengthening their positions; it is likely that debate about programs will increasingly have the evaluation—perhaps competing evaluations—as their focal points.[8] Although some evaluators—anxious to use evaluations as a means of implementing the rational-comprehensive decision model—may believe this development is secondary, it may in fact be the most significant contribution evaluators can hope to make to the public policy process.

---

[8]We venture to predict that in-house, internal evaluations will become less readily accepted as the suspicion that self-evaluations are likely to be self-justifications becomes more widespread. Perhaps evaluators will be given the sort of semiautonomous status auditors now have in some agencies; perhaps evaluation units that serve several agencies but are not subordinate to the agencies will be created.

Output measurement in urban government*

Donald M. Fisk and Richard E. Winnie

The emphasis that we have placed on the need to design evaluation efforts properly is a frequent theme of the literature on program evaluation: vast sums of money have been wasted on improperly designed evaluation projects, projects that could not have answered the research questions even if perfectly executed. In addition to design, evaluators have other concerns; an important one is the difficulty of measuring program accomplishment. Unless it is possible to devise means of telling just what the program is accomplishing in relation to its goals, evaluation is impossible.

Cities are an excellent laboratory for examining the problems and possibilities of measuring the quantity and quality of services they provide for citizens. Through their work for the Urban Institute, the authors of this article have been deeply involved in such efforts. In collaboration with other organizations, including some individual cities, the Institute has studied the problems of measuring the outputs of programs and has assisted cities in devising improved measures. As this article shows, the problems are legion, but progress is being made. Critical to further progress, Fisk and Winnie believe, is the willingness of city governments to devote resources to establishing data-collection systems. Because the return on such investments usually is not immediate, competition with service-providing programs is strong. If evaluation is to assume an important place in the local policy process, a case for funding data systems will have to be made.

Output measurement is not new to local government.[1] As early as the late 1920s efforts were being made to improve data on the consequences of local government services. Within the past decade, though, urban government output measurement has advanced rapidly. Efforts both within local governments and by outside researchers have improved the measurements available.

*Reprinted from Donald M. Fisk and Richard E. Winnie, "Output Measurement in Urban Government: Current Status and Likely Prospects," *Social Science Quarterly* 54 (March 1974): 725–740, by permission of the publisher, University of Texas Press. Copyright, 1973 by the Southwestern Social Science Association.

[1]Revision of a paper presented at the annual meeting of the Americal Political Science Association, September 1973.

More important, local governments have expanded their data collection efforts and their use of such data in decision making.

This paper summarizes the present status of output measurement in urban government—the state of the art as well as the use being made of it—and discusses briefly prospects for its use and further development in the immediate future.

The first, but most difficult, task in describing the current status of output measurement is defining the term, *output measure* itself. The maze of terminology in this area is enough to stop short any meaningful discussions of the subject. Indeed, output measurement techniques are developing so fast and from so many sources that the same terms often connote different meanings when used by authorities on the subject.

For instance, "output," as used by Davis in an International City Management report, is a quantitative characteristic of a service. It describes what was produced or what happened as a result of government activity: acres of park maintained and street line-miles painted. He distinguishes output from *effectiveness*. Effectiveness is a comparison of the actual result (output) with the ideal result, as defined by the goals or objectives of the service. Examples of effectiveness measurements are the percent of stolen cars recovered (100 percent recovered being the objective), the school dropout rate (objective: to minimize), and phosphate reduction in sewage treatment (percent of an achievable standard).[2]

Other writings in the field don't define output quite so narrowly. Hatry defines "output" to include "measures of effectiveness," "evaluation criteria," and "program effects." For Hatry measures of effectiveness describe how well government activities are meeting their end purposes.[3]

The field of evaluation research has produced a slightly different set of terms. Suchman uses such terms as "effort," "performance," "adequacy of performance," "efficiency," and "process." Performance refers to the result of the effort—the number of cases found, number hospitalized, and number cured. "Adequacy of performance" is the degree to which some goal or objective is achieved.[4]

For purposes of this discussion Ostrom has defined "output" as the transformation which occurs when resources are combined to "produce something." "Impact" is the consequence that output has on affected individuals, and "performance" is evaluation of that impact.

Despite these apparent differences, the terminology focuses upon two dimensions of the service which are of concern in this paper: quantitative (the level of effort; work load; or work product in numerical terms) and qualitative (the effect or consequence of the program when acting upon a population group or the community as a whole; the degree to which the output fulfills needs or expectations for the service). Street cleaning services, for example, have quantitative characteristics such as cubic yards or tons of litter collected

---

[2]Robert H. Davis, "Measuring the Effectiveness of Municipal Services," *Management Information Service* (Washington, D.C.: International City Management Association, Aug., 1970), pp. 3–4.

[3]Harry P. Hatry, "Measuring the Effectiveness of Non-Defense Public Programs," *Operations Research* 18 (Sept.–Oct., 1970): 722.

[4]Edward A. Suchman, *Evaluation Research* (New York: Russell Sage Foundation, 1967), pp. 60–67.

Exhibit 1.   Illustrative set of quantitative and qualitative measures[a]

Selected service functions	Illustrative quantity measures	Illustrative quality factors (i.e. Measures of citizen impact)
Solid waste collection	Tons of solid waste collected	Visual appearance of streets Fire/health hazard conditions from solid waste accumulations Service delays
Liquid waste treatment (sewage)	Gallons of sewage treated	Quality level of effluent, e.g. "BOD" removed and remaining after treatment Water quality level resulting where dumped
Law enforcement (police)	Number of surveillance-hours Number of calls Number of crimes investigated	Reduction in crime and victimization rates Crime clearance rates, preferably including court disposition Response times Citizen feeling of security
Health and hospital	Number of patient-days	Reduced number and severity of illnesses Conditions of patients after treatment Duration of treatment Pleasantness of care Accessibility of low-income groups to care
Water treatment	Gallons of water treated	Water quality indices such as for hardness and taste Amount of impurities removed
Recreation	Acres of recreational activities Attendance figures	Participation rates Accessibility to recreational opportunities Variety of opportunities available Crowdedness indices Citizens' perceptions of adequacy of recreational opportunities
Street maintenance	Square yards of repairs made	Smoothness/"bumpiness" of streets Travel time Community disruption: amount and duration Dust and noise during repairs
Fire control	Fire calls Number of inspections	Fire damage Injuries and lives lost

Exhibit 1.   (continued)

Selected service functions	Illustrative quantity measures	Illustrative quality factors (i.e. Measures of citizen impact)
Primary and secondary education	Pupil-days Number of pupils	Achievement test scores and grade levels Continuation/dropout rates

[a]See Harry P. Hatry and Donald M. Fisk, *Improving Productivity and Productivity Measurement in Local Government* (Washington, D.C.: National Commission on Productivity, June 1971), pp. xvi–xvii.

and qualitative characteristics such as the street cleanliness which occurs as a result of the activity. Water supply, another example, has a quantitative dimension as measured by the gallons treated and a qualitative dimension as measured by its taste and color. Additional examples are shown in Exhibit 1.

This paper is concerned with measurement of both the quantitative and qualitative aspects of local government services. Therefore, we focus on what Ostrom calls output and impact; Suchman calls performance; and Hatry calls output and effectiveness. In the real world where public services are delivered, they are variously described by all these terms and, in addition, called "work load."

The next section summarizes the current use of output measurement in local government. Two services, solid waste collection and recreation, are then used to illustrate problems of measuring output and how they are being resolved. The final section contains a brief discussion of some of the prospects for further development of output measurement.

Current use of output measurement

Throughout this century there have been sporadic attempts to improve the data compiled about local government services. The Research Committee on Social Trends appointed by President Hoover in 1928 was perhaps the first major effort by government. It recognized the need to develop more reliable data on local government services as a basis for formulating national policy. Through its Committee on Municipal Standards it attempted to develop ways to measure the effectiveness of local government services.[5]

---

[5]See G. Lyons, *The Uneasy Partnership: Social Science and the Federal Government* (New York: Russell Sage Foundation, 1969), p. 313 and p. 21; and W. C. Mitchell, *Recent Social Trends* (New York: McGraw-Hill Company, 1933).

Table 1. Local government use of measures in reviewing operating budgets, fall, 1971[a]

Measure	Cities		Counties	
	Number reporting	Percent of total	Number reporting	Percent of total
Workload measures				
Total, all jurisdictions	215		118	
None	75	35	51	43
Some	101	47	46	39
Many	39	18	21	18
Efficiency measures				
Total, all jurisdictions	212		119	
None	102	48	59	50
Some	92	43	54	45
Many	18	9	6	5
Population-served measures				
Total, all jurisdictions	214		117	
None	77	36	52	44
Some	113	53	56	48
Many	24	11	9	8
Effectiveness measures				
Total, all jurisdictions	208		118	
None	94	45	57	48
Some	90	43	47	40
Many	24	12	14	12

[a]See Richard E. Winnie, "Local Government Budgeting, Program Planning, and Evaluation," *Urban Data Service* (Washington, D.C.: The International City Management Association, May 1972).

Following this committee's report, most efforts focused on improving data sources within the federal government. One important exception was a study aimed at local governments which was undertaken by Ridley and Simon of the International City Management Association. Their 1936 study resulted in a published set of measurements for assessing local government effectiveness and efficiency. This report was reprinted in 1943, and parts have since been reprinted in other books and pamphlets.[6]

Starting in the mid-1960s a number of new efforts have been directed toward improving local government output measurement. However, local governments are so numerous and varied in their mix of public services, size, and level of professionalism that generalization about them is difficult and somewhat risky. This danger is certainly present when attempting to provide

[6]Clarence E. Ridley and Herbert A. Simon, *Measuring Municipal Activities: A Survey of Suggested Criteria for Appraising Administration* (Washington, D.C.: The International City Management Association, 1943).

an overall picture of the current status of output measurement. Nevertheless, there are a few sources to which we can turn.

In the fall of 1971 the International City Management Association and The Urban Institute jointly conducted a survey of local government budgeting, program planning, and evaluation capabilities and activities.[7] Cities with populations greater than 50,000 and counties of more than 100,000 population were contacted. Approximately 700 governments were surveyed, and 51 percent completed and returned the questionnaire.

Table 1 shows the frequency with which responding jurisdictions replied that they used output measurements, defined to include workload, population served, efficiency, and effectiveness in preparing their operating budgets. About 60 percent of the respondents said that they used work-load or population-served measurements, and approximately 55 percent mentioned using effectiveness measurements.

Such measurements appear to be used much less frequently in preparing capital budgets. Only 18 percent of responding governments reported that they used output measurements in preparing capital budgets.

A greater proportion of the jurisdictions with the largest populations use output measurement in operating and capital budgeting, and a greater proportion of responding cities than counties use output measurements.

Unfortunately, no comparable data are available for other time periods, so it is not possible to determine whether or at what rate the use of these measurements by local governments is changing.

In 1973 the Urban Institute examined budget documents from forty-one local governments (thirty cities, nine counties, and two consolidated cities and counties). The International City Management Association survey questionnaire (discussed above) had been self-administered by local governments, and so its data undoubtedly reflected some differences in the connotations which respondents placed upon terms such as effectiveness, workload, and output. The Urban Institute survey reviewed measurements contained in budget documents themselves, so the same definition of terms was used throughout the analysis. Undoubtedly, other measurements are used in department work sheets, but these were not reviewed in this survey. The governments surveyed included most of the larger jurisdictions of the United States.

This survey revealed that local governments alternatively referred to the output measurements which they use as "work-load indicators," "measures of effectiveness," "measures of service," "informational data," "program activity," "work activity," and "service indices." The output measurements presently used by local governments most often indicate the quantity of output such as tons of garbage collected, number of fires extinguished, amount of sewage treated, and number of pot holes filled. As shown in table 2 four-fifths of the budgets examined have some quantitative output measurements listed. Approximately half of the budgets examined contain some type of quality measures, but in most instances, these measures are few in number and restricted to a few service areas such as water and sewage treatment.

---

[7]Richard E. Winnie, "Local Government Budgeting, Program Planning, and Evaluation," *Urban Data Service* (Washington, D.C.: The International City Management Association, May, 1972).

Public administration and program evaluation/

397

Table 2. Use of quantity and quality measures by a select group of local governments, June 1973[a]

	Total jurisdictions examined	Jurisdictions using measures	
		Number of jurisdictions	Percent of total jurisdictions examined
Quantity-oriented measures	41	34	83
Quality-oriented measures	41	21	51

[a]Based on an examination of budget documents conducted by the Urban Institute in June 1973.

A few governments have progressed so far as to estimate future outputs, set output targets for certain services, or compare actual output against performance projected the previous year. Most of these deal with quantity of output, but a few jurisdictions make such comparisons with quality factors also.

Three general conclusions regarding the present state of output measurement in local governments emerge from these two surveys. First, most governments collect some data on quantitative outputs. Second, some local governments collect data on qualitative aspects of output. And third, the state of measurements varies dramatically by service or program area.

Two examples

These surveys suggest that for some engineering-oriented services such as water and sewage treatment, for instance, there are reasonably good measurements of both quantity and quality. The product of such services is tangible and its effect on the public definable. For other engineering-oriented services, such as solid waste collection, there are relatively good measures of service quantity but few measures of service quality. However, for some services, such as recreation, the product and its effect on the public is more difficult to define. Measurements of its quantity and quality characteristics are poor or entirely lacking. This section reviews recent efforts by several governments to come to grips with the problem of service measurement in the areas of solid waste collection and recreation.

Solid waste collection provides a tangible product to the public—removal of garbage and trash. For this aspect of the service there are fairly good measurements of at least the quantity of its output. Most municipalities regularly collect data on the tons or cubic yards of waste collected, number of residences or businesses serviced, curb miles swept, and abandoned cars removed.

The service also has other important objectives which are qualitative, including maintenance of street cleanliness, abatement of hazards to health or

Moderate/infrequent use		High degree of use	
Number of jurisdictions	Percent of total jurisdictions examined	Number of jurisdictions	Percent of total jurisdictions examined
14	35	20	49
18	44	3	7

physical injury, and avoidance of negative side effects such as noise, inconvenience or property damage to private citizens. These are more difficult to measure. While we may know the street miles swept, this is little help in assessing how clean the streets are. We usually know how many residents are served; but we lack knowledge of citizen satisfaction with the service or detrimental effects such as spillage of trash by collectors, missed collections, or unreported damage to private property. While we know how many abandoned automobiles have been removed, we do not have information on how many continue to clutter public thoroughfares. As crucial as are these quality characteristics, they are seldom assessed because of the difficulty in measurement.

Recreation presents an even more imposing problem. Its "product" is much more difficult to define. Recreation services relate to such intangibles as personal "enjoyment" and "variety" of leisure opportunities. Measurements which can directly indicate either quantity or quality of this service's output are difficult to develop and are presently scarce among local governments.

A 1972 survey of cities over 100,000 and counties over 250,000 population asked about the type of data which they used to measure recreation services. The responses showed that local governments relied most heavily upon counts of total number of visitors and, to a lesser extent, upon the hours of participation to indicate service output.[8] Recreation, however, is a service where qualitative characteristics, the pleasantness and enjoyment of the activities, are crucial. Quantitative statistics, such as the number of visits, are, at best, proxies for the service's quality outputs. Direct measures of the service's quality are lacking. Local governments seldom collect data on citizen satisfaction with the mix of activities offered; attractiveness, cleanliness, maintenance, safety, or availability of facilities; or the helpfulness of the staff.

Recently, we have seen a number of governments expressing interest in

---

[8]Robert Brown and Donald Fisk, "Recreation Planning and Analysis in Local Government," *The Municipal Yearbook* (Washington, D.C.: The International City Management Association, 1973), pp. 53–60.

Table 3. Illustrative data showing effects of cleanup program on street litter ratings[a]

| | Average litter rating[b] for sample | | Inspector ratings | |
| | Before clean sweep | After clean sweep | Change in litter rating (+ shows improvement) | Statistically significant change |
Service area				
1	2.43	2.11	+.32	Yes
2	1.80	1.79	+.01	No
3	3.13	2.53	+.60	Yes
4	2.10	2.32	−.22	No
5	1.58	1.44	+.14	No
6	2.71	2.76	−.05	No
Total city	2.38	2.27	+.11	

[a]See Louis H. Blair and Alfred I. Schwartz, *How Clean Is Our City?* (Washington, D.C.: The Urban Institute, 1972), p. 48.

[b]The actual comparison made in the District of Columbia was more complex.

wrestling with the problems of output measurement. Washington, D.C. has been working to improve output measurement in both solid waste collection and recreation.

Solid waste collection

An important quality factor of solid waste collection is the resulting cleanliness. To measure this output the Washington, D.C. government has implemented a method of inspector ratings of street and alley litter conditions. Inspectors are currently driving the streets and alleys in systematic patterns rating conditions on a numerical scale standardized according to photographic examples of various degrees of litter accumulations.

Two other types of qualitative measures in the solid waste collection field depend on the direct experience of citizens with the service. One is a function of citizen perceptions of conditions resulting from the service such as overall neighborhood cleanliness and odors from uncollected solid waste. The other type of citizen impact is based on detrimental incidents which the citizen has experienced during the course of the service: missed collection, noise, spillage, and property damage. Both these types of data have been collected from a representative sample of Washington, D.C. residents.

Statistics from both inspector ratings and citizen survey are being collected, arrayed, and analyzed by service area periodically.

Citizen survey data

Percent of streets Rating 2.5 or Worse		Change percentage points (+shows improvement)	Statistically significant change
Before C.S.	**After C.S.**		
15	7	+ 8	No
0	0	0	No
61	22	+39	Yes
10	25	−15	Yes
0	0	0	No
31	38	− 7	No
29	25	+ 4	

Table 3 illustrates use of these data. This particular display is modeled after one used to evaluate the effects of an intensive solid waste clean-up program conducted in the District of Columbia late in 1971. In that evaluation, citizen survey data were collected three months before and three months after the program, using essentially the same questionnaire. Inspector ratings were made one week prior to and one week after the cleanup to measure the short term effects on cleanliness of streets and alleys. A third inspection was made approximately two months after the program to test its long-term effects.

This system has enabled the government to compare various aspects of service output among districts of the city and thereby identify areas which have the most serious litter problems. It has also enabled the government to set a level of street cleanliness as a citywide standard and deploy solid waste collection crews geographically to achieve that standard. Parts of the Washington, D.C. rating system have been used elsewhere.

In early 1973 inspector ratings of solid waste conditions served as a basis of a study of solid waste conditions in seven United States cities (Chicago, Detroit, East St. Louis, Newark, New York, Philadelphia, and Washington, D.C.) undertaken for the Environmental Protection Agency.[9] The resulting data

---

[9]*Investigation and Evaluation of Inner-City Solid Waste Problems,* Final Report (New York: Dimpex Associates, May 1973).

provided a basis for making both inter- and intra-city comparisons as well as various other types of correlations:

> *Inter-city comparison:* "A difference of 27 percent in street conditions exists between the best and worst of the cities surveyed (Washington, D.C. and Detroit, Michigan), based upon the litter ratings."

> *Intra-city comparison:* " . . . in individual cities the difference ranges as high as 76 percent between census tracts."

> *Correlation of street cleanliness with other factors:* " . . . in three cities . . . a negative correlation exists between median income and litter ratings." "Correlations between owner-occupancy and litter ratings are not as strong as those for median income and litter ratings, although (in two cities) there were significant correlations."[10]

Other relationships were also tested between cleanliness ratings and collection practices, condition and type of buildings, and population density per residential unit.

At least two other cities, Savannah and St. Petersburg, have used inspector ratings to assess the cleanliness of their cities. In both instances a sample of city streets and alleys was examined. In addition, St. Petersburg has collected data on the number of missed collections, spillage, damage to property, and the like through a citywide citizen survey. Also St. Petersburg plans an annual assessment of its solid waste collection activities using the visual inspection and citizen survey.

Recreation

As noted above both the quantitative and qualitative aspects of local government recreation services raise severe problems for the recreation manager. To measure recreation outputs, the District of Columbia government has focused on the variety, enjoyableness, accessibility, and safety of the program. The total number of participants and number of programs are retained to indicate output in quantitative terms, but it was necessary to develop new measurements of qualitative aspects to complete the picture.

Here also the government relied heavily upon a citizen attitude survey. The data gathered included not only citizen perception of conditions at facilities (crowdedness, cleanliness, helpfulness of staff) and suitability of program (satisfaction with hours of operation), but also factual data not otherwise obtainable (rates of individual participation). Much of the data collected related to a specific recreation facility to serve as a guide for improvements.

An important feature of the survey was that it separated responses from persons who do not participate in recreation services, showing their reasons for nonuse. This allows analysis of the suitability of activities offered to groups with particular needs or limitations. It also can reveal sources of public dissatisfac-

---

10Ibid., pp. 8–9.

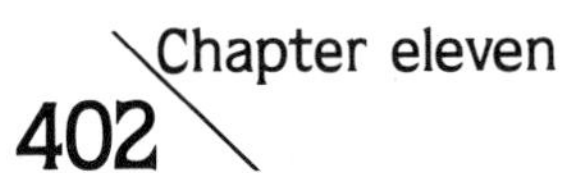

Table 4. Reasons for nonuse of facilities by years residence in neighborhood (percent of total responses) Washington, D.C., May, 1972

Reason	Total	Length of residence in neighborhood	
		Less than 3 years	3 or more years
Causes potentially within government control	48	61	45
Didn't know about facility	26	40	22
Too far away	10	9	11
Activities not interesting	5	5	5
Too dangerous	3	3	3
Too crowded	2	2	2
Wrong hours	1	1	1
Not attractive	1	1	1
Costs too much	—	—	—
Causes probably beyond government control	31	23	33
Too busy	18	17	19
Bad personal health	6	2	6
Too old	5	2	6
Do not like other users	2	2	2
No opinion—other	21	18	22
Other—misc.	11	11	11
No opinion	10	7	11

Source: U.S. Department of the Interior, Bureau of Outdoor Recreation, *How Effective Are Your Community Recreation Services?* (Washington, D.C., April 1973), p. 13.

tion with the service. Table 4 shows responses gathered by the citizen survey from nonparticipants.

Data on another quality characteristic, physical accessibility of residents to recreation facilities, was assembled by mapping. Calculations were also made of program variety by facility and service area of the city. Safety statistics were also collected by service area and compared with citizen perceptions of safety.

Some of the same procedures have been used by the Rockford, Illinois, Park and Recreation District, and the cities of Palo Alto, St. Petersburg, and Nashville. In the case of the latter two governments, there are plans to continue to collect qualitative and quantitative measurement data on an annual basis so as to monitor the progress of programs.

Future prospects

Efforts of local government to measure service outputs comprehensively and systematically are now relatively limited. As noted above, part of the current undeveloped state of output measurement is due to technical problems of how to measure output. However, a more important part of the problem has been a lack of interest on the part of local government in output measurement. This situation is changing.

There has been a sharp increase in the interest of local governments in improving output measurement techniques in the past ten years. The stimulus for this interest is hard to pinpoint exactly, but three possible influences can be cited: the federal government's use of the analytical approach and interest in output measurement, pressure on local governments from community and public interest groups, and professionalism within local government. To varying degrees these forces seem to have provided much of the impetus for current advances, and it is likely they will continue to be influential at least in the immediate future.

First, the federal government's interest and efforts toward PPBS, management by objective, productivity measurement, and program evaluation seem to have had a spillover effect, encouraging local governments to adopt new budgeting and analytical methods. The International City Management Association survey, discussed in the second section, showed a sharp increase in the rate of adoption of program budgets by local governments beginning in the late 1960s. This followed shortly after similar efforts by the federal government.[11]

The federal government has provided direct encouragement in other ways. Many cities have used comprehensive planning grants (HUD-701 program) to support development of program evaluation and analysis staffs and to improve their data systems. Adoption of revenue sharing has led to the publication of *Standards for Audit of Government Organizations, Programs, Activities and Functions* by the Controller General's Office.[12] These guidelines authorize auditors to monitor the use of federal funds by local agencies not only based upon the legality of their use, but also upon whether the programs are meeting their objectives. Thus, output has become a criterion for judging the expenditure of federal funds by local jurisdictions. On another front the National Science Foundation—in particular its Research Applied to National Needs program—has supported research into improved ways of measuring local government output. Finally, the National Commission on Productivity has recently supported projects to identify improved measurements of productivity and to recommend ways of improving the productivity of various local government services.

The activity of citizen groups is also stimulating interest in improved output measurement among many jurisdictions. One aspect of this is pressure upon governments in the form of court suits such as *Hawkins* v. *Town of Shaw, Beal* v. *Lindsay* and *Burner* v. *Washington,* to equalize service levels among neighborhoods or various population groups. This pressure reveals the inability of governments to justify the present distribution of services among areas or groups. Another aspect of this pressure is being generated by businessmen such as the Waterbury, Connecticut Chamber of Commerce and independent citizen groups such as the Minneapolis Citizens League.

Legislators too have begun to demand better information. Difficult budget-

---

11Winnie, "Local Government Budgeting, Program Planning, and Evaluation."

12U.S. General Accounting Office, Office of the Comptroller General, *Standards for Audit of Governmental Organizations, Programs, Activities and Functions* (Washington, D.C.: U.S. General Accounting Office, 1972).

ary choices increasingly evoke requests by legislators that program managers predict the results of various policy alternatives. Furthermore, some city councils, such as St. Petersburg, have set output objectives for their city managers to meet.

Finally, professional staffs within local governments are increasingly becoming interested in the need to improve output measurement. This is evidenced by the report adopted by the International City Management Association at its September, 1973 business meeting. That report recommends to local government managers that they work toward better measurement of service quality, including both "efficiency" and "effectiveness." More specifically, the report suggests that:

> *Communities should concentrate their efforts on effectiveness improvement (based on consumer-oriented objectives) . . . [and] communities of all sizes should undertake programs of measuring the effectiveness of key service areas.*
> *Professional administrators should first concentrate on intra-city comparisons of service levels. . . .*
> *[The International City Management Association] should develop and disseminate—both formally and informally—models of service level measurement, [and] techniques of measurement and quality improvement.*
> *[The Federal government should provide] encouragement of research, development and dissemination of measurement concepts and techniques related to program service levels and for the application of these concepts and techniques to improving local government service quality.*[13]

Given this increasing interest by local government in improved output measurement, what types of improvements are likely to result? In the immediate future concentration will probably be on three deficiencies which presently exist.

First, of course, for most services there is room for vast improvement in measurements of both the quantitative and qualitative outputs of services, and in finding data collection methods which are practical for regular use by local governments. Some local governments already have independent efforts underway to improve their output measurement capabilities. Dallas, Charlotte, and other cities, for example, have developed detailed statements of program objectives and are actively working to identify output measurements which will indicate progress toward these goals. Menlo Park and Palo Alto also recently commenced eighteen-month projects to develop measurements of effectiveness for their services.

More difficult even than identification of output measures is development of methods of gathering data which are practical in light of the limited technical and fiscal resources of local governments. The cost of regular inspector ratings of street and alley conditions and analysis of data are estimated as $9,000–$16,000 for a city of moderate size (100,000–250,000) to $24,000–$52,000 for a large city

---

[13]International City Management Association Committee on the Quality of Municipal Services, "Achieving Quality of Local Government," *Public Management* 55 (September 1973): 19–23.

Public administration and program evaluation/

(over 1,000,000 population), depending on the size of the sample rated.[14] While such costs would be considered small by federal standards, they are exceedingly large for local government.

Presently a major deficiency is the lack of a method of measuring citizen attitudes which is inexpensive enough for regular use by local governments. Advances are now being made in this area, however. A leader has been the Public Opinion Center of Dayton. Established in September 1970 as a nonprofit agency to provide citizen attitude survey assistance to the local governments and community groups of the Dayton-Miami Valley, Ohio area, it has measured community attitudes on public services including mass transit, police, public schools, housing, and health care. One of the side benefits of the center's work is the refinement of survey methods, such as random dial telephone sampling, which can provide governments with citizen attitude and behavioral data at a relatively low cost.

The Dallas city government is cooperating with a nearby university to conduct the first of what is planned to be a regular systematic survey of citizens to test perceptions of city services. Survey results will be reported citywide and for thirty-one separate communities into which the city is divided.

Second, to indicate the quality of many services it is important to separate output data by various population groups. Currently most output data are presented for the city at large only. Some population groups, such as the elderly, have a level of need for service different from the population as a whole or a particular characteristic limiting their access to the service. To measure qualitative service output it is often important to consider population group characteristics such as these.

Disaggregation of output data by income, racial group, or geographical area might enhance local government's ability to make policy decisions regarding equity in the distribution of public services among such groups.[15] As discussed in the previous section, the District of Columbia presently uses its street cleanliness data as a basis for judging equity among districts. Another example is a 1972 court case in which output data were used to test plaintiff's contention that county and state road maintenance services were not equally distributed among racial groups.[16] Data on the surface quality of roads were systematically collected and grouped to test for possible correlations between the quality of road maintenance service (road surface smoothness) and the variables, racial groups, housing value (a proxy for household income), and population density.

Third, improvement is needed in the standardization of data to allow comparison among different points in time. Longitudinal data on local government services has, for the most part, been lacking. This prevents multiyear comparison of service levels, clientele served, and other factors which could be useful both in government decision making and to outside researchers. Claremont,

---

[14]Louis H. Blair and Alfred I. Schwartz, *How Clean Is Our City?* (Washington, D.C.: The Urban Institute, 1972).

[15]Martin H. Krieger, *Social Reporting for a City: A Perspective and Some Problems* (New York: RAND Corporation, May 1971), pp. 12–13.

[16]Andrew J. Boots et al., *Inequality in Local Government Services: A Case Study in Neighborhood Roads* (Washington, D.C.: The Urban Institute, 1972).

\Chapter eleven

California has attempted to standardize statistics which it collects. The city publishes an annual report which features interyear comparisons of service performance.

To pull together the above three components and thereby provide a working example for other cities, the International City Management Association and The Urban Institute are presently working with the cities of St. Petersburg and Nashville. The objective of this effort is to work with city officials to develop measurements of citizen-related impacts and other outputs of government services, as well as productivity. Emphasis is on finding measurements of both quantity and quality characteristics for major city services. Where pertinent, data will be separated by population subgroup or geographical area. Data collection procedures are being developed which are inexpensive enough so that comparable data can be collected at regular intervals.

It appears that the technical aspects of identifying and measuring outputs of local government services are advancing. Furthermore, those factors mentioned early in this paper—the federal government's interest in output measurement, demand from citizen groups for government accountability and the increasing professionalism—should stimulate greater use of output data by local governments.

So, it appears that data on local government services, not previously available without ad hoc efforts by researchers, will increasingly be available from local governments themselves. The rate of this growth, though, will not depend on technical advances in output measurement so much as it will depend on the technical and fiscal resources of local governments. Their work in defining outputs specifically appropriate to the service within the particular jurisdiction, and the level of effort which they apply to data collection will, in the end, determine the usefulness and abundance of output data from local governments.

Study questions for selection sixteen

1. The accomplishments of certain programs are easier to measure than are those of others; for example, Fisk and Winnie note that there are reasonably good quantitative and qualitative measures of "engineering-oriented" services, but that other services, such as recreation, are difficult to measure. What impact might this difference have on the distribution of resources? Why?

2. After looking at the list of "illustrative quality factors" suggested for the selected service functions in exhibit 1, please rate each of the quality factors on the list as (1) difficult to measure, or (2) readily measurable.

3. Based on your consideration of question 2, please formulate a statement that reflects your view of the features that should be contained in a satisfactory measure of program accomplishment.

What can we actually get from program evaluation?*

Joseph S. Wholey

It is appropriate that this chapter conclude with an evaluation of program evaluation. The following paper, written by a member of the Urban Institute's staff, assesses the role evaluation can play in assisting decisions on public programs. That role may vary, of course, depending upon the character of the evaluation. As Joseph Wholey indicates, an important distinction can be made between evaluation as an aid in policy formulation and evaluation as an aid in management.

Several evaluations have received much attention by administrators and, especially, by students of evaluation. (One such student remarked to us that more effort seems to be devoted to writing *about* evaluation than to doing actual evaluations.) The Head Start and negative income tax evaluations are frequently cited and criticized. As Wholey notes, these were of different types; the former was a study of an ongoing program, and the latter was a limited experiment to test the possible impact a new program might have if adopted nationally. Both types are evaluations, but they must be approached differently by those conducting them and those using them.

The concluding portion of the paper raises a few of the political problems confronting evaluators, some of which are of their own making. Many evaluators have been drawn from outside of government circles and have had difficulty adjusting to the norms of public agencies. For example, there is the problem of "freedom of the press": Just how much information should be released about an experiment? Closely related is the "right of privacy": How extensive should be the access of evaluators to school records, police records, health records, etc.? These questions are being answered step by step as evaluations are made, but conflicts occur between evaluators and administrators, and between these groups and other political actors.

Introduction

As an analyst and as a public official, I have been interested for some time in the role that quantitative analysis can play in assisting decisions on public

---

*Reprinted with permission from *Policy Sciences* 3 (1972): 361–369.

programs—in particular, in the role that evaluation of program results can play.

The essence of *program evaluation,* as I use the term today, is the assessment of program *outcome*—what happened that would not have happened in the absence of the program?—and *relative effectiveness* within national programs—what individual local projects or types of projects work best? The purpose of evaluation is to provide objective feedback to program managers and policy makers on the cost and effects of national programs and local projects, to assist effective management and efficient allocation of limited resources.

Evaluation has come into its own over the past few years. There has been rather wide acknowledgement by public officials of the need to evaluate social programs. Federal legislation has called for it, money has been provided, evaluation staffs have been created or strengthened, and some major evaluation studies have been undertaken.

During this time, we have all learned that evaluation is difficult, takes a lot of time to carry out, and can be very expensive. We have discovered that the information generated by evaluation studies is often incomplete, suspect, and unrelated to the problems at hand. We have found bureaucratic and organizational constraints so formidable that today, after investment of significant resources and effort, *not one* federal agency has an overall evaluation system and few programs are able to make any use of the evaluations produced. On the whole, *federal evaluation efforts have not been cost-effective* in terms of impact on policy or program development.

In this paper, I consider the points of view of decision makers at two levels: *policy makers* concerned with legislative changes and budget levels, and *program managers* at various levels. What can policy makers and what can program managers actually *get* from program evaluation?

Evaluation for policy makers: national program impact evaluation

First, what can policy makers get from evaluation? Two major types of evaluation are of interest to policy makers: national program impact evaluation, which may throw light on the effects of a national program, and evaluation of field experiments and demonstration projects, which may throw light on the desirability of new operating programs while there is still time to learn from experience.

Head Start

The Westinghouse-Ohio University evaluation of the national Head Start program is a leading example of program impact evaluation.[1] The Westinghouse study design was not perfect, but the results of the study probably furnished a correct assessment of the impact of the national Head Start program. It revealed

---

[1]Westinghouse Learning Corporation-Ohio University (1969), "The Impact of Head Start: Evaluation of the Effects of Head Start on Children's Cognitive and Affective Development."

that one, two, and three years after children from low-income families had gone through the Head Start program, there was little or no improvement in their cognitive achievement or motivational attitudes (when compared with similar children in the same communities).

The Westinghouse evaluation of the Head Start program therefore produced generally negative findings. The negative findings, however, did not significantly reduce the budget level of Head Start. Powerful constituencies would have fought any reduction in funding for Head Start. Results that seem to have come from the Westinghouse Head Start evaluation are (1) the "hold" placed on the program—increased funding levels would not be sought; (2) the diversion of some Head Start program funds into experimental child development programs, "planned variations," designed to test whether there are better approaches than those that were being used in the national Head Start program; and (3) the reduction of the proportion of Head Start funds now going into *summer* Head Start (the Head Start component with the *least* apparent value).

Manpower training

Perhaps a more typical outcome of national program impact studies can be seen in the manpower area. The Department of Labor spends $4 million per year on evaluation of manpower programs. Yet a recent Urban Institute study for the Joint Economic Committee concluded: "Differences in research design and wide natural variations within programs have led to unreliable cost and effectiveness findings for manpower training programs.... The manpower training benefit/cost studies reviewed had methodological limitations which made it impossible to be sure that the true average results of the manpower programs were measured."[2]

Cost-benefit studies of national impact programs consume a large share of the Labor Department's evaluation resources. But the results of these studies play almost no part in the administration of Labor Department programs. *Even if* reliable and valid data *were* being generated in the national program impact studies being done, such studies are not appropriate support for the types of decisions actually made within the Labor Department. National program impact evaluation studies circulate from office to office in the Labor Department without being acted upon or in most cases even read, because Labor Department administrators do not make the types of decisions which these studies are designed to support. There is room for well-designed cost-benefit studies, but not to the exclusion of other, more relevant types of evaluation.

Title I, ESEA

Another area in which we have examined the feasibility and desirability of national program impact evaluations is that of compensatory education. The federal government spends $1.5 billion per year on education of disadvantaged children, under Title I of the Elementary and Secondary Education Act. It might

---

[2]Joe Nay, et al., *Benefits and Costs of Manpower Training Programs: A Synthesis of Previous Studies with Reservations and Recommendations,* (Washington, D.C.: The Urban Institute, 1971).

Chapter eleven

410

seem important to evaluate the national impact of these large expenditures. Yet, a year ago, the Urban Institute urged the Office of Education not to put $800,000 of its scarce evaluation funds into a national impact evaluation of Title I. The argument concluded:

> *While Title I program impact evaluation is feasible, it faces severe methodological problems in sample selection, in defining the treatments provided, in designation of comparison groups, and in dealing with student mobility. . . . As a result of both our inability to distinguish Title I services from other services provided to program participants (by local funds) and the fact that Title I accounts for a relatively small proportion of total per pupil expenditures, it will be very difficult to attribute observed changes in student achievement to Title I. . . .*
>
> *A national program impact evaluation of Title I, even if methodologically feasible, seems undesirable in comparison with more constructive uses of the evaluation funds available. . . . The Office of Education can and should work with those states that are interested to develop better monitoring systems, to improve local evaluation, to locate and document successful compensatory education projects, to distinguish better from worse Title I projects. . . . The Office of Education can also work through State Educational Agencies to improve the usefulness of local project evaluation efforts by subsidizing cooperative local evaluations which utilize at least some common output measures. . . .*[3]

We are not saying that national program impact studies are never appropriate. What we *do* suggest is that this type of evaluation is too often done for people who need other types of information to help them select among the options in their decision space. Evaluations have been too willing to accept neat, over simplified decision-making models. While evaluators have always recognized the need to understand thoroughly the programs being evaluated, rarely if ever is evaluation preceded by an analysis of the decision-making process and the constraints on the options open to the decision makers for whom the evaluation is being done. If evaluation results are expected to affect policy or program management decisions, then an analysis of the *planning-management-control* process to be affected and the development of realistic models of this process must become integral parts of evaluation planning and design.

Evaluation for policy makers: experimentation

A second type of evaluation important to the policy maker, but less often carried out, is evaluation of demonstration projects and field experiments—

---

[3]Joseph S. Wholey and Bayla F. White, letter to Dr. John W. Evans, Assistant Commissioner of Education, 18 November, 1970. See Joseph S. Wholey, et al., *Title I Evaluation and Technical Assistance: Assessment and Prospects,* (Washington, D.C.: The Urban Institute, 1971).

areas in which evaluation is politically and technically more feasible—and may have more chance to influence decisions. The typical demonstration projects demonstrate only that it is possible to spend public funds in a particular way. The results of the "demonstration" usually go unevaluated.

Police fleet plan

The Urban Institute's study of the Indianapolis Police Fleet Plan is an interesting example of an evaluation of a demonstration program.[4] In the Indianapolis Police Fleet Plan, police patrolmen are allowed to take their police cars home with them for their private use in off-duty hours—thus putting a lot more police cars on the city streets. The Urban Institute worked with the city of Fort Worth, which had some interest in possibly adopting the Police Fleet Plan. While the evaluation results were quite positive in favor of the Police Fleet Plan (auto thefts went down, auto accidents went down, outdoor crime, purse snatching, and robbery went down),[5] the study's sponsor (the Fort Worth city manager) chose not to implement the findings of the study. After the study was published, however, at least one other local government did decide to implement a police fleet plan based on the results of the evaluation study.

Experiments

In the past few years, there has been a new trend in the development of federal programs. Instead of beginning major new programs or demonstration projects designed to be entering wedges for such programs, the federal government has turned toward using *field experiments* in an attempt to find out what is effective and what is not, *before* a program is implemented nationally. True experiments differ from typical demonstration projects in that those responsible exercise control over inputs and process variables—and carefully measure outputs to determine the extent to which the project reaches its objectives. Five years ago, the idea of conducting large-scale social experiments was neither practical nor realistic, for political reasons. The fact that income maintenance experiments are successfully underway and that money has been earmarked for a housing allowance experiment indicates that federal administrators are increasingly willing to take the political risks involved in running a carefully controlled set of experiments.

Outstanding examples of field experiments are OEO's negative income tax experiment now under way in New Jersey; HEW's income maintenance experiments in Gary, Seattle, and Denver; and OEO's experiments with performance contracting in elementary school education. OEO's experiments in performance contracting and the proposed experiments with education vouchers are beginning to break some new ground which may prove important in a number of ways. Private sector agencies will be tested and given a chance to develop new educational program models.

---

[4]See Donald M Fisk, *The Indianapolis Police Fleet Plan: An Example of Program Evaluation for Local Government* (Washington, D.C.: The Urban Institute, 1970).

[5]It's worth noting that the Police Fleet Plan study was done primarily using existing effectiveness data on crime rates, accidents, etc., together with development of cost data from city records. It took only a month or two of an analyst's time to put this study together.

There are two ways to introduce the experimental approach into public programs—or two times at which experiments can be introduced: (1) before a major operating program is undertaken; (2) simultaneously with a major operating program. An experimental program may be started as a possible forerunner of a larger social program; or it may be set up to run alongside a large operating program, to learn things that might improve the operating program. (See, for example, the Office of Education's Follow Through program, in which a dozen or more approaches to the education of disadvantaged children are simultaneously being tested—each in several communities.) There is growing support in Washington for both of these approaches.

Evaluation for program managers

Let's turn our attention now to evaluation for program managers, those at federal, state, or local level who have responsibility for operating major programs. Over the past two years, members of the evaluation group at the Urban Institute have become more and more convinced that the primary evaluation payoff (in terms of decisions actually influenced) may be in evaluation that is done in enough detail to get at the effects of operational changes within operating programs. Many program managers really want to know *what works best, under what conditions.* There is a market, a use, for this type of detailed evaluation.

Following are three examples (or two-and-one-half examples) of evaluation systems designed to help program managers.

Solid waste collection

The Urban Institute recently developed a monitoring system for the District of Columbia Sanitation Department.[6] Inspectors, supplied with reference photographs, drive along city streets and alleyways with a tape recorder microphone in hand. For each block covered, they rate the cleanliness of the block as 1, 2, 3, or 4 (by comparing the street or alleyway with the reference photographs). This system therefore produces data on the *outputs* of services, not simply inputs or estimates of outputs.[7] One can imagine this system being used to assess the results of operational changes in Sanitation Department activities (as is now being done in the District of Columbia) or to justify budget requests (once it is determined that particular additional inputs in the way of increased services can in fact produce differences in outputs, for example, moving a neighborhood's streets and alleys from an average condition 3 or 4 [dirty] to a condition 2 [relatively clean]).

---

[6]See Louis Blair and Alfred Schwartz, *Improving the Measurement of the Effectiveness of D.C. Solid Waste Collection Activities* (Washington, D.C.: The Urban Institute, 1971).

[7]It turned out that the ratings for streets and alleyways were relatively stable within a census tract and over time. Therefore, it was possible to develop an efficient monitoring system using sampling techniques.

Public schools

Urban public school systems have increasingly been called upon to address and correct major inequities in our society while providing quality education to large, heterogeneous school populations. School personnel are bombarded with numbers, which are supposed to be useful in making decisions affecting the operations of the school system. Rarely, however, are the data which pour out of large school systems relevant to the needs of school system decision makers. If, in the future, school systems are to respond to the challenges they face, then the objectives of education must be clarified and information about the performance of the school system in meeting those objectives must be improved and used effectively.

At present, most local educational evaluation focuses on analysis of special projects that occupy only a small fraction of the input to a particular school, while opportunities are ignored to make comparisons of input and output across the entire school system. Experience has shown that these local project evaluations, usually carried out to fulfill federal requirements, are of little use to local decision makers because their results are neither timely nor comparable. Project evaluations also operate under severe methodological constraints, which often make their results inconclusive.

The Urban Institute is now working with the Atlanta Public School System trying to develop a system for estimating the relative effectiveness of different public schools in the city.[8] In this project, Atlanta schools are being classified by the economic level of the students (currently measured by proportions of children receiving free lunches or reduced-price lunches) and by the amount of pupil turnover in the school during the year. The Institute is testing the notion that information on the relative effectiveness of schools serving comparable student populations could be useful to the superintendent and his staff. This work is still in the research and development phase.

Legal services

Some federal agencies are giving attention to improved systems for program monitoring, where evaluation feedback is used directly to assist management decisions (for example, decisions on the refunding of individual projects and decisions on provision of technical assistance or training to projects performing below expectations). The Urban Institute designed, for the OEO Office of Legal Services, a systematic monitoring system that classifies local Legal Services projects into groups according to the kinds of communities in which they are operating, so that projects operating in similar circumstances can be compared with one another.[9] (Projects are classified by budget size, type of population served, and type of community in which the projects operate). When feasible, the same evaluators visit the projects within the same class, to enhance

---

[8]See Bayla F. White, *Design for a School Rating or Classification System* (Washington, D.C.: The Urban Institute, 1970), and Bayla F. White, et al., *The Atlanta Urban Institute School Classification Project,* (Washington, D.C.: The Urban Institute, 1971).

[9]See Hugh G. Duffy, et al., *Design of an On-Site Evaluation System for the Office of Legal Services,* (Washington, D.C.: The Urban Institute, 1971).

the prospects of making valid comparative judgments among projects that are in fact comparable.

The Office of Legal Services monitoring system rates the quality and quantity of the work being done by local Legal Services staff attorneys and provides Office of Legal Services management with estimates of the results achieved by every one of these projects toward Legal Services program goals (to promote economic development, to reform laws and administrative regulations bearing unfairly on the poor, and to provide individual legal services).

Hard work is required to get evaluative information in enough detail and with enough reliability to help program managers—but that's where real pay offs for evaluation can occur. And this kind of evaluation is also more acceptable to program managers, who after all are the people who have to provide much of the data required for evaluation studies.

The Legal Services monitoring system and the D.C. Sanitation monitoring system are alike in their emphasis on outputs. For the Legal Services program, all that could be obtained through the on–site evaluations were relatively soft data on *estimated* outputs. The D.C. solid waste collection monitoring system adds the collection of hard output data on the effectiveness of solid waste collection activities—new data not available in any city records.[10]

Problems with evaluation

Lets's turn now to some of the real problems in getting useful evaluation. From the point of view of decision makers, evaluation is a dangerous weapon. They don't want evaluation if it will yield the "wrong" answers about programs in which they are interested.[11] On the other hand, decision makers are more advanced in their ability to ask pertinent questions than evaluators are in their ability to provide timely answers at reasonable cost. Valid, reliable evaluation is very hard to perform and can cost a lot of money.[12] Evaluators have real problems in detecting causal connections between inputs and outputs—and in doing so in timely enough fashion to be useful to decision makers. The structure of a program can have an important influence on the technical feasibility of separating the effects of the program from the effects of other, often more powerful, forces *not* under control of the program. To the extent that a program is run as a controlled experiment, for example, the evaluator's chances of separating out causal connections may be greater.

Our reviews have found typical federal program evaluation studies marked by certain design characteristics which severely restrict their reliability and usefulness:

---

[10]The Legal Services monitoring system was developed for less than $50,000 and is now being used by the OEO Legal Services program to keep track of their 260-odd local projects. The D.C. solid waste collection monitoring system was developed for approximately $70,000 and is now being implemented in the District of Columbia.

[11]In some cases, political pressures will simply override the empirical evidence without the formality of a methodological argument. Here, the only recourse open to the evaluator is to publish the results and hope that some other more enlightened or less pressured decision maker with similar problems will make use of the results.

[12]The Stanford Research Institute evaluation of the Office of Education Follow Through program, for example, has already cost approximately $7 million.

a. They have been one-shot, one-time efforts, when we need *continuous* evaluation of programs.

b. They have been carried out in terms of national programs and are very weak on process data.

c. They have been small sample studies working with gross averages, when we need studies large enough to allow analysis of the wide variations we know exist in costs and performance among projects within programs.

These studies have often been accompanied by conclusions and recommendations based on unsupportable or unmeasured assumptions and weak, and often confusing data. In these cases, the evaluation results *should* be ignored by policy makers. Other evaluation studies, while competently conceived, are so severly constrained by time, money, and an inadequate data base that the results at best have only limited significance for policy changes or program improvement.

Experimentation presents new opportunities for the evaluator—and a new set of problems. There are important tensions between the evaluator and the program official, tensions which arise out of the very notion of experimentation. The criteria for selection of sites, the carefully controlled design of the experiments, and the random assignment of participants (or communities) to treatments are basic to experimental design. The program administrator may not see the utility of such ideas, however. What is so wrong, he may wonder, about calling an existing exemplary program an "experiment"? Or why not choose the people most in need of housing to participate in a housing allowance experiment? The evaluator must woo and win the administrator to the need for preserving the experimental character of the experiment.

Time also presents an enormous problem for the evaluator of experimental programs. As soon as there is sufficient legislative support to fund a series of experiments, there may be enough support to enact such a program nationwide. The concern that legislation will be enacted before the experiments have had time to produce reliable results may lead to pressures for the release of early, less reliable findings. The New Jersey Income Maintenance experiments experienced this pressure. Some early tentative results from the study were released with reluctance and heavy qualifications. If experimentation is to become a major vehicle in policy research, then ways must be found to anticipate and deal with these types of pressures.

Despite the differences, evaluation of experiments has a great deal in common with the evaluation of on-going programs. In both cases, the evaluator must resist the temptation to search for answers to questions that interest *him,* but which may not be high on the list of questions the *decision maker* wants answered. Decision makers will be convinced of the worth of evaluation only if evaluation meets the needs of the decision maker and provides information useful to him.

Conclusion

What can we actually get from program evaluation? From the point of view of a skeptical, but interested policy maker or program manager, evaluation has a mixed record. From the point of view of the analyst, the problems in doing useful evaluation are formidable. Over the past few years, however, there has been some progress, enough to indicate that certain directions in evaluation have promise.

Study questions for selection seventeen

1. Having read the Wholey article as well as other material in this chapter, how would you answer the question his title poses?

2. Wholey provides very brief descriptions of notable evaluation efforts. Take one of these (or another program of your own choosing) and outline an evaluation research design. What data problems would you encounter? How could you be sure that the changes you measured were results of the program? How would you convince an administrator that the evaluation would be worth the investment? Would yours be an evaluation for policy makers or managers?

Suggested readings for chapter eleven

Brewer, Gary D. *Politicians, Bureaucrats and the Consultant: A Critique of Urban Problem Solving.* New York: Basic Books, 1973.

Campbell, Donald T., and Stanley, Julian C. *Experimental and Quasi-Experimental Design for Research.* Chicago: Rand McNally Publishing Co., 1966.

Freeman, Howard E., and Sherwood, Clarence C. *Social Research and Social Policy.* Englewood Cliffs, N.J.: Prentice-Hall, Inc., 1970.

Garn, Harvey A., et al. *Models for Indicator Development: A Framework for Policy Analysis.* Washington, D.C.: The Urban Institute, 1976.

Hatry, Harry P., et al. *Measuring the Effectiveness of Basic Municipal Services: Initial Report.* Washington, D.C.: The Urban Institute, 1974.

———. *Practical Program Evaluation for State and Local Government Officials.* Washington, D.C.: The Urban Institute, 1973.

Riecken, Henry W., and Boruch, Robert F., eds. *Social Experimentation: A Method for Planning and Evaluating Social Intervention.* New York: Academic Press, 1974.

Rivlin, Alice M. *Systematic Thinking for Social Action.* Washington, D.C.: The Brookings Institution, 1971.

Suchman, Edward A. *Evaluative Research: Principles and Practice in Public Service and Social Action Programs.* New York: The Russell Sage Foundation, 1969.

Weiss, Carol H. *Evaluation Research: Methods of Assessing Program Effectiveness.* Englewood Cliffs, N.J.: Prentice-Hall, Inc., 1972.

The responsibility and the future of American public administration

The previous chapter explored the concept of program evaluation, whereby particular activities of government agencies are assessed according to various criteria. This final chapter broadens the perspective and evaluates whole agencies and the entire system of public administration in the United States. Of course, this brief chapter can only introduce such a large subject. We shall also attempt—with considerable trepidation—to predict some aspects of the future for American public administration.

A. Holding government agencies responsible

Just as one can evaluate the efficiency, the impact on clients, or the cost-effectiveness of particular government programs, such criteria can be utilized for evaluating government agencies in general. But we shall focus instead on a criterion that cuts across others and is clearly normative in character: administrative responsibility. We use responsibility as a broad concept and think of it as encompassing such related notions as bureaucratic accountability and responsiveness.

Responsibility is in essence a *relational* concept; it clearly implies that the objects of attention—in our case, public administrative agencies—are answerable to some individuals or groups for their actions. A list of those to whom modern public agencies are responsible would include the executive, the legislature, the courts, pressure groups, the mass communications media, the electorate, the public at large, and even the unborn generations of future citizens. Thus, enforcing responsibility is a large order, and the interpretations of these various publics as to what constitutes responsible bureaucratic behavior may be contradictory.

Why is bureaucratic responsibility regarded as an important problem for public administration? The simplest answer is that the actions of public agencies have powerful impacts on the lives of citizens, and it is generally accepted that in a democratic polity those who take such influential actions should be held answerable for them. At the beginning of his well-known essay on the subject, Herman Finer goes so far as to argue: "Administrative responsibility is not less important to democratic government than administrative efficiency; it is even a contributor to efficiency in the long run."[1] Since public agencies have become so large and the programs they administer so complex, the enforcement of administrative responsibility has become a project of enormous dimensions. During a single year, for instance, the Department of Health, Education, and Welfare misspent, through waste, fraud, and mismanagement, between \$6.3 and \$7.4 billion.[2] This enormous range—the bottom figure of which is itself

---

[1]Herman Finer, "Administrative Responsibility in Democratic Government," *Public Administration Review* 1 (Summer 1941): 335.

[2]Reported by the Associated Press, 4 April 1978.

more than the gross national product of all but thirty-five of the world's nations—is evidence not only of the size of the problems, but also—assuming that the waste can be substantially reduced—it indicates the potential rewards of enforcing administrative responsibility. After public revelation of this dramatic example of administrative irresponsibility, HEW, of course, was held responsible for its actions. Again assuming that HEW reduces its waste, the example will also illustrate Finer's comment that responsibility can contribute to efficiency.

The accountable administrator

Having introduced the general notion of responsibility, we now turn to a discussion of several of its aspects. In beginning the discussion, we shall look at the subject from the point of view of the administrator and ask in various ways what it means to make responsible public decisions.

Let us begin by examining the concept of *administrative accountability*. In a 1975 article in the *Public Administration Review,* Amitai Etzioni identified four main uses of this concept.[3] First, accountability is sometimes used symbolically in several ways; it may be used as an inauthentic gesture (in the same way that apple pie, patriotism, and motherhood are paid lip service), as a rallying cry for mobilizing others, or as an educational device to make others aware of their moral responsibilities. Second, accountability is sometimes used to draw attention to the *realpolitik* of administrative life; according to this view, there are significant and powerful groups in society and within the organization itself to which an administrator is expected to respond. Third, the formal-legal view of accountability focuses on the checks and balances mechanisms and the formal reporting requirements both within the organization and outside of it. Finally, Etzioni discusses the approach to accountability that he finds most satisfactory, the "guidance" approach, which acknowledges that administrators respond to each of the already listed meanings, but at the same time is aware that they respond also to their internalized notions of right and wrong—their values. The exercise of leadership on accountability questions is an important aspect of the role of what he calls the "creative" administrator.

---

[3]Reprinted from *Public Administration Review* 35 (May/June 1975): 279-286. © 1975 by The American Society for Public Administration, 1225 Connecticut Avenue, N.W., Washington, D.C. All rights reserved.

In grappling with the actual meaning of accountability for practicing administrators, let us consider the position of a hypothetical director of children's summer recreation in a city's Department of Parks and Recreation. This individual is subject to "accountability" requirements in several of its meanings. Perhaps uppermost in the mind of our director is his legal accountability. The director must, by law, account for the use of appropriated funds. In fact, he has even been required to provide a surety bond; should he embezzle city funds, a bonding company would reimburse the city. Additionally, a formal organization chart clearly identifies his legal supervisor, the superintendent of parks and recreation, and requires that he take direction from her; one step farther removed is the city manager, and beyond that official lies the city council. To all of these officials, the director is accountable, although to varying degrees. At the same time, they will share at least some of the blame, should the summer program be a failure.

But what about the children who will take part and their parents? Can our director shunt aside any displeasure they may express by pointing to the organization chart, noting that he is a mere subordinate, and telling them to talk to his superiors if they are not pleased with the program? Of course, legally the director is accountable only to his superiors, but in a democratic system the administrator is normally expected to be responsive to citizens' desires and needs. If only the demands from citizens and superiors were always in accord! Unfortunately, they are not. Further complicating matters, the director may have his own convictions regarding what should be done.

Let us suppose that our director is encouraged—but not directly ordered—by his boss to design the summer program so that most resources go to the wealthier areas of town, where members of the council and their key supporters live. In the superintendent's view, these families pay the most taxes and ought to get the most service. On the other hand, the director knows that needs for recreation are more severe in the poorer areas, and neighborhood groups in those areas are insisting on better programs. In addition, his training as a recreation specialist taught him to stress recreation for the disadvantaged.

What action should the director take for us to judge him properly accountable? Clearly, the answer depends on which understanding of accountability we choose to emphasize. Perhaps Etzioni's final conception, the "guidance" approach to accountability, is most attractive, because it allows for the other views and includes the director's own values.

There remains, however, the critical question of balance. What weight is to be assigned to the various, possibly competing, aspects of accountability? Should all administrators simply decide for themselves? To some extent, they *will* decide for themselves; as a practical matter, it is impossible, as well as undesirable, to prescribe rules so rigidly that each administrator is perfectly responsive and accountable either to superiors or to interest groups. But this relative degree of freedom does not mean that an administrator should be completely allowed to follow his own leanings. Instead, operating under the guidance approach, the administrator is charged to behave responsibly but realistically. As Etzioni puts it,

> *The object is not to fly in the face of reality or power groups, nor to wildly pursue Utopian notions of social justice or accountability—such an administrator is all too likely to be quickly expelled—but to help shape, mobilize, and combine the vectors which determine the unit's direction and accountability model so as to bring them closer to the desired system. To shape these forces requires educating the various groups to definitions and demands which are closer to what is legal and ethical and just. This is probably the most difficult part of the creative administrator's job.*[4]

To accomplish these objectives, the creative administrator must develop specific leadership skills that relate to the various dimensions of accountability.

Administrative values: the "inner check"

Even under the best possible circumstances, then, much depends on the values of the administrators in question. That the values of civil servants are an important aspect of administrative responsibility has been long recognized, and this recognition helps to explain the widespread interest in professionalization of the public service. More than forty years ago, John Gaus predicted as follows: "Certainly, in the system of government which is now emerging, one important kind of responsibility will be that which the individual civil servant recognizes as due to the standards and ideals of his profession. This is 'his

---

[4]Ibid., p. 284.

inner check.' "[5] Since Gaus wrote, the existence of the *inner check* has become increasingly important to citizens, as bureaucracy's intrusion into their lives has expanded.

What are the professional standards and ideals of American civil servants? In briefly addressing this question, we shall examine procedural values only; attention is paid to some important substantive values of civil servants in this chapter's final section.

Because hardly any research has been done on the subject, Americans know surprisingly little about their administrators' values. Opinions about our administrators range widely from those who view them as power-mad, undemocratic minions of satanic, un-American forces to those who view them as all-benevolent, responsive servants of the public, possessing the wisdom of Plato's philosopher-kings. The truth, of course, lies somewhere between these extremes.

In 1974, an article was published in the *Public Administration Review* that applied Herbert McClosky's questionnaire, developed for his pioneering public opinion study, to a sample of high-level (GS 12–15) federal bureaucrats. The article generated considerable controversy, as evidenced by the letters to the editor printed in subsequent issues of the *Review*. One reason for the controversy was that, to a degree considered surprising by some observers, many of the respondents did not subscribe fully to certain of the procedural "rules of the game" which have often been counted as democratic ideals. For example, the bureaucrats were asked to agree or disagree with the following items:

1. "To bring about great changes for the benefit of mankind often requires cruelty and even ruthlessness."

2. "Any person who hides behind the laws when he is being questioned about his activities doesn't deserve much consideration."

3. "When the country is in great danger, we may have to force people to testify against themselves even if it violates their rights."

---

[5]John M. Gaus, "The Responsibility of Public Administration," *The Frontiers of Public Administration* (Chicago: University of Chicago Press, 1936), pp. 39-40; quoted in C. J. Friedrich, "Public Policy and the Nature of Administrative Responsibility," in *Public Policy: A Yearbook of the Graduate School of Public Administration, Harvard University, 1940,* eds. C. J. Friedrich and Edward S. Mason (Cambridge, Mass.: Harvard University Press, 1940), p. 13.

Is it surprising that one-quarter of the respondents *agreed* with each of these three items?[6] Do these results indicate that many federal civil servants harbor highly undemocratic attitudes and that they should be restrained so that they do not take our liberties from us?

Perhaps these results should occasion some concern, but other considerations should be kept in mind. First, the questionnaire items were extreme statements that described abstract theoretical possibilities; they did not describe actual situations that are reasonably close to the work done by most civil servants, and in making decisions, civil servants also are constrained by a number of structural-legal factors. Second, the results are in general remarkably similar to those McClosky got a decade earlier—especially with regard to the findings of the general population survey.[7] After all, is it reasonable to expect that civil servants' values should be markedly different from the values of the population from whom they are drawn? Perhaps the situation is reminiscent of Pogo's proclamation: "We have met the enemy and he is us." Finally, some civil servants are lazy, self-important, imperious purveyors of red tape—and so are some members of the public. But we do not believe that civil servants are conspiring to subvert the liberties traditionally enjoyed by Americans. In this regard, it may be instructive to recall that the Watergate affair, the most serious threat to the American democratic system within living memory, revealed the failings of politicians and their appointees, *not* those of professional civil servants.

What *should be* the professional standards and ideals of American civil servants? This is another question for which we can give no pat answers, but most treatments of the subject suggest that democratic norms should be paramount. Unfortunately, most writers do not make explicit their understanding of democracy or of the moral precepts that flow from it. An exception is Emmette Redford, who in his influential book *Democracy in the Administrative State* says that what he calls "workable democracy" is achieved *"through the interaction of leaders of different types in strategic positions of influence, who are forced by the interaction process, the complexity of interests involved in a decision-making situation, and the access of nonleaders to their positions to give attention to all the interests in the society."*[8] Administrators, Redford says, should attempt to maximize three values:

---

[6]Reprinted from *Public Administration Review* 34 (March/April 1974): 158-59. © 1974 by The American Society for Public Administration, 1225 Connecticut Avenue, N.W., Washington, D.C. All rights reserved.

[7]Herbert McClosky, "Consensus and Ideology in American Politics," *American Political Science Review* 58 (June 1964): 361-82.

[8]Emmette S. Redford, *Democracy in the Administrative State* (New York: Oxford University Press, 1969), pp. 199-200; Redford's italics.

Chapter twelve

424

individual realization, equality, and participation. In combination, these three constitute "democratic morality," which administrators are exhorted to pursue as an ideal. Recognizing, however, that in the real world abstract values sometimes cannot be realized, Redford advises administrators that "responsiveness is the central theme of democratic morality, but wisdom, and tranquility and order are competing claims of political purpose."[9]

Unfortunately, some university and intra-agency training programs fail to sensitize the administrator to important value questions inherent in the government employee's job. Given a limited amount of time and money, it sometimes seems far more important to planners to train administrators to run their agencies efficiently than it is to train them to think about accountability. Some programs are so devoid of such concern that they are indistinguishable from those aimed at private-sector employees. But most programs conducted by agencies and universities do seek to inculcate democratic values so that the "inner check" is created.

The role of bureaucratic monitoring mechanisms

Thus far, we have examined accountability as an important aspect of administrative decision making, and we have examined the normative orientations administrators have toward being accountable. But experience teaches us that administrators do not always *behave* responsibly. In fact, a large and growing literature is very critical of the extent to which the entire administrative process is responsible.

Much of this discussion gives a negative connotation to the word *bureaucracy*. William A. Robson echoes many critics in listing several "persistent maladies" from which he alleges bureaucracy frequently suffers:

> *an excessive sense of self-importance on the part of officials or an undue idea of the importance of their offices; an indifference towards the feelings or the convenience of individual citizens; an obsession with the binding and inflexible authority of departmental decisions, precedents, arrangements or forms, irrespective of how badly or with what injustice or hardship they may work in individual cases; a mania for regulations and formal procedure; a preoccupation with particular units of administration and an inability to consider the government as*

---

[9]Ibid., p. 37.

*a whole; a failure to recognize the relations between the gover-
nors and the governed as an essential part of the democratic
process.*[10]

Although he approaches them from a somewhat different perspective, James Q. Wilson comes to similar conclusions—in describing the
"bureaucracy problem," which he divides into five parts:

*First, there is the problem of accountability or control – getting
the bureaucracy to serve agreed-on national goals. Second is
the problem of equity – getting bureaucrats to treat like cases
alike and on the basis of clear rules, known in advance. Third
is the problem of efficiency – maximizing output for a given
expenditure, or minimizing expenditures for a given output.
Fourth is the problem of responsiveness – inducing bureaucrats
to meet, with alacrity and compassion, those cases which can
never be brought under a single national rule and which, by
common human standards of justice or benevolence, seem to
require that an exception be made or a rule stretched. Fifth is
the problem of fiscal integrity – properly spending and accounting for public money.*[11]

Although the possible defects of bureaucracy specified by Robson
and Wilson may seem inclusive, they are not. Further "malevolent"
characteristics and consequences of bureaucracy could be easily gleaned
from the literature. The following seven, for example, are sometimes
also mentioned or implied:

1. Within bureaucracies, the reliance on rules, regulations, and
   canons of procedure extend so far that goals are displaced and
   means become ends.

2. Bureaucratic overstaffing to handle routine paperwork results in
   cumbersome records and files.

3. Bureaucratic inefficiency and delay prevail in handling both routine business and problems.

4. A protective bureaucratic environment fosters aloofness from public opinion and control.

---

[10]William A. Robson, *The Governors and the Governed* (Baton Rouge: Louisiana
State University Press, 1964), p. 18.

[11]Reprinted with permission of the author, James Q. Wilson, from *The Public Interest*, No. 6 (Winter 1967): 4-5. © 1967 by National Affairs, Inc.

5. There is unwillingness and difficulty in dismissing unproductive and incompetent employees of the bureaucracy.

6. A reluctance to render decisions and to stand accountable makes responsibility difficult to assign within the bureaucracy.

7. Bureaucratic overspecialization leads to narrowness and unresponsiveness.

Even when combined with Robson's and Wilson's, this list of bureaucracy's faults is not an exhaustive catalogue of complaints about bureaucracy. Every writer on the subject comes up with some additional bureaucratic faults—many of which, we might note, restate problems long recognized.[12]

Our purpose here is not to speculate about precisely how responsible or irresponsible bureaucracy really is. The situation would vary from agency to agency within various levels of government and from one part of the country to another; thus, any assessment of the degree of responsibility evidenced by American public bureaucracy would have to be very general in character. Rather than preparing a broad indictment (or an exoneration) of bureaucracy, we draw attention to these maladies and problems because they are potential dangers.

Regardless of how infrequently particular elements of bureaucratic malfeasance and nonfeasance occur, all of those mentioned above occur sometimes. When they do occur, what mechanisms can be brought into play to halt any further damage to the interests of citizens and perhaps even to repair the damage? We shall explore several such mechanisms, which we label *bureaucratic monitoring mechanisms*, but let us first indicate their theoretical place in our conception of the administrative process.

Figure 12-1 summarizes our approach. All official political actors, including the traditional three branches and bureaucracy, are put together in the box labeled *Government*; and all unofficial political actors, including those organized into groups, are put together in the box labeled *Citizens*. The relative positions of the boxes emphasize the great influence of the governors on the lives of the governed; for the same reason, we portray government's *outputs* on the left side of the diagram and citizen *inputs* on the right side, whereas it is conventional

---

[12]For example, Harold Laski opened his now classic article on "Bureaucracy" in the *Encyclopaedia of the Social Sciences* (Vol. 3 [New York: Macmillan, 1930], p. 70) with the following statement: "Bureaucracy is the term usually applied to a system of government the control of which is so completely in the hands of officials that their power jeopardizes the liberties of ordinary citizens. The characteristics of such a regime are a passion for routine in administration, the sacrifice of flexibility to rule, delay in the making of decisions and a refusal to embark upon experiment."

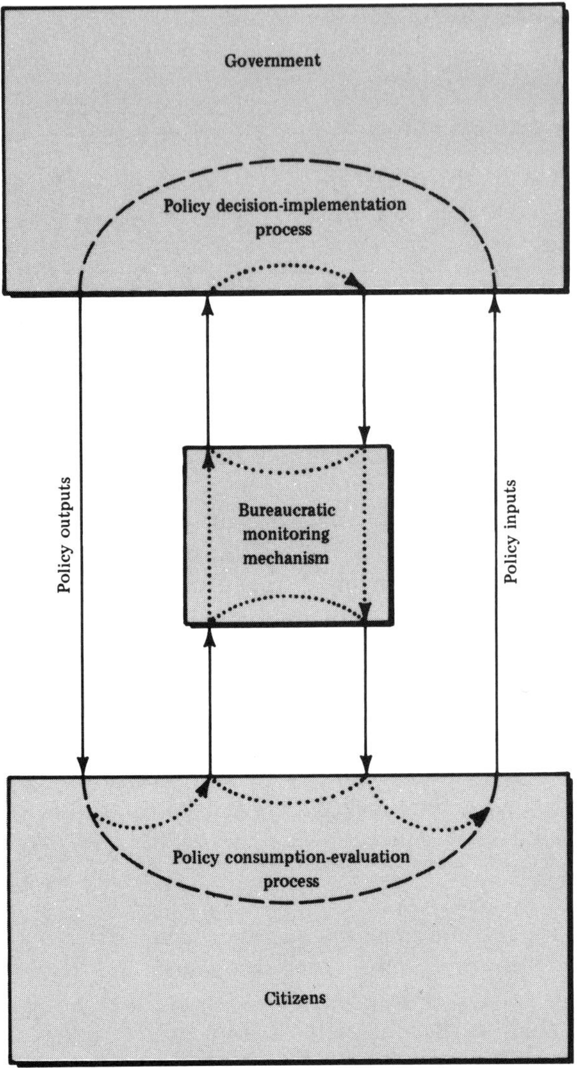

Figure 12–1. **Bureaucratic monitoring mechanisms in the administrative process**

to reverse the positions. Of course, as the preceding chapters indicate, we do not believe the agencies of government are dominant over citizens. Instead, the distribution of power relations varies from time to time and also among various policy sectors. Furthermore, the continuous relationships between those in the two boxes are reciprocal: through whatever processes, elements of government reach *policy* decisions, which are then *implemented* and become outputs; these outputs are consumed and *evaluated* by citizens individually and collectively, and reactions are formulated and become inputs for revising policies or initiating new ones.[13] Since relationships are reciprocal, any point at which the analyst enters the process is arbitrary; one may begin with either the output or the input.

In order to flesh out these abstractions, let us turn to an illustration from the field of social policy. After long deliberation, a federal agency inaugurates a new program providing housing subsidies for the elderly; the conditions governing eligibility are announced and applications are solicited. (Through the policy decision-implementation process, outputs are produced.) Those citizens affected by the program—individual beneficiaries, various organized groups representing retired people, and taxpayers who may not be personally interested—then receive the program's impact and assess it. (The consumption-evaluation process occurs.) Over time, as a result of their assessments and, perhaps, changing conditions, some citizens will press government for changes in the program, while others may endorse the status quo. (Inputs are created.) And a new phase of the policy decision-implementation process begins.

An important aspect of the interaction process between government and citizens is that these reciprocal political processes provide a means for holding bureaucracy accountable. If the National Association of Retired Persons or the Gray Panthers think the housing subsidy program is badly conceived or the regulations implementing it are improper, they can apply lobbying techniques to appropriate pressure points in government and take other actions to hold accountable those responsible for the program.

Thus far in the chapter, nearly all of the analysis has been at the *whole system level.* That is, we have taken the working of the overall political system as our point of reference, and those inputs from citizens that relate to general policy evaluations have been mentioned. For the most part, too, impact has been considered only for aggregates of citizens. In terms of figure 12-1, discussion has focused on the outer ring of indicated relationships. Now we shall change the focus and examine policy from the *citizen level,* the figure's inner ring of relationships. As general policies are implemented, they have an impact on particular individuals. For example, Mr. and Mrs. Brown, a retired couple who are already beneficiaries of another agency housing program, decide to apply for the new subsidy program. Some time after their application

---

[13]Herbert Jacob explores the consumption roles of citizens in *Debtors in Court: The Consumption of Government Services* (Chicago: Rand McNally, 1969), chapter 1.

has been accepted and they have been enrolled in the program, they are told that because of a quirk in the way their income is treated by the regulations, they will receive a lower benefit under the new program than under the old one; furthermore, since they have changed over, they will not be allowed to return to the old program. In terms of figure 12-1, their personal consumption experience has led them to the evaluation that they have been treated badly by the agency, and they want redress. They do not know—nor do they especially care—whether they have been dealt with precisely as they should have been according to the rules, whether a civil servant exercised a discretion, or whether a mistake was made in applying the rules; they know only that they want their grievance rectified.

What options are open to the Browns? Three courses seem possible: they could simply drop their grievance, after making suitably abusive comments about the ancestry of bureaucrats, etc.; they could appeal to the housing agency, hoping that those higher up in the chain of command would overrule the subordinates; or they could complain to a bureaucratic monitoring mechanism. If the Browns are not willing to give up without a fight and if they believe—possibly correctly—that the agency is likely to present a united front and support the original decision (or if their appeal has already been turned down), then they will consider taking their case to one or more monitors of bureaucracy.

We define bureaucratic monitoring mechanisms as those procedures, institutions, or agencies that play significant roles in controlling, regulating, or reviewing the actions of government bureaucracies. Some of the mechanisms are highly specialized as complaint handlers; others perform this function as one aspect of their general accountability role; and yet others are highly unspecialized.

However the monitor may be structured, when a complaint is received it is evaluated and processed (figure 12-1): perhaps further information will be requested from the complainant; perhaps an explanation of the law will satisfy the complainant; or perhaps an investigation, whose scope may depend on the mechanism's authority, will be undertaken into the accused agency's behavior. As the figure indicates, depending upon the results of the initial investigation, the monitoring mechanism may seek further information, or it may take appropriate action on the complaint and communicate the action to the complainant. Of course, for some of the less formally structured mechanisms, these steps might be identifiable in only the most rudimentary form.

In examining briefly the principal bureaucratic monitoring mechanisms, we shall differentiate between those that are unofficial and those that are official. The latter type will be further divided into those internal to the executive and those external to it.

Unofficial bureaucratic monitoring mechanisms

Public opinion

In democracies, public opinion is often described as a general watchdog over government. Thus, although public opinion can be called a mechanism only in a loose sense of the term, it can be said that public opinion is a bureaucratic monitor.[14] If it is a mechanism, public opinion is a crude one, however. Determining even the shape of public opinion on a given issue usually is extremely difficult, if not impossible. We have already mentioned (chapter 5) that elections are very inexact measures of public opinion as it might concern administrators, although the voting on California's Proposition 13 in June of 1978 has been widely interpreted as delivering a message both to elected and to bureaucratic officials. Public opinion polls might provide indicators of some of the public's policy preferences as measured in a certain way at a particular time, but the results usually allow for divergent interpretations, and results are not normally understood to mandate a given course of action. Furthermore, questions directly pertinent to administrative accountability are very seldom asked. Finally, public opinion and the mass media are intimately associated as bureaucratic monitors; it is often assumed that the media reflect public opinion or that the two are practically identical.

Public opinion cannot ordinarily be invoked to investigate an individual's allegation of bureaucratic malfeasance. In fact, upon close examination, it becomes very difficult to determine just how public opinion actually affects the actions of administrators in any particular instances; public opinion tends to develop slowly, whereas administrative action usually must be concluded quickly. Of course, in the long run public opinion affects administrators—who are, after all, members of the public, not a separate class—as they are socialized. Perhaps it is best to view public opinion as an information-generating device that only has impact when it operates through other monitoring mechanisms.

---

[14]Norman John Powell, for example, treats public opinion in this way in *Responsible Public Bureaucracy in the United States* (Boston: Allyn and Bacon, 1967), chapter 3.

The mass media

Both the printed and the electronic media of communication act as governmental watchdogs in various ways. Two important media successes in recent years were the publication of the Pentagon Papers, which had an impact on public images of the war in Vietnam, and the investigative reporting on the Watergate incident, which played a key role in toppling the Nixon administration. These experiences have helped to revitalize the status of the reporter in American society, and schools of journalism are overflowing. But both of these media successes were victories against the political overlords of bureaucracy; although the activities and the advice of professional military officers were revealed in the Pentagon Papers, direction and control came from elected politicians and their appointees.

As Spiro Agnew used to point out to government officials at Richard Nixon's behest, the media are not necessarily as formidable watchdogs as is often supposed. For instance, most reporting is superficial; journalists are often satisfied to rewrite or print official handouts verbatim; when an unfavorable story appears, a denial will virtually always be given "play" and usually accepted by most communications outlets; since fresh and splashy stories are preferred, in an embarrassing situation an agency can simply "stonewall," giving out no other information, and in a short while the media normally will move on to more newsworthy stories. Government agencies also employ large numbers of public relations officers who put the best face on unfortunate incidents, provide briefings for media personnel, and grind out tons of press releases.

Despite the strategic advantages government has over the mass media, the media can be effective mechanisms for enforcing administrative responsibility. As Nixon and Agnew found to their dismay, beyond a certain point, stonewalling may not work; through intensive digging and the cooperation of informants, the media may be able to penetrate the stoutest of defenses.[15] Thus, if a citizen is able to convince a journalist to pursue his grievance against bureaucracy, there is reason for

---

[15]Many representatives of the news media fear that the Supreme Court ruling in the *Stanford Daily* case (delivered on May 31, 1978)—which allows police to enter the offices of news organizations, after obtaining a search warrant, in search for evidence to be used in prosecutions—will weaken the role of the press as a monitor of government. Benjamin C. Bradlee, executive editor of the *Washington Post,* said that under the Stanford ruling the Pentagon Papers could not have been published, because "the police would have entered newspaper offices and seized them before newspapers could bring the facts to the people." Bradley said, "If this decision were in force during Watergate, it requires no stretch of the imagination to see police in these offices on a regular basis on a fishing expedition" (Associated Press, 1 June 1978).

hope. Some limitations of the media should be mentioned. Especially important is the tendency to focus on a single case, simplify it for mass presentation, and generalize from it. Thus, it is very common for the media to treat complex problems superficially and to depict bureaucracy in stereotypical terms (as slow, unresponsive, inefficient) without conducting any real analysis.

Because they do not want the agency or themselves to be publicly criticized, most administrators are much more sensitive to the mass media than they really would have to be if they worried only about the actual power of the media. Virtually all public agencies develop procedures for obtaining clippings of newspaper articles that concern them, and consideration is given to what action the agency should take, if any, in reaction to stories. Many agency leaders have a deep concern, which sometimes seems to border on the pathological, about avoiding a "bad press." This concern is sometimes well grounded, as it is not at all unusual for a series of unfavorable newspaper articles about, let us say, the police department to result in a city council's decision to fire the police chief and perhaps the city manager also. These considerations explain the seriousness with which agencies often take the usually rather minor administrative foul-ups revealed in the "Action Line" columns in many newspapers.[16] At the state and national levels, however, the administrative agencies are considerably more insulated from the direct impact of any particular newspaper, or TV or radio station or network, so agencies at these levels may not be as responsive to media criticisms as those at local levels.

Pressure groups

In chapter 5 we discussed the influence of pressure, or interest, groups of various types in the policy process. Pressure groups also play a role as monitors of government activity, enforcing administrative responsibility; since much of the discussion in chapter 5 is also appropriate here, we shall only treat the topic briefly.

From the citizen-level perspective, many members of some groups—especially of unions and veterans associations—traditionally turn to the group when they have a grievance against bureaucracy. Some groups simply refer the member to the proper grievance channel;

---

[16]A number of television and radio stations have developed "ombudsman" programs in recent years (one of the earliest and apparently most effective is that of station KABC in Los Angeles). Since administrators (along with businessmen, who are usually the objects of most complaints) are sometimes put on the spot and have to formulate an almost immediate verbal response, this kind of program can be a means of making at least a small contribution to administrative responsibility. The Canadian Broadcasting Corporation has an enormously popular national *Ombudsman Program* that airs weekly.

others intervene, on a more or less regular basis, on behalf of their members. Although this process has been hardly studied at all, impressionistic evidence suggests that these approaches can be quite successful, especially when the group and the agency have close relations on a variety of fronts, e.g., the Air Force Association and the Veterans Administration.

From the whole system perspective, whenever an agency initiates a plan that an organized group believes to be politically undesirable or morally wrong, the group is likely to take whatever appropriate actions are available, possibly including informal negotiation, congressional or presidential lobbying, appeals to the mass public, court suits, or organized demonstrations. Of course, agencies may or may not accede to the group's demands, but the knowledge that the groups are watching may keep some administrators on the straight and narrow path.

Assessing the motivation of pressure groups as bureaucratic monitors is difficult. By definition, pressure groups push a predetermined vision of the "truth," whether they are protecting the selfish interests of their members or promoting noble goals that would not benefit their individual members. Thus, the obvious tendency would seem to be for groups to interpret actions favorable to their cause as "responsible" and unfavorable actions as "irresponsible." If this is true, how can we assess those activities of groups which are allegedly designed to hold administrators responsible? Two main answers to this question have been given.

Some argue that the public interest can be defined in objective terms and a group's activities are responsible if they encourage administrative agencies to approximate this public interest. If we assert that a particular social policy (e.g. employing more women and minorities in the public service) is in the public interest, then those activities of a group which encourage administrators to implement such a policy are "responsible."

Others argue that the public interest cannot be determined in any substantive sense. According to this conception, all pressure groups—including those supposedly established to serve the public interest—really follow only their own interpretation of the general good, which is likely to differ from other groups' definitions. Among those who hold to this idea are the "pluralists," who believe that the public interest flows from the competition *among* groups; if a significant number of people are dissatisfied with the status quo, they will form a new group or convince an existing group to add their concern to its program. In this way, an ever-shifting balance of forces is created. It is important to note that the pluralists have a *procedural* rather than a *substantive* notion of administrative responsibility. For example, providing accessibility to the relevant administrators, so that all interested groups would have an opportunity to participate in decision making, is a goal likely to appeal to pluralists.[17]

Internal official bureaucratic monitoring mechanisms

However enterprising a newspaper may be and however hard a pressure group may attempt to right administrative wrongs suffered by its constituents, such unofficial monitors of bureaucracy face important difficulties. Especially noteworthy are their inability to gain access on a regular basis to agency files and documents, which restricts their intelligence capabilities; and their lack of official standing, which means they must convince some outside agency, such as a legislature, that action should be taken to recognize and correct the errors discovered. Official bureaucratic monitoring mechanisms are much less likely to suffer from either limitation. Let us begin by discussing some of the many official monitoring mechanisms that are internal to the executive. Although we recognize that chief executives (from the President of the United States to the mayor or city manager of the smallest town) have a role as bureaucratic monitoring mechanisms, we do not include a separate discussion here (see the treatment of "executive oversight" in chapter 3).

Complaints departments and quasi-ombudsmen

Virtually all agencies have at least rudimentary procedures for dealing with complaints from citizens.[18] In a small agency, complaints may be seen first by a responsible official and then passed on to subordinates for review; perhaps they will even be investigated by those who made the original decision, a procedure that hardly inspires confidence in the objectivity of the review. Larger agencies are more likely to have separate complaints departments. One characteristic of such departments is that they usually deal with complaints on an ad hoc basis and do not develop recommendations that reform the functioning of the

---

[17]Redford's work cited above is in the pluralist tradition.

[18]A survey sponsored by the Administrative Conference of the United States showed that the complaint processes of even many federal agencies were rudimentary indeed. See Victor G. Rosenblum, "Handling Citizen Initiated Complaints: An Introductory Study of Federal Agency Procedures and Practices," *Administrative Law Review* 26 (Winter 1974): 1-45.

Responsibility and future of American public administration/

larger organization. The Securities and Exchange Commission, however, has a Section of Complaints Processing that has won praise for its professional competence and for the extent to which the results of its investigations are applied to the commission's future operations.[19]

In recent years it has become fashionable to attempt to capitalize on the magic of the word *ombudsman,* and several agencies have created officers with this title; for instance, the Commerce Department has an Office of Ombudsman for Business. These complaints officials, which we call *quasi-ombudsmen,* because they lack the independence of true ombudsmen, may well be dedicated to holding administrators responsible for their treatment of citizens. But they are dependent on other executive officials for support; this is why they are often called *executive ombudsmen.* Some of the offices are subordinate to other agency officials; others are subordinate to governors, mayors, or city managers—officials whose purview is wider than the agency whose actions are under review. Quasi-ombudsmen of various types have become increasingly popular. Several states—including Illinois, North Carolina, South Carolina, New Jersey, Maine, New Mexico, Montana, and Oklahoma—have offices of this sort; so also do such cities as Houston, Texas; Columbus, Ohio; Raleigh, North Carolina; Chicago, Illinois; Portland, Oregon; and San Diego, California. Some of these offices have very large caseloads; (the City Services Coordinator for Omaha, Nebraska, receives more than 50,000 citizen contacts per year). It is apparent that, despite their limitations, these kinds of offices help to hold administrators accountable.[20]

Auditors and inspectors general

One of the purposes of auditing is the enforcement of accountability, and for modern auditors accountability means more than fiscal control. Many recent laws, regulations, and guidelines require that attention be paid to performance. A recent review of the literature on the subject concludes: "Hence, the auditor in some instances must review performance matters, because acceptable minimum standards of performance accountability are spelled out in the law."[21] Thus, agencies

---

[19]Ibid., p. 23.

[20]See Alan J. Wyner, ed., *Executive Ombudsmen in the United States* (Berkeley: University of California, Institute of Governmental Studies, 1973).

[21]Peter L. McMickle and Gene Elrod, *Auditing Public Education: Current Status and Future Potential* (Montgomery: The AIDE Staff, Alabama Department of Education, 1974), p. 41.

employ audit staffs that not only monitor the correctness of expenditures, but also develop standards of performance and conduct audits of programs to measure the extent to which the standards are being achieved. Sometimes audit staffs are closely linked components of the agency being investigated (the Army Audit Agency), and sometimes there may be some separation (the Defense Audit Agency may investigate the reports of the Army Audit Agency); but it is usual for the audit department to report to the ultimate head of the macroagency involved.

Also, some agencies have an *inspector general,* who may actually be the head of the audit department or who may handle the performance-based audits. Earlier in the chapter, mention was made of the discovery of several billion dollars of waste within the Department of Health, Education, and Welfare. That situation was revealed by the department's Office of Inspector General, and this can be viewed as an illustration of the contribution that such offices can make to administrative responsibility. The knowledge that a corps of trained investigators with access to all information will, on a more or less regular basis, go through the files and conduct audits of at least randomly selected administrative activities is likely to be an incentive to honesty and probity among individual civil servants and particular administrative units. Such internal monitoring systems have their limits, however; despite the existence of the inspector general, the scandal within HEW occurred. It is also likely that internal monitoring mechanisms normally are more useful in dealing with the minor infractions of an individual civil servant than with the important cases of administrative malfeasance or nonfeasance that concern the organization as a whole.

But the most important limitation of the inspector general as well as of other internal monitoring mechanisms is their lack of independence from the leaders of the agency whose actions they investigate. The agency's leaders exercise hierarchical authority over the monitors; in military jargon, "The commander fills out the IG's [inspector general's] report card." For this reason, it is unrealistic to expect an internal monitoring mechanism to be zealous in pursuing investigations that might seriously embarrass the organization and its leaders. Thus, when we hear of the report of the HEW scandal, the cynic in us expects that the report announcing it was cleared at the secretarial level—and probably higher—before it was released. The following questions also occur as we consider just why the report was released: Were the results of the investigation too hot to keep under cover? Was the report released in order to forestall a comprehensive congressional probe of the entire department? Was all this a ploy to create support for hiring more control personnel for the department? Possibly none of these questions was a factor in the release of the particular report; nevertheless, the dependent status of such offices causes the questions to be raised.[22]

External official bureaucratic monitoring mechanisms

Because several aspects of the roles of legislatures and courts in the accountability process have already been discussed in chapter 4, here we shall deal with only selected features of these two official bureaucratic monitoring mechanisms that are external to the executive, so as to avoid repetition. The final such mechanism we shall examine is the ombudsman.

Legislators

Newspaper reporters and academicians discussing Congress often decry the fact that its members spend so much time on constituents' casework—time, it is argued, that would be better spent on their "real" jobs, writing laws. Much of this criticism is unjust; providing citizens a complaint service, which can result in holding government accountable, is an important way in which legislators perform their representative function. We are critical of our national legislators, however, because so many of them view casework mainly as a way of insuring reelection rather than as a means of monitoring bureaucracy to insure its responsibility, while providing services to citizens.[23]

Congressional offices, which normally are staffed by sixteen to eighteen people, are well equipped to handle the large numbers of contacts from citizens and are very interested in doing so. In fact, it is generally agreed that the main function of most congressional staffs is the

---

[22]Such cynical questions are even more appropriate for some other kinds of internal monitors, most especially for the internal investigation units that handle complaints against most police departments. It is often alleged (sometimes clearly correctly) that the principal purpose of the units is to "whitewash" the police departments involved. Since the elimination of independent police review boards—due to the political power of police organizations—in New York City and Philadelphia during the late 1960s, one can take complaints against most cities' police officers only through internal channels; Berkeley, California is one of the few American cities that still has an independent police review board.

[23]Morris Fiorina, who reviews most of the scant literature on congressional casework, comes to a similar conclusion about the motivation for casework in *Congress: Keystone of the Washington Establishment* (New Haven: Yale University Press, 1977); see especially chapter 5.

processing of casework. What happens when citizens complain? And how well is the casework function performed? There is a great deal of variability in the process, which unfortunately has been studied to only a small degree, and we cannot answer the question with the completeness and assurance that it deserves.

Citizens who write or call congressional offices can normally expect some action on their problem. Incoming mail probably will be scanned by a staff person with considerable professional experience (perhaps by the administrative aide or office manager) and assigned to a caseworker for further action. The action taken will, of course, depend on whether the citizen seeks information, provision of a service, or resolution of a complaint. The action taken also may depend on the experience of the caseworker and the priorities of the congressman.

Describing the quality of staff work as "markedly uneven," Walter Gellhorn concludes: "In the main, however, the personal congressional staffs . . . know little about the matters that cause constituents to write . . . . The caseworkers in some offices do tend to become specialists . . . . But only a few of them appear genuinely knowledgeable about the laws and regulations that bear on their problems."[24] In the summertime, significant amounts of casework in many offices are done by college students acting as interns. Particularly at the beginning of their tenure, these staff members are not likely to know much about the vast federal bureaucracy.

If the caseworker is not very experienced or industrious and if the congressman has not placed a high priority on independent investigation, the constituent's letter is especially likely to be simply passed on to the agency that is the cause of the complaint after adding a "buck slip," a note asking for an investigation and report on the problem. Sometimes this is done automatically, and the following comment from an unusually candid congressman, interviewed by Walter Gellhorn, indicates the reason: "Many of the cases that reach my desk are unmeritorious, and I know it. But, undeserving or not, any request to my office is going to be passed along [to the agency]. It's a necessity for me as a matter of public relations."[25] Being able to quote agency responses or to pass on replies in writing—regardless of content—is hard evidence that the congressman has been working for the citizens—evidence that will be translated, it is hoped, into votes for reelection.

More and more casework is done in local offices in the constituency; about one-third of the personal staffs of congressmen are assigned to district offices, and about half of the members of Congress

---

[24]Walter Gellhorn, *When Americans Complain: Governmental Grievance Procedures* (Cambridge: Harvard University Press, 1966), pp. 82-83.
[25]Ibid., p. 69.

now have *multiple* district offices.[26] In many cases, a letter to the Washington office is rerouted to a district office, and a long-distance telephone caller is asked to contact the office in the constituency. These offices handle much of their casework through telephone calls to the local or regional offices of the administrative agency in question; the casework operation is directed, in more or less coordinated fashion, through the Washington office. From the point of view of administrative accountability, the significance of the emergence of district offices is that, to a small degree at least, the congressman's influence is brought down to federal bureaucrats located in towns and cities across the nation.

How do agencies react to "congressionals," the name given to approaches from the offices of congressmen? This depends on many factors, including the agency traditions, the inclinations of the agency personnel involved, the prestige and committee assignments of the congressmen, and his or her apparent personal interest in the matter. Congressionals are normally given high priority; usually subordinates must have a reply back to the responsible superior within a definite suspense period, such as forty-eight hours. Sometimes the congressional inquiry prompts a reevaluation of the original decision, which may result in a reversal on the merits; sometimes a decision is reversed (or a citizen's application is given priority, etc.) because the agency does not care one way or the other and a reversal would apparently be applauded by the congressman; and sometimes a decision is reversed because the agency fears the congressman, either because he is a powerful member who appears to have a personal interest in the case or because he sits on a committee that controls the agency's budget. But despite the usually quick responses and the occasional reversals of decisions, getting a congressional office to intervene is no guarantee of success.

The conventional estimate, which Gellhorn suspects is inflated, is that about 10 percent of the matters congressmen bring to administrators result in citizens being helped.[27] Often, giving the citizen what he or she wants would be impossible to justify legally or otherwise. In other cases, the agency assumes that so long as it is able to provide a plausible, written rationale for its original decision the congressional office

---

[26]Data compiled by Fiorina, *Congress,* p. 58.

[27]Gellhorn, *When Americans Complain,* p. 79. Not surprisingly, caseworkers have a higher opinion of their efficacy. John R. Johannes found that when 145 members of the House staff were asked, "What proportion of cases result in decisions favorable to the constituent?" the mean respondent thought the office's intervention was effective in nearly two-fifths of the cases (mean equals 37 percent). "Congressional Caseworkers: Attitudes, Orientations, and Operations" (Paper presented at the 1978 Annual Meeting of the Midwest Political Science Association, Chicago, Illinois, April 20-22, 1978), table XV.

Chapter twelve

will be satisfied. Indeed, owing to insufficient information and lack of time to devote to a particular case, the congressional office would seldom have a firm enough grasp of the situation to mount an attack on the agency's response even if it wished to do so.

It is difficult to sum up the contribution made by members of congress in holding administrators accountable.[28] Obviously the role is one of some consequence; if the casework function just described and the general oversight function discussed in chapter 4 were not performed at all or if they were performed much more indifferently than they are, administrators would be considerably less accountable than they now are. But our examination also has revealed enough inconsistencies and other problems with the functions so that we cannot conclude that legislators effectively keep administrators accountable.

Courts

As our treatment in chapter 4 indicated, the courts are involved in the administrative process in several ways, and it can be argued that many, if not all, of a court's administrative-related activities result in holding bureaucracy accountable to at least some extent. In the following discussion we examine the capabilities of the ordinary courts as mechanisms for rectifying the grievances of citizens against bureaucracy.

Administrative law is an exceedingly complex, ever-changing field, whose intricacies are difficult to suggest in a brief treatment. As a vehicle for discussion, let us imagine the following scenario, which is fictional but based on an actual Supreme Court case.[29] The welfare payments of Mary Doe, an unmarried and unemployed mother of four children living in New York City, have been stopped. Her caseworker, seeing what he interpreted as signs of newfound affluence in the apartment during a routine check, challenged her continued eligibility and recommended to his superior that her welfare payments be terminated. This official agreed and notified Ms. Doe that his decision could be

---

[28]The discussion has focused on our most visible legislators, the national Congress, particularly the House of Representatives. Members of state and local legislatures also play roles in helping to assure administrative responsibility for their jurisdictions. Because of the intimacy of local government, members of city and county councils usually are more involved with questions of administrative accountability than are members of state legislatures.

[29]*Goldberg* v. *Kelley,* Supreme Court of the United States, 1970, 397 U.S. 254. The scenario draws upon the discussion of Glen O. Robinson and Ernest Gellhorn of *Goldberg* and related cases *(The Administrative Process* [St. Paul, Minn.: West Publishing Company, 1974], pp. 721-31).

appealed to a higher agency official, but that appeal could only be made through written submissions; there would be no opportunity to present oral evidence, cross-examine witnesses, or be assisted by an attorney. Ms. Doe, who is functionally illiterate, felt that this procedure discriminated against her and feared that the caseworker was prejudiced against her. Nevertheless, she attempted to write out a defense; her appeal was rejected and her benefits terminated. Although a "postdetermination" formal hearing was available, which could result in the restoration of her benefits, Ms. Doe feels she has been wronged by these procedures and seeks redress through the courts. Thus, she files a suit against the welfare department in the federal district court. What are some factors the court will take into account in deciding how to react?[30]

1. In considering whether to review Ms. Doe's suit, the judge will inquire whether she has a "case" or "controversy" in which there is an immediate interest at risk. If the situation facing her were only hypothetical or if the agency only threatened to cut off her welfare payments—however harmful or even illegal the threatened action might be—the court probably would rule that there was no case or controversy. In the present situation a case exists, for her payments have been cut off.

2. The litigant's *standing* is another matter judges scrutinize in determining whether a real case exists. Does the person have a direct and personal interest in the matter protested? Courts have been quick to recognize economic interests, but they hold that the interest of a taxpayer in fiscal economy and responsibility is not sufficient to give standing to question an agency's action. In recent years, courts have expanded the standing doctrine somewhat, particularly to recognize the legitimate interests of consumers and of environmentalists under some circumstances. Since Ms. Doe is dependent upon her welfare payments to provide food, clothing, and shelter for her family, she clearly has standing. In fact, her attorney might well argue that the denial of benefits was causing her "irreparable harm," another catchphrase of the administrative lawyer's lexicon, which could add urgency to her suit.

3. Under the "presumption of reviewability" doctrine, courts assume they have the authority to review cases—whether or not there is express statutory provision for such review, but courts also normally refuse to intervene if some other course of action is available to the defendant or if the case is not "mature" enough to warrant review. Under the "primary jurisdiction" doctrine, it is assumed that the agency authorized to make decisions has exclusive original jurisdiction over

---

[30]The following discussion in points 1-4 relies heavily on Bernard Schwartz and H. W. R. Wade, *Legal Control of Government: Administrative Law in Britain and the United States* (Oxford: Clarendon Press, 1972), pp. 272-80; 286-91.

them. Thus, a court waits until an agency has had an opportunity to act; this was clearly the case in Ms. Doe's situation.

4. Another matter relating to the case's maturity is its *ripeness* for review. Courts want to avoid premature interventions in administrative matters. If an agency is still in the process of making a decision, or even in the preliminary stages of enforcing it, the court is likely to declare that the case is not ripe, because no real conclusion has been reached. Since the agency's action was concluded in Ms. Doe's case, the case was ripe.

5. Another question a judge would ask about a case's maturity is whether the litigant had used up all other available remedies before coming to the court. Normally judges apply the *exhaustion of remedies* doctrine very strictly and require that any existing administrative appeals processes be used before allowing access to the courts. It is common for agencies to have a hierarchy of appeals channels for many kinds of issues. The administrative ruling affecting Ms. Doe could be further appealed within the agency, but only *after* her welfare benefits had been terminated. It could be said that Ms. Doe had exhausted her remedies and final action had been taken on the question of whether to suspend her welfare payments—although they could be restored depending on the results of a final hearing.

6. Finally (although these points would not necessarily be looked at in a particular order), the judge would search for a point of law upon which a review would depend. Courts do not normally review cases in which the central dispute is about facts, and it is uncertain whether they will review cases in which mixtures of fact and law are disputed.[31]

In Ms. Doe's case, the issue was not the factual point of whether her income or assets really should have made her ineligible to continue receiving welfare. Instead, the issue was the following point of law: Did the agency's procedures violate the constitutional guarantees of due process of law, because an evidentiary hearing was not offered *before* the benefits were terminated?[32]

In the 1970 case of *Goldberg* v. *Kelley,* upon which our fictional Ms. Doe's case was based, the Supreme Court affirmed the ruling of the District Court for the Southern District of New York and said that such

---

[31]But the court may review the question of the *reasonableness* of the determination of the facts by the administrator. The "substantial evidence" rule is used in evaluating reasonableness, and the "clear error" test is used in reviewing lower-court decisions. See Robert S. Lorch, *Democratic Process and Administrative Law* (Detroit: Wayne State University Press, 1969), pp. 177-79.

[32]Until rather recently, courts might have disposed of the entire question by asserting that there was no constitutional "right" to welfare benefits, which had the legal status of "privileges." This traditional doctrine is explicitly rejected in *Shapiro* v. *Thompson,* 394 U.S. 618, 627 n. 6 (1969).

procedures did deny due process. Speaking for the Court, Mr. Justice Brennan said that because of the importance of welfare payments to clients "when welfare is discontinued, only a pre-termination evidentiary hearing provides the recipient with procedural due process." He had in mind a *fair hearing,* rather than a judicial or quasi-judicial trial.

Although "fairness" may sound like a vague term, it is one of the most important concepts in administrative law. Courts frequently speak of it as a quality whose presence or absence they can readily determine. Brennan summarizes the elements of a fair hearing as they are normally understood in the field of administrative law and as applied to the case under review: "These principles require that a recipient have timely and adequate notice detailing the reasons for a proposed termination and an effective opportunity to defend by confronting any adverse witnesses and by presenting his own arguments and evidence orally." Also, Brennan ruled, the welfare client should be allowed to be represented by counsel in such a hearing.

Thus, in this expanding area of social policy, the Supreme Court took up an individual's suit and rendered a judgment that had the effect of holding bureaucracy accountable by changing its procedures for dealing with citizens. This case indicates that the courts can be effective monitors of bureaucracy's actions; but it should be noted that for every success story, there are many more failures. Satisfying the technical requirements of ripeness, standing, and exhaustion, for example, can be very frustrating and highly complicated. Delays also are frequent when the courts are used; especially in the case of small businesses, dependent on a particular product or manufacturing process under bureaucratic attack, the time spent in fighting an adverse ruling through the courts can make an eventual victory a hollow one. Too, bringing suit can be very expensive, often beyond the financial resources of individual citizens and small businesses.

One of the principal frustrations of engaging in court action with a government agency is that the agency may have superior information at its command; this situation has been eased somewhat by the 1974 reform of the *Freedom of Information Act,* which makes available to citizens, sometimes only after court suit, many of government's innermost secrets. Lawyers have learned that making a voluminous freedom of information request of an agency can be a useful strategic device, for it ties up important files and personnel. The Freedom of Information Act has become an important aspect of the administrative law process, and the act has become in its own right a significant bureaucratic monitoring mechanism that can be activated by any citizen. In 1977, more than 150,000 requests were made for information, and executive departments estimated they spent at least $16 million in trying to meet the demand.[33]

Ombudsmen

The final bureaucratic monitoring mechanism we shall examine is the ombudsman, originally a Scandinavian office. Although the office is more than 150 years old, it recently has spread throughout much of Europe and to a number of other countries. All of the populous Canadian provinces have ombudsmen, and the government plans to create a national official soon. In the United States, ombudsmen exist in Hawaii, Nebraska, Iowa, and Alaska. In addition, the following localities have ombudsmen: Jamestown, New York; Dayton, Ohio; Seattle-King County, Washington; Wichita, Kansas; Kansas City-Jackson County, Missouri; Anchorage, Alaska; Detroit, Michigan; Lexington-Fayette County, Kentucky; Berkeley, California; and Flint, Michigan.[34] The number of proposals, many of which seem close to success, to create more American ombudsmen at all levels is very large.

What accounts for the institution's popularity? The "bandwagon" effect probably is a factor, but the principal explanation is that many people have become convinced that ombudsmen, who specialize in citizen complaints, are effective monitors of bureaucracy.

In exploring how ombudsmen monitor bureaucracy, let us begin by looking at the institution's purposes and characteristics. The ombudsman's mission is

> *to generate complaints against government administration, to use its extensive powers of investigation in performing a post-decision administrative audit, to form judgments which criticize or vindicate administrators, and to report publicly its findings and recommendations but not to change administrative decisions.*[35]

Earlier in this section, we mentioned that true ombudsmen could be distinguished from quasi-ombudsmen on the basis of the former's independence from other bureaucrats and the political executive. In addition

---

[33]See "Opening Federal Files," *Newsweek,* 19 June 1978, pp. 85-86.

[34]Furthermore, the following states have specialized prison ombudsmen: Minnesota, Connecticut, Kansas, Michigan, and Oregon.

[35]Larry B. Hill, "Institutionalization, the Ombudsman, and Bureaucracy," *American Political Science Review* 68 (September 1974): 1077.

Responsibility and future of American public administration

/445

to being independent, ombudsmen are legally established, functionally autonomous, external to the administration, specialist, expert, nonpartisan, unbiased, client centered but not anti-administration, and both popularly accessible and visible.[36]

The ombudsman shares many of these purposes and characteristics with some other monitoring mechanisms, but the way in which they are combined makes the ombudsman unique. For example, legislators are independent, popularly accessible, and client centered; but they cannot investigate bureaucracy by examining its files, and they may be partisan and biased. So also, courts are independent, expert, nonpartisan, and unbiased; but they are not client centered or popularly accessible, nor do they have investigatory powers. On the other hand, unlike legislators and courts, ombudsmen cannot change laws or deliver summary judgments to enforce their recommendations.

Above all else, ombudsmen can be called "impartial investigators": when fourteen American ombudsmen were asked to choose their principal role model from a list, twelve chose this one. By comparison, only six of sixteen quasi-ombudsmen surveyed chose "impartial investigator." Instead, half of the quasi-ombudsmen chose "enabler-facilitator" as their principal role model; only one true ombudsman made this his choice.[37] That so many quasi-ombudsmen should think of themselves as mainly enablers and facilitators comes as no surprise; their official literature often talks of bringing citizens and government together and of cutting red tape. The results of another question reinforce this difference between the two types of offices. When asked about the relationship in their caseload between requests for government services or information and requests to investigate grievances against bureaucracy, only four ombudsmen said their citizen contacts were mainly requests for services or information, but nine quasi-ombudsmen thought their citizen contacts were mainly of that character.[38]

As they investigate grievances impartially, ombudsmen interact with three groups of constituents: complainants, bureaucrats, and politi-

---

[36]Ibid.

[37]Larry B. Hill, "The Citizen Participation-Representation Roles of American Classical and Quasi-Ombudsmen" (Paper presented at the 1977 annual meeting of the American Political Science Association, Washington, D.C., September 1-4, 1977), table 10. The remaining ombudsman and one of the remaining quasi-ombudsmen chose "broker-negotiator"; the final quasi-ombudsman selected "arbitrator" as his principal role model.

[38]Ibid., table 6.

Chapter twelve

446

cians. Let us briefly examine the nature of the ombudsman's relations with each group.[39]

First, American ombudsmen receive an average of about 2,500 complaints per year, mainly through telephone calls. The Office of Economic Opportunity provided financial aid for the new offices in Seattle-King County, Washington; Nebraska; and Iowa in the late 1960s in the hope that the ombudsman would become an access point to the system for society's unfortunates. Although there are no comprehensive studies of the class origins of the clienteles, these hopes apparently were largely fulfilled. When questioned, all but two of the U.S. ombudsmen reported that their clients were either mainly poor or evenly distributed between the affluent and the poor. Ombudsmen help clients in many ways. They explain seemingly incomprehensible bureaucratic rulings, provide information or referrals, or merely lend a sympathetic ear. Sometimes their investigation results in decisions being changed in the citizen's favor. Just how often American ombudsmen materially help citizens is uncertain, but in a carefully controlled study of the New Zealand office it was found that 13 percent of the complainants received some direct, measurable improvement in their circumstances through the ombudsman's intervention. American ombudsmen probably have a similar success rate. Although the 13 percent figure may not seem high, we suspect that if a truly comparative study could be constructed for other monitoring mechanisms the ombudsman's success rate would compare most favorably with that of other mechanisms.

Second, the ombudsmen's investigations are predominantly targeted against the leaders of those agencies that most frequently touch the lives of citizens—either by providing services or exercising restraints. The ombudsman investigates complaints against most agencies frequently enough to keep them aware of his presence, but interaction with the agency (no other political actors are normally involved in an investigation) is not very extensive for a typical case. From the point of view of the agency, most investigations are not highly threatening: frequently the discretion to decide a case otherwise was not available; in the vast majority of investigations only the resolution of a single case is at issue; and most investigations concern the activities of subordinates rather than the agency's leaders. Ombudsmen usually proceed cautiously against agencies, giving them a full opportunity to explain the action complained of without assuming their guilt in advance; at the

---

[39]The following analysis draws from the works cited above in notes 35 and 37 and also from Larry B. Hill, *The Model Ombudsman: Institutionalizing New Zealand's Democratic Experiment* (Princeton, N.J.: Princeton University Press, 1976).

same time, investigations are as full as necessary, and the files are frequently inspected. Because ombudsmen cannot change decisions (they can only rely on a formal recommendation, backed by the threat of publicity), their negotiating skills and powers of persuasion are crucial.[40] In a behavioral sense, agency-ombudsman relations are normally good: agencies are quick to respond to the ombudsman, almost never challenge his jurisdiction, and readily rectify errors. Studies done thus far indicate that civil servants generally have favorable orientations toward the ombudsman's effectiveness. Alan J. Wyner found that 71 percent of responding Nebraska bureaucrats credited the ombudsman with encouraging either "some" or "significant" improvement in administrative agencies.[41] The improvements resulting from investigations rarely affect the operations of agencies in highly important respects, but over time the policy impacts resulting from ombudsmen's investigations can amount to a significant body of administrative reform. In Hawaii, for example, during seven years the ombudsman has been responsible for at least 181 procedural or substantive reforms of the administrative process.[42]

Third, unlike quasi-ombudsmen, ombudsmen do not owe allegiance to such politicians as governors or mayors. Furthermore, although they are ultimately answerable to the legislature and report to it at least annually, ombudsmen have the status of independent officers of the legislature, which does not ordinarily become involved in the handling of the office's cases. Nonetheless, ombudsmen are dependent on politicians in several respects, and a failure to cultivate political constituents

---

[40]In general, ombudsmen appear to have suffered less from the obvious threat of co-optation than some other rather similar organizations. If this is true (and there is little investigation of the matter), the explanation may be that—unlike the regulatory agencies, for example—ombudsmen ordinarily come into contact with administrators only in an adversary relationship while investigating a complaint; there is, thus, little opportunity to build the close sympathetic relations that can result when organizations work cooperatively to administer a sector of policy (e.g., the FAA and the airline industry).

[41]Alan J. Wyner, "Political and Administrative Constituencies," in *American Ombudsmen,* ed. Larry B. Hill, forthcoming; computed from data in table 2. Similarly, in the Canadian province of Alberta, which has had an ombudsman since 1967, Karl A. Friedmann found that 85 percent of the bureaucrats responding to the question approved of the ombudsman idea and that only 4 percent had a negative "general impression of the Ombudsman's performance." See "Controlling Bureaucracy: Attitudes in the Alberta Public Service towards the Ombudsman," *Canadian Public Administration* 19 (Spring 1976): tables 10 and 12.

[42]Larry B. Hill and Patton N. Morrison, "Administrative Reform," in Hill, ed., *American Ombudsmen.* The most frequent reforms concerned the following kinds of agencies: police, prison, employment, licensing, health, and welfare.

Chapter twelve

448

could be costly.[43] It is widely accepted that the principal factor inhibiting the faster adoption of the office, especially in the United States, is the fear of legislators that the ombudsman might siphon off casework, which is viewed as electorally invaluable. The fear that the ombudsman might usurp this traditional role is understandable, but the evidence from other countries is that this does not happen; informal discussions with legislators in several U.S. jurisdictions that have ombudsmen support a similar conclusion. In fact, most legislators are highly supportive of the ombudsman. When asked their "general impression of the Ombudsman's office," 88 percent of the Nebraska legislators surveyed by Alan J. Wyner replied "very favorable." Ninety-seven percent of them rated the quality of service provided when the legislator referred complaints to the ombudsman office as "very good."[44] In some cases, relations between ombudsmen and local councils appear to have been somewhat more strained, however, than those between ombudsmen and state legislatures.

While the ombudsman institution has a number of attractive structural features as a monitoring mechanism and most American ombudsmen appear to be generally successful, this should not be taken to mean that the office is a panacea for all of bureaucracy's ills. Problems in the ombudsman's relationship with each of the three constituencies just discussed can be identified. For instance, the Nebraska ombudsman keeps a low profile, so that few complaints are generated; the reports of the Detroit ombudsman do not give evidence that he achieves very much bureaucratic change; and the relations between the Seattle-King County ombudsman and his political constituents are sometimes acrimonious (perhaps because he has a divided responsibility to both the city and the county councils). As is true of every other bureaucratic monitoring mechanism, the success of the ombudsman is contingent upon not only the structural configuration of the office, but also upon the professional competence and political skills of those who serve in the office and the political environment in which it exists. After as much as a decade of experience with several ombudsmen, (the Hawaiian office was created in 1969), at least it can be said that the question of the office's success in the United States is now a matter for empirical investigation rather than for speculation.

---

[43]Patricia Hoban-Moore and Charles Moore report that largely because of the incumbent's political ineptitude, the Atlanta, Georgia, ombudsman was killed by eliminating its appropriation, even though the office's statute remained in effect. "A Death in Atlanta," in Hill, ed., *American Ombudsmen.*

[44]Wyner, "Political and Administrative Constituencies," table 1.

Whether there will ever be a national ombudsman (or ombudsman system) and whether such an office could work remains highly speculative. For many years, Congressman Henry S. Reuss has proposed that an Administrative Counsel of the Congress be appointed who would have many of the ombudsman's characteristics but who could investigate only those complaints referred to it by members of Congress.[45] (Such systems have been in operation in Britain and France for some years now under the names of Parliamentary Commissioner for Administration and *Médiateur.*) Because of the large population and geographic extent of the United States, creating a national ombudsman office in the classical sense obviously is a project that would face important organizational problems, but they probably are not insurmountable; perhaps ombudsmen could be appointed for various policy sectors or regions or some combination of the two.

The political problems of creating national ombudsmen are probably more important than the structural ones. In recent years the funding for congressional offices has increased enormously so that they may hire up to eighteen staff members and are given a payroll of up to nearly a quarter of a million dollars.[46] The principal justification for this funding is that it is necessary in order for congressmen to perform their "ombudsman" function, and if true national ombudsmen existed, it would be somewhat more difficult to justify this large expenditure (and any increases). Even though this might seem a slight threat, it may be regarded as a highly ominous one by congressmen, because the large staffs constantly work for the members' reelection and give them a tremendous advantage over any opponents. Nonetheless, interest in the ombudsman and related concepts continues to grow at the national level. For example, in 1978 the Carter administration approved an experimental federal complaint-handling program operated through the Federal Information Centers in the state of Florida.

In conclusion: when Americans complain, they have access to a wide variety of bureaucratic monitoring mechanisms. Each possesses certain advantages and disadvantages that may make it more or less attractive for a particular situation, but there is no one, ideal monitoring mechanism. We cannot even conclude that because of their independence, official external mechanisms are necessarily superior to other types. In some situations, appealing to such unofficial mechanisms as newspapers or professional associations could be more effective than appealing to legislators, courts, or ombudsmen. Can we conclude from

---

[45]See Henry S. Reuss and Stanley V. Anderson, "The Ombudsman: Tribune of the People," *Annals of the American Academy of Political and Social Science* 363 (January 1966): 44-51.

[46]Fiorina, *Congress,* p. 57.

Chapter twelve

450

this survey of American monitoring mechanisms that, even though each
has some faults, in combination they constitute a comprehensive system
upon which citizens can rely for protection from bureaucratic excess?
Sad to say, no. In many situations, a citizen with a justifiable complaint
might have recourse to several of these mechanisms without getting a
fundamental review of his or her problem.

Fortunately, as awareness of the growth of government bureaucracy has expanded in recent years, interest in the general concept of
administrative responsibility—at both the whole system level and the
citizen level—as well as in particular mechanisms for enforcing it also
has expanded. Fortunately, too, the "inner check" usually operates, so
that our civil servants usually are more "civil" to us than they are
required to be. And the inner check and the external ones are mutually
reinforcing.

B.   Public administration's future

Earlier chapters have suggested possible future developments:
more extensive unionization is likely, as are further efforts to reform
the budget process; organizational development programs will continue,
as will administrators' contacts with a widening variety of interest
groups.

Here we want to step back and look at some significant long-term
trends in public administration from a different perspective. Our predictions are necessarily speculative; no one knows what the future holds
for American public administration. Time will prove us right or wrong,
and should we be asked five years from now to comment on our predictions, we would be surprised if some modifications were not
necessary.

The slowing of bureaucratic growth

Most of the forces described in chapter 1 that have encouraged
expansion of the public sector are still with us, although one important
force has changed slightly: population growth has slowed. This is
largely offset, though, by continuing increases in the technological complexity of American life and continuing concentration of Americans in
urban areas, especially in suburbs. Furthermore, America's role in the
world remains large, although the reemergence of Western Europe
makes us less dominant in the non-Communist world; developing
nations, too, are assuming greater responsibility in world affairs.

"Think of it! Presidents come and go, but WE go on forever!"
© 1976 by NEA, Inc.

Americans probably will continue to be suspicious of government bureaucracy, but, at the same time, they are likely to continue to demand that government solve the most difficult problems, from natural resource shortages to urban decay. Much will be heard about the need to increase self-reliance and to depend more on the private sector, but doing so will prove difficult. To overcome this difficulty, some propose (and California recently adopted) rigid limits on government's taxing ability. Adoption of such limits decrees, in effect, a slowing of bureaucratic growth but leaves unresolved the question of just what services or programs will be curtailed.

Because most of the developments that led to governmental expansion continue, we expect the expansion to continue. But with alterations in some of these forces and some shifting of public attitudes, it seems likely that expansion will occur at a slower rate than in the recent past.

Bureaucracy under attack

Recent elections have demonstrated the popularity of criticism leveled against "big government." Such rhetoric probably will continue, and we shall see additional serious attempts to alter the ways government agencies are organized and function. Already there have been efforts by federal agencies to decentralize, to assign greater responsibility to regional offices. The hope is that these offices can cope with problems, especially those concerning state and local officials, better than can administrators in far-off Washington. In 1969, *Federal Regional Councils* were created to coordinate the activities of federal agencies on a regional basis.[47] While the councils did not assume major decision-making authority, they were one step toward greater decentralization.

Even more complicated reforms of bureaucracy may be attempted. The most likely are attempts to reduce the hierarchical nature of agencies. In carrying out the space program, NASA used innovative organizational arrangements. Basically, these involved having administrators work alongside technical personnel, providing administrative support rather than serving as superiors. This scheme has been referred to as a *matrix organization* in contrast to a *hierarchical* organization. With this organizational form, NASA made considerable use of the "project team" approach. Small groups were assigned responsibilities and given considerable discretion in deciding how to accomplish their tasks. The notion that coordination requires a rigid hierarchy, with communication flowing only vertically, was clearly disproved. We will probably see more such efforts.

Further attempts to simplify bureaucratic arrangements will be made by developing *self-executing programs*. The most frequently cited example of such a program is the *negative income tax,* which has been discussed as a replacement for the present public welfare system. The program would eliminate many of the complicated eligibility criteria presently used to qualify families for welfare assistance. Instead of having an array of government employees examining the needs and resources of clients, aid would automatically be made available to those with low incomes reported on income tax returns. The eligibility criteria would be simplified and the welfare bureaucracy reduced.

Using *revenue sharing* instead of complicated grant-in-aid programs is another application of the self-executing formula. As originally proposed by President Nixon, shared revenues were to be distributed to

---

[47]Melvin B. Mogulof, "Federal Interagency Action and Inaction: The Regional Council Experience," *Public Administration Review* 32 (May/June 1972): 232-40.

states and localities in lieu of money made available through grants. Although few grant programs were eliminated, the availability of automatically distributed shared revenues has decreased the pressure for additional grants and probably will continue to do so.

Another likely development is an effort to institutionalize change. Agencies will be encouraged to systematically reexamine their programs and activities in order to modify them to meet emerging demands and needs. So called "sunset" legislation has been adopted in several states. These laws provide that on set dates particular programs or agencies will cease to exist unless the legislature specifically continues them. Zero-base budgeting is aimed at the same target—assuring that programs are not perpetuated beyond their usefulness—and it, too, attempts to institutionalize change. Furthermore, some states have made reorganization easier by permitting the governor to shift responsibilities from agency to agency—subject only to legislative veto.

During the next decade there will be still more efforts to respond to attacks on bureaucracy. Attacks from the political right insist that government bureaucracies usurp responsibilities that should remain in the private sphere; those from the left complain that agencies fail to respond to the real needs of the nation and dehumanize both their employees and citizens at large. The challenge to administrators will be to continue providing their programs and services while, at the same time, making modifications that respond to developing needs.

A closer interface of the private and the public sectors

In 1970 Congress eliminated the United States Post Office Department and replaced it with the U.S. Postal Service. The nation hoped that better (and cheaper) mail handling would result from making a *public* organization into an independent *quasi-private* one. Conversely, in the same year Congress determined that, rather than allowing rail passenger transportation to vanish from the American scene, responsibility for this service should be assumed by a National Railroad Passenger Corporation, AMTRAK. The nation hoped that better transportation would result from making *private* rail operations into *quasi-public* ones.

However one may evaluate the success or failure of these large-scale ventures, there are many other examples of the blending of the private and public spheres. Private firms have become quite conscious of their public responsibilities, thanks in large part to the prodding and threats of such public-sector organizations as the Equal Employment

Opportunity Commission, the Occupational Safety and Health Administration, and the Environmental Protection Agency. Corporations actively recruit women and minorities, for example, and make large investments in equipment to reduce noise levels within the workplace and to eliminate pollution, especially of air and water. Similarly, at the insistence of those who believe that the public sector should model itself on the private sector, public agencies have grown more concerned about their own productivity and their "return" on dollars invested.

This convergence of the private and public sectors, which can be traced at least as far back as the creation of the Interstate Commerce Commission in 1887, is increasing rapidly. Administrators who are skilled at working at the points of intersection between the two sectors will have an advantage in the future. It is likely that the movement of administrators between the public and private sectors will increase as the differences between the two become less extreme.

International administration

We are witnessing an explosion of international contacts in both the private and public spheres, an explosion that creates a strong demand for administrators capable of filling positions under authority of international organizations. These range from such multipurpose organizations as the United Nations and the European Economic Community to special purpose structures operating in education, health, agriculture, and other fields.

Working in organizations of these types can be at once exhilarating and frustrating.[48] The opportunity to contribute to a project that will have substantive impact on the lives of people (building a vocational-technical school, planning a sanitation system, training farmers to increase crop yields) can be highly rewarding. But frustrations also may arise from many sources: apart from overcoming linguistic barriers and making adaptations to what may be a radically different cultural context, the international administrator may be exasperated by such problems as red tape emanating from the host country's government, by the apparent indolence of his native workers (who may not have internalized the "protestant work ethic"), and by fundamental ideological disagreements with key political forces. Coping with these problems (as well as others, including geographical isolation and uncertainties about career development) can be upsetting, but opportunities for travel and

---

[48]Thomas George Weise, *International Bureaucracy* (Lexington, Mass.: Lexington Books, 1975).

for widely varied experiences may compensate. One thing is certain: the interdependence of the world will increase, and the future will see further expansion of employment opportunities in international administration.

The continuing professionalization of public administration

Both the federal Civil Service Commission and state and local merit system agencies have recognized the need for highly skilled employees. These bodies actively recruit engineers, accountants, physicians, lawyers, and a wide variety of others who have the education or training required. As is true in society generally, specialization is an important feature of public service, and we expect that the trend toward specialization will become even more pronounced in the future, especially as our dependence on new technologies continues. Assuming that public agencies will be increasingly staffed by technical specialists, who will manage, lead, and even control these people? There seem to be two possibilities: either managers could be drawn from the ranks of the experts; or managers could be drawn from those trained as general administrators. Both options are, in fact, exercised.

First, in administrative agencies today, it is not at all uncommon for personnel who have developed particular skills to find themselves thrust into general administrative roles. For example, after fifteen years' work in his field, an engineer might find himself no longer *doing* engineering work. Instead, he becomes a *manager* of others who perform the engineering tasks. What is this individual now—a professional engineer or a professional administrator? If we examine his formal education and background, he is clearly an engineer, but if we look at the content of his job, he is a general administrator. How well do competent technicians perform as managers? Some do an excellent job; others fail because the skills required of an administrator simply are not the same skills that were part of the expert's technical training. In recognition of the problems, an important trend today is the encouragement given to specialist-trained managers to seek out generalist training in the skills of administration. In chapter 7 we mentioned the scheduling flexibility available in some programs in higher education. In the future, it is probable that even larger numbers of specialist-trained public administrators will take advantage of such opportunities to develop themselves further as professional administrators.

Second, the option of putting capable generalists in charge of specialists is often followed. Until quite recently, this has been the preferred choice of British writers, who often have contended: "The expert should be on tap, not on top." Apart from the possible inefficiencies and

other managerial problems to which specialist-trained public administrators might fall prey, many theorists feel that for political reasons,
people with such backgrounds ought not to be put in important policy-
making positions within public agencies. Asserting that specialists are
narrowly trained and often do not have a broad view of the public implications of decisions that they may make on technical grounds, these
theorists contend that specialists, who may identify more closely with
the norms of their profession than with the goals of their employing
organization, need to be watched and controlled by outsiders. In this
view, the proper role of the specialist is to provide information and
alternative courses of action for the decision maker. Historically, in the
United States there has been an inclination to prefer that people with
specialist backgrounds be in charge of specialists. There appears to be,
however, a growing willingness among public agencies to employ
generalists.

Although some civil servants have backgrounds in the humanities,
American public agencies have not followed the British tradition of
actually preferring people with degrees in classical languages and history. Instead, to an increasing extent, the generalists recruited as civil
servants have professional training and degrees in the field of public
administration. To stimulate this trend, standards have been developed
by the National Association of Schools of Public Affairs and Administration (NASPAA) to serve as guidelines encouraging greater uniformity
among college and university programs in public administration. A feature common to most professions is a widely recognized core educational
experience, shared by members of the profession. The courses taken by
physicians, accountants, or engineers are fairly standard, regardless of
the school attended. The NASPAA guidelines, while not requiring particular courses, encourage exposure to such a core of material.

In taking this step and later ones leading toward evaluation of
public administration programs, NASPAA is providing a more precise
definition of public administration as a profession. In a Matrix of Professional Competencies, NASPAA suggested that each masters degree program should include the following components:

1. political, social and economic context of administration,

2. quantitative and nonquantitative analytical tools,

3. individual, group, and organizational dynamics,

4. policy analysis, and

5. administrative/management processes.[49]

---

[49]National Association of Schools of Public Affairs and Administration, *Guidelines
and Standards for Professional Masters Degree Programs in Public Affairs/Public
Administration* (Washington, D.C.: National Association of Schools of Public Affairs
and Administration, 1974), p. 7.

Responsibility and future of American public administration/

457

The public administrator should acquire knowledge and develop skills in each of these areas, as well as develop public interest values with regard to each. Finally, the program should equip the budding administrator to participate in the processes represented by these areas.

Thus, whether managers of the future are substantive specialists who have been given generalist training in administration or whether their specialized training is in the process of administration itself, it does appear that the smaller number of positions becoming available in the future are increasingly likely to be filled by those who have undergone formal training in the administrative process.

The future and administrators' democratic values

Throughout this book, the values held by administrators and other political actors have been examined. This critical aspect of administrative life has been explored as questions were raised about the role of interest groups and legislators in public administration, about the goal of efficiency (so often proclaimed as being supremely important), and about administrators' internalization of values thought to be basic to the functioning of a democratic system.

But what of the future? Are there developments that provoke or necessitate changes in the values administrators hold? In earlier times, when administration and politics were treated as inherently separate phenomena, there was a suppression of concern for democratic values. It was thought to be sufficient for administrators to pursue efficiently the goals set by others. But this book has established that administrators do more than this, and they must be concerned about values other than efficiency.

In the early 1970s the New Public Administration movement was an attempt to get administrators to recognize other values. Specifically, they were urged to show greater concern for social equity, to be more concerned with the results of their programs—who benefits and how—and less concerned with the mechanics of operating programs.[50] This

---

[50]See Frank Marini, ed., *Toward a New Public Administration: The Minnowbrook Perspective* (Scranton, Penn.: Chandler, 1971). From the intraorganizational perspective, the New Public Administration movement also strongly endorsed steps to make public agencies more humane places in which to work: increasing the scope of participation in decision making, reducing reliance on hierarchically based authority, and bringing more women and minorities into the organization (and giving them well-paid and responsible positions)—all were seen as ways of encouraging democracy and equity in public administration.

challenge emerged from the political ferment of the 1960s, the struggles of racial and ethnic groups and the controversy surrounding the war in Vietnam. For a time it seemed that the results would be a dramatic shift in the way administrators viewed themselves. Without doubt, some change has occurred—for example, most agencies are much more concerned with establishing good relations with their clients than they were only a few years ago—but striving for efficiency has not been abandoned, nor has the goal of social equity come to center stage. Nonetheless, administrators today—and those who teach public administration—are more sensitive to value alternatives. The Watergate affair and related events made clear to all Americans that the values held by our political leaders are crucial. The values of administrators should be given the same concern.

Emerging technologies available to today's and tomorrow's public administrators give rise to new value questions. Vast amounts of data can now be collected on every citizen, and increasingly sophisticated retrieval systems permit the recall and analysis of those data. While such mechanisms can be highly beneficial when used to determine needs for public programs and to design those programs, it is also apparent that they can be misused to invade the privacy and limit the liberties of citizens. While the various bureaucratic monitoring mechanisms will help prevent such developments, Americans will be dependent, as well, upon administrators' own predispositions not to misuse information technology.

Another development of recent years has been the emergence of truly worldwide mass communications. Agencies can use these facilities to make the public aware of programs available, but they can also be misused for propagandistic purposes, or through mismanagement they can create misunderstanding.

Finally, administrators of today are struggling to decide whether to centralize or decentralize operations. Arguments center on emphasizing efficiency through centralization or emphasizing citizen participation through decentralization. Once again, just what path future developments take will depend upon values administrators hold.

In looking to the future, many other actual or potential developments could be mentioned. These few are sufficient, though, to emphasize the importance of administrators' values. To summarize what has been said here and elsewhere, public administrators must emphasize the word *public*. They will continue to have responsibilities that reach beyond their particular programs or agencies, responsibilities to the democratic political system and, more fundamentally, to the citizens who make up that system.

Suggested readings for chapter twelve

Anderson, Stanley V., ed. *Ombudsmen for American Government?* Englewood Cliffs, N.J.: Prentice-Hall, 1968.

Etzioni, Amitai. "Alternative Conceptions of Accountability." *Public Administration Review* 35 (May/June 1975): 279–86.

Finer, Herman. "Administrative Responsibility in Democratic Government." *Public Administration Review* 1 (Summer 1941): 335.

Fiorina, Morris. *Congress: Keystone of the Washington Establishment.* New Haven: Yale University Press, 1977.

Friedmann, Karl A. "Controlling Bureaucracy: Attitudes in the Alberta Public Service towards the Ombudsman." *Canadian Public Administration* 19 (Spring 1976): 51–87.

Friedrich, C. J. "Public Policy and the Nature of Administrative Responsibility." In *Public Policy: A Yearbook of the Graduate School of Public Administration, Harvard University, 1940.* Edited by C. J. Friedrich and Edward S. Mason. Cambridge, Mass.: Harvard University Press, 1940.

Gaus, John M. "The Responsibility of Public Administration." In *The Frontiers of Public Administration.* Edited by John M. Gaus, Leonard D. White, and Marshall E. Dimock. Chicago: University of Chicago Press, 1936.

Gellhorn, Walter. *When Americans Complain: Governmental Grievance Procedures.* Cambridge, Mass.: Harvard University Press, 1966.

Hill, Larry B. *American Ombudsmen.* Forthcoming.

______. "Institutionalization, the Ombudsman, and Bureaucracy." *American Political Science Review* 68 (September 1974): 1075–85.

______. *The Model Ombudsman: Institutionalizing New Zealand's Democratic Experiment.* Princeton, N.J.: Princeton University Press, 1976.

Jacob, Herbert. *Debtors in Court: The Consumption of Government Services.* Chicago: Rand McNally, 1969.

Kaufman, Herbert. *Red Tape: Its Origins, Uses, and Abuses.* Washington, D.C.: Brookings Institution, 1977.

Laski, Harold. "Bureaucracy." *Encyclopaedia of the Social Sciences.* Vol. 3. New York: Macmillan, 1930.

Lorch, Robert S. *Democratic Process and Administrative Law.* Detroit: Wayne State University Press, 1969.

Marini, Frank, ed. *Toward a New Public Administration: The Minnowbrook Perspective.* Scranton, Penn.: Chandler, 1971.

Mogulof, Melvin B. "Federal Interagency Action and Inaction: The Regional Council Experience." *Public Administration Review* 32 (May/June 1972): 232–40.

"Opening Federal Files." *Newsweek,* 19 June 1978, pp. 85–86.

Powell, Norman John. *Responsible Public Bureaucracy in the United States.* Boston: Allyn and Bacon, 1967.

Redford, Emmette S. *Democracy in the Administrative State.* New York: Oxford University Press, 1969.

Reuss, Henry S., and Anderson, Stanley V. "The Ombudsman: Tribune of the People." *Annals of the American Academy of Political and Social Science* 363 (January 1966): 44–51.

Robinson, Glen O., and Gellhorn, Ernest. *The Administrative Process.* St. Paul, Minn.: West Publishing Company, 1974.

Robson, William A. *The Governors and the Governed.* Baton Rouge: Louisiana State University Press, 1964.

Rosenblum, Victor G. "Handling Citizen Initiated Complaints: An Introductory Study of Federal Agency Procedures and Practices." *Administrative Law Review* 26 (Winter 1974): 1–45.

Rowat, Donald C., ed. *The Ombudsman: Citizen's Defender.* 2d ed. Toronto: University of Toronto Press, 1968.

Schwartz, Bernard, and Wade, H. W. R. *Legal Control of Government: Administrative Law in Britain and the United States.* Oxford: Clarendon Press, 1972.

Waldo, Dwight, ed. *Public Administration in a Time of Turbulence.* Scranton: Chandler Publishing Co., 1971.

Weise, Thomas George. *International Bureaucracy.* Lexington, Mass.: Lexington Books, 1975.

Wilson, James Q. "The Bureaucracy Problem." *The Public Interest.* No. 6 (Winter 1967): 4–5.

Wyner, Alan J., ed. *Executive Ombudsmen in the United States.* Berkeley: University of California, Institute of Governmental Studies, 1973.

__________. *The Nebraska Ombudsman: Innovation in State Government.* Berkeley: Institute of Governmental Studies, University of California, 1974.

Wynia, Bob. L. "Federal Bureaucrats' Attitudes Toward a Democratic Ideology." *Public Administration Review* 34 (March/April 1974): 158–59.

Appendix

How to get a government job

The first question the job seeker might ask is, "Do I have the education or training needed for a government job?" Almost definitely, the answer will be Yes. Governments (federal, state, and the wide variety of local ones) employ people prepared for virtually every occupation in the private sector plus some that are unique to government. Thus, the problem is to find the job that fits your preparation—whatever that preparation might be.

Teaching and the military

Of the 17 million employees of all levels of government, 3.5 million are teachers, and 2 million are military personnel. We begin by briefly considering these two important career fields.

Since about 20 percent of all government employees are teachers (most of whom work at the elementary and secondary levels), the chances are good that some of you intend to follow this path. If so, you must begin as early as possible in your college career to take the courses necessary for teacher certification. Looking ahead, you should also prepare yourself for master's degree work in order to obtain advancement after you begin teaching. Although school enrollments are declining now, the demographic figures indicate that this will reverse at the elementary level in 1982. At the secondary level, the upturn will, of course, come later. In the meantime, there will probably be something of an oversupply of teachers at both levels, but with over 3 million teaching positions, there is always turnover and consequent opportunities.[1] Nearly everywhere, the road to getting a teaching job is through local school district offices. It is usually possible to apply for a position at a certain level or in a certain subject and to be considered for any such positions that become available in the district. It is wise to make application to several districts in the area where you would prefer to live and even to some in areas that might not be your first choice. Furthermore, as is also important for other government jobs, a personal visit with the superintendent, or as high a level person as you can see at the district office, is a wise investment of your time. Finally, the placement services offered by many colleges of education should be used, but do not rely completely on such a service. Get out and seek an opening yourself.

Although the armed forces do not always come to mind when one thinks of public agencies, their members are, of course, government workers. And within the Army, Navy, Air Force, Marines, and Coast Guard, there are opportunities to use the education you have already acquired, regardless of what your college major may have been. Furthermore, the military provides an opportunity to obtain additional education, training, and experience. The new all-volunteer forces now offer salaries competitive with private sector and other government employers in many fields. Of course, the armed forces also offer some unique fringe and retirement benefits. You can find out more about this employment track by visiting a local recruiter.

Other government jobs

In addition to teaching and military jobs, there are 11.5 million other government jobs. There are a number of advantages to government employment, and many of the jobs available are desirable. Whereas most jobs in private industry are blue collar rather than white collar, the situation is reversed in government: 58 percent of government jobs are white collar. As indicated in table 7–1, the pay rates for government employees often seem quite attractive in comparison with other possibilities.

For those already sold on the virtues of government employment, the only question may be: How can I get a job in government? It may be useful to begin by asking how your background fits certain fields. Table A-1, which presents a list of college majors and some of the federal government job categories that might be appropriate for them, indicates that the range of academic preparations useful to government agencies is very wide. The table concerns only the federal government; state and local governments may have similar jobs for people with these backgrounds.

---

[1] U.S., Department of Labor, *Occupational Outlook Handbook, 1978–79 Edition* (Washington, D.C.: U.S. Government Printing Office, 1978), pp. 211–15. This useful volume provides projections of job opportunities for various public and private sector occupations through 1985.

How to get a government job/

Table A-1   Major fields of study and related government positions

Any college major

Administrative assistant
Alcohol and tobacco tax inspector
Alcohol, tobacco, and firearms
   special investigator
Budget officer
Budget analyst
Computer specialist
Correctional officer
Criminal investigator
Customs inspector
Immigration inspector
Intelligence research specialist
Internal security inspector
Management analyst
Museum curator
Narcotics agent
Personnel management specialist
Personnel staffing specialist
Public information specialist
Quality assurance specialist
Revenue officer
Safety officer
Veterans claims examiner
Writer and editor

Accounting

Accountant
Budget officer
Contract negotiator
Financial institution examiner
Industrial labor relations specialist
Internal revenue agent

Agriculture or agricultural services

Agricultural commodity grader
Agricultural marketing specialist
Entomologist
Hydrologist
Range conservationist
Soil conservationist
Wildlife biologist

Anthropology (Social or cultural)

Anthropologist
Sociologist

Archaeology

Anthropologist
Archaeologist
Park ranger

Architecture

Architect and marine architect
Realty specialist

Astronomy

Astronomer
Cartographer
Geodesist

Banking

Financial institution examiner
Loan specialist

Biology or Biological sciences

Biologist
Consumer safety inspector
Entomologist
Environmentalist
Medical technologist
Microbiologist
Park ranger
Pharmacologist
Plant scientist
Statistician
Wildlife biologist
Zoologist

Botany

Entomologist
Forest products technologist
Park ranger

Botany (Continued)

Plant scientist
Wildlife biologist

Business administration

Administrative assistant
Budget analyst
Contract negotiator
Financial institution examiner
Industrial relations specialist
Loan specialist
Personnel management specialist
Quality assurance specialist
Revenue officer
Supply management specialist
Traffic manager and traffic
  management specialist

Chemistry

Agricultural commodity grader
Alcohol and tobacco tax inspector
Chemist
Consumer safety inspector
Medical technologist
Microbiologist
Patent examiner
Pharmacologist

Commercial art

Illustrator
Printing and publication officer
Visual information specialist

Dramatic arts

Recreation specialist

Economics

Agricultural market reporter
Alcohol and tobacco tax inspector
Budget officer
Economist

Economics (Continued)

Financial institution examiner
Industrial relations specialist
Loan specialist
Operations research analyst
Revenue officer
Supply management specialist
Tax law specialist

Education

Educator
Recreation specialist
Sociologist
Statistician

Engineering

Engineer (various branches)
Environmentalist
Geodesist
Geologist
Hydrologist
Industrial specialist
Oceanographer
Patent examiner
Quality assurance specialist
Statistician

English

Printing and publications officer
Public information specialist
Writer-Editor

Finance

Alcohol and tobacco tax inspector
Financial institution examiner
Industrial relations specialist
Investigator (general)
Loan specialist
Realty specialist
Revenue officer
Tax law specialist

Table A-1   Major fields of study and related government positions

Fine arts

Illustrator
Recreation specialist
Visual information specialist

Forestry

Forester
Forest products technologist
Park ranger
Realty specialist

Geography

Cartographer
Meteorologist
Oceanographer

Geology

Cartographer
Geologist
Geophysicist
Hydrologist
Oceanographer
Park ranger

Geophysics

Cartographer
Geodesist
Geophysicist
Meteorologist
Oceanographer
Physicist

History

Archivist
Historian
Park ranger

Home economics

Agricultural commodity grader
Home economist

Hospital administration

Hospital administration assistant
Public health program specialist

Industrial management

Administrative assistant
Budget analyst
Industrial relations specialist
Industrial specialist
Printing and publications officer
Supply management specialist

Languages (Modern)

Translator analyst

Law

Alcohol and tobacco tax inspector
Attorney
Contract negotiator
Investigator (general)
Revenue officer
Special agent (IRS)
Tax law specialist

Marketing

Agricultural commodity grader
Agricultural marketing specialist
Agricultural market reporter
Statistician

Mathematics

Cartographer
Geophysicist
Mathematician
Operations research analyst
Statistician

Medicine

Medical officer (physician)
Pharmacologist

Table A-1   Major fields of study and related government positions

Metallurgy

Metallurgist
Quality assurance specialist

Meteorology

Cartographer
Meteorologist
Oceanographer

Music

Recreation specialist

Natural sciences

Meteorologist
Oceanographer
Park ranger
Range conservationist

Oceanography

Cartographer
Fishery biologist
Oceanographer

Pharmacy

Food and drug assistant
Pharmacist
Pharmacologist

Physical sciences

Aerospace technologist
Biomedical engineer
Chemist
Environmentalist
Meteorologist
Oceanographer
Patent examiner
Statistician

Physics

Consumer safety inspector

Physics (Continued)

Engineer
Forest products technologist
Geodesist
Geophysicist
Hydrologist
Oceanographer
Patent examiner
Physicist
Quality assurance specialist

Physiology

Pharmacologist
Physiologist

**Police administration or
law enforcement**

Border patrol agent
Criminal investigator
Customs inspector
Park ranger
Special agent

Political science

Administrative assistant
Archivist
Budget officer
Historian
Industrial relations specialist
Personnel management specialist
Personnel staffing specialist

Psychology

Personnel management specialist
Personnel staffing specialist
Psychologist
Public health program specialist
Statistician

Public administration

Administrative assistant

Table A-1   Major fields of study and related government positions

Public administration (Continued)

Archivist
Budget officer
Industrial relations specialist
Investigator (general)
Personnel management specialist
Personnel staffing specialist
Public health program specialist
Management analyst
Community planner
Hospital management specialist

Social sciences

Investigator (general)
Park ranger
Personnel management specialist
Personnel staffing specialist
Sociologist
Statistician

Social welfare

Social work associate
Social worker
Sociologist

Sociology

Personnel management specialist
Public health program specialist

Sociology (Continued)

Recreation specialist
Sociologist
Statistician

Speech

Speech pathologist and audiologist

Statistics

Agricultural marketing specialist
Loan specialist
Operations research analyst
Statistician
Supply management specialist
Traffic manager and traffic
  management specialist

Veterinary medicine

Pharmacologist
Veterinary medical officer

Zoology

Entomologist
Fishery biologist
Physiologist
Range conservationist
Wildlife biologist
Zoologist

Source: Abridged from U.S. Civil Service Commission, *Federal Career Directory,
1976-77* (Washington, D.C.: U.S. Government Printing Office, 1976),
pp. 144-50.

Job-getting strategies

What are some good strategies to use in trying to get one of these jobs?
The answer is not so easy to give as it was for the armed forces or the teaching profession. First, recall the description of merit system procedures in
chapter 7: you apply, are examined, have your name certified to agencies
seeking employees with your qualifications, and (if you are lucky) are offered
a job. This is the procedure you should follow for federal employment and for

state and local employment where merit systems operate. *But do not stop there.* Very often (strong defenders of the merit system would say "much too often") these procedures do not lead to the job you might like as quickly as you would prefer—especially if you are getting hungry! What is absolutely essential is that you begin making contacts with agencies that might offer employment opportunities. One author refers to this procedure as "camping out."[2] It might also be called "pounding the pavement." The point is the same. You need to make yourself known to those who will be hiring. Unlike private employers, governments rarely send recruiters to college campuses, and when they do, the recruiters often can do little more than distribute information. As with prospective teachers' visits to school board offices, your visits to other agencies should be to persons with authority to hire—or as close to them as you can get.

How can you get such access? One way, of course, is just to walk in, introduce yourself, and ask to see Mr. or Ms. X, the director. There are, however, some steps that might make this easier and your success more likely. An important one is to seek part-time employment while a student. This can be especially attractive if your school awards internship credit for the employment. You are, of course, likely to be required to do some extra academic work—possibly a term paper—to earn the credit. Regardless of your major, you may find that the Public Administration Department, School of Management, or Political Science Department will be willing to help you work out an internship. Credit you earn might then count as an elective. The exact procedures to follow in internship programs vary widely from school to school, but from the job-search perspective the value is the same: you have gained experience and a contact in a public agency. Perhaps you will decide after a semester that you have no intention of working with that agency on a permanent basis. Nonetheless, you may have met people there who will be happy to help you get access to administrators in other agencies, and you may have developed contacts yourself with people in other agencies.

Another point to remember is to take advantage of opportunities to meet with public officials throughout your college years. They may be guest speakers in your classes or at campuswide events; they may be candidates for public office. In fact, you probably can enhance your job opportunities by participating in a political campaign or two. (You will, additionally, learn much about an important part of the environment in which public agencies operate.) Remember the people you meet and, when you look for a job, try to make them remember you.

Do all of these recommendations for establishing informal contacts suggest that you violate merit rules or encourage employers to do so? Certainly not. Even if the position you want is filled by competitive examination (remember many are not), the hiring official is permitted to choose from the three or five individuals at the top of the list. If that official should know you and respect your initiative and competencies, you would have a deserved advantage.

---

[2]Michael A. Murray, "Strategies for Placing Public Administration Graduates," *Public Administration Review* 35 (November/December 1975): 632.

How to get a government job/

/**469**

Civil service examinations

However good your contacts may be, many positions you apply for will require that you do reasonably well on civil service examinations. Remember from chapter 7 that not all of these are pencil-and-paper, assembled examinations. For example, many federal government positions available in engineering and physical sciences are filled on the basis of scores computed from an evaluation of experience, education, and training reflected in your application and supplementary materials. The same is true for many applicants with bachelor's degrees or equivalent experience in the life sciences.

An important additional opportunity is available through the Professional and Administrative Career examination (PACE). This can be taken by anyone with a bachelor's degree or equivalent experience, regardless of major or field, and is especially important for students in the humanities. The positions filled through this process, which does include a written examination, are those that can lead to higher-level professional and administrative jobs. Under PACE, as well as many of the specialized entrance procedures, hiring occurs at the GS 5 or GS 7 levels. Persons with more extensive education or experience may qualify for higher levels. (You may wish to refer to the salary scale in chapter 7.)

It is difficult to generalize about state and local examinations; they vary too greatly from place to place. We do urge you to apply early for state and local examinations as well as federal ones. Some examinations are given only once or twice a year. In most cases you may apply at the beginning of your senior year and—if a written examination is required—take it during that year. If you have not planned ahead, and if you graduate from college in May or June, waiting until, say, the next October can seem a very long wait.

Final advice

Be as flexible as you can. Opportunities for particular jobs in a certain location fluctuate—sometimes wildly. You may find it necessary to accept a position other than your first choice. While it would not be advisable to tell the administrator hiring you that you would accept the job he offers only as a temporary expedient until you find a better job, there is nothing to prevent you from adopting such a strategy. It can be a good strategy to use the experience you gain and contacts you establish to move to a more satisfactory position or location; perhaps you will get a promotion in the process. Nonetheless, it is not a good idea to flit from job to job; if you do, it cannot be hidden on your resume. Since recruitment is a demanding chore and training is expensive, prospective employers want to hire people who appear likely to stay around long enough to justify the investment.

We offer a final caution. Your performance in every job will be evaluated on both formal and informal bases. Purely in strategic terms (without mentioning moralistic or other standards), it is likely to be a mistake not to perform up to your potential simply because you feel that the position is not worthy of your best effort. Doing a good job in such a situation can earn you the opportunity for a better position.

Glossary

Administrative accountability. A part of the general process of administrative responsibility by which public officials are held answerable to such general notions as democratic morality and to such constituencies as the legislature, the courts, and the citizens.

Administrative discretion. The element of choice that laws, rules, regulations, and agency policies and procedures leave to the individual administrator. Legislators and theorists constantly debate the proper position of the thin line that separates too much discretion, which creates unfairness and inequality, from too little discretion, which creates rigidity and inflexibility.

Administrative law judges. Created by the Administrative Procedure Act (vide) as "hearing examiners," the names of these officials were changed to "administrative law judges" in 1972. They perform judicial functions at administrative hearings, but are often only partially independent from an agency; nonetheless, their existence means that an individual is not both prosecuted by and judged by the same person.

Administrative Procedure Act (APA). Passed in 1946, the federal APA created uniform rule making and adjudicatory procedures among agencies and improved the procedures. Several states have adopted APAs modeled after the federal act.

Affirmative action. Employers' efforts to increase the percentages of minority-group members and women hired and promoted. Included have been changes in experience and education requirements, modifications of tests, recruitment efforts directed at target groups, and use of goals to guide selection.

American Society for Public Administration (ASPA). Founded in 1939, ASPA, which has its headquarters in Washington, D.C., is the main professional association for academics and practitioners in public administration.

Appropriation bills.   Legislative proposals to grant agencies authority to obligate the federal government and to make payments. If passed, agencies create obligations by such activities as employing personnel, signing contracts, and ordering materials.

Bakke case.   Legally cited as *The Regents of the University of California* v. *Allan Bakke,* this case produced a ruling of the U.S. Supreme Court that upheld the use of affirmative action plans to expand minority enrollment in higher education institutions, but declared that—in the absence of a past history of discrimination by that institution—rigid quotas may not be used.

Bureaucracy.   A formal organization in which authority is based upon law, authority is depersonalized (that is, it is professionalized, official and unofficial roles are separated, and universally applicable norms are employed), and authority is hierarchical.

Bureaucratic monitoring mechanisms.   Those procedures, institutions, or agencies (such as public interest groups, inspectors general, legislators, or ombudsmen) that have as a main function the control or regulation or review of the actions of government agencies.

Civil Service Commission.   Created by the Civil Service Act of 1883, the commission made rules and regulations for federal employment and heard workers' appeals concerning alleged violations of merit system procedures. The office of Personnel Management and the Merit System Protection Board replaced the Commission in 1978.

Clientele groups.   Interest groups (vide) composed of the organizations or individuals that receive an agency's services.

Client-processing agencies.   Agencies that deal with individuals but not to provide them services. Law enforcement agencies, for example, process those suspected of crimes, and tax agencies separate people from their money.

Client-serving agencies.   Agencies that provide goods or services directly to individuals or organizations.

Comparative Administration Group (CAG).   Organization of scholars, mainly political scientists, interested in theoretical and practical studies of development administration from the comparative viewpoint in the non-Western world; CAG was most active during the 1960s.

Compensation plan.   A statement that specifies salaries or wages to be received by persons holding various positions shown in the position classification (vide) scheme.

Congressional Budget and Impoundment Control Act.   Passed in 1974, this act created a mechanism through which Congress can monitor the economic impact of its decisions. Established were the House and Senate Budget Committees and the Congressional Budget Office. The act also restricted presidential powers to impound funds.

Equifinality.   A principle of systems theory holding that an open system's fate is not determined by its condition at any given time. Two open systems, though quite different at one time, may later be quite similar as each adjusts to circumstances.

Executive budget. A statement of planned expenditures and income for a future period (normally one or two years) prepared in the name of the chief executive for presentation to the legislature as a request for action on appropriation and revenue matters.

Executive ombudsman. A subtype of quasi-ombudsman (vide) that is dependent upon either the elected or appointed executive.

Executive oversight. The process by which the chief executive attempts to exercise control over administrative agencies and hold them accountable for implementing his programs—most often accomplished by depending on information from a cadre of long-time advisors.

Exhaustion of remedies. Administrative law concept under which, before deciding whether to review a case, the court asks if the litigant has tried all other available appeals and remedies before coming to the court.

"Fair hearing". Important administrative law doctrine, whose elements include adequate notice of a proposed action, a statement of reasons for it, and the opportunity to defend by confronting adverse witnesses and presenting oral arguments and evidence. Such administrative hearings are less formal than proceedings in a court.

Federal Executive Institute. A school located in Charlottesville, Virginia, operated by the U.S. Civil Service Commission to provide managerial training to upper-level federal employees.

Federal Regional Councils. Organizations of high-level regional federal officials created in 1969 as a means of decentralizing the federal government by coordinating the activities of agencies on a regional basis.

Freedom of Information Act. Substantially strengthened in 1974, the act allows citizens to make a Freedom of Information Request (FOIR) for documents in the possession of federal agencies, which must comply unless the documents requested fall under one of nine exempted categories, in which case one may appeal to the courts. Several states have similar laws to combat administrative secrecy.

General Systems Theory (GST). An approach originated by Ludwig von Bertalanffy, holding that all branches of science are concerned with the operation of systems not understandable by examination of individual parts and that the properties of systems of different types at various levels are very similar.

Hawthorne effect. Also called the "experimental effect," this refers to the observation that in experiments involving people as subjects, those subjects sometimes respond to being part of an experiment. Such response may be indistinguishable from responses to the treatment: job counseling, a pill, soft music, or whatever.

Hierarchy of needs. Suggested by Abraham Maslow, a list of categories of human needs. From lowest to highest, they are physiological needs, safety and security needs, belonging needs, esteem needs, and self-actualization needs. Maslow concludes that ability to motivate an individual is improved by recognition of the needs that have been satisfied and those that have not.

Horizontal conflict. The type of interbureaucratic conflict that occurs between subgroups of an agency at similar hierarchical levels.

Human relations. An approach to organization theory emphasizing the presence of an informal organization, norms that may conflict with formal rules, and workers who can be motivated through social rewards and sanctions.

Incremental decision making. A process that permits policies to evolve through a series of small changes, usually resulting from bargaining and negotiation among those desiring to influence the decision.

Independent regulatory commissions. Agencies (such as the Interstate Commerce Commission, the Federal Trade Commission, the Civil Aeronautics Board, and the Federal Communications Commission) created to implement general legal directives in various policy sectors. These agencies have broad discretion in making and enforcing rules, and the courts seldom interfere with their decisions.

"Inner check." The idea that civil servants are restrained from acting irresponsibly by their internalized conceptions of democratic values. Some theorists believe this inner check is more important than external checks in holding administrators accountable.

Inspector General (IG). A bureaucratic monitoring mechanism (vide), having military origins, which is internal to the executive branch; leaders of the agency exercise hierarchical control over the IG.

Interest groups. Groups that attempt to influence the political system and especially public policies, without seeking election of their own members to public office.

Job actions. Steps employees take, short of striking, to interfere with normal work processes and thereby to pressure the employer to meet employee demands. Examples are slow-downs, rigid adherence to rules, and sick-ins.

Legislative oversight. The process by which the legislature keeps watch over agencies to see that the laws are properly implemented. Legislative committees—especially those concerned with agencies' budgets—are very important to the oversight function; individual legislators also may play a role—especially in performing the casework function.

Matrix organization. Innovative, nonhierarchical organizational form developed by NASA in which administrators work alongside technical personnel, providing administrative support rather than serving as superiors.

Management by objectives (MBO). An approach focusing attention on objectives that subordinates set in consultation with superiors. Subordinates are given resources and considerable autonomy to pursue their objectives, and their performance evaluations are based on the degree to which objectives are accomplished.

Managerial Grid. A two-dimensional classification of managerial style developed by R. R. Blake and J. L. Mouton. The two dimensions are "concern for production" and "concern for people." Managers may show high concern for production and little for people, high concern for people and little for production, little concern for either, moderate concern for both, or high concern for both.

Merit system. A set of procedures governing public employment which, in large measure, requires that hiring and promotion decisions be based on competence of individuals to meet job requirements. Merit systems normally provide disciplinary procedures but restrict the employer's ability to dismiss employees.

Mixed scanning. An approach to decision making suggested by Amitai Etzioni that attempts to combine features of the incremental and rational-comprehensive modes. It involves collection and evaluation of general data on a broad range of topics and detailed analysis of particular issues.

National Association of Schools of Public Affairs and Administration (NASPAA). An affiliate of the American Society for Public Administration composed of university programs in the field and dedicated to advancing training and education in public affairs and administration.

Negative entropy. A property of open systems that enables them to persist by importing energy from the environment, whereas closed systems move toward entropy—random arrangement of the parts.

Negative income tax. Rather than the present welfare assistance program, with its complex eligibility requirements, this program—favored by many neoconservatives—would be self-executing (vide). It would eliminate the necessity for many caseworkers by making aid available to those with low incomes, as reported on tax returns, according to a formula.

New Public Administration. A movement of the late 1960s and early 1970s reacting against the value-free positivism and the continued commitment to efficiency and economy within public administration. Instead, the movement suggested that such values as social equity should be emphasized by public organizations, both in dealing with workers in the organization and in dealing with clients and others outside the organization.

Non-client-oriented agencies. Agencies that are not mainly concerned with providing services to individuals nor processing individuals but, rather, function to meet needs of the public in general. The Department of State, for example, serves the public as it participates in treaty negotiations.

Office of Management and Budget (OMB). A unit within the Executive Office of the President responsible for aiding the president in preparing the executive budget, reviewing proposals agencies wish to make to Congress, and monitoring managerial processes in the federal government.

Ombudsman. A citizens-complaint-handling official who reports to the legislature, but is independent from the bureaucracy and the political executive. Ombudsmen are also legally established, functionally autonomous, external to the administration, specialist, expert, nonpartisan, unbiased, client-centered but not antiadministration, and both popularly accessible and visible.

Organization development (OD). The application of behavioral science findings to an organization, usually with the purpose of intervening in organizational functioning and making the organization and its members more responsive to internal and external changes. Outside consultants are often used.

Organizational humanism. An approach to organizations and leadership based on the assumptions that employees can enjoy work, that work can be rewarding, and that employees can be motivated by being given considerable autonomy and opportunity to seek self-actualization.

Organization theory. An interdisciplinary field of academic study that concentrates on such matters as the definition of organizations, patterns of authority within organizations, and relationships among organizations.

Participatory management. Important idea of the organizational humanism (vide) theoretical school, which holds that employees can be motivated to greater productivity if they become involved with and have a say in goal setting and other organizational decision-making activities.

Pendleton Act. Named after a senator from Ohio, the Civil Service Act of 1883 established the Civil Service Commission and was the basis of the present "merit" system of federal employment.

Performance examination. A portion of the total process of examining applicants for some civil service positions. This requires demonstration of particular skills such as typing or lathe operation.

Planning Programming Budgeting System (PPB). Introduced in the federal government in 1965, this was an effort to require that budgetary decisions be made in the rational-comprehensive mode employing multiyear projections and detailed program analyses. Although partially copied by several states with limited success, federal PPB was terminated in 1971.

Politics-administration dichotomy. Now generally discredited, this doctrine suggested that a sharp distinction could be drawn between the task of the elected executive, which was concerned with policy making, and the task of the appointed administrator, which was to carry out the political mandate in an efficient and apolitical fashion.

POSDCORB. An acronym much used in the administrative management period of the 1930s. It refers to *P*lanning, *O*rganizing, *S*taffing, *D*irecting, *CO*ordinating, *R*eporting, and *B*udgeting.

Position classification. The grouping together of jobs with similar responsibilities and education, experience, and skill requirements to form classes. The presentation of these classes is the position classification scheme.

Pressure groups. *See* Interest groups.

Principles of public administration. Advocates of this mechanistic approach searched for universal principles—such as hierarchy, functional differentiation, and coordination—that could be used to promote administrative efficiency.

Professional and Administrative Career Examination (PACE). An entrance examination for federal civil service that can be taken by most college graduates and persons with equivalent experience. It is the basis for employment in a wide variety of positions at the GS 5 and the GS 7 levels.

Program authorization. A statutory provision granting an agency permission to carry out a particular program and establishing procedures to be followed, but normally not providing funds; they must be provided in a separate appropriation bill.

Program evaluation.   The systematic assessment of the contribution a program makes to achievement of the purposes for which it was established. This has become both an academic and a professional specialty in recent years.

Proposition 13.   A state constitutional amendment approved by California voters in June of 1978, which sharply reduced property taxes and which has been viewed as an important step in a national tax-relief movement.

Public interest groups.   Interest groups that claim to be representative of a large segment of the public and of "the public interest." They claim to speak for no narrow economic or social group, but, rather, for the general public. And the goals sought by the groups are not likely to benefit the members in their individual capacities, but are consumable only by society as a whole.

Public policy analysis.   An academic and administrative specialization in which attention is focused on such matters as the development and evaluation of policy options and the study of the implementation and effects of policy choices made. Most practitioners adopt a rational-comprehensive approach to the policy process. Another use is the determination of political, economic, and social variables that seem to influence public policies.

Quasi-judicial authority.   This authority, given to the independent regulatory commissions (vide) by the Congress and affirmed by the Supreme Court, allows the agencies to bring charges, hold hearings, and render judgments—in general, to perform courtlike functions—in the course of enforcing the rules created by the agencies.

Quasi-ombudsman.   A citizens-complaint-handling official who lacks an important characteristic of the ombudsman (vide); perhaps the office is not legally established, unbiased, or independent from the executive (*see* Executive ombudsman).

Rational-comprehensive decision making.   Attempt to apply more "scientific" techniques to the making of public decisions than is done under the incremental decision-making (vide) model. Under the rational-comprehensive model, the decision maker would approach a problem by defining it comprehensively, by developing precise and measurable objectives, by generating decisional alternatives, by determining the costs and effectiveness of each alternative, and by selecting the "best" alternative.

Representative bureaucracy.   The idea that the bureaucracy, as a central decision-making body in a democracy, should generally reflect society as a whole in its social composition. Various minority and women's groups have taken the finding that bureaucracies underrepresent their members as evidence that more should be hired.

Revenue sharing.   A self-executing program (vide) begun during the Nixon administration that distributes tax moneys collected by the federal government to state and local governments. This differs from previous categorical grant programs in that recipient governments are allocated funds for discretionary use according to a formula and do not have to propose specific projects to which the federal aid would apply, meet eligibility requirements, and provide matching funds.

Ripeness.   Administrative law concept under which, before deciding whether to review a case, the courts inquire about its maturity. In order to avoid premature intervention, the courts ask whether final administrative action has been taken and a decision rendered.

Scientific management.   Approach developed by Frederick Taylor, an engineer, who insisted that work should be accomplished in the most efficient way possible and that through the use of certain rational techniques, management could be made into a true science.

Self-executing programs.   Programs, such as the negative income tax (vide), designed to be administered almost automatically; favored by neoconservatives who want to reduce the number of government employees.

Standing.   Administrative law concept under which, before deciding whether to review a case, the courts inquire if the litigant has a direct and personal interest in the matter protested. The interests of consumers and environmentalists are now considered sufficient to be given standing under some circumstances, but the interest of a taxpayer is considered insufficient.

Sunset laws.   Provisions enacted in several states to require that agencies and programs automatically terminate after a certain period (usually five years) unless they are renewed.

Theory X and theory Y.   Two contrasting views managers may have of employees and their approaches to work. Each view leads to a different approach to the leadership task. Theory X assumes workers find work distasteful, prefer close supervision, and are motivated as individuals by threat or punishment. Theory Y assumes workers can find work as natural as play, prefer self-control, and are motivated as groups by ego and social rewards.

Unassembled examination.   The process of assigning an examination score to applicants for civil service positions on the basis of education and experience described in application materials, without administering a test.

Vertical conflict.   The type of interbureaucratic conflict between hierarchical levels of the agency. The informal hierarchy may not be the same as the formal one.

Veterans' preference.   The practice of giving veterans special treatment in civilian government employment. It includes the adding of bonus points to examination scores and the providing of greater job security than is available to nonveterans.

Zero-base budgeting (ZBB).   A set of budgetary procedures introduced to the federal government by President Carter and to many states and local governments that purports to give old programs as careful scrutiny as new ones. It requires a division of each program into decision packages that can be ranked in order of importance. After the amount of funds available is known, the ranking is used to determine the decision units that will be supported.

Index

Accountability: 53, 157, 376–378, 391, 418–459, 471; auditing and, 436–437; bureaucratic monitoring and, 425–451; courts and, 441–445; inspectors general and, 437–438; legislators and, 438–441; mass media and, 432–433; ombudsmen and, 435–436, 445–451; pressure groups and, 433–435; public opinion and, 431; values and, 422–425, 474

Acheson, Dean: 92, 94

Activism: judicial, 132; of 1960s, 3

Adaptation: 194, 198, 199

Adjudication: 124–125, 126. *See also* Courts

Administrative: behavior, 174–175; management, 173–174. *See also* Public administration

Administrative Procedure Act (APA): 123, 124, 149, 152, 153, 471

Affirmative action: 207–208, 232–236, 455, 471

AFL-CIO: 219

AFSCME: 219, 220

AFT: 219

Aged: programs for, 26

Agencies: client-serving, 137–138, 139–144, 472; and courts, 121–125; management of, 280–324; non-client-oriented, 138; Nader and, 156–157; regulatory, 142–144; suppliers and contractors of, 144–145

Agnew, Spiro: and mass media, 432

Agriculture, Department of (USDA): and Army Corps of Engineers, 78–79; clients of, 139; Food Stamp Program of, 140–141; history of, 20; jobs in, 464; policies of, 242, 272; and zero base budgeting, 359–360

Air quality laboratory: and zero base budgeting, 347–352

Air transport: 24, 26

Alabama: courts in, 130, 131

Allison, Graham: *Essence of Decision*, 97

American Association of University Professors: 144

American Legion: and Veterans Administration, 139, 142

American Library Association: 144

American Municipal Association: 48

American Public Works Association: 48

American Society for Public Administration (ASPA): 48, 471

Americans for Democratic Action: 145

AMTRAK: 454
Analysis: 249, 259, 267; cost-benefit, 344, 357, 360, 361, 362, 410; cross cultural, 52; empirical, 268–270; and program evaluation, 381–382; public policy, 53, 477; systems, 251–264; time series, 384, 385
Anderson papers: 96, 99
Antitrust Division of Justice Department: 25
Appropriations: 329, 332–333, 334, 472, 476
Argyris, Chris: 293
Armed forces: jobs in, 462–463; and standing army, 82
Army Corps of Engineers: 78–79, 178
Atomic Energy Commission: 138
Attitudes, citizen: 406; and civil servants, 423–425; toward government, 30–38, 128; and taxes, 31–32
Auditing: 335; and bureaucratic monitoring, 436–437
Austin, Warren: 96
Authoritarian leadership style: 284, 285
Authoritative implementaion: 1
Automobiles: and air bags, 78; impact of, 26; Nader and, 155n; and public interest groups, 156

Bakke case: 208, 472
Ball, George: 98
Banfield, Edward C.: 268
Barnard, Chester I.: 167, 168
Bay of Pigs: 82, 92, 93, 95, 99
Beal v. *Lindsay*: 404
Beard, Charles A.: 49
Behavioral movement: 52, 53
Bennis, Warren: 190, 294
Bissell, Richard: 93
Blake, Robert: 286–287, 474
Branch method: 267–268, 275
Brennan, Justice: on fair hearing, 444
Buck, A. E.: 356
Buckle, Thomas: 263
Budget, Bureau of the: 327
Budgetary process: 87, 315–316, 318–319, 326–372, 473; alternative system, 364–365; appropriations, 329, 332–333, 334; auditing, 335; budget cycle, 328–335; cuts, 336, 337, 368; decision making, 335–337, 337–338, 339; execution, 329, 334–335; padding, 336–337; performance budgeting, 362–363, 364, 367; planning programming budgeting, 338–339; preparation, 328–329; presidential control, 71–72; reform of, 337–340; wage settlements, 221; zero base budgeting, 339–372
Bureaucracy: 4–5, 171, 472; bureaucratic imperialism, 79–80; bureaucrats and, 4–5, 36–38; definition of, 40; foreign affairs, 91–100; and human behavior, 187; and Industrial Revolution, 199; and interrelationships, 80; monitoring mechanisms, 425–451, 472; office holding, 183–187; problems, 194, 197, 425–427; reform, 453–454; representative, 215–216, 477; slowing of growth, 451–452; technical advantages, 187–189; Weber on, 41, 42, 181–189, 192
Burkhead, Jesse: 362
Burner v. *Washington*: 404
Burns, Arthur F.: 343–344, 356–357
Burns, James M.: 88
Business: and consumerism, 54–55; and courts, 130; and defense contractors, 145; and government, 197; historical, 17; regulation of, 54, 143–144, 150–151
Busing of school children: 380

Cabinet, the: 73, 83
Calculable rules: 189
California: Proposition 13, 33–34, 452
Canals: 20
Capitalism: and bureaucracy, 188–189
Caplow, Theodore: 167–168; *Principles of Organization*, 167
Carter, Jimmy: civil service reform, 212–213; complaint-handling procedures, 450; detente, 105; executive appointments, 68–70; Griffin firing, 77; human rights, 53; White House staff, 81; zero base budgeting, 340–341, 343, 356, 369, 478
Case study system: 50; constructed case study, 315–324

Casework, legislative: 118, 439–441, 474; and oversight, 117

CATV: 157

Celler, Emanuel: 113

Census, Bureau of: and expenditures, 14; history of, 16; and population, 191

Center for Analysis of Public Issues: 157

Center for Auto Safety: 155n

Center for Law and Social Policy: 148

Center for the Study of Responsive Law: 145, 154

Charlotte, S.C.: program evaluation in, 405

Chayes, Abram: 130, 133

CIA: 91; and Bay of Pigs, 93, 95; as organization, 178

Cities: bankruptcy of, 226; public works projects in, 20; reform in, 47–48

Citizens: and agencies, 138; attitudes, 30–38; and legislators, 439–440; lobbies, 150–151, 429; participation of, 45, 140–141, 459; pressure groups, 433–434; and program evaluation, 404; use of government services by, 32–33. *See also* Clients

Citizens for Clean Air: 145

Civil Aeronautics Board (CAB): 24, 121, 474; and lobbyists, 143

Civil Rights Act: 232

Civil rights movement: 113, 311; and courts, 120; and jobs, 236; and media, 132

Civil Service Act of 1883: 46, 49, 476

Civil Service Assembly: 48

Civil Service Commission: 46, 209, 214, 221, 456, 472, 476; and affirmative action, 232

Civil service system: exams, 233, 470; executive appointment, 68; reform, 212–213

Civil War: expenditures, 20

Claremont, CA.: program evaluation, 406–407

Classification: functional, 14–16; of public programs, 12–16

Clients: 137–138, 139–141; and budget, 367; client-processing agencies, 472; groups, 145–146, 472; non-client-oriented agencies, 475; and ombudsmen, 447; and regulatory agencies, 142–144; relations, 459

Clifford, Clark: 92

Coal Mine Health and Safety Act: 153

Coding process: 179

Cold War: 82

Collective bargaining: 216–226; pros and cons of, 225–226; and public interest, 224–225

Colleges: administration of, 4, 125–126; and evaluation research, 383–388; and foundation grants, 198; professional associations, 144; public programs, 16–17; systems analysis, 261, 262

Colonial era: public administration in, 43–44

Committee on Municipal Standards: 395

Common Cause: 145, 151, 154

Communication: employee, 299; system, 17

Community Action Programs (CAP): 140

Comparative Administration Group (CAG): 51–52

Complaint-handling procedures: 107, 430, 435–436, 450–451, 475, 477; and ombudsmen, 446–447

Comprehensive Employment and Training Act (CETA): 228

Comprehensive Occupational Safety Act: 153

Computers: and systems analysis, 255

Conflict: and decision making, 244; horizontal, 77–79, 474; vertical, 77–79, 478

Congress: and budgetary process, 327–328, 329, 330–333; committees in, 114–115, 117–118; historical powers, 17; legislative oversight, 107–119; policy formulation, 61; policy preferences, 113; and presidential powers, 82–83, 85–86; staff workers, 118–119. *See also* Legislature

Congressional Budget Office: 108

Congressional Budget and Impoundment Control Act: 72, 329, 472

Constitution: changes in, 129; and due

process, 123; Fifth Amendment, 123;
Fourteenth Amendment, 123; Eigh-
teenth Amendment, 380
Consultants: 476
Consumer Product Safety Commission:
4–5
Consumerism: 53, 54–55, 311. *See also*
Public interest
Contractors: 144–145
Control activities: 14
Corrections system: 20, 131
Corruption: 45, 143
Cost-benefit analysis: 344, 362, 410; and
zero base budgeting, 357, 360, 361
Council of Economic Advisers: 82
Council of Environmental Quality: 82
Courts: 19; bureaucratic monitoring by,
441–445; and employee recruitment,
207–208; judicial review by, 128–129;
procedural matters, 123–124; and
public administration, 54, 119–134;
public litigation, 130; regulatory
agencies and, 143, 150, 474
Cramton, Roger C.: 126–127
Cronin, Thomas E.: 81–90
Cross-cultural analysis: 52
Cuba: Bay of Pigs, 82, 92, 93, 95, 99;
missile crisis, 94, 97
Customs Service: 18, 178

Dallas, Texas: program evaluation, 405,
406
Davis, Kenneth Culp: 104–105
Davis, Robert H.: 393
Dayton-Miami Valley, Ohio: citizen
attitudes, 406
DDT: 263–264
Decentralization: 317, 459
Decision making: 53, 239–278; autonomy, 316; budgetary, 335–337, 337–
338, 339; and confidence in science
and technology, 248–249; controversial decisions, 2; decentralization and,
317; decision packages, 345–347, 348,
349, 350, 351–352, 354, 357–358; decision units, 345; divided authority,
247–248; evaluation, 268–270, 411;
and "good" policy, 271; incrementalism, 240–247, 272–273, 367, 474; and
leadership, 301–309; means-end rela-

tionship, 270–271; mixed scanning,
475; primacy of representation, 248;
procedures, 264–278; rational-comprehensive school, 240–247, 272, 477;
successive limited comparisons, 267–
268, 272, 273, 275–276, 277–278; systems analysis, 251–264; theorists and
practitioners, 276–277; and values,
249–250, 269–270, 273–274
Defense, Department of: contractors,
144; expenditures, 14, 15; McNamara
and, 251, 338–339; policy implementation, 61; reforms, 244; systems analysis, 252, 253, 256, 260
Delegation of responsibility: 304–305
Democracy: and bureaucracy, 228
Democratic leadership style: 284, 285,
301, 305
Demonstration projects: 411–412
Depression: 82
Desegregation: school, 132, 133
Developing countries: 52
Differentiation: 179
Discretion: 104, 105, 153, 471, 474
Discrimination: job, 209, 210, 227, 229,
231, 232, 234, 235; racial, 235;
reverse, 235–236
District of Columbia: sanitation moni-
toring project, 400–402, 406, 413,
415
Division of power: 250
Downs, Anthony: 168
Drucker, Peter: 197–198, 295
Due process: 123, 129, 151, 444
Dulles, Allen: 93
Dulles, John Foster: 95
Dynamics: 164–165

Education: back to basics, 377–378;
compensatory, 410–411; continuing,
213–214; degrees, 290; and desegregation, 132, 133; employment in, 13,
462–463; evaluation of, 395; expenditures on, 12, 14, 15, 26, 28; Follow
Through program, 413; history of, 20;
as job requirement, 227, 234; performance contracting, 412; of population,
197–198; in public administration,
48–53; public school system, 414;
teachers' strikes, 218. *See also*

Colleges

Efficiency: 459, 475; budgetary process, 362; and decision making, 241

Eisenhower, Dwight D.: 99; highway construction, 26; military industrial complex, 145; and Quemoy, 95; staff of, 82; and troops in Europe, 92, 95–96

Elections: 138, 185–186

Elementary and Secondary Education Act (ESEA): 381, 410–411

Emergency Employment Program (EEP): 228

Empirical analysis: 268–270

Employment: government, 3, 13, 21–22, 23, 24, 28–29, 462–470; and civil service system, 46; employer-employee relationship, 203; executive appointment, 67–71; history, 45; job-getting strategies, 468–470; merit system, 68; professional associations, 48. *See also* Personnel management

Employment Act of 1946: 273

Energy shortages: 249

Enthoven, Alain C.: 251–264

Entropy, negative: 178–179, 475

Environmental impact statements: 141

Environmental Protection Agency: 141, 455

Environmentalism: 53, 121, 151, 311

Equal Employment Opportunity Act (EEO): 140, 232, 233; and commission, 454–455

Equal protection clause: 129

Equality: of services, 37

Equifinality principle: 179, 472

Equity: job, 215–216, 227–230, 231–236; social, 459, 475

Erie Canal: 20

Ethics: 55, 139, 196. *See also* Values

Etzioni, Amitai: 168; on accountability, 420, 421, 422; on decision making, 247, 475

European Economic Community: 455

Evaluation Quarterly: 381

Evaluations: 375–378; budgetary, 367, 370; and decision making, 249; empirical analysis, 268–270; of employee performance, 211, 233, 323, 457, 470; by General Accounting Office, 108;

program, 241, 379–416, 477; zero base budgeting, 346, 352, 353

Examinations: civil service, 233, 470; employment, 208–209, 235; and job discrimination, 234; performance, 476; unassembled, 478

Exception principle: 320

Executive powers: oversight, 72–73; and public visibility, 72. *See also* Presidency

Exhaustion of remedies: 443, 473

Expenditures, government: 12–13, 14, 15, 18–20; and presidency, 71–72; twentieth century, 21–30

Experimentation: 249; design, 385–388; experimental effect, 473; and program evaluation, 411–413, 416

Fair hearing: 444, 473

Family: changes in, 26

FBI: and executive appointments, 69; and leaks, 96

Federal Communications Commission (FCC): 24–25, 121, 474; and CATV, 157

Federal Executive Institute: 213, 473

Federal Information Centers: complaint handling procedures, 450

Federal Maritime Commission: 24

Federal Regional Councils: 453, 473

Federal system: 43

Federal Trade Commission (FTC): 25, 121, 474; and Nader, 153–154

Federalists: 17–18

Feedback: 294, 316; and systems analysis, 259

Fiedler, Fred: on leadership, 288, 289

Finer, Herman: on accountability, 419–420

Fire control: evaluation of, 394

Fisk, Donald M.: 392

Follow Through program: 413

Food and Drug Administration (FDA): 26; and Nader, 154

Food shortages: 249

Food Stamp program: 140

Ford, Gerald: and detente, 105; White House staff of, 81

Foreign affairs; 82; bureaucracy, 91–100; expenditures, 24; and govern-

ment expansion, 30
Fort Worth: police fleet plan, 412
Foundations: and organizations, 198; and public interest advocacy, 157
Franklin, Benjamin: 131
Free speech clause: 129
Freedom: concept of, 43–44
Freedom of Information Act: 55, 152, 153, 444, 473

Garfield, James: 46
Garland, Texas: zero base budgeting, 349, 363
Gaus, John: on accountability, 422–423
Gelb, Leslie H.: 91
Gellhorn, Walter: 439, 440
General Accounting Office (GAO): 108, 335; oversight by, 115
General Motors: and Nader, 154, 155n
General Services Administration (GSA): 77
General systems theory (GST): 473
Generalists: and specialists, 456–457, 458
Georgia: zero base budgeting, 340, 341, 343, 347–352, 356, 357, 358, 361–362, 363, 364, 365, 370, 371
Gibbon, Edward: 192
Glazer, Nathan: 127
Goals: 198, 309–310, 320, 321, 339; and accountability, 376–377; in decision making, 241; management by objectives, 295–298; setting of, 315, 316–318, 389
Goldberg v. *Kelley:* 443–444
Goodnow, Frank J.: *Politics and Administration,* 47
Government: attitudes toward, 30–38; and divided authority, 247–248; history, 17–19, 29–30, 44; organizational structure, 74, 75; primacy of representation, 248; reform, 46–48; and science and technology, 248–249. *See also* Congress; Expenditures; Presidency
Government Economy and Spending Reform Act: 343
Grant, Ulysses: 46
Grants: 12–13, 477; grant-in-aid programs, 453, 454

Great Britain: budget cycle, 355–356; civil service system, 46; public administration professionals, 456, 457
Great Society programs: 83
Griffin, Robert: 77
Griggs decision: 231–232, 234
Gronouski, John: 112
Gross national product (GNP): 28
Group: effectiveness, 308; management functions, 313
Growth rate: 23–24; and expenditures, 28
Gulick and Urwick: *Papers on the Science of Administration,* 173–174

Halperin, Morton H.: 91
Hammann, Arthur: 359–360
Harvard Business School: case study program, 50; and Nixon, 296
Hatry, Harry P.: 393
Hawkins v. *Town of Shaw:* 404
Hawthorne effect: 175–176, 388, 473
Head Start: program evaluation, 408, 409–410
Health care: evaluation, 394; government, 26, 28
Health, Education and Welfare, Department of (HEW): and citizen participation, 141; income maintenance, 412; mismanagement, 419–420, 437; organizational structure, 74, 76; student loans, 178
Hearing examiners: 123, 471
Hearings: 118; and citizen participation, 141; judicial, 123–124, 125–126; legislative, 107; and regulatory agencies, 143
Hebert, F. Ted: 355
Herzberg, Frederick: 293
Hierarchy: of authority, 294; of needs, 293–294, 473; principle of, 74–77
Highway construction: 12, 15, 17, 20, 26
Hitch, Charles: 252, 262, 266
Holden, Matthew, Jr.: 79-80
Homeostasis: 179
Hoover, Herbert: 86; program evaluation, 395
Hoover Commission: 359
Hospitals: construction, 30; grants for,

12, 15; public, 20
House Judiciary Committee: and civil rights, 113
Housing and Urban Development, Department of (HUD): program evaluation, 404; zero base budgeting, 369, 370
Human relations: 474; and leadership styles, 283; management, 299; movement, 292, 295; and organization theory, 175–176; training, 301–302
Human rights: 53
Humanism, organizational: 476

Immunization programs: 380
Impartial investigators: 446
Income: definition, 104; maintenance, 412
Incompetency: of government employees, 116
Incrementalism: 159, 272–273; and budget process, 337–338; and decision making, 240–241, 368; and policy formulation, 274–276; and rational comprehensive approach, 241–247; and zero base budgeting, 340
India-Pakistan crisis: 96, 99
Indianapolis: police fleet plan, 412
Indicators: development of, 317
Industrial democracy: 313
Industrial Revolution: 46, 199, 249
Industry. *See* Business
"Infeasibility" technique: 94
Inflation: 28
Information inputs: 179
"Informational data": 397
Inspectors General: 437–438, 474
Institute of Public Administration: 49
Institute of Public Policy Analysis: 49
Insurance: no fault, 156
Intentional communities: 313
Interest groups: 136–137, 274, 474; and budget process, 337, 367; and clients, 138, 139; and decision making, 241; and professional associations, 144; promotional groups, 145–146. *See also* Lobbies; Pressure groups
Interfaces: 319
Intergovernmental Personnel Act: 213
Interior, Department of; and Army

Corps of Engineers, 78–79
Internal Revenue Code: 154, 155
Internal Revenue Service: and executive appointments, 69; and public interest groups, 154, 155. *See also* Taxation
International administration: 51, 53
International City Management Association: 48, 396–397, 404, 405, 407
Interstate Commerce Commission (ICC): 24, 121, 142, 455, 474
Israel: and Truman, 92

Jackson, Andrew: 45; personnel management, 205–206
Javits, Jacob: and systems analysis, 251, 262–264
Jefferson, Thomas: 30, 43
Jeffersonian Republicans: 45
Job actions: 474
Jobs. *See* Employment
John Birch Society: 26
Johnson, Frank: 130, 131
Johnson, Lyndon B.: and budget reform, 338; and Vietnam, 92, 93–94, 99
Judges: and public administration, 121–122, 123–124, 130–133, 134, 471
Judicial review: 128–129, 150
Justice Department: Antitrust Division, 25; and civil rights, 113

Kahn, Robert: organization, theory of, 177
Katz, Daniel: organization, theory of, 177
Kaufman, Herbert: 79, 179
Kennedy, John F.: Bay of Pigs, 92, 93, 95, 99; Cuban missile crisis, 94, 97; and Laos, 94–95; policies of, 88; staff of, 82
Kerr, Clark: 195
Key, V. O.: 89
Kissinger, Henry: 96; on bureaucracy, 97, 99
Kitchen cabinet: 73
Kohlmeir, Louis, Jr.: 143
Korean War: 30
Kranz, Harry: 227
Kurzman, Dan: *Genesis 1948*, 92

Labor, Department of: manpower evaluations, 410
Laissez-faire leadership style: 284, 285
Laos: and Kennedy, 94-95
Law, administrative: 120-134
Law enforcement: 14, 15; evaluation of, 394; expenditures, 12. *See also* Corrections system; Police
Lawyers: public interest, 155, 157
Leadership: 280–324; and decision making, 301–309; and expected behavior, 307; identifying, 281; and organizational humanism, 292–294; and pay schedules, 291–292; problems, 280–324; selection of leadership pattern, 300–314; situational character of, 287–289; strategies of, 290–291, 309–310; styles, 282–287; and time pressures, 309; traits, 281–282, 289–290, 310; and values, 306, 308
League of Women Voters: 145
Leaks: 96, 98, 99
Lee, James A.: 292
Legal Services: program evaluation, 414–415
Legislative Organization Act of 1946: 110
Legislative Reorganization Act of 1970: 115
Legislature: and bureaucratic monitoring, 438–441; and courts, 132; oversight by, 72–73, 107–119; as policy implementor, 106–119; proposals 4
Leone, Richard C.: 146, 147
Lewin, Kurt: on leadership styles, 283–285
Lewis, Anthony: 133
Lewis, Verne B.: 364, 365
Licensing: 144
Likert, Rensis: 293
Lindblom, Charles E.: 264
Liquor stores: 14, 15
Lobbies: 143, 144; business, 150; citizen, 429; public interest, 154–155; union, 219; veterans', 213. *See also* Interest groups
Lorch, Robert: 125
Louisiana: budgetary process, 363
Lovett, Robert: 92

McCloskey, Herbert: on accountability, 423, 424
McClure's magazine: 158
McGregor, Douglas: 292–293
Machlup, Fritz: 195
McNamara, Robert: and budget, 338–339; and Cuban missile crisis, 97; and Defense Department, 244, 251; and military assistance, 97–98; and systems analysis, 252
Madison, James: on public administration, 67
Management by objectives (MBO): 295–298, 299, 315–324, 404, 474
Management systems: 54; managerial grid, 286–287; and organization development, 294–295; and organizational humanism, 292–294; participatory management, 293; and program evaluation, 381–382. *See also* Leadership; Scientific management
Managerial grid: 286–287, 474–475
Manhattan Bail Bond Experiment: 383
Manpower program: 228
Maritime policies: 242
Marshall, George: 92
Maslow, Abraham: 293–294, 473
Matrix organization: 453, 474
Maxwell School of Citizenship and Public Affairs: 49
Mayo, Elton: Hawthorne study, 175–176
Measures: of effectiveness, 397; output measurements, 397; quantitative and qualitative, 393–395; of service, 397
Media, mass: 4–5, 24–25; and bureaucratic monitoring, 432–433, 459; and ombudsmen, 448; and Supreme Court, 132. *See also* Press; Publicity
Medicare: 14, 30, 263
Meetings: employee, 299; open, 55
Meier, Kenneth: 216
Menlo Park: program evaluation, 405
Merewitz, Leonard: 365
Merit system: 203–204, 212, 227, 228, 230–231, 232–236, 316, 475, 476
Meyerson, Martin: 268
MHRM: 292
Military: assistance, 97–98; -industrial

complex, 145; jobs in, 462–463; standing army, 82
Minmier, George: and zero base budgeting, 356, 358, 364
Minneapolis Citizens League: 404
Mismanagement: 5; HEW, 419–420, 437
Mixed scanning: 247, 475
Model Cities Program: 140
Modern Human Resources Management (MHRM): 292
Mondale, Walter: 77
Monitoring: bureaucratic, 425–451. *See also* Accountability
Mooney, James D.: 170–171; and Alan C. Reiley, 173
Morale: employee, 211, 214
Mosher, Frederick C.: 55
Motivation, employee: 199–200, 214, 292, 294, 309, 476
Motor Vehicle Safety Act: 153
Mouton, Jane: 286–287, 474
Muckraking: 47, 158; and public interest groups, 156–157
Municipal services: employment in, 13
Murphy, George: 251, 254, 262
Muskie, Edmund: 343

Nader, Ralph: 145; public interest groups, 146–147, 153–159
Narcotics arrest procedures: 104–105
NASA: matrix organization, 453, 474
National Association for the Advancement of Colored People: 145
National Association of Schools of Public Affairs and Administration (NASPAA): 53, 457, 475
National Civil Service League: 221
National Commission on Productivity: 404
National debt: 18–19
National Defense Education Loans: 26
National Education Association (NEA): 144, 219
National Farm Bureau Federation: 141
National Labor Relations Board: 212
National Organization for Women: 145
National Science Foundation: 178; and program evaluation, 404
National security: 92

National Security Council: 82, 86
National Welfare Rights Organization (NWRO): 140
NATO: 95–96, 252
Natural Gas Pipeline Safety Act: 153
Navy, U.S.: and Cuban missile crisis, 97
Negative feedback: 179
Negative income tax: 380, 408, 412, 453, 475, 478
Nelson, Gaylord: 251–264
New public administration movement: 52–53, 458, 475
New York City: Bureau of Municipal Research, 47, 49; corrections system, 130; history, 18, 19; public employees of, 217, 219–220, 220–221, 224
Newsletters: employee, 299
Nigro, Felix: 216, 217
Nixon, Richard: and budget, 72; and bureaucracy, 99; and China, 93; and CIA, 91; and detente, 105; Family Assistance Program, 88–89; FTC investigation, 153–154; and Indian affairs, 88; and management by objective, 296; and merit system, 203–204; and OEO, 79, 140; and revenue sharing, 453–454; staff of, 83; and Vietnam, 92; and Watergate, 81, 432

Objectives. *See* Goals
O'Brien, Lawrence: 112
Occupational Safety and Health Administration: 455
Odiorne, George S.: 315
Office of Economic Opportunity (OEO): 140; legal services, 414–415; negative income tax, 412; and Nixon, 79; and ombudsmen, 447
Office of International Security Affairs: 97
Office of Management and Budget (OMB): 296, 327–329, 475; and budgetary process, 330–331, 334; and zero base budgeting, 340, 341, 342, 343, 369–370
Ogul, Morris: 109
Oklahoma City: zero base budgeting, 371

Old Age, Survivors, Disability and Health Insurance: 14, 15

Ombudsmen: 435–436, 473, 475, 477; and bureaucratic monitoring, 445–451

O'Neill, Thomas "Tip": 77

Open-meeting legislation: 55

Open-system theory: 312

Oppenheimer, J. Robert: 191

Organization development (OD): 294–295, 475–476

Organization theory: 54, 166–200; adaptation, 194, 198, 199; administrative behavior, 174–175; administrative management, 173–174; bureaucracy, 171, 181–189; collaboration, 194, 196–197; coordinative principle, 170; definition of organization, 167–168; and future, 197–200; hierarchical principle, 170; human relations approach, 175–176; integration, 194, 196; motivation, 176, 199–200; organic adaptive structure, 190, 199; organizational change, 199–200; principle of functional differentiation, 170–171; revitalization, 193, 194, 196, 197; scientific management, 171–173; systems theories, 176–180

Organizational humanism: 292–294, 476

Output measurement: 392–407

Oversight: executive, 473; legislative, 107–119, 474

Palo Alto: program evaluation, 405

PAR: 223–224

Parks: public, 20

Participation: 295; employee, 308, 311

Participatory: decision making, 301, 304; management, 293, 476

Party system: and policy formulation, 273

Pay schedules: 291–292

Payoffs: 316

Pendleton Act: 46, 213, 476

Pentagon Papers: 432

Pennsylvania Economy League: 145

Performance budgeting: 362–363, 364, 367

Performance contracting: 412

Personnel management: 202–236; affirmative action, 207–208; changing of system, 232–236; collective bargaining, 216–226; compensation plan, 205; continuing education, 213–214; discipline, 211; equity, 215, 227–230, 231–236; evaluation, 211, 233, 234; examinations, 208–209; job requirements, 233; merit system, 203–204, 212, 227, 228, 230–231, 232–236; morale and motivation, 214; position classification, 205; probationary period, 210; promotion, 231, 232, 233, 235, 236; recruitment, 205–208, 233; reverse discrimination, 235–236; selection of personnel, 209–210, 232, 234–235; unionization, 215; veterans' preference, 209–210, 213, 227, 231. *See also* Civil service system; Leadership

Pesticides: 263–264

Phenomenarchy: 313

Philadelphia: history, 19

Planning procedures: 120–121

Planning programming budgeting (PPB): 338–339, 340, 360, 361, 362, 366, 404, 476; and budget cuts, 368, 369

Pluralism: 434–435

Points: job, 235. *See also* Veterans' preference

Police: clientele of, 138; expenditures, 28; Fraternal Order of, 144; narcotics arrests, 104–105; Police Fleet Plan, 412; procedures, 242–243

Policy formulation: 60–61, 266–267, 273; by administrators, 103–106; incrementalism, 274–276; successive comparisons, 277–278

Policy implementation: 60–61, 89, 105; by legislators, 106–119

Politics-administration dichotomy: 476

Pollution: 263; water, 242

Population: characteristics, 197–198; projections, 261; U.S., 191

Populism: 158

PODSCORB: 174, 476

Position classification: 476

Postal Service: 112, 454; merit system, 204

Pound, Roscoe: 127
Poverty Program: 140
Power: concept of, 196
Powers, General: 98
Presidency: appointment of personnel, 67–71, 99; budgetary control, 71–72, 327–328, 330–331; executive oversight, 72–74; growth of power of, 81–90; job description, 86–90; powers of, 65–100; and succession, 42
Press: muckraking, 47, 158; and public administration, 54; and public interest groups, 155, 156–157; and regulatory agencies, 149–150. *See also* Media, mass; Publicity
Pressure groups: 84, 136–137; bureaucratic monitoring, 433–435. *See also* Interest groups
Presumption of reviewability doctrine: 442
Principles: approach, 50–51; of public administration, 476
Productivity measurement: 404
Professional and Administrative Career Examination (PACE): 209, 470, 476
Professionalism: and accountability, 376–378; and public administration, 456–458
Professional associations: 48, 139–140, 144; and complaint handling, 450
Professionals for Auto Safety: 155
Professions: regulation of, 144
Profit: 54
Program: activity, 397; authorization, 329, 334, 476
Program evaluation: 379–416, 477; experimentation, 411–413; manpower training, 410; measures, 393–394; output measurement, 392–407; political considerations, 388–391; research, 380–381, 383–388
Project for Corporate Responsibility: 155
Project team approach: 453
Promotional groups: 145–146
Proposition 13: 33–34, 477
Proxmire, William: and military-industrial complex, 145
Psychology: 51
Public administration: as academic

discipline, 48–53, 54; definition, 1–2; future of, 451–459; history, 40–41, 43–48; image of, 36–38; impact of, 3; international, 455–456; and policy formulation, 103–106; as political game, 62–64; and professionalism, 456–458; and vertical and horizontal conflict, 77–79; values, 258–259
Public Administration Service (PAS): 48
Public interest: concept of, 54; and collective bargaining, 224–225; funding of advocacy, 157–159; groups, 145, 146–159, 477
Public Interest Research Groups: 154, 157
Public opinion: 138; and bureaucratic monitoring, 431
Public Opinion Center of Dayton: 406
Public Personnel Administration: 48
Public policy analysis: 53, 477
Public programs: classification of, 12–16; history of, 16–30
Public Service Careers: 228
Public works projects: 20
Publicity: and business interests, 151; and consumerism, 54–55; and controversy, 2, 11; and discretionary powers, 153; and executive powers, 72; and presidency, 89. *See also* Leaks; Media, mass
Pyhrr, Peter A.: 342; and zero base budgeting, 356, 357, 358, 361, 362, 364, 365, 366

Quemoy: 95

Radiation Control for Health and Safety Act: 153
Railroads: regulation of, 20, 24
Ralph Nader, Public Citizen, Inc.: 154–155
Rand Corporation: 266; and decision making, 241; and systems analysis, 254
Rap sessions: 299
Raskin, Abe: 224–225
Rate regulation: 150
Rational-comprehensive approach: 53, 267–268; and analysis, 272; to deci-

sion making, 240–241, 337, 338, 477;
and evaluation, 391; and incrementalism, 241–247; and systems analysis,
251–264; value implications of,
249–250
Rationality: definition of, 49
Recreation programs: and accountability, 421–422; evaluation of, 394, 399,
402–403
Redford, Emmette: *Democracy in the
Administrative State,* 424–425
Referenda: public, 225
Reform: budgetary, 337–340, 355, 359,
361–366, 367, 368, 372; bureaucratic,
453–454; by courts, 131; of Defense
Department, 244; governmental, 46–
48; and public interest advocacy, 158,
159; regulatory, 148–149
Regulation: government, 20, 24–25, 54;
of health care and hospitals, 14, 26; of
liquor industry, 14
Regulatory agencies: clients of, 142–
144; and public interest groups,
146–159
Regulatory commissions: 121, 474;
quasi-judicial authority, 477
Reiley, Alan C.: 167, 170–171
Representative: bureaucracy, 228–230;
system, 250
Research: evaluation, 380–381, 383–
388, 410; and systems analysis,
259–260
Research Applied to National Needs
program: 404
Research Committee on Social Needs:
395
Reuss, Henry S.: and ombudsmen, 450
Revenue sharing programs: 380, 453–
454, 477
Revenues: 28
Revolutionary War: and public pro-
grams, 16–19
Rewards: 291–292, 294, 322–323
Rickover, Admiral Hyman G.: and
atomic aircraft carrier, 244–245
Ridgeway, General Matthew B.: 98
Ridley, Clarence E.: 396
Rifkind, Simon: 129, 133
Riggs, Fred W.: 52
Ripeness for review doctrine: 443, 478

Rizzo, Mayor: 134
Robinson, Donald: 82
Robson, William: on bureaucracy, 425–
426, 427
Roman Empire: public administration
in, 40, 41
Roosevelt, Franklin D.: 86, 88, 173
Root method: 267–268, 275
Rose, Richard: 296–297
Rowen, Henry B.: 241–242
Rule making administration: 124–126
Rule of rigor: 318

St. Petersburg, Fla.: solid waste collec-
tion evaluation, 402, 405, 407
Salary: 187, 198, 206, 207; incentive
pay, 322–323; pay schedules,
291–292
Salisbury, Harrison: 195
Savannah, Ga.: solid waste collection,
402
Schick, Allen: 359, 360, 363, 367, 368
Schmidt, Warren H.: 300
Science: and government, 248–249
Scientific management: 50, 53, 171–173,
291, 296, 298-299, 367, 478
Scientific method: and systems analysis,
255–257
Securities and Exchange Commission:
436
Selection process: of public employees,
290
Self-actualization: 294, 476
Self-control: 320
Self-executing programs: 453, 478
Service: activities, 14; indices, 397
Services, public: equal level of, 31; and
tax reductions, 34
Sewage treatment: evaluation of, 394
Shapiro, Martin: 121, 122
Sierra Club: 145
Simon, Herbert: 51, 396; *Administrative
Behavior,* 174–175; on decision mak-
ing, 53, 246–247; and personnel man-
agement, 203
Sine ira al studio principle: 189
Social Security Act: 141
Social Security System: 14, 31; clients
of, 137; history, 26
Social Workers, National Association of:

139–140

Sociology: and organization theory, 167; and public administration, 51

Solid waste collection: evaluation of, 394, 398–399, 400–402, 413; and zero base budgeting, 349

Solomon, Jay: 77

Sosnick, Stephen H.: 365

Soviet Union: Cuban missile crisis, 94, 97; detente, 105; organizations, 195

Specialists: and generalists, 456–457, 458

Spoils system: 46, 206

Sputnik: 82

Standards of performance: 322–323

Standing: legal concept of, 150, 442, 478

State: courts, 120–121; governments, 44; regulation of professions, 144

State, Department of: 138

Statutes: and adjudication, 125; ambiguity of, 106; changing of, 106–107

Steady state: 179

Steffens, Lincoln: 47

Stogdill, Ralph: 169

Strategic Air Command: 254

Street maintenance: evaluation of, 394

Strikes: 220; teachers', 218

Subordinate: use of, 312–313

Successive limited comparisons: 272, 273, 275–276, 277–278

Suchman, Edward A.: 393

Sunset laws: 79, 108, 342, 389, 454, 478

Suppliers and contractors: 144–145

Supreme Court: 132; v6 and civil rights movement, 126; and compensatory preferential treatment, 235

Syracuse University: public administration studies, 49

Systems theory: 176–180; coding process, 179; and cycles of events, 178; differentiation, 179; equifinality, 179–180; general systems theory, 177; homeostasis, 179; importation of energy, 178; information input, 179; negative entropy, 178–179; negative feedback, 179; output, 178; steady state, 179; systems analysis, 251–264; through-put, 178

Taft-Hartley Act: 220

Taiwan: military assistance to, 97–98

Talent Inventory Process (TIP): 68–69

Tannenbaum, Robert: 300

Taxation: 61; and clientele contact, 138; collection, 42; history, 17, 19; limitations on, 452; Proposition 13, 33–34; reform, 225–226; taxpayers' revolt, 31–32, 33–34

Taylor, Frederick W.: 175; and scientific management, 49–51, 171–173, 291, 478

Taylor, General Maxwell: 98

Team: building, 295; management, 287

Technology: and government, 248–249

Television, cable: 157

Tenure: 186

Tenure of Office Act: 45

Texas Instruments: and zero base budgeting, 343

T-groups: 294

Theory X and Theory Y: 292–293, 478

"1313" group: 48

Time: and goal setting, 317; and motion studies, 173; and program evaluation, 416; series analysis, 384, 385

Tocqueville, Alexis de: 136–137, 191, 200

Toffler, Alvin: *Future Shock*, 190

Training: 233, 236

Training groups: 294–295

Training School for Public Service: 49

Transportation: 242; regulation of, 24; systems, 454

Transportation, Department of: 78

Treasury Department: and budget, 334; and Congress, 327; history, 17, 18

Triandis, Henry: 169

Truman, Harry S.: 99; and Israel, 92, 96–97

Turkey: U.S. missiles in, 97

Unions: collective bargaining, 216–226; public sector, 215

United Nations: and public administration, 455

United States: history of public administration in, 43–48; history of public programs in, 16–30

Urban Institute: 392, 397, 407, 408;

education program evaluation, 414;
legal services program evaluation,
414; manpower training evaluation,
410; police fleet plan evaluation, 412;
program evaluation, 411; solid waste
collection evaluation, 413
Urban programs: 30
USDA. *See* Agriculture, Department of

Values: 198, 458–459, 475; and accountability, 422–425, 474; and courts, 132;
and decision making, 249–250, 269–270, 273–274; and leadership style,
306, 308
Veterans Administration: and American Legion, 139, 142; clients of, 137;
educational benefits, 26; Vietnam
War benefits, 106
Veterans of Foreign Wars: 139
Veterans' preference: 209–210, 213, 227,
231, 478
Vietnam War: 30, 86, 92, 93–94, 98, 99,
128; effect of, 52, 459; and media, 432;
and military-industrial complex, 145;
and VA programs, 106; veterans of,
139
Virginia v. *Charles R. Pfizer and Co.:*
155
von Bertalanffy, Ludwig: 177, 179, 473

Waldo, Dwight: 52
Warren, Earl: 126
Washington, George: 17–19, 44–45, 191
Washington, D.C.: solid waste collection
evaluation, 400–402, 406, 413, 415
Waste: in HEW, 437
Water: resource projects, 78, 242; treatment evaluation, 394
Waterbury, Ct.: Chamber of Commerce,
404
Watergate: effect of, 53, 73, 128, 131;
and ethics, 55; and legislative power,
109; and media, 432; and Nixon, 81;
and values, 459
Weber, Max: on bureaucracy, 41, 42, 49,
171, 181–189, 192, 294

Weizmann, Chaim: 96
Welfare: clients, 139, 140; demonstrations, 141; expenditures, 12–13, 15;
interest groups, 142; negative income
tax, 475
West Germany: government of, 18
Westinghouse-Ohio University: Head
Start evaluation, 409–410
White, Kevin: 134
White House staff: 73, 81, 83–84, 86,
89
Whitehead, Alfred North: 197
Wholesome Meat Act: 153
Wholey, Joseph S.: 408
Wildavsky, Aaron: *Politics of the Budgetary Process*, 335–336, 337, 338; and
zero base budgeting, 359–360, 366,
367, 368
Wilson, James Q.: 426, 427
Wilson, Woodrow: 46–47, 103
Winnie, Richard E.: 392
Wirtz, W. Willard: 198
Women: and job discrimination, 207–208, 209, 210, 227, 229, 231, 232, 234;
recruiting of, 455
Women's rights movement: 145
Work: activity, 397; load indicators,
397; units, 367
World War I: and growth rate, 24
World War II: and growth rate, 24; and
presidential powers, 82
Wurf, Jerry: 220
Wyner, Alan J.: 448, 449

Young, E. Hilton: 355–356
Young, N. E.: 355–356
Youth revolution: 311

Zeidler, Frank P.: 225
Zero base budgeting: 339–372, 454, 478;
and air quality lab, 347–352; decision
packages, 345–347, 348, 349, 350,
351–352, 354, 357–358; ranking
process, 350–352, 357–358
Zoning: 120 121